Schroer

THIRD EDITION

Research Methods in Psychology

EVALUATING A WORLD OF INFORMATION

Research Methods in Psychology

EVALUATING A WORLD OF INFORMATION

Beth Morling

UNIVERSITY OF DELAWARE

W. W. NORTON & COMPANY, INC.
NEW YORK · LONDON

W. W. Norton & Company has been independent since its founding in 1923, when William Warder Norton and Mary D. Herter Norton first published lectures delivered at the People's Institute, the adult education division of New York City's Cooper Union. The firm soon expanded its program beyond the Institute, publishing books by celebrated academics from America and abroad. By midcentury, the two major pillars of Norton's publishing program—trade books and college texts—were firmly established. In the 1950s, the Norton family transferred control of the company to its employees, and today—with a staff of four hundred and a comparable number of trade, college, and professional titles published each year—W. W. Norton & Company stands as the largest and oldest publishing house owned wholly by its employees.

Editor: Sheri L. Snavely
Project Editor: David Bradley
Editorial Assistant: Eve Sanoussi
Manuscript/Development Editor: Betsy Dilernia
Managing Editor, College: Marian Johnson
Managing Editor, College Digital Media: Kim Yi
Production Manager: Jane Searle
Media Editor: Scott Sugarman
Associate Media Editor: Victoria Reuter
Media Assistant: Alex Trivilino
Marketing Manager, Psychology: Ashley Sherwood
Design Director and Text Design: Rubina Yeh
Photo Editor: Travis Carr
Photo Researcher: Dena Digilio Betz
Permissions Manager: Megan Schindel
Composition: CodeMantra
Illustrations: Electragraphics
Manufacturing: Transcontinental Printing

Permission to use copyrighted material is included in the Credits section beginning on page 603.

Library of Congress Cataloging-in-Publication Data

Names: Morling, Beth, author.
Title: Research methods in psychology : evaluating a world of information /
    Beth Morling, University of Delaware.
Description: Third Edition. | New York : W. W. Norton & Company, [2017] |
    Revised edition of the author's Research methods in psychology, [2015] |
    Includes bibliographical references and index.
Identifiers: LCCN 2017030401 | **ISBN 9780393617542 (pbk.)**
Subjects: LCSH: Psychology—Research—Methodology—Textbooks. | Psychology,
    Experimental—Textbooks.
Classification: LCC BF76.5 .M667 2017 | DDC 150.72—dc23 LC
record available at https://lccn.loc.gov/2017030401

Text-Only ISBN 978-0-393-63017-6

W. W. Norton & Company, Inc., 500 Fifth Avenue, New York, NY 10110
wwnorton.com
W. W. Norton & Company Ltd., 15 Carlisle Street, London W1D 3BS

1 2 3 4 5 6 7 8 9 0

For my parents

Brief Contents

About the Author

BETH MORLING is Professor of Psychology at the University of Delaware. She attended Carleton College in Northfield, Minnesota, and received her Ph.D. from the University of Massachusetts at Amherst. Before coming to Delaware, she held positions at Union College (New York) and Muhlenberg College (Pennsylvania). In addition to teaching research methods at Delaware almost every semester, she also teaches undergraduate cultural psychology, a seminar on the self-concept, and a graduate course in the teaching of psychology. Her research in the area of cultural psychology explores how cultural practices shape people's motivations. Dr. Morling has been a Fulbright scholar in Kyoto, Japan, and was the Delaware State Professor of the Year (2014), an award from the Council for Advancement and Support of Education (CASE) and the Carnegie Foundation for the Advancement of Teaching.

Preface

Students in the psychology major plan to pursue a tremendous variety of careers—not just becoming psychology researchers. So they sometimes ask: Why do we need to study research methods when we want to be therapists, social workers, teachers, lawyers, or physicians? Indeed, many students anticipate that research methods will be "dry," "boring," and irrelevant to their future goals. This book was written with these very students in mind—students who are taking their first course in research methods (usually sophomores) and who plan to pursue a wide variety of careers. Most of the students who take the course will never become researchers themselves, but they can learn to systematically navigate the research information they will encounter in empirical journal articles as well as in online magazines, print sources, blogs, and tweets.

I used to tell students that by conducting their own research, they would be able to read and apply research later, in their chosen careers. But the literature on learning transfer leads me to believe that the skills involved in designing one's own studies will not easily transfer to understanding and critically assessing studies done by others. If we want students to assess how well a study supports its claims, we have to teach them to assess research. That is the approach this book takes.

Students Can Develop Research Consumer Skills

To be a systematic consumer of research, students need to know what to prioritize when assessing a study. Sometimes random samples matter, and sometimes they do not. Sometimes we ask about random assignment and confounds, and sometimes we do not. Students benefit from having a set of systematic steps to help them prioritize their questioning when they interrogate quantitative information. To provide that, this book presents a framework of **three claims and four validities**, introduced in Chapter 3. One axis of the framework is the three kinds of claims researchers (as well as journalists, bloggers, and commentators) might make: frequency claims (some percentage of people do X), association claims (X is associated with Y), and causal claims (X changes Y). The second axis of the framework is the four validities that are generally agreed upon by methodologists: internal, external, construct, and statistical.

The three claims, four validities framework provides a scaffold that is reinforced throughout. The book shows how almost every term, technique, and piece of information fits into the basic framework.

The framework also helps students set priorities when evaluating a study. Good quantitative reasoners prioritize different validity questions depending on the claim. For example, for a frequency claim, we should ask about measurement (construct validity) and sampling techniques (external validity), but not about random assignment or confounds, because the claim is not a causal one. For a causal claim, we prioritize internal validity and construct validity, but external validity is generally less important.

Through engagement with a consumer-focused research methods course, students become systematic interrogators. They start to ask more appropriate and refined questions about a study. By the end of the course, students can clearly explain why a causal claim needs an experiment to support it. They know how to evaluate whether a variable has been measured well. They know when it's appropriate to call for more participants in a study. And they can explain when a study must have a representative sample and when such a sample is not needed.

What About Future Researchers?

This book can also be used to teach the flip side of the question: How can producers of research design better studies? The producer angle is presented so that students will be prepared to design studies, collect data, and write papers in courses that prioritize these skills. Producer skills are crucial for students headed for Ph.D. study, and they are sometimes required by advanced coursework in the undergraduate major.

Such future researchers will find sophisticated content, presented in an accessible, consistent manner. They will learn the difference between mediation (Chapter 9) and moderation (Chapters 8 and 9), an important skill in theory building and theory testing. They will learn how to design and interpret factorial designs, even up to three-way interactions (Chapter 12). And in the common event that a student-run study fails to work, one chapter helps them explore the possible reasons for a null effect (Chapter 11). This book provides the basic statistical background, ethics coverage, and APA-style notes for guiding students through study design and execution.

Organization

The fourteen chapters are arranged in six parts. Part I (Chapters 1–3) includes introductory chapters on the scientific method and the three claims, four validities framework. Part II (Chapters 4–5) covers issues that matter for any study: research ethics and good measurement. Parts III–V (Chapters 6–12) correspond to each of the three claims (frequency, association, and causal). Part VI (Chapters 13–14) focuses on balancing research priorities.

Most of the chapters will be familiar to veteran instructors, including chapters on measurement, experimentation, and factorial designs. However, unlike some methods books, this one devotes two full chapters to correlational research (one on bivariate and one on multivariate studies), which help students learn how to interpret, apply, and interrogate different types of association claims, one of the common types of claims they will encounter.

There are three supplementary chapters, on Descriptive Statistics, Inferential Statistics, and APA-Style Reports and Conference Posters. These chapters provide a review for students who have already had statistics and provide the tools they need to create research reports and conference posters.

Two appendices—Random Numbers and How to Use Them, and Statistical Tables—provide reference tools for students who are conducting their own research.

Support for Students and Instructors

The book's pedagogical features emphasize active learning and repetition of the most important points. Each chapter begins with high-level learning objectives—major skills students should expect to remember even "a year from now." Important terms in a chapter are introduced in boldface. The Check Your Understanding questions at the end of each major section provide basic questions that let students revisit key concepts as they read. Each chapter ends with multiple-choice Review Questions for retrieval practice, and a set of Learning Actively exercises that encourage students to apply what they learned. (Answers are provided at the end of the book.) A master table of the three claims and four validities appears inside the book's front cover to remind students of the scaffold for the course.

I believe the book works pedagogically because it spirals through the three claims, four validities framework, building in repetition and depth. Although each chapter addresses the usual core content of research methods, students are always reminded of how a particular topic helps them interrogate the key validities. The interleaving of content should help students remember and apply this questioning strategy in the future.

I have worked with W. W. Norton to design a support package for fellow instructors and students. The online Interactive Instructor's Guide offers in-class activities, models of course design, homework and final assignments, and chapter-by-chapter teaching notes, all based on my experience with the course. The book is accompanied by other ancillaries to assist both new and experienced research methods instructors, including a new InQuizitive online assessment tool, a robust test bank with over 750 questions, updated lecture and active learning slides, and more; for a complete list, see p. xix.

Teachable Examples on the Everyday Research Methods Blog

Students and instructors can find additional examples of psychological science in the news on my regularly updated blog, Everyday Research Methods (www.everydayresearchmethods.com; no password or registration required). Instructors can use the blog for fresh examples to use in class, homework, or exams. Students can use the entries as extra practice in reading about research studies in psychology in the popular media. Follow me on Twitter to get the latest blog updates (@bmorling).

Changes in the Third Edition

Users of the first and second editions will be happy to learn that the basic organization, material, and descriptions in the text remain the same. The third edition provides several new studies and recent headlines. Inclusion of these new examples means that instructors who assign the third edition can also use their favorite illustrations from past editions as extra examples while teaching.

In my own experience teaching the course, I found that students could often master concepts in isolation, but they struggled to bring them all together when reading a real study. Therefore, the third edition adds new Working It Through sections in several chapters (Chapters 3, 4, 5, 8, and 11). Each one works though a single study in depth, so students can observe how the chapter's central concepts are integrated and applied. For instance, in Chapter 4, they can see how ethics concepts can be applied to a recent study that manipulated Facebook newsfeeds. The Working It Through material models the process students will probably use on longer class assignments.

Also new in the third edition, every figure has been redrawn to make it more visually appealing and readable. In addition, selected figures are annotated to help students learn how to interpret graphs and tables.

Finally, W. W. Norton's InQuizitive online assessment tool is available with the third edition. InQuizitive helps students apply concepts from the textbook to practice examples, providing specific feedback on incorrect responses. Some questions require students to interpret tables and figures; others require them to apply what they're learning to popular media articles.

Here is a detailed list of the changes made to each chapter.

CHAPTER	MAJOR CHANGES IN THE THIRD EDITION
1. Psychology Is a Way of Thinking	The heading structure is the same as in the second edition, with some updated examples. I replaced the facilitated communication example (still an excellent teaching example) with one on the Scared Straight program meant to keep adolescents out of the criminal justice system, based on a reviewer's recommendation.
2. Sources of Information: Why Research Is Best and How to Find it	I simplified the coverage of biases of intuition. Whereas the second edition separated cognitive biases from motivated reasoning, the biases are now presented more simply. In addition, this edition aims to be clearer on the difference between the availability heuristic and the present/present bias. I also developed the coverage of Google Scholar.
3. Three Claims, Four Validities: Interrogation Tools for Consumers of Research	The three claims, four validities framework is the same, keeping the best teachable examples from the second edition and adding new examples from recent media. In response to my own students' confusion, I attempted to clarify the difference between the type of study conducted (correlational or experimental) and the claims made about it. To this end, I introduced the metaphor of a gift, in which a journalist might "wrap" a correlational study in a fancy, but inappropriate, causal claim.

When introducing the three criteria for causation, I now emphasize that covariance is about the study's results, while temporal precedence and internal validity are determined from the study's method.

Chapter 3 includes the first new Working It Through section. |
4. Ethical Guidelines for Psychology Research	I updated the section on animal research and removed the full text of APA Standard 8. There's a new figure on the difference between plagiarism and paraphrasing, and a new example of research fabrication (the notorious, retracted *Lancet* article on vaccines and autism). A new Working It Through section helps students assess the ethics of a recent Facebook study that manipulated people's newsfeeds.
5. Identifying Good Measurement	This chapter retains many of the teaching examples as the second edition. For clarity, I changed the discriminant validity example so the correlation is only weak (not both weak and negative). A new Working It Through section helps students apply the measurement concepts to a self-report measure of gratitude in relationships.
6. Surveys and Observations: Describing What People Do	Core examples are the same, with a new study illustrating the effect of leading questions (a poll on attitudes toward voter ID laws). Look for the new "babycam" example in the Learning Actively exercises.
7. Sampling: Estimating the Frequency of Behaviors and Beliefs	Look for new content on MTurk and other Internet-based survey panels. I updated the statistics on cell-phone-only populations, which change yearly. Finally, I added clarity on the difference between cluster and stratified samples and explained sample weighting.

I added the new keyword *nonprobability sample* to work in parallel with the term *probability sample*. A new table (Table 7.3) helps students group related terms. |

CHAPTER	MAJOR CHANGES IN THE THIRD EDITION
8. Bivariate Correlational Research	This chapter keeps most of the second edition examples. It was revised to better show that association *claims* are separate from correlational *methods*. Look for improved moderator examples in this chapter. These new examples, I hope, will communicate to students that moderators change the relationship between variables; they do not necessarily reflect the level of one of the variables.
9. Multivariate Correlational Research	I replaced both of the main examples in this chapter. The new example of cross-lag panel design, on parental overpraise and child narcissism, has four time periods (rather than two), better representing contemporary longitudinal studies. In the multiple regression section, the recess example is replaced with one on adolescents in which watching sexual TV content predicts teen pregnancy. The present regression example is student-friendly and also has stronger effect sizes.

Look for an important change in Figure 9.13 aimed to convey that a moderator can be thought of as *vulnerability*. My own students tend to think something is a moderator when the subgroup is simply higher on one of the variables. For example, boys might watch more violent TV content *and* be higher on aggression, but that's not the same as a moderator. Therefore, I have updated the moderator column with the moderator "parental discussion." I hope this will help students come up with their own moderators more easily. |
| 10. Introduction to Simple Experiments | The red/green ink example was replaced with a popular study on notetaking, comparing the effects of taking notes in longhand or on laptops. There is also a new example of pretest/posttest designs (a study on mindfulness training). Students sometimes are surprised when a real-world study has multiple dependent variables, so I've highlighted that more in the third edition. Both of the chapter's opening examples have multiple dependent variables.

I kept the example on pasta bowl serving size. However, after Chapter 10 was typeset, some researchers noticed multiple statistical inconsistencies in several publications from Wansink's lab (for one summary of the issues, see the *Chronicle of Higher Education* article, "Spoiled Science"). At the time of writing, the pasta study featured in Chapter 10 has not been identified as problematic. Nevertheless, instructors might wish to engage students in a discussion of these issues. |
| 11. More on Experiments: Confounding and Obscuring Variables | The content is virtually the same, with the addition of two Working It Through sections. The first one is to show students how to work through Table 11.1 using the mindfulness study from Chapter 10. This is important because after seeing Table 11.1, students sometimes think their job is to find the flaw in any study. In fact, most published studies do not have major internal validity flaws. The second Working It Through shows students how to analyze a null result. |
| 12. Experiments with More Than One Independent Variable | Recent work has suggested that context-specific memory effects are not robust, so I replaced the Godden and Baddeley factorial example on context-specific learning with one comparing the memory of child chess experts to adults. |

CHAPTER	MAJOR CHANGES IN THE THIRD EDITION
13. Quasi-Experiments and Small-*N* Designs	I replaced the Head Start study for two reasons. First, I realized it's not a good example of a nonequivalent control group posttest-only design, because it actually included a pretest! Second, the regression to the mean effect it meant to illustrate is rare and difficult to understand. In exchange, there is a new study on the effects of walking by a church.
	In the small-*N* design section, I provided fresh examples of multiple baseline design and alternating treatment designs. I also replaced the former case study example (split-brain studies) with the story of H.M. Not only is H.M.'s story compelling (especially as told through the eyes of his friend and researcher Suzanne Corkin), the brain anatomy required to understand this example is also simpler than that of split- brain studies, making it more teachable.
14. Replication, Generalization, and the Real World	A significant new section and table present the so-called "replication crisis" in psychology. In my experience, students are extremely engaged in learning about these issues. There's a new example of a field experiment, a study on the effect of radio programs on reconciliation in Rwanda.
Supplementary Chapters	In the supplementary chapter on inferential statistics, I replaced the section on randomization tests with a new section on confidence intervals. The next edition of the book may transition away from null hypothesis significance testing to emphasize the "New Statistics" of estimation and confidence intervals. I welcome feedback from instructors on this potential change.

Acknowledgments

Working on this textbook has been rewarding and enriching, thanks to the many people who have smoothed the way. To start, I feel fortunate to have collaborated with an author-focused company and an all-around great editor, Sheri Snavely. Through all three editions, she has been both optimistic and realistic, as well as savvy and smart. She also made sure I got the most thoughtful reviews possible and that I was supported by an excellent staff at Norton: David Bradley, Jane Searle, Rubina Yeh, Eve Sanoussi, Victoria Reuter, Alex Trivilino, Travis Carr, and Dena Diglio Betz. My developmental editor, Betsy Dilernia, found even more to refine in the third edition, making the language, as well as each term, figure, and reference, clear and accurate.

I am also thankful for the support and continued enthusiasm I have received from the Norton sales management team: Michael Wright, Allen Clawson, Ashley Sherwood, Annie Stewart, Dennis Fernandes, Dennis Adams, Katie Incorvia, Jordan Mendez, Amber Watkins, Shane Brisson, and Dan Horton. I also wish to thank the science and media specialists for their creativity and drive to ensure my book reaches a wide audience, and that all the media work for instructors and students.

I deeply appreciate the support of many colleagues. My former student Patrick Ewell, now at Kenyon College, served as a sounding board for new examples and authored the content for InQuizitive. Eddie Brummelman and Stefanie Nelemans provided additional correlations for the cross-lag panel design in Chapter 9. My friend Carrie Smith authored the Test Bank for the past two editions and has made it an authentic measure of quantitative reasoning (as well as sending me things to blog about). Catherine Burrows carefully checked and revised the Test Bank for the third edition. Many thanks to Sarah Ainsworth, Reid Griggs, Aubrey McCarthy, Emma McGorray, and Michele M. Miller for carefully and patiently fact-checking every word in this edition. My student Xiaxin Zhong added DOIs to all the references and provided page numbers for the Check Your Understanding answers. Thanks, as well, to Emily Stanley and Jeong Min Lee, for writing and revising the questions that appear in the Coursepack created for the course management systems. I'm grateful to Amy Corbett and Kacy Pula for reviewing the questions in InQuizitive. Thanks to my students Matt Davila-Johnson and Jeong Min Lee for posing for photographs in Chapters 5 and 10.

The book's content was reviewed by a cadre of talented research method professors, and I am grateful to each of them. Some were asked to review; others cared enough to send me comments or examples by e-mail. Their students are lucky to have them in the classroom, and my readers will benefit from the time they spent in improving this book:

Eileen Josiah Achorn, *University of Texas, San Antonio*
Sarah Ainsworth, *University of North Florida*
Kristen Weede Alexander, *California State University, Sacramento*
Leola Alfonso-Reese, *San Diego State University*
Cheryl Armstrong, *Fitchburg State University*
Jennifer Asmuth, *Susquehanna University*
Kristin August, *Rutgers University, Camden*

Jessica L. Barnack-Tavlaris, *The College of New Jersey*

Gordon Bear, *Ramapo College*

Margaret Elizabeth Beier, *Rice University*

Jeffrey Berman, *University of Memphis*

Brett Beston, *McMaster University*

Alisa Beyer, *Northern Arizona University*

Julie Boland, *University of Michigan*

Marina A. Bornovalova, *University of South Florida*

Caitlin Brez, *Indiana State University*

Shira Brill, *California State University, Northridge*

J. Corey Butler, *Southwest Minnesota State University*

Ricardo R. Castillo, *Santa Ana College*

Alexandra F. Corning, *University of Notre Dame*

Kelly A. Cotter, *California State University, Stanislaus*

Lisa Cravens-Brown, *The Ohio State University*

Victoria Cross, *University of California, Davis*

Matthew Deegan, *University of Delaware*

Kenneth DeMarree, *University at Buffalo*

Jessica Dennis, *California State University, Los Angeles*

Nicole DeRosa, *SUNY Upstate Golisano Children's Hospital*

Rachel Dinero, *Cazenovia College*

Dana S. Dunn, *Moravian College*

C. Emily Durbin, *Michigan State University*

Russell K. Espinoza, *California State University, Fullerton*

Patrick Ewell, *Kenyon College*

Iris Firstenberg, *University of California, Los Angeles*

Christina Frederick, *Sierra Nevada College*

Alyson Froehlich, *University of Utah*

Christopher J. Gade, *University of California, Berkeley*

Timothy E. Goldsmith, *University of New Mexico*

Jennifer Gosselin, *Sacred Heart University*

AnaMarie Connolly Guichard, *California State University, Stanislaus*

Andreana Haley, *University of Texas, Austin*

Edward Hansen, *Florida State University*

Cheryl Harasymchuk, *Carleton University*

Richard A. Hullinger, *Indiana State University*

Deborah L. Hume, *University of Missouri*

Kurt R. Illig, *University of St. Thomas*

Jonathan W. Ivy, *Pennsylvania State University, Harrisburg*

W. Jake Jacobs, *University of Arizona*

Matthew D. Johnson, *Binghamton University*

Christian Jordan, *Wilfrid Laurier University*

Linda Juang, *San Francisco State University*

Victoria A. Kazmerski, *Penn State Erie, The Behrend College*

Heejung Kim, *University of California, Santa Barbara*

Greg M. Kim-Ju, *California State University, Sacramento*

Ari Kirshenbaum, Ph.D., *St. Michael's College*

Kerry S. Kleyman, *Metropolitan State University*

Penny L. Koontz, *Marshall University*

Christina M. Leclerc, Ph.D., *State University of New York at Oswego*

Ellen W. Leen-Feldner, *University of Arkansas*

Carl Lejuez, *University of Maryland*

Marianne Lloyd, *Seton Hall University*

Stella G. Lopez, *University of Texas, San Antonio*

Greg Edward Loviscky, *Pennsylvania State University*

Sara J. Margolin, Ph.D., *The College at Brockport, State University of New York*

Azucena Mayberry, *Texas State University*

Christopher Mazurek, *Columbia College*

Peter Mende-Siedlecki, *University of Delaware*

Molly A. Metz, *Miami University*

Dr. Michele M. Miller, *University of Illinois Springfield*

Daniel C. Molden, *Northwestern University*

J. Toby Mordkoff, *University of Iowa*

Elizabeth Morgan, *Springfield College*

Katie Mosack, *University of Wisconsin, Milwaukee*

Erin Quinlivan Murdoch, *George Mason University*

Stephanie C. Payne, *Texas A&M University*

Anita Pedersen, *California State University, Stanislaus*

Elizabeth D. Peloso, *University of Pennsylvania*

M. Christine Porter, *College of William and Mary*

Joshua Rabinowitz, *University of Michigan*

Elizabeth Riina, *Queens College, City University of New York*

James R. Roney, *University of California, Santa Barbara*

Richard S. Rosenberg, Ph.D., *California State University, Long Beach*

Carin Rubenstein, *Pima Community College*

Silvia J. Santos, *California State University, Dominguez Hills*

Pamela Schuetze, Ph.D., *The College at Buffalo, State University of New York*

John N. Schwoebel, Ph.D., *Utica College*

Mark J. Sciutto, *Muhlenberg College*

Elizabeth A. Sheehan, *Georgia State University*

Victoria A. Shivy, *Virginia Commonwealth University*

Leo Standing, *Bishop's University*

Harold W. K. Stanislaw, *California State University, Stanislaus*

Kenneth M. Steele, *Appalachian State University*

Mark A. Stellmack, *University of Minnesota, Twin Cities*

Eva Szeli, *Arizona State University*

Lauren A. Taglialatela, *Kennesaw State University*

Alison Thomas-Cottingham, *Rider University*

Chantal Poister Tusher, *Georgia State University*

Allison A. Vaughn, *San Diego State University*

Simine Vazire, *University of California, Davis*

Jan Visser, *University of Groningen*

John L. Wallace, Ph.D., *Ball State University*

Shawn L. Ward, *Le Moyne College*

Christopher Warren, *California State University, Long Beach*

Shannon N. Whitten, *University of Central Florida*

Jelte M. Wicherts, *Tilburg University*

Antoinette R. Wilson, *University of California, Santa Cruz*

James Worthley, *University of Massachusetts, Lowell*

Charles E. (Ted) Wright, *University of California, Irvine*

Guangying Wu, *The George Washington University*

David Zehr, *Plymouth State University*

Peggy Mycek Zoccola, *Ohio University*

I have tried to make the best possible improvements from all of these capable reviewers.

My life as a teaching professor has been enriched during the last few years because of the friendship and support of my students and colleagues at the University of Delaware, colleagues I see each year at the SPSP conference, and all the faculty I see regularly at the National Institute for the Teaching of Psychology, affectionately known as NITOP.

Three teenage boys will keep a person both entertained and humbled; thanks to Max, Alek, and Hugo for providing their services. I remain grateful to my mother-in-law, Janet Pochan, for cheerfully helping on the home front. Finally, I want to thank my husband Darrin for encouraging me and for always having the right wine to celebrate (even if it's only Tuesday).

Beth Morling

Media Resources for Instructors and Students

INTERACTIVE INSTRUCTOR'S GUIDE
Beth Morling, *University of Delaware*

The Interactive Instructor's Guide contains hundreds of downloadable resources and teaching ideas, such as a discussion of how to design a course that best utilizes the textbook, sample syllabus and assignments, and chapter-by-chapter teaching notes and suggested activities.

POWERPOINTS

The third edition features three types of PowerPoints. The Lecture PowerPoints provide an overview of the major headings and definitions for each chapter. The Art Slides contain a complete set of images. And the Active Learning Slides provide the author's favorite in-class activities, as well as reading quizzes and clicker questions. Instructors can browse the Active Learning Slides to select activities that supplement their classes.

TEST BANK
C. Veronica Smith, *University of Mississippi,* **and Catherine Burrows,** *University of Miami*

The Test Bank provides over 750 questions using an evidence-centered approach designed in collaboration with Valerie Shute of Florida State University and Diego Zapata-Rivera of the Educational Testing Service. The Test Bank contains multiple-choice and short-answer questions classified by section, Bloom's taxonomy, and difficulty, making it easy for instructors to construct tests and quizzes that are meaningful and diagnostic. The Test Bank is available in Word RTF, PDF, and *ExamView*® Assessment Suite formats.

INQUIZITIVE
Patrick Ewell, *Kenyon College*

InQuizitive allows students to practice applying terminology in the textbook to numerous examples. It can guide the students with specific feedback for incorrect answers to help clarify common mistakes. This online assessment tool gives students the repetition they need to fully understand the material without cutting into valuable class time. InQuizitive provides practice in reading tables and figures, as well as identifying the research methods used in studies from popular media articles, for an integrated learning experience.

EVERYDAY RESEARCH METHODS BLOG: *www.everydayresearchmethods.com*

The *Research Methods in Psychology* blog offers more than 150 teachable moments from the web, curated by Beth Morling and occasional guest contributors. Twice a month, the author highlights examples of psychological science in the news. Students can connect these recent stories with textbook concepts. Instructors can use blog posts as examples in lecture or assign them as homework. All entries are searchable by chapter.

COURSEPACK
Emily Stanley, *University of Mary Washington,* **and Jeong Min Lee,** *University of Delaware*

The Coursepack presents students with review opportunities that employ the text's analytical framework. Each chapter includes quizzes based on the Norton Assessment Guidelines, Chapter Outlines created by the textbook author and based on the Learning Objectives in the text, and review flashcards. The APA-style guidelines from the textbook are also available in the Coursepack for easy access.

Contents

PART I   Introduction to Scientific Reasoning

PART III   Tools for Evaluating Frequency Claims

PART V Tools for Evaluating Causal Claims

THIRD EDITION

Research Methods in Psychology

EVALUATING A WORLD OF INFORMATION

PART I

Introduction to Scientific Reasoning

Your Dog Hates Hugs

NYMag.com, 2016

Mindfulness May Improve Test Scores

Scientific American, 2015

1

Psychology Is a Way of Thinking

THINKING BACK TO YOUR introductory psychology course, what do you remember learning? You might remember that dogs can be trained to salivate at the sound of a bell or that people in a group fail to call for help when the room fills up with smoke. Or perhaps you recall studies in which people administered increasingly stronger electric shocks to an innocent man although he seemed to be in distress. You may have learned what your brain does while you sleep or that you can't always trust your memories. But how come you *didn't* learn that "we use only 10% of our brain" or that "hitting a punching bag can make your anger go away"?

The reason you learned some principles, and not others, is because psychological science is based on studies—on research—by psychologists. Like other scientists, psychologists are empiricists. Being an empiricist means basing one's conclusions on systematic observations. Psychologists do not simply think intuitively about behavior, cognition, and emotion; they know what they know because they have conducted studies on people and animals acting in their natural environments or in specially designed situations. Research is what tells us that most people will administer electric shock to an innocent man in certain situations, and it also tells us that people's brains are usually fully engaged—not just 10%. If you are to think like a psychologist, then you must think like a researcher, and taking a course in research methods is crucial to your understanding of psychology.

This book explains the types of studies psychologists conduct, as well as the potential strengths and limitations of each type of study. You will learn not only how to plan your own studies but

A year from now, you should still be able to:

1.
Explain what it means to reason empirically.

2.
Appreciate how psychological research methods help you become a better producer of information as well as a better consumer of information.

3.
Describe five practices that psychological scientists engage in.

also how to find research, read about it, and ask questions about it. While gaining a greater appreciation for the rigorous standards psychologists maintain in their research, you'll find out how to be a systematic and critical consumer of psychological science.

RESEARCH PRODUCERS, RESEARCH CONSUMERS

Some psychology students are fascinated by the research process and intend to become *producers* of research. Perhaps they hope to get a job studying brain anatomy, documenting the behavior of dolphins or monkeys, administering personality questionnaires, observing children in a school setting, or analyzing data. They may want to write up their results and present them at research meetings. These students may dream about working as research scientists or professors.

Other psychology students may not want to work in a lab, but they do enjoy reading about the structure of the brain, the behavior of dolphins or monkeys, the personalities of their fellow students, or the behavior of children in a school setting. They are interested in being *consumers* of research information—reading about research so they can later apply it to their work, hobbies, relationships, or personal growth. These students might pursue careers as family therapists, teachers, entrepreneurs, guidance counselors, or police officers, and they expect psychology courses to help them in these roles.

In practice, many psychologists engage in both roles. When they are planning their research and creating new knowledge, they study the work of others who have gone before them. Furthermore, psychologists in both roles require a curiosity about behavior, emotion, and cognition. Research producers and consumers also share a commitment to the practice of empiricism—to answer psychological questions with direct, formal observations, and to communicate with others about what they have learned.

Why the Producer Role Is Important

For your future coursework in psychology, it is important to know how to be a producer of research. Of course, students who decide to go to graduate school for psychology will need to know all about research methods. But even if you do not plan to do graduate work in psychology, you will probably have to write a paper following the style guidelines of the American Psychological Association (APA) before you graduate, and you may be required to do research as part of a course lab section. To succeed, you will need to know how to randomly assign people to groups, how to measure attitudes accurately, or how to interpret results from a graph. The skills you acquire by conducting research can teach you how psychological scientists ask questions and how they think about their discipline.

As part of your psychology studies, you might even work in a research lab as an undergraduate (**Figure 1.1**). Many psychology professors are active researchers, and if you are offered the opportunity to get involved in their laboratories, take it! Your faculty supervisor may ask you to code behaviors, assign participants to different groups, graph an outcome, or write a report. Doing so will give you your first taste of being a research producer. Although you will be supervised closely, you will be expected to know the basics of conducting research. This book will help you understand why you have to protect the anonymity of your participants, use a coding book, or flip a coin to decide who goes in which group. By participating as a research producer, you can expect to deepen your understanding of psychological inquiry.

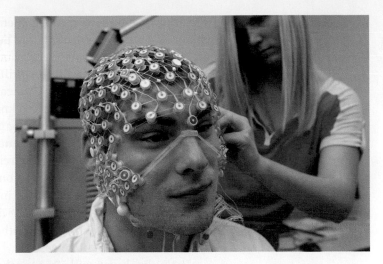

FIGURE 1.1
Producers of research.
As undergraduates, some psychology majors work alongside faculty members as producers of information.

Why the Consumer Role Is Important

Although it is important to understand the psychologist's role as a producer of research, most psychology majors do not eventually become researchers. Regardless of the career you choose, however, becoming a savvy consumer of information is essential. In your psychology courses, you will read studies published by psychologists in scientific journals. You will need to develop the ability to read about research with curiosity—to understand it, learn from it, and ask appropriate questions about it.

Think about how often you encounter news stories or look up information on the Internet. Much of the time, the stories you read and the websites you visit will present information based on research. For example, during an election year, Americans may come across polling information in the media almost every day. Many online newspapers have science sections that include stories on the latest research. Entire websites are dedicated to psychology-related topics, such as treatments for autism, subliminal learning tapes, or advice for married couples. Magazines such as *Scientific American*, *Men's Health*, and *Parents* summarize research for their readers. While some of the research—whether online or printed—is accurate and useful, some of it is dubious, and some is just plain wrong. How can you tell the good research information from the bad? Understanding research methods enables you to ask the appropriate questions so you can evaluate information correctly. Research methods skills apply not only to research studies but also to much of the other types of information you are likely to encounter in daily life.

Finally, being a smart consumer of research could be crucial to your future career. Even if you do not plan to be a researcher—if your goal is to be a social worker, a teacher, a sales representative, a human resources professional, an entrepreneur, or a parent—you will need to know how to interpret published research with a critical eye. Clinical psychologists, social workers, and family therapists must read research to know which therapies are the most effective. In fact, licensure in these helping professions requires knowing the research behind **evidence-based treatments**—that is, therapies that are supported by research. Teachers also use research to find out which teaching methods work best. And the business world runs on quantitative information: Research is used to predict what sales will be like in the future, what consumers will buy, and whether investors will take risks or lie low. Once you learn how to be a consumer of information—psychological or otherwise—you will use these skills constantly, no matter what job you have.

In this book, you will often see the phrase "interrogating information." A consumer of research needs to know how to ask the right questions, determine the answers, and evaluate a study on the basis of those answers. This book will teach you systematic rules for interrogating research information.

The Benefits of Being a Good Consumer

What do you gain by being a critical consumer of information? Imagine, for example, that you are a correctional officer at a juvenile detention center, and you watch a TV documentary about a crime-prevention program called Scared Straight. The program arranges for teenagers involved in the criminal justice system to visit prisons, where selected prisoners describe the stark, violent realities of prison life (**Figure 1.2**). The idea is that when teens hear about how tough it is in prison, they will be scared into the "straight," law-abiding life. The program makes a lot

FIGURE 1.2
Scared straight.

Although it makes intuitive sense that young people would be scared into good behavior by hearing from current prisoners, such intervention programs have actually been shown to cause an increase in criminal offenses.

of sense to you. You are considering starting a partnership between the residents of your detention center and the state prison system.

However, before starting the partnership, you decide to investigate the efficacy of the program by reviewing some research that has been conducted about it. You learn that despite the intuitive appeal of the Scared Straight approach, the program doesn't work—in fact, it might even cause criminal activity to get worse! Several published articles have reported the results of randomized, controlled studies in which young adults were assigned to either a Scared Straight program or a control program. The researchers then collected criminal records for 6–12 months. None of the studies showed that Scared Straight attendees committed fewer crimes, and most studies found an *increase* in crime among participants in the Scared Straight programs, compared to the controls (Petrosino, Turpin-Petrosino, & Finckenauer, 2000). In one case, Scared Straight attendees had committed 20% *more* crimes than the control group.

At first, people considering such a program might think: If this program helps even one person, it's worth it. However, we always need empirical evidence to test the efficacy of our interventions. A well-intentioned program that seems to make sense might actually be doing harm. In fact, if you investigate further, you'll find that the U.S. Department of Justice officially warns that such programs are ineffective and can harm youth, and the Juvenile Justice and Delinquency Prevention Act of 1974 was amended to prohibit youth in the criminal justice system from interactions with adult inmates in jails and prisons.

Being a skilled consumer of information can inform you about other programs that might work. For example, in your quest to become a better student, suppose you see this headline: "Mindfulness may improve test scores." The practice of mindfulness involves attending to the present moment, on purpose, with a nonjudgmental frame of mind (Kabat-Zinn, 2013). In a mindful state, people simply observe and let go of thoughts rather than elaborating on them. Could the practice of mindfulness really improve test scores? A study conducted by Michael Mrazek and his colleagues assigned people to take either a 2-week mindfulness training course or a 2-week nutrition course (Mrazek, Franklin, Philips, Baird, & Schooner, 2013). At the end of the training, only the people who had practiced mindfulness showed improved GRE scores (compared to their scores beforehand). Mrazek's group hypothesized that mindfulness training helps people attend to an academic task without being distracted. They were better, it seemed, at controlling their minds from wandering. The research evidence you read about here appears to support the use of mindfulness for improving test scores.

By understanding the research methods and results of this study, you might be convinced to take a mindfulness-training course similar to the one used by Mrazek and his colleagues. And if you were a teacher or tutor, you might consider advising your students to practice some of the focusing techniques. (Chapter 10 returns to this example and explains why the Mrazek study stands up to interrogation.) Your skills in research methods will help you become a better consumer of studies like this one, so you can decide when the research supports some programs (such as mindfulness for study skills) but not others (such as Scared Straight for criminal behavior).

CHECK YOUR UNDERSTANDING

1. Explain what the consumer of research and producer of research roles have in common, and describe how they differ.

2. What kinds of jobs would use consumer-of-research skills? What kinds of jobs would use producer-of-research skills?

1. See pp. 6–7. 2. See pp. 7–8.

HOW SCIENTISTS APPROACH THEIR WORK

Psychological scientists are identified not by advanced degrees or white lab coats; they are defined by what they do and how they think. The rest of this chapter will explain the fundamental ways psychologists approach their work. First, they act as empiricists in their investigations, meaning that they systematically observe the world. Second, they test theories through research and, in turn, revise their theories based on the resulting data. Third, they take an empirical approach to both applied research, which directly targets real-world problems, and basic research, which is intended to contribute to the general body of knowledge. Fourth, they go further: Once they have discovered an effect, scientists plan further research to test why, when, or for whom an effect works. Fifth, psychologists make their work public: They submit their results to journals for review and respond to the opinions of other scientists. Another aspect of making work public involves sharing findings of psychological research with the popular media, who may or may not get the story right.

Scientists Are Empiricists

» For more on the contrast between empiricism and intuition, experience, and authority, see Chapter 2, pp. 26–31.

Empiricists do not base conclusions on intuition, on casual observations of their own experience, or on what other people say. **Empiricism**, also referred to as the *empirical method* or *empirical research*, involves using evidence from the senses (sight, hearing, touch) or from instruments that assist the senses (such as thermometers, timers, photographs, weight scales, and questionnaires) as the basis for conclusions. Empiricists aim to be systematic, rigorous, and to make their work independently verifiable by other observers or scientists. In Chapter 2, you will learn more about why empiricism is considered the most reliable basis for conclusions when compared with other forms of reasoning, such as experience or intuition. For now, we'll focus on some of the practices in which empiricists engage.

Scientists Test Theories: The Theory-Data Cycle

In the theory-data cycle, scientists collect data to test, change, or update their theories. Even if you have never been in a formal research situation, you have probably tested ideas and hunches of your own by asking specific questions that are grounded in theory, making predictions, and reflecting on data.

For example, let's say you need to take your bike to work later, so you check the weather forecast on your tablet (**Figure 1.3**). The application opens, but you see a blank screen. What could be wrong? Maybe your entire device is on the blink: Do the other apps work? When you test them, you find your calculator is working, but not your e-mail. In fact, it looks as if only the apps that need wireless are not working. Your wireless indicator looks low, so you ask your roommate, sitting nearby, "Are you having wifi problems?" If she says no, you might try resetting your device's wireless connection.

Notice the series of steps in this process. First, you asked a particular set of questions, all of which were guided by your theory about how such devices work. The questions (Is it the tablet as a whole? Is it only the wifi?) reflected your theory that the weather app requires a working electronic device as well as a wireless connection. Because you were operating under this theory, you chose not to ask other kinds of questions (Has a warlock cursed my tablet? Does my device have a bacterial infection?). Your theory set you up to ask certain questions and not others. Next, your questions led you to specific predictions, which you tested by collecting data. You tested your first idea about the problem (My device can't run any apps) by making a specific prediction (If I test any application, it won't work). Then you set up a situation to test your prediction (Does the calculator work?). The data (The calculator does work) told you your initial prediction was wrong. You used that outcome to change your idea about the problem (It's only the wireless-based apps that aren't working). And so on. When you take systematic steps to solve a problem, you are participating in something similar to what scientists do in the theory-data cycle.

THE CUPBOARD THEORY VS. THE CONTACT COMFORT THEORY

A classic example from the psychological study of attachment can illustrate the way researchers similarly use data to test their theories. You've probably observed that animals form strong attachments to their caregivers. If you have a dog, you know he's extremely happy to see you when you come home, wagging his tail and jumping all over you. Human babies, once they are able to crawl, may follow their parents or caregivers around, keeping close to them. Baby monkeys exhibit similar behavior, spending hours clinging tightly to the mother's fur. Why do animals form such strong attachments to their caregivers?

FIGURE 1.3
Troubleshooting a tablet.

Troubleshooting an electronic device is a form of engaging in the theory-data cycle.

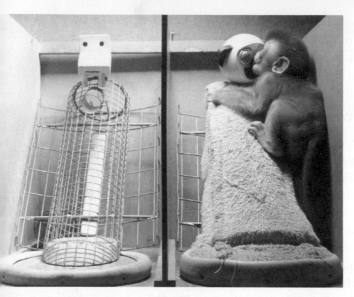

FIGURE 1.4
The contact comfort theory.

As the theory hypothesized, Harlow's baby monkeys spent most of their time on the warm, cozy cloth mother, even though she did not provide any food.

One theory, referred to as the cupboard theory of mother-infant attachment, is that a mother is valuable to a baby mammal because she is a source of food. The baby animal gets hungry, gets food from the mother by nursing, and experiences a pleasant feeling (reduced hunger). Over time, the sight of the mother is associated with pleasure. In other words, the mother acquires positive value for the baby because she is the "cupboard" from which food comes. If you've ever assumed your dog loves you only because you feed it, your beliefs are consistent with the cupboard theory.

An alternative theory, proposed by psychologist Harry Harlow (1958), is that hunger has little to do with why a baby monkey likes to cling to the warm, fuzzy fur of its mother. Instead, babies are attached to their mothers because of the comfort of cozy touch. This is the contact comfort theory. (In addition, it provides a less cynical view of why your dog is so happy to see you!)

In the natural world, a mother provides both food and contact comfort at once, so when the baby clings to her, it is impossible to tell why. To test the alternative theories, Harlow had to separate the two influences—food and contact comfort. The only way he could do so was to create "mothers" of his own. He built two monkey foster "mothers"—the only mothers his lab-reared baby monkeys ever had. One of the mothers was made of bare wire mesh with a bottle of milk built in. This wire mother offered food, but not comfort. The other mother was covered with fuzzy terrycloth and was warmed by a lightbulb suspended inside, but she had no milk. This cloth mother offered comfort, but not food.

Note that this experiment sets up three possible outcomes. The contact comfort theory would be supported if the babies spent most of their time clinging to the cloth mother. The cupboard theory would be supported if the babies spent most of their time clinging to the wire mother. Neither theory would be supported if monkeys divided their time equally between the two mothers.

When Harlow put the baby monkeys in the cages with the two mothers, the evidence in favor of the contact comfort theory was overwhelming. Harlow's data showed that the little monkeys would cling to the cloth mother for 12–18 hours a day (**Figure 1.4**). When they were hungry, they would climb down, nurse from the wire mother, and then at once go back to the warm, cozy cloth mother. In short, Harlow used the two theories to make two specific predictions about how the monkeys would interact with each mother. Then he used the data he recorded (how much time the monkeys spent on each mother) to support only one of the theories. The theory-data cycle in action!

THEORY, HYPOTHESIS, AND DATA

A **theory** is a set of statements that describes general principles about how variables relate to one another. For example, Harlow's theory, which he developed in light of extensive observations of primate babies and mothers, was about the overwhelming importance of bodily contact (as opposed to simple nourishment) in forming attachments. Contact comfort, not food, was the primary basis for a baby's attachment to its mother. This theory led Harlow to investigate particular kinds of questions—he chose to pit contact comfort against food in his research. The theory meant that Harlow also chose *not* to study unrelated questions, such as the babies' food preferences or sleeping habits.

The theory not only led to the questions; it also led to specific hypotheses about the answers. A **hypothesis**, or *prediction*, is the specific outcome the researcher expects to observe in a study if the theory is accurate. Harlow's hypothesis related to the way the baby monkeys would interact with two kinds of mothers he created for the study. He predicted that the babies would spend more time on the cozy mother than the wire mother. Notably, a single theory can lead to a large number of hypotheses because a single study is not sufficient to test the entire theory—it is intended to test only part of it. Most researchers test their theories with a series of empirical studies, each designed to test an individual hypothesis.

Data are a set of observations. (Harlow's data were the amount of time the baby monkeys stayed on each mother.) Depending on whether the data are consistent with hypotheses based on a theory, the data may either support or challenge the theory. Data that match the theory's hypotheses strengthen the researcher's confidence in the theory. When the data do not match the theory's hypotheses, however, those results indicate that the theory needs to be revised or the research design needs to be improved. **Figure 1.5** shows how these steps work as a cycle.

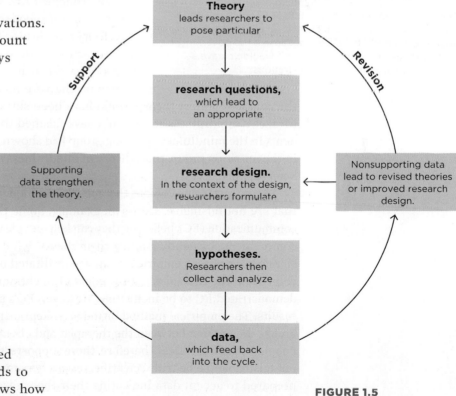

FIGURE 1.5
The theory-data cycle.

FIGURE 1.6
An example of a theory that is not falsifiable.

Certain people might wear a tinfoil hat, operating under the idea that the hat wards off government mental surveillance. But like most conspiracy theories, this notion of remote government mindreading is not falsifiable. If the government has been shown to read people's minds, the theory is supported. But if there is no physical evidence, that also supports the theory because if the government does engage in such surveillance, it wouldn't leave a detectable trace of its secret operations.

FEATURES OF GOOD SCIENTIFIC THEORIES

In scientific practice, some theories are better than others. The best theories are supported by data from studies, are falsifiable, and are parsimonious.

Good Theories Are Supported by Data. The most important feature of a scientific theory is that it is supported by data from research studies. In this respect, the contact comfort theory of infant attachment turned out to be better than the cupboard theory because it was supported by the data. Clearly, primate babies need food, but food is not the source of their emotional attachments to their mothers. In this way, good theories, like Harlow's, are consistent with our observations of the world. More importantly, scientists need to conduct multiple studies, using a variety of methods, to address different aspects of their theories. A theory that is supported by a large quantity and variety of evidence is a good theory.

Good Theories Are Falsifiable. A second important feature of a good scientific theory is **falsifiability**. A theory must lead to hypotheses that, when tested, could actually fail to support the theory. Harlow's theory was falsifiable: If the monkeys had spent more time on the *wire* mother than the cloth mother, the contact-comfort theory would have been shown to be incorrect. Similarly, Mrazek's mindfulness study could have falsified the researchers' theory: If students in the mindfulness training group had shown *lower* GRE scores than those in the nutrition group, their theory of mindfulness and attention would not have been supported.

In contrast, some dubious therapeutic techniques have been based on theories that are not falsifiable. Here's an example. Some therapists practice facilitated communication (FC), believing they can help people with developmental disorders communicate by gently guiding their clients' hands over a special keyboard. In simple but rigorous empirical tests, the facilitated messages have been shown to come from the therapist, not the client (Twachtman-Cullen, 1997). Such studies demonstrated FC to be ineffective. However, FC's supporters don't accept these results. The empirical method introduces skepticism, which, the supporters say, breaks down trust between the therapist and client and shows a lack of faith in people with disabilities. Therefore, these supporters hold a belief about FC that is not falsifiable. To be truly scientific, researchers must take risks, including being prepared to accept data indicating their theory is not supported. Even practitioners must be open to such risk, so they can use techniques that actually work. For another example of an unfalsifiable claim, see **Figure 1.6**.

Good Theories Have Parsimony. A third important feature of a good scientific theory is that it exhibits **parsimony**. Theories are supposed to be simple. If two theories explain the data equally well, most scientists will opt for the simpler, more parsimonious theory.

Parsimony sets a standard for the theory-data cycle. As long as a simple theory predicts the data well, there should be no need to make the theory more complex. Harlow's theory was parsimonious because it posed a simple explanation for infant attachment: Contact comfort drives attachment more than food does. As long as the data continue to support the simple theory, the simple theory stands. However, when the data contradict the theory, the theory has to change in order to accommodate the data. For example, over the years, psychologists have collected data showing that baby monkeys do not always form an attachment to a soft, cozy mother. If monkeys are reared in complete social isolation during their first, critical months, they seem to have problems forming attachments to anyone or anything. Thus, the contact comfort theory had to change a bit to emphasize the importance of contact comfort for attachment *especially in the early months of life*. The theory is slightly less parsimonious now, but it does a better job of accommodating the data.

THEORIES DON'T PROVE ANYTHING

The word *prove* is not used in science. Researchers never say they have proved their theories. At most, they will say that some data *support* or *are consistent with* a theory, or they might say that some data *are inconsistent with* or *complicate* a theory. But no single confirming finding can prove a theory (**Figure 1.7**). New information might require researchers, tomorrow or the next day, to change and improve current ideas. Similarly, a single, disconfirming finding does not lead researchers to scrap a theory entirely. The disconfirming study may itself have been designed poorly. Or perhaps the theory needs to be modified, not discarded. Rather than thinking of a theory as proved or disproved by a single study, scientists evaluate their theories based on the **weight of the evidence**, for and against. Harlow's theory of attachment could not be "proved" by the single study involving wire and cloth mothers. His laboratory conducted dozens of individual studies to rule out alternative explanations and test the theory's limits.

《

For more on weight of the evidence, see Chapter 14, p. 436.

Science proves what you suspected: hiking's good for your mental health

FIGURE 1.7
Scientists don't say "prove."

When you see the word *prove* in a headline, be skeptical. No single study can prove a theory once and for all. A more scientifically accurate headline would be: "Study Supports the Hypothesis that Hiking Improves Mental Health." (Source: Netburn, LAtimes.com, 2015.)

FIGURE 1.8
Basic, applied, and translational research.
Basic researchers may not have an applied context in mind, and applied researchers may be less familiar with basic theories and principles. Translational researchers attempt to translate the findings of basic research into applied areas.

Scientists Tackle Applied and Basic Problems

The empirical method can be used for both applied and basic research questions. **Applied research** is done with a practical problem in mind; the researchers conduct their work in a particular real-world context. An applied research study might ask, for example, if a school district's new method of teaching language arts is working better than the former one. It might test the efficacy of a treatment for depression in a sample of trauma survivors. Applied researchers might be looking for better ways to identify those who are likely to do well at a particular job, and so on.

Basic research, in contrast, is not intended to address a specific, practical problem; the goal is to enhance the general body of knowledge. Basic researchers might want to understand the structure of the visual system, the capacity of human memory, the motivations of a depressed person, or the limitations of the infant attachment system. Basic researchers do not just gather facts at random; in fact, the knowledge they generate may be applied to real-world issues later on.

Translational research is the use of lessons from basic research to develop and test applications to health care, psychotherapy, or other forms of treatment and intervention. Translational research represents a dynamic bridge from basic to applied research. For example, basic research on the biochemistry of cell membranes might be translated into new drug for schizophrenia. Or basic research on how mindfulness changes people's patterns of attention might be translated into a study skills intervention. **Figure 1.8** shows the interrelationship of the three types of research.

Scientists Dig Deeper

Psychological scientists rarely conduct a single investigation and then stop. Instead, each study leads them to ask a new question. Scientists might start with a simple effect, such as the effect of comfort on attachment, and then ask, "Why does this occur?" "When does this happen the most?" "For whom does this apply?" "What are the limits?"

Mrazek and his team did not stop after only one study of mindfulness training and GRE performance. They dug deeper. They also asked whether mindfulness training was especially helpful for people whose minds wander the most. In other studies, they investigated if mindfulness training influenced skills such as people's insight about their own memory (Baird, Mrazek, Phillips, & Schooler, 2014). And they have contrasted mindfulness with mind-wandering, attempting to find both the benefits and the costs of mind-wandering (Baird et al., 2012). This research team has conducted many related studies of how people can and cannot control their own attention.

Scientists Make It Public: The Publication Process

When scientists want to tell the scientific world about the results of their research, they write a paper and submit it to a scientific **journal**. Like magazines, journals usually come out every month and contain articles written by various qualified contributors. But unlike popular newsstand magazines, the articles in a scientific journal are *peer-reviewed*. The journal editor sends the submission to three or four experts on the subject. The experts tell the editor about the work's virtues and flaws, and the editor, considering these reviews, decides whether the paper deserves to be published in the journal.

The peer review process in the field of psychology is rigorous. Peer reviewers are kept anonymous, so even if they know the author of the article professionally or personally, they can feel free to give an honest assessment of the research. They comment on how interesting the work is, how novel it is, how well the research was done, and how clear the results are. Ultimately, peer reviewers are supposed to ensure that the articles published in scientific journals contain innovative, well-done studies. When the peer-review process works, research with major flaws does not get published. However, the process continues even after a study is published. Other scientists can cite an article and do further work on the same subject. Moreover, scientists who find flaws in the research (perhaps overlooked by the peer reviewers) can publish letters, commentaries, or competing studies. Through publishing their work, scientists make the process of their research transparent, and the scientific community evaluates it.

Scientists Talk to the World: From Journal to Journalism

One goal of this textbook is to teach you how to interrogate information about psychological science that you find not only in scientific journals, but also in more mainstream sources that you encounter in daily life. Psychology's scientific journals are read primarily by other scientists and by psychology students; the general public almost never reads them. **Journalism**, in contrast, includes the kinds of news and commentary that most of us read or hear on television, in magazines and newspapers, and on Internet sites—articles in *Psychology Today* and *Men's Health*, topical blogs, relationship advice columns, and so on. These sources are usually written by journalists or laypeople, not scientists, and they are meant to reach the general public; they are easy to access, and understanding their content does not require specialized education.

How does the news media find out about the latest scientific findings? A journalist might become interested in a particular study by reading the current issue of a scientific journal or by hearing scientists talk about their work at a conference. The journalist turns the research into a news story by summarizing it for a popular audience, giving it an interesting headline, and writing about it using nontechnical terms. For example, the journal article by Mrazek and his colleagues on the effect of mindfulness on GRE scores was summarized by a journalist in the magazine *Scientific American* (Nicholson, 2013).

BENEFITS AND RISKS OF JOURNALISM COVERAGE

Psychologists can benefit when journalists publicize their research. By reading about psychological research in the newspaper, the general public can learn what psychologists really do. Those who read or hear the story might also pick up important tips for living: They might understand their children or themselves better; they might set different goals or change their habits. These important benefits of science writing depend on two things, however. First, journalists need to report on the most important scientific stories, and second, they must describe the research accurately.

Is the Story Important? When journalists report on a study, have they chosen research that has been conducted rigorously, that tests an important question, and that has been peer-reviewed? Or have they chosen a study simply because it is cute or eye-catching? Sometimes journalists do follow important stories, especially when covering research that has already been published in a selective, peer-reviewed journal. But sometimes journalists choose the sensational story over the important one.

For example, one spring, headlines such as "Your dog hates hugs" and "You need to stop hugging your dog, study finds" began popping up in newsfeeds. Of course, this topic is clickbait, and dozens of news outlets shocked readers and listeners with these claims. However, the original claim had been made by a psychology professor who had merely reported some data in a blog post. The study he conducted had not been peer-reviewed or published in an empirical journal. The author had simply coded some Internet photographs of people hugging their dogs; according to the author, 82% of the dogs in the sample were showing signs of stress (Coren, 2016). Journalists should not have run with this story before it had been peer-reviewed. Scientific peer reviewers might have criticized the study because it didn't include a comparison group of photos of dogs that weren't being hugged.

The author also left out important details, such as how the photographs were selected and whether the dogs' behavior actually meant they were stressed. In this case, journalists were quick to publish a headline that was sensational, but not necessarily important.

Is the Story Accurate? Even when journalists report on reliable, important research, they don't always get the story right. Some science writers do an excellent, accurate job of summarizing the research, but not all of them do (**Figure 1.9**). Perhaps the journalist does not have the scientific training, the motivation, or the time before deadline to understand the original science very well. Maybe the journalist dumbs down the details of a study to make it more accessible to a general audience. And sometimes a journalist wraps up the details of a study with a more dramatic headline than the research can support.

FIGURE 1.9
Getting it right.

Cartoonist Jorge Cham parodies what can happen when journalists report on scientific research. Here, an original study reported a relationship between two variables. Although the University Public Relations Office relates the story accurately, the strength of the relationship and its implications become distorted with subsequent retellings, much like a game of "telephone."

FIGURE 1.10
The Mozart effect.

Journalists sometimes misrepresent research findings. Exaggerated reports of the Mozart effect even inspired a line of consumer products for children.

Media coverage of a phenomenon called the "Mozart effect" provides an example of how journalists might misrepresent science when they write for a popular audience (Spiegel, 2010). In 1993, researcher Frances Rauscher found that when students heard Mozart music played for 10 minutes, they performed better on a subsequent spatial intelligence test when compared with students who had listened to silence or to a monotone speaking voice (Rauscher, Shaw, & Ky, 1993). Rauscher said in a radio interview, "What we found was that the students who had listened to the Mozart sonata scored significantly higher on the spatial temporal task." However, Rauscher added, "It's very important to note that we did not find effects for general intelligence . . . just for this one aspect of intelligence. It's a small gain and it doesn't last very long" (Spiegel, 2010). But despite the careful way the scientists described their results, the media that reported on the story exaggerated its importance:

> The headlines in the papers were less subtle than her findings: "Mozart makes you smart" was the general idea. . . . But worse, says Rauscher, was that her very modest finding started to be wildly distorted. "Generalizing these results to children is one of the first things that went wrong. Somehow or another the myth started exploding that children that listen to classical music from a young age will do better on the SAT, they'll score better on intelligence tests in general, and so forth." (Spiegel, 2010)

Perhaps because the media distorted the effects of that first study, a small industry sprang up, recording child-friendly sonatas for parents and teachers (**Figure 1.10**). However, according to research conducted since the first study was published, the effect of listening to Mozart on people's intelligence test scores is not very strong, and it applies to most music, not just Mozart (Pietschnig, Voracek, & Formann, 2010).

The journalist Ben Goldacre (2011) catalogs examples of how journalists and the general public misinterpret scientific data when they write about it for a popular audience. Some journalists create dramatic stories about employment statistics that show, for example, a 0.9% increase in unemployment claims. Journalists may conclude that these small increases show an upward trend—when in fact, they may simply reflect sampling error. Another example comes from a happiness survey of 5,000 people in the United Kingdom. Local journalists picked up on tiny city-to-city differences, creating headlines about, for instance, how the city of Edinburgh is the "most miserable place in the country." But the differences the survey found between the various places were not statistically significant (Goldacre, 2008). Even though there were slight differences in happiness from Edinburgh to London, the differences were small enough to be caused by random variation. The researcher who conducted the study said, "I tried to explain issues of [statistical] significance to the journalists who interviewed me. Most did not want to know" (Goldacre, 2008).

How can you prevent being misled by a journalist's coverage of science? One idea is to find the original source, which you'll learn to do in Chapter 2. Reading the original scientific journal article is the best way to get the full story. Another approach is to maintain a skeptical mindset when it comes to popular sources. Chapter 3 explains how to ask the right questions before you allow yourself to accept the journalist's claim.

« To learn about sampling error, see Chapter 7, pp. 196–197.

CHECK YOUR UNDERSTANDING

1. What happens to a theory when the data do not support the theory's hypotheses? What happens to a theory when the data do support the theory's hypotheses?

2. Explain the difference between basic research and applied research, and describe how the two interact.

3. Why can't theories be proved in science?

4. When scientists publish their data, what are the benefits?

5. Describe two ways journalists might distort the science they attempt to publicize.

1. See the discussion of Harlow's monkey experiment on p. 13. 2. See p. 16. 3. See p. 15. 4. See p. 17. 5. See pp. 18–21.

CHAPTER REVIEW

Summary

Thinking like a psychologist means thinking like a scientist, and thinking like a scientist involves thinking about the empirical basis for what we believe.

Research Producers, Research Consumers

- Some students need skills as producers of research; they develop the ability to work in research laboratories and make new discoveries.
- Some students need skills as consumers of research; they need to be able to find, read, and evaluate the research behind important policies, therapies, and workplace decisions.
- Having good consumer-of-research skills means being able to evaluate the evidence behind the claims of a salesperson, journalist, or researcher, and making better, more informed decisions by asking the right questions.

How Scientists Approach Their Work

- As scientists, psychologists are empiricists; they base their conclusions on systematic, unbiased observations of the world.
- Using the theory-data cycle, researchers propose theories, make hypotheses (predictions), and collect data. A good scientific theory is supported by data, is falsifiable, and is parsimonious. A researcher might say that a theory is well supported or well established, rather than proved, meaning that most of the data have confirmed the theory and very little data have disconfirmed it.

- Applied researchers address real-world problems, and basic researchers work for general understanding. Translational researchers attempt to translate the findings of basic research into applied areas.
- Scientists usually follow up an initial study with more questions about why, when, and for whom a phenomenon occurs.
- The publication process is part of worldwide scientific communication. Scientists publish their research in journals, following a peer-review process that leads to sharper thinking and improved communication. Even after publication, published work can be approved or criticized by the scientific community.
- Journalists are writers for the popular media who are skilled at transforming scientific studies for the general public, but they don't always get it right. Think critically about what you read online, and when in doubt, go directly to the original source—peer-reviewed research.

Key Terms

evidence-based treatment, p. 8
empiricism, p. 10
theory, p. 13
hypothesis, p. 13
data, p. 13

falsifiability, p. 14
parsimony, p. 15
weight of the evidence, p. 15
applied research, p. 16
basic research, p. 16

translational research, p. 16
journal, p. 17
journalism, p. 18

To see samples of chapter concepts in the popular media, visit www.everydayresearchmethods.com and click the box for Chapter 1.

Review Questions

1. Which of the following jobs most likely involves producer-of-research skills rather than consumer-of-research skills?

   a. Police officer

   b. University professor

   c. Physician

   d. Journalist

2. To be an empiricist, one should:

   a. Base one's conclusions on direct observations.

   b. Strive for parsimony.

   c. Be sure that one's research can be applied in a real-world setting.

   d. Discuss one's ideas in a public setting, such as on social media.

3. A statement, or set of statements, that describes general principles about how variables relate to one another is a(n) _____.

   a. prediction

   b. hypothesis

   c. empirical observation

   d. theory

4. Why is publication an important part of the empirical method?

   a. Because publication enables practitioners to read the research and use it in applied settings.

   b. Because publication contributes to making empirical observations independently verifiable.

   c. Because journalists can make the knowledge available to the general public.

   d. Because publication is the first step of the theory-data cycle.

5. Which of the following research questions best illustrates an example of basic research?

   a. Has our company's new marketing campaign led to an increase in sales?

   b. How satisfied are our patients with the sensitivity of the nursing staff?

   c. Does wearing kinesio-tape reduce joint pain?

   d. Can 2-month-old human infants tell the difference between four objects and six objects?

Learning Actively

1. To learn more about the theory-data cycle, look in the textbooks from your other psychology courses for examples of theories. In your introductory psychology book, you might look up the James Lange theory or the Cannon-Bard theory of emotion. You could look up Piaget's theory of cognitive development, the Young-Helmholz theory of color vision, or the stage theory of memory. How do the data presented in your textbook show support for the theory? Does the textbook present any data that do not support the theory?

2. Go to an online news website and find a headline that is reporting the results of a recently published study. Read the story, and ask: Has the research in the story been published yet? Does the journalist mention the name of a journal in which the results

appeared? Or has the study only been presented at a research conference? Then, use the Internet to find examples of how other journalists have covered the same story. What variation do you notice in their stories?

3. See what you can find online that has been written about the Mozart effect, about whether people should hug their dogs, or whether people should begin a mindfulness practice in their lives. Does the source you found discuss research evidence? Does the source provide the names of scientists and the journals in which data have been published? On the downside, does the coverage suggest that you purchase a product or that science has "proved" the effectiveness of a certain behavior or technique?

Six Great Ways to Vent Your Frustrations
Lifehack.org, n.d.

Houston's "Rage Room" a Smash as Economy Struggles
The Guardian, 2016

2

Sources of Information: Why Research Is Best and How to Find It

HAVE YOU EVER LOOKED online for a stress-relief technique? You might have found aggressive games such as *Kick the Buddy* or downloaded an app such as *Vent*. Maybe you've considered a for-profit "rage room" that lets you destroy plates, computers, or teddy bears. Perhaps a friend has suggested posting your complaints publicly and anonymously on Yik Yak. But does venting anger really make people feel better? Does expressing aggression make aggression go away?

Many sources of information promote the idea that venting your frustrations works. You might try one of the venting apps yourself and feel good while you're using it. Or you may hear from guidance counselors, friends, or online sources that venting negative feelings is a healthy way to manage anger. But is it accurate to base your conclusions on what authorities—even well-meaning ones—say? Should you believe what everyone else believes? Does it make sense to base your convictions on your own personal experience?

This chapter discusses three sources of evidence for people's beliefs—experience, intuition, and authority—and compares them to a superior source of evidence: *empirical research*. We will focus on evaluating a particular type of response to the question about handling anger: the idea of cathartically releasing bottled-up tension by hitting a punching

A year from now, you should still be able to:

1.
Explain why all scientists, including psychologists, value research-based conclusions over beliefs based on experience, intuition, or authority.

2.
Locate research-based information, and read it with a purpose.

FIGURE 2.1
Anger management.
Some people believe that venting physically or emotionally the best way to work through anger. But what does the research suggest?

FIGURE 2.2
Your own experience.
You may think you feel better when you wear kinesio-tape. But does placing stretchy tape on your body really reduce pain, prevent injury, or improve performance?

bag, screaming, or expressing your emotions (**Figure 2.1**). Is catharsis a healthy way to deal with feelings of anger and frustration? How could you find credible research on this subject if you wanted to read about it? And why should you trust the conclusions of researchers instead of those based on your own experience or intuition?

THE RESEARCH VS. YOUR EXPERIENCE

When we need to decide what to believe, our own experiences are powerful sources of information. "I've used tanning beds for 10 years. No skin cancer yet!" "My knee doesn't give out as much when I use kinesio-tape." "When I'm mad, I feel so much better after I vent my feelings online." Often, too, we base our opinions on the experiences of friends and family. For instance, suppose you're considering buying a new car. You want the most reliable one, so after consulting *Consumer Reports*, you decide on a Honda Fit, a top-rated car based on its objective road testing and a survey of 1,000 Fit owners. But then you hear about your cousin's Honda Fit, which is always in the shop. Why shouldn't you trust your own experience—or that of someone you know and trust—as a source of information?

Experience Has No Comparison Group

There are many reasons not to base beliefs solely on personal experience, but perhaps the most important is that when we do so, we usually don't take a comparison group into account. Research, by contrast, asks the critical question: Compared to what? A **comparison group** enables us to compare what would happen both with and without the thing we are interested in—both with and without tanning beds, online games, or kinesio-tape (**Figure 2.2**).

Here's a troubling example of why a comparison group is so important. Centuries ago, Dr. Benjamin Rush drained blood from people's wrists or ankles as part of a "bleeding," or bloodletting, cure for illness (Eisenberg, 1977). The practice emerged from the belief that too much blood was the cause of illness. To restore an "appropriate" balance, a doctor might remove up to 100 ounces of blood from a patient over the course of a week. Of course, we now know that draining blood is one of the last things a doctor would want to do to a sick patient. Why did Dr. Rush, one of the most respected physicians of his time, keep on using such a practice? Why did he believe bloodletting was a cure?

In those days, a doctor who used the bleeding cure would have noticed that some of his patients recovered and some died; it was the doctor's personal experience. Every patient's recovery from yellow fever after bloodletting *seemed* to support Rush's theory that the treatment worked. But Dr. Rush never set up a systematic comparison because doctors in the 1700s were not collecting data on their treatments. To test the bleeding cure, doctors would have had to systematically count death rates among patients who were bled versus those who received some comparison treatment (or no treatment). How many people were bled and how many were not? Of each group, how many died and how many recovered? Putting all the records together, the doctors could have come to an empirically derived conclusion about the effectiveness of bloodletting.

Suppose, for example, Dr. Rush had kept records and found that 20 patients who were bled recovered, and 10 patients who refused the bleeding treatment recovered. At first, it might look like the bleeding cure worked; after all, twice as many bled patients as untreated patients improved. But you need to know *all* the numbers—the number of bled patients who died and the number of untreated patients who died, in addition to the number of patients in each group who recovered. **Tables 2.1**, **2.2**, and **2.3** illustrate how we need all the data to draw the correct conclusion. In the first example (**Table 2.1**), there is no relationship at all between treatment and improvement. Although twice as many bled patients as untreated patients recovered, twice as many bled patients as untreated patients died, too. If you calculate the percentages, the recovery rate among people who were bled was 20%, and the recovery rate among people who were not treated was also 20%: The proportions are identical. (Remember, these data were invented for purposes of illustration.)

TABLE 2.1

Baseline Comparisons

At first, it looks like more patients who were bled survived (20 vs. 10), but when we divide by the total numbers of patients, survival rates were the same.

	BLED	NOT BLED
Number of patients who recovered	20 ←	10
Number of patients who died	80	40
(Number recovered divided by total number of patients)	20/100	10/50
Percentage recovered	**20%**	**20%** ←

TABLE 2.2

One Value Decreased

If we change the value in one cell (in red), survival rates change, and the bleeding cure is very ineffective.

	BLED	NOT BLED
Number of patients who recovered	20	10
Number of patients who died	80	1 ←
(Number recovered divided by total number of patients)	20/100	10/11
Percentage recovered	**20%**	**91%** ←

TABLE 2.3

One Value Increased

If we change the value in the same cell (in red), now the bleeding cure looks effective.

	BLED	NOT BLED
Number of patients who recovered	20	10
Number of patients who died	80	490 ←
(Number recovered divided by total number of patients)	20/100	10/500
Percentage recovered	**20%**	**2%** ←

To reach the correct conclusion, we need to know *all* the values, including the number of untreated patients who died. **Table 2.2** shows an example of what might happen if the value in only that cell changes. In this case, the number of untreated patients who died is much lower, so the treatment is shown to have a *negative* effect. Only 20% of the treated patients recovered, compared with 91% of the untreated patients. In contrast, if the number in the fourth cell were increased drastically, as in **Table 2.3**, the treatment would be shown to have a *positive* effect. The recovery rate among bled patients is still 20%, but the recovery rate among untreated patients is a mere 2%.

Notice that in all three tables, changing only one value leads to dramatically different results. Drawing conclusions about a treatment—bloodletting, ways of venting anger, or using stretchy tape—requires comparing data systematically from all four cells: the treated/improved cell, the treated/unimproved cell, the untreated/improved cell, and the untreated/unimproved cell. These comparison cells show the relative rate of improvement when using the treatment, compared with no treatment.

FIGURE 2.3
Bloodletting in the eighteenth century.
Describe how Dr. Rush's faulty attention to information led him to believe the bleeding treatment was effective.

Because Dr. Rush bled every patient, he never had the chance to see how many would recover without the bleeding treatment **(Figure 2.3)**. Similarly, when you rely on personal experience to decide what is true, you usually don't have a systematic comparison group because you're observing only one "patient": yourself. The tape you've been using may seem to be working, but what would have happened to your knee pain *without* it? Maybe it would have felt fine anyway. Or perhaps you try an online brain-training course and get higher grades later that semester. But what kind of grades would you have gotten if you hadn't taken the course? Or you might think using the *Kick the Buddy* game makes you feel better when you're angry, but would you have felt better anyway, even if you had played a nonviolent game? What if you had done nothing and just let a little time pass?

Basing conclusions on personal experience is problematic because daily life usually doesn't include comparison experiences. In contrast, basing conclusions on systematic data collection has the simple but tremendous advantage of providing a comparison group. Only a systematic comparison can show you whether your knee improves when you use a special tape (compared with when you do not), or whether your anger goes away when you play a violent online game (compared with doing nothing).

Experience Is Confounded

Another problem with basing conclusions on personal experience is that in every-day life, too much is going on at once. Even if a change has occurred, we often can't be sure what caused it. When a patient treated by Dr. Rush got better, that patient might also have been stronger to begin with, or may have been eating special foods or drinking more fluids. Which one caused the improvement? When you notice a difference in your knee pain after using kinesio-tape, maybe you also took it easy that day or used a pain reliever. Which one caused your knee pain to improve? If you play *Kick the Buddy*, it provides violent content, but you might also be distract-ing yourself or increasing your heart rate. Is it these factors, or the game's violence that causes you to feel better after playing it?

In real-world situations, there are several possible explanations for an outcome. In research, these alternative explanations are called **confounds**. Confounded can also mean confused. Essentially, a confound occurs when you think one thing caused an outcome but in fact other things changed, too, so you are confused about what the cause really was. You might think online brain-training exercises are making your grades better than last year, but because you were also taking differ-ent classes and have gained experience as a student, you can't determine which of these factors (or combination of factors) caused the improvement.

« For more on confounds and how to avoid them in research designs, see Chapter 10, pp. 281–286.

What can we do about confounds like these? For a personal experience, it is hard to isolate variables. Think about the last time you had an upset stomach. Which of the many things you ate that day made you sick? Or your allergies—which of the blossoming spring plants are you allergic to? In a research setting, though, scientists can use careful controls to be sure they are changing only one factor at a time.

Research Is Better Than Experience

What happens when scientists set up a systematic comparison that controls for potential confounds? For example, by using controlled, systematic comparisons, several groups of researchers have tested the hypothesis that venting anger is ben-eficial (e.g., Berkowitz, 1973; Bushman, Baumeister, & Phillips, 2001; Feshbach, 1956; Lohr, Olatunji, Baumeister, & Bushman, 2007). One such study was con-ducted by researcher Brad Bushman (2002). To examine the effect of venting, or catharsis, Bushman systematically compared the responses of angry people who were allowed to vent their anger with the responses of those who did not vent their anger.

First, Bushman needed to make people angry. He invited 600 undergraduates to arrive, one by one, to a laboratory setting, where each student wrote a political essay. Next, each essay was shown to another person, called Steve, who was actually a **confederate**, an actor playing a specific role for the experimenter. Steve insulted the writer by criticizing the essay, calling it "the worst essay I've ever read," among other unflattering comments. (Bushman knew this technique made students angry because he had used it in previous studies, in which students whose essays were criticized reported feeling angrier than those whose essays were not criticized.)

Bushman then randomly divided the angry students into three groups, to systematically compare the effects of venting and not venting anger. Group 1 was instructed to sit quietly in the room for 2 minutes. Group 2 was instructed to punch a punching bag for 2 minutes, having been told it was a form of exercise. Group 3 was instructed to punch a punching bag for 2 minutes while imagining Steve's face on it. (This was the important catharsis group.) Finally, all three groups of students were given a chance to get back at Steve. In the course of playing a quiz game with him, students had the chance to blast Steve's ears with a loud noise. (Because Steve was a confederate, he didn't actually hear the noises, but the students thought he did.)

Which group gave Steve the loudest, longest blasts of noise? The catharsis hypothesis predicts that Group 3 should have calmed down the most, and as a result, this group should not have blasted Steve with very much noise. This group, however, gave Steve the loudest noise blasts of all! Compared with the other two groups, those who vented their anger at Steve through the punching bag continued to punish him when they had the chance. In contrast, Group 2, those who hit the punching bag for exercise, subjected him to less noise (not as loud or as long). Those who sat quietly for 2 minutes punished Steve the least of all. So much for the catharsis hypothesis. When the researchers set up the comparison groups, they found the opposite result: People's anger subsided more quickly when they sat in a room quietly than if they tried to vent it. **Figure 2.4** shows the study results in graph form.

Notice the power of systematic comparison here. In a controlled study, researchers can set up the conditions to include at least one comparison group. Contrast the researcher's larger view with the more subjective view, in which each person consults only his or her own experience. For example, if you had asked some of the students in the catharsis group whether using the punching bag helped their anger subside, they could only consider their own, idiosyncratic experiences. When Bushman looked at the pattern overall—taking into account all three groups—the results indicated that the catharsis group still felt

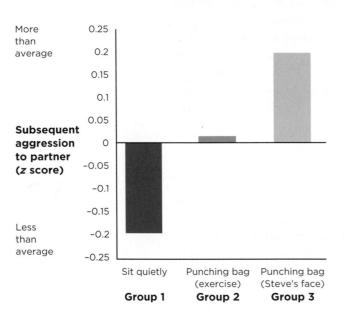

FIGURE 2.4
Results from controlled research on the catharsis hypothesis.

In this study, after Steve (the confederate) insulted all the students in three groups by criticizing their essays, those in Group 1 sat quietly for 2 minutes, Group 2 hit a punching bag while thinking about exercise, and Group 3 hit a punching bag while imagining Steve's face on it. Later, students in all three groups had the chance to blast Steve with loud noise. (Source: Adapted from Bushman, 2002, Table 1.)

the angriest. The researcher thus has a privileged view—the view from the outside, including all possible comparison groups. In contrast, when you are the one acting in the situation, yours is a view from the inside, and you only see one possible condition.

Researchers can also control for potential confounds. In Bushman's study, all three groups felt equally angry at first. Bushman even separated the effects of aggression only (using the punching bag for exercise) from the effects of aggression toward the person who made the participant mad (using the punching bag as a stand-in for Steve). In real life, these two effects—exercise and the venting of anger—would usually occur at the same time.

Bushman's study is, of course, only one study on catharsis, and scientists always dig deeper. In other studies, researchers have made people angry, presented them with an opportunity to vent their anger (or not), and then watched their behavior. Research results have repeatedly indicated that people who physically express their anger at a target actually become *more* angry than when they started. Thus, practicing aggression only seems to teach people how to be aggressive (Berkowitz, 1973; Bushman et al., 2001; Feshbach, 1956; Geen & Quanty, 1977; Lohr et al., 2007; Tavris, 1989).

« For more on the value of conducting multiple studies, see Chapter 14, pp. 425–433.

The important point is that the results of a single study, such as Bushman's, are certainly better evidence than experience. In addition, consistent results from several similar studies mean that scientists can be confident in the findings. As more and more studies amass evidence on the subject, *theories* about how people can effectively regulate their anger gain increasing support. Finally, psychologist Todd Kashdan applied this research when he was interviewed for a story about the "rage room" concept, in which people pay to smash objects. He advised the journalist that "it just increases your arousal and thus makes you even more angry. What you really need is to reduce or learn to better manage that arousal" (Dart, 2016).

Research Is Probabilistic

Although research is usually more accurate than individual experience, sometimes our personal stories contradict the research results. Personal experience is powerful, and we often let a single experience distract us from the lessons of more rigorous research. Should you disagree with the results of a study when your own experience is different? Should you continue to play online games when you're angry because you believe they work for you? Should you disregard *Consumer Reports* because your cousin had a terrible experience with her Honda Fit?

At times, your experience (or your cousin's) may be an exception to what the research finds. In such cases, you may be tempted to conclude: The research must be wrong. However, behavioral research is **probabilistic**, which means that its findings are not expected to explain all cases all of the time. Instead, the conclusions of research are meant to explain a certain proportion (preferably a high proportion) of the possible cases. In practice, this means scientific conclusions are based on patterns that emerge only when researchers set up comparison groups and test many people. Your own experience is only one point in that overall pattern. Thus, for instance, even though bloodletting does not cure illness, some sick patients did recover after being bled. Those exceptional patients who recovered do not change the conclusion derived from all of the data. And even though your cousin's Honda needed a lot of repairs, her case is only one out of 1,001 Fit owners, so it doesn't invalidate the general trend. Similarly, just because there is a strong general trend (that Honda Fits are reliable), it doesn't mean your Honda will be reliable too. The research may suggest there is a *strong probability* your Honda will be reliable, but the prediction is not perfect.

CHECK YOUR UNDERSTANDING

1. What are two general problems with basing beliefs on experience? How does empirical research work to correct these problems?
2. What does it mean to say that research is probabilistic?

1. See pp. 26–31. 2. See pp. 31–32.

THE RESEARCH VS. YOUR INTUITION

Personal experience is one way we might reach a conclusion. Another is intuition—using our hunches about what seems "natural," or attempting to think about things "logically." While we may believe our intuition is a good source of information, it can lead us to make less effective decisions.

Ways That Intuition Is Biased

Humans are not scientific thinkers. We might be aware of our potential to be biased, but we often are too busy, or not motivated enough, to correct and control for these biases. What's worse, most of us think we aren't biased at all! Fortunately, the formal processes of scientific research help prevent these biases from affecting our decisions. Here are five examples of biased reasoning.

BEING SWAYED BY A GOOD STORY

One example of a bias in our thinking is accepting a conclusion just because it makes sense or feels natural. We tend to believe good stories—even ones that are false. For example, to many people, bottling up negative emotions seems unhealthy, and expressing anger is sensible. As with a pimple or a boiling kettle of water, it might seem better to release the pressure. One of the early proponents of catharsis was the neurologist Sigmund Freud, whose models of mental distress focused on the harmful effects of suppressing one's feelings and the benefits of expressing them. Some biographers have speculated that Freud's ideas were influenced by the industrial technology of his day (Gay, 1989). Back then, engines used the power of steam to create vast amounts of energy. If the steam was too compressed, it could have devastating effects on a machine. Freud seems to have reasoned that the human psyche functions the same way. Catharsis makes a good story, because it draws on a metaphor (pressure) that is familiar to most people.

The Scared Straight program is another commonsense story that turned out to be wrong. As you read in Chapter 1, such programs propose that when teenagers susceptible to criminal activity hear about the difficulties of prison from actual inmates, they will be scared away from committing crimes in the future. It certainly makes sense that impressionable young people would be frightened and deterred by such stories. However, research has consistently found that Scared Straight programs are ineffective; in fact, they sometimes even cause *more* crime. The intuitive appeal of such programs is strong (which accounts for why many communities still invest in them), but the research warns against them. One psychologist estimated that the widespread use of the program in New Jersey might have "caused 6,500 kids to commit crimes they otherwise would not have committed" (Wilson, 2011, p. 138). Faulty intuition can even be harmful.

Sometimes a good story will turn out to be accurate, of course, but it's important to be aware of the limitations of intuition. When empirical evidence contradicts what your common sense tells you, be ready to adjust your beliefs on the basis of the research. Automatically believing a story that may seem to make sense can lead you astray.

BEING PERSUADED BY WHAT COMES EASILY TO MIND

Another bias in thinking is the **availability heuristic**, which states that things that pop up easily in our mind tend to guide our thinking (Tversky & Kahneman, 1974). When events or memories are vivid, recent, or memorable, they come to mind more easily, leading us to overestimate how often things happen.

Here's a scary headline: "Woman dies in Australian shark attack." Dramatic news like this might prompt us to change our vacation plans. If we rely on our intuition, we might think shark attacks are truly common. However, a closer look at the frequency of reported shark attacks reveals that they are incredibly rare. Being killed by a shark (1 in 3.7 million) is less likely than dying from the flu (1 in 63) or in a bathtub (1 in 800,000; Ropeik, 2010).

Why do people make this mistake? Death by shark attack is certainly more memorable and vivid than getting the flu or taking a bath, so people talk about it

FIGURE 2.5
The availability heuristic.

Look quickly: Which color candy is most common in this bowl? You might have guessed yellow, red, or orange, because these colors are easier to see—an example of the availability heuristic. Blue is the most prevalent, but it doesn't stand out in this context.

more. It comes to mind easily, and we inflate the associated risk. In contrast, more common methods of dying don't get much press. Nevertheless, we are too busy (or too lazy) to think beyond the easy answer. We decide the answer that comes to mind easily must be the correct one. We avoid swimming in the ocean, but neglect to get the flu vaccine.

The availability heuristic might lead us to wrongly estimate the number of something or how often something happens. For example, if you visited my campus, you might see some women wearing a headcovering (hijab), and conclude there are lots of Muslim women here. The availability heuristic could lead you to overestimate, simply because Muslim women stand out visually. People who practice many other religions do not stand out, so you may underestimate their frequency.

Our attention can be inordinately drawn to certain instances, leading to overestimation. A professor may complain that "everybody" uses a cell phone during his class, when in fact only one or two students do so; it's just that their annoying behavior stands out. You might overestimate how often your kid sister leaves her bike out in the rain, only because it's harder to notice the times she put it away. When driving, you may complain that you always hit the red lights, only because you spend more time at them; you don't notice the green lights you breeze through. What comes to mind easily can bias our conclusions about how often things happen (**Figure 2.5**).

FAILING TO THINK ABOUT WHAT WE CANNOT SEE

The availability heuristic leads us to overestimate events, such as how frequently people encounter red lights or die in shark attacks. A related problem prevents us from seeing the relationship between an event and its outcome. When deciding if there's a pattern, for example, between bleeding a patient and the patient's recovery, or between using kinesio-tape and feeling better, people forget to seek out the information that *isn't* there.

In the story "Silver Blaze," the fictional detective Sherlock Holmes investigates the theft of a prize racehorse. The horse was stolen at night while two stable hands and their dog slept, undisturbed, nearby. Holmes reflects on the dog's "curious" behavior that night. When the other inspectors protest that "the dog did nothing in the night-time," Holmes replies, "That was the curious incident." Because the dog did *not* bark, Holmes deduces that the horse was stolen by someone familiar to the dog at the stable (Doyle, 1892/2002, p. 149; see Gilbert, 2005). Holmes solves the crime because he notices the *absence* of something.

When testing relationships, we often fail to look for absences; in contrast, it is easy to notice what is present. This tendency, referred to as the

present/present bias, is a name for our failure to consider appropriate comparison groups (discussed earlier). Dr. Rush may have fallen prey to the present/present bias when he was observing the effects of bloodletting on his patients. He focused on patients who *did* receive the treatment and *did* recover (the first cell in Table 2.1 where bleeding treatment was "present" and the recovery was also "present"). He did not fully account for the untreated patients or those who did *not* recover (the other three cells back in Table 2.1 in which treatment was "absent" or recovery was "absent").

Did you ever find yourself thinking about a friend and then get a text message or phone call from him? "I must be psychic!" you think. No; it's just the present/present bias in action. You noticed the times when your thoughts coincided with a text message and concluded there was a psychic relationship. But you forgot to consider all the times you thought of people who didn't subsequently text you or the times when people texted you when you weren't thinking about them.

In the context of managing anger, the present/present bias means we will easily notice the times we *did* express frustration at the gym, at the dog, or in an e-mail, and subsequently felt better. In other words, we notice the times when both the treatment (venting) and the desired outcome (feeling better) are present but are less likely to notice the times when we didn't express our anger and just felt better anyway; in other words, the treatment was absent but the outcome was still present (**Table 2.4**). When thinking intuitively, we tend to focus only on experiences that fall in the present/present cell, the instances in which catharsis seemed to work. But if we think harder and look at the whole picture, we would conclude catharsis doesn't work well at all.

The availability heuristic plays a role in the present/present bias because instances in the "present/present" cell of a comparison stand out. But the present/present bias adds the tendency to ignore "absent" cells, which are essential for testing relationships. To avoid the present/present bias, scientists train themselves always to ask: Compared to what?

TABLE 2.4

The Present/Present Bias

	EXPRESSED FRUSTRATION (TREATMENT PRESENT)	DID NOTHING (TREATMENT ABSENT)
Felt better (outcome present)	5 Present/present	10 Absent/present
Felt worse (outcome absent)	10 Present/absent	5 Absent/absent

Note: The number in each cell represents the number of times the two events coincided. We are more likely to focus on the times when two factors were both present or two events occurred at the same time (the red present/present cell), rather than on the full pattern of our experiences.

FOCUSING ON THE EVIDENCE WE LIKE BEST

During an election season, you might check opinion polls for your favorite candidate. What if your candidate lags behind in the first opinion poll you see? If you're like most people, you will keep looking until you find a poll in which your candidate has the edge (Wolfers, 2014).

The tendency to look only at information that agrees with what we already believe is called the **confirmation bias**. We "cherry-pick" the information we take in—seeking and accepting only the evidence that supports what we already think. A lyric by the songwriter Paul Simon captures this well: "A man sees what he wants to see and disregards the rest."

One study specifically showed how people select only their preferred evidence. The participants took an IQ test and then were told their IQ was either high or low. Shortly afterward, they all had a chance to look at some magazine articles about IQ tests. Those who were told their IQ was low spent more time looking at articles that *criticized* the validity of IQ tests, whereas those who were told their IQ was high spent more time looking at articles that *supported* IQ tests as valid measures of intelligence (Frey & Stahlberg, 1986). They all wanted to think they were smart, so they analyzed the available information in biased ways that supported this belief. People keep their beliefs intact (in this case, the belief that they are smart) by selecting only the kinds of evidence they want to see.

One way we enact the confirmation bias is by asking questions that are likely to give the desired or expected answers. Take, for example, a study in which the researchers asked students to interview fellow undergraduates (Snyder & Swann, 1978). Half the students were given the goal of deciding whether their target person was extroverted, and the other half were given the goal of deciding whether their target person was introverted.

Before the interview, the students selected their interview questions from a prepared list. As it turned out, when the students were trying to find out whether their target was extroverted, they chose questions such as "What would you do if you wanted to liven things up at a party?" and "What kind of situations do you seek out if you want to meet new people?" You can see the problem: Even introverts will look like extroverts when they answer questions like these. The students were asking questions that would tend to confirm that their targets were extroverted. The same thing happened with the students who were trying to find out if their target was introverted. They chose questions such as "In what situations do you wish you could be more outgoing?" and "What factors make it hard for you to really open up to people?" Again, in responding to these questions, wouldn't just about anybody seem introverted? Later, when the students asked these questions of real people, the targets gave answers that supported the expectations. The researchers asked some judges to listen in on what the targets said during the interviews. Regardless of their personality, the targets who were being tested for extroversion acted extroverted, and the targets who were being tested for introversion acted introverted.

Unlike the hypothesis-testing process in the theory-data cycle (see Chapter 1), confirmation bias operates in a way that is decidedly not scientific. If interviewers were testing the hypothesis that their target was an extrovert, they asked the questions that would confirm that hypothesis and did not ask questions that might disconfirm that hypothesis. Indeed, even though the students could have chosen neutral questions (such as "What do you think the good and bad points of acting friendly and open are?"), they hardly ever did. In follow-up studies, Snyder and Swann found that student interviewers chose hypothesis-confirming questions even if they were offered a big cash prize for being the most objective interviewer, suggesting that even when people are trying to be accurate, they cannot always be.

FIGURE 2.6
Confirmation bias.

This therapist suspects her client has an anxiety disorder. What kinds of questions should she be asking that would both potentially confirm and potentially disconfirm her hypothesis?

Without scientific training, we are not very rigorous in gathering evidence to test our ideas. Psychological research has repeatedly found that when people are asked to test a hypothesis, they tend to seek the evidence that supports their expectations (Copeland & Snyder, 1995; Klayman & Ha, 1987; Snyder & Campbell, 1980; Snyder & White, 1981). As a result, people tend to gather only a certain kind of information, and then they conclude that their beliefs are supported. This bias is one reason clinical psychologists and other therapists are required to get a research methods education (**Figure 2.6**).

BIASED ABOUT BEING BIASED

Even though we read about the biased ways people think (such as in a research methods textbook like this one), we nevertheless conclude that those biases do not apply to *us*. We have what's called a **bias blind spot**, the belief that we are unlikely to fall prey to the other biases previously described (Pronin, Gilovich, & Ross, 2004; Pronin, Lin, & Ross, 2002). Most of us think we are less biased than others, so when we notice our own view of a situation is different from that of somebody else, we conclude that "I'm the objective one here" and "you are the biased one."

In one study, researchers interviewed U.S. airport travelers, most of whom said the average American is much more biased than themselves (Pronin et al., 2002). For example, the travelers said that while most others would take

personal credit for successes, the travelers themselves would not. Respondents believed other Americans would say a person is smart and competent, just because he is nice; however, they themselves do not have this bias. People believed other Americans would tend to "blame the victim" of random violence for being in the wrong place at the wrong time, even though they would do no such thing themselves (**Figure 2.7**).

The bias blind spot might be the sneakiest of all of the biases in human thinking. It makes us trust our faulty reasoning even more. In addition, it can make it difficult for us to initiate the scientific theory-data cycle. We might say, "I don't need to test this conclusion; I already know it is correct." Part of learning to be a scientist is learning not to use feelings of confidence as evidence for the truth of our beliefs. Rather than thinking what they want to, scientists use data.

FIGURE 2.7
The bias blind spot.

A physician who receives a free gift from a pharmaceutical salesperson might believe she won't be biased by it, but she may also believe other physicians will be persuaded by such gifts to prescribe the drug company's medicines.

The Intuitive Thinker vs. the Scientific Reasoner

When we think intuitively rather than scientifically, we make mistakes. Because of our biases, we tend to notice and actively seek information that confirms our ideas. To counteract your own biases, try to adopt the empirical mindset of a researcher. Recall from Chapter 1 that empiricism involves basing beliefs on systematic information from the senses. Now we have an additional nuance for what it means to reason empirically: To be an empiricist, you must also strive to interpret the data you collect in an objective way; you must guard against common biases.

Researchers—scientific reasoners—create comparison groups and look at all the data. Rather than base their theories on hunches, researchers dig deeper and generate data through rigorous studies. Knowing they should not simply go along with the story everyone believes, they train themselves to test their intuition with systematic, empirical observations. They strive to ask questions objectively and collect potentially disconfirming evidence, not just evidence that confirms their hypotheses. Keenly aware that they have biases, scientific reasoners allow the data to speak more loudly than their own confidently held—but possibly biased—ideas. In short, while researchers are not perfect reasoners themselves, they have trained themselves to guard against the many pitfalls of intuition—and they draw more accurate conclusions as a result.

CHECK YOUR UNDERSTANDING

1. This section described several ways in which intuition is biased. Can you name all five?

2. Why might the bias blind spot be the most sneaky of all the intuitive reasoning biases?

3. Do you think you can improve your own reasoning by simply learning about these biases? How?

1. See pp. 32–38. 2. See pp. 37–38. 3. Answers will vary.

TRUSTING AUTHORITIES ON THE SUBJECT

You might have heard statements like these: "We only use 10% of our brains" and "People are either right-brained or left-brained." People—even those we trust—make such claims as if they are facts. However, you should be cautious about basing your beliefs on what everybody says—even when the claim is made by someone who is (or claims to be) an authority. In that spirit, how reliable is the advice of guidance counselors, TV talk show hosts, or psychology professors? All these people have some authority—as cultural messengers, as professionals with advanced degrees, as people with significant life experience. But should you trust them?

Let's consider this example of anger management advice from a person with a master's degree in psychology, several published books on anger management, a thriving workshop business, and his own website. He's certainly an authority on the subject, right? Here is his advice:

> Punch a pillow or a punching bag. Yell and curse and moan and holler. . . . If you are angry at a particular person, imagine his or her face on the pillow or punching bag, and vent your rage. . . . You are not hitting a person, you are hitting the ghost of that person . . . a ghost alive in you that must be exorcised in a concrete, physical way. (Lee, 1993, p. 96)

Knowing what you know now, you probably do not trust John Lee's advice. In fact, this is a clear example of how a self-proclaimed "expert" might be wrong.

Before taking the advice of authorities, ask yourself about the source of their ideas. Did the authority systematically and objectively compare different conditions, as a researcher would do? Or maybe they have read the research and

FIGURE 2.8
Which authority to believe?
Jenny McCarthy (left), an actress and celebrity, claims that giving childhood vaccines later in life would prevent autism disorders. Dr. Paul Offit (right), a physician-scientist who has both reviewed and conducted scientific research on childhood vaccines, says that early vaccines save lives and that there is no link between vaccination and autism diagnosis.

are interpreting it for you; they might be practitioners who are basing their conclusions on empirical evidence. In this respect, an authority with a scientific degree may be better able to accurately understand and interpret scientific evidence (**Figure 2.8**). If you know this is the case—in other words, if an authority refers to research evidence—their advice might be worthy of attention. However, authorities can also base their advice on their own experience or intuition, just like the rest of us. And they, too, might present only the studies that support their own side.

Keep in mind, too, that not all research is equally reliable. The research an expert uses to support his or her argument might have been conducted poorly. In the rest of this book, you will learn how to interrogate others' research and form conclusions about its quality. Also, the research someone cites to support an argument may not accurately and appropriately support that particular argument. In Chapter 3, you'll learn more about what kinds of research support different kinds of claims. **Figure 2.9** shows a concept map illustrating the sources of information reviewed in this chapter. Conclusions based on research, outlined in black on the concept map, are the most likely to be correct.

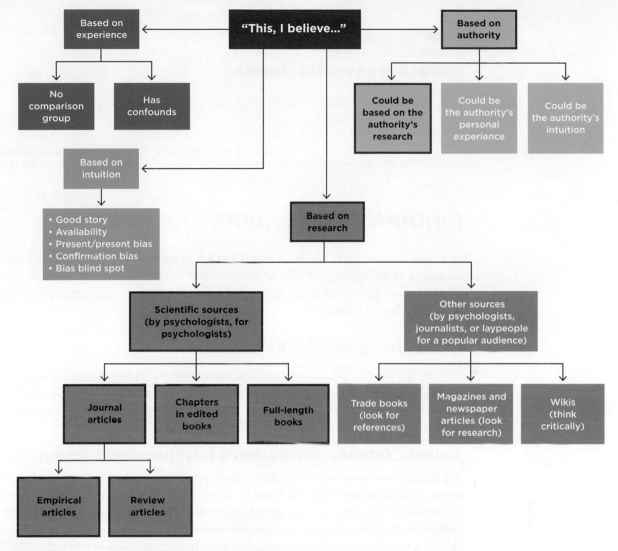

FIGURE 2.9

A concept map showing sources of information.

People's beliefs can come from several sources. You should base your beliefs about psychological phenomena on research, rather than experience, intuition, or authority. Research can be found in a variety of sources, some more dependable than others. Ways of knowing that are mentioned in outlined boxes are more trustworthy.

CHECK YOUR UNDERSTANDING

1. When would it be sensible to accept the conclusions of authority figures? When might it not?

1. See p. 40. When authorities base their conclusions on well-conducted research (rather than experience or intuition), it may be reasonable to accept them.

FINDING AND READING THE RESEARCH

In order to base your beliefs on empirical evidence rather than on experience, intuition, or authority, you will, of course, need to read about that research. But where do you find it? What if you wanted to read studies on venting anger? How would you locate them?

Consulting Scientific Sources

Psychological scientists usually publish their research in three kinds of sources. Most often, research results are published as articles in scholarly journals. In addition, psychologists may describe their research in single chapters within edited books. Some researchers also write full-length scholarly books.

JOURNAL ARTICLES: PSYCHOLOGY'S MOST IMPORTANT SOURCE

Scientific journals come out monthly or quarterly, as magazines do. Unlike popular magazines, however, scientific journals usually do not have glossy, colorful covers or advertisements. You are most likely to find scientific journals in college or university libraries or in online academic databases, which are generally available through academic libraries. For example, the study by Bushman (2002) described earlier was published in the journal *Personality and Social Psychology Bulletin*.

Journal articles are written for an audience of other psychological scientists and psychology students. They can be either empirical articles or review articles. **Empirical journal articles** report, for the first time, the results of an (empirical) research study. Empirical articles contain details about the study's method, the statistical tests used, and the results of the study. **Figure 2.10** is an example of an empirical journal article.

Review journal articles provide a summary of all the published studies that have been done in one research area. A review article by Anderson and his colleagues (2010), for example, summarizes 130 studies on the effects of playing violent video games on the aggressive behavior of children. Sometimes a review article uses a quantitative technique called **meta-analysis**, which combines the

» For a full discussion of meta-analysis, see Chapter 14, pp. 433–437.

Does Venting Anger Feed or Extinguish the Flame? Catharsis, Rumination, Distraction, Anger, and Aggressive Responding

Brad J. Bushman
Iowa State University

Does distraction or rumination work better to diffuse anger? Catharsis theory predicts that rumination works best, but empirical evidence is lacking. In this study, angered participants hit a punching bag and thought about the person who had angered them (rumination group) or thought about becoming physically fit (distraction group). After hitting the punching bag, they reported how angry they felt. Next, they were given the chance to administer loud blasts of noise to the person who had angered them. There also was a no punching bag control group. People in the rumination group felt angrier than did people in the distraction or control groups. People in the rumination group were also most aggressive, followed respectively by people in the distraction and control groups. Rumination increased rather than decreased anger and aggression. Doing nothing at all was more effective than venting anger. These results directly contradict catharsis theory.

The belief in the value of venting anger has become widespread in our culture. In movies, magazine articles, and even on billboards, people are encouraged to vent their anger and "blow off steam." For example, in the movie *Analyze This*, a psychiatrist (played by Billy Crystal) tells his New York gangster client (played by Robert De Niro), "You know what I do when I'm angry? I hit a pillow. Try that." The client promptly pulls out his gun, points it at the couch, and fires several bullets into the pillow. "Feel better?" asks the psychiatrist. "Yeah, I do," says the gunman. In a *Vogue* magazine article, female model Shalom concludes that boxing helps her release pent-up anger. She said,

> I found myself looking forward to the chance to pound out the frustrations of the week against Carlos's (her trainer) mitts. Let's face it: A personal boxing trainer has advantages over a husband or lover. He won't look at you accusingly and say, "I don't know where this irritation is

coming from." ...Your boxing trainer knows it's in there. And he wants you to give it to him. ("Fighting Fit," 1993, p. 179)

In a *New York Times Magazine* article about hate crimes, Andrew Sullivan writes, "Some expression of prejudice serves a useful purpose. It lets off steam; it allows natural tensions to express themselves incrementally; it can siphon off conflict through words, rather than actions" (Sullivan, 1999, p. 113). A large billboard in Missouri states, "Hit a Pillow, Hit a Wall, But Don't Hit Your Kids!"

Catharsis Theory

The theory of catharsis is one popular and authoritative statement that venting one's anger will produce a positive improvement in one's psychological state. The word *catharsis* comes from the Greek word *katharsis*, which literally translated means a cleansing or purging. According to catharsis theory, acting aggressively or even viewing aggression is an effective way to purge angry and aggressive feelings.

Sigmund Freud believed that repressed negative emotions could build up inside an individual and cause psychological symptoms, such as hysteria (nervous outbursts). Breuer and Freud (1893-1895/1955) proposed that the treatment of hysteria required the discharge of the emotional state previously associated with trauma. They claimed that for interpersonal traumas, such as

Author's Note: I would like to thank Remy Reinier for her help scanning photo IDs of students and photographs from health magazines. I also would like to thank Angelica Bonacci for her helpful comments on an early [...] should [...] Iowa St[...] iastate.e[...]

PSPB, V[...]
© 2002 [...]

724

FIGURE 2.10
Bushman's empirical article on catharsis.

The first page is shown here, as it appeared in *Personality and Social Psychology Bulletin*. The inset shows how the article appears in an online search in that journal. Clicking "Full Text pdf" takes you to the article shown. (Source: Bushman, 2002.)

FIGURE 2.11
The variety of scientific sources.

You can read about research in empirical journal articles, review journal articles, edited books, and full-length books.

results of many studies and gives a number that summarizes the magnitude, or the **effect size**, of a relationship. In the Anderson review (2010), the authors computed the average effect size across all the studies. This technique is valued by psychologists because it weighs each study proportionately and does not allow cherry-picking particular studies.

Before being published in a journal, both empirical articles and review articles must be peer-reviewed (see Chapter 1). Both types are considered the most prestigious forms of publication because they have been rigorously peer-reviewed.

CHAPTERS IN EDITED BOOKS

An edited book is a collection of chapters on a common topic; each chapter is written by a different contributor. For example, Michaela Riedeger and Kathrin Klipker published a chapter entitled "Emotional Regulation in Adolescence" in an edited book, *The Handbook of Emotion Regulation* (2014). There are over 30 chapters, all written by different researchers. The editor, James Gross, invited all the other authors to contribute. Generally, a book chapter is not the first place a study is reported; instead, the scientist is summarizing a collection of research and explaining the theory behind it. Edited book chapters can therefore be a good place to find a summary of a set of research a particular psychologist has done. (In this sense, book chapters are similar to review articles in journals.) Chapters are not peer-reviewed as rigorously as empirical journal articles or review articles. However, the editor of the book is careful to invite only experts—researchers who are intimately familiar with the empirical evidence on a topic—to write the chapters. The audience for these chapters is usually other psychologists and psychology students (**Figure 2.11**).

FULL-LENGTH BOOKS

In some other disciplines (such as anthropology, art history, or English), full-length books are a common way for scholars to publish their work. However, psychologists do not write many full-length scientific books for an audience of other psychologists. Those books that have been published are most likely to be found in academic libraries. (Psychologists may also write full-length books for a general audience, as discussed below.)

Finding Scientific Sources

You can find trustworthy, scientific sources on psychological topics by starting with the tools in your college or university's library. The library's reference staff can be extremely helpful in teaching you how to find appropriate articles or chapters. Working on your own, you can use databases such as PsycINFO and Google Scholar to conduct searches.

PsycINFO

One comprehensive tool for sorting through the vast number of psychological research articles is a search engine and database called PsycINFO; it is maintained and updated weekly. Doing a search in PsycINFO is like using Google, but instead of searching the Internet, it searches only sources in psychology, plus a few sources from related disciplines, including communication, marketing, and education. PsycINFO's database includes more than 2.5 million records, mostly peer-reviewed articles.

PsycINFO has many advantages. It can show you all the articles written by a single author (e.g., "Brad Bushman") or under a single keyword (e.g., "autism"). It tells you whether each source was peer-reviewed. One of the best features of PsycINFO is that it shows other articles that have cited each target article (listed under "Cited by") and other articles each target article has cited (listed under "References"). If you've found a great article for your project in PsychINFO, the "cited by" and "references" lists can be helpful for finding more papers just like it.

The best way to learn to use PsycINFO is to simply try it yourself. Or, a reference librarian can show you the basic steps in a few minutes.

One disadvantage is that you cannot use PsycINFO unless your college or university library subscribes to it. Another challenge—true for any search—is translating your curiosity into the right keywords. Sometimes the search you run will give you too many results to sort through easily. Other times your search words won't yield the kinds of articles you were expecting to see. **Table 2.5** presents some strategies for turning your questions into successful searches.

TABLE 2.5

Tips for Turning Your Question into a Successful Database Search

1. Find out how psychologists talk about your question.
Use the Thesaurus tool in the PsycINFO search window to help you find the proper search term:

Example question: *Do eating disorders happen more frequently in families that eat dinner together?*

Instead of "eating disorders," you may need to be more specific. The Thesaurus tool suggests "binge-eating disorder" or "binge eating."

Instead of "eating dinner together," you may need to be more broad. Thesaurus terms include "family environment" and "home environment."

Example question: *What motivates people to study?*

Search terms to try: "achievement motivation," "academic achievement motivation," "academic self concept," "study habits," "homework," "learning strategies."

Example question: *Is the Mozart effect real?*

Search terms to try: "Mozart-effect," "music," "performance," "cognitive processes," "reasoning."

2. An asterisk can help you get all related terms:
Example: "adolescen*" searches for "adolescence" and "adolescents" and "adolescent."

3. If you get too few hits, combine terms using "or" (*or* gives you *more*):
Example: "anorexia" or "bulimia" or "eating disorder."
Example: "false memory" or "early memory."

4. If you get too many hits, restrict using "and" or by using "not":
Example: "anorexia" and "adolescen*."
Example: "repressed memory" and "physical abuse."
Example: "repressed memory" not "physical abuse."

5. Did you find a suitable article? Great! Find similar others by looking through that article's <u>References</u> and by clicking on <u>Cited by</u> to find other researchers who have used it.

GOOGLE SCHOLAR

If you want to find empirical research but don't have access to PsycINFO, you can try the free tool Google Scholar. It works like the regular Google search engine, except the search results are only in the form of empirical journal articles and scholarly books. In addition, by visiting the User Profile for a particular scientist, you can see all of that person's publications. The User Profile list is updated automatically, so you can easily view each scientist's most recent work, as well as his or her most cited publications.

One disadvantage of Google Scholar is that it doesn't let you limit your search to specific fields (such as the abstract). In addition, it doesn't categorize the articles it finds, for example, as peer-reviewed or not, whereas PsycINFO does. And while PsycINFO indexes only psychology articles, Google Scholar contains articles from all scholarly disciplines. It may take more time for you to sort through the articles it returns because the output of a Google Scholar search is less well organized.

When you find a good source in Google Scholar, you might be able to immediately access a PDF file of the article for free. If not, then look up whether your university library offers it. You can also request a copy of the article through your college's interlibrary loan office, or possibly by visiting the author's university home page.

Reading the Research

Once you have found an empirical journal article or chapter, then what? You might wonder how to go about reading the material. At first glance, some journal articles contain an array of statistical symbols and unfamiliar terminology. Even the titles of journal articles and chapters can be intimidating. Take this one, for example: "Object Substitution Masking Interferes with Semantic Processing: Evidence from Event-Related Potentials" (Reiss & Hoffman, 2006). How is a student supposed to read this sort of thing? It helps to know what you will find in an article and to read with a purpose.

COMPONENTS OF AN EMPIRICAL JOURNAL ARTICLE

Most empirical journal articles (those that report the results of a study for the first time) are written in a standard format, as recommended by the *Publication Manual of the American Psychological Association* (APA, 2010). Most empirical journal articles include certain sections in the same order: abstract, introduction, method, results, discussion, and references. Each section contains a specific kind of information. (For more on empirical journal articles, see Presenting Results: APA-Style Reports at the end of this book.)

Abstract. The abstract is a concise summary of the article, about 120 words long. It briefly describes the study's hypotheses, method, and major results. When you are collecting articles for a project, the abstracts can help you quickly decide whether each article describes the kind of research you are looking for, or whether you should move on to the next article.

Introduction. The introduction is the first section of regular text, and the first paragraphs typically explain the topic of the study. The middle paragraphs lay out the background for the research. What theory is being tested? What have past studies found? Why is the present study important? Pay attention to the final paragraph, which states the specific research questions, goals, or hypotheses for the current study.

Method. The Method section explains in detail how the researchers conducted their study. It usually contains subsections such as Participants, Materials, Procedure, and Apparatus. An ideal Method section gives enough detail that if you wanted to repeat the study, you could do so without having to ask the authors any questions.

Results. The Results section describes the quantitative and, as relevant, qualitative results of the study, including the statistical tests the authors used to analyze the data. It usually provides tables and figures that summarize key results. Although you may not understand all the statistics used in the article (especially early in your psychology education), you might still be able to understand the basic findings by looking at the tables and figures.

Discussion. The opening paragraph of the Discussion section generally summarizes the study's research question and methods and indicates how well the results of the study supported the hypotheses. Next, the authors usually discuss the study's importance: Perhaps their hypothesis was new, or the method they used was a creative and unusual way to test a familiar hypothesis, or the participants were unlike others who had been studied before. In addition, the authors may discuss alternative explanations for their data and pose interesting questions raised by the research.

References. The References section contains a full bibliographic listing of all the sources the authors cited in writing their article, enabling interested readers to locate these studies. When you are conducting a literature search, reference lists are excellent places to look for additional articles on a given topic. Once you find one relevant article, the reference list for that article will contain a treasure trove of related work.

READING WITH A PURPOSE: EMPIRICAL JOURNAL ARTICLES

Here's some surprising advice: Don't read every word of every article, from beginning to end. Instead, *read with a purpose*. In most cases, this means asking two questions as you read: (1) What is the argument? (2) What is the evidence to support the argument? The obvious first step toward answering these questions is to read the abstract, which provides an overview of the study. What should you read next?

Empirical articles are stories from the trenches of the theory-data cycle (see Figure 1.5 in Chapter 1). Therefore, an empirical article reports on data that are generated to test a hypothesis, and the hypothesis is framed as a test of a particular theory. After reading the abstract, you can skip to the end of the introduction to find the primary goals and hypotheses of the study. After reading the goals and hypotheses, you can read the rest of the introduction to learn more about the theory that the hypotheses are testing. Another place to find information about the argument of the paper is the first paragraph of the Discussion section, where most authors summarize the key results of their study and state how well the results supported their hypotheses.

Once you have a sense of what the argument is, you can look for the evidence. In an empirical article, the evidence is contained in the Method and Results sections. What did the researchers do, and what results did they find? How well do these results support their argument (i.e., their hypotheses)?

READING WITH A PURPOSE: CHAPTERS AND REVIEW ARTICLES

While empirical journal articles use predetermined headings such as Method, Results, and Discussion, authors of chapters and review articles usually create headings that make sense for their particular topic. Therefore, a way to get an overview of a chapter or review article is by reading each heading.

As you read these sources, again ask: What is the argument? What is the evidence? The argument will be the purpose of the chapter or review article—the author's stance on the issue. In a review article or chapter, the argument often presents an entire theory (whereas an empirical journal article usually tests only one part of a theory). Here are some examples of arguments you might find in chapters or review articles:

- Playing violent video games causes children to be more aggressive (Anderson et al., 2010).
- While speed reading is possible, it comes at the cost of comprehension of the text (Rayner, Schotter, Masson, Potter, & Treiman, 2016).
- "Prolonged exposure therapy" is effective for treating most people who suffer from posttraumatic stress disorder, though many therapists do not yet use this therapy with their clients (Foa, Gillihan, & Bryant, 2013).

In a chapter or review article, the evidence is the research that the author reviews. How much previous research has been done? What have the results been? How strong are the results? What do we still need to know? With practice, you will get better at reading efficiently. You'll learn to categorize what you read as argument or evidence, and you will be able to evaluate how well the evidence supports the argument.

Finding Research in Less Scholarly Places

Reading about research in its original form is the best way to get a thorough, accurate, and peer-reviewed report of scientific evidence. There are other sources for reading about psychological research, too, such as nonacademic books written for the general public, websites, and popular newspapers and magazines. These can be good places to read about psychological research, as long as you choose and read your sources carefully.

THE RETAIL BOOKSHELF

If you browse through the psychology section in a bookstore, you will mostly find what are known as trade books about psychology, written for a general audience (**Figure 2.12**). Unlike the scientific sources we've covered, these books are written for people who do not have a psychology degree. They are written to help people, to inform, to entertain, and to make money for their authors.

FIGURE 2.12
Finding research in a popular bookstore.

You can find some good descriptions of psychology at your local bookstore. Be sure to choose books that contain a long list of scientific sources in their reference section.

The language in trade books is much more readable than the language in most journal articles. Trade books can also show how psychology applies to your everyday life, and in this way they can be useful. But how well do trade books reflect current research in psychology? Are they peer-reviewed? Do they contain the best research, or do they simply present an uncritical summary of common sense, intuition, or the author's own experience?

One place to start is flipping to the end of the book, where you should find footnotes or references documenting the research studies on which the arguments are based. For example, *The Secret Life of Pronouns*, by psychologist James Pennebaker (2011), contains 54 pages of notes—mostly citations to research discussed in the rest of the book. Gabriele Oettingen's *Rethinking Positive Thinking* (2014) contains 17 pages of citations and notes. A book related to this chapter's theme, *Anger: The Misunderstood Emotion* (Tavris, 1989), contains 25 pages of references. These are examples of trade books based on research that are written by psychologists for a general audience.

In contrast, if you flip to the end of some other trade books, you may not find any references or notes. For example, *The Everything Guide to Narcissistic Personality Disorder*, by Cynthia Lechan and Barbara Leff (2011), suggests a handful of books, but includes no reference section. *Healing ADD: The Breakthrough Program that Allows You to See and Heal the 6 Types of ADD*, by Daniel Amen (2002), cites no research. The book *Why Mars and Venus Collide: Improving Relationships by Understanding How Men and Women Cope Differently with Stress*, by John Gray (2008), has four pages of references. Four pages is better than nothing but seems a little light, given that literally thousands of journal articles have been devoted to the scientific study of gender differences.

Vast, well-conducted bodies of literature exist on such topics as self-esteem, ADHD, gender differences, mental illnesses, and coping with stress, but some authors ignore this scientific literature and instead rely on hand-selected anecdotes from their own clinical practice. So if you find a book that claims to be about psychology but does not have any references, consider it to be light entertainment (at best) or irresponsible (at worst). By now, you know that you can do better.

WIKIS AS A RESEARCH SOURCE

Wikis can provide quick, easy-to-read facts about almost any topic. What kind of animal is a narwhal? What years were the *Hunger Games* movies released? How many Grammy awards has Shakira received? Wikis are democratic encyclopedias. Anybody can create a new entry, anybody can contribute to the content of a page, and anybody can log in and add details to an entry. Theoretically, wikis are self-correcting: If one user posts an incorrect fact, another user would come along and correct it.

If you're like most students, you've used wikis for research even though you've been warned not to. If you use Wikipedia for psychology research, for example, sometimes you will find a full review of a psychological phenomenon; sometimes you won't. Searching for the term *catharsis* provides an illustration. If you look up that term on Wikipedia, the first article that comes up is not related to psychology at all; it's about the role of catharsis in classical drama.

You probably know about other disadvantages. First, wikis are not comprehensive in their coverage: You cannot read about a topic if no one has created a page for it. Second, although wiki pages might include references, these references are not a comprehensive list; they are idiosyncratic, representing the preferences of wiki contributors. Third, the details on the pages might be incorrect, and they will stay incorrect until somebody else fixes them. Finally, vandalism is a potential problem (sometimes people intentionally insert errors into pages); however, Wikipedia has developed digital robots to detect and delete the most obvious errors—often within seconds (Nasaw, 2012).

Now that more scientists make a point of contributing to them, wikis may become more comprehensive and accurate (Association for Psychological Science, n.d.). But be careful. Wikis may be written only by a small, enthusiastic, and not necessarily expert group of contributors. Although Wikipedia may be your first hit from a Google search, you should always double-check the information found there. And be aware that many psychology professors do not accept wikis as sources in academic assignments.

THE POPULAR MEDIA

Overall, popular media coverage is good for psychology. Journalists play an important role in telling the public about exciting findings in psychological science. Psychological research is covered in online magazines (such as *Slate* and *Vox*), in news outlets, and in podcasts and blogs. Some outlets, such as *Psychology Today*

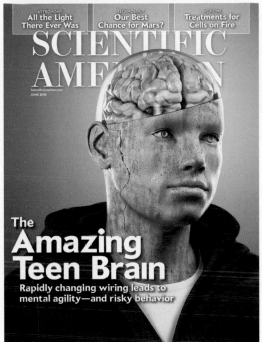

FIGURE 2.13

Examples of sources for reading about psychological science, directed at a popular audience.

A variety of sources cover psychological science in a reader-friendly format.

and the *Hidden Brain* podcast, are devoted exclusively to covering social science research for a popular audience (**Figure 2.13**).

Chapter 1 explained that journalists who specialize in science writing are trained to faithfully represent journal articles for a popular audience, but journalists who are not trained in science writing might not correctly summarize a journal article. They may oversimplify things and even make claims that the study did not support. When you read popular media stories, plan to use your skills as a consumer of information to read the content critically. Delve into the topic the journalist is covering by using PsycINFO or Google Scholar to locate the original article and read the research at its source.

CHECK YOUR UNDERSTANDING

1. How are empirical journal articles different from review journal articles? How is each type of article different from a chapter in an edited book?

2. What two guiding questions can help you read any academic research source?

3. Describe the advantages and disadvantages of using PsycINFO and Google Scholar.

4. If you encounter a psychological trade book, what might indicate that the information it contains is research-based?

1. See pp. 42–44. 2. See p. 47. 3. See pp. 45–46. 4. See pp. 49–50.

CHAPTER REVIEW

Summary

People's beliefs can be based on their own experience, their intuition, on authorities, or on controlled research. Of these, research information is the most accurate source of knowledge.

The Research vs. Your Experience

- Beliefs based on personal experience may not be accurate. One reason is that personal experience usually does not involve a comparison group. In contrast, research explicitly asks: Compared to what?

- In addition, personal experience is often confounded. In daily life, many things are going on at once, and it is impossible to know which factor is responsible for a particular outcome. In contrast, researchers can closely control for confounding factors.

- Research has an advantage over experience because researchers design studies that include appropriate comparison groups.

- Conclusions based on research are probabilistic. Research findings are not able to predict or explain all cases all the time; instead, they aim to predict or explain a high proportion of cases. Individual exceptions to research findings will not nullify the results.

The Research vs. Your Intuition

- Intuition is a flawed source of information because it is affected by biases in thinking. People are likely to accept the explanation of a story that makes sense intuitively, even if it is not true.

- People can overestimate how often something happens if they consider only readily available thoughts, those that come to mind most easily.

- People find it easier to notice what is present than what is absent. When people forget to look at the

information that would falsify their belief, they may see relationships that aren't there.

- Intuition is also subject to confirmation bias. We tend to focus on the data that support our ideas and criticize or discount data that disagree. We ask leading questions whose answers are bound to confirm our initial ideas.

- We all seem to have a bias blind spot and believe we are less biased than everyone else.

- Scientific researchers are aware of their potential for biased reasoning, so they create special situations in which they can systematically observe behavior. They create comparison groups, consider all the data, and allow the data to change their beliefs.

Trusting Authorities on the Subject

- Authorities may attempt to convince us to accept their claims. If their claims are based on their own experience or intuition, we should probably not accept them. If they use well-conducted studies to support their claims, we can be more confident about taking their advice.

Finding and Reading the Research

- Tools for finding research in psychology include the online database PsycINFO, available through academic libraries. You can also use Google Scholar or the websites of researchers.

- Journal articles, chapters in edited books, and full-length books should be read with a purpose by asking: What is the theoretical argument? What is the evidence—what do the data say?

- Trade books, wikis, and popular media articles can be good sources of information about psychology research, but they can also be misleading. Such sources should be evaluated by asking whether they are based on research and whether the coverage is comprehensive, accurate, and responsible.

Key Terms

comparison group, p. 26
confound, p. 29
confederate, p. 29
probabilistic, p. 31

availability heuristic, p. 33
present/present bias, p. 35
confirmation bias, p. 36
bias blind spot, p. 37

empirical journal article, p. 42
review journal article, p. 42
meta-analysis, p. 42
effect size, p. 44

 To see examples of chapter concepts in the popular media, see www.everydayresearchmethods.com and click the box for Chapter 2.

Review Questions

1. Destiny concluded that her new white noise machine helped her fall asleep last night. She based this conclusion on personal experience, which might have confounds. In this context, a confound means:

   a. Another thing might have also occurred last night to help Destiny fall asleep.

   b. Destiny's experience has left her puzzled or confused.

   c. Destiny has not compared last night to times she didn't use the white noise machine.

   d. Destiny will have trouble thinking of counterexamples.

2. What does it mean to say that research is probabilistic?

   a. Researchers refer to the probability that their theories are correct.

   b. Research predicts all possible results.

   c. Research conclusions are meant to explain a certain proportion of possible cases, but may not explain all.

   d. If there are exceptions to a research result, it means the theory is probably incorrect.

3. After two students from his school commit suicide, Marcelino concludes that the most likely cause of death in teenagers is suicide. In fact, suicide is not the most likely cause of death in teens. What happened?

   a. Marcelino was probably a victim of the bias blind spot.

   b. Marcelino was probably influenced by the availability heuristic; he was too influenced by cases that came easily to mind.

   c. Marcelino thought about too many examples of teens who died from other causes besides suicide.

   d. Marcelino did not consider possible confounds.

4. When is it a good idea to base conclusions on the advice of authorities?

   a. When authorities have an advanced degree, such as a Ph.D. or a master's degree.

   b. When authorities based their advice on research that systematically and objectively compares different conditions.

   c. It is never a good idea to base conclusions on the advice of authorities.

   d. When authorities have several years of experience in their specialty area.

5. Which of the following is not a place where psychological scientists publish their research?

   a. Scientific journals

   b. Online podcasts

   c. Chapters in edited books

   d. Full-length books

6. In reading an empirical journal article, what are the two questions you should be asking as you read?

   a. What is the argument? What is the evidence to support the argument?

   b. Why was this research done? Were there any significant findings?

   c. How reputable is (are) the author(s)? Did the findings include support for the hypotheses?

   d. How does this research relate to other research? What are ways to extend this research further?

Learning Actively

1. Each of the examples below is a statement, based on experience, that does not take a comparison group into account:

   a. A bath at bedtime helps my baby sleep better.

   b. My meditation practice has made me feel more peaceful.

   c. The GRE course I took really improved my scores!

   For each statement: (a) Ask: Compared to what? Write a comparison group question that would help you evaluate the conclusion. (b) Get all the information. Draw a 2x2 matrix for systematically comparing outcomes. (c) Address confounds. Assuming there is a relationship, write down possible confounds for the proposed relationship.

   Example: "Since I cut sugar from their diets, I've noticed the campers in my cabin are much more cooperative!"

   (a) Compared to what? Would the campers have improved anyway, without the change in diet?

   (b) A systematic comparison should be set up as follows:

	REDUCE SUGAR IN DIET (TREATMENT)	NO CHANGE IN DIET (NO TREATMENT)
Kids are cooperative (outcome present)		
Kids are not cooperative (outcome absent)		

   (c) Possible confounds: What other factor might have changed at the same time as the low-sugar diet and also caused more cooperativeness? Possible confounds include that the campers may simply have gotten used to camp and settled down. Maybe the new swimming program started at the same time and tired the campers out.

2. Using what you have learned in this chapter, write a sentence or two explaining why the reasoning reflected in each of the following statements is sound or unsound. (a) What are you being asked to believe in each case? (b) What further information might you need to determine the accuracy of the speaker's conclusions? (c) On what is the speaker basing her claim—experience, intuition, or authority?

   a. "I'm positive my cousin has an eating disorder! She's always eating diet bars."

   b. A friend tells you, "I read something cool in the paper this morning: They said violent video games don't cause aggression when they are played cooperatively as team games. They were talking about some research somebody did."

   c. "It's so clear that our candidate won that debate! Did you hear all the zingers he delivered?"

   d. "I read online that doing these special puzzles every day helps grow your brain. It's been proven by neuropsychology."

   e. "Binge drinking is totally normal on my campus. Everybody does it almost every weekend."

   f. "I'm afraid of flying—planes are so dangerous!"

   g. Decluttering your closets makes a huge difference in your happiness. I did it last week, and I feel so much happier when I am in my room.

   h. "Wow—look at how many happy couples got married after meeting on Match.com! I think I'm going to try it, too."

3. Finding sources on PsycINFO means figuring out the right search terms. Use the PsycINFO Thesaurus tool to find keywords that will help you do searches on these research questions. Table 2.5 has some suggestions for turning research questions into helpful searches.

   a. Are adults with autism more violent than typical adults?

   b. Does having PTSD put you at risk for alcoholism?

   c. Can eating more protein make you smarter?

   d. How do we measure narcissism?

   e. What kinds of managers do employees like the best?

4. Choose one of the search terms you worked on in Question 3. Try doing the same search using three platforms: a general search engine, then Google Scholar, then PsycINFO.

   a. What kind of information did you get from the general search engine you chose? Were the results based on research, or do you see more commercial websites or blogs? How might you refine your search to get more research-based hits?

   b. Which of the three search platforms is the easiest to use when you want a general overview of a topic? Which platforms will give you the most up-to-date research? Which of the three makes it easiest to know if information has been peer-reviewed?

People with Higher Incomes Spend Less Time Socializing

Huffington Post, 2016

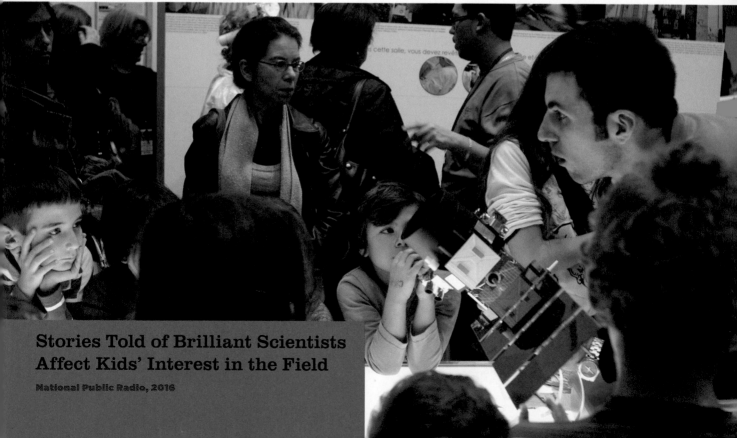

Stories Told of Brilliant Scientists Affect Kids' Interest in the Field

National Public Radio, 2016

3

Three Claims, Four Validities: Interrogation Tools for Consumers of Research

ARTICLES ABOUT PSYCHOLOGY RESEARCH written for a general audience regularly appear in the popular media. Headlines about psychology attract readers because people are interested in such topics as happiness, social interaction, and school achievement among many others. As a psychology student, you're probably interested in these subjects as well. But to what extent should you believe the information you read online? Journalists who write about psychological science should simply report what the researchers did and why the study was important, but sometimes they misrepresent or overstate the research findings. They may do so either unintentionally, because they lack the appropriate training to properly critique the findings, or intentionally, to draw readers' attention. Even an empirical journal article could overstate a study's findings. When writers make unsupported claims about what a particular study means, it's kind of like wrapping an unexciting gift in fancy paper (**Figure 3.1**).

Your research methods course will help you understand both popular and research-based articles at a more sophisticated level. You can learn how to raise the appropriate questions for interrogating the study that is being used to support a writer's claims about

LEARNING OBJECTIVES

A year from now, you should still be able to:

1.
Differentiate the three types of claims: frequency, association, and causal.

2.
Ask appropriate questions to help you interrogate each of the four big validities: construct validity, statistical validity, external validity, and internal validity.

3.
Explain which validities are most relevant for each of the three types of claims.

4.
State which kind of research study is required to support a causal claim.

FIGURE 3.1
Studies may not match the claims made about them.

Journalists and researchers sometimes make claims about the meaning of research results. When a study has been "wrapped up" in a dramatic headline, the research inside might not live up to the expectations. Does the study support the headline in which a writer has wrapped it?

human behavior. By extension, the skills you use to evaluate information behind the research will also help you plan your own studies if you intend to become a producer of information.

Think of this chapter as a scaffold. All the research information in later chapters will have a place in the framework of three claims and four validities presented here. The three types of claims—frequency claims, association claims, and causal claims—make statements about variables or about relationships between variables. Therefore, learning some basics about variables comes first.

VARIABLES

Variables are the core unit of psychological research. A **variable**, as the word implies, is something that varies, so it must have at least two **levels**, or *values*.

Take this headline: "72% of the world smiled yesterday." Here, "whether a person smiled yesterday" is the variable, and its levels are a person smiling yesterday and a person not smiling yesterday. Similarly, the study that inspired the statement "People with higher incomes spend less time socializing" contains two variables: income (whose levels might be low, medium, and high) and the amount of time people spend socializing (with levels ranging from 0 to 7 evenings per week). In contrast if a study concluded that "15% of Americans smoke," nationality is not a variable because everyone in the study is American. In this example, nationality would be a constant, not a variable. A **constant** is something that could potentially vary but that has only one level in the study in question. (In this example, "smoking" would be a variable, and its levels would be smoker and nonsmoker.)

Measured and Manipulated Variables

The researchers in any study either measure or manipulate each variable. The distinction is important because some claims are tested with measured variables, while other claims must be tested with both measured and manipulated variables. A **measured variable** is one whose levels are simply observed and recorded. Some variables, such as height and IQ, are measured using familiar tools (a ruler, a test). Other variables, such as gender and hair color, are also said to be "measured." To measure abstract variables, such as depression and stress, researchers might devise a special set of questions to represent the various levels. In each case, measuring a variable is a matter of recording an observation, a statement, or a value as it occurs naturally.

In contrast, a **manipulated variable** is a variable a researcher controls, usually by assigning study participants to the different levels of that variable. For example, a researcher might give some participants 10 milligrams of a medication, others 20 mg, and still others 30 mg. Or a researcher might assign some people to take a test in a room with many other people and assign others to take the test alone.

In both examples, the participants could end up at any of the levels because the researchers do the manipulating, assigning participants to be at one level of the variable or another.

Some variables cannot be manipulated—they can only be measured. Age can't be manipulated because researchers can't assign people to be older or younger; they can only measure what age they already are. IQ is another variable that can't be manipulated; researchers cannot assign some people to have a high IQ and others to have a low IQ; they can only measure each person's IQ. Even if the researchers choose the 10% of people with the highest IQ and the 10% with the lowest IQ, it is still a measured variable because people cannot be assigned to the highest or lowest 10%.

Other variables cannot be manipulated because it would be unethical to do so. For example, in a study on the long-term effects of elementary education, you could not ethically assign children to "high-quality school" and "low-quality school" conditions. Nor could you ethically assign people to conditions that put their physical or emotional well-being at risk.

« For a complete discussion of ethical guidelines in research, see Chapter 4.

Some variables, however, can be either manipulated or measured, depending on the goals of a study. If childhood extracurricular activities were the variable of interest, you could *measure* whether children already take music or drama lessons, or you could *manipulate* this variable if you assigned some children to take music lessons and others to take drama lessons. If you wanted to study hair color, you could *measure* this trait by recording whether people have, for instance, blond, brown, or black hair. You could also *manipulate* this variable if you assigned some willing people to dye their hair one color or the other.

From Conceptual Variable to Operational Definition

Each variable in a study can be described in two ways (**Table 3.1**). When researchers are discussing their theories and when journalists write about research, they use concept-level language. **Conceptual variables** are abstract concepts, such as "spending time socializing" and "school achievement." A conceptual variable is sometimes called a **construct**. Conceptual variables must be carefully defined at the theoretical level, and these definitions are called **conceptual definitions**. To test hypotheses, researchers have to do something specific in order to gather data. When testing their hypotheses with empirical research, they create **operational definitions** of variables, also known as **operational variables**, or *operationalizations*. To **operationalize** means to turn a concept of interest into a measured or manipulated variable.

For example, a researcher's interest in the conceptual variable "spending time socializing" might be operationalized as a structured question, in which people tell an interviewer how often they spend an evening alone, socialize with friends, or see relatives in a typical week. Alternatively, the same concept might

TABLE 3.1

Describing Variables

VARIABLE NAME (CONCEPTUAL VARIABLE)	OPERATIONAL DEFINITION (ONE POSSIBILITY)	LEVELS OF THIS VARIABLE	IS THE VARIABLE MEASURED OR MANIPULATED IN THIS CONTEXT?
Car ownership	Researchers asked people to circle "I own a car" or "I do not" on their questionnaire.	2 levels: own a car or not	Measured
Expressing gratitude to romantic partner	Researchers asked people in relationships the extent to which they agree with items such as "I tell my partner often that s/he is the best."	7 levels, from 1 (strongly disagree) to 7 (strongly agree)	Measured
Type of story told about a scientist	Researchers assigned participants to read stories about Einstein and Curie, which related either their work struggles or their achievements.	2 levels: a story about a scientist's struggles and a story about a scientist's achievements	Manipulated
What time children eat dinner	Using a daily food diary, researchers had children write down what time they ate dinner each evening.	Researchers divided children into two groups: those who ate dinner between 2 P.M. and 8 P.M., and those who ate after 8 P.M.	Measured

be operationalized by having people keep a diary for one month, recording which nights they spent with relatives or friends and which nights they were alone.

Sometimes this operationalization step is simple and straightforward. For example, a researcher interested in a conceptual variable such as "weight gain" in laboratory rats would probably just weigh them. Or a researcher who was interested in the conceptual variable "income" might operationalize this variable by asking each person about their total income last year. In these two cases, the researcher can operationalize the conceptual variable of interest quite easily.

Often, however, concepts researchers wish to study are difficult to see, touch, or feel, so they are also harder to operationalize. Examples are personality traits, states such as "argumentativeness," and behavior judgments such as "attempted suicide." The more abstract nature of these conceptual variables does not stop psychologists from operationalizing them; it just makes studying them a little harder. In such cases, researchers spend extra time clarifying and defining the conceptual variables they plan to study. They might develop creative or elegant operational definitions to capture the variable of interest.

Most often, variables are stated at the conceptual level. To discover how the variable "school achievement" was operationalized, you need to ask: How did the researchers measure "school achievement" in this study? To determine how a

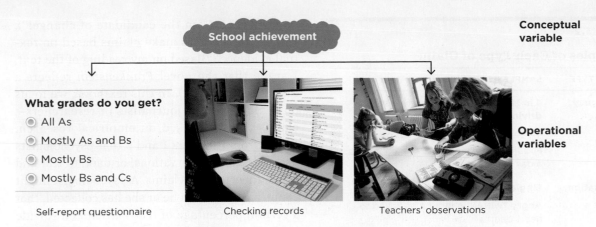

School achievement

What grades do you get?

- ○ All As
- ○ Mostly As and Bs
- ○ Mostly Bs
- ○ Mostly Bs and Cs

Self-report questionnaire

Checking records

Teachers' observations

Operational variables

FIGURE 3.2
Operationalizing "school achievement."
A single conceptual variable can be operationalized in a number of ways.

variable such as "frequency of worrying" was operationalized, ask: How did researchers measure "worrying" in this research? **Figure 3.2** shows how the first variable might be operationalized.

CHECK YOUR UNDERSTANDING

1. What is the difference between a variable and its levels? What might be the levels of the variable "favorite color"?

2. Explain why some variables can only be measured, not manipulated. Can "gender" be a manipulated variable? Can "frequency of worrying" be a manipulated variable?

3. What is the difference between a conceptual variable and the operational definition of a variable? How might the conceptual variables "frequency of worrying," "intelligence," and "stress" be operationalized by a researcher?

1. See p. 58. 2. See pp. 58–59. "Gender" is probably not a manipulated variable, but "frequency of worrying" might be manipulated if researchers assigned some people to purposely worry about something. 3. See pp. 59–61.

THREE CLAIMS

A **claim** is an argument someone is trying to make. Internet bloggers might make claims based on personal experience or observation ("The media coverage of congressional candidates has been sexist"). Politicians might make claims based

TABLE 3.2

Examples of Each Type of Claim

CLAIM TYPE	SAMPLE HEADLINES
Frequency claims	**4 in 10 teens admit to texting while driving** 42% of Europeans never exercise Middle school kids see 2–4 alcohol ads a day
Association claims	**Single people eat fewer vegetables** Angry Twitter communities linked to heart deaths Girls more likely to be compulsive texters Suffering a concussion could triple the risk of suicide
Causal claims	**Music lessons enhance IQ** Babysitting may prime brain for parenting Family meals curb eating disorders Why sleep deprivation makes you crabby

on rhetoric ("I am the candidate of change!"). Literature scholars make claims based on textual evidence ("Based on my reading of the text, I argue that the novel *Frankenstein* reflects a fear of technology"). In this textbook, we focus on claims made by journalists or researchers—claims that are based on empirical research. Recall from Chapters 1 and 2 that psychologists use systematic observations, or data, to test and refine theories and claims. A psychologist might claim, based on data he or she has collected, that a certain percentage of teens attempted suicide last year, or that higher-income people spend less time socializing, or that music lessons can improve a child's IQ.

Notice the different wording in the boldface headlines in **Table 3.2**. In particular, the first claim merely gives a percentage of teens who texted while driving; this is a *frequency claim*. The claim in the middle, about single people eating fewer vegetables, is an *association claim*: It suggests that the two variables go together, but does not claim that being single causes people to eat fewer vegetables or that eating fewer vegetables causes people to be single. The last boldface claim, however, is a *causal claim*: The verb *enhance* indicates that the music lessons actually cause improved IQ. The kind of claim a psychological scientist makes must be backed up by the right kind of study. How can you identify the types of claims researchers make, and how can you evaluate whether their studies are able to support each type of claim? If you conduct research yourself, how will you know what kind of study will support the type of claim you wish to make?

Frequency Claims

Two Out of Five Americans Say They Worry Every Day
Just 15% of Americans Smoke
72% of the World Smiled Yesterday
4 in 10 Teens Admit to Texting While Driving

Frequency claims describe a particular rate or degree of a single variable. In the first example above, "two out of five" is the frequency of worrying among people in the United States. In the second example, "15%" is the rate (the proportion) of American adults who smoke. These headlines claim how frequent or common something is. Claims that mention the percentage of a variable, the number of people who engage in some activity, or a certain group's level on a variable can all be called frequency claims.

The best way to identify frequency claims is that they focus on only one variable—such as frequency of worrying, rate of smiling, or amount of texting. In addition, in studies that support frequency claims, the variables are always measured, not manipulated. In the examples above, the researchers have measured the frequency of worrying by using a questionnaire or an interview and have reported the results.

Some reports give a list of single-variable results, all of which count as frequency claims. Take, for example, the recent report from Gallup stating that 72% of the world smiled yesterday (Gallup.com, 2016). The same report also found that 51% of people said they learned something interesting yesterday. These are two separate frequency claims—they each measured a single variable one at a time. The researchers were not trying to show an association between these single variables; the report did not claim the people who learned something interesting were more likely to smile. It simply stated that a certain percentage of the world's people smiled and a certain percentage learned something interesting.

Association Claims

People with Higher Incomes Spend Less Time Socializing
Romantic Partners Who Express Gratitude Are Three Times More Likely to Stay
    Together
People Who Multitask the Most Are the Worst at It
A Late Dinner Is Not Linked to Childhood Obesity, Study Shows

These headlines are all examples of association claims. An **association claim** argues that one level of a variable is likely to be associated with a particular level of another variable. Variables that are associated are sometimes said to **correlate**, or *covary*, meaning that when one variable changes, the other variable tends to change, too. More simply, they may be said to be *related*.

Notice that there are two variables in each example above. In the first, the variables are income and spending time socializing: Having a higher income is associated with spending less time socializing (and therefore having a lower income goes with spending more time socializing). In the second example, the variables are the frequency of expressing gratitude and the likelihood of staying together: More frequent gratitude goes with a longer relationship.

An association claim states a relationship between at least two variables. In order to support an association claim, the researcher usually measures the two variables and determines whether they're associated. This type of study, in which the variables are measured and the relationship between them is tested, is called

《
For more on correlation patterns, see Chapter 8.

FIGURE 3.3
Correlational studies support association claims.

When a journalist makes an association claim, it's usually based on a correlational study, in which two or more variables were measured.

a **correlational study**. Therefore, when you unwrap an association claim, you should find a correlational study supporting it (**Figure 3.3**).

There are three basic types of associations among variables: positive associations, negative associations, and zero associations.

POSITIVE ASSOCIATION

The headline "Romantic partners who express gratitude are three times more likely to stay together" is an association in which high goes with high and low goes with low, and it's called a **positive association**, or *positive correlation*. Stated another way, high scores on gratitude go with staying together longer, and low scores on gratitude go with a shorter time together.

One way to represent an association is to use a **scatterplot**, a graph in which one variable is plotted on the y-axis and the other variable is plotted on the x-axis; each dot represents one participant in the study, measured on the two variables. **Figure 3.4** shows what scatterplots of the associations in three of the example headlines would look like. (Data are fabricated for illustration purposes, and numbers are arbitrary units.) Notice that the dots in **Figure 3.4A** form a cloud of points, as opposed to a straight line. If you drew a straight line through the center of the cloud of points, however, the line would incline upward; in other words, the mathematical slope of the line would be positive.

NEGATIVE ASSOCIATION

The study behind the claim "People who multitask the most are the worst at it" obtained a negative association. In a **negative association** (or *negative correlation*), high goes with low and low goes with high. In other words, high rates of multitasking go with a low ability to multitask, and low rates of multitasking go with a high ability to multitask.

A scatterplot representing this association would look something like the one in **Figure 3.4B**. Each dot represents a person who has been measured on two variables. However, in this example, a line drawn through the cloud of points would slope downward; it would have a negative slope.

Keep in mind that the word *negative* refers only to the slope; it does not mean the association is somehow bad. In this example, the reverse of the association—that people who multitask the least are the best at it—is another way to phrase this negative association. To avoid this kind of confusion, some people prefer the term *inverse association*.

ZERO ASSOCIATION

The study behind the headline "A late dinner is not linked to childhood obesity, study shows" is an example of a **zero association**, or no association between the variables (*zero correlation*). In a scatterplot, both early and late levels of dinner time are associated with all levels of obesity (**Figure 3.4C**). This cloud of points has

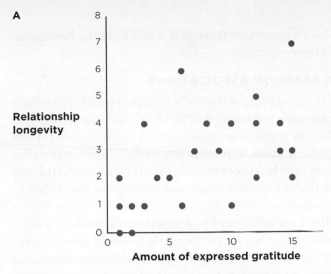

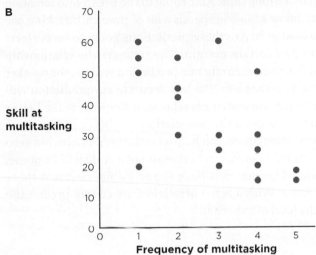

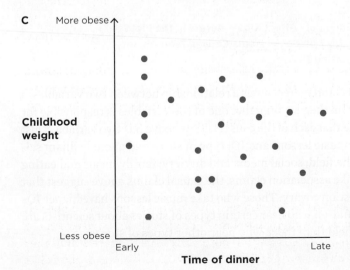

FIGURE 3.4
**Scatterplots showing three types
of associations.**

(A) Positive association: "Romantic partners who express gratitude are more likely to stay together." (B) Negative association: "People who multitask the most are the worst at it." (C) Zero association: "A late dinner is not linked to childhood obesity, study shows." Data are fabricated for illustration purposes.

no slope—or more specifically, a line drawn through it would be nearly horizontal, and a horizontal line has a slope of zero.

MAKING PREDICTIONS BASED ON ASSOCIATIONS

Some association claims are useful because they help us make predictions. Which couples are going to stay together the longest? Who's likely to have poor multitasking skill? With a positive or negative association, if we know the level of one variable, we can more accurately guess, or predict, the level of the other variable. Note that the word *predict*, as used here, does not necessarily mean predicting into the future. It means predicting in a mathematical sense—using the association to make our estimates more accurate.

To return to the headlines, according to the positive association described in the first example, if we know how much gratitude a couple is showing, we can predict how long they will stay together, and if a couple expresses a lot of gratitude, we might predict they'll be together a long time. According to the negative association in the second example, if we know someone spends a lot of time multitasking, we can predict she'll be less skilled at it. Are these predictions going to be perfect? No—they will usually be off by a certain margin. The stronger the relationship between the two variables, the more accurate our prediction will be; the weaker the relationship between the two variables, the less accurate our prediction will be. But if two variables are even somewhat correlated, it helps us make better predictions than if we didn't know about this association.

Both positive and negative associations can help us make predictions, but zero associations cannot. If we wanted to predict whether or not a child will be obese, we could not do so just by knowing what time he or she eats dinner because these two variables are not correlated. With a zero correlation, we cannot predict the level of one variable from the level of the other.

» For more on predictions from correlations, see Chapter 8, pp. 212–213.

Causal Claims

Music Lessons Enhance IQ

Stories Told of Brilliant Scientists Affect Kids' Interest in the Field

Pressure to Be Available 24/7 on Social Media Causes Teen Anxiety

Family Meals Curb Teen Eating Disorders

Whereas an association claim merely notes a relationship between two variables, a **causal claim** goes even further, arguing that one of the variables is responsible for changing the other. Note that each of the causal claims above has two variables, just like association claims: music lessons and IQ; type of story told about brilliant scientists and interest in the field; social media and anxiety; family meals and eating disorders. In addition, like association claims, the causal claims above suggest that the two variables in question covary: Those who take music lessons have higher IQs that those who don't; children who hear certain types of stories about scientists are more interested in the field than those who hear other types of stories.

Causal claims start with a positive or negative association. Music lessons are positively associated with IQ, and social media pressure is associated with anxiety. Occasionally you might also see a causal claim based on a zero association; it would report lack of cause. For example, you might read that vaccines do not cause autism or that daycare does not cause behavior problems.

Causal claims, however, go beyond a simple association between the two variables. They use language suggesting that one variable causes the other—verbs such as *cause*, *enhance*, *affect*, and *change*. In contrast, association claims use verbs such as *link*, *associate*, *correlate*, *predict*, *tie to*, and *being at risk for*. In **Table 3.3**, notice the difference between these types of verbs and verb phrases. Causal verbs tend to be more exciting; they are active and forceful, suggesting that one variable comes first in time and acts on the other variable. It's not surprising, then, that journalists may be tempted to describe family dinners as *curbing* eating disorders, for example, because it makes a better story than family meals just *being associated with* eating disorders.

TABLE 3.3

Verb Phrases That Distinguish Association and Causal Claims

ASSOCIATION CLAIM VERBS	CAUSAL CLAIM VERBS	
is linked to	causes	promotes
is at higher risk for	affects	reduces
is associated with	may curb	prevents
is correlated with	exacerbates	distracts
prefers	changes	fights
are more/less likely to	may lead to	worsens
may predict	makes	increases
is tied to	sometimes makes	trims
goes with	hurts	adds

Here's another important point: A causal claim that contains tentative language—*could*, *may*, *seem*, *suggest*, *sometimes*, *potentially*—is still considered a causal claim. If the first headline read "Music lessons *may* enhance IQ," it would be more tentative, and you should assume a causal claim. The verb *enhance* makes it a causal claim, regardless of any softening or qualifying language.

Advice is also a causal claim; it implies that if you do X, then Y will happen. For example: "Best way to deal with jerks? Give them the cold shoulder." "Want to boost brain power? Do yoga."

Causal claims are a step above association claims. Because they make a stronger statement, we hold them to higher standards. To move from the simple language of association to the language of causality, a study has to satisfy three criteria. First, it must establish that the two variables (the causal variable and the outcome variable) are correlated; the relationship cannot be zero. Second, it must show that the causal variable came first and the outcome variable came later. Third, it must establish that no other explanations exist for the relationship. Therefore, when we unwrap a causal claim, we must be sure the study inside can support it. Later in this chapter, you will learn that only one type of study, an experiment, can enable researchers to support a causal claim because it meets all three criteria.

Not All Claims Are Based on Research

Besides the types of claims mentioned above, you may also encounter stories in the popular media that are not based on research, even if they are related to psychology. For instance:

12-Year-Old's Insight on Autism and Vaccines Goes Viral
Living in the Shadow of Huntington's Disease
Baby Born Without Skull in the Back of His Head Defies Odds

Such headlines do not report the results of research. They may describe a person's solution to a problem, an inspiring story, or an expert's advice, but they don't say anything about the frequency of a problem or what research has been shown to work. The Huntington's piece is about a single person's experience with an inherited condition that involves the breakdown of nerve cells in the brain, but it is not suggesting a treatment. The account of the baby's survival is uplifting, but it doesn't report systematic research about the outcomes of babies with different birth conditions. Stories like these show what *can* happen, but not how often it happens, or when, or why.

These kinds of headlines may be interesting, and they might be related to psychology, but they are not frequency, association, or causal claims, in which a writer summarizes the results of a poll, survey, or other research study. Such anecdotes are about isolated experiences, not empirical studies. And as you read in Chapter 2, experience is not as good a source of information as empirical research.

CHECK YOUR UNDERSTANDING

1. How many variables are there in a frequency claim? An association claim? A causal claim?

2. Which part of speech in a claim can help you differentiate between association and causal claims?

3. How are causal claims special, compared with the other two claim types?

4. What are the three criteria causal claims must satisfy?

1. See pp. 62–64 and 66–67. 2. The verbs matter; see pp. 66–67 3. See Table 3.3. 4. See p. 67.

INTERROGATING THE THREE CLAIMS USING THE FOUR BIG VALIDITIES

You now have the tools to differentiate the three major claims you'll encounter in research journals and the popular media—but your job is just beginning. Once you identify the kind of claim a writer is making, you need to ask targeted questions as a critically minded consumer of information. The rest of this chapter will sharpen your ability to evaluate the claims you come across, using what we'll call the four big validities: construct validity, external validity, statistical validity, and internal validity. **Validity** refers to the appropriateness of a conclusion or decision, and in general, a *valid* claim is reasonable, accurate, and justifiable. In psychological research, however, we do not say a claim is simply "valid." Instead, psychologists specify which of the validities they are applying. As a psychology student, you will learn to pause before you declare a study to be "valid" or "not valid," and to specify which of the four big validities the study has achieved.

Although the focus for now is on how to evaluate other people's claims based on the four big validities, you'll also be using this same framework if you plan to conduct your own research. Depending on whether you decide to test a frequency claim, an association claim, or a causal claim, it is essential to plan your research carefully, emphasizing the validities that are most important for your goals.

Interrogating Frequency Claims

To evaluate how well a study supports a frequency claim, you will focus on two of the big validities: construct validity and external validity. You may decide to ask about statistical validity, too.

CONSTRUCT VALIDITY OF FREQUENCY CLAIMS

Construct validity refers to how well a conceptual variable is operationalized. When evaluating the construct validity of a frequency claim, the question is how well the researchers measured their variables. Consider this claim: "4 in 10 teens admit to texting while driving." There are several ways to measure this variable. You could ask teenagers to tell you on an online survey how often they engage in text messaging while they're behind the wheel. You could stand near an intersection and record the behaviors of teenage drivers. You could even use cell phone records to see if a text was sent at the same time a person was known to be driving. In other words, there are a number of ways to operationalize such a variable, and some are better than others.

When you ask how well a study measured or manipulated a variable, you are interrogating the construct validity: how accurately a researcher has operationalized each variable—be it smiling, exercising, texting, gender identity, body mass index, or self-esteem. For example, you would expect a study on obesity rates to use an accurate scale to weigh participants. Similarly, you should expect a study about texting among teenagers to use an accurate measure, and observing behavior is probably a better way than casually asking, "Have you ever texted while driving?" To ensure construct validity, researchers must establish that each variable has been measured reliably (meaning the measure yields similar scores on repeated testings) and that different levels of a variable accurately correspond to true differences in, say, depression or happiness. (For more detail on construct validity, see Chapter 5.)

EXTERNAL VALIDITY OF FREQUENCY CLAIMS

The next important questions to ask about frequency claims concern **generalizability**: How did the researchers choose the study's participants, and how well do those participants represent the intended population? Consider the example "72% of the world smiled yesterday." Did Gallup researchers survey every one of the world's 7 billion people to come up with this number? Of course not. They surveyed only a small sample of people. Next you ask: Which people did they survey, and how did they choose their participants? Did they include only people in major urban areas? Did they ask only college students from each country? Or did they attempt to randomly select people from every region of the world?

Such questions address the study's **external validity** how well the results of a study generalize to, or represent, people or contexts besides those in the original study. If Gallup researchers had simply asked people who visited the Gallup website whether they smiled yesterday, and 72% of them said they did, the researcher cannot claim that 72% of the entire world smiled. The researcher cannot even argue that 72% of Gallup website visitors smiled because the people who choose to answer such questions may not be an accurate representation. Indeed, to claim that 72% of the world smiled yesterday, the researchers would have needed to ensure that the participants in the sample adequately represented all people in the world—a daunting task! Gallup's Global Emotions Report states that their sample included adults in each of 140 countries who were interviewed by phone or in person (Gallup.com, 2016). The researchers attempted to obtain representative samples in each country (excluding very remote or politically unstable areas of certain countries).

» For more on the procedures that researchers use to ensure external validity, see Chapter 7, pp. 186–191.

STATISTICAL VALIDITY OF FREQUENCY CLAIMS

Researchers use statistics to analyze their data. **Statistical validity**, also called *statistical conclusion validity*, is the extent to which a study's statistical conclusions are accurate and reasonable. How well do the numbers support the claim?

Statistical validity questions will vary depending on the claim. Asking about the statistical validity of a frequency claim involves reminding yourself that the number associated with the claim is an estimate, and it has a specific amount of error associated with it. The percentage reported in a frequency claim is usually accompanied by a **margin of error of the estimate**. This is a statistical figure, based on sample size for the study, that attempts to include the true value in the population. For example, in the report about how many teenagers text while driving, the Centers for Disease Control's 41% value was accompanied by this note: "The margin of error is +/–2.6 percentage points" (CDC, n.d.). The margin of error helps us describe how well our sample estimates the true percentage. Specifically, the range, 38.4–43.6%, is highly likely to contain the true percentage of teens who text while driving.

Interrogating Association Claims

As mentioned earlier, studies that are able to support association claims are called correlational studies: They measure two variables instead of just one. Such studies describe how these variables are related to each other. To interrogate an association claim, you ask how well the correlational study behind the claim supports construct, external, and statistical validities.

CONSTRUCT VALIDITY OF ASSOCIATION CLAIMS

To support an association claim, a researcher measures two variables, so you have to assess the construct validity of *each* variable. For the headline "People who multitask the most are the worst at it," you should ask how well the researchers measured the frequency of multitasking and how well they measured the ability to multitask. The first variable, frequency of multitasking, could be measured accurately by asking people to document their day or by observing people during the day and recording times when they are multitasking. The second variable, ability to multitask, could be measured accurately using a computer-scored exercise that involves doing two things at once; a less accurate measure would be obtained by asking people how good they are at multitasking.

In any study, measuring variables is a fundamental strength or weakness—and construct validity questions assess how well such measurements were conducted. If you conclude one of the variables was measured poorly, you would not be able to trust the conclusions related to that variable. However, if you conclude the construct validity in the study was excellent, you can have more confidence in the association claim being reported.

EXTERNAL VALIDITY OF ASSOCIATION CLAIMS

You might also interrogate the external validity of an association claim by asking whether it can generalize to other populations, as well as to other contexts, times, or places. For the association between expressing gratitude and relationship length, you would ask whether the results from this study's participants, 194 California college students currently in a romantic relationship, would generalize to other people and settings. Would the same results be obtained if all of the participants were midwestern couples 45 or older? You can evaluate generalizability to other contexts by asking, for example, whether the link between gratitude and relationship length also exists in friendships. (**Table 3.4** summarizes the four big validities used in this text.)

STATISTICAL VALIDITY OF ASSOCIATION CLAIMS: STRENGTH AND SIGNIFICANCE

When applied to an association claim, statistical validity is the extent to which the statistical conclusions are accurate and reasonable. One aspect of statistical validity is strength: How strong is the association? Some associations—such as the association between height and shoe size—are quite strong. People who are tall almost always have larger feet than people who are short, so if you predict shoe size from height, you will predict fairly accurately. Other associations—such as the

TABLE 3.4

The Four Big Validities

TYPE OF VALIDITY	DESCRIPTION
Construct validity	How well the variables in a study are measured or manipulated.
	The extent to which the operational variables in a study are a good approximation of the conceptual variables.
External validity	The extent to which the results of a study generalize to some larger population (e.g., whether the results from this sample of children apply to all U.S. schoolchildren), as well as to other times or situations (e.g., whether the results based on this type of music apply to other types of music).
Statistical validity	The extent to which the data support the conclusions. Among many other questions, it is important to ask about the strength of an association and its statistical significance (the probability that the results could have been obtained by chance if there really is no relationship).
Internal validity	In a relationship between one variable (A) and another (B), the extent to which A, rather than some other variable (C), is responsible for changes in B.

association between height and income—might be very weak. In fact, because of a stereotype that favors tall people (tall people are more admired in North America), taller people do earn more money than short people, but the relationship is not very strong. Though you can predict income from height, your prediction will be less accurate than predicting shoe size from height.

Another question worth interrogating is the statistical significance of a particular association. Some associations obtained in a study might simply be due to chance connections in that particular sample caused by a few individuals. However, if an association is statistically significant, it is probably *not* due to chance characteristics in that one sample. For example, because the association between gratitude and relationship length is statistically significant, it means the association is probably not a chance result from that sample alone.

» For more about association strength and statistical significance, see Chapter 8, pp. 205–207 and pp. 214–217.

STATISTICAL VALIDITY OF ASSOCIATION CLAIMS: AVOIDING TWO MISTAKEN CONCLUSIONS

As you might imagine, evaluating statistical validity can be complicated. Full training in how to interrogate statistical validity requires a separate, semester-long statistics class. This book introduces you to the basics, and we will focus mainly on asking about statistical significance and the strength of an effect.

It's also worth mentioning that statistical validity involves two kinds of mistakes. First, a study might mistakenly conclude, based on the results from a sample of people, that there is an association between two variables (e.g., gratitude and relationship length), when there really is *no* association in the full population. Careful researchers try to minimize the chances of making this kind of mistake, known as a "false positive," or **Type I error**. They want to increase the chances of finding associations only when they are really there.

Second, a study might mistakenly conclude from a sample that there is no association between two variables (e.g., dinner time and obesity), when there really *is* an association in the full population. Careful researchers try to minimize the chances of making this kind of mistake, too; it's known as a "miss," or **Type II error**. Obviously, they want to reduce the chances of missing associations that are really there.

«

For more on Type I and Type II errors, see Statistics Review: Inferential Statistics. pp. 484–490.

In sum, when you come across an association claim, you should ask about three validities: construct, external, and statistical. You can ask how well the two variables were measured (construct validity). You can ask whether you can generalize the result to a population (external validity). And you can evaluate the strength and significance of the association (statistical validity).

Table 3.5 gives an overview of the three claims, four validities framework. Before reading about how to interrogate causal claims, use the table to review what we've covered so far.

TABLE 3.5

Interrogating the Three Types of Claims Using the Four Big Validities

TYPE OF VALIDITY	FREQUENCY CLAIMS ("4 IN 10 TEENS ADMIT TO TEXTING WHILE DRIVING")	ASSOCIATION CLAIMS ("PEOPLE WITH HIGHER INCOMES SPEND LESS TIME SOCIALIZING")	CAUSAL CLAIMS ("MUSIC LESSONS ENHANCE IQ")
	Usually based on a survey or poll, but can come from other types of studies	Usually supported by a correlational study	Must be supported by an experimental study
Construct validity	How well has the researcher measured the variable in question?	How well has the researcher measured each of the two variables in the association?	How well has the researcher measured or manipulated the variables in the study?
Statistical validity	What is the margin of error of the estimate?	What is the effect size? How strong is the association? Is the association statistically significant? If the study finds a relationship, what is the probability the researcher's conclusion is a false positive? If the study finds no relationship, what is the probability the researcher is missing a true relationship?	What is the effect size? Is there a difference between groups, and how large is it? Is the difference statistically significant?
Internal validity	Frequency claims are usually not asserting causality, so internal validity is not relevant.	People who make association claims are not asserting causality, so internal validity is not relevant to interrogate. A researcher should avoid making a causal claim from a simple association, however (see Chapter 8).	Was the study an experiment? Does the study achieve temporal precedence? Does the study control for alternative explanations by randomly assigning participants to groups? Does the study avoid several internal validity threats (see Chapters 10 and 11)?
External validity	To what populations, settings, and times can we generalize this estimate? How representative is the sample—was it a random sample?	To what populations, settings, and times can we generalize this association claim? How representative is the sample? To what other problems might the association be generalized?	To what populations, settings, and times can we generalize this causal claim? How representative is the sample? How representative are the manipulations and measures?

Interrogating Causal Claims

An association claim says that two variables are related, but a causal claim goes beyond, saying that one variable causes the other. Instead of using such verb phrases as *is associated with, is related to,* and *is linked to,* causal claims use directional verbs such as *affects, leads to,* and *reduces.* When you interrogate such a claim, your first step will be to make sure it is backed up by research that fulfills the three criteria for causation: covariance, temporal precedence, and internal validity.

THREE CRITERIA FOR CAUSATION

Of course, one variable usually cannot be said to cause another variable unless the two are related. **Covariance**, the extent to which two variables are observed to go together, is determined by the results of a study. It is the first criterion a study must satisfy in order to establish a causal claim. But to justify using a causal verb, the study must not only have results showing that two variables are associated. The research method must also satisfy two additional criteria: temporal precedence and internal validity (**Table 3.6**).

To say that one variable has **temporal precedence** means it comes first in time, before the other variable. To make the claim "Music lessons enhance IQ," a study must show that the music lessons came first and the higher IQ came later. Although this statement might seem obvious, it is not always so. In a simple association, it might be the case that music lessons made the children smart, but it is also possible that children who start out smart are more likely to want to take music lessons. It's not always clear which one came first. Similarly, to make the claim "Pressure to be available 24/7 on social media causes teen anxiety," the study needs to show that social media pressure came first and the anxiety came later.

Another criterion, called **internal validity**, or the *third-variable criterion,* is an indication of a study's ability to eliminate alternative explanations for the

---

TABLE 3.6

Three Criteria for Establishing Causation Between Variable A and Variable B

CRITERION	DEFINITION
Covariance	The study's results show that as A changes, B changes; e.g., high levels of A go with high levels of B, and low levels of A go with low levels of B.
Temporal precedence	The study's method ensures that A comes first in time, before B.
Internal validity	The study's method ensures that there are no plausible alternative explanations for the change in B; A is the only thing that changed.

association. For example, to say "Music lessons enhance IQ" is to claim that music lessons *cause* increased IQ. But an alternative explanation could be that certain kinds of parents both encourage academic achievement (leading to higher IQ scores) *and* encourage their kids to take music lessons. In other words, there could be an internal validity problem: It is a certain type of parent, not the music lessons, that causes these children to score higher on IQ tests. In Chapter 2 you read that basing conclusions on personal experience is subject to confounds. Such confounds are also called internal validity problems.

EXPERIMENTS CAN SUPPORT CAUSAL CLAIMS

What kind of study can satisfy all three criteria for causal claims? Usually, to support a causal claim, researchers must conduct a well-designed **experiment**, in which one variable is manipulated and the other is measured.

Experiments are considered the gold standard of psychological research because of their potential to support causal claims. In daily life, people tend to use the word *experiment* casually, referring to any trial of something to see what happens ("Let's experiment and try making the popcorn with olive oil instead"). In science, including psychology, an experiment is more than just "a study." When psychologists conduct an experiment, they *manipulate* the variable they think is the cause and *measure* the variable they think is the effect (or outcome). In the context of an experiment, the manipulated variable is called the **independent variable** and the measured variable is called the **dependent variable**. To support the claim that music lessons enhance IQ, the researchers in that study would have had to manipulate the music lessons variable and measure the IQ variable.

« For examples of independent and dependent variables, see Chapter 10, p. 277.

Remember: To *manipulate* a variable means to assign participants to be at one level or the other. In the music example, the researchers might assign some children to take music lessons, others to take another kind of lesson, and a third group to take no lessons. In an actual study that tested this claim in Toronto, Canada, researcher Glen Schellenberg (2004) manipulated the music lesson variable by having some children take music lessons (either keyboard or voice lessons), others take drama lessons, and still others take no lessons. After several months of lessons, he measured the IQs of all the children. At the conclusion of his study, Schellenberg found that the children who took keyboard and voice lessons gained an average of 3.7 IQ points more than the children who took drama lessons or no lessons (**Figure 3.5**). This

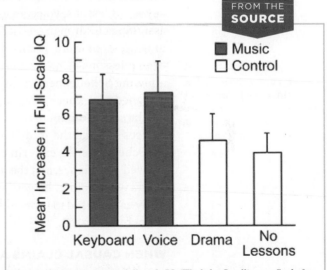

STRAIGHT FROM THE SOURCE

Fig. 1. Mean increase in full-scale IQ (Wechsler Intelligence Scale for Children–Third Edition) for each group of 6-year-olds who completed the study. Error bars show standard errors.

FIGURE 3.5
Interrogating a causal claim.

What key features of Schellenberg's study of music lessons and IQ made it possible for him to claim that music lessons increase children's IQ? (Source: Schellenberg, 2004.)

was a statistically significant gain, and the result therefore established the first part of a causal claim: covariance.

A Study's Method Can Establish Temporal Precedence and Internal Validity. Why does the method of manipulating one variable and measuring the other help scientists make causal claims? For one thing, manipulating the independent variable—the causal variable—ensures that it comes first. By manipulating music lessons and measuring IQ, Schellenberg ensured temporal precedence in his study.

In addition, when researchers manipulate a variable, they have the potential to control for alternative explanations; that is, they can ensure internal validity. When Schellenberg was investigating whether music lessons could enhance IQ, he did not want the children in the music lessons groups to have more involved parents than those in the drama lessons group or the no-lessons group because then parental involvement would have been a plausible alternative explanation for why the music lessons enhanced IQ. He didn't want the children in the music lessons groups to come from a different school district than those in the drama lessons group or the no-lessons group because then the school curriculum or teacher quality might have been an alternative explanation.

Therefore, Schellenberg used a technique called **random assignment** to ensure that the children in all the groups were as similar as possible. He used a method, such as rolling a die, to decide whether each child in his study would take keyboard lessons, voice lessons, drama lessons, or no lessons. Only by randomly assigning children to one of the groups could Schellenberg ensure those who took music lessons were as similar as possible, in every other way, to those who took drama lessons or no lessons. Random assignment increased internal validity by allowing Schellenberg to control for potential alternative explanations. He also designed the experiment so the children were engaged in their respective lessons for the same amount of time, over the same number of weeks. These methodology choices secured the study's internal validity.

» For more on how random assignment helps ensure that experimental groups are similar, see Chapter 10, pp. 284–286.

Schellenberg's experiment met all three criteria of causation. The results showed covariance, and the method established temporal precedence and internal validity. Therefore, he was justified in making a causal claim from his data. His study can be used to support the claim that music lessons really do enhance—*cause* an increase in—IQ.

WHEN CAUSAL CLAIMS ARE A MISTAKE

Let's use two other examples to illustrate how to interrogate causal claims made by writers and journalists.

Do Family Meals Really Curb Eating Disorders? To interrogate the causal claim "Family meals curb teen eating disorders," we start by asking about covariance in the study behind this claim. Is there an association between family meals and eating disorders? Yes: The news report says 26% of girls who ate with their families fewer than five times a week had eating-disordered behavior (e.g., the use of laxatives or diuretics, or self-induced vomiting), and only 17% of girls who ate with their families five or more times a week engaged in eating-disordered behaviors (Warner, 2008). The two variables are associated.

What about temporal precedence? Did the researchers make sure family meals had increased before the eating disorders decreased? The best way to ensure temporal precedence is to assign some families to have more meals together than others. Sure, families who eat more meals together may have fewer daughters with eating-disordered behavior, but the temporal precedence is not clear from this association. In fact, one of the symptoms of an eating disorder is embarrassment about eating in front of others, so perhaps the eating disorder came first and the decreased family meals came second. Daughters with eating disorders may simply find excuses to avoid eating with their families.

Internal validity is a problem here, too. Without an experiment, we cannot rule out many alternative, third-variable explanations. Perhaps girls from single-parent families are less likely to eat with their families and are vulnerable to eating disorders, whereas girls who live with both parents are not. Maybe high-achieving girls are too busy to eat with their families and are also more susceptible to eating-disordered behavior. These are just two possible alternative explanations. Only a well-run experiment could have controlled for these internal validity problems (the alternative explanations), using random assignment to ensure that the girls who had frequent family dinners and those who had less-frequent family dinners were comparable in all other ways: high versus low scholastic achievement, single-parent versus two-parent households, and so on. However, it would be impractical and probably unethical to conduct such an experiment.

Although the study's authors reported the findings appropriately, the journalist wrapped the study's results in an eye-catching causal conclusion by saying that family dinners *curb* eating disorders (**Figure 3.6**). The journalist should probably have wrapped the study in the association claim, "Family dinners *are linked to* eating disorders."

Does Social Media Pressure Cause Teen Anxiety? Another example of a dubious causal claim is this headline: "Pressure to be available 24/7 on social media causes teen anxiety" In the story, the journalist reported on a study that measured two variables in a set of teenagers; one variable was social media use (especially the degree of pressure to respond to texts and posts) and the other was level of anxiety (Science News, 2015). The researchers found that those who felt pressure to respond immediately also had higher levels of anxiety.

Let's see if this study's design is adequate to support the journalist's conclusion—that social media pressure *causes* anxiety in teenagers. The study certainly does have covariance; the results showed that teens who felt more pressure to respond immediately to social media were also more anxious. However, this was a correlational study, in which both variables were measured at the same time, so there was no temporal precedence. We cannot know if the pressure to respond to social media increased first, thereby leading to increased anxiety, or

FIGURE 3.6
Only experiments should be wrapped in causal language.

When a journalist or researcher makes a causal claim, you need to be sure the right kind of study—an experiment—was conducted.

FIGURE 3.7

Support for a causal claim?

Without conducting an experiment, researchers cannot support the claim that social media pressure causes teen anxiety.

if teens who were already anxious expressed their anxiety through social media use, by putting pressure on themselves to respond immediately.

In addition, this study did not rule out possible alternative explanations (internal validity) because it was not an experiment. Several outside variables could potentially correlate with both anxiety and responding immediately to social media. One might be that teens who are involved in athletics are more relaxed (because exercise can reduce anxiety) and less engaged in social media (because busy schedules limit their time). Another might be that certain teenagers are vulnerable to emotional disorders in general; they are already more anxious *and* feel more pressure about the image they're presenting on social media (**Figure 3.7**).

An experiment could potentially rule out such alternative explanations. In this example, though, conducting an experiment would be hard. A researcher cannot randomly assign teens to be concerned about social media or to be anxious. Because the research was not enough to support a causal claim, the journalist should have packaged the description of the study under an association claim headline: "Social media pressure and teen anxiety are linked."

OTHER VALIDITIES TO INTERROGATE IN CAUSAL CLAIMS

A study can support a causal claim only if the results demonstrate covariance, and only if it used the experimental method, thereby establishing temporal precedence and internal validity. Therefore, internal validity is one of the most important validities to evaluate for causal claims. Besides internal validity, the other three validities discussed in this chapter—construct validity, statistical validity, and external validity—should be interrogated, too.

Construct Validity of Causal Claims. Take the headline, "Music lessons enhance IQ." First, we could ask about the construct validity of the measured variable in this study. How well was IQ measured? Was an established IQ test administered by trained testers? Then we would need to interrogate the construct validity of the manipulated variable as well. In operationalizing manipulated variables, researchers must create a specific task or situation that will represent each level of the variable. In the current example, how well did the researchers manipulate music lessons? Did students take private lessons for several weeks or have a single group lesson?

» For more on how researchers use data to check the construct validity of their manipulations, see Chapter 10, pp. 298–301.

External Validity of Causal Claims. We could ask, in addition, about external validity. If the study used children in Toronto, Canada, as participants, do the results generalize to Japanese children? Do the results generalize to rural Canadian children? If Japanese students or rural students take music lessons, will their IQs go up, too? What about generalization to other settings—could the results generalize to other music lessons? Would flute lessons and violin lessons also work? (In Chapters 10 and 14, you'll learn more about how to evaluate the external validity of experiments and other studies.)

Statistical Validity of Causal Claims. We can also interrogate statistical validity. To start, we would ask: How strong is the relationship between music lessons and IQ? In our example study, participants who took music lessons gained 7 points in IQ, whereas students who did not gained an average of 4.3 points in IQ—a net gain of about 3.7 IQ points (Schellenberg, 2004). Is this a large gain? (In this case, the difference between these two groups is about 0.35 of a standard deviation, which, as you'll learn, is considered a moderate difference between the groups.) Next, asking whether the differences among the lessons groups were statistically significant helps ensure that the covariance criterion was met; it helps us be more sure that the difference is not just due to a chance difference in this sample alone. (In Chapter 10, you'll learn more about interrogating the statistical validity of causal claims.)

« For more on determining the strength of a relationship between variables, see Statistics Review: Descriptive Statistics, pp. 468–472.

Prioritizing Validities

Which of the four validities is the most important? It depends. When researchers plan studies to test hypotheses and support claims, they usually find it impossible to conduct a study that satisfies all four validities at once. Depending on their goals, sometimes researchers don't even try to satisfy some of them. They decide what their priorities are—and so will you, when you participate in producing your own research.

External validity, for instance, is not always possible to achieve—and sometimes it may not be the researcher's priority. As you'll learn in Chapter 7, to be able to generalize results from a sample to a wide population requires a representative sample from that population. Consider the Schellenberg study on music lessons and IQ. Because he was planning to test a causal claim, he wanted to emphasize internal validity, so he focused on making his different groups—music lessons, drama lessons, or no lessons—absolutely equivalent. He was not prioritizing external validity and did not try to sample children from all over Canada. However, his study is still important and interesting because it used an internally valid experimental method—even though it did not achieve external validity. Furthermore, even though he used a sample of children from Toronto, there may be no theoretical reason to assume music lessons would not improve the IQs of rural children, too. Future research could confirm that music works for other groups of children just as well, but there is no obvious reason to expect otherwise.

In contrast, if some researchers were conducting a telephone survey and did want to generalize its results to the entire Canadian population—to maximize external validity—they would have to randomly select Canadians from all ten provinces. One approach would be using a random-digit telephone dialing system to call people in their homes, but this technology is expensive. When researchers do use formal, randomly sampled polls, they often have to pay the polling company a fee to administer each question. Therefore, a researcher who wants to evaluate, say, depression levels in a large population may be economically forced to use a short questionnaire or survey. A 2-item measure might not be as good as a 15-item measure, but the longer one would cost more. In this example, the researcher might sacrifice some construct validity in order to achieve external validity.

You'll learn more about these priorities in Chapter 14. The point, for now, is simply that in the course of planning and conducting a study, researchers weigh the pros and cons of methodology choices and decide which validities are most important. When you read about a study, you should not necessarily conclude it is faulty just because it did not meet one of the validities.

CHECK YOUR UNDERSTANDING

1. What question(s) would you use to interrogate a study's construct validity?
2. In your own words, describe at least two things that statistical validity addresses.
3. Define external validity, using the term *generalize* in your definition.
4. Why is a correlational study not able to support a causal claim?
5. Why don't researchers usually aim to achieve all four of the big validities at once?

1. See pp. 69, 71, and 78. 2. See pp. 71–72. 3. See pp. 70–71 and 78–79. 4. See pp. 74–75 and Table 3.4. 5. See pp. 79–80.

REVIEW: FOUR VALIDITIES, FOUR ASPECTS OF QUALITY

As a review, let's apply the four validities discussed in this chapter to another headline from a popular news source: "Stories told of brilliant scientists affect kids' interest in the field." The journalist's story was reported on the radio (Vedantam, 2016), and the original research was published in the *Journal of Educational Psychology* (Lin-Siegler, Ahn, Chen, Fang, & Luna-Lucero, 2016). Should we consider this a well-designed study? How well does it hold up on each of the four validities? At this stage in the course, your focus should be on asking the right questions for each validity. In later chapters, you will also learn how to evaluate the answers to those questions. You can see how we might interrogate this study by reading the Working It Through section.

Does Hearing About Scientists' Struggles Inspire Young Students?

Educational psychologists conducted a study in which children were told different kinds of stories about scientists, and the researchers tracked the children's interest in being scientists themselves (Lin-Siegler et al., 2016). We will work through this example to demonstrate how to apply the concepts from Chapter 3.

QUESTIONS TO ASK	CLAIMS, QUOTES, OR DATA	INTERPRETATION AND EVALUATION
What kind of claim is in the headline? What are the variables in the headline? Which validities should we interrogate for this claim?	"Stories told of brilliant scientists affect kids' interest in the field" (Vedantam 2016).	This is a causal claim because *affect* is a causal verb. One variable is the type of story told. The other variable is kids' level of interest in the field. We should interrogate a causal claim on all four validities, especially internal validity.
Construct validity How well did the researchers manipulate "Stories told of brilliant scientists"?	The journalist reports that "some kids were told very conventional genius stories [such as] Albert Einstein, brilliant physicist, won the Nobel Prize. He's such a genius. Others were told how hard Einstein had to struggle. At one point, apparently Einstein was having such trouble working out the math in his theories that he turned to his friend Max Planck and said, this is driving me crazy. Can you please help me with the math?" (Vedantam, 2016).	These two stories do seem to differ in focus in the way the researchers intended, with one emphasizing genius and the other Einstein's troubles. The manipulation seems well done.

(Continued)

QUESTIONS TO ASK	CLAIMS, QUOTES, OR DATA	INTERPRETATION AND EVALUATION
Construct Validity *(continued)* How well did they measure "kids' interest in the field"?	The journalist lists several ways interest in the field was operationalized, reporting, "Lin-Siegler and her colleagues then measured how well students who read the struggle stories did in science tests. She also measured how engaged the students felt about science and how much persistence they demonstrated when they faced obstacles" (Vedantam, 2016).	Classroom science tests seem a clear way to operationalize performance. We might want to find out more about how engagement and persistence were measured, such as the kinds of items used. Note that science performance and motivation may not be the same as what the journalist's headline called it, "interest in the field."
Statistical validity How large was the difference in science performance and motivation between the different story groups? Was the difference in science performance and motivation between the different story groups statistically significant?	The journalist interviewed one of the researchers, who was quoted as saying, "people who read struggle stories improved their science grades significantly more than people who read the achievement story" (Vedantam, 2016).	This quote indicates the difference was statistically significant, but does not mention how far apart the groups' science grades were. Although the headline indicated "interest in the field" was a main outcome of the study, only science grades (not motivation beliefs) showed a statistically significant difference.
Internal validity Was this study an experiment? Are there alternative explanations, other than the struggle aspect of the science stories, that could have caused the improvement in students' grades?	The fact that students heard one of two stories suggests the study is probably an experiment, in which some students heard about struggles and others heard about genius. The journalist reports that both stories were about the same scientist, but they differed in focus. The journalist did not indicate if students were randomly assigned to the different stories or not.	If researchers randomly assigned students to stories, we can assume the students who heard struggle stories and those who heard achievement stories were equivalent in background, ability level, original interest in science, gender, age, and so on. If the stories were the same length, reading level, and tone, we can assume it was the struggle aspect of the story, rather than anything else, that caused grades to improve.
External validity Can we generalize from the 9th and 10th graders in this sample to other students? Would students also benefit from hearing about the struggles of people in other fields, such as law or art?	The journalist does not indicate whether the people in this study were a representative sample. The subjects in this study heard only about scientists, not other fields.	The study's ability to generalize to students in other cities or other grades is unknown. However, when researchers conduct experiments to support causal claims, their priority is usually internal validity, not external validity. We don't yet know if the pattern generalizes to other disciplines. A future study could test this idea.

CHAPTER REVIEW

Summary

The three claims, four validities framework enables you to systematically evaluate any study you read, in a journal article or a popular media story. It can also guide you in making choices about research you might conduct yourself.

Variables

- Variables, concepts of interest that vary, form the core of psychological research. A variable has at least two levels.

- Variables can be measured or manipulated.

- Variables in a study can be described in two ways: as conceptual variables (elements of a theory) and as operational definitions (specific measures or manipulations in order to study them).

Three Claims

- As a consumer of information, you will identify three types of claims that researchers, journalists, and other writers make about research: frequency, association, and causal claims.

- Frequency claims make arguments about the level of a single, measured variable in a group of people.

- Association claims argue that two variables are related to each other. An association can be positive, negative, or zero. Association claims are usually supported by correlational studies, in which all variables are measured. When you know how two variables are associated, you can use one to predict the other.

- Causal claims state that one variable is responsible for changes in the other variable. To support a causal claim, a study must meet three criteria—covariance, temporal precedence, and internal validity—which is accomplished only by an experimental study.

Interrogating the Three Claims Using the Four Big Validities

- To interrogate a frequency claim, ask questions about the study's construct validity (quality of the measurements), external validity (generalizability to a larger population), and statistical validity (degree of error in the percentage estimate).

- To interrogate an association claim, ask about its construct, external, and statistical validity. Statistical validity addresses the strength of a relationship, and whether or not a finding is statistically significant.

- To interrogate a causal claim, ask whether the study conducted was an experiment, which is the only way to establish internal validity and temporal precedence. If it was an experiment, further assess internal validity by asking whether the study was designed with any confounds, and whether the researchers used random assignment for making participant groups. You can also ask about the study's construct, external, and statistical validity.

- Researchers cannot usually achieve all four validities at once in an experiment, so they prioritize them. Their interest in making a causal statement means they may sacrifice external validity to ensure internal validity.

Key Terms

 To see samples of chapter concepts in the popular media, visit www.everydayresearchmethods.com and click the box for Chapter 3.

Review Questions

1. Which of the following variable or variables is manipulated, rather than measured? (Could be more than one.)

   a. Number of pairs of shoes owned, in pairs.

   b. A person's height, in cm.

   c. Amount of aspirin a researcher gives a person to take, either 325 mg or 500 mg.

   d. Degree of happiness, rated on a scale from 1 to 10.

   e. Type of praise a researcher uses in groups of dogs: verbal praise or a clicking sound paired with treats.

2. Which of the following headlines is an association claim?

   a. Chewing gum can improve your mood and focus.

   b. Handling money decreases helpful behavior in young children.

   c. Workaholism is tied to psychiatric disorders.

   d. Eating kiwis may help you fall asleep.

3. Which of the following headlines is a frequency claim?

   a. Obese kids are less sensitive to tastes.

   b. 80% of women feel dissatisfied with how their bodies look.

   c. Feeling fat? Maybe Facebook is to blame.

   d. Daycare and behavior problems are not linked.

4. Which of the following headlines is a causal claim?

   a. Taking a deep breath helps minimize high blood pressure, anxiety, and depression.

   b. Younger people can't read emotions on wrinkled faces.

   c. Strange but true: Babies born in the autumn are more likely to live to 100.

   d. Check the baby! Many new moms show signs of OCD.

5. Which validity would you be interrogating by asking: How well did the researchers measure sensitivity to tastes in this study?

   a. Construct validity

   b. Statistical validity

   c. External validity

   d. Internal validity

6. Which validity would you be interrogating by asking: How did the researchers get their sample of people for this survey?

   a. Construct validity

   b. Statistical validity

   c. External validity

   d. Internal validity

7. In most experiments, trade-offs are made between validities because it is not possible to achieve all four at once. What is the most common trade-off?

a. Internal and external validity.

b. Construct and statistical validity.

c. Statistical and internal validity.

d. External and statistical validity.

Learning Actively

1. For each boldfaced variable below, indicate the variable's levels, whether the variable is measured or manipulated, and how you might describe the variable conceptually and operationally.

VARIABLE IN CONTEXT	CONCEPTUAL VARIABLE NAME	OPERATIONALIZATION OF THIS VARIABLE	LEVELS OF THIS VARIABLE	MEASURED OR MANIPULATED
A questionnaire study asks for various demographic information, including participants' **level of education.**	Level of education	Asking participants to circle their highest level of education from this list: High school diploma Some college College degree Graduate degree	High school diploma Some college College degree Graduate degree	Measured
A questionnaire study asks about **anxiety**, measured on a 20-item Spielberger Trait Anxiety Inventory.				
A study of readability has people read a passage of text printed in one of two **fonts: sans-serif or serif.**				
A study of **school achievement** asks each participant to report his or her SAT score, as a measure of college readiness.				
A researcher studying self-control and **blood sugar levels** gives participants one of two glasses of sweet-tasting lemonade: one has sugar, the other is sugar-free.				

2. Imagine you encounter each of the following headlines. What questions would you ask if you wanted to understand more about the quality of the study behind the headline? For each question, indicate which of the four validities it is addressing. Follow the model in the Working It Through section.

a. Chewing gum can improve your mood and focus.

b. Workaholism is tied to psychiatric disorders.

c. 80% of women feel dissatisfied with how their bodies look.

3. Suppose you want to test the causal claim about chewing gum improving your mood and focus. How could you design an experiment to test this claim? What would the variables be? Would each be manipulated or measured? What results would you expect? Sketch a graph of the outcomes you would predict. Would your experiment satisfy the three criteria for supporting a causal statement?

PART II

Research Foundations for Any Claim

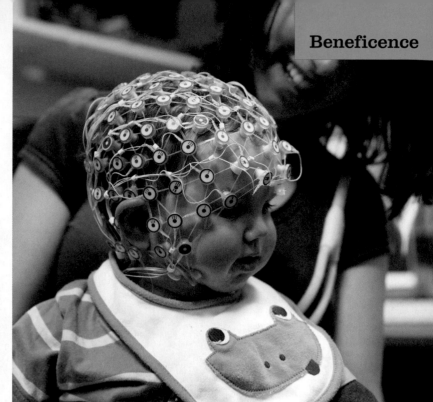

4

Ethical Guidelines for Psychology Research

NO MATTER WHAT TYPE of claim researchers are investigating, they are obligated—by law, by morality, and by today's social norms—to treat the participants in their research with kindness, respect, and fairness. In the 21st century, researchers are expected to follow basic ethical principles in the treatment of humans and other animals. Researchers are also expected to produce research that is meaningful and helpful to society. How can we know when a study is conducted ethically? This chapter introduces the criteria for evaluating whether a set of research was conducted appropriately.

HISTORICAL EXAMPLES

In the past, researchers may have held different ideas about the ethical treatment of study participants. Two examples of research, one from medicine and one from psychology, follow. The first one clearly illustrates several ethics violations. The second demonstrates the difficult balance of priorities researchers might face when evaluating a study's ethics.

The Tuskegee Syphilis Study Illustrates Three Major Ethics Violations

In the late 1920s and early 1930s, about 35% of poor Black men living in the southern United States were infected with syphilis. Because the disease was largely untreatable at the time, it interfered with their ability to work, contribute to society, and climb their way out of poverty. The available treatment involved infusions of toxic metals; when it worked at all, this method had serious—even fatal—side effects (CDC, 2016). In 1932, the U.S. Public Health Service (PHS), cooperating with the Tuskegee (Alabama) Institute, began a study of 600 Black men. About 400 were already infected with syphilis, and about 200 were not. The researchers wanted to study the effects of untreated syphilis on the men's health over the long term. At the time, no treatment was a reasonable choice because the risky methods available in 1932 were not likely to work (Jones, 1993). The men were recruited in their community churches and schools, and many of them were enthusiastic about participating in a project that would give them access to medical care for the first time in their lives (Reverby, 2009). However, there is little evidence that the men were told the study was actually about syphilis.

Early in the project, the researchers decided to follow the men infected with syphilis until each one had died, to obtain valuable data on how the disease progresses when untreated. The study lasted 40 years, during which the researchers made a long series of unethical choices (**Figure 4.1**). Infected men were told they had "bad blood" instead of syphilis. The researchers told them they were being treated, and all of them were required to come to the Tuskegee clinic for evaluation and testing. But they were never given any beneficial treatment. At one point, in fact, the researchers had to conduct a painful, potentially dangerous spinal tap procedure on every participant, in order to follow the progression of the disease. To ensure that they would come in for the procedure, the researchers lied, telling the men it was a "special free treatment" for their illness (Jones, 1993).

As the project continued, 250 of the men registered to join the U.S. Armed Forces, which were then engaged in World War II. As part of the draft process, the men were diagnosed (again) with syphilis and told to reenlist after they had been treated. Instead of following these instructions, however, the researchers interfered by preventing the men from being treated. As a result, they could not serve in the armed forces or receive subsequent G. I. benefits (Final Report of the Tuskegee Study Ad Hoc Advisory Panel, 1973).

In 1943, the PHS approved the use of penicillin for treating syphilis, yet the Tuskegee Institute did not provide information about this new cure to the participants in their study. In 1968, PHS employee Peter Buxtun raised concerns with officials at the CDC. However, the researchers decided to proceed

FIGURE 4.1
The Tuskegee Syphilis Study.

A doctor takes a blood sample from a participant. What unethical decisions were made by the researchers who conducted this study?

as before. The study continued until 1972, when Buxtun told the story to the Associated Press (Gray, 1998; Heller, 1972), and the study was widely condemned. Over the years, many men got sicker, and dozens died. Several men inadvertently infected their partners, thereby causing, in some cases, congenital syphilis in their children (Jones, 1993; Reverby, 2009).

In 1974, the families of the participants reached a settlement in a lawsuit against the U.S. government. In 1997, President Bill Clinton formally apologized to the survivors on behalf of the nation (**Figure 4.2**). Nonetheless, the Tuskegee Syphilis Study has contributed to an unfortunate legacy. As a result of this study, some African Americans are suspicious of government health services and research participation (McCallum, Arekere, Green, Katz, & Rivers, 2006).

FIGURE 4.2
An official apology in 1997.
The U.S. government issued an apology to survivors of the Tuskegee Syphilis Study.

UNETHICAL CHOICES

The researchers conducting this infamous study made a number of choices that are unethical from today's perspective. Later writers have identified these choices as falling into three distinct categories (Childress, Meslin, & Shapiro, 2005; Gray, 1998). First, the men were *not treated respectfully*. The researchers lied to them about the nature of their participation and withheld information (such as penicillin as a cure for the disease); in so doing, they did not give the men a chance to make a fully informed decision about participating in the study. If they had known in advance the true nature of the study, some might still have agreed to participate but others might not. After the men died, the doctors offered a generous burial fee to the families, but mainly so they could be sure of doing autopsy studies. These low-income families may have felt coerced into agreeing to an autopsy only because of the large payment.

Second, the men in the study were *harmed*. They and their families were not told about a treatment for a disease that, in the later years of the study, could be easily cured. (Many of the men were illiterate and thus unable to learn about the penicillin cure on their own.) They were also subjected to painful and dangerous tests. Third, the researchers *targeted a disadvantaged social group* in this study. Syphilis affects people from all ethnicities and social backgrounds, yet all the men in this study were poor and African American (Gray, 1998; Jones, 1993).

The Milgram Obedience Studies Illustrate a Difficult Ethical Balance

The Tuskegee Syphilis Study provides several clear examples of ethics violations, but decisions about ethical matters are usually more nuanced. Social psychologist Stanley Milgram's series of studies on obedience to authority, conducted in the early 1960s, illustrates some of the difficulties of ethical decision making.

Imagine yourself as a participant in one of Milgram's studies. You are told there will be two participants: you, the "teacher," and another participant, the "learner." As teacher, your job is to punish the learner when he makes mistakes in a learning task. The learner slips into a cubicle where you can't see him, and the session begins (Milgram, 1963, 1974).

As the study goes on, you are told to punish the learner for errors by administering electric shocks at increasingly higher intensities, as indicated on an imposing piece of equipment in front of you: the "shock generator." At first, while receiving the low-voltage shocks, the learner does not complain. But he keeps making mistakes on a word association test he is supposed to be learning, and you are required by the rules of the study to deliver shocks that are 15 volts higher after each mistake (**Figure 4.3**). As the voltage is increased, the learner begins to grunt with pain. At about 120 volts, the learner shouts that the shocks are very painful and says he wants to quit the experiment. At 300 volts, the learner screams that he will no longer respond to the learning task; he stops responding. The experimenter, sitting behind you in a white lab coat, tells you to keep delivering shocks—15 volts more each time, until the machine indicates you're delivering 450-volt shocks. Whereas before the learner screamed in pain with each new shock, after 300 volts you now hear nothing from him. You can't tell whether he is even conscious in his cubicle.

If you protest (and you probably would), the experimenter behind you says calmly, "Continue." If you protest again, the experimenter says, again calmly, "The experiment requires that you continue," or even, "You have no choice, you must go on." What would you do now?

You may believe you would have refused to obey the demands of this inhumane experimenter. However, in the original study, fully 65% of the participants obeyed, following the experimenter's instructions and delivering the 450-volt shock to the learner. Only two or three participants (out of hundreds) refused to give even the first, 15-volt shock. Virtually all participants subjected another person to one or more electric shocks—or at least they thought they did. Fortunately, the learner was actually a confederate of the experimenter; he

FIGURE 4.3
The Milgram obedience studies.

In one version, the experimenter (right) and the true participant, or "teacher" (left) help connect the "learner" to the electrodes that would supposedly shock him. Was it ethical for the researchers to invent this elaborate situation, which ultimately caused participants so much stress?

was a paid actor playing a role, and he did not actually receive any shocks. The participants did not know this; they thought the learner was an innocent, friendly man.

Milgram conducted 18 or more variations of this study. Each time, 40 new participants were asked to deliver painful shocks to the learner. In one variation, the learner mentioned he had a heart condition; this made no difference, and the level of obedience remained at about 65%. In another variation, the learner sat right in the room with the teacher-participant; this time the obedience level dropped to 40% (**Figure 4.4**). Another time, the experimenter supervised the situation from down the hall, giving his instructions ("Continue," "The experiment requires that you continue") over the phone. The obedience level also dropped, and only 20% of participants delivered all the shocks.

BALANCING RISK TO PARTICIPANTS WITH BENEFIT TO SOCIETY

Was Milgram acting ethically in conducting this research? One psychologist at the time criticized the study because it was extremely stressful to the teacher-participants (Baumrind, 1964). Milgram relayed this observation from one of his research assistants:

FIGURE 4.4
Balancing ethical concerns.

In one variation of the Milgram obedience studies, participants were required to force the learner's arm onto a (fake) electric plate. How do you balance potential harm to participants with the benefit to society in this research?

> I observed a mature and initially poised businessman enter the laboratory smiling and confident. Within 20 minutes he was reduced to a twitching, nervous wreck, who was rapidly approaching a point of nervous collapse. He constantly pulled on his earlobe, and twisted his hands. At one point he pushed his fist into his forehead and muttered, "Oh, God, let's stop it." And yet he continued to respond to every word of the experimenter, and obeyed to the very end. (Milgram, 1963, p. 377)

Was it ethical or unethical to put unsuspecting volunteers through such a stressful experience?

Some writers have questioned how Milgram's participants coped with their involvement over time. In an interview after the study, the participants were **debriefed**; they were carefully informed about the study's hypotheses. They shook hands with the learner, who reassured them he was unharmed. However, in order to avoid influencing potential future participants, the debriefing never mentioned that the learner did not receive shocks (Perry, 2013). In interviews years later, some participants reported worrying for weeks about the learner's welfare (Perry, 2013).

Milgram claimed that his results—65% obedience—surprised him (Milgram, 1974; but see Perry, 2013). Experts at the time predicted that only 1–2% of people would obey the experimenter up to 450 volts. After the first variation of the study, however, Milgram knew what kind of behavior to expect, and he had already seen firsthand the stress the participants were under. Once he knew that many of the people in the study would experience anxiety and stress, Milgram might have taken steps to stop, or modify, the procedure, and yet he did not.

An ethical debate about the Milgram studies must also weigh the lessons learned, and Milgram himself emphasized their social impact. Some argue they contributed crucial lessons about obedience to authority and the "power of the situation"—lessons we would not have learned without his research (Blass, 2002). The research may have benefitted individual participants: Milgram had an associate call some of the participants at home, months later, to ask about their current state of well-being. Some of them felt they had learned something important. For example, one participant reported: "What appalled me was that I could possess this capacity for obedience and compliance. . . . I hope I can deal more effectively with future conflicts of values I encounter" (Milgram, 1974, p. 54). Thus, there is a fundamental conundrum in deciding whether this research is ethical—trying to balance the potential *risks to participants* and *the value of the knowledge* gained. In cases like the Milgram studies, it is not an easy decision.

CHECK YOUR UNDERSTANDING

1. What three categories of ethics violations are illustrated by the Tuskegee Syphilis Study?

2. What concerns have been raised against the Milgram obedience studies?

1. See pp. 89–91. 2. See pp. 92–94.

CORE ETHICAL PRINCIPLES

Organizations around the world have developed formal statements of ethics. Following World War II, the Nuremberg Trials revealed the horror of medical experiments conducted on concentration camp victims in Nazi-occupied Europe and resulted in the Nuremberg Code. Although it is not a formal law in any nation, the ten-point Nuremberg Code influences the ethical research laws of many countries (Shuster, 1997). In addition, many national leaders have signed the Declaration of Helsinki, which guides ethics in medical research and practice. Within the United States, ethical systems are also based on the Belmont Report, which defines the ethical guidelines researchers should follow. All of these ethical statements are grounded in the same core principles.

The Belmont Report: Principles and Applications

In 1976, a commission of physicians, ethicists, philosophers, scientists, and other citizens gathered at the Belmont Conference Center in Eldridge, Maryland, at the request of the U.S. Congress. They got together for an intensive discussion of basic ethical principles researchers should follow when conducting research with human participants. The commission was created partly in response to the serious ethics violations of the Tuskegee Syphilis Study (Jonsen, 2005). The contributors produced a short document called the Belmont Report, which outlines three main principles for guiding ethical decision making: respect for persons, beneficence, and justice. Each principle has standard applications. The guidelines are intended for use in many disciplines, including medicine, sociology, anthropology, and basic biological research, as well as psychology.

THE PRINCIPLE OF RESPECT FOR PERSONS

In the Belmont Report, the **principle of respect for persons** includes two provisions. First, individuals potentially involved in research should be treated as autonomous agents: They should be free to make up their own minds about whether they wish to participate in a research study. Applying this principle means that every participant is entitled to the precaution of **informed consent**; each person learns about the research project, considers its risks and benefits, and decides whether to participate.

In obtaining informed consent, researchers are not allowed to mislead people about the study's risks and benefits. Nor may they coerce or unduly influence a person into participating; doing so would violate the principle of respect for persons. Coercion is an implicit or explicit suggestion that those who do not participate will suffer a negative consequence; for example, a professor implying that students' grades will be lower if they don't participate in a particular study. Undue influence is offering an incentive too attractive to refuse, such as an irresistible amount of money in exchange for participating. The report notes that financially poor individuals may be more easily swayed into participating if a research study provides a large payment.

The second application of respect for persons states that some people have less autonomy, so they are entitled to special protection when it comes to informed consent. For example, children, people with intellectual or developmental disabilities, and prisoners should be protected, according to the Belmont Report. Children and certain other individuals might be unable to give informed consent because of not understanding the procedures involved well enough to make a responsible decision (**Figure 4.5**). Prisoners are especially susceptible to coercion, according to the Belmont Report, because they may perceive requests to participate in research as demands, rather than as invitations. All these populations should be treated with special consideration.

THE PRINCIPLE OF BENEFICENCE

To comply with the **principle of beneficence**, researchers must take precautions to protect participants from harm and to ensure their well-being. To apply this principle, researchers need to carefully assess the risks and benefits of the study they plan to conduct. In addition, they must consider how the community might benefit or be harmed. Will a community gain something of value from the knowledge this research is producing? Will there be costs to a community if this research is not conducted?

FIGURE 4.5
Vulnerable populations in research.

Why might children be considered a vulnerable population that requires special ethical consideration?

The Tuskegee Syphilis Study failed to treat the participants in accordance with the principle of beneficence. The researchers harmed participants through risky and invasive medical tests, and they harmed the participants' families by exposing them to untreated syphilis. The researchers also withheld benefits from the men in the study. Today, researchers may not withhold treatments that are known to be helpful to study participants. For example, if preliminary results indicate, halfway through a study, that a treatment is advantageous for an experimental group, the researcher must give the participants in the control group the opportunity to receive that treatment, too.

A potential risk is having people's personal information (their behavior, mental health information, or private reactions) revealed to others. To prevent harm, researchers usually make participant information either anonymous or confidential. In an **anonymous study,** researchers do not collect any potentially identifying information, including names, birthdays, photos, and so on. Anonymous online surveys will even strip away the identifiers of the computer used. In a **confidential study**, researchers collect some identifying information (for contacting people at a later date if needed), but prevent it from being disclosed. They may save data in encrypted form or store people's names separately from their other data.

Risks and benefits are generally easy to assess when it comes to physical health, the type measured in medical research. Is a person's health getting worse or better? Is the community going to be healthier because of this research, or not? In contrast, some psychological studies can expose participants to emotional or psychological harm, such as anxiety, stress, depression, or mental strain, and these may be harder to evaluate.

Consider the participants in the Milgram studies, who were clearly experiencing stress. How might you assess the harm done in this situation? Would you measure the way participants felt at that time? Would you ask how they felt about it a year later? Would you measure what they say about their own stress, or what an observer would say? Just as it's hard to evaluate emotional or psychological harm, it is difficult to evaluate how damaging a study like Milgram's might be. However, the principle of beneficence demands that researchers consider such risks (and benefits) before beginning each study. As a point of reference, some institutions ask researchers to estimate how stressful a study's situation would be compared with the normal stresses of everyday life.

The other side of the balance—the benefits of psychological research to the community—may not be easy to assess either. One could argue that Milgram's results are valuable, but their value is impossible to quantify in terms of lives or dollars saved. Nevertheless, to apply the principle of beneficence, researchers must attempt to predict the risks and benefits of their research—to both participants and the larger community.

THE PRINCIPLE OF JUSTICE

The **principle of justice** calls for a fair balance between the kinds of people who participate in research and the kinds of people who benefit from it. For example, if a research study discovers that a procedure is risky or harmful, the participants, unfortunately, "bear the burden" of that risk, while other people—those not in the study—are able to benefit from the research results (Kimmel, 2007). The Tuskegee Syphilis Study illustrates a violation of this principle of justice: Anybody, regardless of race or income, can contract syphilis and benefit from research on it, but the participants in the study—who bore the burden of untreated syphilis—were all poor, African American men. Therefore, these participants bore an undue burden of risk.

When the principle of justice is applied, it means that researchers might first ensure that the participants involved in a study are representative of the kinds of people who would also benefit from its results. If researchers decide to study a sample from only one ethnic group or only a sample of institutionalized individuals, they must demonstrate that the problem they are studying is especially prevalent in that ethnic group or in that type of institution. For example, it might violate the justice principle if researchers studied a group of prisoners mainly because they were convenient. However, it might be perfectly acceptable to study only institutionalized people for a study on tuberculosis because tuberculosis is particularly prevalent in institutions, where people live together in a confined area.

ETHICAL PRINCIPLES IN PRACTICE

Just as panels of judges interpret a country's laws, panels of people interpret the guidelines in the Belmont Report (Jonsen, 2005). Most universities and research hospitals have committees who decide whether research and practice are complying with ethical guidelines. In the United States, federally funded agencies must follow the Common Rule, which describes detailed ways the Belmont Report should be applied in research (U.S. Department of Health and Human Services, 2009). For example, it explains informed consent procedures and ways to approve research before it is conducted.

At many colleges and universities, policies require anyone involved in research with human participants (professors, graduate students, undergraduates, or research staff) to be trained in ethically responsible research. Perhaps your institution requires you to complete online training, such as the course Responsible Conduct of Research, administered by the CITI program. By learning the material in this chapter, you will be better prepared for CITI courses, if you're required to take them.

CHECK YOUR UNDERSTANDING

1. Name and describe the three main principles of the Belmont Report.

2. Each principle in the Belmont Report has a particular application. The principle of respect for persons has its application in the informed consent process. What are the applications of the other two principles?

1. See pp. 94–95 for principles and pp. 95–97 for definitions. 2. See pp. 95–97.

GUIDELINES FOR PSYCHOLOGISTS: THE APA ETHICAL PRINCIPLES

In addition to the Belmont Report, local policies, and federal laws, American psychologists can consult another layer of ethical principles and standards written by the American Psychological Association (2002), the Ethical Principles of Psychologists and Code of Conduct (**Figure 4.6**). This broad set of guidelines governs the three most common roles of psychologists: research scientists, educators, and practitioners (usually as therapists). Psychological associations in other countries have similar codes of ethics, and other professions have codes of ethics as well (Kimmel, 2007).

Belmont Plus Two: APA's Five General Principles

The APA outlines five general principles for guiding individual aspects of ethical behavior. These principles are intended to protect not only research participants, but also students in psychology classes and clients of professional therapists. As you can see in **Table 4.1**, three of the APA principles (A, D, and E in the table) are identical to the three main principles of the Belmont Report (beneficence, justice, and respect for persons). Another principle is *fidelity and responsibility* (e.g., a clinical psychologist teaching in a university may not serve as a therapist to one of his or her classroom students, and psychologists must avoid sexual relationships with their students or clients). The last APA principle is *integrity* (e.g., professors are obligated to teach accurately, and therapists are required to stay current on the empirical evidence for therapeutic techniques).

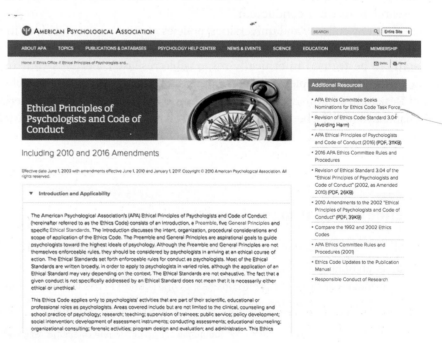

FIGURE 4.6
The APA website.
The full text of the APA's ethical principles can be found on the website.

TABLE 4.1

The Belmont Report's Basic Principles and the APA's Five General Principles Compared

BELMONT REPORT (1979)	APA ETHICAL PRINCIPLES (2002)	DEFINITION
Beneficence	**A. Beneficence and nonmaleficence**	Treat people in ways that benefit them. Do not cause suffering. Conduct research that will benefit society.
	B. Fidelity and responsibility	Establish relationships of trust; accept responsibility for professional behavior (in research, teaching, and clinical practice).
	C. Integrity	Strive to be accurate, truthful, and honest in one's role as researcher, teacher, or practitioner.
Justice	**D. Justice**	Strive to treat all groups of people fairly. Sample research participants from the same populations that will benefit from the research. Be aware of biases.
Respect for persons	**E. Respect for people's rights and dignity**	Recognize that people are autonomous agents. Protect people's rights, including the right to privacy, the right to give consent for treatment or research, and the right to have participation treated confidentially. Understand that some populations may be less able to give autonomous consent, and take precautions against coercing such people.

Note: The principles in boldface are shared by both documents and specifically involve the treatment of human participants in research. The APA guidelines are broader; they apply not only to how psychologists conduct research, but also to how they teach and conduct clinical practice.

Ethical Standards for Research

In addition to the five general principles, the APA lists ten specific ethical standards. These standards are similar to enforceable rules or laws. Psychologist members of the APA who violate any of these standards can lose their professional license or may be disciplined in some other way by the association.

Of its ten ethical standards, Ethical Standard 8 is the one most relevant in a research methods book, it is written specifically for psychologists in their role as researchers. (The other standards are more relevant to their roles as therapists, consultants, and teachers.) The next sections outline the details of the APA's Ethical Standard 8, noting how it works together with other layers of guidance a researcher must follow.

The website of the APA Ethics Office provides the full text of the APA's ethics documents. If you are considering becoming a therapist or counselor someday, you may find it interesting to read the other ethical standards that were written specifically for practitioners.

INSTITUTIONAL REVIEW BOARDS (STANDARD 8.01)

An **institutional review board** (**IRB**) is a committee responsible for interpreting ethical principles and ensuring that research using human participants is conducted ethically. Most colleges and universities, as well as research hospitals, have an IRB. In the United States, IRBs are mandated by federal law. If an institution uses federal money (such as government grants) to carry out research projects, a designated IRB is required. However, in the United States, research conducted by private businesses does not have to use an IRB or follow any particular ethical guidelines (though businesses may write their own ethics policies).

An IRB panel in the U.S. includes five or more people, some of whom must come from specified backgrounds. At least one member must be a scientist, one has to have academic interests outside the sciences, and one (or more) should be a community member who has no ties to the institution (such as a local pastor, a community leader, or an interested citizen). In addition, when the IRB discusses a proposal to use prison participants, one member must be recruited as a designated prisoner advocate. The IRB must consider particular questions for any research involving children. IRBs in most other countries follow similar mandates for their composition.

At regular meetings, the IRB reviews proposals from individual scientists. Before conducting a study, researchers must fill out a detailed application describing their study, its risks and benefits (to both participants and society), its procedures for informed consent, and its provisions for protecting people's privacy. The IRB then reviews each application.

Different IRBs have different procedures. In some universities, when a study is judged to be of little or no risk (such as a completely anonymous questionnaire), the IRB might not meet to discuss it in person. In most institutions, though, any study that poses risks to humans or that involves vulnerable populations must be reviewed by an in-person IRB meeting. In many cases, IRB oversight provides a neutral, multiperspective judgment on any study's ethicality. An effective IRB should not permit research that violates people's rights, research that poses unreasonable risk, or research that lacks a sound rationale. However, an effective IRB should not obstruct research, either. It should not prevent controversial—but still ethical—research questions from being investigated. Ideally, the IRB attempts to balance the welfare of research participants and the researchers' goal of contributing important knowledge to the field.

INFORMED CONSENT (STANDARD 8.02)

As mentioned earlier, informed consent is the researcher's obligation to explain the study to potential participants in everyday language and give them a chance to decide whether to participate. In most studies, informed consent is obtained by providing a written document that outlines the procedures, risks, and benefits of the research, including a statement about any treatments that are experimental. Everyone who wishes to participate signs two copies of the document—one for the researcher to store, and one for the participant to take home.

In certain circumstances, the APA standards (and other federal laws that govern research) indicate that informed consent procedures are not necessary. Specifically, researchers may not be required to have participants sign informed consent forms if the study is not likely to cause harm and if it takes place in an educational setting. Written informed consent might not be needed when participants answer a completely anonymous questionnaire in which their answers are not linked to their names in any way. Written consent may not be required when the study involves naturalistic observation of participants in low-risk public settings, such as a museum, classroom, or mall—where people can reasonably expect to be observed by others anyway. The individual institution's regulations determine whether written informed consent is necessary in such situations, and those studies still must be approved by an IRB. However, the IRB will allow the researcher to proceed without obtaining formal, written consent forms from every participant. Nevertheless, researchers are always ethically obliged to respect participants' rights.

According to Ethical Standard 8 (and most other ethical guidelines), obtaining informed consent also involves informing people whether the data they provide in a research study will be treated as private and confidential. Nonconfidential data might put participants at some risk. For example, in the course of research people might report on their health status, political attitudes, test scores, or study habits—information they might not want others to know. Therefore, informed consent procedures ordinarily outline which parts of the data are confidential and which, if any, are not. If data are to be treated as confidential, researchers agree to remove names and other identifiers. Such things as handwriting, birthdays, and photographs might reveal personal data, and researchers must be careful to protect that information if they have promised to do so. At many institutions, confidentiality procedures are not optional. Many institutions require researchers to store any identifiable data in a locked area or on secure computers.

DECEPTION (STANDARD 8.07)

You may have read about psychological research in which the researchers lied to participants. Consider some of the studies you've learned about in your psychology courses. In the Milgram obedience studies described earlier, the participants did not know the learner was not really being shocked. In another study, an experimental confederate posed as a thief, stealing money from a person's bag while an unsuspecting bystander sat reading at a table (**Figure 4.7**). In some versions of this study, the "thief," the "victim," and a third person who sat calmly nearby, pretending to read, were all experimental confederates. That makes three confederates and a fake crime—all in one study (Shaffer, Rogel, & Hendrick, 1975).

Even in the most straightforward study, participants are not told about all the comparison conditions. For example, in the study described in Chapter 3, some participants might have been aware they were reading a story about a scientist, but didn't know others were reading a different story (Lin-Siegler, Ahn, Chen, Fang, & Luna-Lucero, 2016). All these studies contained an element of **deception**. Researchers withheld some details of the study from participants—deception through *omission*; in some cases, they actively lied to them—deception through *commission*.

FIGURE 4.7
Deception in research.

A study on bystander action staged a theft at a library table.

Consider how these studies might have turned out if there had been no such deception. Suppose the researchers had said, "We're going to see whether you're willing to help prevent a theft. Wait here. In a few moments, we will stage a theft and see what you do." Or "We want to know whether reading about Einstein's struggles will make you more motivated in science class. Ready?" Obviously, the data would be useless. Deceiving research participants by lying to them or by withholding information is, in many cases, necessary in order to obtain meaningful results.

Is deception ethical? In a deception study, researchers must still uphold the principle of respect for persons by informing participants of the study's activities, risks, and benefits. The principle of beneficence also applies: What are the ethical costs and benefits of doing the study with deception, compared with the ethical costs of not doing it this way? It's important to find out what kinds of situational factors influence someone's willingness to report a theft and to test hypotheses about what motivates students in school. Because most people consider these issues to be important, some researchers argue that the gain in knowledge seems worth the cost of lying (temporarily) to the participants (Kimmel, 1998). Even then, the APA principles and federal guidelines require researchers to avoid using deceptive research designs except as a last resort and to debrief participants after the study.

Despite such arguments, some psychologists believe that deception undermines people's trust in the research process and should never be used in a study design (Ortmann & Hertwig, 1997). Still others suggest deception is acceptable in certain circumstances (Bröder, 1998; Kimmel, 1998; Pittenger, 2002). Researchers have investigated how undergraduates respond to participating in a study that uses deception. Results indicate students usually tolerate minor deception and even some discomfort or stress, considering them necessary parts of research. When students do find deception to be stressful, these negative effects are diminished when the researchers fully explain the deception in a debriefing session (Bröder, 1998; Sharpe, Adair, & Roese, 1992; Smith & Richardson, 1983).

DEBRIEFING (STANDARD 8.08)

When researchers have used deception, they must spend time after the study talking with each participant in a structured conversation. In a debriefing session, the researchers describe the nature of the deception and explain why it was necessary. Emphasizing the importance of their research, they attempt to restore an honest relationship with the participant. As part of the debriefing process, the researcher describes the design of the study, thereby giving the participant some insight about the nature of psychological science.

Nondeceptive studies often include a debriefing session, too. At many universities, all student participants in research receive a written description of the study's goals and hypotheses, along with references for further reading. The intention is to make participation in research a worthwhile educational experience, so students can learn more about the research process in general, understand how their participation fits into the larger context of theory testing, and learn how their participation might benefit others. In debriefing sessions, researchers might also offer to share results with the participants. Even months after their participation, people can request a summary of the study's results.

RESEARCH MISCONDUCT

Most discussions of ethical research focus on protection and respect for participants, and rightly so. However, the publication process also involves ethical decision making. As an example, it is considered ethical to publish one's results. After participants have spent their time in a study, it is only fair to make the results known publicly for the benefit of society. Psychologists must also treat their data and their sources accurately.

Data Fabrication (Standard 8.10) and Data Falsification. Two forms of research misconduct involve manipulating results. **Data fabrication** occurs when, instead of recording what really happened in a study (or sometimes instead of running a study at all), researchers invent data that fit their hypotheses. **Data falsification** occurs when researchers influence a study's results, perhaps by selectively deleting observations from a data set or by influencing their research subjects to act in the hypothesized way.

A recent case exemplifies both of these breaches. In 2012, social psychologist Diederik Stapel was fired from his job as a professor at Tilburg University in the Netherlands because he fabricated data in dozens of his studies (Stapel Investigation, 2012). Three graduate students became suspicious of his actions and bravely informed their department head. Soon thereafter, committees at the three universities where he had worked began documenting years of fraudulent data collection by Stapel. In written statements, he admitted that at first, he changed occasional data points (data falsification), but that later he found himself typing in entire datasets to fit his and his students' hypotheses (data fabrication). The scientific journals that published his fraudulent data have retracted over 58 articles to date.

Creating fabricated or falsified data is clearly unethical and has far-reaching consequences. Scientists use data to test their theories, and they can do so only if they know that previously reported data are true and accurate. When people fabricate data, they mislead others about the actual state of support for a theory. Fabricated data might inspire other researchers to spend time (and, often, grant money) following a false lead or to be more confident in theories than they should be. In the case of Stapel, the fraud cast a shadow over the careers of the graduate students and coauthors he worked with. Even though investigators stated the collaborators did not know about or participate in the fabrication, Stapel's collaborators subsequently found many of their own published papers on the retraction

<<
For more on the theory-data cycle, see Chapter 1, pp. 11–13.

list. Psychologists are concerned that Stapel's fraud could potentially harm psychology's reputation, even though psychology as a field is not uniquely vulnerable to fraud (Stroebe, Postmes, & Spears, 2012).

The costs were especially high for a fraudulent study that suggested a link between the measles, mumps, rubella (MMR) vaccine and autism (Wakefield et al., 1998, cited in Sathyanarayana Rao & Andrade, 2011). The study, though conducted on only 12 children, was discussed worldwide among frightened parents. Some parents refuse to vaccinate their children, even though the paper has been retracted from the journal *The Lancet* because the authors admitted fraud (**Figure 4.8**). Even now, there are measles outbreaks in the U.K. and the U.S. attributable to inadequate vaccination rates.

Why might a researcher fabricate or falsify data? In many universities, the reputations, income, and promotions of professors are based on their publications and their influence in the field. In such high-pressure circumstances, the temptation might be great to delete contradictory data or create supporting data (Stroebe, Postmes, & Spears, 2012). In addition, some researchers may simply be convinced of their own hypotheses and believe that any data that do not support their predictions must be inaccurate. Writing about his first instance of falsification, Stapel said: "I changed an unexpected 2 into a 4 . . . I looked at the [office] door. It was closed. When I saw the new results, the world had returned to being logical" (quoted in Borsboom & Wagenmakers, 2013). Unethical scientists may manipulate their data to coincide with their intuition rather than with formal observations, as a true empiricist would.

» To review the quality of different sources of information, see Chapter 2, pp. 42–52 and Figure 2.9.

FIGURE 4.8
Fabricated and falsified data.

This paper on vaccines was retracted from *The Lancet* after the authors admitted to fabricating results, selectively reporting data (falsification), and failing to report their financial interest. The cost of this fraud can be measured in loss of life from reduced vaccination rates and increased rates of diseases like measles. (Source: Wakefield et al., 1998, cited in Sathyanarayana Rao & Andrade, 2011. Originally published in *The Lancet*.)

Most recent cases of research fraud have been detected not by the peer review process, but by people who work with the perpetrator (Stroebe, Postmes, & Spears, 2012). If colleagues or students of a researcher in the U.S. suspect such misconduct, they may report it to the scientist's institution. If the research project is federally funded, suspected misconduct can be reported to the Office of Research Integrity, a branch of the Department of Health and Human Services, which then has the obligation to investigate.

Plagiarism (Standard 8.11). Another form of research misconduct is **plagiarism**, usually defined as representing the ideas or words of others as one's own. A formal definition, provided by the U.S. Office of Science and Technology Policy, states that plagiarism is "the appropriation of another person's ideas, processes, results, or words without giving appropriate credit" (Federal Register, 2000). Academics and researchers consider plagiarism a violation of ethics because it is unfair for a researcher to take credit for another person's intellectual property: It is a form of stealing.

To avoid plagiarism, a writer must cite the sources of all ideas that are not his or her own, to give appropriate credit to the original authors. Psychologists usually follow the style guidelines for citations in the *Publication Manual of the American Psychological Association* (APA, 2010). When a writer describes or paraphrases another person's ideas, the writer must cite the original author's last name and the year of publication. Writers must be careful not to paraphrase the original text too closely; failure to put the original source in one's own words is a form of plagiarism. To avoid plagiarizing when using another person's exact words, the writer puts quotation marks around the quoted text and indicates the page number where the quotation appeared in the original source. Complete source citations are included in the References section of the publication for all quoted or paraphrased works. **Figure 4.9** presents examples of these guidelines.

Plagiarism is a serious offense—not only in published work by professional researchers, but also in papers students submit for college courses. Every university and college has plagiarism policies that prohibit students from copying the words or ideas of others without proper credit. Students who plagiarize in their academic work are subject to disciplinary action—including expulsion, in some cases.

« For further discussion of plagiarism in writing and the APA guidelines, see Presenting Results at the end of this book.

ANIMAL RESEARCH (STANDARD 8.09)

In some branches of psychology, research is conducted almost entirely on animal subjects: rats, mice, cockroaches, sea snails, dogs, rabbits, cats, chimpanzees, and others. The ethical debates surrounding animal research can be just as complex as those for human participants. Most people have a profound respect for animals and compassion for their well-being. Psychologists and nonpsychologists alike want to protect animals from undue suffering.

Legal Protection for Laboratory Animals. In Standard 8.09, the APA lists ethical guidelines for the care of animals in research laboratories. Psychologists who use animals in research must care for them humanely, must use as few animals

Even Einstein Struggled: Effects of Learning About Great Scientists' Struggles on High School Students' Motivation to Learn Science

Xiaodong Lin-Siegler and Janet N. Ahn
Teachers College, Columbia University

Jondou Chen
University of Washington

Fu-Fen Anny Fang and Myra Luna-Lucero
Teachers College, Columbia University

Students' beliefs that success to learn. For example, such t taking science and math cou story-based instruction that n emphasizing the achievements of these scientists, or (c) the control condition, providing more content instruction in physics that the student were studying in school.

Students in the struggle story condition perceived scientists as individuals, like themselves, who needed to overcome obstacles to succeed. In contrast, students in the achievement story condition expressed views that scientists are innately talented individuals who are endowed with a special aptitude for science. Learning about scientists' struggles not only sparked interest among students who initially displayed little interest for science but also improved students' retention of theoretical material and performance in solving more complex tasks based on the lesson material.

Paraphrasing too close to the original.

The absence of quote marks around the highlighted areas presents the authors' words as the writer's own; passage is plagiarized even though it is cited.

Correct presentation of a direct quotation from the article	**Correct presentation of a paraphrase**	
The authors explained that "students in the struggle story condition perceived scientists as individuals, like themselves, who needed to overcome obstacles to succeed. In contrast, students in the achievement story condition expressed views that scientists are innately talented individuals who are endowed with a special aptitude for science" (Lin-Siegler, Ahn, Chen, Fang, & Luna-Lucero, 2016, p. 317).	The authors explained that the two stories led students to think about scientists in different ways. When they'd read a struggle story, they tended to think scientists were regular people. But when they'd read an achievement story, they tended to think scientists were more special and talented (Lin-Siegler, Ahn, Chen, Fang, & Luna-Lucero, 2016).	The authors explained that students in the struggle condition considered scientists as individuals like themselves. On the other hand, students in the achievement story condition thought that scientists are innately talented individuals with a special aptitude for science (Lin-Siegler, Ahn, Chen, Fang, & Luna-Lucero, 2016).

References

Lin-Siegler, X. D., Ahn, J., Chen, J., Fang, A., & Luna-Lucero, M. (2016). Even Einstein struggled: Effects of learning about great scientists' struggles on high school students' motivation to learn science. *Journal of Educational Psychology, 108,* 314–328.

FIGURE 4.9

Avoiding plagiarism.

Writers must cite direct quotations using quote marks, author name, year of publication, and page number. Paraphrasing must be cited with the author name and year. Paraphrasing that is too close to the original is plagiarism, even when it is cited.

as possible, and must be sure the research is valuable enough to justify using animal subjects.

In addition to these APA standards, psychologists must follow federal and local laws for animal care and protection. In the United States, the Animal Welfare Act (AWA) outlines standards and guidelines for the treatment of animals (Animal Welfare Act, 1966). The AWA applies to many species of animals in research laboratories and other contexts, including zoos and pet stores.

The AWA mandates relevant research institutions to have a local board called the Institutional Animal Care and Use Committee (IACUC, pronounced "EYE-a-kuk"). Similar to an IRB, the IACUC must approve any animal research project before it can begin (Animal Welfare Act, 1966). It must contain at least three members: a veterinarian, a practicing scientist who is familiar with the goals and procedures of animal research, and a member of the local community who is unconnected with the institution. The IACUC requires researchers to submit an extensive protocol specifying how animals will be treated and protected. The IACUC application also includes the scientific justification for the research: Applicants must demonstrate that the proposed study has not already been done and explain why the research is important. The AWA does not cover mice, rats, and birds, but such species are included in the oversight of IACUC boards.

After approving a research project, the IACUC monitors the treatment of animals throughout the research process. It inspects the labs every 6 months. If a laboratory violates a procedure outlined in the proposal, the IACUC or a government agency can stop the experiment, shut the lab down, or discontinue government funding. In European countries and Canada, similar laws apply.

Animal Care Guidelines and the Three Rs. Animal researchers in the United States use the resources of the *Guide for the Care and Use of Laboratory Animals*, which focuses on what's known as the Three Rs: replacement, refinement, and reduction (National Research Council, 2011).

- *Replacement* means researchers should find alternatives to animals in research when possible. For example, some studies can use computer simulations instead of animal subjects.
- *Refinement* means researchers must modify experimental procedures and other aspects of animal care to minimize or eliminate animal distress.
- *Reduction* means researchers should adopt experimental designs and procedures that require the fewest animal subjects possible.

In addition, the manual provides guidelines for housing facilities, diet, and other aspects of animal care in research. The guide indicates which species must be housed in social groups and specifies cage sizes, temperature and humidity ranges, air quality, lighting and noise conditions, sanitation procedures, and enrichments such as toys and bedding.

THIS IS ANIMAL EXPERIMENTATION

Don't let anyone tell you different.
PeTA

FIGURE 4.10
A poster opposing animal research.

Attitudes of Scientists and Students Toward Animal Research. In surveys, the majority of psychology students and faculty support the use of animals in research (Plous, 1996a). Nationally, about 47% of Americans favor the use of animals in research; the more education people have, the more likely they are to back it (Pew Research Center, 2015). In fact, when people read about the requirements stated in the AWA, they become more supportive of animal research (Metzger, 2015). In other words, people seem to favor animal research more if they know it protects the welfare of animal subjects.

Attitudes of Animal Rights Groups. Since the mid-1970s in the United States, some groups have increased their visibility and have assumed a more extreme position—arguing for animal rights, rather than animal welfare (**Figure 4.10**). Groups such as People for the Ethical Treatment of Animals (PETA), as well as other groups, both mainstream and marginal, violent and nonviolent, have tried to discover and expose cruelty to animals in research laboratories.

Animal rights groups generally base their activities on one of two arguments (Kimmel, 2007). First, they may believe animals are just as likely as humans to experience suffering. They feel humans should not be elevated above other animals: Because all kinds of animals can suffer, all of them should be protected from painful research procedures. According to this view, a certain type of research with animals could be allowed, but only if it might also be permitted with human participants.

Second, some groups also believe animals have inherent rights, equal to those of humans. These activists argue that most researchers do not treat animals as creatures with rights; instead, animals are treated as resources to be used and discarded (Kimmel, 2007). In a way, this argument draws on the principle of justice, as outlined in the Belmont Report and the APA Ethical Principles: Animal rights activists do not believe animals should unduly bear the burden of research that benefits a different species (humans). Both arguments lead animal rights groups to conclude that many research practices using animals are morally wrong. Some activists accuse researchers who study animals of conducting cruel and unethical experiments (Kimmel, 2007).

The members of these groups may be politically active, vocal, and sincerely devoted to the protection of animals. In a survey, Herzog (1993) concluded they are "intelligent, articulate, and sincere . . . [and] eager to discuss their views about the treatment of animals" with a scientist (quoted in Kimmel, 2007, p. 118). Consistent with this view, Plous (1998) polled animal rights activists and found most to be open to compromise via a respectful dialogue with animal researchers.

Ethically Balancing Animal Welfare, Animal Rights, and Animal Research. Given the laws governing animal welfare and given the broad awareness (if not universal endorsement) of animal rights arguments, you can be sure that today's research with animals in psychological science is not conducted lightly or irresponsibly. On the contrary, though research with animals is widespread, animal researchers are generally thoughtful and respectful of animal welfare.

Animal researchers defend their use of animal subjects with three primary arguments. The first and central argument is that animal research has resulted in numerous benefits to humans and animals alike (**Figure 4.11**). Animal research has contributed countless valuable lessons about psychology, biology, and neuroscience; discoveries about basic processes of vision, the organization of the brain, the course of infection, disease prevention, and therapeutic drugs. Animal research has made fundamental contributions to both basic and applied science, for both humans and animals.

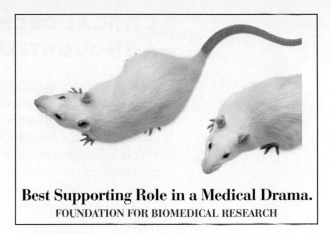

Best Supporting Role in a Medical Drama.
FOUNDATION FOR BIOMEDICAL RESEARCH

FIGURE 4.11
How do researchers achieve an ethical balance between concern for animal welfare and the benefits to society from research using animals?

Therefore, as outlined in the Belmont Report and APA Ethical Principles, ethical thinking means that research scientists and the public must evaluate the costs and benefits of research projects—in terms of both the subjects used and the potential outcomes.

Second, supporters argue that animal researchers are sensitive to animal welfare. They think about the pain and suffering of animals in their studies and take steps to avoid or reduce it. The IACUC oversight process and the *Guide for the Care and Use of Laboratory Animals* help ensure that animals are treated with care. Third, researchers have successfully reduced the number of animals they need to use because of new procedures that do not require animal testing (Kimmel, 2007). Some animal researchers even believe animal rights groups have exaggerated (or fabricated, in some cases) the cruelty of animal research (Coile & Miller, 1984) and that some activists have largely ignored the valuable scientific and medical discoveries that have resulted from animal research.

CHECK YOUR UNDERSTANDING

1. What are the five ethical principles outlined by the APA? Which two are not included in the three principles of the Belmont Report?

2. Name several ways the Animal Welfare Act, IACUC boards, and the *Guide for the Care and Use of Laboratory Animals* influence animal research.

1. See p. 98 and Table 4.1. 2. See pp. 105–109.

ETHICAL DECISION MAKING: A THOUGHTFUL BALANCE

Ethical decision making, as you have learned, does not involve simple yes-or-no decisions; it requires a balance of priorities. When faced with a study that could possibly harm human participants or animals, researchers (and their IRBs) consider the potential benefits of the research: Will it contribute something important to society? Many people believe that research with some degree of risk is justified, if the benefit from the knowledge gained from the results is great. In contrast, if the risk to participants becomes too high, the new knowledge may not be valuable enough to justify the harm.

Another example of this careful balance comes from the way researchers implement the informed consent process. On the one hand, researchers may want to demonstrate their gratitude and respect for participants by compensating them with money or some other form of reward or credit. Paying participants might help ensure that the samples represent a variety of populations, as the principle of justice requires, because some people might not participate in a study without a financial incentive. On the other hand, if the rewards researchers offer are too great, they could tip the balance. If monetary rewards become too influential, potential participants may no longer be able to give free consent.

Although in some cases it is easy to conduct important research that has a low degree of risk to participants, other ethical decisions are extremely difficult. Researchers try to balance respect for animal subjects and human participants, protections from harm, benefits to society, and awareness of justice. As this chapter has emphasized, they do not weigh the factors in this balance alone. Influenced by IRBs, IACUCs, peers, and sociocultural norms, they strive to conduct research that is valuable to society and to do it in an ethical manner.

Ethical research practice is not performed according to a set of permanent rules. It is an evolving and dynamic process that takes place in historical and cultural contexts. Researchers refine their ethical decision making in response to good and bad experiences, changing social norms (even public opinion), and scientific discoveries. By following ethical principles, researchers make it more likely that their work will benefit, and be appreciated by, the general public.

The Working it Through section shows how ethical principles can be applied to a controversial research example.

CHECK YOUR UNDERSTANDING

1. Give some examples from the preceding discussion of how the ethical practice of research balances priorities.

1. Answers will vary.

Did a Study Conducted on Facebook Violate Ethical Principles?

A few years ago, researchers from Facebook and Cornell University collaborated to test the effect of emotional contagion through online social networks (Kramer, Guillory, & Hancock, 2014). Emotional contagion is the tendency for emotions to spread in face-to-face interactions. When people express happiness, people around them become happier, too. Researchers randomly selected over 600,000 Facebook users and withheld certain posts from their newsfeeds. From one group, they withheld posts with positive emotion words (such as *happy* and *love*). From a second group, they withheld posts at random (not altering their emotional content). A third group had negative posts withheld. The researchers measured how many positive and negative emotion words people used on their own Facebook timelines. The results showed the group who'd seen fewer positive posts tended to use fewer positive and more negative emotion words on their own pages. The effect size was extremely small, but the researchers concluded that emotional contagion can happen even through online text. After the media publicized the study's results, commentators raised an alarm. Facebook manipulated people's newsfeeds? Is that ethical? We can organize the critiques of this study around the topics in Chapter 4.

QUESTIONS TO ASK	DETAILS FROM THE STUDY	INTERPRETATION AND EVALUATION
Institutional review board		
Was the study reviewed by an IRB?	The study's lead scientist was employed by Facebook, and as a private company, Facebook is not required to follow federal ethical guidelines such as the Common Rule.	This example highlights that private businesses sometimes conduct research on people who use their products and such research might not be reviewed for ethics.
	The other two scientists had the study reviewed by Cornell University's IRB, as required. The Cornell IRB decided the study did not fall under its program because the data had been collected by Facebook.	

(Continued)

QUESTIONS TO ASK	DETAILS FROM THE STUDY	INTERPRETATION AND EVALUATION
Informed consent Did Facebook users get to decide if they wanted to participate?	The study's authors reported that when people create a Facebook account, they agree to a Data Use Policy, and this constituted informed consent.	Not all critics agreed. The journal in which the study was published attached an Editorial Statement of Concern stating that, though it had agreed to publish the paper, it was concerned that the study did not allow participants to opt out.
Deception and debriefing Were participants told in full about the study after they participated?	Participants were not told their newsfeeds might have been manipulated for research purposes.	Participants were deceived through omission of information. In addition, people were not debriefed afterwards; even now, people cannot find out whether they had participated in this study or not.
If an IRB had considered this study in advance, they would have evaluated it, first, in terms of **respect for persons**.	The application of respect for persons is informed consent. Participants did not consent to this particular study.	Although people did not provide informed consent for this particular study, informed consent might not be deemed necessary when a study takes place in a public place where people can reasonably expect to be observed. Do you think the Facebook study falls into the same category?
An IRB would also ask about **beneficence**: Did the research harm anyone, and did it benefit society?	The study itself demonstrated that people felt worse when positive emotion posts were removed. The researchers argued that the study benefited society. Social media plays a role in most people's daily lives, and emotions are linked to well-being.	People may have suffered a bit, but was their distress any greater than it might have been in daily life? (Perhaps not, because the effect size was so small.) In addition, some argued that Facebook already manipulates newsfeeds. For example, your own newsfeed's stories and posts have been selected according to a computerized algorithm. The results did show that social media is a source of emotional contagion that could potentially improve public health. Do you find this study to be beneficial to society?
An IRB would consider whether the principle of **justice** was met. Were the people who participated in the study representative of the people who can benefit from its findings?	The study randomly selected hundreds of thousands of people who read Facebook in English.	Because the sample was selected at random, it appears that the people who "bore the burden" of research participation were the same types who could benefit from its findings. The principle of justice has probably been met.

CHAPTER REVIEW

Summary

Whether psychologists are testing a frequency, association, or causal claim, they strive to conduct their research ethically. Psychologists are guided by standard ethical principles as they plan and conduct their research.

Historical Examples

- The Tuskegee Syphilis Study, which took place in the U.S. during the 1930s through the 1970s, illustrates the ethics violations of harming people, not asking for consent, and targeting a particular group in research.

- The Milgram obedience studies illustrate the gray areas in ethical research, including how researchers define harm to participants and how they balance the importance of a study with the harm it might do.

Core Ethical Principles

- Achieving an ethical balance in research is guided by standards and laws. Many countries' ethical policies are governed by the Nuremberg Code and the Declaration of Helsinki. In the U.S., federal ethical policies are based on the Common Rule, which is grounded in the Belmont Report.

- The Belmont Report outlines three main principles for research: respect for persons, beneficence, and justice. Each principle has specific applications in the research setting.

- Respect for persons involves the process of informed consent and the protection of special groups in research, such as children and prisoners.

- Beneficence involves the evaluation of risks and benefits, to participants in the study and to society as a whole.

- Justice involves the way participants are selected for the research. One group of people should not bear an undue burden for research participation, and participants should be representative of the groups that will also benefit from the research.

Guidelines for Psychologists: The APA Ethical Principles

- The APA guides psychologists by providing a set of principles and standards for research, teaching, and other professional roles.

- The APA's five general principles include the three Belmont Report principles, plus two more: the principle of fidelity and responsibility, and the principle of integrity.

- The APA's Ethical Standard 8 provides enforceable guidelines for researchers to follow. It includes specific information for informed consent, institutional review boards, deception, debriefing, research misconduct, and animal research.

Ethical Decision Making: A Thoughtful Balance

- For any type of claim psychologists are investigating, ethical decision making requires balancing a variety of priorities.

- Psychologists must balance benefits to society with risks to research participants, and balance compensation for participants with undue coercion for their involvement.

Key Terms

debriefed, p. 93
principle of respect for
    persons, p. 95
informed consent, p. 95
principle of beneficence, p. 95

anonymous study, p. 96
confidential study, p. 96
principle of justice, p. 96
institutional review board
    (IRB), p. 99

deception, p. 101
data fabrication, p. 103
data falsification, p. 103
plagiarism, p. 105

 **To see samples of chapter concepts in the popular media,
visit www.everydayresearchmethods.com and click the box for Chapter 4.**

Review Questions

1. Which of the following is not one of the three principles of the Belmont Report?

   a. Respect for persons

   b. Justice

   c. Beneficence

   d. Fidelity and responsibility

2. In a study of a new drug for asthma, a researcher
   finds that the group receiving the drug is doing much
   better than the control group, whose members are
   receiving a placebo. Which principle of the Belmont
   Report requires the researcher to also give the control group the opportunity to receive the new drug?

   a. Informed consent

   b. Justice

   c. Beneficence

   d. Respect for persons

3. In order to study a sample of participants from only
   one ethnic group, researchers must first demonstrate
   that the problem being studied is especially prevalent
   in that ethnic group. This is an application of which
   principle from the Belmont Report?

   a. Respect for persons

   b. Beneficence

   c. Special protection

   d. Justice

4. Following a study using deception, how does the
   researcher attempt to restore an honest relationship
   with the participant?

   a. By apologizing to the participant and offering mon-
      etary compensation for any discomfort or stress.

   b. By debriefing each participant in a structured
      conversation.

   c. By reassuring the participant that all names and
      identifiers will be removed from the data.

   d. By giving each participant a written description
      of the study's goals and hypotheses, along with
      references for further reading.

5. What type of research misconduct involves representing the ideas or words of others as one's own?

   a. Plagiarism

   b. Obfuscation

   c. Suppression

   d. Data falsification

6. Which of the following is not one of the Three R's
   provided by the *Guide for the Care and Use of
   Laboratory Animals*?

   a. Reduction

   b. Replacement

   c. Restoration

   d. Refinement

Learning Actively

1. A developmental psychologist applies to an institutional review board (IRB), proposing to observe children ages 2–10 playing in the local McDonald's play area. Because the area is public, the researcher does not plan to ask for informed consent from the children's parents. What ethical concerns exist for this study? What questions might an IRB ask?

2. A social psychologist plans to hand out surveys in her 300-level undergraduate class. The survey asks about students' study habits. The psychologist does not ask the students to put their names on the survey; instead, students will put completed surveys into a large box at the back of the room. Because of the low risk involved in participation and the anonymous nature of the survey, the researcher requests to be exempted from formal informed consent procedures. What ethical concerns exist for this study? What questions might an IRB ask?

3. Consider the use of deception in psychological research. Does participation in a study involving deception (such as the Milgram obedience studies) necessarily cause harm? Recall that when evaluating the risks and benefits of a study, the researcher considers both the participants in the study and society as a whole—anyone who might be affected by the research. What might be some of the costs and benefits to participants who are deceived? What might be some of the costs and benefits to society of studies involving deception?

4. Use the Internet to look up your college's definition of plagiarism. Does it match the one given in APA Ethical Standard 8.11? If not, what does it exclude or add? What are the consequences for plagiarism at your college?

5. Use the Internet to find out the procedures of the IRB at your college. According to your college's policies, do undergraduates like you need special ethics training before they can conduct research? Does research conducted in a research methods class need formal IRB approval? Does your college categorize studies that are "exempt" from IRB review versus "Expedited" versus "Full board" review? If so, what kinds of studies are considered exempt?

Who Are the Happiest People in the World?

Gallup, 2016

Can Money Buy You Happiness?

Wall Street Journal, 2014

Gratitude Is for Lovers

Greater Good, 2013

5

Identifying Good Measurement

WHETHER STUDYING THE NUMBER of polar bears left in the Arctic Circle, the strength of a bar of steel, the number of steps people take each day, or the level of human happiness, every scientist faces the challenge of measurement. When researchers test theories or pursue empirical questions, they have to systematically observe the phenomena by collecting data. Such systematic observations require measurements, and these measurements must be good ones—or else they are useless.

Measurement in psychological research can be particularly challenging. Many of the phenomena psychologists are interested in—motivation, emotion, thinking, reasoning—are difficult to measure directly. Happiness, the topic of much research, is a good example of a construct that could be hard to assess. Is it really possible to quantify how happy people are? Are the measurements accurate? Before testing, for example, whether people who make more money are happier, we might ask whether we can really measure happiness. Maybe people misrepresent their level of well-being, or maybe people aren't aware of how happy they are. How do we evaluate who is really happy and who isn't? This chapter explains how to ask questions about the quality of a study's measures—the construct validity of quantifications of things like happiness, gratitude, or wealth. Construct validity, remember, refers to how well a study's variables are measured or manipulated.

Construct validity is a crucial piece of any psychological research study—for frequency, association, or causal claims. This chapter focuses on the construct validity of *measured variables*. You will learn, first, about different ways researchers operationalize

LEARNING OBJECTIVES

A year from now, you should still be able to:

1.
Interrogate the construct validity of a study's variables.

2.
Describe the kinds of evidence that support the construct validity of a measured variable.

» For a review of measured and manipulated variables, see Chapter 3, pp. 58–59.

measured variables. Then you'll learn how you can evaluate the reliability and validity of those measurements. The construct validity of *manipulated variables* is covered in Chapter 10.

WAYS TO MEASURE VARIABLES

The process of measuring variables involves some key decisions. As researchers decide how they should operationalize each variable in a study, they choose among three common types of measures: self-report, observational, and physiological. They also decide on the most appropriate scale of measurement for each variable they plan to investigate.

More About Conceptual and Operational Variables

In Chapter 3, you learned about operationalization, the process of turning a construct of interest into a measured or manipulated variable. Much psychological research requires two definitions of each variable. The conceptual definition, or construct, is the researcher's definition of the variable in question at a theoretical level. The operational definition represents a researcher's specific decision about how to measure or manipulate the conceptual variable.

OPERATIONALIZING "HAPPINESS"

Let's take the variable "happiness," for example. One research team, led by Ed Diener, began the study of happiness by developing a precise conceptual definition. Specifically, Diener's team reasoned that the word *happiness* might have a variety of meanings, so they explicitly limited their interest to "subjective well-being" (or well-being from a person's own perspective).

After defining happiness at the conceptual level, Diener and his colleagues developed an operational definition. Because they were interested in people's perspectives on their own well-being, they chose to operationalize subjective well-being, in part, by asking people to report on their own happiness in a questionnaire format. The researchers decided people should use their own criteria to describe what constitutes a "good life" (Pavot & Diener, 1993). They worded their questions so people could think about the interpretation of life satisfaction that was appropriate for them. These researchers operationally defined, or measured, subjective well-being by asking people to respond to five items about their satisfaction with life using a 7-point scale; 1 corresponded to "strongly disagree" and 7 corresponded to "strongly agree":

_____ 1. In most ways my life is close to my ideal.

_____ 2. The conditions of my life are excellent.

_____ 3. I am satisfied with my life.

_____ 4. So far I have gotten the important things I want in life.

_____ 5. If I could live my life over, I would change almost nothing.

The unhappiest people would get a total score of 5 on this self-report scale because they would answer "strongly disagree," or 1, to all five items (1 + 1 + 1 + 1 + 1 = 5). The happiest people would get a total score of 35 on this scale because they would answer "strongly agree," or 7, to all five items (7 + 7 + 7 + 7 + 7 = 35). Those at the neutral point would score 20—right in between satisfied and dissatisfied (4 + 4 + 4 + 4 + 4 = 20). Diener and Diener (1996) reported some data based on this scale, concluding that most people are happy, meaning most people scored above 20. For example, 63% of high school and college students scored above 20 in one study, and 72% of disabled adults scored above 20 in another study.

In choosing this operational definition of subjective well-being, the research team started with only one possible measure, even though there are many other ways to study this concept. Another way to measure happiness is to use a single question called the Ladder of Life (Cantril, 1965). The question goes like this:

> Imagine a ladder with steps numbered from 0 at the bottom to 10 at the top. The top of the ladder represents the best possible life for you and the bottom of the ladder represents the worst possible life for you. On which step of the ladder would you say you personally stand at this time?

On this measure, participants respond by giving a value between 0 and 10. The Gallup polling organization uses the Ladder of Life scale in its daily Gallup-Healthways Well-Being Index.

You might be thinking one of these operational definitions seems like a better measure of happiness than the other. Which one do you think is best? We'll see that they both do a good job of measuring the construct. Diener's research team and Gallup have both learned their measures of happiness are accurate because they have collected data on them, as we'll see later in this chapter.

OPERATIONALIZING OTHER CONCEPTUAL VARIABLES

To study conceptual variables other than happiness, researchers follow a similar process: They start by stating a definition of their construct (the conceptual variable) and then create an operational definition. For example, to measure the association between wealth and happiness, researchers need to measure not only happiness, but also wealth. They might operationally define wealth by asking about salary in dollars, by asking for bank account balances, or even by observing the kind of car people drive.

Consider another variable that has been studied in research on relationships: gratitude toward one's partner. Researchers who measure gratitude toward a relationship partner might operationalize it by asking people how often they thank their partner for something they did. Or they might ask people how appreciative

TABLE 5.1

Variables and Operational Definitions

VARIABLE	ONE POSSIBLE OPERATIONAL DEFINITION (OPERATIONALIZATION)	ANOTHER POSSIBLE OPERATIONAL DEFINITION
Gratitude toward one's relationship partner	Asking people if they agree with the statement: "I appreciate my partner."	Watching couples interact and counting how many times they thank each other.
Gender	Asking people to report on a survey whether they identify as male or female.	In phone interviews, a researcher guesses gender through the sound of the person's voice.
Wealth	Asking people to report their income on various ranges (less than $20,000, between $20,000 and 50,000, and more than $50,000).	Coding the value of a car from 1 (older, lower-status vehicle) to 5 (new, high-status vehicle in good condition).
Intelligence	An IQ test that includes problem-solving items, memory and vocabulary questions, and puzzles.	Recording brain activity while people solve difficult problems.
Well-being (happiness)	10-point Ladder of Life scale.	Diener's 5-item subjective well-being scale.

they usually feel. Even a simple variable such as gender must be operationalized. As **Table 5.1** shows, any conceptual variable can be operationalized in a number of ways. In fact, operationalizations are one place where creativity comes into the research process, as researchers work to develop new and better measures of their constructs.

Three Common Types of Measures

The types of measures psychological scientists typically use to operationalize variables generally fall into three categories: self-report, observational, and physiological.

SELF-REPORT MEASURES

A **self-report measure** operationalizes a variable by recording people's answers to questions about themselves in a questionnaire or interview. Diener's five-item scale and the Ladder of Life question are both examples of self-report measures about life satisfaction. Similarly, asking people how much they appreciate their partner and asking about gender identity are both self-report measures. If stress was the variable being studied, researchers might ask people to self-report on the frequency of specific events they've experienced in the past year, such as marriage, divorce, or moving (e.g., Holmes & Rahe, 1967).

   In research on children, self-reports may be replaced with parent reports or teacher reports. These measures ask parents or teachers to respond to a series of questions, such as describing the child's recent life events, the words the child knows, or the child's typical classroom behaviors. (Chapter 6 discusses situations when self-report measures are likely to be accurate and when they might be biased.)

OBSERVATIONAL MEASURES

An **observational measure**, sometimes called a *behavioral measure*, operationalizes a variable by recording observable behaviors or physical traces of behaviors. For example, a researcher could operationalize happiness by observing how many times a person smiles. Intelligence tests can be considered observational measures, because the people who administer such tests in person are observing people's intelligent behaviors (such as being able to correctly solve a puzzle or quickly detect a pattern). Coding how much a person's car cost would be an observational measure of wealth (Piff, Stancato, Côté, Mendoza-Denton, & Keltner, 2012).

Observational measures may record physical traces of behavior. Stress behaviors could be measured by counting the number of tooth marks left on a person's pencil, or a researcher could measure stressful events by consulting public legal records to document whether people have recently married, divorced, or moved. (Chapter 6 addresses how an observer's ratings of behavior might be accurate and how they might be biased.)

PHYSIOLOGICAL MEASURES

A **physiological measure** operationalizes a variable by recording biological data, such as brain activity, hormone levels, or heart rate. Physiological measures usually require the use of equipment to amplify, record, and analyze biological data. For example, moment-to-moment happiness has been measured using facial electromyography (EMG)—a way of electronically recording tiny movements in the muscles in the face. Facial EMG can be said to detect a happy facial expression because people who are smiling show particular patterns of muscle movement around the eyes and cheeks.

Other constructs might be measured using a brain scanning technique called functional magnetic resonance imaging, or fMRI. In a typical fMRI study, people engage in a carefully structured series of psychological tasks (such as looking at three types of photos or playing a series of rock-paper-scissors games) while lying in an MRI machine. The MRI equipment records and codes the relative changes in blood flow in particular regions of the brain, as shown in **Figure 5.1**. When more

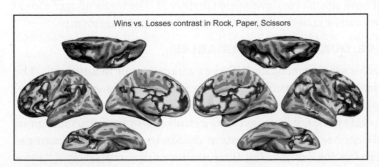

Wins vs. Losses contrast in Rock, Paper, Scissors

FIGURE 5.1

Images from fMRI scans showing brain activity.

In this study of how people respond to rewards and losses, the researchers tracked blood flow patterns in the brain when people had either won, lost, or tied a rock-paper-scissors game played with a computer. They found that many regions of the brain respond more to wins than to losses, as indicated by the highlighted regions. (Source: Vickery, Chun, & Lee, 2011.)

blood flows to a brain region while people perform a certain task, researchers conclude that brain area is activated because of the patterns on the scanned images.

Some research indicates a way fMRI might be used to measure intelligence in the future. Specifically, the brains of people with higher intelligence are more efficient at solving complex problems; their fMRI scans show relatively less brain activity for complex problems (Deary, Penke, & Johnson, 2010). Therefore, future researchers may be able to use the efficiency of brain activity as a physiological measure of intelligence. A physiological measure from a century ago turned out to be flawed: People used head circumference to measure intelligence, under the mistaken impression that smarter brains would be stored inside larger skulls (Gould, 1996).

A physiological way to operationalize stress might be to measure the amount of the hormone cortisol released in saliva because people under stress show higher levels of cortisol (Carlson, 2009). Skin conductance, an electronic recording of the activity in the sweat glands of the hands or feet, is another way to measure stress physiologically. People under more stress have more activity in these glands. Another physiological measure used in psychology research is the detection of electrical patterns in the brain using electroencephalography (EEG).

WHICH OPERATIONALIZATION IS BEST?

A single construct can be operationalized in several ways, from self-report to behavioral observation to physiological measures. Many people erroneously believe physiological measures are the most accurate, but even their results have to be validated by using other measures. For instance, as mentioned above, researchers used fMRI to learn that the brain works more efficiently relative to level of intelligence. But how was participant intelligence established in the first place? Before doing the fMRI scans, the researchers gave the participants an IQ test—an observational measure (Deary et al., 2010). Similarly, researchers might trust an fMRI pattern to indicate when a person is genuinely happy. However, the only way a researcher could know that some pattern of brain activity was associated with happiness is by asking each person how happy he or she feels (a self-report measure) at the same time the brain scan was being done. As you'll learn later in this chapter, it's best when self-report, observational, and physiological measures show similar patterns of results.

Scales of Measurement

All variables must have at least two levels (see Chapter 3). The levels of operational variables, however, can be coded using different scales of measurement.

CATEGORICAL VS. QUANTITATIVE VARIABLES

Operational variables are primarily classified as categorical or quantitative. The levels of **categorical variables**, as the term suggests, are categories. (Categorical variables are also called *nominal variables*.) Examples are sex, whose levels are male and female; and species, whose levels in a study might be rhesus macaque, chimpanzee, and bonobo. A researcher might decide to assign numbers to the levels of a categorical variable (e.g., using "1" to represent rhesus macaques, "2" for chimps, and "3" for bonobos) during the data-entry process. However, the numbers do not have numerical meaning—a bonobo is different from a chimpanzee, but being a bonobo ("3") is not quantitatively "higher" than being a chimpanzee ("2").

In contrast, the levels of **quantitative variables** are coded with *meaningful* numbers. Height and weight are quantitative because they are measured in numbers, such as 170 centimeters or 65 kilograms. Diener's scale of subjective well-being is quantitative too, because a score of 35 represents more happiness than a score of 7. IQ score, level of brain activity, and amount of salivary cortisol are also quantitative variables.

THREE TYPES OF QUANTITATIVE VARIABLES

For certain kinds of statistical purposes, researchers may need to further classify a quantitative variable in terms of ordinal, interval, or ratio scale.

An **ordinal scale** of measurement applies when the numerals of a quantitative variable represent a ranked order. For example, a bookstore's website might display the top 10 best-selling books. We know that the #1 book sold more than the #2 book, and that #2 sold more than #3, but we don't know whether the number of books that separates #1 and #2 is equal to the number of books that separates #2 and #3. In other words, the intervals may be unequal. Maybe the first two rankings are only 10 books apart, and the second two rankings are 150,000 books apart. Similarly, a professor might use the order in which exams were turned in to operationalize how fast students worked. This represents ordinal data because the fastest exams are on the bottom of the pile—ranked 1. However, this variable has not quantified *how much* faster each exam was turned in, compared with the others.

An **interval scale** of measurement applies to the numerals of a quantitative variable that meet two conditions: First, the numerals represent equal intervals (distances) between levels, and second, there is no "true zero" (a person can get a score of 0, but the 0 does not really mean "nothing"). An IQ test is an interval scale—the distance between IQ scores of 100 and 105 represents the same as the distance between IQ scores of 105 and 110. However, a score of 0 on an IQ test does not mean a person has "no intelligence." Body temperature in degrees Celsius is another example of an interval scale—the intervals between levels are equal; however, a temperature of 0 degrees does not mean a person has "no temperature." Most researchers assume questionnaire scales like Diener's (scored from 1 = *strongly disagree* to 7 = *strongly agree*) are interval scales. They do not have a true zero but we assume the distances between numerals, from 1 to 7, are equivalent. Because they do not have a true zero, interval scales cannot allow a researcher to say things like "twice as hot" or "three times happier."

Finally, a **ratio scale** of measurement applies when the numerals of a quantitative variable have equal intervals and when the value of 0 truly means "none" or "nothing" of the variable being measured. On a knowledge test, a researcher might measure how many items people answer correctly. If people get a 0, it truly represents "nothing correct" (0 answers correct). A researcher might measure how frequently people blink their eyes in a stressful situation; number of eyeblinks is a

TABLE 5.2

Measurement Scales for Operational Variables

TYPE OF VARIABLE	CHARACTERISTICS	EXAMPLES
Categorical	Levels are categories.	Nationality. Type of music. Kind of phone people use.
Quantitative	Levels are coded with meaningful numbers.	
Ordinal	A quantitative variable in which numerals represent a rank order. Distance between subsequent numerals may not be equal.	Order of finishers in a swimming race. Ranking of 10 movies from most to least favorite.
Interval	A quantitative variable in which subsequent numerals represent equal distances, but there is no true zero.	IQ score. Shoe size. Degree of agreement on a 1–7 scale.
Ratio	A quantitative variable in which numerals represent equal distances and zero represents "none" of the variable being measured.	Number of exam questions answered correctly. Number of seconds to respond to a computer task. Height in cm.

ratio scale because 0 would represent zero eyeblinks. Because ratio scales do have a true zero, one can meaningfully say something like "Miguel answered twice as many problems as Diogo." **Table 5.2** summarizes all the above variations.

CHECK YOUR UNDERSTANDING

1. Explain why a variable will usually have only one conceptual definition but can have multiple operational definitions.

2. Name the three common ways in which researchers operationalize their variables.

3. In your own words, describe the difference between categorical and quantitative variables. Come up with new examples of variables that would fit the definition of ordinal, interval, and ratio scales.

1. See pp. 118–120. 2. See pp. 120–122. 3. See pp. 122–124.

RELIABILITY OF MEASUREMENT: ARE THE SCORES CONSISTENT?

Now that we've established different types of operationalizations, we can ask the important construct validity question: How do you know if a study's operationalizations are good ones? The construct validity of a measure has two aspects.

Reliability refers to how consistent the results of a measure are, and **validity** concerns whether the operationalization is measuring what it is supposed to measure. Both are important, and the first step is reliability.

Introducing Three Types of Reliability

Before deciding on the measures to use in a study, researchers collect their own data or review data collected by others. They use data because establishing the reliability of a measure is an empirical question. A measure's reliability is just what the word suggests: whether or not researchers can rely on a particular score. If an operationalization is reliable, it will yield a consistent pattern of scores every time.

Reliability can be assessed in three ways, depending on how a variable was operationalized, and all three involve consistency in measurement. With **test-retest reliability**, the researcher gets consistent scores every time he or she uses the measure. With **interrater reliability**, consistent scores are obtained no matter who measures the variable. With **internal reliability** (also called *internal consistency*), a study participant gives a consistent pattern of answers, no matter how the researcher has phrased the question.

TEST-RETEST RELIABILITY

To illustrate test-retest reliability, let's suppose a sample of people took an IQ test today. When they take it again 1 month later, the pattern of scores should be consistent: People who scored the highest at Time 1 should also score the highest at Time 2. Even if all the scores from Time 2 have increased since Time 1 (due to practice or training), the pattern should be consistent: The highest-scoring Time 1 people should still be the highest scoring people at Time 2. Test-retest reliability can apply whether the operationalization is self-report, observational, or physiological, but it's most relevant when researchers are measuring constructs (such as intelligence, personality, or gratitude) they expect to be relatively stable. Happy mood, for example, may reasonably fluctuate from month to month or year to year for a particular person, so less consistency would be expected in this variable.

INTERRATER RELIABILITY

With interrater reliability, two or more independent observers will come up with consistent (or very similar) findings. Interrater reliability is most relevant for observational measures. Suppose you are assigned to observe the number of times each child smiles in 1 hour at a daycare playground. Your lab partner is assigned to sit on the other side of the playground and make his own count of the same children's smiles. If, for one child, you record 12 smiles during the first hour, and your lab partner also records 12 smiles in that hour for the same child, there is interrater reliability. Any two observers watching the same children at the same time should agree about which child has smiled the most and which child has smiled the least.

INTERNAL RELIABILITY

The third kind of reliability, internal reliability, applies only to self-report scales with multiple items. Suppose a sample of people take Diener's five-item subjective well-being scale. The questions on his scale are worded differently, but each item is intended to be a measure of the same construct. Therefore, people who agree with the first item on the scale should also agree with the second item (as well as with Items 3, 4, and 5). Similarly, people who disagree with the first item should also disagree with Items 2, 3, 4, and 5. If the pattern is consistent across items in this way, the scale has internal reliability.

Using a Scatterplot to Quantify Reliability

Before using a particular measure in a study they are planning, researchers collect data to see if it is reliable. Researchers may use two statistical devices for data analysis: scatterplots (see Chapter 3) and the correlation coefficient r (discussed below). In fact, evidence for reliability is a special example of an association claim—the association between one version of the measure and another, between one coder and another, or between an earlier time and a later time.

Here's an example of how correlations are used to document reliability. Years ago, when people thought smarter people had larger heads, they may have tried to use head circumference as an operationalization of intelligence. Would this measure be reliable? Probably. Suppose you record the head circumference, in centimeters, for everyone in a classroom, using an ordinary tape measure. To see if the measurements were reliable, you could measure all the heads twice (test-retest reliability) or you could measure them first, and then have someone else measure them (interrater reliability).

Figure 5.2 shows how the results of such a measurement might look, in the form of a data table and a scatterplot. In the scatterplot, the first measurements of head circumference for four students are plotted on the y-axis. The circumferences as measured the second time—whether by you again (test-retest) or by a second observer (interrater)—are plotted on the x-axis. In this scatterplot, each dot represents a person measured twice.

We would expect the two measurements of head circumference to be about the same for each person. They are, so the dots on the scatterplot all fall almost exactly on the sloping line that would indicate perfect agreement. The two measures won't always be exactly the same because there is likely to be some measurement error that will lead to slightly different scores even for the same person (such as variations in the tape measure placement for each trial).

SCATTERPLOTS CAN SHOW INTERRATER AGREEMENT OR DISAGREEMENT

In a different scenario, suppose ten young children are being observed at a playground. Two independent observers, Mark and Matt, rate how happy each child appears to be, on a scale of 1 to 10. They later compare notes to see how well their

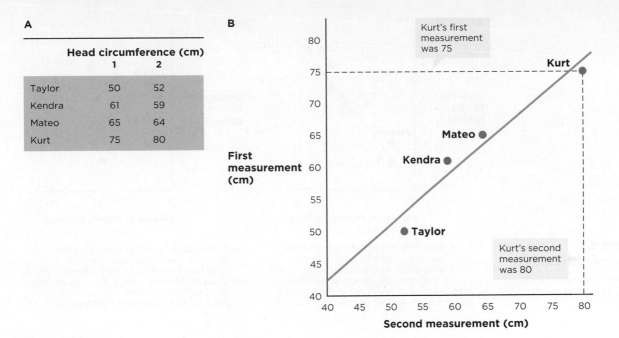

A

| | Head circumference (cm) | |
	1	2
Taylor	50	52
Kendra	61	59
Mateo	65	64
Kurt	75	80

FIGURE 5.2
Two measurements of head circumference.

(A) The data for four participants in table form. (B) The same data presented in a scatterplot.

ratings agree. From these notes, they create a scatterplot, plotting Observer Mark's ratings on the x-axis and Observer Matt's ratings on the y-axis.

If the data looked like those in **Figure 5.3A**, the ratings would have high interrater reliability. Both Mark and Matt rate Jay's happiness as 9—one of the happiest kids on the playground. Observer Mark rates Jackie a 2—one of the least happy kids; Observer Matt agreed because he rates her 3, and so on. The two observers do not show perfect agreement, but there are no great disagreements about the happiest and least happy kids. Again, the points are scattered around the plot a bit, but they hover close to the sloping line that would indicate perfect agreement.

In contrast, suppose the data looked like **Figure 5.3B**, which shows much less agreement. Here, the two observers are Mark and Peter, and they are watching the same children at the same time, but Mark gives Jay a rating of 9 and Peter thinks he rates only a 6. Mark considers Jackie's behavior to be shy and withdrawn and rates her a 2, but Peter thinks she seems calm and content and rates her a 7. Here the interrater reliability would be considered unacceptably low. One reason could be that the observers did not have a clear enough operational definition of "happiness" to work with. Another reason could be that one or both of the coders has not been trained well enough yet.

A scatterplot can thus be a helpful tool for visualizing the agreement between two administrations of the same measurement (test-retest reliability) or between two coders (interrater reliability). Using a scatterplot, you can see whether the

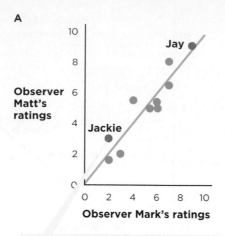

A

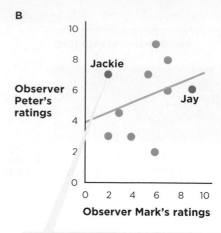

B

FIGURE 5.3
Interrater reliability.

(A) Interrater reliability is high. (B) Interrater reliability is low.

If the data show this pattern, it means Matt and Mark have good interrater reliability. Mark rated Jackie as one of the least happy children in the sample, and so did Matt. Mark rated Jay as one of the happiest children in the sample, and so did Matt.

If the data show this pattern, it means Mark and Peter have poor interrater reliability. For example, they disagree about Jackie—Mark rated Jackie as one of the least happy children in the sample, but Peter rated her as one of the happiest.

two ratings agree (if the dots are close to a straight line drawn through them) or whether they disagree (if the dots scatter widely from a straight line drawn through them).

Using the Correlation Coefficient *r* to Quantify Reliability

Scatterplots can provide a picture of a measure's reliability. However, a more common and efficient way to see if a measure is reliable is to use the correlation coefficient. Researchers can use a single number, called a **correlation coefficient**, or *r*, to indicate how close the dots, or points, on a scatterplot are to a line drawn through them.

»
For more on the slope of a scatterplot, see Chapter 3, pp. 63–66.

Notice that the scatterplots in **Figure 5.4** differ in two important ways. One difference is that the scattered clouds of points slope in different directions. In Figure 5.4A and Figure 5.4B the points slope upward from left to right, in Figure 5.4C they slope downward, and in Figure 5.4D they do not slope up or down at all. This slope is referred to as the direction of the relationship, and the **slope direction** can be positive, negative, or zero—that is, sloping up, sloping down, or not sloping at all.

The other way the scatterplots differ is that in some, the dots are close to a straight, sloping line; in others, the dots are more spread out. This spread corresponds to the **strength** of the relationship. In general, the relationship is strong when dots are close to the line; it is weak when dots are spread out.

The numbers below the scatterplots are the correlation coefficients, or *r*. The *r* indicates the same two things as the scatterplot: the direction of the relationship and the strength of the relationship, both of which psychologists use in evaluating reliability evidence. Notice that when the slope is positive, *r* is positive; when the slope is negative, *r* is negative. The value of *r* can fall only between 1.0 and –1.0. When the relationship is strong, *r* is close to either 1 or –1; when the relationship is weak, *r* is closer to zero. An *r* of 1.0 represents the strongest possible positive relationship, and an *r* of –1.0 represents the strongest possible negative relationship. If there is no relationship between two variables, *r* will be .00 or close to .00 (i.e., .02 or –.04).

Those are the basics. How do psychologists use the strength and direction of *r* to evaluate reliability evidence?

«
For more on how to compute *r*, see Statistics Review: Descriptive Statistics, pp. 470–472.

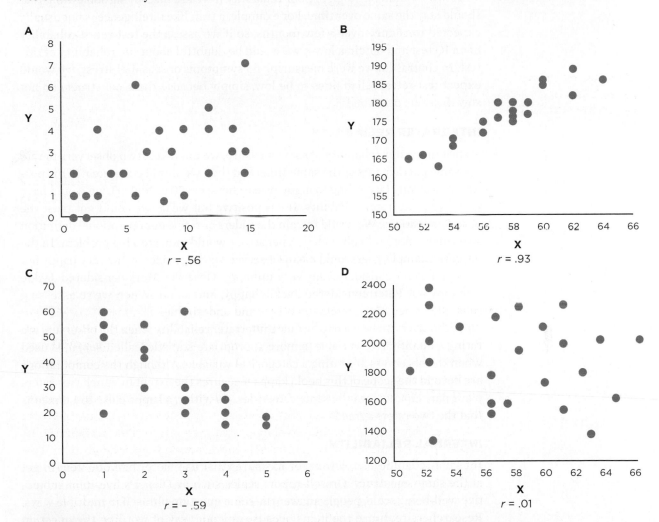

FIGURE 5.4
Correlation coefficients.

Notice the differences in the correlation coefficients (*r*) in these scatterplots. The correlation coefficient describes both the direction and the strength of the association between the two variables, regardless of the scale on which the variables are measured.

TEST-RETEST RELIABILITY

To assess the test-retest reliability of some measure, we would measure the same set of participants on that measure at least twice. First we'd give the set of participants the measure at Time 1. Then we'd wait a while (say, 2 months), and contact the same set of people again, at Time 2. After recording each person's score at Time 1 and Time 2, we could compute r. If r turns out to be positive and strong (for test-retest, we might expect .5 or above), we would have very good test-retest reliability. If r is positive but weak, we would know that participants' scores on the test changed from Time 1 to Time 2.

A low r would be a sign of poor reliability if we are measuring something that should stay the same over time. For example, a trait like intelligence is not usually expected to change over a few months, so if we assess the test-retest reliability of an IQ test and obtain a low r, we would be doubtful about the reliability of this test. In contrast, if we were measuring flu symptoms or seasonal stress, we would expect test-retest reliabilities to be low, simply because these constructs do not stay the same over time.

INTERRATER RELIABILITY

To test interrater reliability of some measure, we might ask two observers to rate the same participants at the same time, and then we would compute r. If r is positive and strong (according to many researchers, $r = .70$ or higher), we would have very good interrater reliability. If r is positive but weak, we could not trust the observers' ratings. We would retrain the coders or refine our operational definition so it can be more reliably coded. A negative r would indicate a big problem. In the daycare example, that would mean Observer Mark considered Jay very happy but Observer Peter considered Jay very unhappy, Observer Mark considered Jackie unhappy but Peter considered Jackie happy, and so on. When we're assessing reliability, a negative correlation is rare and undesirable.

Although r can be used to evaluate interrater reliability when the observers are rating a quantitative variable, a more appropriate statistic, called *kappa*, is used when the observers are rating a categorical variable. Although the computations are beyond the scope of this book, kappa measures the extent to which two raters place participants into the same categories. As with r, a kappa close to 1.0 means that the two raters agreed.

INTERNAL RELIABILITY

Internal reliability is relevant for measures that use more than one item to get at the same construct. On self-report scales such as Diener's five-item subjective well-being scale, people answer the same question phrased in multiple ways. Researchers rephrase the items because any one way of wording the question might introduce measurement error. Researchers predict any such errors will cancel each other out when the items are summed up to form each person's score.

Before combining the items on a self-report scale, researchers need to assess the scale's internal reliability to evaluate whether people responded consistently to each item, despite the different wordings. Internal reliability means people gave consistent answers every time, no matter how the researchers asked the questions.

Let's consider the following version of Diener's well-being scale. Would a group of people give consistent responses to all five items? Would people who agree with Item 1 also agree with Items 2, 3, and 4?

_____ 1. In most ways my life is close to my ideal.
_____ 2. The conditions of my life are excellent.
_____ 3. I am fond of polka dots.
_____ 4. I am a good swimmer.
_____ 5. If I could live my life over, I would change almost nothing.

Obviously, these items do not seem to go together, so we could not average them together for a meaningful well-being score. Items 1 and 2 are probably correlated, since they are similar to each other, but Items 1 and 3 are probably not correlated, since people can like polka dots whether or not they are living their ideal lives. Item 4 doesn't seem to go with any other item, either. But how could we quantify these intuitions about internal reliability?

Researchers typically will run a correlation-based statistic called **Cronbach's alpha** (or *coefficient alpha*) to see if their measurement scales have internal reliability. First, they collect data on the scale from a large sample of participants, and then they compute all possible correlations among the items. The formula for Cronbach's alpha returns one number, computed from the average of the inter-item correlations and the number of items in the scale. The closer the Cronbach's alpha is to 1.0, the better the scale's reliability. (For self-report measures, researchers are looking for Cronbach's alpha of .70 or higher.) If Cronbach's alpha is high, there is good internal reliability and researchers can sum all the items together. If Cronbach's alpha is less than .70, then internal reliability is poor and the researchers are not justified in combining all the items into one scale. They have to go back and revise the items, or they might select only those items that were found to correlate strongly with one another.

Reading About Reliability in Journal Articles

Authors of empirical journal articles usually present reliability information for the measures they are using. One example of such evidence is in **Figure 5.5**, which comes from an actual journal article. According to the table, the subjective well-being scale, called Satisfaction with Life (SWL), was used in six studies. The table shows the internal reliability (labeled as coefficient alpha) from each of these studies, as well as test-retest reliability for each one. The table did not present interrater reliability because the scale is a self-report measure, and interrater reliability is relevant only when two or more observers are doing the ratings. Based on the evidence in this table, we can conclude the subjective well-being scale has excellent internal reliability and excellent test-retest reliability. You'll see another example of how reliability is discussed in a journal article in the Working It Through section at the end of this chapter.

**FIGURE 5.5
Reliability of the
well-being scale.**

The researchers created this table
to show how six studies supported
the internal reliability and test-retest
reliability of their SWL scale.
(Source: Pavot & Diener, 1993, Table 2.)

Table 2
*Estimates of Internal Consistency and Temporal Reliability
for the Satisfaction with Life Scale*

Sample	Coefficient alpha	Test–retest	Temporal interval
Alfonso & Allison (1992a)	.89	.83	2 weeks
Pavot et al. (1991)	.85	.84	1 month
Blais et al. (1989)	.79–.84	.64	2 months
Diener et al. (1985)	.87	.82	2 months
Yardley & Rice (1991)	.80, .86	.50	10 weeks
Magnus, Diener, Fujita, & Pavot (1992)	.87	.54	4 years

Authors of study
using SWL scale.

Coefficient (Cronbach's)
alpha above .70 means
SWL scale has good
internal reliability.

High correlation of *r* = .83
for retesting 2 weeks apart
means scale has good
test-retest reliability.

CHECK YOUR UNDERSTANDING

1. Reliability is about consistency. Define the three kinds of reliability, using the
word *consistent* in each of your definitions.

2. For each of the three common types of operationalizations—self-report,
observational, and physiological—indicate which type(s) of reliability would
be relevant.

3. Which of the following correlations is the strongest: $r = .25$, $r = -.65$, $r = -.01$,
or $r = .43$?

1. See pp. 125-126. 2. Self-report: test-retest and internal may be relevant; observational: interrater
would be relevant; physiological: interrater may be relevant. 3. $r = -.65$.

VALIDITY OF MEASUREMENT: DOES IT MEASURE WHAT IT'S SUPPOSED TO MEASURE?

Before using particular operationalizations in a study, researchers not only check
to be sure the measures are reliable; they also want to be sure they get at the
conceptual variables they were intended for. That's construct validity. You might

ask whether the five-item well-being scale Diener's team uses really reflects how subjectively happy people are. You might ask if a self-report measure of gratitude really reflects how thankful people are. You might ask if recording the value of the car a person drives really reflects that person's wealth.

Measurement reliability and measurement validity are separate steps in establishing construct validity. To demonstrate the difference between them, consider the example of head circumference as an operationalization of intelligence. Although head size measurements may be very reliable, almost all studies have shown that head circumference is not related to intelligence (Gould, 1996). Therefore, like a bathroom scale that always reads too light (**Figure 5.6**), the head circumference test may be reliable, but it is not valid as an intelligence test: It does not measure what it's supposed to measure.

Measurement Validity of Abstract Constructs

Does anyone you know use an activity monitor? Your friends may feel proud when they reach a daily steps goal or boast about how many miles they've covered that day (**Figure 5.7**). How can you know for sure these pedometers are accurate? Of course, it's straightforward to evaluate the validity of a pedometer: You'd simply walk around, counting your steps while wearing one, then compare your own count to that of your device. If you're sure you walked 200 steps and your pedometer says you walked 200, then your device is valid. Similarly, if your pedometer counted the correct distance after you've walked around a track or some other path with a known mileage, it's probably a valid monitor.

In the case of an activity monitor, we are lucky to have concrete, straightforward standards for accurate measurement. But psychological scientists often want to measure abstract constructs such as happiness, intelligence, stress, or self-esteem, which we can't simply count (Cronbach & Meehl, 1955; Smith, 2005a, 2005b). Construct validity is therefore important in psychological research, especially when a construct is not directly observable. Take happiness: We have no means of directly measuring how happy a person is. We could estimate it in a number of ways, such as scores on a well-being inventory, daily smile rate, blood pressure, stress hormone levels, or even the activity levels of certain brain regions. Yet each of these measures of happiness is indirect. For some abstract constructs, there is no single, direct measure. And that is the challenge: How can we know if indirect operational measures of a construct are really measuring happiness and not something else?

We know by collecting a variety of data. Before using a measure in a study, researchers evaluate the measure's validity, by either collecting their own data or reading about the data collected by others. Furthermore, the evidence for construct validity is always a matter of degree. Psychologists do not say a particular measure is or is not valid. Instead, they ask: What is the weight of evidence in favor of this measure's validity? There are a number of kinds of

FIGURE 5.6
Reliability is not the same as validity.

This person's bathroom scale may report that he weighs 50 pounds (22.7 kg) every time he steps on it. The scale is certainly reliable, but it is not valid.

FIGURE 5.7
Are activity monitors valid?

A friend wore a pedometer during a hike and recorded these values. What data could you collect to know whether or not it accurately counted his steps?

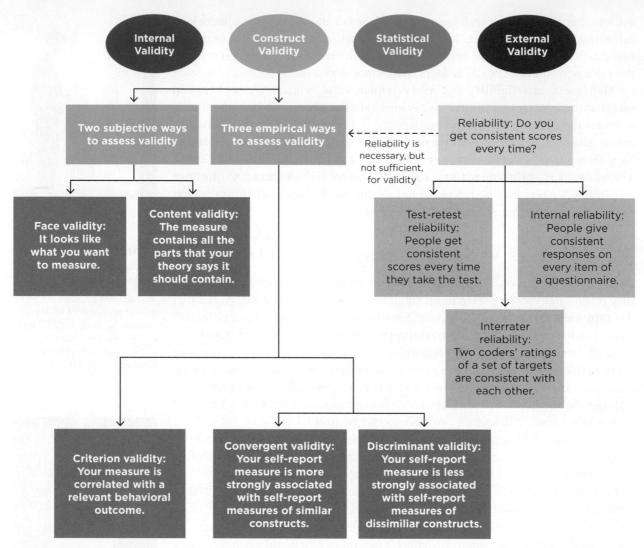

FIGURE 5.8
A concept map of measurement reliability and validity.

evidence that can convince a researcher, and we'll discuss them below. First, take a look at **Figure 5.8**, an overview of the reliability and validity concepts covered in this chapter.

Face Validity and Content Validity: Does It Look Like a Good Measure?

A measure has **face validity** if it is subjectively considered to be a plausible operationalization of the conceptual variable in question. If it looks like a good measure, it has face validity. Head circumference has high face validity as a measurement of hat size, but it has low face validity as an operationalization of intelligence. In contrast, speed of problem solving, vocabulary size, and creativity have higher face validity as operationalizations of intelligence. Researchers generally check face validity by consulting experts. For example, we might assess the face validity of Diener's well-being scale by asking a panel of judges (such as personality psychologists) their opinion on how reasonable the scale is as a way of estimating happiness.

Content validity also involves subjective judgment. To ensure **content validity**, a measure must capture all parts of a defined construct. For example, consider this conceptual definition of intelligence, which contains distinct elements, including the ability to "reason, plan, solve problems, think abstractly, comprehend complex ideas, learn quickly, and learn from experience" (Gottfredson, 1997, p. 13). To have adequate content validity, any operationalization of intelligence should include questions or items to assess each of these seven components. Indeed, most IQ tests have multiple categories of items, such as memory span, vocabulary, and problem-solving sections.

Criterion Validity: Does It Correlate with Key Behaviors?

To evaluate a measurement's validity, face and content validity are a good place to start, but most psychologists rely on more than a subjective judgment: They prefer to see empirical evidence. There are several ways to collect data on a measure, but in all cases, the point is to make sure the measurement is associated with something it theoretically *should* be associated with. In some cases, such relationships can be illustrated by using scatterplots and correlation coefficients. They can be illustrated with other kinds of evidence too, such as comparisons of groups with known properties.

CORRELATIONAL EVIDENCE FOR CRITERION VALIDITY

Criterion validity evaluates whether the measure under consideration is associated with a concrete behavioral outcome that it should be associated with, according to the conceptual definition. Suppose you work for a company that wants to predict how well job applicants would perform as salespeople. Of the several commercially available tests of sales aptitude, which one should the company use? You have two choices, which we'll call Aptitude Test A and Aptitude Test B. Both have items that look good in terms of face validity—they ask about a candidate's motivation, optimism, and interest in sales. But do the test scores correlate with a key behavior: success in selling? It's an empirical question. Your company can collect data to tell them how well each of the two aptitude tests is correlated with success in selling.

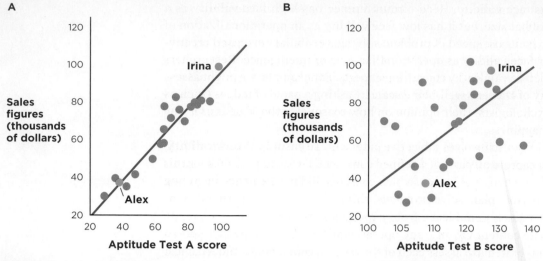

FIGURE 5.9

Correlational evidence for criterion validity.

(A) Aptitude Test A strongly predicts sales performance, so criterion validity is high. (B) Aptitude Test B does not predict sales as well, so criterion validity is lower. A company would probably want to use Test A for identifying potential selling ability when selecting salespeople.

Spread-out dots indicate lower correlation between Test B scores and sales figures, so this test has lower criterion validity as a measure of sales performance.

To assess criterion validity, your company could give each sales test to all the current sales representatives and then find out each person's sales figures—a measure of their selling performance. You would then compute two correlations: one between Aptitude Test A and sales figures, and the other between Aptitude Test B and sales figures. **Figure 5.9A** shows scatterplot results for Test A. The score on Aptitude Test A is plotted on the x-axis, and actual sales figures are plotted on the y-axis. (Alex scored 39 on the test and brought in $38,000 in sales, whereas Irina scored 98 and brought in $100,000.) **Figure 5.9B**, in contrast, shows the association of sales performance with Aptitude Test B.

Looking at these two scatterplots, we can see that the correlation in the first one is much stronger than in the second one. In other words, future sales performance is correlated more strongly with scores on Aptitude Test A than with scores on Aptitude Test B. If the data looked like this, the company would conclude that Aptitude Test A has better criterion validity as a measure of selling ability, and this is the one they should use for selecting salespeople. In contrast, the other data show that scores on Aptitude Test B are a poorer indicator of future sales performance; it has poor criterion validity as a measure of sales aptitude.

Criterion validity is especially important for self-report measures because the correlation can indicate how well people's self-reports predict their actual behavior. Criterion validity provides some of the strongest evidence for a measure's construct validity.

Here's another example. Most colleges in the United States use standardized tests, such as the SAT and ACT, to measure the construct "aptitude for college-level work." To demonstrate that these tests have criterion validity, an educational psychologist might want to show that scores on these measures are correlated with college grades (a behavioral outcome that represents "college-level work").

Gallup presents criterion validity evidence for the 10-point Ladder of Life scale they use to measure happiness. They report that Ladder of Life scores correlate with key behavioral outcomes, such as becoming ill and missing work (Gallup, n.d.).

If an IQ test has criterion validity, it should be correlated with behaviors that capture the construct of intelligence, such as how fast people can learn a complex set of symbols (an outcome that represents the conceptual definition of intelligence). Of course, the ability to learn quickly is only one component of that definition. Further criterion validity evidence could show that IQ scores are correlated with other behavioral outcomes that are theoretically related to intelligence, such as the ability to solve problems and indicators of life success (e.g., graduating from college, being employed in a high-level job, earning a high income).

KNOWN-GROUPS EVIDENCE FOR CRITERION VALIDITY

Another way to gather evidence for criterion validity is to use a **known-groups paradigm**, in which researchers see whether scores on the measure can discriminate among two or more groups whose behavior is already confirmed. For example, to validate the use of salivary cortisol as a measure of stress, a researcher could compare the salivary cortisol levels in two groups of people: those who are about to give a speech in front of a classroom, and those who are in the audience. Public speaking is recognized as being a stressful situation for almost everyone. Therefore, if salivary cortisol is a valid measure of stress, people in the speech group should have higher levels of cortisol than those in the audience group.

Lie detectors are another good example. These instruments record a set of physiological measures (such as skin conductance and heart rate) whose levels are supposed to indicate which of a person's statements are truthful and which are lies. If skin conductance and heart rate are valid measures of lying, we could conduct a known-groups test in which we know in advance which of a person's statements are true and which are false. The physiological measures should be elevated only for the lies, not for the true statements. (For a review of the mixed evidence on lie detection, see Saxe, 1991.)

The known-groups method can also be used to validate self-report measures. Psychiatrist Aaron Beck and his colleagues developed the Beck Depression Inventory (BDI), a 21-item self-report scale with items that ask about major symptoms of depression (Beck, Ward, Mendelson, Mock, & Erbaugh, 1961). Participants circle one of four choices, such as the following:

0   I do not feel sad.
1   I feel sad.
2   I am sad all the time and I can't snap out of it.
3   I am so sad or unhappy that I can't stand it.

0   I have not lost interest in other people.
1   I am less interested in other people than I used to be.
2   I have lost most of my interest in other people.
3   I have lost all of my interest in other people.

A clinical scientist adds up the scores on each of the 21 items for a total BDI score, which can range from a low of 0 (not at all depressed) to a high of 63.

To test the criterion validity of the BDI, Beck and his colleagues gave this self-report scale to two known groups of people. They knew one group was suffering from clinical depression and the other group was not because they had asked psychiatrists to conduct clinical interviews and diagnose each person. The researchers computed the mean BDI scores of the two groups and created a bar graph, shown in **Figure 5.10**. The evidence supports the criterion validity of the BDI. The graph shows the expected result: the average BDI score of the known group of depressed people was higher than the average score of the known group who were not depressed. Because its criterion validity was established in this way, the BDI is still widely used today when researchers need a quick and valid way to identify new people who are vulnerable to depression.

Beck also used the known-groups paradigm to calibrate low, medium, and high scores on the BDI. When the psychiatrists interviewed the people in the sample, they evaluated not only whether they were depressed but also the level of depression in each person: none, mild, moderate, or severe. As expected, the BDI scores of the groups rose as their level of depression (assessed by psychiatrists) was more severe (**Figure 5.11**). This result was even clearer evidence that the BDI was a valid measure of depression. With the BDI, clinicians and researchers can confidently use specific ranges of BDI scores to categorize how severe a person's depression might be.

Diener's subjective well-being (SWB) scale is another example of using the known-groups paradigm for criterion validity. In one review article, he and his colleague presented the SWB scale averages from several different studies. Each study had given the SWB scale to different groups of people who could be

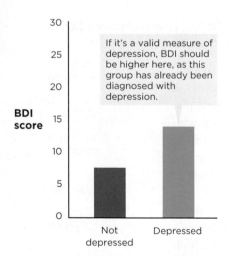

FIGURE 5.10
BDI scores of two known groups.

This pattern of results provides evidence for the criterion validity of the BDI using the known-groups method. Clients judged to be depressed by psychiatrists also scored higher. (Source: Adapted from Beck et al., 1961.)

expected to vary in happiness level (Pavot & Diener, 1993). For example, male prison inmates, a group that would be expected to have low subjective well-being, showed a lower mean score on the scale, compared with Canadian college students, who averaged much higher—indicated by the *M* column in **Table 5.3**. Such known-groups patterns provide strong evidence for the criterion validity of the SWB scale. Researchers can use this scale in their studies with confidence.

What about the Ladder of Life scale, the measure of happiness used in the Gallup-Healthways Well-Being Index? This measure also has some known-groups evidence to support its criterion validity. For one, Gallup reported that Americans' well-being was especially low in 2008 and 2009, a period corresponding to a significant downturn in the U.S. economy. Well-being is a little bit higher in American summer months, as well. These results fit what we would expect if the Ladder of Life is a valid measure of well-being.

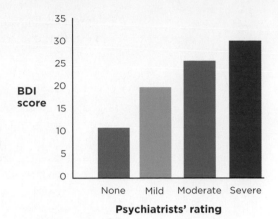

FIGURE 5.11

BDI scores of four known groups.

This pattern of results means it is valid to use BDI cutoff scores to decide if a person has mild, moderate, or severe depression. (Source: Adapted from Beck et al., 1961.)

Convergent Validity and Discriminant Validity: Does the Pattern Make Sense?

Criterion validity examines whether a measure correlates with key behavioral outcomes. Another form of validity evidence is whether there is a meaningful pattern of similarities and differences among self-report measures. A self-report measure should correlate more strongly with self-report measures of similar constructs than it does with those of dissimilar constructs. The pattern of correlations with measures of theoretically similar and dissimilar constructs is called **convergent validity** and **discriminant validity** (or *divergent validity*), respectively.

CONVERGENT VALIDITY

As an example of convergent validity, let's consider Beck's depression scale, the BDI, again. One team of researchers wanted to test the convergent and discriminant validity of the

TABLE 5.3

Subjective Well-Being (SWB) Scores for Known Groups from Several Studies

SAMPLE CHARACTERISTICS	N	M	SD	STUDY REFERENCE
American college students	244	23.7	6.4	Pavot & Diener (1993)
French Canadian college students (male)	355	23.8	6.1	Blais et al. (1989)
Korean university students	413	19.8	5.8	Suh (1993)
Printing trade workers	304	24.2	6.0	George (1991)
Veterans Affairs hospital inpatients	52	11.8	5.6	Frisch (1991)
Abused women	70	20.7	7.4	Fisher (1991)
Male prison inmates	75	12.3	7.0	Joy (1990)

Note: N = Number of people in group. *M* = Group mean on SWB.
SD = Group standard deviation.
Source: Adapted from Pavot & Diener, 1993, Table 1.

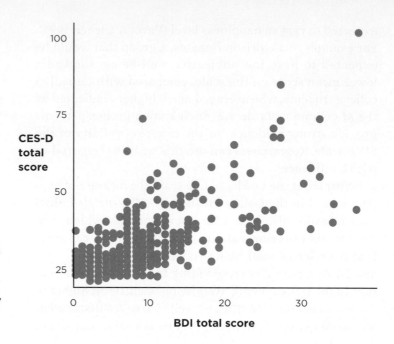

FIGURE 5.12

Evidence supporting the convergent validity of the BDI.

The BDI is strongly correlated with another measure of depression, the CES-D (*r* = .68), providing evidence for convergent validity. (Source: Segal et al., 2008.)

BDI (Segal, Coolidge, Cahill, & O'Riley, 2008). If the BDI really quanitfies depression, the researchers reasoned, it should be correlated with (should converge with) other self-report measures of depression. Their sample of 376 adults completed the BDI and a number of other questionnaires, including a self-report instrument called the Center for Epidemiologic Studies Depression scale (CES-D).

As expected, BDI scores were positively, strongly correlated with CES-D scores (*r* = .68). People who scored as depressed on the BDI also scored as depressed on the CES-D; likewise, those who scored as not depressed on the BDI also scored as not depressed on the CES-D. **Figure 5.12** shows a scatterplot of the results. (Notice that most of the dots fall in the lower left portion of the scatterplot because most people in the sample are not depressed; they score low on both the BDI and the CES-D.) This correlation between similar self-report measures of the same construct (depression) provided good evidence for the convergent validity of the BDI.

Testing for convergent validity can feel circular. Even if researchers validate the BDI with the CES-D, for instance, there is no assurance that the CES-D measure is a gold standard. Its validity would need to be established, too! The researchers might next try to validate the CES-D with a third measure, but that measure's validity would also need to be supported with evidence. Eventually, however, they might be satisfied that a measure is valid after evaluating the *weight* and *pattern* of the evidence. Many researchers are most convinced when measures are shown to predict actual behaviors (using criterion validity). However, no single definitive outcome will establish validity (Smith, 2005a).

» For more on the strength of correlations, see Chapter 8, Table 8.4, and Statistics Review: Descriptive Statistics, pp. 468–472.

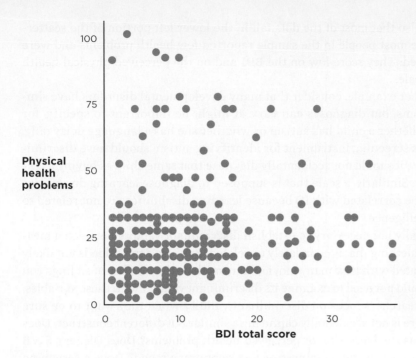

FIGURE 5.13
Evidence supporting the discriminant validity of the BDI.

As expected, the BDI is only weakly correlated with perceived health problems (r = .16), providing evidence for discriminant validity. (Source: Segal et al., 2008.)

This example of convergent validity is somewhat obvious: A measure of depression should correlate with a different measure of the same construct—depression. But convergent validity evidence also includes *similar* constructs, not just the same one. The researchers showed, for instance, that the BDI scores were strongly correlated with a score quantifying psychological well-being (r = -.65). The observed strong, negative correlation made sense as a form of convergent validity because people who are depressed are expected to also have lower levels of well-being (Segal, Coolidge, Cahill, & O'Riley, 2008).

DISCRIMINANT VALIDITY

The BDI should *not* correlate strongly with measures of constructs that are very different from depression; it should show discriminant validity with them. For example, depression is not the same as a person's perception of his or her overall physical health. Although mental health problems, including depression, do overlap somewhat with physical health problems, we would not expect the BDI to be strongly correlated with a measure of perceived physical health problems. More importantly, we would expect the BDI to be more strongly correlated with the CES-D and well-being than it is with physical health problems. Sure enough, Segal and his colleagues found a correlation of only r = .16 between the BDI and a measure of perceived physical health problems. This weak correlation shows that the BDI is different from people's perceptions of their physical health, so we can say that the BDI has discriminant validity with physical health problems. **Figure 5.13** shows a scatterplot of the results.

Notice also that most of the dots fall in the lower left portion of the scatterplot because most people in the sample reported few health problems and were not depressed: They score low on the BDI and on the perceived physical health problems scale.

As another example, consider that many developmental disorders have similar symptoms, but diagnoses can vary. It might be important to specify, for instance, whether a child has autism or whether she has a language delay only. Therefore, a screening instrument for identifying autism should have discriminant validity; it should not accidentally diagnose that same child as having a language delay. Similarly, a scale that is supposed to diagnose learning disabilities should not be correlated with IQ because learning disabilities are not related to general intelligence.

It is usually not necessary to establish discriminant validity between a measure and something that is completely unrelated. Because depression is not likely to be associated with how many movies you watch or the number of siblings you have, we would not need to examine its discriminant validity with these variables. Instead, researchers focus on discriminant validity when they want to be sure their measure is not accidentally capturing a similar but different construct. Does the BDI measure depression or perceived health problems? Does Diener's SWB scale measure enduring happiness or just temporary mood? Does a screening technique identify autism or language delay?

Convergent validity and discriminant validity are usually evaluated together, as a pattern of correlations among self-report measures. A measurement should have higher correlations (higher r values) with similar traits (convergent validity) than it does with dissimilar traits (discriminant validity). There are no strict rules for what the correlations should be. Instead, the overall pattern of convergent and discriminant validity helps researchers decide whether their operationalization really measures the construct they want it to measure.

The Relationship Between Reliability and Validity

One essential point is worth reiterating: The validity of a measure is not the same as its reliability. A journalist might boast that some operationalization of behavior is "a very reliable test," but to say that a measure is "reliable" is only half the story. Determining head circumference might be extremely reliable, but it still may not be valid for assessing intelligence.

Although a measure may be less valid than it is reliable, it cannot be more valid than it is reliable. Intuitively, this statement makes sense. Reliability has to do with how well a measure correlates with itself. For example, an IQ test is reliable if it is correlated with itself over time. Validity, however, has to do with how well a measure is associated with something else, such as a behavior that indicates intelligence. An IQ test is valid if it is associated with another variable, such as school grades or life success. If a measure does not even correlate with itself, then how can it be more strongly associated with some other variable?

As another example, suppose you used your pedometer to count how many steps there are in your daily walk from your parking spot to your building. If the pedometer reading is very different day to day, then the measure is unreliable—and of course, it also cannot be valid because the true distance of your walk has not changed. Therefore, reliability is necessary (but not sufficient) for validity.

CHECK YOUR UNDERSTANDING

1. What do face validity and content validity have in common?

2. Many researchers believe criterion validity is more important than convergent and discriminant validity. Can you see why?

3. Which requires stronger correlations for its evidence: convergent validity or discriminant validity? Which requires weaker correlations?

4. Can a measure be reliable but not valid? Can it be valid but unreliable?

1. See pp. 134–135. 2. Because only criterion validity establishes how well a measure correlates with a behavioral outcome, not simply with other self-report measures; see pp. 135–142. 3. Convergent validity. 4. It can be reliable but not valid, but a measure cannot be valid if it is unreliable; see pp. 142–143.

REVIEW: INTERPRETING CONSTRUCT VALIDITY EVIDENCE

Before using a stopwatch in a track meet, a coach wants to be sure the stopwatch is working well. Before taking a patient's blood pressure, a nurse wants to be sure the cuff she's using is reliable and accurate. Similarly, before conducting a study, researchers want to be sure the measures they plan to use are reliable and valid ones. When you read a research study, you should be asking: Did the researchers collect evidence that the measures they are using have construct validity? If they didn't do it themselves, did they review construct validity evidence provided by others?

In empirical journal articles, you'll usually find reliability and validity information in the Method section, where the authors describe their measures. How do you recognize this evidence, and how can you interpret it? The Working It Through section shows how such information might be presented, using a study conducted by Gordon, Impett, Kogan, Oveis, & Keltner (2012) as an example.

Item

1. I tell my partner often that s/he is the best.
2. I often tell my partner how much I appreciate her/him.
3. At times I take my partner for granted. (reverse scored item)
4. I appreciate my partner.
5. Sometimes I don't really acknowledge or treat my partner like s/he is someone special. (reverse scored item)
6. I make sure my partner feels appreciated.
7. My partner sometimes says that I fail to notice the nice things that s/he does for me. (reverse scored item)
8. I acknowledge the things that my partner does for me, even the really small things.
9. I am sometimes struck with a sense of awe and wonder when I think about my partner being in my life.

FIGURE 5.14

Items in the Appreciation in Relationships (AIR) Scale.

These items were used by the researchers to measure how much people appreciate their relationship partner. Do you think these items have face validity as a measure of appreciation? (Source: Gordon et al., 2012.)

The evidence reported by Gordon et al. (2012) supports the AIR scale as a reliable and valid scale (**Figure 5.14**). It has internal and test-retest reliability, and there is evidence of its convergent, discriminant, and criterion validity. The researchers were confident they could use AIR when they later tested their hypothesis that more appreciative couples would have healthier relationships. Many of their hypotheses about gratitude (operationalized by the AIR scale) were supported. One of the more dramatic results was from a study that followed couples over time. The authors reported: "We found that people who were more appreciative of their partners were significantly more likely to still be in their relationships at the 9-month follow-up" (Gordon et al., 2012, p. 268).

This empirical journal article illustrates how researchers use data to establish the construct validity of the measure they plan to use ahead of time, before going on to test their hypotheses. Their research helps support the headline, "Gratitude is for lovers."

How Well Can We Measure the Amount of Gratitude Couples Express to Each Other?

What do partners bring to a healthy romantic relationship? One research team proposed that gratitude toward one's partner would be important (Gordon et al., 2012). They predicted that when people are appreciative of their partners, close relationships are happier and last longer. In an empirical journal article, the researchers reported how they tested this hypothesis. But before they could study how the concept of gratitude contributes to relationship health, they needed to be able to measure the variable "gratitude" in a reliable and valid way. They created and tested the AIR scale, for Appreciation in Relationships. We will work through ways this example illustrates concepts from Chapter 5.

QUESTIONS TO ASK	CLAIMS, QUOTES, OR DATA	INTERPRETATION AND EVALUATION
Conceptual and Operational Definitions		
How did they operationalize the conceptual variable "gratitude"?	"In the first step, we created an initial pool of items based on lay knowledge, theory, and previous measures of appreciation and gratitude. . . . These items were designed to capture a broad conceptualization of appreciation by including items that assess the extent to which people recognize and value their partner as a person as well as the extent to which they are grateful for a partner's kind deeds. . . ." (p. 260).	This quoted passage describes how Gordon and her colleagues developed and selected the AIR items. Notice how they wrote items to capture their conceptual definition of gratitude.

(Continued)

QUESTIONS TO ASK	CLAIMS, QUOTES, OR DATA	INTERPRETATION AND EVALUATION
Was the AIR scale reliable? Did the scale give consistent scores?		
Internal Reliability When a self-report scale has multiple items, it should have good internal reliability. Did the AIR scale have good internal reliability?	"In the initial online survey, participants completed a questionnaire with basic demographic information. Participants completed the AIR scale ... $\alpha = .87$" (p. 266).	In this passage, the authors report the internal reliability of the AIR scale. The value $\alpha = .87$ indicates that people in the Gordon study answered all the AIR items consistently. A Cronbach's alpha of .87 is considered good internal reliability because it is close to 1.0.
Test-Retest Reliability We might expect the AIR scale to have test-retest reliability because gratitude should be stable over time. Were the AIR scores stable over time?	"The AIR scale had strong test-retest reliability from baseline to the 9-month follow-up (... $r = .61$, $p = .001$)" (p. 267).	This passage reports the test-retest correlation, which was $r = .61$. Those who were the most appreciative at Time 1 were also the most appreciative at Time 2; similarly, those who were least appreciative at Time 1 were also least appreciative at Time 2.
Interrater Reliability Because the AIR scale is a self-report measure, the researchers do not need to report interrater reliability evidence.		
The evidence indicates the AIR scale has adequate internal and test-retest reliability. What evidence is there for its validity? Is the scale really measuring the concept of gratitude?		
Convergent and Discriminant Validity Do AIR scores correlate more strongly with measures similar to gratitude and less strongly with measures dissimilar to gratitude?	In a section on convergent and discriminant validity, the authors write: "As expected, . . . [the AIR scale was] positively correlated with the extent to which people had a grateful disposition [$r = .25$], as well as with people's gratitude in response to their partners' kind acts [$r = .60$]. In contrast, [the AIR scale was not] associated with people's feelings of indebtedness to their partners [$r = .19$]" (p. 262).	In this passage, the authors give convergent and discriminant validity evidence. The AIR scale has convergent validity with other measures of gratitude, and discriminant validity with a measure of indebtedness. In other words, there was a pattern of higher correlations with gratitude than with indebtedness.
Criterion Validity Does the AIR scale predict relevant behavioral outcomes?	The "final study allowed us to provide additional evidence for the validity of the AIR scale by examining cross-partner associations. . . . [P]eople who reported feeling more appreciative of their partners had partners who felt more appreciated by them, $\beta = .50$, $t(66) = 5.87$, $p < .001$, . . . suggesting that the AIR scale is capturing the interpersonal transmission of appreciation from one partner to the other" (p. 269).	In this passage, the authors present criterion validity evidence. If the AIR scale is a valid measure, you'd expect partners with higher AIR scores to also have partners who notice this appreciation. Because the results showed that AIR scores were associated with this relevant outcome, there is evidence for the AIR scale's criterion validity.

CHAPTER REVIEW

Summary

The construct validity of a study's measured variables is something you will interrogate for any type of claim.

Ways to Measure Variables

- Psychological scientists measure variables in every study they conduct. Three common types of measures are self-report, in which people report on their own behaviors, beliefs, or attitudes; observational measures, in which raters record the visible behaviors of people or animals; and physiological measures, in which researchers measure biological data, such as heart rate, brain activity, and hormone levels.

- Depending on how they are operationalized, variables may be categorical or quantitative. The levels of categorical variables are categories. The levels of quantitative variables are meaningful numbers, in which higher numbers represent more of some variable.

- Quantitative variables can be further classified in terms of ordinal, interval, or ratio scales.

Reliability of Measurement: Are the Scores Consistent?

- Both measurement reliability and measurement validity are important for establishing a measure's construct validity.

- Researchers use scatterplots and correlation coefficients (among other methods) to evaluate evidence for a measure's reliability and validity.

- To establish a measure's reliability, researchers collect data to see whether the measure works consistently. There are three types of measurement reliability.

- Test-retest reliability establishes whether a sample gives a consistent pattern of scores at more than one testing.

- Interrater reliability establishes whether two observers give consistent ratings to a sample of targets.

- Internal reliability is established when people answer similarly worded items in a consistent way.

- Measurement reliability is necessary but not sufficient for measurement validity.

Validity of Measurement: Does It Measure What It's Supposed to Measure?

- Measurement validity can be established with subjective judgments (face validity and content validity) or with empirical data.

- Criterion validity requires collecting data that show a measure is correlated with expected behavioral outcomes.

- Convergent and discriminant validity require collecting data that show a self-report measure is correlated more strongly with self-report measures of similar constructs than with measures of dissimilar constructs.

Review: Interpreting Construct Validity Evidence

- Measurement reliability and validity evidence are reported in the Method section of empirical journal articles. Details may be provided in the text, as a table of results, or through cross-reference to a longer article that presents full reliability and validity evidence.

Key Terms

self-report measure, p. 120
observational measure, p. 121
physiological measure, p. 121
categorical variable, p. 122
quantitative variable, p. 123
ordinal scale, p. 123
interval scale, p. 123
ratio scale, p. 123

reliability, p. 125
validity, p. 125
test-retest reliability, p. 125
interrater reliability, p. 125
internal reliability, p. 125
correlation coefficient r, p. 128
slope direction, p. 128
strength, p. 128

Cronbach's alpha, p. 131
face validity, p. 134
content validity, p. 135
criterion validity, p. 135
known-groups paradigm, p. 137
convergent validity, p. 139
discriminant validity, p. 139

 To see samples of chapter concepts in the popular media, visit www.everydayresearchmethods.com and click the box for Chapter 5.

Review Questions

1. Classify each operational variable below as categorical or quantitative. If the variable is quantitative, further classify it as ordinal, interval, or ratio.

   a. Degree of pupil dilation in a person's eyes in a study of romantic couples (measured in millimeters).

   b. Number of books a person owns.

   c. A book's sales rank on Amazon.com.

   d. The language a person speaks at home.

   e. Nationality of the participants in a cross-cultural study of Canadian, Ghanaian, and French students.

   f. A student's grade in school.

2. Which of the following correlation coefficients best describes the pictured scatterplot?

   a. $r = .78$

   b. $r = -.95$

   c. $r = .03$

   d. $r = .45$

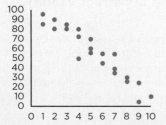

3. Classify each of the following results as an example of internal reliability, interrater reliability, or test-retest reliability.

   a. A researcher finds that people's scores on a measure of extroversion stay stable over 2 months.

   b. An infancy researcher wants to measure how long a 3-month-old baby looks at a stimulus on the right and left sides of a screen. Two undergraduates watch a tape of the eye movements of ten infants and time how long each baby looks to the right and to the left. The two sets of timings are correlated $r = .95$.

   c. A researcher asks a sample of 40 people a set of five items that are all capturing how extroverted they are. The Cronbach's alpha for the five items is found to be .75.

4. Classify each result below as an example of face validity, content validity, convergent and discriminant validity, or criterion validity.

   a. A professor gives a class of 40 people his five-item measure of conscientiousness (e.g., "I get chores done right away," "I follow a schedule," "I do not make a mess of things"). Average scores are correlated ($r = -.20$) with how many times each student has been late to class during the semester.

   b. A professor gives a class of 40 people his five-item measure of conscientiousness (e.g., "I get chores done right away," "I follow a schedule," "I do not make a mess of things"). Average scores are more highly correlated with a self-report measure of tidiness (r = .50) than with a measure of general knowledge (r = .09).

c. The researcher e-mails his five-item measure of conscientiousness (e.g., "I get chores done right away," "I follow a schedule," "I do not make a mess of things") to 20 experts in personality psychology, and asks them if they think his items are a good measure of conscientiousness.

d. The researcher e-mails his five-item measure of conscientiousness (e.g., "I get chores done right away." "I follow a schedule," "I do not make a mess of things") to 20 experts in personality psychology, and asks them if they think he has included all the important aspects of conscientiousness.

Learning Actively

1. For each measure below, indicate which kinds of reliability would need to be evaluated. Then, draw a scatterplot indicating that the measure has good reliability and another one indicating the measure has poor reliability. (Pay special attention to how you label the axes of your scatterplots.)

    a. Researchers place unobtrusive video recording devices in the hallway of a local high school. Later, coders view tapes and code how many students are using cell phones in the 4-minute period between classes.

    b. Clinical psychologists have developed a seven-item self-report measure to quickly identify people who are at risk for panic disorder.

    c. Psychologists measure how long it takes a mouse to learn an eyeblink response. For 60 trials, they present a mouse with a distinctive blue light followed immediately by a puff of air. The 5th, 10th, and 15th trials are test trials, in which they present the blue light alone (without the air puff). The mouse is said to have learned the eyeblink response if observers record that it blinked its eyes in response to a test trial. The earlier in the 60 trials the mouse shows the eyeblink response, the faster it has learned the response.

    d. Educational psychologists use teacher ratings of classroom shyness (on a nine-point scale, where 1 = "not at all shy in class" and 9 = "very shy in class") to measure children's temperament.

2. Consider how you might validate the nine-point classroom shyness rating example in question 1d. First, what behaviors might be relevant for establishing this rating's criterion validity? Draw a scatterplot showing the results of a study in which the classroom shyness rating has good criterion validity (be careful how you label the axes). Second, come up with ways to evaluate the convergent and discriminant validity of this rating system. What traits should correlate strongly with shyness? What traits should correlate only weakly or not at all? Explain why you chose those traits. Draw a scatterplot showing the results of a study in which the shyness rating has good convergent or discriminant validity (be careful how you label the axes).

3. This chapter included the example of a sales ability test. Search online for "sales ability assessment" and see what commercially available tests you can find. Do the websites present reliability or validity evidence for the measures? If so, what form does the evidence take? If not, what kind of evidence would you like to see? You might frame your predictions in this form: "If this sales ability test has convergent validity, I would expect it to be correlated with . . . ."; "If this sales ability test has discriminant validity, I would expect it *not* to be correlated with . . . ."; "If this sales ability test has criterion validity, I would expect it to be correlated with . . . ."

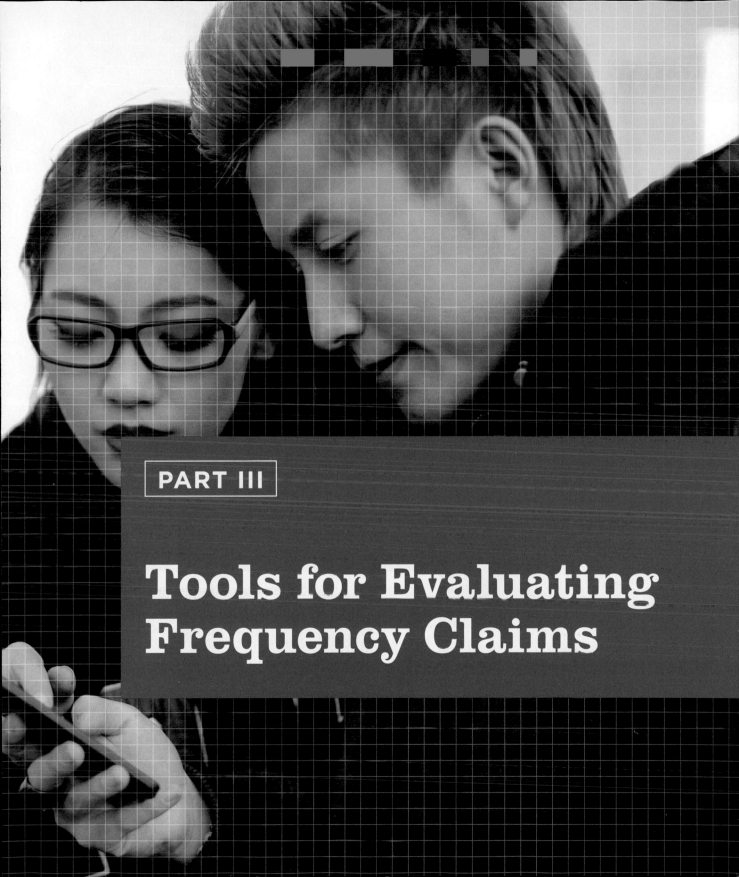

PART III

Tools for Evaluating Frequency Claims

"Should we eat at this restaurant? It got almost 5 stars on Yelp."

7 Secrets of Low-Stress Families
WebMD.com, 2010

"Should I take this class? The professor has a green smiley face on RateMyProfessors.com."

6

Surveys and Observations: Describing What People Do

YOU SHOULD BE ABLE to identify the three statements that open this chapter as single-variable frequency claims. Each claim is based on data from one variable: the rated quality of a restaurant, opinions about a professor, or the habits of families. Where do the data for such claims come from? This chapter focuses on the construct validity of surveys and polls, in which researchers ask people questions, as well as observational studies, in which researchers watch the behavior of people or other animals, often without asking them questions at all. Researchers use surveys, polls, and observations to measure variables for any type of claim. However, in this chapter and the next, many of the examples focus on how surveys and observations are used to measure one variable at a time—for frequency claims.

CONSTRUCT VALIDITY OF SURVEYS AND POLLS

Researchers use surveys and polls to ask people questions over the telephone, in door-to-door interviews, through the mail, or over the Internet. You may have been asked to take surveys in various situations. Perhaps after you purchased an item from an Internet retailer,

A year from now, you should still be able to:

1.
Explain how carefully prepared questions improve the construct validity of a poll or survey.

2.
Describe how researchers can make observations with good construct validity.

you got an e-mail asking you to post a review. While you were reading an online newspaper, maybe a survey popped up. A polling organization, such as Gallup or Pew Research Center, may have called you at home.

The word *survey* is often used when people are asked about a consumer product, whereas the word *poll* is used when people are asked about their social or political opinions. However, these two terms can be interchangeable, and in this book, **survey** and **poll** both mean the same thing: a method of posing questions to people on the phone, in personal interviews, on written questionnaires, or online. Psychologists might conduct national polls as part of their research, or they may use the polling information they read (as consumers of information) to inspire further research.

How much can you learn about a phenomenon just by asking people questions? It depends on how well you ask. As you will learn, researchers who develop their questions carefully can support frequency, association, or causal claims that have excellent construct validity.

Choosing Question Formats

Survey questions can follow four basic formats. Researchers may ask **open-ended questions** that allow respondents to answer any way they like. They might ask people to name the public figure they admire the most, or ask a sample of people to describe their views on immigration. Departing overnight guests might be asked to submit comments about their experience at a hotel. Their various responses to open-ended questions provide researchers with spontaneous, rich information. The drawback is that the responses must be coded and categorized, a process that is often difficult and time-consuming. In the interest of efficiency, therefore, researchers in psychology often restrict the answers people can give.

One specific way to ask survey questions uses **forced-choice questions**, in which people give their opinion by picking the best of two or more options. Forced-choice questions are often used in political polls, such as asking which of two or three candidates respondents plan to vote for.

An example of a psychology measure that uses forced-choice questions is the Narcissistic Personality Inventory (NPI; Raskin & Terry, 1988). This instrument asks people to choose one statement from each of 40 pairs of items, such as the following:

1. _____ I really like to be the center of attention.
   _____ It makes me uncomfortable to be the center of attention.
2. _____ I am going to be a great person.
   _____ I hope I am going to be successful.

To score a survey like this, the researcher adds up the number of times people choose the "narcissistic" response over the "non-narcissistic" one (in the example items above, the narcissistic response is the first option).

In another question format, people are presented with a statement and are asked to use a rating scale to indicate their degree of agreement. When such a scale contains more than one item and each response value is labeled with the specific terms *strongly agree, agree, neither agree nor disagree, disagree,* and *strongly disagree*, it is often called a **Likert scale** (Likert, 1932). If it does not follow this format exactly (e.g., if it has only one item, or if its response labels are a bit different from the original Likert labels) it may be called a *Likert-type scale*. Here is one of the ten items from the Rosenberg self-esteem inventory, a commonly used measure of self-esteem (Rosenberg, 1965). It can be considered a Likert scale:

I am able to do things as well as most other people.

1	2	3	4	5
Strongly disagree				Strongly agree

Instead of degree of agreement, respondents might be asked to rate a target object using a numeric scale that is anchored with adjectives; this is called a **semantic differential format**. For example, on the Internet site RateMyProfessors.com, students assign ratings to a professor using the following adjective phrases:

Overall Quality:

Profs get F's too	1	2	3	4	5	A real gem

Level of Difficulty:

Show up and pass	1	2	3	4	5	Hardest thing I've ever done

The five-star rating format that Internet rating sites (like Yelp) use is another example of this technique (**Figure 6.1**). Generally one star means "poor" or "I don't like it," and five stars means "outstanding" or even "Woohoo! As good as it gets!"

There are other question types, of course, and researchers might combine formats on a single survey. The point is that the format of a question (open-ended, forced-choice, or Likert scale) does not make or break its construct validity. The way the questions are worded, and the order in which they appear, are much more important.

Writing Well-Worded Questions

As with other research findings, when you interrogate a survey result, your first question is about construct validity: How well was that variable measured? The way a question is worded and presented in a survey can make a tremendous

El Diablo Burritos

212 reviews   Details

$ · Mexican   Edit

FIGURE 6.1
A five-star restaurant rating on the Internet.

Ratings of the products and services people might consult online are examples of frequency claims. Is a five-star rating a valid indicator of a restaurant's quality?

difference in how people answer. It is crucial that each question be clear and straightforward. Poll and survey creators work to ensure that the wording and order of the questions do not influence respondents' answers.

QUESTION WORDING MATTERS

An example of the way question wording can affect responses comes from survey research on a random sample of Delaware voters (Wilson & Brewer, 2016). The poll asked about people's support for voter identification laws, which require voters to show a photo ID before casting a ballot. Participants heard one of several different versions of the question. Here are three of them:

1. What is your opinion? Do you strongly favor, mostly favor, mostly oppose, or strongly oppose voter ID laws?
2. Opponents of voter ID laws argue that they will prevent people who are eligible to vote from voting. What is your opinion? Do you strongly favor, mostly favor, mostly oppose, or strongly oppose voter ID laws?
3. Opponents of voter ID laws argue that they will prevent people who are eligible to vote from voting, and that the laws will affect African American voters especially hard. What is your opinion? Do you strongly favor, mostly favor, mostly oppose, or strongly oppose voter ID laws?

As you can see, the first version of the question simply asks people's opinion about voter ID laws, but the second question is potentially a **leading question**, one whose wording leads people to a particular response because it explains why some people oppose the law. The third question specifies a group (African American voters) that will be affected by voter ID laws. The researchers found that presenting potentially leading information did, in fact, affect people's support. Without the additional wording, 79% of people supported voter ID laws. In the second version, 69% supported them, and when African Americans were specified, 61% supported such laws. The study shows that the wording matters; when people answer questions that suggest a particular viewpoint, at least some people change their answers.

In general, if the intention of a survey is to capture respondents' true opinions, the survey writers might attempt to word every question as neutrally as possible. When researchers want to measure how much the wording matters for their topic, they word each question more than one way. If the results are the same regardless of the wording, they can conclude that question wording does not affect people's responses to that particular topic. If the results are different, then they may need to report the results separately for each version of the question.

DOUBLE-BARRELED QUESTIONS

The wording of a question is sometimes so complicated that respondents have trouble answering in a way that accurately reflects their opinions. In a survey, it is always best to ask a simple question. When people understand the question, they can give a clear, direct, and meaningful answer, but sometimes survey writers forget this basic guideline. For example, an online survey from the National Rifle Association asked this question:

Do you agree that the Second Amendment to our United States Constitution guarantees your individual right to own a gun and that the Second Amendment is just as important as your other Constitutional rights?

○   Support

○   Oppose

○   No opinion

This is called a **double-barreled question**; it asks two questions in one. Double-barreled questions have poor construct validity because people might be responding to the first half of the question, the second half, or both. Therefore, the item could be measuring the first construct, the second construct, or both. Careful researchers would have asked each question separately:

Do you agree that the Second Amendment guarantees your individual right to own a gun?

○   Support

○   Oppose

○   No opinion

Do you agree that the Second Amendment is just as important as your other Constitutional rights?

○   Support

○   Oppose

○   No opinion

NEGATIVE WORDING

Negatively worded questions are another way survey items can be unnecessarily complicated. Whenever a question contains negative phrasing, it can cause confusion, thereby reducing the construct validity of a survey or poll (Schwarz & Oyserman, 2001).

A classic example comes from a survey on Holocaust denial, which found that 20% of Americans denied that the Nazi Holocaust ever happened. In the months that followed the publication of this survey's results, writers and journalists criticized and analyzed the "intensely disturbing" news (Kagay, 1994).

Upon further investigation, the Roper polling organization reported that the people in the original telephone poll had been asked, "Does it seem possible or does it seem impossible to you that the Nazi extermination of the Jews never happened?" Think for a minute about how you would answer that question. If you wanted to convey the opinion that the Holocaust did happen, you would have to say, "It's impossible that it never happened." In order to give your opinion about the Holocaust accurately, you must also be able to unpack the double negative of *impossible* and *never*. So instead of measuring people's beliefs, the question may be measuring people's working memory or their motivation to pay attention.

We know that this negatively worded question may have affected people's responses because the same polling organization repeated the survey less than a year later, asking the question more clearly, with less negativity: "Does it seem possible to you that the Nazi extermination of the Jews never happened, or do you feel certain that it happened?" This time, only 1% responded that the Holocaust might not have happened, 8% did not know, and 91% said they were certain it happened (Kagay, 1994). This new result, as well as other polls reflecting similarly low levels of Holocaust denial, indicates that because of the original wording, the question had poor construct validity: It probably did not measure people's true beliefs.

Sometimes even one negative word can make a question difficult to answer. For example, consider the following question:

Abortion should never be restricted.

1	2	3	4	5
Disagree				Agree

To answer this question, those who oppose abortion must think in the double negative ("I *disagree* that abortion should *never* be restricted"), while those who support abortion rights would be able to answer more easily ("I agree—abortion should never be restricted").

When possible, negative wording should be avoided, but researchers sometimes ask questions both ways, like this:

Abortion should never be restricted.

1	2	3	4	5
Disagree				Agree

I favor strong restrictions on abortion.

1	2	3	4	5
Disagree				Agree

After asking the question both ways, the researchers can study the items' internal consistency (using Cronbach's alpha) to see whether people respond similarly to both questions (in this case, agreement with the first item should correlate with disagreement with the second item). Like double-barreled questions, negatively worded ones can reduce construct validity because they might capture people's ability or motivation to figure out the question rather than their true opinions.

QUESTION ORDER

The order in which questions are asked can also affect the responses to a survey. The earlier questions can change the way respondents understand and answer the later questions. For example, a question on a parenting survey such as "How often do your children play?" would have different meanings if the previous questions had been about sports versus music versus daily activities.

Consider this example: Political opinion researcher David Wilson and his colleagues asked people whether they supported affirmative action for different groups (Wilson, Moore, McKay, & Avery, 2008). Half the participants were asked two forced-choice questions in this order:

1. Do you generally favor or oppose affirmative action programs for women?
2. Do you generally favor or oppose affirmative action for racial minorities?

The other half were asked the same two questions, but in the opposite order:

1. Do you generally favor or oppose affirmative action for racial minorities?
2. Do you generally favor or oppose affirmative action programs for women?

Wilson found that Whites reported more support for affirmative action for minorities when they had first been asked about affirmative action for women. Presumably, most Whites support affirmative action for women more than they do for minorities. To appear consistent, they might feel obligated to express support for affirmative action for racial minorities if they have just indicated their support for affirmative action for women.

The most direct way to control for the effect of question order is to prepare different versions of a survey, with the questions in different sequences. If the results for the first order differ from the results for the second order, researchers can report both sets of results separately. In addition, they might be safe in assuming that people's endorsement of the first question on any survey is unaffected by previous questions.

Encouraging Accurate Responses

Careful researchers pay attention to how they word and order their survey questions. But what about the people who answer them? Overall, people can give meaningful responses to many kinds of questions (Paulhus & Vazire, 2007; Schwarz & Oyserman, 2001). In certain situations, however, people are less likely to respond accurately. It's not because they are intentionally being dishonest. People might give inaccurate answers because they don't make an effort to think about each question, because they want to look good, or because they are simply unable to report accurately about their own motivations and memories.

PEOPLE CAN GIVE MEANINGFUL RESPONSES

Some students are skeptical that people can *ever* report accurately on surveys. Despite what you might think, though, self-reports are often ideal. People are able to report their own gender identity, socioeconomic status, ethnicity, and so on; there is no need to use expensive or difficult measures to collect such information. More importantly, self-reports often provide the most meaningful information you can get. Diener and his colleagues, in their studies of well-being (see Chapter 5), were specifically interested in subjective perspectives on happiness, so it made sense to ask participants to self-report on aspects of their life satisfaction (Diener, Emmons, Larsen, & Griffin, 1985).

In some cases, self-reports might be the only option. For example, researchers who study dreaming can monitor brain activity to identify *when* someone is dreaming, but they need to use self-reports to find out the *content* of the person's dreams because only the dreamer experiences the dream. Other traits are not very observable, such as how anxious somebody is feeling. Therefore, it is meaningful and effective to ask people to self-report on their own subjective experiences (Vazire & Carlson, 2011).

SOMETIMES PEOPLE USE SHORTCUTS

Response sets, also known as *nondifferentiation*, are a type of shortcut respondents can take when answering survey questions. Although response sets do not cause many problems for answering a single, stand-alone item, people might adopt a consistent way of answering all the questions—especially toward the end of a long questionnaire (Lelkes, Krosnick, Marx, Judd, & Park, 2012). Rather than thinking carefully about each question, people might answer all of them positively, negatively, or neutrally. Response sets weaken construct validity because these survey respondents are not saying what they really think.

One common response set is **acquiescence**, or *yea-saying*; this occurs when people say "yes" or "strongly agree" to every item instead of thinking carefully about each one. For example, a respondent might answer "5" to every item on Diener's scale of subjective well-being—not because he is a happy person, but because he is using a yea-saying shortcut (**Figure 6.2**). People apparently have a bias to agree with (say "yes" to) any item—no matter what it states (Krosnick, 1999). Acquiescence can threaten construct validity because instead of measuring the construct of true feelings of well-being, the survey could be measuring the tendency to agree, or the lack of motivation to think carefully.

How can researchers tell the difference between a respondent who is yea-saying and one who really does agree with all the items? The most common way is by including reverse-worded items. Diener might have changed the wording of some items to mean their opposite, for instance,

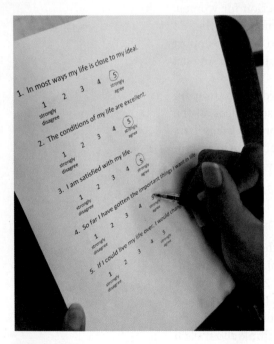

FIGURE 6.2
Response sets.

When people use an acquiescent response set, they agree with almost every question or statement. It can be hard to know whether they really mean it, or whether they're just using a shortcut to respond to the questions.

"If I had my life to live over, I'd change almost *everything*." One benefit is that reverse-worded items might slow people down so they answer more carefully. (Before computing a scale average for each person, the researchers rescore only the reverse-worded items such that, for example, "strongly disagree" becomes a 5 and "strongly agree" becomes a 1.) The scale with reverse-worded items would have more construct validity because high or low averages would be measuring true happiness or unhappiness, instead of acquiescence. A drawback of reverse-wording is that sometimes the result is negatively worded items, which are more difficult to answer.

Another specific response set is **fence sitting**—playing it safe by answering in the middle of the scale, especially when survey items are controversial. People might also answer in the middle (or say "I don't know") when a question is confusing or unclear. Fence sitters can weaken a survey's construct validity when middle-of-the-road scores suggest that some responders don't have an opinion, when they actually do. Of course, some people honestly may have no opinion on the questions; in that case, they choose the middle option for a valid reason. It can be difficult to distinguish those who are unwilling to take a side from those who are truly ambivalent.

Researchers may try to jostle people out of this tendency. One approach is to take away the neutral option. Compare these two formats:

Race relations are going well in this country.

    ○   ○   ○   ○   ○

Strongly   Strongly

disagree   agree

Race relations are going well in this country.

    ○   ○   ○   ○

Strongly   Strongly

disagree   agree

When a scale contains an even number of response options, the person has to choose one side or the other because there is no neutral choice. The drawback of this approach is that sometimes people really do not have an opinion or an answer, so for them, having to choose a side is an invalid representation of their truly neutral stance. Therefore, researchers must carefully consider which format is best.

Another common way to get people off the fence is to use forced-choice questions, in which people must pick one of two answers. Although this reduces fence sitting, again it can frustrate people who feel their own opinion is somewhere in the middle of the two options. In some telephone surveys, interviewers will write down a response of "I don't know" or "No opinion" if a person volunteers that response. Thus, more people get off the fence, but truly ambivalent people can also validly report their neutral opinions.

TRYING TO LOOK GOOD

Most of us want to look good in the eyes of others, but when survey respondents give answers that make them look better than they really are, these responses decrease the survey's construct validity. This phenomenon is known as **socially desirable responding**, or **faking good**. The idea is that because respondents are embarrassed, shy, or worried about giving an unpopular opinion, they will not tell the truth on a survey or other self-report measure. A similar, but less common, phenomenon is called **faking bad**.

To avoid socially desirable responding, a researcher might ensure that the participants know their responses are anonymous—perhaps by conducting the survey online, or in the case of an in-person interview, reminding people of their anonymity right before asking sensitive questions (Schwarz & Oyserman, 2001). However, anonymity may not be a perfect solution. Anonymous respondents may treat surveys less seriously. In one study, anonymous respondents were more likely to start using response sets in long surveys. In addition, anonymous people were less likely to accurately report a simple behavior, such as how many candies they had just eaten, which suggests they were paying less attention to things (Lelkes, Krosnik, Marx, Judd, & Park, 2012).

One way to minimize this problem is to include special survey items that identify socially desirable responders with target items like these (Crowne & Marlowe, 1960):

My table manners at home are as good as when I eat out in a restaurant.

I don't find it particularly difficult to get along with loud-mouthed, obnoxious people.

If people agree with many such items, researchers may discard that individual's data from the final set, under suspicion that they are exaggerating on the other survey items, or not paying close attention in general.

Researchers can also ask people's friends to rate them. When it comes to domains where we want to look good (e.g., on how rude or how smart we are), others know us better than we know ourselves (Vazire & Carlson, 2011). Thus, researchers might be better off asking people's friends to rate them on traits that are observable but desirable.

Finally, researchers increasingly use special, computerized measures to evaluate people's implicit opinions about sensitive topics. One widely used test, the Implicit Association Test, asks people to respond quickly to positive and negative words on the right and left of a computer screen (Greenwald, Nosek, & Banaji, 2003). Intermixed with the positive and negative words may be faces from different social groups, such as Black and White faces. People respond to all possible combinations, including positive words with Black faces, negative words with White faces, negative words with Black faces, and positive words with White faces. When people respond more efficiently to the White-positive/Black-negative combination than to the White-negative/Black-positive combination, researchers infer that the person may hold negative attitudes on an implicit, or unconscious, level.

SELF-REPORTING "MORE THAN THEY CAN KNOW"

As researchers strive to encourage accurate responses, they also ask whether people are *capable* of reporting accurately on their own feelings, thoughts, and actions. Everyone knows his or her opinions better than anyone else does, right? Only *I* know my level of support for a political candidate. Only *you* know how much you liked a professor. Only *the patron* knows how much she liked that restaurant. In some cases, however, self-reports can be inaccurate, especially when people are asked to describe *why* they are thinking, behaving, or feeling the way they do. When asked, most people willingly provide an explanation or an opinion to a researcher, but sometimes they unintentionally give inaccurate responses.

Psychologists Richard Nisbett and Timothy Wilson (1977) conducted a set of studies to demonstrate this phenomenon. In one study, they put six pairs of nylon stockings on a table and asked female shoppers in a store to tell them which of the stockings they preferred. As it turned out, almost everyone selected the last pair on the right. The reason for this preference was something of a mystery—especially since all the stockings were exactly the same! Next, the researchers asked each woman why she selected the pair she did. Every participant reported that she selected the pair on the right for its excellent quality. Even when the researchers suggested they might have chosen the pair because it was on the far right side of the table, the women insisted they made their choices based on the quality of the stockings. In other words, the women easily formulated answers for the researchers, but their answers had nothing to do with the real reason they selected the one pair of stockings (**Figure 6.3**). Moreover, the women did not seem to be aware they were inventing a justification for their preference. They gave a sincere, reasonable response—one that just happened to be wrong. Therefore, researchers cannot assume the reasons people give for their own behavior are their actual reasons. People may not be able to accurately explain why they acted as they did.

SELF-REPORTING MEMORIES OF EVENTS

Even if people can't always accurately report the reasons behind their behaviors, surely they know what those behaviors were, right? In fact, psychological research has shown that people's memories about events in which they participated are not very accurate. For example, many American adults can say exactly where they were when they heard the news that two planes had crashed into New York's World Trade Center on September 11, 2001, and their memories are often startlingly vivid. Cognitive psychologists have checked the accuracy of such "flashbulb memories."

FIGURE 6.3
The accuracy of self-reports.

If you ask this shopper why she chooses one of these items, she will probably give you a reasonable answer. But does her answer represent the true reason for making her choice?

To conduct such a study, researchers administer a short questionnaire to their students on the day after a dramatic event, asking them to recall where they were, whom they were with, and so forth. A few years later, the researchers ask the same people the same questions as before, and also ask them to rate their confidence in their memories. Such studies have shown that overall accuracy is very low: For example, years later, about 73% of students recalling their memories of the 9/11 attacks remembered seeing the first plane hit the World Trade Center on TV, when in fact no such footage was available at that time (Pezdek, 2003).

The other important finding from these studies is that people's confidence in the accuracy of their memories is virtually unrelated to how accurate the memories actually are. Three years later, people who are extremely confident in their memories are about as likely to be wrong as people who report their memories with little or no confidence. In one study, when researchers showed participants what they wrote years ago, on the day after significant events, they were genuinely stumped, saying, "I still think of it as the other way around" or "I mean, like I told you, I have no recollection of [that version] at all" (Neisser & Harsch, 1992, p. 21). Studies like these remind us to question the construct validity of even the most vivid and confidently held "memories" of the past. In other words, asking people what they remember is probably not the best operationalization for studying what really happened to them.

RATING PRODUCTS

What about the special case of online product ratings? Online ratings constitute data that support frequency claims. Are consumers able to make good judgments about products they have purchased and used? One study found little correspondence between five-star ratings on Amazon.com and the ratings of the same products by Consumer Reports, an independent product rating firm (De Langhe, Fernbach, & Lichtenstein, 2016). The researchers found that consumers' ratings were, instead, correlated with the cost of the product and the prestige of its brand. Studies like these suggest that people may not always be able to accurately report on the quality of products they buy (**Figure 6.4**).

FIGURE 6.4
Do consumer ratings match expert ratings?

This camera's online reviews were positive, but Consumer Reports (an independent rating firm) ranked it second to last. While consumers may be able to report their subjective experience with a product, their ratings might not accurately predict product quality.

CONSTRUCT VALIDITY OF BEHAVIORAL OBSERVATIONS

Survey and poll results are among the most common types of data used to support a frequency claim—the kind you read most often in newspapers or on websites. Researchers also study people simply by watching them in action. When a researcher watches people or animals and systematically records how they behave or what they are doing, it is called **observational research**. Some scientists believe observing behavior is better than collecting self-reports through surveys, because people cannot always report on their behavior or past events accurately, as we've discussed. Given the potential for the effect of question order, response sets, socially desirable responding, and other problems, many psychologists trust behavioral data more than survey data, at least for some variables.

Observational research can be the basis for frequency claims. Researchers might record how much people eat in fast-food restaurants or observe drivers, counting how many will stop for a pedestrian in a crosswalk. They might test the balance of athletes who have been hit on the head during practice, listen in on the comments of parents watching a hockey game, or watch families as they eat dinner. Observational research is not just for frequency claims: Observations can also be used to operationalize variables in association claims and causal claims. Regardless of the type of claim, it is important that observational measures have good construct validity.

Some Claims Based on Observational Data

Self-report questions can be excellent measures of what people *think* they are doing, and of what they *think* is influencing their behavior. But if you want to know what people are *really* doing or what *really* influences behavior, you should

≪

For more detail on statistical significance, see Chapter 3, pp. 71–72, and Statistics Review: Inferential Statistics, pp. 499–501.

A

B

Table 1. Estimated number of words spoken per day for female and male study participants across six samples. $N = 396$. Year refers to the year when the data collection started; duration refers to the approximate number of days participants wore the EAR; the weighted average weighs the respective sample group mean by the sample size of the group.

Sample	Year	Location	Duration	Age range (years)	Sample size (N) Women	Sample size (N) Men	Estimated average number (SD) of words spoken per day Women	Estimated average number (SD) of words spoken per day Men
1	2004	USA	7 days	18–29	56	56	18,443 (7460)	16,576 (7871)
2	2003	USA	4 days	17–23	42	37	14,297 (6441)	14,060 (9065)
3	2003	Mexico	4 days	17–25	31	20	14,704 (6215)	15,022 (7864)
4	2001	USA	2 days	17–22	47	49	16,177 (7520)	16,569 (9108)
5	2001	USA	10 days	18–26	7	4	15,761 (8985)	24,051 (10,211)
6	1998	USA	4 days	17–23	27	20	16,496 (7914)	12,867 (8343)
					Weighted average		16,215 (7301)	15,669 (8633)

FIGURE 6.5

Observational research on daily spoken words.

(A) Study participants wore a small recording device to measure how many words they spoke per day. (B) This table shows the study's results, as they were reported in the original empirical journal article. (Source: Mehl et al., 2007, Table 1.)

probably watch them. Here are three examples of how observational methods have been used to answer research questions in psychology.

OBSERVING HOW MUCH PEOPLE TALK

Matthias Mehl and his colleagues kept track of what people say in everyday contexts (Mehl, Vazire, Ramirez-Esparza, Slatcher, & Pennebaker, 2007). The researchers recruited several samples of students and asked them to wear an electronically activated recorder (EAR) for 2–10 days (depending on the sample). This device contains a small, clip-on microphone and a digital sound recorder similar to an iPod (**Figure 6.5A**). At 12.5-minute intervals throughout the day, the EAR records 30 seconds of ambient sound. Later, research assistants transcribe everything the person says during the recorded time periods. The published data demonstrate that on average, women speak 16,215 words per day, while men speak 15,669 words per day (**Figure 6.5B**). This difference is not statistically significant, so despite stereotypes of women being the chattier gender, women and men showed the same level of speaking.

OBSERVING HOCKEY MOMS AND DADS

Canadian researchers investigated popular media stories about parents who had acted violently at youth ice hockey games (Bowker et al., 2009). To see how widespread this "problem" was, the researchers decided to watch a sample of hockey games and record the frequency of violent, negative behavior (as well as positive, supportive behavior) by parents. Although the media has reported dramatic stories about fights among parents at youth hockey games, these few instances seem to have been an exception. After sitting in the stands at 69 boys' and girls' hockey games in one Canadian city, the researchers found that 64% of the parents' comments were positive, and only 4% were negative. The authors concluded that their results were "in stark contrast to media reports, which paint a grim picture of aggressive spectators and out-of-control parents" (Bowker et al., 2009, p. 311).

OBSERVING FAMILIES IN THE EVENING

A third example comes from a study of families in which both parents work (Campos et al., 2013). The researchers had camera crews follow both parents from a sample of 30 dual-earner families, from the time they got home from work until 8:00 P.M. Later, teams of assistants coded a variety of behaviors from the resulting videotapes. The researchers studied two aspects of family life: the emotional tone of the parents, and the topics of conversation during dinner.

To code emotional tone, they watched the videos, rating each parent on a 7-point scale. The rating scale went from 1 (cold/hostile) to 4 (neutral) to 7 (warm/happy) (**Figure 6.6**). The results from the Campos study showed that emotional tone in the families was slightly positive in the evening hours (around 4.2 on the 7-point scale). In addition, they found that kids and parents differed in

> ***Emotional tone.*** To measure emotional tone, coders rated the extent to which the behavior of each parent was marked by verbal and nonverbal markers of coldness/hostility or warmth/happiness on a Likert scale (1 = *cold/hostile*; 4 = *neutral*; 7 = *warm/happy*). Cold/hostile emotional tone was defined as short communication, flat or angry affect, and no evidence of positive affect. Neutral tone was defined as a task oriented, practical tone that was neither cold/hostile nor warm/happy. Warm/happy emotional tone was defined as warm voice tones, smiles, laughter, and head nods with no evidence of negative affect. Coders independently rated a parent's emotional tone when they appeared in the video (a) alone, (b) with their partner (if present), or (c) with their 7- to 12-year-old child (if present). The latter rating was restricted to the 7- to 12-year-old child that all families were required to have to standardize interaction that might otherwise vary with stage of child development. Thus, up to three emotional tone variables could be rated for each parent in each 30-s video slice. Interrater reliabilities for emotional tone alone (ICC = .92), with partner (ICC = .91), and with child (ICC = .95) were high.

STRAIGHT FROM THE SOURCE

Interrater reliability of this observation.

FIGURE 6.6
Coding emotional tone.

Here is how researchers reported the way they coded emotional tone in the Method section of their article. (Source: Adapted from Campos et al., 2013.)

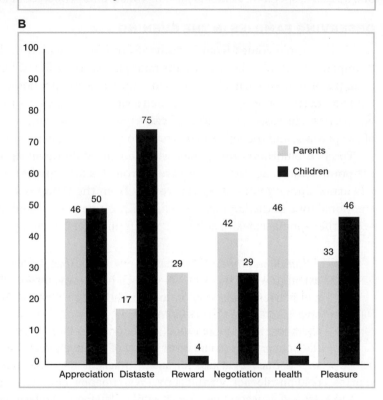

Dinnertime talk. Coders documented whether each family member present engaged in each of the following six types of food-related talk: (a) expressions of appreciation, (b) expressions of distaste, (c) reference to health, (d) reference to pleasure, (e) reference to food as a reward, and (f) negotiation over the terms of food rewards or penalties.

FIGURE 6.7
Coding dinnertime topics.

(A) The coders assigned each piece of dinnertime conversation to one of six categories. (B) The results showed that children were most likely to express distaste at the food their parents had prepared. (Source: Adapted from Campos et al., 2013.)

what they discussed at dinnertime. The kids were more likely to express distaste at the food, while the parents talked about how healthy it was (**Figure 6.7**). In addition to these frequency estimates, the researchers also studied associations. For example, they found that mothers' (but not fathers') emotional tone was more negative when children complained about the food at dinner.

OBSERVATIONS CAN BE BETTER THAN SELF-REPORTS

The previous examples illustrate a variety of ways researchers have conducted observational studies—either through direct means, such as sitting in the stands during a hockey game, or by using technology, such as an EAR or a video camera. Let's reflect on the benefits of behavioral observation in these cases. What might have happened if the researchers had asked the participants to self-report? The college students certainly would not have been able to state how many words they spoke each day. The hockey parents might have reported that their own comments at the rink were mostly positive, but they might have exaggerated their reports of other parents' degree of negativity. And while parents could report on how they were feeling in the evening and at dinner, they might not have been able to describe how emotionally warm their expressions appeared to others—the part that matters to their partners and children. Observations can sometimes tell a more accurate story than self-reporting (Vazire & Carlson, 2011).

Making Reliable and Valid Observations

Observational research is a way to operationalize a conceptual variable, so when interrogating a study we need to ask about the construct validity of any observational measure. We ask: What is the variable of interest, and did the observations accurately measure that variable? Although observational research may seem straightforward, researchers must work quite diligently to be sure their observations are reliable and valid.

The construct validity of observations can be threatened by three problems: observer bias, observer effects, and reactivity. Observations have good construct validity to the extent that they can avoid these three problems.

OBSERVER BIAS: WHEN OBSERVERS SEE WHAT THEY EXPECT TO SEE

Observer bias occurs when observers' expectations influence their interpretation of the participants' behaviors or the outcome of the study. Instead of rating behaviors objectively, observers rate behaviors according to their own expectations or hypotheses. In one study, psychoanalytic therapists were shown a videotape of a 26-year-old man talking to a professor about his feelings and work experiences (Langer & Abelson, 1974). Some of the therapists were told the young man was a patient, while others were told he was a job applicant. After seeing the videotape, the clinicians were asked for their observations. What kind of person was this young man?

Although all the therapists saw the same videotape, their reactions were not the same. Those who thought the man was a job applicant described him with such terms such as "attractive," "candid," and "innovative." Those who saw the videotape thinking the young man was a patient described him as a "tight, defensive person," "frightened of his own aggressive impulses" (Langer & Abelson, 1974, p. 8). Since everyone saw the same tape, these striking differences can only have reflected the biases of the observers in interpreting what they saw.

OBSERVER EFFECTS: WHEN PARTICIPANTS CONFIRM OBSERVER EXPECTATIONS

It is problematic when observer biases affect researchers' own interpretations of what they see. It is even worse when the observers inadvertently change the behavior of those they are observing, such that participant behavior changes to match observer expectations. Known as **observer effects**, or *expectancy effects,* this phenomenon can occur even in seemingly objective observations.

Bright and Dull Rats. In a classic study of observer effects, researchers Rosenthal and Fode (1963) gave each student in an advanced psychology course five rats to test as part of a final lab experience in the course. Each student timed how long it took for their rats to learn a simple maze, every day for several days. Although each student actually received a randomly selected group of rats, the researchers told half of them that their rats were bred to be "maze-bright" and the other half that their rats were bred to be "maze-dull."

Even though all the rats were genetically similar, those that were believed to be maze-bright completed the maze a little faster each day and with fewer mistakes. In contrast, the rats believed to be maze-dull did not improve their performance over the testing days. This study showed that observers not only see what they expect to see; sometimes they even cause the behavior of those they are observing to conform to their expectations.

Clever Hans. A horse nicknamed Clever Hans provides another classic example of how observers' subtle behavior changed a subject's behavior, and how scientifically minded observers corrected the problem (Heinzen, Lillienfeld, & Nolan, 2015). More than 100 years ago, a retired schoolteacher named William von Osten tutored his horse, Hans, in mathematics. If he asked Hans to add 3 and 2, for example, the horse would tap his hoof five times and then stop. After 4 years of daily training, Clever Hans could perform math at least as well as an average fifth-grader, identify colors, and read German words (**Figure 6.8**). Von Osten allowed many scientists to test his horse's abilities, and all were satisfied that von Osten was not giving Hans cues on the sly because he apparently could do arithmetic even when his owner was not even present.

FIGURE 6.8
William von Osten and Clever Hans.

The horse Clever Hans could detect nonverbal gestures from anybody—not just his owner—so his behavior even convinced a special commission of experts in 1904.

Just when other scientists had concluded Clever Hans was truly capable of doing math, an experimental psychologist, Oskar Pfungst, came up with a more rigorous set of checks (Pfungst, 1911). Suspecting the animal was sensing subtle nonverbal cues from his human questioners, Pfungst showed the horse a series of cards printed with numbers. He alternated situations in which the questioner could or could not see each card. As Pfungst suspected, Hans was correct only when his questioner saw the card.

As it turned out, the horse *was* extremely clever—but not at math. He was smart at detecting the subtle head movements of the questioner. Pfungst noticed that a questioner would lean over to watch Hans tap his foot, raising his head a bit at the last correct tap. Clever Hans had learned this slight move was the cue to stop tapping (Heinzen et al., 2015).

Positive, General (Pg).   These comments were defined as positive in tone and as directed at the team in general, with no instructional content (e.g., "Go Crusaders"; 'Nice try"; "Good work").

Positive, Specific (Ps).   These comments were defined as being positive, but directed at a specific player (e.g., "Nice play JD"; "Way to go LJ").

Corrective/Instructional (Cor).   These comments were defined as including a specific action or play that the player was instructed to do. They included comments which were positive in nature (e.g., "Go after it"), and those with a more negative tone (e.g., "Get back"; "You've got to cover him").

Negative (Neg).   These comments were defined as those meant to criticize the target in some way (usually directed toward the referee). Much of the time, the negativity of the comment was due to a sarcastic tone (e.g., "What kind of call is that?"; "Come on ref, you call that a penalty?").

Neutral (Neu).   These comments were defined as those not fitting into any of the other categories, and/or were unrelated to the game (e.g., "Did you book your hotel room for the tournament?").

Each remark was coded for intensity, based on a three-point scale: 1 = spoken relatively quietly, with little to no emotion; 2 = louder, more intense speech, stronger emotion, but controlled; 3 = loud, intense speech, extreme emotional content.

FIGURE 6.9
Clear codebooks can improve the construct validity of observations.

This information was included in the empirical journal article's Method section. (Source: Adapted from Bowker et al., 2009.)

PREVENTING OBSERVER BIAS AND OBSERVER EFFECTS

Researchers must ensure the construct validity of observational measures by taking steps to avoid observer bias and observer effects. First and foremost, careful researchers train their observers well. They develop clear rating instructions, often called *codebooks,* so the observers can make reliable judgments with less bias. Codebooks are precise statements of how the variables are operationalized, and the more precise and clear the codebook statements are, the more valid the operationalizations will be. **Figure 6.9** shows an example of how the parents' comments were coded in the hockey games study.

Researchers can assess the construct validity of a coded measure by using multiple observers. Doing so allows the researchers to assess the interrater reliability of their measures. Refer to Figure 6.6, the excerpt from the Campos et al. (2013) article, in which the researchers discuss the interrater reliability of the emotional tone ratings. The abbreviation ICC is a correlation that quantifies degree of agreement. The closer the correlation is to 1.0, the more the observers agreed with one another. The coders in this case showed acceptable interrater reliability.

« For more on interrater reliability, see Chapter 5, pp. 125–132.

Using multiple observers does not eliminate anyone's biases, of course, but if two observers of the same event agree on what happened, the researchers can be more confident. If there is disagreement, the researchers may need to train their observers better, develop a clearer coding system for rating the behaviors, or both.

Even when an operationalization has good interrater reliability, it still might not be valid. When two observers agree with each other, they might share the same biases, so their common observations are not necessarily valid. Think about the therapists in the Langer and Abelson (1974) study. Those who were told the man in the videotape was a patient might have showed interrater reliability in their descriptions of how defensive or frightened he appeared. But because they shared similar biases, their reliable ratings were not valid descriptions of the man's behavior. Therefore, interrater reliability is only half the story; researchers should employ methods that minimize observer bias and observer effects.

Masked Research Design. The Rosenthal and Fode (1963) study and the Clever Hans effect both demonstrate that observers can give unintentional cues influencing the behavior of their subjects. A common way to prevent observer bias and observer effects is to use a **masked design**, or *blind design*, in which the observers are unaware of the purpose of the study and the conditions to which participants have been assigned.

If Rosenthal and Fode's students had not known which rats were expected to be bright and dull, the students would not have evoked different behavior in their charges. Similarly, when Clever Hans' observers did not know the right answer to the questions they were asking, the horse acted differently; he looked much less intelligent. These examples make it clear that coders and observers should not be aware of a study's hypotheses, or should take steps to mask the conditions they are observing.

REACTIVITY: WHEN PARTICIPANTS REACT TO BEING WATCHED

Sometimes the mere presence of an outsider is enough to change the behavior of those being observed. Suppose you're visiting a first-grade classroom to observe the children. You walk quietly to the back of the room and sit down to watch what the children do. What will you see? A roomful of little heads swiveled around looking at you! Do first graders usually spend most of their time staring at the back of the room? Of course not. What you are witnessing is an example of reactivity.

Reactivity is a change in behavior when study participants know another person is watching. They might react by being on their best behavior—or in some cases, their worst—rather than displaying their typical behavior. Reactivity occurs not only with human participants but also with animal subjects. Psychologist Robert Zajonc once demonstrated that even cockroaches behave differently in the presence of other cockroaches (Zajonc, Heingartner, & Herman, 1969). If people and animals can change their behavior just because they are being watched, what should a careful researcher do?

Solution 1: Blend In. One way to avoid observer effects is to make **unobtrusive observations**—that is, make yourself less noticeable. A developmental psychologist doing research might sit behind a one-way mirror, like the one shown in **Figure 6.10**, in order to observe how children interact in a classroom without letting them know. In a public setting, a researcher might act like a casual onlooker—another face in the crowd—to watch how other people behave. In the Bowker hockey games study, observers collected data in plain sight by posing as fans in the stands. In 69 hockey games, only two parents ever asked the observer what he or she was doing, suggesting that the researcher's presence was truly unobtrusive.

Solution 2: Wait It Out. Another solution is to wait out the situation. A researcher who plans to observe at a school might let the children get used to his or her presence until they forget they're being watched. The anthropologist Jane Goodall, in her studies of chimpanzees in the wild, used a similar tactic. When she began introducing herself to the chimps in the Gombe National Park in Africa, they fled, or stopped whatever else they were doing to focus on her. After several months, the chimps got used to having her around and were no longer afraid to go about their usual activities in her presence. Similarly, participants in the Mehl EAR study reported that after a couple of days of wearing the device, they did not find it to be invasive (Mehl & Pennebaker, 2003).

Solution 3: Measure the Behavior's Results. Another way to avoid reactivity is to use unobtrusive data. Instead of observing behavior directly, researchers measure the traces a particular behavior leaves behind. For example, in a museum, wear-and-tear on the flooring can signal which areas of the museum are the most popular, and the height of smudges on the windows can indicate the age of visitors. The number of empty liquor bottles in residential garbage cans indicates how much alcohol is being consumed in a community (Webb, Campbell, Schwartz, & Sechrest, 1966). Researchers can measure behavior without doing any direct participant observation.

FIGURE 6.10
Unobtrusive observations.
This one-way mirror lets the researcher unobtrusively record the behaviors of children in a preschool classroom.

OBSERVING PEOPLE ETHICALLY

Is it ethical for researchers to observe the behaviors of others? It depends. Most psychologists believe it is ethical to watch people in museums, classrooms, hockey games, or even at the sinks of public bathrooms because in those settings people can reasonably expect their activities to be public, not private. Of course, when psychologists report the results of such observational studies, they do not specifically identify any of the people who were observed.

More secretive methods, such as one-way mirrors and covert video recording, are also considered ethical in some conditions. In most cases, psychologists doing research must obtain permission in advance to watch or to record people's private behavior. If hidden video recording is used, the researcher must explain the procedure at the conclusion of the study. If people object to having been recorded, the researcher must erase the file without watching it.

Certain ethical decisions may be influenced by the policies of a university where a study is conducted. As discussed in Chapter 4, institutional review boards (IRBs) assess each study to decide whether it can be conducted ethically.

CHECK YOUR UNDERSTANDING

1. Sketch a concept map of observer bias, observer effects, and reactivity, and indicate the approaches researchers can take to minimize each problem.

2. Explain why each of these three problems can threaten construct validity, using this sentence structure for each issue:

   If an observational study suffers from _____, then the researcher might be measuring _____ instead of _____.

1. See pp. 169–173. 2. See pp. 169 and 172.

CHAPTER REVIEW

Summary

- Surveys, polls, and observational methods are used to support frequency claims, but they also measure variables for association and causal claims. When interrogating a claim based on data from a survey or an observational study, we ask about the construct validity of the measurement.

- Surveys are efficient and accurate ways to assess people's subjective feelings and opinions; they may be less appropriate for assessing people's actual behavior, motivations, or memories.

Construct Validity of Surveys and Polls

- Survey question formats include open-ended, forced-choice, Likert scale, and semantic differential.

- Sometimes the way a survey question is worded can lead people to be more likely or less likely to agree with it.

- Double-barreled and negatively worded questions are difficult to answer in a valid way.

- People sometimes answer survey questions with an acquiescent or fence-sitting response tendency or in a way that makes them look good. Researchers can add items to a survey or change the way questions are written, in order to avoid some of these problems.

Construct Validity of Behavioral Observations

- Observational studies record people's true behavior, rather than what people say about their behavior.

- Well-trained coders and clear codebooks help ensure that observations will be reliable and not influenced by observer expectations.

- Some observational studies are susceptible to reactivity. Masked designs and unobtrusive observations make it more likely that observers will not make biased ratings, and that participants will not change their behavior in reaction to being observed.

- Local IRB guidelines may vary, but in general, it is considered ethical to conduct observational research in public settings where people expect to be seen by others.

Key Terms

To see samples of chapter concepts in the popular media, visit www.everydayresearchmethods.com and click the box for Chapter 6.

Review Questions

1. The following item appears on a survey: "Was your cell phone purchased within the last two years, and have you downloaded the most recent updates?" What is the biggest problem with this wording?

   a. It is a leading question.

   b. It involves negative wording.

   c. It is a double-barreled question.

   d. It is not on a Likert scale.

2. When people are using an acquiescent response set they are:

   a. Trying to give the researcher the responses they think he or she wants to hear.

   b. Misrepresenting their views to appear more socially acceptable.

   c. Giving the same, neutral answer to each question.

   d. Tending to agree with every item, no matter what it says.

3. In which of the following situations do people most accurately answer survey questions?

   a. When they are describing the reasons for their own behavior.

   b. When they are describing what happened to them, especially after important events.

   c. When they are describing their subjective experience; how they personally feel about something.

   d. People almost never answer survey questions accurately.

4. Which of the following makes it more likely that behavioral observations will have good interrater reliability?

   a. A masked study design

   b. A clear codebook

   c. Using naive, untrained coders

   d. Open-ended responses

5. Which one of the following is a means of controlling for observer bias?

   a. Using unobtrusive observations.

   b. Waiting for the participants to become used to the observer.

   c. Making sure the observer does not know the study's hypotheses.

   d. Measuring physical traces of behavior rather than observing behavior directly.

6. Which of the following is a way of preventing reactivity?

   a. Waiting for the participants to become used to the observer.

   b. Making sure the observers do not know the study's hypotheses.

   c. Making sure the observer uses a clear codebook.

   d. Ensuring the observers have good interrater reliability.

Learning Actively

1. Consider the various survey question formats: open-ended, forced-choice, Likert scale, and semantic differential. For each of the following research topics, write a question in each format, keeping in mind some of the pitfalls in question writing. Which of the questions you wrote would have the best construct validity, and why?

   a. A study that measures attitudes about women serving in combat roles in the military.

   b. A customer service survey asking people about their satisfaction with their most recent shopping experience.

   c. A poll that asks people which political party they have supported in the past.

2. As part of their Well-Being Index, the Gallup organization asks a daily sample of Americans, "In the last seven days, on how many days did you exercise

for 30 or more minutes?" If people say they have exercised three or more days, Gallup classifies them as "frequent exercisers." Gallup finds that between about 47% (in the winter months) and 55% (in the summer) report being frequent exercisers (Gallup, n.d.). What kind of question is this: forced-choice, Likert scale, semantic differential, or some other format? Does the item appear to be leading, negatively worded, or double-barreled? Do you think it leads to accurate responses?

3. Plan an observational study to see which kind of drivers are more likely to stop for a pedestrian in a crosswalk: male or female drivers. Think about how to maximize your construct validity. Will observers be biased about what they record? How might they influence the people they're watching, if at all? Where should they stand to observe driver behavior? How will you evaluate the interrater reliability of your observers? Write a two- to three-sentence operational definition of what it means to "stop for a pedestrian in a crosswalk." The definition should be clear enough that if you asked two friends to use it to code "stopping for pedestrian" behavior, it would have good reliability and validity.

4. To study the kinds of faces babies usually see, researchers asked parents to place tiny video cameras on their 1-month-old and 3-month-old infants during their waking hours (Sugden, Mohamed-Ali, & Moulson, 2013). Coders viewed the resulting video footage frame by frame, categorizing the gender, race, and age of the faces each baby saw. The results revealed that babies are exposed to faces 25% of their waking hours. In addition, the babies in the sample were exposed to female faces 70% of the time, and 96% of the time they were exposed to faces that were the same race as themselves. What questions might you ask to decide whether the observational measures in this study were susceptible to observer bias, observer effects, or reactivity?

8 out of 10 Drivers Say They Experience Road Rage

CBS Local, 2016

Three in Four Women Worldwide Rate Their Lives as "Struggling" or "Suffering"

Gallup, 2015

61% Said This Shoe "Felt True to Size"

Zappos.com

Fit Survey: **61%** Felt true to size

7

Sampling: Estimating the Frequency of Behaviors and Beliefs

THE CLAIMS THAT OPEN this chapter address a variety of topics: driving behavior, well-being, and the fit of a pair of shoes. The target population in each case is different. One example is about American drivers, one applies to women around the world, and the last represents online shoppers. In all three claims, we are being asked to believe something about a larger group of people (e.g., all U.S. drivers or all the world's women—more than 3.5 billion), based on data from a smaller sample that was actually studied. In this chapter, you'll learn about when we can use a sample to generalize to a population, and when we cannot. In addition, you'll learn when we really care about being able to generalize to a population, and when it's less important.

GENERALIZABILITY: DOES THE SAMPLE REPRESENT THE POPULATION?

When interrogating external validity, we ask whether the results of a particular study can be generalized to some larger population of interest. External validity is often extremely important for frequency claims. To interrogate the external validity of frequency

LEARNING OBJECTIVES

A year from now, you should still be able to:

1.
Explain why external validity is often essential for frequency claims.

2.
Describe which sampling techniques allow generalizing from a sample to a population of interest, and which ones do not.

claims such as those discussed in Chapter 6 and also presented here, we might ask the following types of questions:

> "Do the students who rated the professor on this website adequately represent all the professor's former students?"

> "Does the sample of drivers who were asked about road rage adequately represent American drivers?"

> "Can feelings of the women in the sample generalize to all the world's women?"

> "Do the people who reviewed the fit of these shoes represent the population of people who wear them?"

and even . . .

> "Can we predict the results of the presidential election if the polling sample consisted of 1,500 people?"

Recall that external validity concerns both *samples* and *settings*. A researcher may intend the results of a study to generalize to the other members of a certain population, as in the questions above. Or a researcher may intend the results to generalize to other settings, such as other shoes from the same manufacturer, other products, or other classes taught by the same professor. However, this chapter focuses primarily on the external validity of samples.

Populations and Samples

Have you ever been offered a free sample in a grocery store? Say you tried a sample of spinach mini-quiche and you loved it. You probably assumed that all 50 in the box would taste just the same. Maybe you liked one baked pita chip and assumed all the chips in the bag would be good, too. The single bite you tried is the sample. The box or bag it came from is the population. A **population** is the entire set of people or products in which you are interested. The **sample** is a smaller set, taken from that population. You don't need to eat the whole bag (the whole population) to know whether you like the chips; you only need to test a small sample. If you did taste every chip in the population, you would be conducting a **census**.

Researchers usually don't need to study every member of the population either—that is, they do not need to conduct a census. Instead, they study a sample of people, assuming that if the sample behaves a certain way, the population will do the same. The external validity of a study concerns whether the sample used in the study is adequate to represent the unstudied population. If the sample can generalize to the population, there is good external validity. If the sample is biased in some way, there is not. Therefore, when a sample has good external validity, we also say the sample "generalizes to" or "is representative of," a population of interest.

WHAT IS THE POPULATION OF INTEREST?

The world's population is around 7.5 billion people, but researchers only rarely have that entire population in mind when they conduct a study. Before researchers can decide whether a sample is biased or unbiased, they have to specify a population to which they want to generalize: the *population of interest*. Instead of "the population" as a whole, a research study's intended population is more limited. A population of interest might be laboratory mice. It might be undergraduate women. It might be men with dementia. At the grocery store, the population of interest might be the 50 mini-quiches in the box, or the 200 pita chips in the bag.

If a sample of people rated a style of shoe on how well they fit, we might be interested in generalizing to the population of people who have worn those shoes. If we are interrogating the results of a national election poll, we might care primarily about the population of people who will vote in the next election in the country. In order to say that a sample generalizes to a population, we have to first decide which population we are interested in.

COMING FROM A POPULATION VS. GENERALIZING TO THAT POPULATION

For a sample to be representative of a population, the sample must come from the population. However, coming from the population is not sufficient by itself; that is, just because a sample *comes from* a population does not mean it *generalizes to* that population. Just because a sample consists of American drivers does not mean it represents all American drivers. Just because a sample contains women doesn't mean the sample can generalize to the population of the world's women.

Samples are either biased or representative. In a **biased sample**, also called an *unrepresentative sample*, some members of the population of interest have a much higher probability of being included in the sample compared to other members. In an **unbiased sample**, also called a *representative sample*, all members of the population have an equal chance of being included in the sample. Only unbiased samples allow us to make inferences about the population of interest. **Table 7.1** lists a few examples of biased and unbiased samples.

TABLE 7.1

Biased and Unbiased Samples of Different Populations of Interest

POPULATION OF INTEREST	BIASED SAMPLING TECHNIQUE	UNBIASED SAMPLING TECHNIQUE
Democrats in Texas	Recruiting people sitting in the front row at the Texas Democratic Convention.	Obtaining a list of all registered Texas Democrats from public records, and calling a sample of them through randomized digit dialing.
Drivers	Asking drivers to complete a survey when they stop to add coins to a parking meter.	Obtaining a list of licensed drivers in each state, and selecting a sample using a random number generator.
Students who have taken a class with Professor A	Including only students who have written comments about Professor A on an online website.	Obtaining a list of all of Professor A's current and former students, and selecting every fifteenth student for study.

When Is a Sample Biased?

Let's return to the food examples to explore biased and unbiased samples further. If you reached all the way to the bottom of the bag to select your sample pita chip, that sample would be *biased,* or *unrepresentative.* Broken chips at the bottom of the bag are not representative of the population, and choosing a broken chip would cause you to draw the wrong conclusions about the quality of that bag of chips. Similarly, suppose the box of 50 quiches was a variety pack, containing various flavors of quiche. In that case, a sample spinach quiche would be unrepresentative, too. If the other types of quiche are not as tasty as the spinach, you would draw incorrect conclusions about the varied population.

In a consumer survey or an online opinion poll, a biased sample could be like getting a handful from the bottom of the bag, where the broken pita chips are more likely to be. In other words, a researcher's sample might contain too many of the most *unusual* people. For instance, the students who rate a professor on a website might tend to be the ones who are angry or disgruntled, and they might not represent the rest of the professor's students very well. A biased study sample could also be like an unrepresentative spinach quiche. A researcher's sample might include only one kind of people, when the population of interest is more like a variety pack. Imagine a poll that sampled only Democrats when the population of interest contains Republicans, Democrats, and people with other political views (**Figure 7.1**). Or imagine a study that sampled only men when the population of interest contains both men and women.

Of course, the population of interest is what the researcher says it is, so if the population is only Democrats, it is appropriate to use only people who are registered Democrats

FIGURE 7.1
Biased, or unrepresentative, samples.

If the population of interest includes members of all political parties, a sample from a single party's political convention would not provide a representative sample.

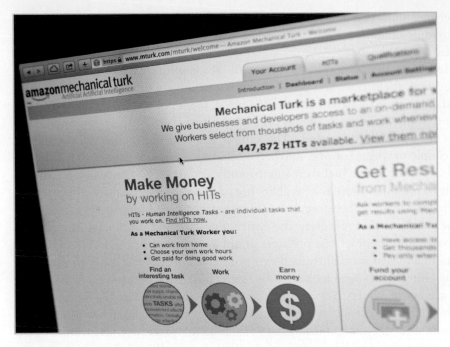

FIGURE 7.2

Online studies normally use convenience samples.

People who participate in online research for payment, such as at the MTurk website, are considered a convenience sample. How do they differ from college student samples, or from representative samples of people from the same country? (Source: MTurk.com.)

in the sample. Even then, the researcher would want to be sure the Democrats in the sample are representative of the population of Democrats.

WAYS TO GET A BIASED SAMPLE

A sample could be biased in at least two ways: Researchers might study only those they can contact conveniently, or only those who volunteer to respond. These two biases can threaten the external validity of a study because people who are convenient or more willing might have different opinions from those who are less handy and less willing.

Sampling Only Those Who Are Easy to Contact. Many studies incorporate **convenience sampling**, using a sample of people who are easy to contact and readily available to participate. Psychology studies are often conducted by psychology professors, and they find it handy to use college students as participants. The Mehl study on how much people talk is an example (see Chapter 6). However, those easy-to-reach college students may not be representative of other populations that are less educated, older, or younger (e.g., Connor, Snibbe & Markus, 2005).

Another form of convenience sampling is used in online studies. In the last 10 years, psychologists have been conducting research through websites such as Amazon's Mechanical Turk and Prolific Academic (**Figure 7.2**). People who want to earn money for participating in research can do so online. Even though these samples are convenient, those who complete studies on websites sometimes show personality traits and political beliefs that differ slightly from other adult samples (Clifford, Jewell, & Waggoner, 2015; Goodman, Cyrder, & Cheema, 2013).

Here's another example. Imagine you are conducting an exit poll during a presidential election, and you've hired interviewers to ask people who they voted for as they're leaving the polling place. (Exit polls are widely used in the United States to help the media predict the results of an election before the votes are completely counted.) The sample for your exit poll might be biased in a couple of ways. For one, maybe you had only enough money to send pollsters to polling places that were nearby and easy to reach. The resulting sample might be biased because the neighboring precincts might be different from the district as a whole. Therefore, it would be better to send interviewers to a sample of precincts that represent the entire population of precincts. In addition, at a particular precinct, the pollsters might approach the population of exiting voters in a biased way. Untrained exit poll workers may feel most comfortable approaching voters who look friendly, look similar to themselves, or look as if they are not in a hurry. For instance, younger poll workers might find it easiest to approach younger voters. Yet because younger voters tend to be more liberal, that sample's result might lead you to conclude the voters at that location voted for a Democratic candidate more often than they really did. In this case, sampling only the people who are convenient would lead to a biased sample. Effective pollsters train their staff to interview exiting voters according to a strict (usually randomized) schedule.

Researchers might also end up with a convenience sample if they are *unable* to contact an important subset of people. They might not be able to study those who live far away, who don't show up to a study appointment, or who don't answer the phone. Such circumstances may result in a biased sample when the people the researchers *can* contact are different from the population to which they want to generalize.

Many years ago, for instance, people conducting surveys in the U.S. selected their samples from landline telephone numbers. At the time, this approach made sense because almost all Americans had telephones in their homes. Yet the number of people who use only cell phones increases every year. If wireless-only people are different from people who have landlines, then a survey or poll that excluded wireless numbers could have inaccurate results.

The U.S. government's Centers for Disease Control and Prevention conducts monthly surveys of people's health behavior. They use the data to estimate important health indicators, such as psychological distress, vaccination rates, smoking, and alcohol use. They have found that wireless-only citizens (at last estimate, 48.3% of households) differ from those with both types of phones (41.2%), landline-only (7.2%), or no phones (3.1%) (Blumberg & Luke, 2015). People in wireless-only households tend to be younger, renting rather than owning their homes, and living in poverty.

TABLE 7.2

Health Behaviors of Samples with Different Phone Ownership

It's important to include cell phone numbers in survey and poll samples.

HEALTH INDICATOR (DECEMBER 2015)	LANDLINE-ONLY OR LANDLINE + WIRELESS HOUSEHOLD (48.4%)	WIRELESS-ONLY HOUSEHOLD (48.3%)	NO PHONE AT ALL HOUSEHOLD (3.1%)
Current smoker	11.5	18.8	20.8
At least one heavy drinking day in the past year	17.2	29.6	24.0
Received influenza vaccine in the past year	49.8	33.9	38.1

Note: N = 15,988
Source: U.S. Department of Health and Human Services, 2016. Data collected from July 2015 to December 2015.

As **Table 7.2** shows, some of their health behaviors also differ. If the CDC estimated the American population's smoking behavior simply from calling landline phones, their estimates would be incorrect; they would be biased toward underestimating. Fortunately, the CDC calls both wireless and landline numbers for its monthly survey.

Sampling Only Those Who Volunteer. Another way a sample might be biased is through **self-selection**, a term used when a sample is known to contain only people who volunteer to participate. Self-selection is ubiquitous in online polls, and it can cause serious problems for external validity.

When Internet users choose to rate something—a product on Amazon.com, an online quiz on BuzzFeed.com, a professor on RateMyProfessors.com—they are self-selecting when doing so (**Figure 7.3**). This could lead to biased estimates because the people who rate the items are not necessarily representative of the population of all people who have bought the product, visited the website, or taken the class. Researchers do not always know how online "raters" differ from "nonraters," but they speculate that the people who take the time to rate things might have stronger opinions or might be more willing to share ideas with others.

Not all Internet-based surveys are subject to self-selection bias. An example is the road rage survey conducted by the American Automobile Association (**Figure 7.4**). A panel of people were randomly selected by a market research firm to complete weekly surveys online. Members of the panel could not self-select; they were invited only if their home address had been randomly selected. In addition, the small portion of participants who did not have Internet access were provided with a laptop and Internet service so they could be represented in the sample.

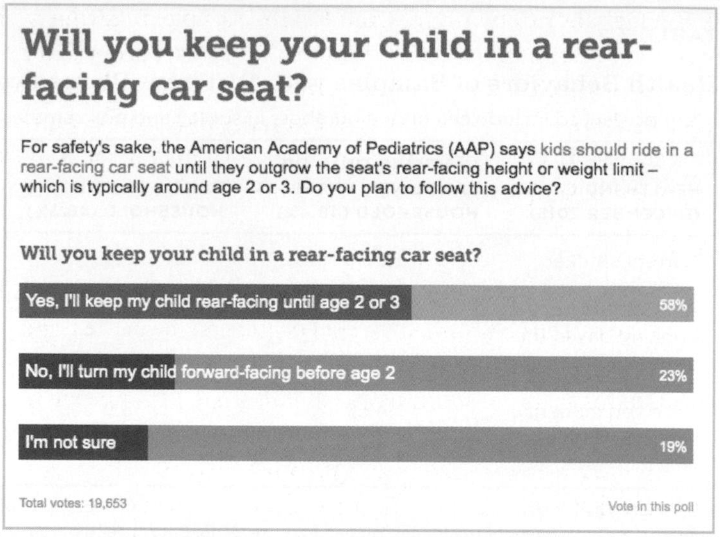

Will you keep your child in a rear-facing car seat?
For safety's sake, the American Academy of Pediatrics (AAP) says kids should ride in a rear-facing car seat until they outgrow the seat's rear-facing height or weight limit – which is typically around age 2 or 3. Do you plan to follow this advice?
Will you keep your child in a rear-facing car seat?
Yes, I'll keep my child rear-facing until age 2 or 3
58%
No, I'll turn my child forward-facing before age 2
23%
I'm not sure
19%
Total votes: 19,653
Vote in this poll

FIGURE 7.3
Some Internet polls are based on self-selected samples.
This online poll invited readers to vote on their plans for child car seats. Why can't we generalize from this sample of 17,153 to the population of parents of small children? (Source: babycenter.com)

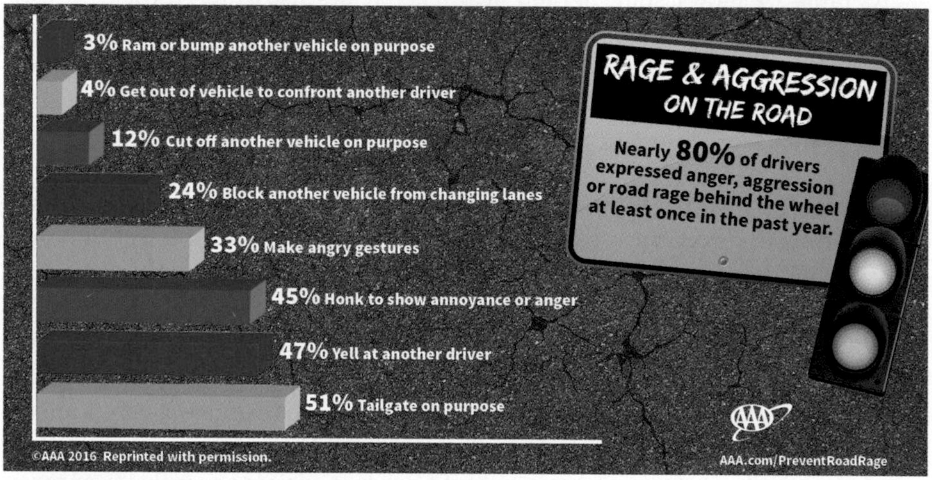

3% Ram or bump another vehicle on purpose
4% Get out of vehicle to confront another driver
12% Cut off another vehicle on purpose
24% Block another vehicle from changing lanes
33% Make angry gestures
45% Honk to show annoyance or anger
47% Yell at another driver
51% Tailgate on purpose
RAGE & AGGRESSION
ON THE ROAD
Nearly 80% of drivers expressed anger, aggression or road rage behind the wheel at least once in the past year.
©AAA 2016 Reprinted with permission.
AAA.com/PreventRoadRage

FIGURE 7.4
Some Internet polls are based on random samples.
The data in this figure came from an online survey on road rage. Respondents had been randomly sampled and invited to respond, so we can probably generalize from this poll to the population of American drivers. Respondents could endorse multiple behaviors on the list. (Source: AAA.com.)

Obtaining a Representative Sample: Probability Sampling Techniques

Samples that are convenient or self-selected are not likely to represent the population of interest. In contrast, when external validity is vital and researchers need an unbiased, representative sample from a population, probability sampling is the best option. There are several techniques for probability sampling, but they all involve an element of random selection. In **probability sampling**, also called *random sampling*, every member of the population of interest has an equal and known chance of being selected for the sample, regardless of whether they are convenient or motivated to volunteer. Therefore, probability samples have excellent external validity. They can generalize to the population of interest because all members of the population are equally likely to be represented. In contrast, **nonprobability sampling** techniques involve nonrandom sampling and result in a biased sample.

SIMPLE RANDOM SAMPLING

The most basic form of probability sampling is **simple random sampling**. To visualize this process, imagine that each member of the population of interest has his or her name written on a plastic ball. The balls are rolled around in a bowl, then a mechanism spits out a number of balls equal to the size of the desired sample. The people whose names are on the selected balls will make up the sample.

Another way to create a simple random sample is to assign a number to each individual in a population, and then select certain ones using a table of random numbers. Professional researchers use software to generate random numbers (**Figure 7.5**). When pollsters need a random sample, they program computers to randomly select telephone numbers from a database of eligible cell phones and landlines.

« For a sample table of random numbers, see Appendix A, pp. 547–550.

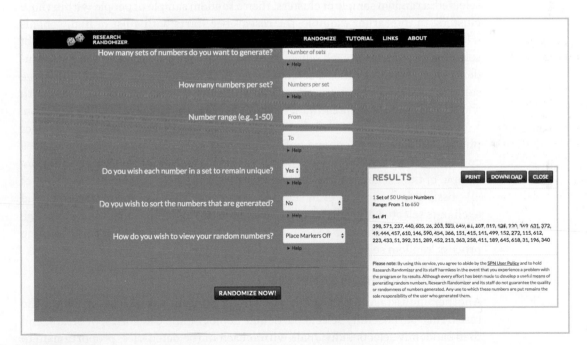

FIGURE 7.5
Computerized randomizers.
This website generates lists of random numbers. In this example, the user requested a list of 50 random members of a population of 650. Each individual in the original population must first be assigned a number from 1 to 650. The randomizer tool determines which of the 50 individuals should be in the random sample. (Source: randomizer.org.)

Although simple random sampling works well in theory, it can be surprisingly difficult and time consuming. It can be nearly impossible to find and enumerate every member of the population of interest, so researchers usually use variants of the basic technique. The variants below are just as externally valid as simple random sampling because they all contain an element of random selection.

CLUSTER SAMPLING AND MULTISTAGE SAMPLING

Cluster sampling is an option when people are already divided into arbitrary groups. Clusters of participants within a population of interest are randomly selected, and then all individuals in each selected cluster are used. If a researcher wanted to randomly sample high school students in the state of Pennsylvania, for example, he could start with a list of the 952 public high schools (clusters) in that state, randomly select 100 of those high schools (clusters), and then include every student from each of those 100 schools in the sample. The Bowker hockey games study (2009) used a version of cluster sampling (see Chapter 6). The researchers selected 69 games at random out of 630 possible hockey games in Ottawa, Canada, that they could have attended during the season. They then sampled every single comment at each game. Each game was a cluster, and every comment at the game was sampled.

In the related technique of **multistage sampling**, two random samples are selected: a random sample of clusters, then a random sample of people within those clusters. In the earlier example, the researcher starts with a list of high schools (clusters) in the state and selects a random 100 of those schools. Then, instead of selecting all students at each school, the researcher selects a random sample of students from each of the 100 selected schools. Both cluster sampling and multistage sampling are easier than sampling from all Pennsylvania high schools, and both should still produce a representative sample because they involve random selection.

Professional pollsters might use three-stage multistage sampling to select phone numbers for telephone polls. They first select a random sample of area codes out of all possible area codes in the country. Next, they select a random sample of the exchanges (the middle three digits of a U.S. phone number) out of all possible exchanges in each selected area code. Then, for each area code and exchange selected, they dial the last four digits at random, using a computer. The area codes and exchanges are considered clusters. At each stage of this sampling process, random selection is used.

STRATIFIED RANDOM SAMPLING

Another multistage technique is **stratified random sampling**, in which the researcher purposefully selects particular demographic categories, or strata, and then randomly selects individuals within each of the categories, proportionate to their assumed membership in the population. For example, a group of researchers might want to be sure their sample of 1,000 Canadians includes people of South Asian descent in the same proportion as in the Canadian population (which is 4%). Thus, they might have two categories (strata) in their population: South Asian Canadians and other Canadians. In a sample of 1,000, they would make sure to include at least

40 members of the category of interest (South Asian Canadians). Importantly, however, all 1,000 members of both categories are selected at random.

Stratified random sampling differs from cluster sampling in two ways. First, strata are meaningful categories (such as ethnic or religious groups), whereas clusters are more arbitrary (any random set of hockey games or high schools would do). Second, the final sample sizes of the strata reflect their proportion in the population, whereas clusters are not selected with such proportions in mind.

OVERSAMPLING

A variation of stratified random sampling is called **oversampling**, in which the researcher intentionally overrepresents one or more groups. Perhaps a researcher wants to sample 1,000 people, making sure to include South Asians in the sample. Maybe the researcher's population of interest has a low percentage of South Asians (say, 4%). Because 40 individuals may not be enough to make accurate statistical estimates, the researcher decides that of the 1,000 people she samples, a full 100 will be sampled at random from the Canadian South Asian community. In this example, the ethnicities of the participants are still the categories, but the researcher is oversampling the South Asian population: The South Asian group will constitute 10% of the sample, even though it represents only 4% of the population. A survey that includes an oversample adjusts the final results so members in the oversampled group are weighted to their actual proportion in the population. However, this is still a probability sample because the 100 South Asians in the final sample were sampled randomly from the population of South Asians.

SYSTEMATIC SAMPLING

In **systematic sampling**, using a computer or a random number table, the researcher starts by selecting two random numbers—say, 4 and 7. If the population of interest is a roomful of students, the researcher would start with the fourth person in the room and then count off, choosing every seventh person until the sample was the desired size. Mehl and his colleagues (2007) used the EAR device to sample conversations every 12.5 minutes (see Chapter 6). Although they did not choose this value (12.5 min) at random, the effect is essentially the same as being a random sample of participants' conversations. (Note that although external validity often involves generalizing to populations of *people*, researchers may also generalize to settings—in this case, to a population of conversations.)

« For more on random numbers and how to use them, see Appendix A, pp. 545–546.

COMBINING TECHNIQUES

When reading about studies in the news or in empirical journal articles, you'll probably come across methods of sampling that combine the techniques described here. Researchers might do a combination of multistage sampling and oversampling, for example. As long as clusters or individuals were selected at random, the sample will represent the population of interest. It will have good external validity.

In addition, to control for bias, researchers might supplement random selection with a statistical technique called *weighting*. If they determine that the final sample

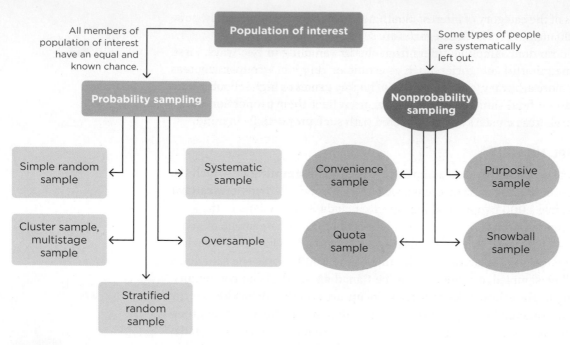

FIGURE 7.6
Probability and nonprobability sampling techniques.
Probability sampling techniques all involve an element of random selection, and result in samples that resemble the population. Nonprobability sampling techniques are biased because they exclude systematic subsets of individuals; they cannot be generalized to the population.

contains fewer members of a subgroup than it should (such as fewer wireless-only respondents or fewer young adults), they adjust the data so responses from members of underrepresented categories count more, and overrepresented members count less.

In sum, there are many acceptable ways to obtain a representative sample. Because all these probability sampling techniques involve a component of randomness, they all ensure that each individual, cluster, or systematic interval has an equal and known chance of being selected. In other words, people are not excluded from the sample for any of the reasons that might lead to bias. **Figure 7.6** provides a visual overview of the probability and nonprobability sampling techniques.

RANDOM SAMPLING AND RANDOM ASSIGNMENT

In conversation you might hear, "I have a random question . . ." for an unexpected comment. But in research, *random* has a more precise meaning: occurring without any order or pattern. Each coin flip in a series is random because you cannot predict (beyond 50% certainty) whether it will come up heads or tails; there's no predictable order.

In the context of research methods, it's important not to confuse random sampling and random assignment. With random sampling (probability sampling), researchers create a sample using some random method, such as drawing names from a hat or using a random-digit phone dialer, so that each member of the population has an equal chance of being in the sample. Random sampling enhances *external validity*.

Random assignment is used only in experimental designs. When researchers want to place participants into two different groups (such as a treatment group and a comparison group), they usually assign them at random. Random assignment enhances *internal validity* by helping ensure that the comparison group and the treatment group have the same kinds of people in them, thereby controlling for alternative explanations. For example, in an experiment testing how exercise affects one's well-being, random assignment would make it likely that the people in the treatment and comparison groups are about equally happy at the start. (For more detail on random assignment, see Chapters 3 and 10.)

Settling for an Unrepresentative Sample: Nonprobability Sampling Techniques

Samples obtained through random selection achieve excellent external validity, but such samples can be difficult to obtain. For example, the Gallup organization really does survey people in 160 countries, either by calling random samples of people in each country or traveling in person to randomly selected remote villages. You can appreciate the expense required to obtain the estimate that "three in four women worldwide rate their lives as 'struggling' or 'suffering.'"

In cases where external validity is *not* vital to a study's goals, researchers might be content with a nonprobability sampling technique. Depending on the type of study, they can choose among a number of techniques for gathering such a sample.

CONVENIENCE SAMPLING

The most common sampling technique in behavioral research, convenience sampling (introduced earlier) uses samples that are chosen merely on the basis of who is easy to reach. Many psychologists study students on their own campuses because they are nearby. The researchers may ask for volunteers in an introductory psychology class or among residents of a dormitory.

PURPOSIVE SAMPLING

If researchers want to study only certain kinds of people, they recruit only those particular participants. When this is done in a nonrandom way, it is called **purposive sampling**. Researchers wishing to study, for example, the effectiveness of a specific intervention to quit smoking would seek only smokers for their sample. Notice that limiting a sample to only one type of participant does not make a sample purposive. If smokers are recruited by phoning community members at random, that sample would not be considered purposive because it is a random sample. However, if researchers recruit the sample of smokers by posting flyers at a local tobacco store, that action makes it a purposive sample, because only smokers will participate, and because the smokers are not randomly selected. Researchers studying a weight management program might study only people in a diabetes clinic. Such a sample would not be, and might not need to be, representative of the population of obese people in some area.

SNOWBALL SAMPLING

One variation on purposive sampling that can help researchers find rare individuals is **snowball sampling**, in which participants are asked to recommend a few acquaintances for the study. For a study on coping behaviors in people who have Crohn's disease, for example, a researcher might start with one or two who have the condition, and then ask them to recruit people from their support groups. Each of them might, in turn, recruit one or two more acquaintances, until the sample is large enough. Snowball sampling is unrepresentative because people are recruited via social networks, which are not random. You might be familiar with this approach from online surveys that urge you to forward the survey link to a few more people. (Many Facebook quizzes work like this, even though they are created for entertainment, not for research.)

QUOTA SAMPLING

Similar to stratified random sampling, in **quota sampling** the researcher identifies subsets of the population of interest and then sets a target number for each category in the sample (e.g., 80 Asian Americans, 80 African Americans, and 80 Latinos). Next, the researcher samples from the population of interest nonrandomly until the quotas are filled. As you can see, both quota sampling and stratified random sampling specify subcategories and attempt to fill targeted percentages or numbers for each subcategory. However, in quota sampling the participants are selected nonrandomly (perhaps through convenience or purposive sampling), and in stratified random sampling they are selected using a random selection technique.

CHECK YOUR UNDERSTANDING

1. What are five techniques for selecting a probability sample of a population of interest? Where does randomness enter into each of these five selection processes?

2. In your own words, define the word *random* in the research methods context. Then describe the difference between random sampling and random assignment.

3. What are four ways of selecting a nonprobability sample? What types of people might be more likely to be selected in each case?

4. Why are convenience, purposive, snowball, and quota sampling *not* examples of representative sampling?

1. See pp. 186–191. 2. See pp. 190–191. 3. See pp. 191–192. 4. Because none of them involve selecting participants at random.

INTERROGATING EXTERNAL VALIDITY: WHAT MATTERS MOST?

A sample is either externally valid for a population of interest, or it has unknown external validity. **Table 7.3** organizes synonymous terms from this chapter under the two descriptors.

Although external validity is crucial for many frequency claims, it might not always matter. When researchers study association claims or causal claims, they are often comfortable with unknown external validity.

In a Frequency Claim, External Validity Is a Priority

Frequency claims, as you know, are claims about how often something happens in a population. When you read headlines like these—"8 out of 10 Drivers Say They Experience Road Rage" and "Three in Four Women Worldwide Rate Their Lives as 'Struggling' or 'Suffering' "—it might be obvious to you that external validity is important. If the driving study used sampling techniques that contained mostly urban residents, the road rage estimate might be too high because urban driving may be more stressful. If the Gallup poll included too few women from impoverished countries, the three-in-four estimate might be too low. In such claims, external validity, which relies on probability sampling techniques, is crucial.

In certain cases, the external validity of surveys based on random samples can actually be confirmed. In political races, the accuracy of pre-election opinion polling can be compared with the final voting results. In most cases, however, researchers are not able to check the accuracy of their samples' estimates because they hardly ever complete a full census of a population on the variable of interest. For example, we could never evaluate the well-being of all the women in the world to find out the true percentage of those who are struggling or suffering. Similarly, a researcher can't find all the owners of a particular style of shoe to ask them whether their shoes "fit true to size." Because you usually cannot directly check

TABLE 7.3

Synonymous Sampling Terms Used in This Chapter

EXTERNALLY VALID	UNKNOWN EXTERNAL VALIDITY
Unbiased sample	Biased sample
Probability sample	Nonprobability sample
Random sample	Nonrandom sample
Representative sample	Unrepresentative sample

accuracy when interrogating a frequency claim, the best you can do is examine the method the researchers used. As long as it was a probability sampling technique, you can be more confident in the external validity of the result.

When External Validity Is a Lower Priority

Even though you need a probability sample to support a frequency claim, many associations and causes can still be accurately detected even in a non-probability sample. Researchers might not have the funds to obtain random samples for their studies, and their priorities lie elsewhere. For example, as you will learn, random assignment is prioritized over random sampling when conducting an experiment.

»
For more on when external validity may not be a priority, see Chapter 8, pp. 226–227; Chapter 10, pp. 301–303; and Chapter 14.

What about a frequency claim that is *not* based on a probability sample? It might matter a lot, or it might not. You will need to carefully consider whether the reason for the sample's bias is relevant to the claim.

NONPROBABILITY SAMPLES IN THE REAL WORLD

Consider whether self-selection affects the results of an online shopping rating, as in the Zappos.com headline, "61% said this shoe felt true to size." You can be pretty sure the people who rated the fit of these shoes are self-selected and therefore don't represent all the people who own that model. The raters obviously have Internet access, whereas some of the shoe owners might not; the raters probably do more online shopping, whereas some of the shoe owners used bricks-and-mortar stores. More importantly, the raters cared enough to rate the shoes online; while many of them probably responded because they either loved or hated the shoes, those who are in-between might not be motivated enough to bother rating their new shoes online.

Another reason people respond might be that they are conscientious. They like to keep others informed, so they tend to rate everything they buy. In this case, the shopping rating sample is self-selected to include people who are more helpful than average.

The question is: Do the opinions of these nonrandom shoppers apply to other shoppers, and to how the shoes will fit *you*? Are the feet of opinionated or conscientious raters likely to be very different from those of the general population? Probably not, so their opinions about the fit of the shoes might generalize. The raters' fashion sense might even be the same as yours. (After all, they were attracted to the same image online.) If you believe the characteristics of this self-selected sample are roughly the same as others who bought them, their ratings might be valid for you after all.

Here's another example. Let's say a driver uses the Waze navigation app to report heavy traffic on a specific highway (**Figure 7.7**). This driver is not a randomly selected sample of drivers on that stretch of road; in fact, she is more conscientious and thus more likely to report problems. However, these traits are not that relevant. Traffic is the same for everybody, conscientious or not, so even though this driver is a nonrandom sample, her traffic report can probably generalize to the

FIGURE 7.7
Nonprobability samples might not matter.
A driver who reports traffic is probably not representative of all the drivers on that stretch of road. Nevertheless, the report from this nonrandom sample might be accurate.

other drivers on that road. The feature that has biased the sample (being conscientious) is not relevant to the variable being measured (being in traffic).

In short, when you know a sample is not representative, you should think carefully about how much it matters. Are the characteristics that make the sample biased actually relevant to what you are measuring? In certain cases, it's reasonable to trust the reports of unrepresentative samples.

NONPROBABILITY SAMPLES IN RESEARCH STUDIES

Let's use this reasoning to work through a couple of other examples. Recall from Chapter 6 the 30 dual-earner families who allowed the researchers to videotape their evening activities (Campos et al., 2013). Only certain kinds of families will let researchers walk around the house and record everyone's behavior. Does this affect the conclusions of the study? It seems possible that a family that volunteers for such intrusion has a warmer emotional tone than the full population of dual-earning families. Without more data on families who do not readily agree to be videotaped, we cannot know for sure. The researchers may have to live with some uncertainty about the generalizability of their data.

Now we'll return to the Mehl study in Chapter 6 on how many words people speak in a day (Mehl, Vazire, Ramirez-Esparza, Slatcher, & Pennebaker, 2007). The sample of participants was not drawn randomly from a population of college students; instead, it was a convenience sample who participated because they were trying to earn class credit or a few extra dollars. Could the qualities that make these students volunteer for the study also be qualities that affect how many words they would say? Probably not, but it is possible. Again, we live with some uncertainty about whether the Mehl findings would generalize—not only to other college students, but to other populations outside the college setting as well. We know that Mehl found the same results among college students in Mexico, but we don't know whether those results apply to samples of middle-aged or older adults. However, just because we don't know whether the finding generalizes to other populations doesn't mean Mehl's results from college students are wrong or even uninteresting. Indeed, future research by Mehl and his colleagues could investigate this question in new populations.

Larger Samples Are Not More Representative

In research, is a bigger sample always a better sample? The answer may surprise you: not necessarily. The idea that larger samples are more externally valid than smaller samples is perhaps one of the hardest misconceptions to dispel in a research methods course.

When a phenomenon is rare, we do need a large sample in order to locate enough instances of that phenomenon for valid statistical analysis. For example, in a study of religion in American life, the Pew Research Center phoned a random sample of 35,071 adults. The large size enabled them to obtain and analyze sufficiently large samples of small religious groups, such as Jehovah's Witnesses, who comprise less than 1% of Americans (Pew Research Center, 2015). But for most variables, when researchers are striving to generalize from a sample to a population, the size of a sample is in fact much less important than how that sample was selected. When it comes to the external validity of the sample, it's *how*, not *how many*.

Suppose you want to try to predict the outcome of the U.S. presidential election by polling 4,000 people at the Republican National Convention. You would have a grand old sample, but it would not tell you anything about the opinions of the entire country's voting population because everyone you sampled would be a member of one political party. Similarly, many Internet polls are so popular that thousands of people choose to vote in them. Even so, 100,000 self-selected people are not likely to be representative of the population. Look back at the BabyCenter poll about car seats (see Figure 7.3). More than 17,000 people chose to vote, yet we have no idea to whom the results generalize.

When researchers conduct public opinion polls, it turns out that 1,000–2,000 randomly selected people are all they usually need—even for populations as large as the U.S. population of 319 million. For reasons of statistical accuracy, many polls shoot for, at most, a sample of 2,000. A researcher chooses a sample size for the poll in order to optimize the margin of error of the estimate. As introduced in Chapter 3, the margin of error of the estimate (or just margin of error) is a statistic that quantifies the degree of sampling error in a study's results. For instance, you might read that 46% of Canadians in some poll support the Liberal Party, plus or minus 3%. In this example, the margin of error ("plus or minus 3%") means that if the researchers conducted the same poll many times and computed margins of error, 95% of the ranges would include the true value of support. In other words, it would mean that the range, 43% to 49%, probably contains the true percentage of Canadians who support the Liberal Party.

Table 7.4 shows the margin of error for samples of different sizes. You can see in the table that the larger the sample size, the smaller the margin of error—that is, the more accurately the sample's results reflect the views of the population. However, after a random sample size of 1,000, it takes many more people to gain just a little more accuracy in the margin of error. That's why many researchers consider 1,000 to be an optimal balance between statistical accuracy and polling effort. A sample of 1,000 people, *as long as it is random*, allows them to generalize to the population (even a population of 319 million) quite accurately. In effect, sample size is not an external validity issue; it is a statistical validity issue.

TABLE 7.4

Margins of Error Associated with Different Random Sample Sizes

IF THE PERCENTAGE IS ESTIMATED ON A RANDOM SAMPLE OF SIZE	MARGIN OF ERROR ON THE PERCENTAGE IS
2,000	Plus or minus 2%
1,500	Plus or minus 3%
1,000	Plus or minus 3%
500	Plus or minus 4%
200	Plus or minus 7%
100	Plus or minus 10%
50	Plus or minus 10%

Note: Margin of error varies as a function of sample size and the percentage result of the poll. In this table, estimates were based on a 50% polling result (e.g., if 50% of people supported a candidate).

CHECK YOUR UNDERSTANDING

1. When might researchers decide to use a nonprobability sample, even though a probability sample would ensure external validity?

2. For what type of claim will it be most important for a researcher to use a representative sample?

3. Which of these samples is more likely to be representative of a population of 100,000?
   a. A snowball sample of 50,000 people
   b. A cluster sample of 500 people

4. Explain why a larger sample is not necessarily more externally valid than a smaller one.

1. See pp. 194–196. 2. A frequency claim; see p. 193. 3. b. 4. See pp. 196–197.

CHAPTER REVIEW

Summary

When a claim makes a statement about a population of interest, you can ask how well the sample that was studied (such as a sample of online shoppers) represents the population in the claim (all online shoppers).

Generalizability: Does the Sample Represent the Population?

- The quality of a frequency claim usually depends on the ability to generalize from the sample to the population of interest. Researchers use samples to estimate the characteristics of a population.

- When a sample is externally valid, we can also say it is unbiased, generalizable or representative.

- When generalization is the goal, random sampling techniques—rather than sample size—are vital because they lead to unbiased estimates of a population.

- Nonrandom and self-selected samples do not represent the population. Such biased samples may be obtained when researchers sample only those who are easy to reach or only those who are more willing to participate.

- Probability sampling techniques can result in a representative sample; they include simple random sampling, cluster sampling, multistage sampling, stratified random sampling, oversampling, systematic sampling, and combinations of these. All of them select people or clusters at random, so all members

of the population of interest are equally likely to be included in the sample.

- Nonprobability sampling techniques include convenience sampling, purposive sampling, snowball sampling, and quota sampling. Such sampling methods do not allow generalizing from the sample to a population.

Interrogating External Validity: What Matters Most?

- When researchers intend to generalize from the sample to the population, probability sampling (random sampling) is essential.

- Random samples are crucial when researchers are estimating the frequency of a particular opinion, condition, or behavior in a population. Nonprobability (nonrandom) samples can occasionally be appropriate when the cause of the bias is not relevant to the survey topic. Representative samples may be of lower priority for association and causal claims.

- For external validity, the size of a sample is not as important as whether the sample was selected randomly.

Key Terms

To see samples of chapter concepts in the popular media, visit www.everydayresearchmethods.com and click the box for Chapter 7.

Review Questions

1. Which of the following four terms is not synonymous with the others?

   a. Generalizable sample

   b. Externally valid sample

   c. Representative sample

   d. Biased sample

2. A researcher's population of interest is New York City dog owners. Which of the following samples is most likely to generalize to this population of interest?

   a. A sample of 25 dog owners visiting dog-friendly New York City parks.

   b. A sample of 25 dog owners who have appointments for their dogs at veterinarians in the New York City area.

   c. A sample of 25 dog owners selected at random from New York City pet registration records.

   d. A sample of 25 dog owners who visit New York City's ASPCA website.

3. Which of the following samples is most likely to generalize to its population of interest?

   a. A convenience sample of 12,000.

   b. A quota sample of 120.

   c. A stratified random sample of 120.

   d. A self-selected sample of 120,000.

4. Externally valid samples are more important for some research questions than for others. For which of the following research questions will it be most important to use an externally valid sampling technique?

   a. Estimating the proportion of U.S. teens who are depressed.

   b. Testing the association between depression and illegal drug use in U.S. teens.

   c. Testing the effectiveness of support groups for teens with depression.

Learning Actively

1. During a recent U.S. election, the news media interviewed a group of women in Florida. Although opinion polls supported the liberal candidate, these conservative women were still optimistic that their own side would win. One woman said, "I don't think those polls are very good—after all, they've never called *me.* Have they called any of you ladies?" Is this woman's critique of polling techniques appropriate? Why or why not?

2. Imagine you're planning to estimate the price of the average book at your college bookstore. The bookstore carries 13,000 titles, but you plan to sample only 200 books. You will select a sample of 200 books, record the price of each book, and use the average of the 200 books in the sample to estimate the average price of the 13,000 titles in the bookstore. Assume the bookstore can give you access to a database that lists all 13,000 titles it carries. Based on this information, answer the following questions:

   a. What is the sample in this study, and what is the population of interest?

   b. How might you collect a simple random sample of books?

   c. How might you collect a stratified random sample? (What would your strata be?)

   d. How might you collect a convenience sample?

   e. How might you collect a systematic random sample?

   f. How might you collect a cluster sample?

   g. How might you collect a quota sample?

PART IV

Tools for Evaluating Association Claims

Meaningful Conversations Linked to Happier People

Scientific American, 2010

Couples Who Meet Online Have Better Marriages

Freakonomics, 2013

8

Bivariate Correlational Research

THE TWO STATEMENTS ON the opposite page are examples of association claims that are supported by correlational studies. Each one is an association claim because it describes a relationship between variables: meaningful conversations and happiness; where people met their spouse and marriage quality.

The verbs used in each case are weaker, association verbs. In the first claim, the verb is *linked*, and the second claim's verb is *have*. Neither statement argues that X *causes* Y, or X *makes Y happen*, or X *increases rates of* Y. (If they did, they would be causal claims, not association claims.)

What about the studies behind these statements? Even without reading the full details of each study, we might guess that the variables were all measured. Researchers can evaluate people's meaningful conversations and their levels of happiness, but they can't easily assign people to have deep conversations or assign people to have certain levels of happiness. Researchers can measure where people met their spouses, but they can't reasonably assign people to meet their spouse either online or in person. They can measure marital satisfaction, but they can't assign people to be satisfied or not. Because it's a plausible assumption that the two variables in each claim were measured (rather than manipulated), we suspect the studies behind the claims are correlational.

LEARNING OBJECTIVES

A year from now, you should still be able to:

1.
Explain that measured variables, not any particular statistic, make a study correlational.

2.
Interrogate the construct validity and statistical validity (and, of lower priority, external validity) of an association claim.

3.
Explain why a correlational study can support an association claim, but not a causal claim.

This chapter describes the kinds of studies that can support association claims, explains what kinds of graphs and statistics are used to describe the associations, and shows how you can systematically interrogate an association claim using the four big validities framework. What kinds of questions should you ask when you encounter an association claim? What should you keep in mind if you plan to conduct a study to test such a claim?

INTRODUCING BIVARIATE CORRELATIONS

An association claim describes the relationship found between two measured variables. A **bivariate correlation**, or *bivariate association*, is an association that involves exactly two variables. Chapter 3 introduced the three types of associations: positive, negative, and zero. To investigate associations, researchers need to measure the first variable and the second variable—in the same group of people. Then they use graphs and simple statistics to describe the type of relationship the variables have with each other.

To investigate the association between meaningful, substantive conversations and happiness, Matthias Mehl and his colleagues (2010) measured people's happiness by combining Pavot and Diener's (1993) subjective well-being (SWB) scale (see Chapter 5) with a measure of overall happiness. Then they measured people's level of "deep talk" by having them wear an electronically activated recorder (EAR) for 4 days. (The EAR, introduced in Chapter 6, is an observational measurement device, an unobtrusive microphone worn by a participant that records 30 seconds of ambient sound every 12.5 minutes.) After people's daily conversations were recorded and transcribed, researchers coded the extent to which the recorded snippets represented "deep talk" or "substantive conversation." Each participant was assigned a value representing the percentage of time spent on substantive conversation. Those with deeper conversations had higher well-being scores.

To test the relationship between meeting one's spouse online and marital satisfaction, researcher John Cacioppo and his colleagues had e-mail surveys sent to thousands of people who participate in uSamp, an online market research project (Cacioppo, Cacioppo, Gozaga, Ogburn, & VanderWeele, 2013). Respondents answered questions about where they met their spouse—online or not. Then, to evaluate marital satisfaction, the researchers used a 4-item measure called the Couples Satisfaction Index (CSI), which asks questions such as "Indicate the degree of happiness, all things considered, of your marriage," with a 7-point rating scale from 1 ("extremely unhappy") to 7 ("perfect"). People who met online scored a little higher on the CSI.

Another correlational study investigated this claim: "People who multitask the most are the worst at it" (introduced in Chapter 3). David Sanbonmatsu and his colleagues tested people on two variables: their frequency of media multitasking and their ability to do it (Sanbonmatsu, Strayer, Medeiros-Ward, & Watson, 2013). To measure frequency, the researchers had participants complete a Media Multitasking Inventory (MMI) indicating how many hours a day they spent using each of 12 kinds of media (such as web surfing, text messaging, music, computer video, TV) and also how often they used each one at the same time as doing another task. To measure multitasking ability, they gave participants the OSPAN (operation span) task. In this difficult task, participants had to alternately read letters on the computer screen and solve basic math problems in their heads. When prompted, they had to report all the letters and give the answers to all the math problems they'd recently seen. In the Sanbonmatsu study, those who reported doing the most media multitasking had the lowest ability on the OSPAN task.

Sample data from these three studies appear in **Tables 8.1**, **8.2**, and **8.3**. Notice that each row shows one person's scores on two measured variables. Even though each study measured more than two variables, an analysis of bivariate correlations looks at only two variables at a time. Therefore, a correlational study might have measured multiple variables, but the authors present the bivariate correlations between different pairs of variables separately.

Review: Describing Associations Between Two Quantitative Variables

After recording the data, the next step in testing an association claim is to describe the relationship between the two measured variables using scatterplots and the correlation coefficient *r*. We could create a scatterplot for the relationship between deep talk and well-being, for example, by placing scores on the well-being scale on the x-axis and percentage

TABLE 8.1

Sample Data from the Mehl Study on Well-Being and Deep Talk

PERSON	SCORE ON WELL-BEING SCALE	PERCENTAGE OF CONVERSATIONS RATED AS DEEP TALK
A	4.5	80
B	3.0	52
C	3.2	35
D	4.1	42
...	...	...
ZZ	2.8	16

Note: Data are fabricated for illustration purposes.
Source: Adapted from Mehl et al., 2010.

TABLE 8.2

Sample Data from the Cacioppo Study on Marital Satisfaction

RESPONDENT	WHERE DID YOU MEET SPOUSE?	MARITAL SATISFACTION RATING
a	Online	6.2
b	Offline	5.5
c	Online	7.0
d	Offline	4.2
...	...	...
yy	Online	7.0

Note: Data are fabricated for illustration purposes.
Source: Adapted from Cacioppo et al., 2013.

TABLE 8.3

Sample Data from the Sanbonmatsu Study on Multitasking Frequency and Ability

STUDENT	MMI SCORE FOR MULTITASKING FREQUENCY	ACCURACY SCORE ON OSPAN TASK FOR MULTITASKING ABILITY
Alek	3.65	27
Jade	4.21	48
Deangie	2.06	62
Max	8.44	25
...		...
Xiaxin	4.56	32

Source: Adapted from Sanbonmatsu et al., 2013.

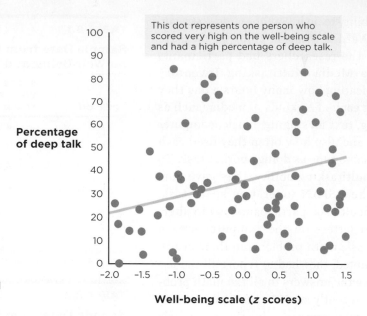

This dot represents one person who scored very high on the well-being scale and had a high percentage of deep talk.

Percentage of deep talk

Well-being scale (*z* scores)

FIGURE 8.1
Scatterplot of the association between deep talk and well-being.

(Source: Adapted from Mehl et al., 2010.)

of conversations that include deep talk on the y-axis, placing a dot on the graph to represent each person (**Figure 8.1**).

In addition to creating the scatterplot, Mehl and his team computed the correlation coefficient for their data and came up with an *r* of .28. As discussed in Chapter 3, a positive *r* means that the relationship is positive: High scores on one variable go with high scores on the other. In other words, high percentages of substantive conversation go with high levels of well-being, and low percentages of substantive conversation go with low levels of well-being. The magnitude of *r* is .28, which indicates a relationship that is moderate in strength.

The reason we consider an association of .28 to be moderate is that psychology researchers typically follow a set of conventions once provided by the psychological statistician Jacob Cohen (1992). Recall that *r* has two qualities: direction and strength. Direction refers to whether the association is positive, negative, or zero; strength refers to how closely related the two variables are—how close *r* is to 1 or −1. Cohen provided benchmarks for labeling association strength, as shown in **Table 8.4**. According to these conventions, the magnitude of the deep talk/well-being association is medium. (These guidelines are discussed in more detail later in the chapter.)

TABLE 8.4

Cohen's Guidelines for Evaluating Strength of Association (Based on *r*)

AN *r* OF APPROXIMATELY	WOULD BE CONSIDERED TO HAVE AN EFFECT SIZE THAT IS
.10 (or −.10)	Small, or weak
.30 (or −.30)	Medium, or moderate
.50 (or −.50)	Large, or strong

Source: Cohen, 1992.

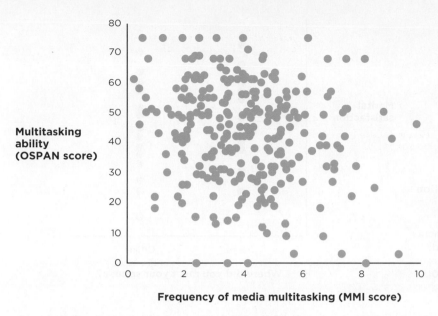

FIGURE 8.2
Scatterplot of the association between the frequency and ability of media multitasking.
Does this cloud of points slope up or down? Is it a strong or a weak relationship? (Source: Adapted from Sanbonmatsu et al., 2013.)

Figure 8.2 shows a scatterplot for the study correlating the frequency and ability of multitasking. When Sanbonmatsu's team computed the correlation coefficient between those two variables, they found an *r* of −.19. The negative *r* means that more frequent media multitasking is associated with lower scores on multitasking ability, and less frequent media multitasking is associated with higher ability. According to Cohen's conventions, the size of the correlation, .19, would be interpreted as small to medium in strength.

Describing Associations with Categorical Data

In the examples we have discussed so far, the nature of the association can be described with scatterplots and the correlation coefficient *r*. For the association between marital satisfaction and online dating, however, the dating variable is *categorical*; its values fall in either one category or another. A person meets his or her spouse either online or offline. The other variable in this association, marital satisfaction, is *quantitative*; 7 means more marital satisfaction than 6, 6 means more than 5, and so on.

« For more on categorical and quantitative variables, see Chapter 5, pp. 122–123.

GRAPHING ASSOCIATIONS WHEN ONE VARIABLE IS CATEGORICAL

When both variables in an association are measured on quantitative scales (as were number of substantive conversations and happiness), a scatterplot is usually the best way to represent the data. But is a scatterplot the best representation of an association in which one of the variables is measured

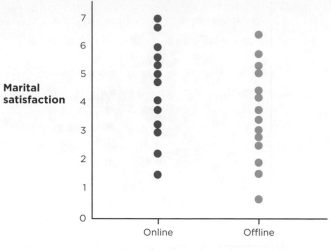

FIGURE 8.3

Scatterplot of meeting location and marital satisfaction.

Do you see an association here between meeting location and marital satisfaction? (Data are fabricated for illustration purposes.) (Source: Adapted from Cacioppo et al., 2013.)

Where did you meet your spouse?

categorically? **Figure 8.3** shows how a scatterplot for the association between meeting location and marital satisfaction might look.

As in all scatterplots, one variable is plotted on the x-axis and the other on the y-axis, and one dot represents one person (in a study with a very large sample, one dot could represent several people who had the same scores). You can even look for an association in this graph: Do the scattered points slope up from right to left, do they slope down, or is the slope flat? If you answered that you see a very slight downward slope, you would be right. You'd conclude there's an association between where people meet their spouse and marital satisfaction, and that those who met online have slightly happier marriages, just as the researchers found when they conducted their study (Cacioppo et al., 2013). If you computed the correlation between these two variables, you would get a very weak correlation: $r = -.06$.

Although you can make a scatterplot of such data, it is far more common for researchers to plot the results of an association with a categorical variable as a bar graph, as in **Figure 8.4**. Each person is not represented by one data point; instead, the graph shows the **mean** marital satisfaction rating (the arithmetic average) for all the people who met their spouses online and the mean marital satisfaction rating for those who met their spouses in person.

When you use a bar graph, you usually examine the *difference* between the group averages to see whether there is an association. In the graph of meeting location and marital satisfaction in Figure 8.4, you can see that the average satisfaction score is slightly higher in the

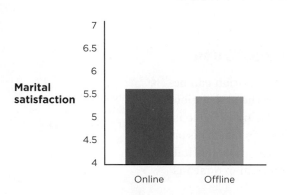

Where did you meet your spouse?

FIGURE 8.4

Bar graph of meeting location and marital satisfaction.

This is the same outcome as in Figure 8.3, graphed differently. Do you see an association here between meeting location and marital satisfaction? (Source: Adapted from Cacioppo et al., 2013.)

online than the offline group. The difference in means indicates an association between where people met their spouse and marital satisfaction. Because the difference is small, the association would be considered weak.

ANALYZING ASSOCIATIONS WHEN ONE VARIABLE IS CATEGORICAL

When at least one of the variables in an association claim is categorical, as in the online dating example, researchers may use different statistics to analyze the data. Although they occasionally use *r*, it is more common to test whether the difference between means (group averages) is statistically significant, usually by using a statistic called the **t test**, or other statistical tests.

≪
For more detail about the *t* test, see Statistics Review: Inferential Statistics, pp. 491–495.

A Study with All Measured Variables Is Correlational

It might seem confusing that association claims can be supported by either scatterplots or bar graphs, using a variety of statistics, such as *r* or *t* tests. It's important to remember that no matter what kind of graph you see, when the method of the study measured both variables, the study is correlational, and therefore it can support an association claim. (In contrast, recall from Chapter 3 that if one of the variables is *manipulated*, it's an experiment, which is more appropriate for testing a causal claim.) An association claim is not supported by a particular kind of statistic or a particular kind of graph; it is supported by a study design—correlational research—in which all the variables are measured (**Figure 8.5**).

Couples who meet online have better marriages.

Correlational study: two measured variables.

Couples who meet online have better marriages.

FIGURE 8.5
Correlational studies support association claims.

When you look for the study behind an association claim, you should find a correlational study.

INTERROGATING ASSOCIATION CLAIMS

With an association claim, the two most important validities to interrogate are construct validity and statistical validity. You might also ask about the external validity of the association. Although internal validity is relevant for causal claims, not association claims, you need to be able to explain why correlational studies do not establish internal validity. We'll now discuss the questions you'll use to interrogate each of the four big validities specifically in the context of association claims.

Construct Validity: How Well Was Each Variable Measured?

An association claim describes the relationship between two measured variables, so it is relevant to ask about the construct validity of *each* variable. How well was each of the two variables measured?

To interrogate the Mehl study, for example, you would ask questions about the researchers' operationalizations of deep talk and well-being. Recall that deep talk in this study was observed via the EAR recordings and coded later by research assistants, while well-being was measured using the SWB scale. Once you know what kind of measure was used for each variable, you can ask questions to assess each one's construct validity: Does the measure have good reliability? Is it measuring what it's intended to measure? What is the evidence for its face validity, its concurrent validity, its discriminant and convergent validity? For example, you could ask whether the 4-item measure of marital satisfaction used in the Caccioppo study had good internal reliability, and whether it had convergent validity. Does it correlate with other measures of marital happiness?

Statistical Validity: How Well Do the Data Support the Conclusion?

When you ask about the statistical validity of an association claim, you are asking about factors that might have affected the scatterplot, correlation coefficient r, bar graph, or difference score that led to your association claim. You need to consider the effect size and statistical significance of the relationship, any outliers that might have affected the overall findings, restriction of range, and whether a seemingly zero association might actually be curvilinear.

STATISTICAL VALIDITY QUESTION 1: WHAT IS THE EFFECT SIZE?

All associations are not equal; some are stronger than others. Recall that the **effect size** describes the strength of a relationship between two or more variables. As an example, **Figure 8.6** depicts two associations: Both are positive, but the one in part B is stronger (its r is closer to 1). In other words, part B depicts a stronger effect size.

Recall the conventions for labeling correlations as small, medium, or large in strength. In the Mehl study, the association between deep talk and well-being was $r = .28$, a relationship of medium strength. In the Sanbonmatsu study, the size of the association between multitasking frequency and ability was $r = -.19$, a relationship of small to medium strength. In the Caccioppo

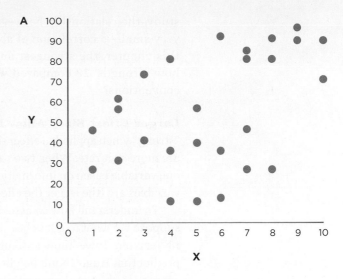

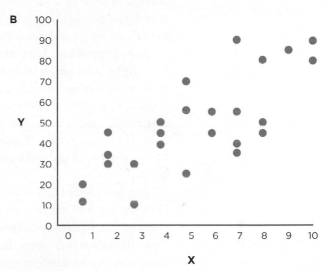

FIGURE 8.6

Two scatterplots depicting different association strengths.

Both of these are positive associations. Which scatterplot shows the stronger relationship, part A or part B?

study, the relationship between meeting location and marital satisfaction was very small—a correlation of about $r = .06$. Therefore, of the three examples in this chapter, the strongest one is the deep talk/well-being relationship. But how strong is .28 compared with −.19 or .06? What is the logic behind these conventions?

Larger Effect Sizes Allow More Accurate Predictions. One meaning of "strong" when applied to effect size is that strong effect sizes enable predictions that are more accurate. When two variables are correlated, we can make predictions of one variable based on information from another. The more strongly correlated two variables are (the larger the effect size), the more accurate our predictions can be.

To understand how an association can help us make more accurate predictions, suppose we want to guess how tall a 2-year-old, we'll call him Hugo, will be as an 18-year-old. If we know absolutely nothing about Hugo, our best bet would be to predict that Hugo's adult height will be exactly average. Hugo might be taller than average or shorter than average, and the mean splits the difference. In the United States, the average height (or 50th percentile) for an 18-year-old man is 175 centimeters, so we should guess that Hugo will be 175 cm tall at age 18.

Now suppose we happen to know that Hugo is a relatively short 2-year-old; his height is 83 cm, within the 25th percentile for that age group. Given this new information, we should lower our prediction of Hugo's adult height accordingly. Why? Because we know there's a strong correlation between 2-year-old height and adult height, and we can use a prediction line generated from this correlation (**Figure 8.7A**). Starting at Hugo's 2-year-old height of 83 cm, we'd read up to the prediction line and predict 172 cm as his 18-year-old height.

Are our predictions of Hugo's adult height likely to be perfect? Of course not. Let's say we find out that Hugo actually grew up to be 170 cm tall at age 18. We guessed 172, so our prediction was off by 2 cm. That's the error of prediction. Our 2 cm difference is an error, but it's a smaller error than the 5 cm error we would have made for him before, using average adult height.

Errors of prediction get larger when associations get weaker. Suppose we want to predict Hugo's adult height but we don't know his 2-year-old height anymore; now all we know is the height of his mother. The correlation between mothers' height and sons' height is positive, but weaker than the correlation between one's 2-year-old height and one's adult height. As shown in **Figure 8.7B**, the scatterplot is more spread out. We can still use the prediction line associated with this correlation, but the fact that the correlation is weaker means our errors of prediction will be larger. If Hugo's mother's height is 163 cm, the prediction line indicates that Hugo's adult height would be 174 cm. Our prediction is now off by 4 cm (recall that Hugo grew up to be 170 cm). Our prediction error was larger than when we used 2-year-old height, in part because the correlation behind our prediction was weaker.

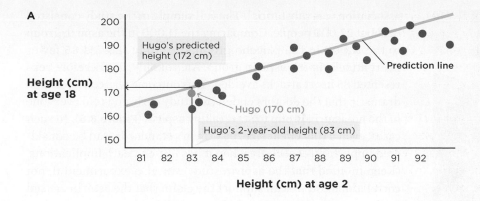

A

Height (cm) at age 18

Hugo's predicted height (172 cm)

Prediction line

Hugo (170 cm)

Hugo's 2-year-old height (83 cm)

Height (cm) at age 2

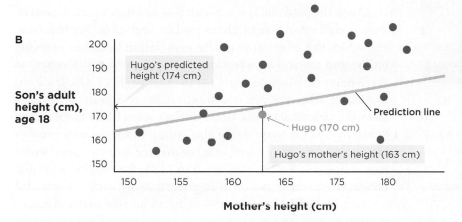

B

Son's adult height (cm), age 18

Hugo's predicted height (174 cm)

Prediction line

Hugo (170 cm)

Hugo's mother's height (163 cm)

Mother's height (cm)

FIGURE 8.7
Stronger correlations mean more accurate predictions.

(A) If we use Hugo's 2-year-old height to predict Hugo's adult height, we would be off by 2 cm. (B) If we use Hugo's mother's height to predict Hugo's adult height, we would be off by 4 cm. Weaker correlations allow predictions, too, but their errors of prediction are larger. (Data are fabricated for illustration purposes.)

In sum, positive and negative associations can allow us to predict one variable from another, and the stronger the effect size, the more accurate, on average, our predictions will be.

Larger Effect Sizes Are Usually More Important. Effect sizes can also indicate the importance of a result. When all else is equal, a larger effect size is often considered more important than a small one. By this criterion, the association between deep talk and happiness is more important than the much weaker one between meeting online and having a happier marriage.

However, there are exceptions to this rule. Depending on the context, even a small effect size can be important. A medical study on heart disease provides one famous example in which a small r was considered extremely important. The study (reported in McCartney & Rosenthal, 2000) found that taking an aspirin a day was associated with a lower rate of heart attacks, though the strength was seemingly tiny: $r = .03$. According to the guidelines in Table 8.4, this is a very weak association, but in terms of the number of lives saved, even this small

FIGURE 8.8
Effect size and importance.

Larger effect sizes are usually more important than smaller ones. In some studies, however, such as those showing that an aspirin a day can reduce heart attack risk, even a very small effect size can be an important result.

association was substantial. The full sample in the study consisted of about 22,000 people. Comparing the 11,000 in the aspirin group to the 11,000 in the placebo group, the study showed 85 fewer heart attacks in the aspirin group. An r of only .03 therefore represented 85 heart attacks avoided. This outcome was considered so dramatic that the doctors ended the study early and told everyone in the no-aspirin group to start taking aspirin (**Figure 8.8**). In such cases, even a tiny effect size, by Cohen's standards, can be considered important, especially when it has life-or-death implications. (Keep in mind that the aspirin study was also experimental, not correlational, so we can support the claim that the aspirin caused the lower rate of heart attacks.)

When the outcome is not as extreme as life or death, however, a very small effect size might indeed be negligible. For instance, at $r = .06$, the effect size of the association between meeting online and marital satisfaction corresponds to a difference on the 7-point satisfaction scale of .16 (5.64 versus 5.48). It's hard to picture what sixteen one-hundredths of a point difference means in practical terms, but it doesn't seem like a large effect. Similarly, the Cacioppo team also collected the divorce rates in the two groups. They found that the divorce rate for couples who met online was 5.87%, compared to 7.73% for couples who met offline, which corresponds to an effect size of $r = .02$. That is also a very small effect size, representing about two extra divorces per 100 people. In your opinion, is it important? What's more, does the effect size correspond to the headlines used by journalists who covered the study in the press?

STATISTICAL VALIDITY QUESTION 2: IS THE CORRELATION STATISTICALLY SIGNIFICANT?

» For more on statistical significance, see Statistics Review: Inferential Statistics, pp. 499–500.

Whenever researchers obtain a correlation coefficient (r), they not only establish the direction and strength (effect size) of the relationship; they also determine whether the correlation is statistically significant. In the present context, **statistical significance** refers to the conclusion a researcher reaches regarding the likelihood of getting a correlation of that size just by chance, assuming there's no correlation in the real world.

The Logic of Statistical Inference. Determining statistical significance is a process of inference. Researchers cannot study everybody in a population of interest, so they investigate one sample at a time, assuming the sample's result mirrors what is happening in the population. If there is a correlation between two variables in a population, we will probably observe the same correlation in the sample, too. And likewise in the case of no association.

Even if, in the full population, there is exactly zero association ($r = .00$) between two variables, a sample's result can easily be a little larger or smaller than zero (such as $r = .03$ or $r = -.08$), just by chance. Therefore, when we find an association in a sample, we can never know for sure whether or not there really is one in the larger population.

Here's an example. A researcher conducts a study on a sample of 310 college students and finds that ability to multitask correlates with frequency of multitasking at $r = -.19$. That correlation might really exist in the whole population of college students. On the other hand, even if there is zero correlation between multitasking ability and frequency in the real world, once in a while a sample may, for reasons of chance alone, find such a correlation as strong as $-.19$.

Statistical significance calculations help researchers evaluate the probability that the result (such as $r = -.19$) came from a population in which the association is really zero. We can estimate the probability that our sample's result is the kind we'd get from a zero-association population, versus a result that is actually quite rare in a zero-association population. The calculations estimate the following: What kinds of r results would we typically get from a zero-correlation population if we (hypothetically) conducted the same study many, many times with samples of the same size? How rarely would we get an r of $-.19$ just by chance, even if there is no association in the population?

What Does a Statistically Significant Result Mean? Statistical significance calculations provide a probability estimate (p, sometimes abbreviated as sig for significance). The p value is the probability that the sample's association came from a population in which the association is zero. If the probability (p) associated with the result is very small—that is, less than 5%—we know that the result is very *unlikely* to have come from a zero-association population (it is rare). The correlation is considered statistically significant. The r of $-.19$ in the Sanbonmatsu study had a low probability of being from a zero-association population ($p < .05$), so we can conclude that their result is statistically significant.

What Does a Nonsignificant Result Mean? By contrast, sometimes we determine that the probability (p) of getting the sample's correlation just by chance would be relatively *high* (i.e., higher than $p = .05$) in a zero-association population. In other words, the result is not that rare. It is considered to be "nonsignificant" (n.s.) or "not statistically significant." This means we cannot rule out the possibility that the result came from a population in which the association is zero.

Effect Size, Sample Size, and Significance. Statistical significance is related to effect size; usually, the stronger a correlation (the larger its effect size), the more likely it will be statistically significant. That's because the stronger an association is, the more rare it would be in a population in which the association is zero. But we can't tell whether a particular correlation is statistically

«
For more detail on effect size, sample size, and statistical significance, see Statistics Review: Inferential Statistics, pp. 487–493 and pp. 499–500.

significant by looking at its effect size alone. We also have to look for the *p* values associated with it.

Statistical significance calculations depend not only on effect size but also on sample size. A very small effect size will be statistically significant if it is identified in a very large sample (1,000 or more). For example, in the Cacioppo study on meeting location and marriage satisfaction, the researchers found a very small effect size ($r = .06$), but it was statistically significant because the sample size was extremely large: more than 20,000. That same small effect size of $r = .06$ would not have been statistically significant if the study used a small sample (say, 30). A small sample is more easily affected by chance events than a large sample is. Therefore, a weak correlation based on a small sample is more likely to be the result of chance variation and is more likely to be judged "not significant."

Reading About Significance in Journal Articles. In an empirical journal article, statistically significant associations are recognizable by their *p* values. Significance information may also be indicated by an asterisk (*), which usually means that an association is significant, or with the word sig, or with a notation such as $p < .05$ or $p < .01$. See, for example, **Figure 8.9**, from the

STRAIGHT FROM THE SOURCE

Correlation (*r*) between happiness and amount of time people were coded as being alone: a moderate, positive correlation. Asterisk directs you to notes below, saying *p* is less than .05, meaning correlation of .27 is statistically significant.

Table 1. Daily Interaction Variables: Reliabilities and Correlations With Well-Being

Interaction variable	Intercoder reliability	Overall correlation with well-being			Correlation with well-being on weekdays	Correlation with well-being on weekends[b]	Correlation with well-being after accounting for personality differences
		Well-being index	Satisfaction with life	Happiness			
Alone[a]	.97	−.35**	−.36**	−.27*	−.29**	−.35**	−.40**
Talking to others[a]	.95	.31**	.31**	.26*	.30**	.30**	.39**
Small talk[a]	.76	−.07	−.03	−.10	−.01	−.09	.08
Small talk as a percentage of all conversations	—[c]	−.33**	−.25*	−.35**	−.30**	−.34**	−.17
Substantive conversations[a]	.84	.31**	.26*	.30**	.27*	.31**	.36**
Substantive conversations as a percentage of all conversations	—[c]	.28**	.20	.31**	.28**	.27*	.22*

Note: *N* = 79. Intercoder reliabilities were computed as intraclass correlations, *ICC*(2, *k*), from a training set of 221 Electronically Activated Recorder (EAR) sound files that were independently coded by all coders. Satisfaction with life was assessed using participants' responses on the Satisfaction With Life Scale (Diener, Emmons, Larsen, & Griffin, 1985); happiness was assessed using self-reports and informant reports on a single item. The happiness and life-satisfaction measures were combined to create the well-being index. Personality was measured using self-reports and informant reports on the Big Five Inventory (John & Srivastava, 1999).
[a]These variables were calculated as the proportion of the total number of sampled sound files in which the indicated activity occurred. [b]The weekend was defined as beginning Friday at 6:00 p.m. and ending Sunday at midnight. [c]No reliability is reported because the variable is a quotient of two coded variables.
*$p \leq .05$ (two-tailed). **$p < .01$ (two-tailed).

FIGURE 8.9
Statistical significance in an empirical journal article.

This table presents a variety of bivariate correlations. It also presents interrater reliability information for the variables that were coded from the EAR. (The last column shows a multiple-regression analysis; see Chapter 9.) (Source: Mehl et al., 2010.)

Mehl et al. (2010) journal article. Some of the correlations have asterisks next to them indicating their statistical significance. In contrast, a popular media article usually will not specify whether a correlation is significant or not. The only way to know for sure is to track down the original study.

STATISTICAL VALIDITY QUESTION 3: COULD OUTLIERS BE AFFECTING THE ASSOCIATION?

An **outlier** is an extreme score—a single case (or a few cases) that stands out from the pack. Depending on where it sits in relation to the rest of the sample, a single outlier can have an effect on the correlation coefficient r. The two scatterplots in **Figure 8.10** show the potential effect of an outlier, a single person who happened to score high on both x and y. Why would a single outlier be a problem? As it turns out, adding that one data point changes the correlation from $r = .26$ to $r = .37$. Depending on where the outlier is, it can make a medium-sized correlation appear stronger, or a strong one appear weaker, than it really is.

Outliers can be problematic because even though they are only one or two data points, they may exert disproportionate influence. Think of an association as a seesaw. If you sit close to the center of the seesaw, you don't have much power to make it move, but if you sit way out on one end, you have a much larger influence on whether it moves. Outliers are like people on the far ends of a seesaw: They can have a large impact on the direction or strength of the correlation.

In a bivariate correlation, outliers are mainly problematic when they involve extreme scores on *both* of the variables. In evaluating the positive correlation between height and weight, for example, a person who is both extremely tall and extremely heavy would make the r appear stronger; a person who is extremely short and extremely heavy would make the r appear weaker. When interrogating an association claim, it is therefore important to ask whether a sample has any outliers. The best way to find them is to look at the scatterplots and see if one or a few data points stand out.

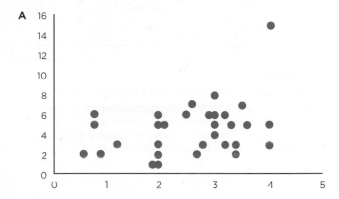

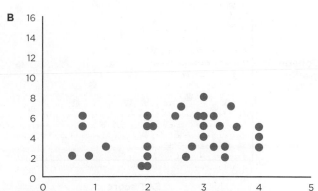

FIGURE 8.10
The effects of an outlier.

These two scatterplots are identical, except for the outlier in the top-right corner of part A. (A) $r = .37$. (B) $r = .26$.

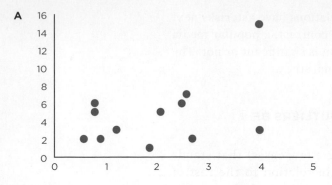

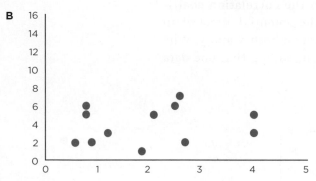

FIGURE 8.11
Outliers matter most when the sample is small.

Again, these two scatterplots are identical except for the outlier. But in this case, removing the outlier changed the correlation from $r = .49$ to $r = .15$; this is a much bigger jump than in Figure 8.10, which has more data points.

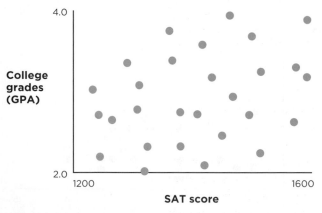

FIGURE 8.12
Correlation between SAT scores and first-year college grades.

College S might observe a scatterplot like this for its enrolled students. (Data are fabricated for illustration purposes.)

Outliers matter the most when a sample is small (**Figure 8.11**). If there are 500 points in a scatterplot (a whole bunch of people sitting in the middle of the seesaw), one outlier is not going to have as much impact. But if there are only 12 points in a scatterplot (only a few people in the middle of the seesaw), an outlier has much more influence on the pattern.

STATISTICAL VALIDITY QUESTION 4: IS THERE RESTRICTION OF RANGE?

In a correlational study, if there is not a full range of scores on one of the variables in the association, it can make the correlation appear smaller than it really is. This situation is known as **restriction of range**.

To understand the problem, imagine a selective college (College S) that admits only students with high SAT scores. To support this admissions practice, the college might claim that SAT scores are associated with academic success. To support their claim with data, they would use the correlation between SAT scores and first-year college grades. (Those grades are an appropriate measure for such a study because for many students, first-year college courses are similar in content and difficulty.)

Suppose College S plots the correlation between its own students' SAT scores and first-year college grades, getting the results shown in **Figure 8.12**. You'll see that the scatterplot shows a wide cloud of points. It has a positive slope, but it does not appear very strong. In fact, in real analyses of similar data, the correlation between SAT and first-year college grades is about $r = .33$ (Camara & Echternacht, 2000). As you have learned, such a correlation is considered moderate in strength. Is this the evidence College S was looking for? Maybe not.

Here's where restriction of range comes in. As you may know, student scores on the SAT currently range from 400 to 1600. But our selective College S admits only students who score 1200 or higher

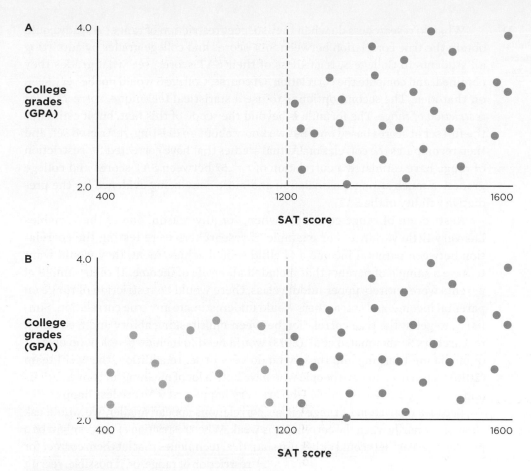

FIGURE 8.13
Restriction of range underestimates the true correlation.
(A) College S admits only those students whose SAT scores are above 1200, so its observed correlation between SAT and GPA is about $r = .33$. (B) If we could include estimates of the scores for students who were not admitted, the correlation between SAT and GPA would be stronger, about $r = .57$. (Data are fabricated for illustration purposes.)

on their SATs, as shown in **Figure 8.13A**. Therefore, the true range of SAT scores is *restricted* in College S; it ranges only from 1200 to 1600 out of a possible 400 to 1600.

If we assume the pattern in Figure 8.12A continues in a linear fashion, we can see what the scatterplot would look like if the range on SAT scores were not restricted, as shown in **Figure 8.13B**. The admitted students' scatterplot points are in exactly the same pattern as they were before, but now we have scatterplot points for the unadmitted students. Compared to the range-restricted correlation in part A, the full sample's correlation in part B appears much stronger. In other words, the restriction of range situation means College S originally *underestimated* the true correlation between SAT scores and grades.

» Restriction of range is similar to ceiling and floor effects; see Chapter 11, pp. 333–334.

What do researchers do when they suspect restriction of range? A study could obtain the true correlation between SAT scores and college grades by admitting all students to College S, regardless of their SAT scores, see what grades they obtained, and compute the correlation. Of course, College S would not be very keen on that idea. The second option is to use a statistical technique, *correction for restriction of range*. The formula is beyond the scope of this text, but it estimates the full set of scores based on what we know about an existing, restricted set, and then recomputes the correlation. Actual studies that have corrected for restriction of range have estimated a correlation of $r = .57$ between SAT scores and college grades—a much stronger association and more convincing evidence for the predictive validity of the SAT.

Restriction of range can apply when, for any reason, one of the variables has very little variance. For example, if researchers were testing the correlation between parental income and child school achievement, they would want to have a sample of parents that included all levels of income. If their sample of parents were entirely upper middle class, there would be restriction of range on parental income, and researchers would underestimate any true correlation. Similarly, to get at the true correlation between multitasking ability and frequency, researchers Sanbonmatsu et al. (2013) would need to include people who do a lot of media multitasking and those who do very little. In addition, the Mehl team (2010) would need to have people who have both a lot of meaningful conversations and very few, as well as people who are very happy and who are less happy.

Because restriction of range makes correlations appear smaller, we would ask about it primarily when the correlation is weak. When restriction of range might be a problem, researchers could either use statistical techniques that let them correct for restriction of range, or, if possible, recruit more people at the ends of the spectrum.

STATISTICAL VALIDITY QUESTION 5: IS THE ASSOCIATION CURVILINEAR?

When a study reports that there is no relationship between two variables, the relationship might truly be zero. In rare cases, however, there might be a **curvilinear association** in which the relationship between two variables is not a straight line; it might be positive up to a point, and then become negative.

A curvilinear association exists, for example, between age and the use of health care services, as shown in **Figure 8.14**. As people get older, their use of the health care system decreases up to

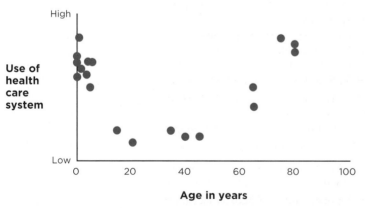

FIGURE 8.14

A curvilinear association.

With increasing age, people's use of the health care system decreases and then increases again. A curvilinear association is not captured adequately by the simple bivariate correlation coefficient r. In these data, $r = .01$, a value that does not describe the relationship. (Data are fabricated for illustration purposes.)

a point. Then, as they approach age 60 and beyond, health care use increases again. However, when we compute a simple bivariate correlation coefficient r on these data, we get only $r = -.01$ because r is designed to describe the slope of the best-fitting *straight line* through the scatterplot. When the slope of the scatterplot goes up and then down (or down and then up), r does not describe the pattern very well. The straight line that fits best through this set of points is flat and horizontal, with a slope of zero. Therefore, if we looked only at the r and not at the scatterplot, we might conclude there is no relationship between age and use of health care. When researchers suspect a curvilinear association, the statistically valid way to analyze it is to compute the correlation between one variable and the square of the other.

Internal Validity: Can We Make a Causal Inference from an Association?

Even though it's not necessary to formally interrogate internal validity for an association claim, we must guard against the powerful temptation to make a causal inference from any association claim we read. We hear that couples who meet online have happier marriages, so we advise our single friends to sign up for Match.com (thinking online dating will *make* their future marriages more happy). In fact, a press release erroneously wrapped the dating study in the causal headline, "Meeting online *leads to* happier, more enduring marriages" (Harms, 2013; emphasis added). Or we hear that deep talk goes with greater well-being, and we vow to have more substantive conversations. A journalist's report on the Mehl et al. (2010) finding included this sentence: "Deep conversations made people happier than small talk, one study found." Oops; the strong verb *made* turned the claim into a causal one (Rabin, 2010). When we read a correlational result, the temptation to make a causal claim can be irresistible.

APPLYING THE THREE CAUSAL CRITERIA

Because the causal temptation is so strong, we have to remind ourselves repeatedly that correlation is not causation. Why is a simple association insufficient to establish causality? As discussed in Chapter 3, to establish causation, a study has to satisfy three criteria:

1. *Covariance of cause and effect.* The results must show a correlation, or association, between the cause variable and the effect variable.
2. *Temporal precedence.* The cause variable must precede the effect variable; it must come first in time.
3. *Internal validity.* There must be no plausible alternative explanations for the relationship between the two variables.

The temporal precedence criterion is sometimes called the **directionality problem** because we don't know which variable came first. The internal validity

1. *Covariance:* Do the results show that the variables are correlated?

2. *Temporal precedence* (directionality problem): Does the method establish which variable came first in time?

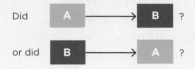

Did A → B ?

or did B → A ?

(If we cannot tell which came first, we cannot infer causation.)

3. *Internal validity* (third-variable problem): Is there a C variable that is associated with both A and B, independently?

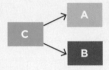

(If there is a plausible third variable, we cannot infer causation.)

FIGURE 8.15
The three criteria for establishing causation.

When variable A is correlated with variable B, does that mean A causes B? To decide, apply the three criteria.

criterion is often called the **third-variable problem**: When we can come up with an alternative explanation for the association between two variables, that alternative is some lurking third variable. **Figure 8.15** provides a shorthand description of these three criteria.

Let's apply these criteria to the deep talk and well-being association, to see whether we can conclude that meaningful conversations *cause* an increase in well-being:

1. *Covariance of cause and effect.* From the study's results, we already know deep talk is associated positively with well-being. As the percentage of deep talk goes up, well-being goes up, thus showing covariance of the proposed cause and the proposed effect.

2. *Temporal precedence.* The study's method meant that deep talk and well-being were measured during the same, short time period, so we cannot be sure whether people used deep talk first, followed by an increase in well-being, or whether people were happy first and later engaged in more meaningful conversations.

3. *Internal validity.* The association between deep talk and well-being could be attributable to some third variable connected to both deep talk and well-being. For instance, a busy, stressful life might lead people to report lower well-being and have less time for substantive talks. Or perhaps in this college sample, having a strong college-preparatory background is associated with both deep conversations and having higher levels of well-being in college (because those students are better prepared). But be careful—not any third variable will do. The third variable, to be plausible, must correlate logically with *both* of the measured variables in the original association. For example, we might propose that income is an alternative explanation, arguing that people with higher incomes will have greater well-being. For income to work as a plausible third variable, though, we would have to explain how higher income is related to more deep talk, too.

As you can see, the bivariate correlation between well-being and deep talk doesn't let us make the causal claim that high levels of substantive conversation cause high levels of well-being. We also cannot make a causal claim in the other direction—that high levels of well-being cause people to engage in more deep conversations. Although the two variables are associated, the study has met only one of the three causal criteria: covariance. Further research using a different kind of study would be needed to establish temporal precedence and internal validity before we would accept this relationship as causal.

What about the press release stating that meeting one's spouse online is associated with a happier marriage? Consider whether this finding justifies the headline, "Meeting online leads to happier, more enduring marriages" (Harms, 2013). Let's see how this study stands up to the three causal criteria:

1. *Covariation of cause and effect.* The study reported an association between meeting online and greater marital satisfaction. As discussed earlier, the association in the original study was very weak, but it was statistically significant.
2. *Temporal precedence.* We can be sure that the meeting location variable came first and marital satisfaction came later. People usually do have to meet somebody (either online or offline) before getting married!
3. *Internal validity.* This criterion is not met by the study. It is possible that certain types of people are more likely to both meet people online and be happier in their marriages. For example, people who are especially motivated to be in a relationship may be more likely to sign up for, and meet their spouses on, online dating sites. And these same relationship-motivated people may be especially prepared to feel happy in their marriages.

In this case, the two variables are associated, so the study has established covariance, and the temporal precedence criterion has also been satisfied. However, the study does not establish internal validity, so we cannot make a causal inference.

MORE ON INTERNAL VALIDITY: WHEN IS THAT POTENTIAL THIRD VARIABLE A PROBLEM?

When we think of a reasonable third variable explanation for an association claim, how do we know if it's an internal validity problem? In the Mehl study (2010) about deep talk and well-being, we thought level of education might be a third variable that explains this association. As mentioned earlier, it could be that better-educated people are both happier *and* have more meaningful conversations, and that's why deep talk is correlated with well-being. Educational level makes a reasonable third variable here because well-educated people might have more substantive conversations, and research also shows that more educated people tend to be happier. But is education really responsible for the relationship the Mehl team found? We have to dig deeper.

What would it look like if education really was the third variable responsible for the correlation between deep talk and well-being? We can use a scatterplot to

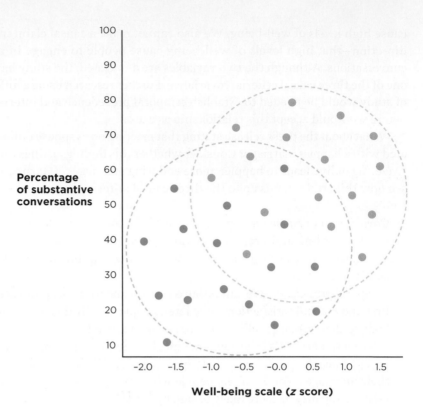

FIGURE 8.16

A third variable, education: an internal validity problem.

More-educated people (green dots) are both higher in happiness and higher in substantive conversations (deep talk), compared to less-educated people (blue dots). Within each educational level, there is no relationship between these two variables. This outcome means level of education is really the reason deep talk and happiness are correlated. (Data are fabricated for illustration purposes.)

(Figure axis labels: Y-axis — Percentage of substantive conversations, from 10 to 100; X-axis — Well-being scale (z score), from -2.0 to 1.5)

illustrate. Looking at **Figure 8.16** overall, we see a moderate, positive relationship between deep talk (substantive conversations) and happiness, just as we know exists. But let's think about separating people who are more and less educated into two subgroups. In the graph, the more-educated people are represented by green dots and the less-educated by blue dots. The more-educated (green dots) are generally higher on both happiness and substantive conversations, and the less-educated (blue dots) are generally lower on both variables.

Furthermore, if we study the scatterplot pattern of just the green dots, we see that *within* the subgroup of well-educated people, there is no positive relationship between deep talk and happiness. The cloud of green dots is spread out and has no positive slope at all. Similarly, if we study the pattern of just the blue dots, the same thing occurs; less-educated people are lower on both happiness and deep talk, and within this subgroup, the cloud of blue dots shows no positive relationship between the two.

The outcome shown in Figure 8.16 means that the only reason deep talk and happiness are correlated is because well-educated people are higher on both of these variables. In other words, education presents a third variable problem. In such situations, the original relationship is referred to as a **spurious association**; the bivariate correlation is there, but only because of some third variable.

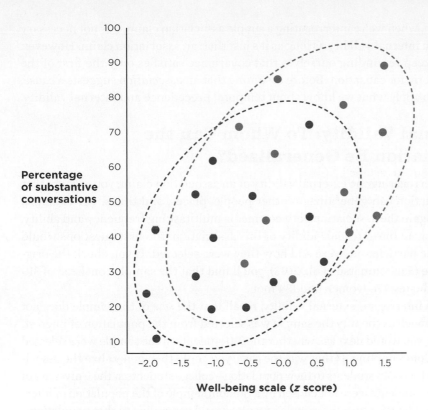

Percentage of substantive conversations

Well-being scale (z score)

FIGURE 8.17

A third variable, leisure time: not an internal validity problem.

People with more leisure time (orange dots) are both higher in happiness and higher in substantive conversations (deep talk), compared to people with less leisure time (dark blue dots). However, within each leisure time group there is still a positive relationship between deep talk and happiness. This outcome means that amount of leisure time does not actually pose an internal validity problem; deep talk and happiness are still correlated even within the two leisure subgroups. (Data are fabricated for illustration purposes.)

Other times, proposed third variables come out differently. Suppose we suspect the relationship between substantive conversations and well-being is attributable to the third variable of leisure time. We might think that people with more leisure time have greater well-being (they're more relaxed) and also have more meaningful conversations (they have more time for thinking). In **Figure 8.17**, the orange dots (more leisure time) are higher on both happiness and substantive conversations and the dark blue dots (less leisure time) are lower on both variables. But this time, when we study just the orange dots, we see that within this subgroup of people, there is still a positive association between deep talk and happiness; the cloud of orange dots still has a positive slope. Similarly, within the dark blue dots alone, there is an overall positive relationship between deep talk and happiness. Therefore, the situation in Figure 8.17 indicates that although we thought amount of leisure time might be a third variable explanation for Mehl's result, a closer look at the data indicates we were wrong: Deep talk and well-being are still correlated within subgroups of people with more and less leisure time.

When we propose a third variable that could explain a bivariate correlation, it's not necessarily going to present an internal validity problem. Instead, it's a reason to dig deeper and ask more questions. We can ask the researchers if their bivariate correlation is still present within potential subgroups.

«

For more on subgroups and third variables, see Chapter 9, pp. 244–247.

In sum, when we're interrogating a simple association claim, it is not necessary to focus on internal validity as long as it's just that: an association claim. However, we must keep reminding ourselves that covariance satisfies only the first of the three criteria for causation. Before assuming that an *association* suggests a *cause*, we have to apply what we know about temporal precedence and internal validity.

External Validity: To Whom Can the Association Be Generalized?

» For more on sampling techniques, see Chapter 7, pp. 183–192.

When interrogating the external validity of an association claim, you ask whether the association can generalize to other people, places, and times. For example, consider again the association between media multitasking frequency and ability. To interrogate the external validity of this association, the first questions would be who the participants were and how they were selected. If you check the original article (Sanbonmatsu et al., 2013), you'll find that the sample consisted of 310 undergraduates: 176 women and 134 men.

As you interrogate external validity, recall that the *size* of the sample does not matter as much as the *way* the sample was selected from the population of interest. Therefore, you would next ask whether the 310 students in the sample were selected using random sampling. If that was the case, you could then generalize the association from these 310 students to their population—college students at the University of Utah. If the students were not chosen by a random sample of the population of interest, you could not be sure the sample's results would generalize to that population.

As it turns out, the Sanbonmatsu team do not say in their article whether the 310 students were a random sample of University of Utah students or not. And of course, because the college students in this sample were from only Utah, we don't know if the study results will generalize to other college students in other areas of the country. Finally, because the sample consisted entirely of college students, the association may not generalize to nonstudents and older people. The external validity of the Sanbonmatsu study is unknown.

HOW IMPORTANT IS EXTERNAL VALIDITY?

What should you conclude when a study does not use a random sample? Is it fair to disregard the entire study? In the case of the Sanbonmatsu study, the construct validity is excellent; the measures of multitasking frequency and ability have been used in other studies and have been shown to be valid and reliable measures of these concepts. In terms of statistical validity, the correlation is statistically significant, and the effect size is moderate. The sample was large enough to avoid the influence of outliers, and there did not seem to be a curvilinear association or restriction of range. The researchers did not make any causal claims that would render internal validity relevant. In most respects, this association claim stands up; it lacks only external validity.

A bivariate correlational study may not have used a random sample, but you should not automatically reject the association for that reason. Instead, you can accept the study's results and leave the question of generalization to the next study, which might test the association between these two variables in some other population.

Furthermore, many associations do generalize—even to samples that are very different from the original one. Imagine a study of college students in the U.S. that found men to be taller than women. Would this finding generalize to people in the Netherlands, who are, overall, taller than Americans? Most likely it would: We'd still find the same *association* between sex and height because Dutch men are taller than Dutch women.

Similarly, you might think the multitasking result would not generalize to older adults, ages 70–80, because you assume they are less likely to multitask with many forms of media, and perhaps they're less capable of multitasking, compared to a younger, college-aged population. You would probably be right about these mean (average) differences between the samples. However, *within* a sample of people in the 70–80 age range, those who *do* tend to multitask the most may still be the ones who are the worst at it. The new sample of people might score lower, on average, on both variables in the association claim, but even so, the association might still hold true within that new sample. In a scatterplot that includes both these samples, the association holds true within each subgroup (**Figure 8.18**).

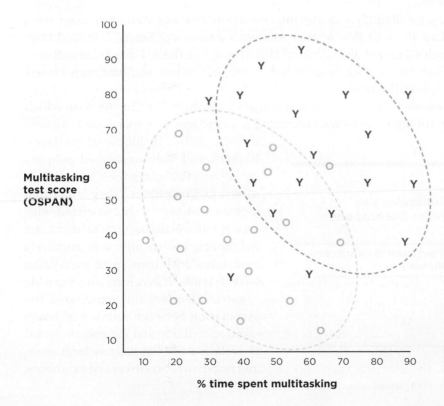

FIGURE 8.18
An association in two different samples.

Older adults (represented by O) might engage in less multitasking than college students (Y), and they might perform worse on multitasking tests, such as OSPAN. But the association between the two variables *within* each sample of people may exist. (Data are fabricated for illustration purposes.)

MODERATING VARIABLES

When the relationship between two variables changes depending on the level of another variable, that other variable is called a **moderator**. Let's consider a study on the correlation between professional sports games attendance and the success of the team. You might expect to see a positive correlation: The more the team wins, the more people will attend the games. However, research by Shige Oishi and his colleagues shows that this association is moderated by the franchise city's level of residential mobility (Oishi et al., 2007). In cities with high residential mobility (such as Phoenix, Arizona), people move in and out of the city frequently. Because they don't develop ties to their community, they theorized, they'd be "fair weather" fans whose interest in the local team depends on whether the team wins. In contrast, in cities with low residential mobility (such as Pittsburgh, Pennsylvania), people live in the city for a long time. They develop strong community ties and are loyal to their sports team even when it loses.

Using data gathered over many major league baseball seasons, Oishi and his team determined that in cities with high residential mobility, there is a positive correlation between success and attendance, indicating a fair-weather fan base. In cities with low residential mobility, there is not a significant correlation between success and attendance. We say that the degree of residential mobility moderates the relationship between success and attendance (**Table 8.5** and **Figure 8.19**).

When we identify a moderator, we are not saying Arizona's team wins more than Pittsburgh's, or that Arizona's games are better attended than Pittsburgh's. Instead, the *relationship* differs: When the Arizona Diamondbacks lose, people are less likely to attend games, but when the Pittsburgh Pirates lose, people still attend.

For another example, consider a study introduced in Chapter 3, in which people with higher incomes were found to spend less time socializing (Bianchi & Vohs, 2016). In follow-up analyses, Bianchi and Vohs separated people's socializing into categories: friends, relatives, and neighbors. They found that income was *negatively* associated with time spent socializing with relatives and neighbors, but income was *positively* associated with time spent socializing with friends. Therefore, the variable "type of relationship" moderated the association between number of hours spent socializing and income, such that the relationship was positive for friends, and negative for relatives and neighbors.

TABLE 8.5

A City's Residential Mobility Moderates the Relationship Between Sports Team Success and Game Attendance

CITY	ASSOCIATION (*r*) BETWEEN TEAM SUCCESS AND GAME ATTENDANCE
Phoenix, AZ (high residential mobility)	.29*
Pittsburgh, PA (low residential mobility)	–.16

Note: **p* < .05; correlation is statistically significant.
Source: Adapted from Oishi et al., 2007.

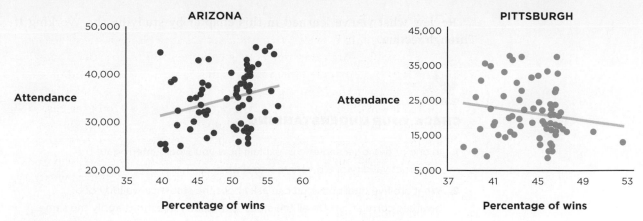

FIGURE 8.19
A moderating variable.

A city's degree of residential mobility moderates the relationship between local sports team success and attendance at games. Each dot represents one major league baseball season. The Arizona Diamondbacks are based in Phoenix, a high residential mobility city; that pattern shows people are more likely to attend games there when the team is having a winning season. Pittsburgh is a low residential mobility city; that pattern shows Pittsburgh Pirates fans attend games regardless of how winning the season is. (Source: Adapted from Oishi et al., 2007.)

Finally, Mehl et al. (2010) looked for moderators in the relationship they found between deep talk and well-being. They wondered if the relationship would differ depending on whether substantive conversations took place on a weekend or a weekday. However, the results suggested that weekend/weekday status did not moderate the relationship between deep talk and well-being: The relationship was positive and of equal strength in both time periods (**Table 8.6**; see also Figure 8.9).

In correlational research, moderators can inform external validity. When an association is moderated by residential mobility, type of relationship, day of the week, or some other variable, we know it does not generalize from one of these situations to the others. For example, in asking whether the association between multitasking frequency and ability would generalize to 70–80-year-olds, you were asking whether that association would be moderated by age. Similarly, the Mehl team found that the association between deep talk and well-being does generalize well from the weekends to weekdays: The strength of the association is almost the same in the two contexts.

« In Chapter 12, you will learn that another way of understanding moderators is to describe them as interactions; see p. 358.

TABLE 8.6

Weekend/Weekday Status Does Not Moderate the Relationship Between Deep Talk and Well-Being

DAY OF WEEK	ASSOCIATION (*r*) BETWEEN PERCENTAGE OF SUBSTANTIVE CONVERSATIONS AND WELL-BEING
Weekday	.28*
Weekend	.27*

Note: Substantive conversations are associated with happiness on both weekdays and weekends. *$p < .05$; result is statistically significant.
Source: Adapted from Mehl et al., 2006.

Review what you've learned in this chapter by studying the Working It Through section.

CHECK YOUR UNDERSTANDING

1. In one or two brief sentences, explain how you would interrogate the construct validity of a bivariate correlation.

2. What are five questions you can ask about the statistical validity of a bivariate correlation? Do all the statistical validity questions apply the same way when bivariate correlations are represented as bar graphs?

3. Which of the three rules of causation is almost always met by a bivariate correlation? Which two rules might not be met by a correlational study?

4. Give examples of some questions you can ask to evaluate the external validity of a correlational study.

5. If we found that gender moderates the relationship between deep talk and well-being, what might that mean?

1. See pp. 210–211. 2. See pp. 211–221; questions about outliers and curvilinear associations may not be relevant for correlations represented as bar graphs. 3. See pp. 221–223. 4. See pp. 226–227. 5. It would mean the relationship between deep talk and well-being is different for men than for women. For example, the relationship might be stronger for women than for men than it is for men.

Are Parents Happier Than People with No Children?

Some researchers have found that people with children are less happy than people who don't have kids. In contrast, a popular media story reports on a study in which parents are, in fact, happier. We will work through this example of a bivariate correlational study to illustrate the concepts from Chapter 8.

QUESTIONS TO ASK	CLAIMS, QUOTES, OR DATA	INTERPRETATION AND EVALUATION
What kind of claim is being made in the journalist's headline?	"Parents are happier than non-parents" (Welsh, 2012).	The simple verb *are* made this an association claim. Parenting goes with being happier.
What are the two variables in the headline?	The journalist reported: "Parents may not be the overtired, overworked and all-around miserable individuals they are sometimes made out to be, suggests new research finding Mom and Dad (particularly fathers) experience greater levels of happiness and meaning from life than nonparents" (Welsh, 2012).	The two variables are "being a parent or not" and "level of happiness."
Association claims can be supported by correlational studies. Why can we assume the study was correlational?		We can assume this is a correlational study because parenting and level of happiness are probably measured variables (it's not really possible to manipulate them). In a correlational study all variables are measured.

The journal article contains three studies on parenting and happiness, and we'll focus on the second study (Nelson, Kushlev, English, Dunn, & Lyubomirsky, 2013)

Are the variables categorical or quantitative?	The Method section described how the researchers distributed pagers to 329 adults, about half of whom were parents. They reported on their happiness (on a 7-point scale) at different times of the day.	One variable is categorical; people were either parents or not.
		The other variable, happiness, was quantitative because people could range from low to high.

(Continued)

QUESTIONS TO ASK	CLAIMS, QUOTES, OR DATA	INTERPRETATION AND EVALUATION
What were the results?	0.3 0.2 0.1 **Happiness** 0 −0.1 −0.2 −0.3 ▪ Parents ▪ Nonparents	Because one variable was categorical and the other was quantitative, the researchers presented the results as a bar graph. Parents had a higher average well-being than nonparents.
Construct Validity How well was each variable measured?	To measure parenting status, the researchers simply asked people if they were parents. To measure happiness, participants wore devices that paged them five times daily. At each page, the participant rated 8 positive emotions (such as pride, joy) and 11 negative emotions (such as anger, guilt). The researchers subtracted the ratings of negative emotions from positive ones at each time point, and averaged across each person's 35 reports for a week.	It seems unlikely that people would lie about their parental status, so we can assume a self-report was a valid measure of parenting. It seems reasonable that people who have positive emotions throughout the day are happier, so this operationalization of happiness has face validity. Notably, happiness was based on an "in-the-moment" response, not a global judgment, so it may be more accurate. However, the researchers don't present any criterion validity or convergent validity evidence for the measure.
Statistical Validity What is the effect size? Is the difference statistically significant?	The researchers reported: "As in Study 1, we first examined the relationship between parenthood and happiness with t tests. Parents reported higher levels of global well-being, including more happiness, $t(325) = 2.68$, $p = .008$, $r = .15$..." (Nelson et al., 2013, p. 7).	The authors report an effect size of $r = .15$, and $p = .008$. Since p is less than .05, we can conclude the difference in happiness between parents and nonparents is statistically significant, and the effect size is small.
Are there outliers? Is the association curvilinear? Could there be restriction of range?		The researchers don't mention outliers, but in a sample this large, outliers are unlikely to have an impact on the overall pattern. Parenting is a two-category variable. Without some middle category we can't have a curvilinear association. We look for restriction of range when the results are smaller than expected. Perhaps because these researchers found a significant effect, they did not test for restriction of range.
Internal Validity Can the study possibly support the claim that parenthood *causes* people to be happy?		We can't support a causal claim. The results show covariance, but temporal precedence is not present because happiness and parenting were measured at the same time. The correlational method could not rule out third variables. For example, parents are more likely to be married, and married people may also be happier.
External Validity To whom can we generalize this association?	The article reports that the sample of 329 adults came from "a study on emotional experience in adulthood" (p. 4).	The authors did not state that the sample was selected at random, so we do not know to whom this association can generalize.

CHAPTER REVIEW

Summary

- Association claims state that two variables are linked, but they do not state that one causes the other.

- Association claims are supported by correlational research, in which both variables are measured in a set of participants. (If either of the variables is manipulated, the study is an experiment, which could potentially support a causal claim.)

Introducing Bivariate Correlations

- The variables in a bivariate correlational study can be either quantitative or categorical. If both variables are quantitative, the data are usually depicted in a scatterplot; if one variable is categorical, the data are usually depicted in a bar graph.

- For a scatterplot, the correlation coefficient r can be used to describe the relationship. For a bar graph, the difference between the two group means is used to describe the relationship.

- Regardless of whether an association is analyzed with scatterplots or bar graphs, if both variables are measured, the study is correlational.

Interrogating Association Claims

- Because a correlational study involves two measured variables, the construct validity of each measure must be interrogated in a bivariate correlation study.

- Interrogating the statistical validity of an association claim involves five areas of inquiry: effect size (strength of r), statistical significance, the presence of outliers, possible restriction of range, and whether the association is curvilinear.

- Internal validity addresses the degree to which a study supports a causal claim. Although it is not necessary to interrogate internal validity for an association claim because it does not make a causal statement, it can be tempting to assume causality from a correlational study.

- Correlational studies do not satisfy all three criteria for a causal claim: They may show covariance but do not usually satisfy temporal precedence, and they cannot establish internal validity.

- Interrogating the external validity of an association claim involves asking whether the sample is representative of some population. If a correlational study does not use a random sample of people or contexts, the results cannot necessarily generalize to the population from which the sample was taken.

- A lack of external validity should not disqualify an entire study. If the study fulfills the other three validities and its results are sound, the question of generalizability can be left for a future investigation.

- A bivariate correlation is sometimes moderated, which means the relationship changes depending on the levels of another variable, such as gender, age, or location.

Key Terms

bivariate correlation, p. 204

mean, p. 208

t test, p. 209

effect size, p. 211

statistical significance, p. 214

outlier, p. 217

restriction of range, p. 218

curvilinear association, p. 220

directionality problem, p. 221

third-variable problem, p. 222

spurious association, p. 224

moderator, p. 228

 To see samples of chapter concepts in the popular media, visit www.everydayresearchmethods.com and click the box for Chapter 8.

Review Questions

1. Suppose you hear that conscientious people are more likely to get regular health checkups. Which of the following correlations between conscientiousness and getting checkups would probably support this claim?

   a. *r* = .03

   b. *r* = .45

   c. *r* = −.35

   d. *r* = −1.0

2. Which of these associations will probably be plotted as a bar graph rather than a scatterplot?

   a. The more conscientious people are, the greater the likelihood they'll get regular health checkups.

   b. Level of depression is linked to the amount of exercise people get.

   c. Students at private colleges get higher GPAs than those at public colleges.

   d. Level of chronic stomach pain in kids is linked to later anxiety as adults.

3. A study found that people who like spicy foods are generally risk takers. Which of the following questions interrogates the construct validity of this correlation?

   a. Is the result statistically significant?

   b. Did the study use a random sample of people?

   c. Were there any outliers in the relationship?

   d. How well did they measure each variable, risk taking and liking spicy foods?

4. Darrin reads a story reporting that students at private colleges get higher GPAs than those at public colleges. He wonders if this means going to a private college causes you to have a higher GPA; if so, he'll go to a private college! Applying the three causal criteria, Darrin knows there is covariance here. He also knows there is temporal precedence because you choose a college first, and then you get your GPA. Which of the following questions would help Darrin ask about the third criterion, internal validity?

   a. Could there be restriction of range?

   b. Is the link between private college and high grades the same for both men and women?

   c. How did they decide what qualifies a college as private or public?

   d. Is there some other reason these two are related? Maybe better students are more likely to go to private colleges, and they are also going to get better grades.

5. Which of the following sentences describes a moderator for the relationship between risk taking and liking spicy foods?

   a. There is a positive relationship between liking spicy foods and risk taking for men, but no relationship for women.

   b. Older adults tend to like spicy foods less than younger adults.

   c. The relationship between liking spicy foods and risk taking is the same for people in cities and in rural areas.

Learning Actively

1. For each of the following examples, sketch a graph of the result (either a bar graph or a scatterplot). Then, interrogate the construct validity, the statistical validity, and the external validity of each association claim. What questions would you ask? What answers would you expect?

   a. "Chronic stomach pain in kids is linked to adult anxiety disorders in later life." In this study, the researchers "followed 332 children between the ages of 8 and 17 who were diagnosed with functional abdominal pain and 147 with no pain for an average of eight years. . . . On follow-up, the researchers interviewed the volunteers—who were on average age 20 at that point—either in person or by phone. . . . Of adults who had abdominal pain as children, 51 percent had experienced an anxiety disorder during their lives, compared to 20 percent of those who didn't experience tummy aches as children" (Carroll, 2013).

   b. "Kids with ADHD may be more likely to bully." In this study, the researchers "followed 577 children—the entire population of fourth graders from a municipality near Stockholm—for a year. The researchers interviewed parents, teachers and children to determine which kids were likely to have ADHD. Children showing signs of the disorder were then seen by a child neurologist for diagnosis. The researchers also asked the kids about bullying. [The study found that] children with attention deficit hyperactivity disorder are almost four times as likely as others to be bullies" (Carroll, 2008).

2. A researcher conducted a study of 34 scientists (Grim, 2008). He reported a correlation between the amount of beer each scientist drank per year and the likelihood of that scientist publishing a scientific paper. The correlation was reported as $r = -.55$, $p < .01$.

   a. What does a negative correlation mean in this example? Is this relationship strong or weak?

   b. What does $p < .01$ mean in this result?

   c. Draw a scatterplot of this association. What might happen to this correlation if you added one person in the sample who drank much more beer than other scientists and also published far fewer papers than other scientists?

   d. A popular media report about this article was headlined, "Suds seem to skew scientific success" (*San Diego Union-Tribune*, 2008). Is such a causal claim justified?

   e. Perhaps scientific discipline is a moderator of this relationship. Create a moderator table, using Table 8.5 as a model, showing that the association between beer drinking and publications is stronger for female scientists (perhaps because alcohol affects women more strongly) than for male scientists.

The Origins of Narcissism:
Children More Likely to
Be Self-Centered If They
Are Praised Too Much

Independent, 2015

Study Links
Teen Pregnancy
to Sex on
TV Shows

Newsmax.com, 2008

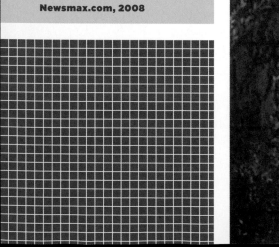

9

Multivariate Correlational Research

CORRELATIONAL STUDIES CAN PROVIDE interesting new information in their own right. The opening headlines provide examples. It might interest us to read that children who are praised too much are also self-centered or narcissistic. We might be surprised to learn that watching sex on TV shows is linked to teen pregnancy. Often, however, a correlational result is an early step in establishing a causal relationship between two variables. Psychological scientists (among many others) want to know about causes and effects, not just correlations, because they may suggest treatments. If praise is linked to narcissism, we might wonder whether or not the praise *makes* kids narcissistic. If it does, parents might change how they express approval. When reading that sexual content on TV is linked to teenage pregnancy, we may wonder whether watching sexual material *causes* behavior that leads to pregnancy. If it does, then pediatricians, teachers, or advocacy groups could argue for restricting teens' exposure to certain kinds of TV shows. However, if the relationships are not causal, such interventions would not work.

Because correlation is not causation, what are the options? Researchers have developed some techniques that enable them to test for cause. The best of these is experimentation: Instead of measuring both variables, researchers manipulate one variable and measure the other. (Experimental designs are covered in Chapters 10–12.) Even without setting up an experiment, however,

LEARNING OBJECTIVES

A year from now, you should still be able to:

1.
State why simple bivariate correlations are not sufficient for establishing causation.

2.
Explain how longitudinal correlational designs can establish temporal precedence.

3.
Explain how multiple-regression analyses help address internal validity (the third-variable problem).

4.
Describe the value of pattern and parsimony, in which a variety of research results support a single, parsimonious causal theory.

5.
Explain the function of a mediating variable.

researchers can use some advanced correlational techniques to get a bit closer to making a causal claim. This chapter outlines three such techniques: longitudinal designs, which allow researchers to establish temporal precedence in their data; multiple-regression analyses, which help researchers rule out certain third-variable explanations; and the "pattern and parsimony" approach, in which the results of a variety of correlational studies all support a single, causal theory. In the three techniques, as in all correlational studies, the variables are measured—that is, none are manipulated.

REVIEWING THE THREE CAUSAL CRITERIA

Unlike the bivariate examples in Chapter 8, which involved only two measured variables, longitudinal designs, multiple-regression designs, and the pattern and parsimony approach are **multivariate designs**, involving more than two measured variables. While these techniques are not perfect solutions to the causality conundrum, they are extremely useful and widely used tools, especially when experiments are impossible to run.

Remember that the three criteria for establishing causation are covariance, temporal precedence, and internal validity. We might apply these criteria to correlational research on the association between parental praise and narcissism.

In the research you'll read about in this chapter, narcissism is studied as a personality trait in which people feel superior to others, believe they deserve special treatment, and respond strongly when others put them down; narcissists are difficult relationship partners. Parental overpraise, the other variable discussed in this example, is telling kids they are exceptional or more special than other children. It's important to note that childhood narcissism is different from high self-esteem (a trait that is considered healthy). Similarly, overpraising is different from parents expressing warmth and love for their children.

Let's examine the three criteria:

1. *Is there covariance?* One study did find covariance (Otway & Vignoles, 2006). Adults who were narcissistic remembered their parents praising them for almost everything they did. The correlation was weak, but statistically significant (r values around .20).
2. *Is there temporal precedence?* A correlational study like Otway and Vignoles' does not establish temporal precedence. Adults reflected on their parents' behavior during childhood, so their current self-views could have colored their recall of the past. It's not clear which variable came first in time.
3. *Is there internal validity?* The association between parental praise and child narcissism might be explained by a third variable. Perhaps parents praise boys more than girls, and boys are also more likely to have narcissistic traits. Or perhaps parents who are themselves narcissistic simply overpraise their children and, independently, tend to be mimicked by their kids.

CHECK YOUR UNDERSTANDING

1. Why can't a simple bivariate correlational study meet all three criteria for establishing causation?

1. See p. 238.

ESTABLISHING TEMPORAL PRECEDENCE WITH LONGITUDINAL DESIGNS

A **longitudinal design** can provide evidence for temporal precedence by measuring the same variables in the same people at several points in time. Longitudinal research is used in developmental psychology to study changes in a trait or an ability as a person grows older. In addition, this type of design can be adapted to test causal claims.

Researchers conducted such a study on a sample of 565 children and their mothers and fathers living in the Netherlands (Brummelman et al., 2015). The parents and children were contacted four times, every 6 months. Each time, the children completed questionnaires in school, responding to items about narcissism (e.g., "Kids like me deserve something extra"). Parents also completed questionnaires about overpraising their children, which was referred to in the study as overvaluation (e.g., "My child is more special than other children").

This study was longitudinal because the researchers measured the *same* variables in the *same* group of people across time—every 6 months. It is also a multivariate correlational study because eight variables were considered: child narcissism at Time 1, 2, 3, and 4, and parental overvaluation at Time 1, 2, 3, and 4.

Interpreting Results from Longitudinal Designs

Because there are more than two variables involved, a multivariate design gives several individual correlations, referred to as cross-sectional correlations, auto-correlations, and cross-lag correlations. The Brummelman researchers conducted their analyses on mothers' and fathers' overvaluation separately, in order to investigate the causal paths for each parent separately. We present the results for mothers here, but the results are similar for fathers.

CROSS-SECTIONAL CORRELATIONS

The first set of correlations are **cross-sectional correlations**; they test to see whether two variables, measured at the same point in time, are correlated. For example, the study reports that the correlation between mothers' overvaluation

FIGURE 9.1
Cross-sectional correlations.

Look at the correlations of the variables when measured at the same time. Within each time period, the mothers' overvaluation is weakly associated with child narcissism. Notice that the arrows point in both directions because in these cross-sectional correlations, the two variables were measured at the same time. The figure shows zero-order (bivariate) correlations. (Source: Adapted from Brummelman et al., 2015.)

at Time 4 and children's narcissism at Time 4 was $r = .099$. This is a weak correlation, but consistent with the hypothesis. However, because both variables in a cross-sectional correlation were measured at the same time, this result alone cannot establish temporal precedence. Either one of these variables might have led to changes in the other. **Figure 9.1** depicts how this study was designed and shows all of the cross-sectional correlations.

AUTOCORRELATIONS

The next step was to evaluate the associations of each variable with itself across time. For example, the Brummelman team asked whether mothers' overvaluation at Time 1 was associated with mothers' overvaluation at Time 2, Time 3, and so on; they also asked whether children's narcissism at Time 1 was associated with their scores at Time 2, Time 3, and so on. Such correlations are sometimes called **autocorrelations** because they determine the correlation of one variable with itself, measured on two different occasions. The results in **Figure 9.2** suggest that both overvaluation and narcissism are fairly consistent over time.

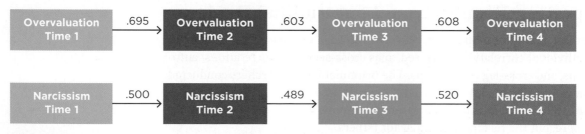

FIGURE 9.2
Autocorrelation.

In a longitudinal study, researchers also investigate the autocorrelations. These results indicate that both variables seem to be relatively stable over time. Notice that the arrows point in only one direction because the Time 1 measurements came before the Time 2 measurements. Overvaluation values are based on mothers' results. (Source: Adapted from Brummelman et al., 2015.)

CROSS-LAG CORRELATIONS

So far so good. However, cross-sectional correlations and autocorrelations are generally not the researchers' primary interest. They are usually most interested in **cross-lag correlations**, which show whether the earlier measure of one variable is associated with the later measure of the other variable. Cross-lag correlations thus address the directionality problem and help establish temporal precedence.

In the Brummelman study, the cross-lag correlations show how strongly mothers' overvaluation at Time 1 is correlated with child narcissism later on, compared to how strongly child narcissism at Time 1 is correlated with mothers' overvaluation later on. By inspecting the cross-lag correlations in a longitudinal design, we can investigate how one variable correlates with another one over time—and therefore establish temporal precedence. In Brummelman's results, only one set of the cross-lag correlations was statistically significant; the other set was not significant (**Figure 9.3**). Mothers who overvalued their children at one time period had children who were higher in narcissism 6 months later. In contrast, children who were higher in narcissism at a particular time period did not have mothers who overvalued them 6 months later. Because the "overvaluation to narcissism" correlations are significant and the "narcissism to overvaluation" correlations are not, this suggests the overvaluation, not the narcissism, came first.

Three Possible Patterns from a Cross-Lag Study. The results of the cross-lag correlations in the Brummelman study could have followed one of three patterns. The study did show that parental overpraise (overvaluation) at earlier time periods was significantly correlated with child narcissism at the later time periods. Such a pattern was consistent with the argument that overpraise leads to increases in narcissism over time. However, the study could have shown the opposite result— that narcissism at earlier time periods was significantly correlated with overpraise later. Such a pattern would have indicated that the childhood narcissistic tendency came first, leading parents to change their type of praise later.

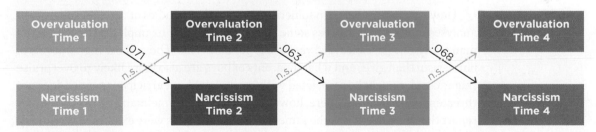

FIGURE 9.3
Results of a cross-lag study.
The cross-lag correlations in this study are consistent with the conclusion that parental overpraise comes before narcissism because overpraise in early time periods significantly predicts later narcissism, but narcissism in earlier time periods was not significantly (n.s.) related to later overpraise. The arrows point in only one direction because in each case the method makes clear which variable came first in time; Time 1 always comes before Time 2, and so on. Values shown are associated with mothers' overpraise. (Source: Adapted from Brummelman et al., 2015.)

Finally, the study could have shown that *both* correlations are significant—that overpraise at Time 1 predicted narcissism at Time 2 *and* that narcissism at Time 1 predicted overpraise at Time 2. If that had been the result, it would mean excessive praise and narcissistic tendencies are mutually reinforcing. In other words, there is a cycle in which overpraise leads to narcissism, which leads parents to overpraise, and so on.

Longitudinal Studies and the Three Criteria for Causation

Longitudinal designs can provide some evidence for a causal relationship by means of the three criteria for causation:

1. *Covariance.* Significant relationships in longitudinal designs help establish covariance. When two variables are significantly correlated (as in the cross-lag correlations in Figure 9.3), there is covariance.
2. *Temporal precedence.* A longitudinal design can help researchers make inferences about temporal precedence. Because each variable is measured in at least two different points in time, they know which one came first. By comparing the relative strength of the two cross-lag correlations, the researchers can see which path is stronger. If only one of them is statistically significant (as in the Brummelman overvaluation and narcissism study), the researchers move a little closer to determining which variable comes first, thereby causing the other.
3. *Internal validity.* When conducted simply—by measuring only the two key variables—longitudinal studies do not help rule out third variables. For example, the Brummelman results presented in Figure 9.3 cannot clearly rule out the possible third variable of socioeconomic status. It's possible that parents in higher income brackets overpraise their children, and also that children in upper-income families are more likely to think they're better than other kids.

However, researchers can sometimes design their studies or conduct subsequent analyses in ways that address some third variables. For example, in the Brummelman study, one possible third variable is gender. What if boys show higher levels of narcissism than girls, and what if parents of boys are also more likely to overpraise them? Gender might be associated with both variables. Participant gender does not threaten internal validity here, however, because Brummelman and his colleagues report that the pattern was the same when boys and girls were examined separately. Thus, gender is a potential third variable, but by studying the longitudinal patterns of boys and girls separately, the Brummelman team was able to rule it out.

Why Not Just Do an Experiment?

Why would Brummelman and his team go to the trouble of tracking children every 6 months for 2 years? Why didn't they just do an experiment? After all, conducting experiments is the only certain way to confirm or disconfirm causal claims. The problem is that in some cases people cannot be randomly assigned to a causal variable of interest. For example, we cannot manipulate personality traits, such as narcissism in children. Similarly, while parents might be able to learn new ways to praise their children, they can't easily be assigned to daily parenting styles, so it's hard to manipulate this variable.

In addition, it could be unethical to assign some people, especially children, to a condition in which they receive a certain type of praise, especially over a long time period. Particularly if we suspect that one type of praise might make children narcissistic, it would not be ethical to expose children to it in an experimental setting. Similarly, if researchers suspect that smoking causes lung cancer or sexual content on TV causes pregnancy, it would be unethical (and difficult) to ask study participants to smoke cigarettes or watch certain TV shows for several years. When an experiment is not practical or ethical, a longitudinal correlational design is a good option.

Nevertheless, researchers who investigate how children react to different types of praise have not relied solely on correlational data. They have developed ethical experiments to study such reactions, at least over a short time period (Brummelman, Crocker, & Bushman, 2016; Mueller & Dweck, 1998). By randomly assigning children to receive praise for who they are (e.g., "You are so smart") versus praise for how hard they worked (e.g., "You must have worked hard at these problems"), researchers have produced some solid evidence that children really do change their behavior and attitudes in response to adult praise (**Figure 9.4**). Because it is ethically questionable to expose children to potentially harmful feedback, such studies had to pass strict ethical review and approval before they were conducted (see Chapter 4). In addition, the exposure time was short (only one instance of praise per study, and no instances of criticism). It would be much more challenging to do an ethical experimental study of the effects of long-term exposure to potentially maladaptive praise at home. That makes longitudinal correlational designs an attractive alternative.

FIGURE 9.4
Praising children.

Correlational and experimental studies suggest that when adults praise children's learning strategies and efforts (compared to praising the type of person they are), kids respond favorably and continue to work hard.

CHECK YOUR UNDERSTANDING

1. Why is a longitudinal design considered a multivariate design?

2. What are the three kinds of correlations obtained from a longitudinal design? What does each correlation represent?

3. Describe which patterns of temporal precedence are indicated by different cross-lag correlational results.

1. See p. 239. 2. See pp. 239–242. 3. See p. 241.

RULING OUT THIRD VARIABLES WITH MULTIPLE-REGRESSION ANALYSES

> Groundbreaking research suggests that pregnancy rates are much higher among teens who watch a lot of TV with sexual dialogue and behavior than among those who have tamer viewing tastes. (CBSNews, 2008)

This news item, referring to a study on TV content and teenage pregnancy, reports a simple association between the amount of sexual content teens watch on TV and their likelihood of becoming pregnant (Chandra et al., 2008). But is there a causal link? Does sexual TV content *cause* pregnancy? Apparently there is covariance: According to the published study, teens who watched more sexual material on TV were more likely to get pregnant. What about temporal precedence? Did the TV watching come before the pregnancy? According to the report, this study did establish temporal precedence because first they asked teens to report the types of TV shows they like to watch, and followed up with the very same teens 3 years later to find out if they had experienced a pregnancy.

What about internal validity? Third variables could explain the association. Perhaps one is age: Older teenagers might watch more mature TV programs, and they're also more likely to be sexually active. Or perhaps parenting is a third variable: Teens with stricter parents might monitor their TV use and also put tighter limits on their behavior.

How do we know whether one of these variables—or some other one—is the true explanation for the association? This study used a statistical technique called **multiple regression** (or *multivariate regression*), which can help rule out some third variables, thereby addressing some internal validity concerns.

Measuring More Than Two Variables

In the sexual TV content and pregnancy study, the researchers investigated a sample of 1,461 teenagers on the two key variables (Chandra et al., 2008). To measure the amount of sexual TV content viewed, they had participants report how often they watched 23 different programs popular with teens. Then coders watched 14 episodes of each show, counting how many scenes involved sex, including passionate kissing, sexually explicit talk, or intercourse. To assess pregnancy rates 3 years later, they asked girls "Have you ever been pregnant?" and asked boys "Have you ever gotten a girl pregnant?" The two variables were positively correlated: Higher amounts of sex on TV were associated with a higher risk of pregnancy (**Figure 9.5**).

If the researchers had stopped there and measured only these two variables, they would have conducted a bivariate correlational study. However, they also measured several other variables, including the total amount of time teenage

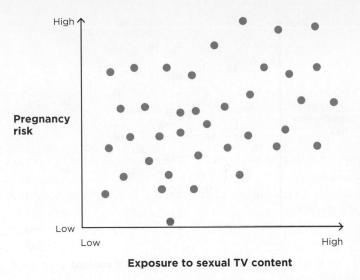

FIGURE 9.5
Correlating sexual TV content with pregnancy risk.

Higher rates of sexual content on TV go with higher risk of pregnancy, and lower rates of sexual content go with lower risk of pregnancy. (Data are fabricated for illustration purposes.)

participants watched any kind of TV, their age, their academic grades, and whether they lived with both parents. By measuring all these variables instead of just two (with the goal of testing the interrelationships among them all), they conducted a multivariate correlational study.

USING STATISTICS TO CONTROL FOR THIRD VARIABLES

By conducting a multivariate design, researchers can evaluate whether a relationship between two key variables still holds when they **control for** another variable. To introduce what "controlling for" means, let's focus on one potential third variable: age. Perhaps sexual content and pregnancy are correlated only because older teens are both more likely to watch more mature shows and more likely to be sexually active. If this is the case, all three variables are correlated with one another: Viewing sex on TV and getting pregnant are correlated, as we already determined, but sex on TV and age are also correlated with each other, and age and pregnancy are correlated, too. The researchers want to know whether age, as a third variable correlated with both the original variables, can account for the relationship between sexual TV content and pregnancy rates. To answer the question, they see what happens when they control for age.

You'll learn more about multiple-regression computations in a full-semester statistics course; this book will focus on a conceptual understanding of what these analyses mean. The most statistically accurate way to describe the phrase "control for age" is to talk about proportions of variability. Researchers are asking whether, after they take the relationship between age and pregnancy into account, there is still a portion of variability in pregnancy that is attributable to watching sexy TV. But this is extremely abstract language. The meaning is a bit like asking about the overall movement (the variance) of your wiggling, happy dog when you return home. You can ask, "What portion of the variability in my dog's overall movement

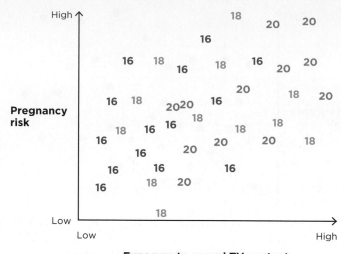

FIGURE 9.6

The association between sexual TV content and pregnancy remains positive, even controlling for age.

The overall relationship shown here is positive, and this holds even within the three subgroups: age 20, age 18, and age 16. (Data are fabricated for illustration purposes.)

is attributable to his tail moving? To his shoulders moving? To his back legs moving?" You can ask, "Will the dog still be moving when he greets me, even if I were to hold his tail constant—hold it still?"

An easier way to understand "controlling for" is to recognize that testing a third variable with multiple regression is similar to identifying subgroups. We can think of it like this: We start by looking only at the oldest age group (say, 20-year-olds) and see whether viewing sexual TV content and pregnancy are still correlated. Then we move to next oldest group (age 18), then the youngest group (age 16). We ask whether the bivariate relationship still holds at all levels.

There are a couple of possible outcomes from such a subgroup analysis, and one is shown in the scatterplot in **Figure 9.6**. Here, the overall association is positive—the more sexual TV programs teens watch, the higher the chance of getting pregnant. In addition, the oldest teens (the 20 symbols) are, overall, higher on sexual TV content and higher in chance of pregnancy. The youngest teens (16 symbols) are, overall, lower on sexual TV content and lower in chance of pregnancy. If we look *only* at the 20-year-olds, or *only* at the 16-year-olds, however, we still find the key relationship between sexy TV and pregnancy: It remains positive even within these age subgroups. Therefore, the relationship is still there, even when we hold age constant.

In contrast, the second possible outcome is shown in **Figure 9.7**. Here, the *overall* relationship is still positive, just as before—the more sexual content teens watch on TV, the higher the chance of pregnancy. In addition, just as before, the 20-year-olds watch more sexy TV and are more likely to become pregnant. However, this time, when we look *only* at the age 20 subgroup or *only* the age 16 subgroup, the key relationship between sexy TV and pregnancy is absent. The scatterplots *within* the age subgroups do not show the relationship anymore.

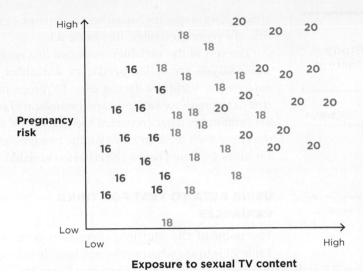

High

Pregnancy
risk

Low

Low   High

Exposure to sexual TV content

FIGURE 9.7
The association between sexual TV content and pregnancy goes away, controlling for age.

The overall association shown here is positive, but if we separately consider the subgroups of age 20, age 18, or age 16, there is no relationship between the two variables. (Data are fabricated for illustration purposes.)

Therefore, the association between watching sexual TV content and getting pregnant goes away when we control for age. In this case, age was, indeed, the third variable that was responsible for the relationship.

Regression Results Indicate If a Third Variable Affects the Relationship

Which one of the two scatterplots, Figure 9.6 or Figure 9.7, best describes the relationship between sexual content on TV and pregnancy? The statistical technique of multiple regression can tell us. When researchers use regression, they are testing whether some key relationship holds true even when a suspected third variable is statistically controlled for.

As a consumer of information, you'll probably work with the end result of this process, when you encounter regression results in tables in empirical journal articles. Suppose you're reading an article and you come across a table showing what the regression results would look like for the sexy TV/pregnancy example. What do the numbers mean? What steps did the researchers follow to come up with them?

CRITERION VARIABLES AND PREDICTOR VARIABLES

When researchers use multiple regression, they are studying three or more variables. The first step is to choose the variable they are most interested in understanding or predicting; this is known as the **criterion variable**, or *dependent variable*. The Chandra team were primarily interested in predicting pregnancy, so they chose that as their criterion variable. The criterion (dependent) variable is

TABLE 9.1

Multiple-Regression Results from a Study Predicting Pregnancy from Sexual Content on TV and Age

CRITERION (DEPENDENT) VARIABLE: PREGNANCY RISK	BETA	SIG
Predictor (independent) variables:		
Exposure to sex on TV	0.25	*
Age	0.33	*

Note: Data are fabricated, based on imagined results if the researchers had used only two predictor variables.
*$p < .001$.

almost always specified in either the top row or the title of a regression table, like **Table 9.1**.

The rest of the variables measured in a regression analysis are called **predictor variables**, or *independent variables*. In the sexy TV/pregnancy study, the predictor variables are the amount of sexual content teenagers reported viewing on TV and the age of each teen. In Table 9.1, the two predictor variables are listed below the criterion variable.

USING BETA TO TEST FOR THIRD VARIABLES

The point of the multiple-regression results in Table 9.1 is to see whether the relationship between exposure to sex on TV and pregnancy might be explained by a third variable—age. Does the association remain, even within each age group (as in Figure 9.6)? Or does the relationship between sexy TV and pregnancy go away within each age group (as in Figure 9.7)? The betas in Table 9.1 help answer this central question.

Beta Basics. In a regression table like Table 9.1, there is often a column labeled beta (or β, or even standardized beta). There will be one beta value for each predictor variable. Beta is similar to *r*, but it reveals more than *r* does. A positive beta, like a positive *r*, indicates a positive relationship between that predictor variable and the criterion variable, when the other predictor variables are statistically controlled for. A negative beta, like a negative *r*, indicates a negative relationship between two variables (when the other predictors are controlled for). A beta that is zero, or not significantly different from zero, represents no relationship (when the other predictors are controlled for). Therefore, betas are similar to correlations in that they denote the direction and strength of a relationship. The higher beta is, the stronger the relationship is between that predictor variable and the criterion variable. The smaller beta is, the weaker the relationship.

Within a single regression table, we can usually compare predictor variables that show larger betas to predictor variables with smaller betas—the larger the beta, the stronger the relationship. For example, in Table 9.1 we can say that the beta for the age predictor is stronger than the beta for the exposure to sex on TV predictor. (However, it is not appropriate to compare the strengths of betas from one regression table to the strengths of betas from another one.)

Unlike *r*, there are no quick guidelines for beta to indicate effect sizes that are weak, moderate, or strong. The reason is that betas change, depending on what other predictor variables are being used—being controlled for—in the regression.

Sometimes a regression table will include the symbol *b* instead of beta. The coefficient *b* represents an unstandardized coefficient. A *b* is similar to beta in that the sign of *b*—positive or negative—denotes a positive or negative association (when the other predictors are controlled for). But unlike two betas, we cannot compare two *b* values within the same table to each other. The reason is that *b* values are computed from the original measurements of the predictor variables (such as dollars, centimeters, or inches), whereas betas are computed from predictor variables that have been changed to standardized units. A predictor variable that shows a large *b* may not actually denote a stronger relationship to the criterion variable than a predictor variable with a smaller *b*.

Interpreting Beta. In Table 9.1, notice that the predictor variable "exposure to sex on TV" has a beta of 0.25. This positive beta, like a positive *r*, means higher levels of sex on TV go with higher pregnancy risk (and lower levels of sex on TV go with lower pregnancy risk), *even when we statistically control for the other predictor on this table—age*. In other words, even when we hold age constant statistically, the relationship between exposure to TV sex and pregnancy is still there. This result is consistent with the relationship depicted in Figure 9.6, not the one in Figure 9.7.

The other beta in Table 9.1, the one associated with the age predictor variable, is also positive. This beta means that older age is associated with higher pregnancy rates, *when exposure to sex on TV is controlled for*. In other words, when we hold exposure to sex on TV constant, age predicts pregnancy, too. In sum, the beta that is associated with a predictor variable represents the relationship between that predictor variable and the criterion variable, when the other predictor variables in the table are controlled for.

Statistical Significance of Beta. The regression tables in empirical journal articles often have a column labeled sig or *p*, or an asterisked footnote giving the *p* value for each beta. Such data indicate whether each beta is statistically significantly different from zero. As introduced in Chapter 8, the *p* value gives the probability that the beta came from a population in which the relationship is zero. When *p* is less than .05, the beta (i.e., the relationship between that predictor variable and the criterion variable, when the other predictor variables are controlled for) is considered statistically significant. When *p* is greater than .05, the beta is considered not significant, meaning we cannot conclude beta is different from zero.

In Table 9.1, both of the betas reported are statistically significant. **Table 9.2** gives several appropriate ways to explain what the significant beta for the TV variable means.

« For more on statistical significance, see Statistics Review: Inferential Statistics, pp. 499–500.

TABLE 9.2

Describing the Significant Beta of 0.25 in Table 9.1

EACH OF THESE SENTENCES IS AN APPROPRIATE DESCRIPTION OF THE RELATIONSHIP:

- The relationship between exposure to sex on TV and pregnancy is positive (high levels of sex on TV are associated with higher levels of pregnancy risk), even when age is controlled for.

- The relationship between exposure to sex on TV and pregnancy is positive even when age is controlled for.

- The relationship between exposure to sex on TV and pregnancy is positive (high levels of sex on TV are associated with higher pregnancy risk), and is not attributable to the third variable of age because it holds even when age is held constant.

What If Beta Is Not Significant? To answer this question, we'll use an example from a different line of research: family meals and child academic achievement. When these two variables are studied as a bivariate relationship, researchers find that children in families that eat many meals together (dinners and breakfasts) tend to be more academically successful, compared to kids in families that eat only a few meals together.

Once again, this simple bivariate relationship is not enough to show causation. In many studies, family meal habits and academic success are measured at the same time, so there is a temporal precedence problem: Did family meals come first and reinforce key academic skills, leading to higher achievement? Or did high academic success come first, perhaps making it more pleasant for parents to have meals with their kids? In addition, there are third variables that present an internal validity concern. For instance, more involved parents might arrange more family meals, and more involved parents might also have higher-achieving children.

A multiple-regression analysis could hold parental involvement constant and see if family meal frequency is still associated with academic success. In one such study, the researchers found that when parental involvement was held constant (along with other variables), family meal frequency was no longer a significant predictor of school success (Miller, Waldfogel, & Han, 2012). This pattern of results means that the only reason family meals correlated with academic success was because of the third-variable problem of parental involvement (**Table 9.3**).

In other words, although frequency of family meals and academic success are significantly related in their bivariate relationship, that relationship goes away when potential third variables, such as parental involvement, are controlled for.

TABLE 9.3

Multiple-Regression Results from a Study Predicting Academic Success from Frequency of Family Meals and Parental Involvement

CRITERION (DEPENDENT) VARIABLE: ACADEMIC SUCCESS	BETA	SIG
Predictor (independent) variables:		
Frequency of family meals	−0.01	Not significant
Parental involvement	0.09	*

Note: Data are fabricated, but reflect actual research. The study controlled for not only parental involvement, but also income, family structure, school quality, birth weight, school type, and many other possible third variables. When controlling for all these in a sample of more than 20,000 children, the researchers found that the beta for frequency of family meals was not significant.
*$p < .001$.
Source: Adapted from Miller et al., 2012.

TABLE 9.4

Describing the Nonsignificant Beta of –0.01 in Table 9.3

EACH OF THESE SENTENCES IS AN APPROPRIATE DESCRIPTION OF THE RELATIONSHIP:

- The relationship between family meal frequency and child academic success is not significant when controlling for parental involvement.

- The relationship between family meal frequency and child academic success can be explained by the third variable of parental involvement.

- The relationship between family meal frequency and child academic success goes away when parental involvement is held constant.

When you hold parental involvement constant, there is no longer a relationship between frequency of family meals and academic success (**Table 9.4**).

Adding More Predictors to a Regression

Up to now, when considering the relationship between sexual TV content and pregnancy, we've focused on only one potential internal validity problem—age. But remember there are many other possible third variables. What about participation in school activities? What about living with one versus two parents? In fact, the Chandra team measured each of those third variables and even added a few more, such as parental education, ethnicity, and having a history of problem behaviors (Chandra et al., 2008). **Table 9.5** shows every variable tested, as well as the multiple-regression results for all the other variables.

Even when there are many more predictor variables in the table, beta still means the same thing. The beta for the exposure to sex on TV is positive: High levels of sex on TV are associated with higher pregnancy rate, when the researchers controlled for age, total TV exposure, lower grades, parent education, educational aspirations, and so on, down to intention to have children before age 22. Even after controlling for all variables

TABLE 9.5

Multiple-Regression Results from a Study Predicting Pregnancy from Exposure to Sex on TV and Other Variables

CRITERION (DEPENDENT) VARIABLE: PREGNANCY RISK	BETA	SIG
Predictor (independent) variables:		
Exposure to sex on TV	0.44	*
Total television exposure	–0.42	*
Age	0.28	*
Lower grades	0.21	n.s
Parent education	0.00	n.s.
Educational aspirations (highest level of school you plan to finish)	–0.14	n.s.
Being Hispanic (vs. other ethnicities)	0.86	n.s.
Being Black (vs. other ethnicities)	1.20	*
Being female	1.20	*
Living in a 2-parent household	–1.50	*
History of deviant or problem behavior (e.g., skipping school, stealing, cheating on a test)	0.43	*
Intention to have children before age 22	0.61	n.s.

*$p \leq .001$.
Source: Adapted from Chandra et al., 2008, Table 2.

listed in Table 9.5, the researchers found that more exposure to sex on TV predicts a higher chance of pregnancy.

Adding several predictors to a regression analysis can help answer two kinds of questions. First, it helps control for several third variables at once. In the Chandra study, even after all other variables were controlled for, exposure to sex on TV still predicted pregnancy. A result like that gets the researchers a bit closer to making a causal claim because the relationship between the suspected cause (sexy TV) and the suspected effect (pregnancy) does not appear to be attributable to any of the other variables that were measured.

Second, by looking at the betas for all the other predictor variables, we can get a sense of which factors most strongly predict chance of pregnancy. One strong predictor is gender, which, as you can see, has a beta of 1.20, even when the other variables are controlled for. This result means girls are more likely to report becoming pregnant than boys are to report getting a girl pregnant. (Even though it takes two to cause a pregnancy, presumably boys are sometimes unaware of getting a girl pregnant, whereas a girl is more certain.) We also notice that teens with a history of deviant behavior also have a higher risk of pregnancy, controlling for exposure to sex on TV, age, grades, and the other variables in the table. In fact, the predictive power of history of deviant behavior is about the same magnitude as that of exposure to sex on TV. Even though the authors of this study were most interested in describing the potential risk of viewing sexual content on TV, they were also able to evaluate which other variables are important in predicting pregnancy. (Recall, however, that when a table presents *b* values, or unstandardized coefficients, it is not appropriate to compare their *relative* strength. We can only do so with beta, and even then, remember that betas change depending on what other predictor variables are used.)

Regression in Popular Media Articles

When making association claims in the popular media—magazines, newspapers, websites—journalists seldom discuss betas, *p* values, or predictor variables. Because they're writing for a general audience, they assume most of their readers will not be familiar with these concepts. However, if you read carefully, you can detect when a multiple regression has been used if a journalist uses one of the phrases in the sections that follow.

"CONTROLLED FOR"

The phrase "controlled for" is one common sign of a regression analysis. For example, when journalists covered the story about family meals and academic success, they stated the findings like this:

> Researchers . . . determined that there wasn't any relationship between family meals and a child's academic outcomes or behavior. . . . Miller and his team also

controlled for factors such as parental employment, television-watching, the quality of school facilities, and the years of experience the children's teachers had, among others. (Family Dinner Benefits, Huffingtonpost.com, 2012; emphasis added)

"TAKING INTO ACCOUNT"

Here's another example from an article about a study of male military veterans. This is the headline: "Perk of a good job: aging mind is sharp."

> Mentally demanding jobs come with a hidden benefit: less mental decline with age. Work that requires decision making, negotiating with others, analysis, and making judgments may not necessarily pad your bank account. But it does build up your "cognitive reserve"—a level of mental function that helps you avoid or compensate for age-related mental decline. (DeNoon, 2008)

In this story, the central association is between how mentally demanding a man's job is and his cognitive functioning as he ages. The more demanding the job, the less cognitive decline he suffers. But could there be a third variable, such as intelligence or level of education? Perhaps the veterans in the study who were better educated were more likely to have a mentally challenging job and to experience less cognitive decline. However, the story goes on:

> *After taking into account both intelligence and education*, [the researchers] found that men with more complex jobs—in terms of general intellectual demands and human interaction and communication—performed significantly better on tests of mental function. (DeNoon, 2008; emphasis added)

The phrase "taking into account" means the researchers conducted multiple-regression analyses. Even when they controlled for education and intelligence, they still found a relationship between job complexity and cognitive decline.

"CONSIDERING" OR "ADJUSTING FOR"

When the sexy TV/pregnancy study was reported online, the journalist mentioned the simple relationship between exposure to sexual TV content and getting pregnant, and then wrote:

> Chandra said TV watching was strongly connected with teen pregnancy even when other factors were considered, including grades, family structure, and parents' education level. (CBSnews, 2008)

The phrase "even when other factors were considered" indicates the researchers used multiple regression.

FIGURE 9.8
Multiple regression in the popular media.

This journalist wrote that people who ate more chocolate had lower body mass index, and that the researchers adjusted their results for several variables. The phrase "adjusted for" signals a regression analysis, thereby ruling out those variables as internal validity problems. (Source: O'Connor, 2012.)

The Chocolate Diet?

"Since so many complicating factors can influence results, it is difficult to pinpoint cause and effect. But the researchers adjusted their results for a number of variables, including age, gender, depression, vegetable consumption, and fat and calorie intake."

Similar terminology such as "adjusting for" can also indicate multiple regression. Here's a study that found a relationship between eating chocolate and body mass (**Figure 9.8**):

> The people who ate chocolate the most frequently, despite eating more calories and exercising no differently from those who ate the least chocolate, tended to have lower B.M.I.'s. . . . The researchers *adjusted their results for* a number of variables, including age, gender, depression, vegetable consumption, and fat and calorie intake. "It didn't matter which of those you added, the relationship remained very stably significant." (O'Connor, nytimes.com, 2012; emphasis added)

In sum, journalists can use a variety of phrases to describe a study's use of multiple regression. When you encounter an association claim in a magazine, newspaper, or online, one of your questions should be whether the researchers controlled for possible third variables. If you can't tell from the story what the researchers controlled for, it's reasonable to suspect that certain third variables cannot be ruled out.

Regression Does Not Establish Causation

Multiple regression might seem to be a foolproof way to rule out all kinds of third variables. If you look at the data in Table 9.5 on exposure to TV sex and pregnancy, for example, you might think you can safely make a causal statement now, since the researchers controlled for so many internal validity problems. They seem to have thought of everything! Not so fast. One problem is that even though multivariate designs analyzed with regression statistics can control for third variables, they are not always able to establish temporal precedence. Of course, the Chandra study did measure viewing sexual TV content 3 years before pregnancies occurred. But others, such as the study on family meals and academic achievement, may not.

Even when a study takes place over time (longitudinally), another very important problem is that researchers cannot control for variables they do not measure.

FIGURE 9.9
Possible third variables in the association between sexual TV content and pregnancy.
What additional third variables, not already measured by the researchers, might be associated with both watching sex on TV and pregnancy?

Even though multiple regression controls for any third variables the researchers do measure in the study, some other variable they did not consider could account for the association. In the sexy TV/pregnancy study, some unmeasured variable—maybe the teenagers' level of religiosity or the geographic area where they live—might account for the relationship between watching sex on TV and getting pregnant. But since those possible third variables were not measured (or even considered), there is no way of knowing (**Figure 9.9**).

In fact, some psychological scientists have critiqued media studies like this one, arguing that certain types of teenagers are predisposed to watching sexual TV content, and these same teens are also more likely to be sexually active (Steinberg & Monahan, 2011). These critics contend that the relationship between sexual media content and sexual activity is attributable to this predisposition (see Collins, Martino, Elliott, & Miu, 2011).

This unknown third-variable problem is one reason that a well-run experimental study is ultimately more convincing in establishing causation than a correlational study. An experimental study on TV, for example, would randomly assign a sample of people to watch either sexy TV shows or programs without sexual content. The power of random assignment would make the two groups likely to be equal on any third variables the researchers did not happen to measure, such as religiosity, social class, or parenting styles. But of course, just like randomly assigning children to get one type of praise or another, it is ethically questionable to conduct an experiment on sexual TV content.

A randomized experiment is the gold standard for determining causation. Multiple regression, in contrast, allows researchers to control for potential third variables, but only for the variables they choose to measure.

CHECK YOUR UNDERSTANDING

1. Describe what it means to say that some variable "was controlled for" in a multivariate study.

2. How many criterion variables are there in a multiple-regression analysis? How many predictor variables?

3. What does a significant beta mean? What does a nonsignificant beta mean?

4. Give at least two phrases indicating that a study used a multiple-regression analysis.

5. What are two reasons that multiple-regression analyses cannot completely establish causation?

1. See pp. 245–247. 2. One criterion variable, and at least two predictor variables. See pp. 247–248. 3. See pp. 248–251. 4. See pp. 252–254. 5. See pp. 254–256.

GETTING AT CAUSALITY WITH PATTERN AND PARSIMONY

So far this chapter has focused on two multivariate techniques that help researchers investigate causation, even when they're working with correlations among measured variables. Longitudinal correlational designs can satisfy the temporal precedence criterion. And multiple-regression analyses statistically control for some potential internal validity problems (third variables).

In this section, we explore how researchers can investigate causality by using a variety of correlational studies that all point in a single, causal direction. This approach can be called "pattern and parsimony" because there's a pattern of results best explained by a single, parsimonious causal theory. As discussed in Chapter 1, **parsimony** is the degree to which a scientific theory provides the simplest explanation of some phenomenon. In the context of investigating a causal claim, parsimony means the simplest explanation of a pattern of data—the theory that requires making the fewest exceptions or qualifications.

The Power of Pattern and Parsimony

A great example of pattern and parsimony is the case of smoking and lung cancer. This example was first articulated by the psychological scientist Robert Abelson.

Decades ago, it started becoming clear that smokers had higher rates of lung cancer than nonsmokers (the correlation has been estimated at about $r = .40$). Did the smoking *cause* the cancer? Cigarette manufacturers certainly did not want people to think so. If someone argued that this correlation was causal, a critic might counter that the cigarettes were not the cause; perhaps people who smoked were more stressed, which predisposed them to lung cancer. Or perhaps smokers also drank a lot of coffee, and it was the coffee, not the cigarettes, that caused cancer. The list of third-variable explanations could go on and on. Even though multiple-regression analyses could control for these alternative explanations, critics could always argue that regression cannot control for every possible third variable.

Another problem, of course, is that even though an experiment could rule out third-variable explanations, a smoking experiment would not be ethical or practical. A researcher could not reasonably assign a sample of volunteers to become lifetime smokers or nonsmokers. The only data researchers had to work with were correlational.

The solution to this problem, Abelson explains, is to specify a mechanism for the causal path. Specifically, in the case of cigarettes, researchers proposed that cigarette smoke contains chemicals that are toxic when they come into contact with human tissue. The more contact a person has with these chemicals, the greater the toxicity exposure. This simple theory leads to a set of predictions, all of which could be explained by the single, parsimonious theory that chemicals in cigarettes cause cancer (Abelson, 1995, p. 184):

1. The longer a person has smoked cigarettes, the greater his or her chances of getting cancer.
2. People who stop smoking have lower cancer rates than people who keep smoking.
3. Smokers' cancers tend to be in the lungs and of a particular type.
4. Smokers who use filtered cigarettes have a somewhat lower rate of cancer than those who use unfiltered cigarettes.
5. People who live with smokers would have higher rates of cancer, too, because of their passive exposure to the same chemicals.

This process exemplifies the theory-data cycle (see Chapter 1). A theory—cigarette toxicity—led to a particular set of research questions. The theory also led researchers to frame hypotheses about what the data should show.

Indeed, converging evidence from several individual studies conducted by medical researchers has supported each of these separate predictions (their evidence became part of the U.S. Surgeon General's warning in 1964), and that's where parsimony comes in. Because all five of these diverse predictions are tied back to one central principle (the toxicity of the chemicals in cigarette smoke), there is a strong case for parsimony (**Figure 9.10**).

FIGURE 9.10
Pattern and parsimony.

Many studies, using a variety of methods, provide converging evidence to support the causal claim that cigarettes contain toxic chemicals that are harmful to humans. Although each of the individual studies has methodological weaknesses, taken together, they all support the same, parsimonious conclusion.

»
To review the concept of weight of the evidence, see Chapter 1, p. 15.

Notice, also, that the diversity of these five empirical findings makes it much harder to raise third-variable explanations. Suppose a critic argued that coffee drinking was a third variable. Coffee drinking could certainly explain the first result (the longer one smokes—and presumably drinks coffee, too—the higher the rates of cancer). But it cannot explain the effect of filtered cigarettes or the cancer rates among secondhand smokers. The most parsimonious explanation of this entire pattern of data—and the weight of the evidence—is the toxicity of cigarettes.

It is hard to overstate the strength of the pattern and parsimony technique. In psychology, researchers commonly use a variety of methods and many studies to explore the strength and limits of a particular research question. Another example comes from research on TV violence and aggression. Many studies have investigated the relationship between watching violence on TV and violent behavior. Some studies are correlational; some are experimental. Some are on children; others on adults. Some are longitudinal; others are not. But in general, the evidence all points to a single, parsimonious conclusion that watching violence on TV causes people to behave aggressively (Anderson et al., 2003).

Many psychological scientists build their careers by doing study after study devoted to one research question. As discussed in Chapter 1, scientists dig deeper: They use a variety of methods, combining results to develop their causal theories and to support them with converging evidence.

Pattern, Parsimony, and the Popular Media

When journalists write about science, they do not always fairly represent pattern and parsimony in research. Instead, they may report only the results of the latest study. For example, they might present a news story on the most recent nutrition research, without describing the other studies done in that area. They might report that people who multitask the most are the worst at it, but fail to cover the full pattern of studies on media multitasking. They might report on a single study that showed an association between eating chocolate and body mass, without mentioning the rest of the studies on that same topic, and without tying the results to the theory they are supporting.

When journalists report only one study at a time, they selectively present only a part of the scientific process. They might not describe the context of the research, such as what previous studies have revealed, or what theory the study was testing. Reporting on the latest study without giving the full context can make it seem as though scientists conduct unconnected studies on a whim. It might even give the impression that one study can reverse decades of previous research. In addition, skeptics who read such science stories might find it easy to criticize the results of a single, correlational study. But in fact, science accumulates incrementally. Ideally, journalists should report on the entire body of evidence, as well as the theoretical background, for a particular claim.

CHECK YOUR UNDERSTANDING

1. Why do many researchers find pattern and parsimony an effective way to support a causal claim?

2. What is a responsible way for journalists to cover single studies on a specific topic?

1. See pp. 256–258. 2. See p. 258.

MEDIATION

We have discussed the research designs and statistical tools researchers use to get closer to making causal claims. Once a relationship between two variables has been established, we often want to explore it further by thinking about *why*. For example, we might ask why watching sexual content on TV predicts a higher pregnancy risk, or why people who engage in meaningful conversations are happier. Many times, these explanations suggest a **mediator**, or *mediating variable*. Researchers may propose a mediating step between two of the variables. A study does not have to be correlational to include a mediator; experimental studies can also test them. However, mediation analyses often rely on multivariate tools such as multiple regression, so it makes sense to learn about mediators here.

Consider this example. We know conscientious people are more physically healthy than less conscientious people. But why? The mediator of this relationship might be the fact that conscientious people are more likely to follow medical advice and instructions, and that's why they're healthier. Following doctor's orders would be the mediator of the relationship between the trait, conscientiousness, and the outcome, better health (Hill & Roberts, 2011).

Similarly, we know there's an association between having deep conversations and feelings of well-being (see Chapter 8). Researchers might next propose a reason—a mediator of this relationship. One likely mediator could be social ties: Deeper conversations might help build social connections, which in turn can lead to increased well-being. The researchers could draw this mediation hypothesis, as shown in **Figure 9.11**.

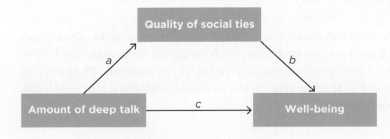

FIGURE 9.11
A proposed mediation model.

We could propose that deep talk leads to stronger social ties, which leads to increased well-being. To test this model, a researcher follows five steps (see text).

They would propose an overall relationship, *c*, between deep talk and well-being. However, this overall relationship exists only because there are two other relationships: *a* (between deep talk and social ties) and *b* (between social ties and well-being). In other words, social ties mediate the relationship between deep talk and well-being. (Of course, there are other possible mediators, such as intellectual growth or taking a break from technology. Those mediators could be tested, too, in another study.)

The researchers could examine this mediation hypothesis by following five steps (Kenny, 2008):

1. Test for relationship *c*. Is deep talk associated with well-being? (If it is not, there is no relationship to mediate.)
2. Test for relationship *a*. Is deep talk associated with the proposed mediator, strength of social ties? Do people who have deeper conversations actually have stronger ties than people who have more shallow conversations? (If social tie strength is the aspect of deep talk that explains why deep talk leads to well-being, then, logically, people who have more meaningful conversations must also have stronger social ties.)
3. Test for relationship *b*. Do people who have stronger social ties have higher levels of well-being? (Again, if social tie strength explains well-being, then, logically, people with stronger social connections must also have higher well-being.)
4. Run a regression test, using both strength of social ties and deep talk as predictor variables to predict well-being, to see whether relationship *c* goes away. (If social tie strength is the mediator of relationship *c*, the relationship between deep talk and well-being should drop when social tie strength is controlled for. Here we would be using regression as a tool to show that deep talk was associated with well-being in the first place because social tie strength was responsible.)

Because mediation hypotheses are causal claims, a fifth important step establishes temporal precedence:

5. Mediation is definitively established only when the proposed causal variable is measured or manipulated first in a study, followed some time later by the mediating variable, followed by the proposed outcome variable.

In other words, to establish mediation in this example, the researchers must conduct a study in which the amount of deep talk is measured (or manipulated) first, followed shortly afterwards by a measure of social tie strength. They have to measure well-being last of all, to rule out the possibility that the well-being led to having deeper conversations.

If researchers want to examine whether following doctor's orders is the mediator of the relationship between conscientiousness and good health, the design of the study should ideally measure conscientiousness first, and then later measure medical compliance, and then later measure health. If the design establishes temporal precedence *and* the results support the steps above, there is evidence for mediation.

Mediators vs. Third Variables

Mediators appear similar to third-variable explanations. Both of them involve multivariate research designs, and researchers use the same statistical tool (multiple regression) to detect them. However, they function differently.

In a third-variable explanation, the proposed third variable is external to the two variables in the original bivariate correlation; it might even be seen as an accident—a problematic "lurking variable" that potentially distracts from the relationship of interest. For example, if we propose that education level is a third variable responsible for the deep talk/well-being relationship, we're saying deep talk and well-being are correlated with each other *only because* each one is correlated separately with education, as shown in **Figure 9.12**. In other words, the relationship between deep talk and well-being is there only because both of those variables happen to vary with the outside third variable, education level. The third variable may seem like a nuisance; it might not be of central interest to the researchers. (If they are really interested in deep talk and well-being, they have to control for education level first.)

In contrast, when researchers propose a mediator, they are interested in isolating which aspect of the presumed causal variable is responsible for that relationship. A mediator variable is *internal* to the causal variable and often of direct interest to the researchers, rather than a nuisance. In the deep talk example, the

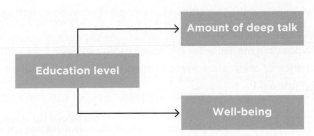

FIGURE 9.12
A third variable.

In a third-variable scenario, the third variable is seen as external to the original two variables. Here, deep talk and higher well-being might both be associated with education level.

researchers believe stronger social ties is the important aspect, or outcome, of deep talk that is responsible for increasing well-being.

Mediators vs. Moderators

Recall that moderators were introduced in Chapter 8. Similar-sounding names can make them confusing at first. However, testing for mediation versus moderation involves asking different questions (Baron & Kenny, 1986). When researchers test for mediating variables, they ask: Why are these two variables linked? When they test for moderating variables, they ask: Are these two variables linked the same way for everyone, or in every situation? Mediators ask: Why? Moderators ask: Who is most vulnerable? For whom is the association strongest?

A mediation hypothesis could propose, for instance, that medical compliance is the reason conscientiousness is related to better health. In contrast, a moderation hypothesis could propose that the link between conscientiousness and good health is strongest among older people (perhaps because their health problems are more severe, and most likely to benefit from medical compliance) and weakest among younger people (whose health problems are less serious anyway).

As the name implies, the mediating variable comes in the middle of the other two variables. The word *moderate* can mean "to change," and a moderating variable can change the relationship between the other two variables (making it more intense or less intense). **Figure 9.13** diagrams the differences between mediation, moderation, and third variables.

CHECK YOUR UNDERSTANDING

1. Explain why each of the five steps examining a mediation hypothesis is important to establishing evidence for a mediator.

2. Think of a possible mediator for the relationship between exposure to sex on TV and chance of pregnancy. Sketch a diagram of the mediator you propose, following Figure 9.11.

1. See pp. 259–261. 2. Diagram should resemble Figure 9.11, with exposure to sex on TV in the left box, pregnancy risk in the right box, and your proposed mediator in the middle box.

Mediation	**Moderation**	**Third-variable Problem**
Definition *Why* are two variables related?	Are there certain groups or situations for which the two variables are more strongly related?	Two variables are correlated, but only because they are both linked to a third variable.

Example

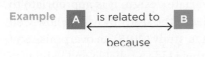

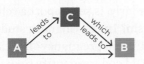

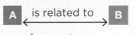

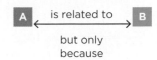

Example

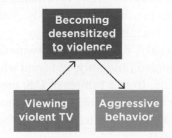

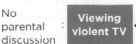

| **Sentence** Level of desensitization mediates the relationship between TV violence and aggressive behavior. | Parental discussion moderates the relationship between TV violence and aggressive behavior. Children are more vulnerable when parents do not discuss TV violence with them. | The relationship between viewing violent TV and aggressive behavior may be attributable to the third variable of parental leniency. |

FIGURE 9.13

Mediation, moderation, and third variables.

How are they different?

MULTIVARIATE DESIGNS AND THE FOUR VALIDITIES

Researchers use multivariate correlational research, such as longitudinal designs and multiple-regression analyses, to get closer to making causal claims. Longitudinal designs help establish temporal precedence, and multiple-regression analysis helps rule out third variables, thus providing some evidence for internal validity. We must remember, however, to interrogate the other three major validities—construct, external, and statistical validity—as well.

For any multivariate design, as for any bivariate design, it is appropriate to interrogate the construct validity of the variables in the study by asking how well each variable was measured. In the Brummelman study (2015) on overpraise and narcissism, is asking parents what they say to their kids a reliable and valid way to measure their actual level of overpraise? Similarly, is self-report a reliable and valid way to measure a child's levels of narcissism? In the Chandra study (2008), what about the measures of exposure to sex on TV and pregnancy? Did the coding of TV show content have interrater reliability? Did coders identify sexual content in a valid way?

We can also interrogate the external validity of a multivariate design. In the Brummelman study on narcissism, the researchers invited all children from 17 schools in the Netherlands to participate, and 565 (75%) of them agreed. Volunteers are not a random sample, so we are uncertain about whether we can generalize from this sample to the population of children in the 17 schools. We might also ask whether the association generalizes to other kinds of praise, such as praise from teachers or other adults.

To interrogate the external validity of the sexual TV content and pregnancy study, we can ask whether the teenagers were sampled randomly, and from what kind of population. In fact, the Chandra study came from a sample of U.S. teens from all states, and the sample's demographic characteristics were similar to those for the entire U.S. However, the researchers do not report whether or not their sample was selected randomly (Chandra et al., 2008).

For interrogating a multivariate correlational research study's statistical validity, we can ask about the effect size and statistical significance (see Chapter 8). In the case of the sexy TV/pregnancy study, we know the beta was 0.44 and was statistically significant. However, there are no guidelines for what constitutes a "large" or "small" beta. The authors of the study also presented the pregnancy risk of low, compared to medium and high, sexual content viewers (**Figure 9.14**). These data show that among 20-year-olds, those who had watched the most sexual TV had a pregnancy risk two times higher than those who had watched the least. Because the risk of pregnancy doubled, it was interpreted as a strong effect size by the authors.

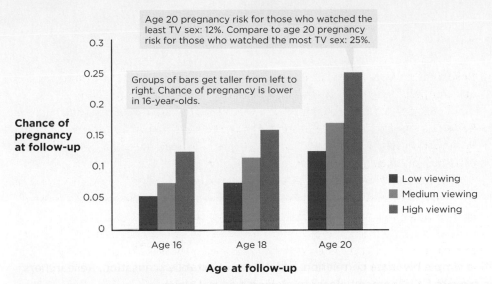

Age 20 pregnancy risk for those who watched the least TV sex: 12%. Compare to age 20 pregnancy risk for those who watched the most TV sex: 25%.

Groups of bars get taller from left to right. Chance of pregnancy is lower in 16-year-olds.

Chance of pregnancy at follow-up

- Low viewing
- Medium viewing
- High viewing

Age 16   Age 18   Age 20

Age at follow-up

FIGURE 9.14
Statistical validity in the sexual TV content and pregnancy study.

The researchers calculated the pregnancy risk among teens who reported watching the lowest levels of sexual content (low viewing), as well as medium and high viewing levels. Different age groups were calculated separately. The graph depicts a large effect size for sexual content because the pregnancy risk for the highest viewers is double that for the lowest viewers. (Source: Adapted from Chandra et al., 2008.)

Other statistical validity questions apply to multivariate designs, too. When researchers use multivariate designs, they need to take precautions to look for subgroups, outliers, and curvilinear associations, all of which can be more complicated to detect when there are more than two variables.

CHECK YOUR UNDERSTANDING

1. Give an example of a question you would ask to interrogate each of the four validities for a multivariate study.

1. See pp. 264-265.

CHAPTER REVIEW

Summary

Research often begins with a simple bivariate correlation, which cannot establish causation. Researchers can use multivariate techniques to help them get closer to making a causal claim.

Reviewing the Three Causal Criteria

- In a multivariate design, researchers measure more than two variables and look for the relationships among them.
- A simple, bivariate correlation indicates that there is covariance, but cannot always indicate temporal precedence or internal validity, so it cannot establish causation.

Establishing Temporal Precedence with Longitudinal Designs

- Longitudinal designs start with two key variables, on which the same group of people are measured at multiple points in time. Researchers can tell which variable came first in time, thus helping establish temporal precedence.
- Longitudinal designs produce cross-sectional correlations (correlations between the two key variables at any one time period) and autocorrelations (correlations between one variable and itself, over time).
- Longitudinal designs also produce cross-lag correlations. By comparing the relative strengths of the two cross-lag correlations, researchers can infer which of the variables probably came first in time (or if they are mutually reinforcing each other).

Ruling Out Third Variables with Multiple-Regression Analyses

- In a regression design, researchers start with a bivariate correlation and then measure other potential third variables that might affect it.

- Using multiple-regression analysis, researchers can see whether the basic relationship is still present, even when they statistically control for one or more third variables. If the beta is still significant for the key variable when the researchers control for the third variables, it means the key relationship is not explained by those third variables.
- If the beta becomes nonsignificant when the researchers control for a third variable, then the key relationship can be attributed to that third variable.
- Even though regression analyses can rule out third variables, they cannot definitively establish causation because they can only control for possible third variables that the researchers happened to measure. An experiment is the only design that definitively establishes causation.

Getting at Causality with Pattern and Parsimony

- Researchers can approach causal certainty through pattern and parsimony; they specify a mechanism for the causal relationship and combine the results from a variety of research questions. When a single causal theory explains all of the disparate results, researchers are closer to supporting a causal claim.

Mediation

- In a mediation hypothesis, researchers specify a variable that comes between the two variables of interest as a possible reason the two variables are associated. After collecting data on all three variables (the original two, plus the mediator), they follow specific steps to evaluate how well the data support the mediation hypothesis.

Multivariate Designs and the Four Validities

- Interrogating multivariate correlational designs involves investigating not only internal validity and temporal precedence, but also construct validity, external validity, and statistical validity. While no single study is perfect, exploring each validity in turn is a good way to systematically assess a study's strengths and weaknesses.

Key Terms

multivariate design, p. 238
longitudinal design, p. 239
cross-sectional correlation, p. 239
autocorrelation, p. 240

cross-lag correlation, p. 241
multiple regression, p. 244
control for, p. 245
criterion variable, p. 247

predictor variable, p. 248
parsimony, p. 256
mediator, p. 259

To see samples of chapter concepts in the popular media, visit www.everydayresearchmethods.com and click the box for Chapter 9.

Review Questions

1. A headline in Yahoo! News made the following (bivariate) association claim: "Facebook users get worse grades in college" (Hsu, 2009). The two variables in this headline are:

   a. Level of Facebook use and college grades.

   b. High grades and low grades.

   c. High Facebook use and low Facebook use.

2. Suppose a researcher uses a longitudinal design to study the relationship between Facebook use and grades over time. She measures both of these variables in Year 1, and then measures both variables again in Year 2. Which of the following is an example of an autocorrelation in the results?

   a. The correlation between Facebook use in Year 1 and Facebook use in Year 2.

   b. The correlation between Facebook use in Year 1 and grades in Year 2.

   c. The correlation between grades in Year 1 and Facebook use in Year 2.

   d. The correlation between grades in Year 1 and Facebook use in Year 1.

3. In the longitudinal study described in question 2, which pattern of cross-lag correlations would indicate

that Facebook use leads to lower grades (rather than the reverse)?

   a. Grades at Year 1 shows a strong correlation with Facebook use at Year 2, but Facebook use at Year 1 shows a weak correlation with grades at Year 2.

   b. Grades at Year 1 shows a weak correlation with Facebook use at Year 2, but Facebook use at Year 1 shows a strong correlation with grades at Year 2.

   c. Grades at Year 1 shows a strong correlation with Facebook use at Year 2, and Facebook use at Year 1 shows a strong correlation with grades at Year 2.

4. Consider this statement: "People who use Facebook got worse grades in college, even when the researchers controlled for the level of college preparation (operationalized by SAT scores) of the students." What does it mean?

   a. Facebook use and grades are correlated only because both of these are associated with SAT score.

   b. SAT score is a third variable that seems to explain the association between Facebook use and grades.

   c. SAT score can be ruled out as a third variable explanation for the correlation between Facebook use and college grades.

5. Which of the following statements is an example of a mediator of the relationship between Facebook use and college grades?

a. Facebook use and college grades are more strongly correlated among nonathletes, and less strongly correlated among athletes.

b. Facebook use and college grades are only correlated with each other because they are both related to the difficulty of the major. Students in more difficult majors get worse grades, and those in difficult majors have less time to use Facebook.

c. Facebook use and college grades are correlated because Facebook use leads to less time studying, which leads to lower grades.

6. A news outlet reported on a study of people with dementia. The study found that among patients with dementia, bilingual people had been diagnosed 3-4 years later than those who were monolingual. What are the variables in this bivariate association?

a. Being bilingual or monolingual

b. Being bilingual or not, and age at dementia diagnosis

c. Age at dementia diagnosis

7. The journalist reported that the relationship between bilingualism and age at diagnosis did not change, even when the researchers controlled for level of education. What does this suggest?

a. That the relationship between bilingualism and dementia onset is probably attributable to the third variable: level of education.

b. That the relationship between bilingualism and dementia onset is not attributable to the third variable: level of education.

c. That being bilingual can prevent dementia.

8. Researchers speculated that the reason bilingualism is associated with later onset of dementia is that bilingual people develop richer connections in the brain through their experiences in managing two languages; these connections help stave off dementia symptoms. This statement describes:

a. A mediator

b. A moderator

c. A third variable

Learning Actively

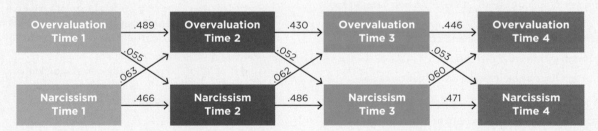

1. The accompanying figure shows the result of a cross-lag panel study on a sample of Dutch children aged 7–11 (Brummelman et al., 2015). The study collected several variables at four time points, each about 6 months apart. At each wave, they measured the child's self-esteem using a self-report measure (a sample item was "Kids like me are happy with themselves as a person"). It also measured the child's perception of each parent's warmth (a sample question was "My father/mother lets me know he/she loves me"). The results in the figure are only for the mother's warmth (as rated by the child). All results in the figure are statistically significant.

a. Point to the autocorrelations in the figure.

b. Are there cross-sectional correlations in the figure?

c. Overall, what do the cross-lag correlations suggest? Does parental warmth lead to higher self-esteem, or does higher self-esteem lead to parental warmth, or is there a mutually reinforcing relationship?

2. Indicate whether each statement below is describing a mediation hypothesis, a third-variable argument, or a moderator result. First, identify the key bivariate relationship. Next, decide whether the extra variable comes between the two key variables or is causing the two key variables simultaneously. Then, draw a sketch of each explanation, following the examples in Figure 9.13.

a. Having a mentally demanding job is associated with cognitive benefits in later years, because people who are highly educated take mentally demanding jobs, and people who are highly educated have better cognitive skills.

b. Having a mentally demanding job is associated with cognitive benefits in later years, but only in men, not women.

c. Having a mentally demanding job is associated with cognitive benefits in later years because cognitive challenges build lasting connections in the brain.

d. Being a victim of sibling aggression is associated with poor mental health in childhood, but the link is especially strong for later-born children and weaker in firstborn children.

e. Sibling aggression is associated with poor childhood mental health because child victims of sibling aggression are more likely to feel lonely at home. Sibling aggression leads to loneliness, which leads to mental health problems.

f. Sibling aggression is associated with poor childhood mental health only because of parental conflict. Sibling aggression is more likely among parents who argue frequently, and arguing also affects kids' mental health.

3. Do victims of sibling aggression suffer worse mental health? A recent study investigated this question (Tucker, Finkelhor, Turner, & Shattuck, 2013). The researchers wondered whether sibling aggression was linked to poor mental health in children, and whether sibling victimization was as bad for kids as peer victimization. In a large sample of children and youths, ages 2–17, they measured several kinds of sibling aggression (e.g., physical assault, taking something away from the child, breaking the child's toys on purpose, calling names). They also measured mental health using a trauma symptom checklist, on which high scores indicate the child has more symptoms of anxiety, depression, and other signs of mental disturbances. The researchers also measured parents' education, child's age, and so on. The regression table in **Table 9.6** comes from their article.

a. What is the criterion (dependent) variable in this study, and where do you find it?

b. How many predictor variables are there in this study?

c. Write a sentence that describes what the beta for the "Total types of sibling victimization" predictor means. (Use the sentences in Table 9.2 as a model.)

d. Write a sentence that describes what the beta for the "Total types of peer victimization" predictor variable means.

TABLE 9.6

Multiple Regression Predicting Children's and Adolescents' Mental Health

PREDICTOR VARIABLE	CRITERION VARIABLE: TRAUMA SYMPTOM CHECKLIST SCORE β
Parent education: some college	−0.02
College degree or more	−0.04
Ethnicity	
Black	−0.05[b]
Hispanic, any race	−0.01
Other or mixed	−0.00
Language of interview in Spanish	−0.01
Child age 10 plus	−0.13[a]
Child gender male	0.00
Child maltreatment	0.15[a]
Sexual victimization	0.06[b]
School victimization	0.05[c]
Internet victimization	0.02
Witness family violence	0.17[a]
Witness community violence	0.07[a]
Total types of sibling victimization	0.15[a]
Total types of peer victimization	0.25[a]
Total sibling × peer types of victimization	−0.02
R^2	0.27

[a] $p < .001$.
[b] $p < .01$.
[c] $p < .05$.
Source: Tucker et al., 2013.

e. Write a sentence that describes what the beta for the "Child maltreatment" predictor variable means.

f. Write a sentence that describes what the beta for the "Internet victimization" predictor means.

g. Using the magnitude of the betas to decide, which of the predictors is most strongly associated with poor childhood mental health? What about the researchers' initial question: Is sibling victimization just as bad for kids as peer victimization?

within groups design

repeated measures

concurrent

Independent groups design

pre-test/ post-test

post-test only

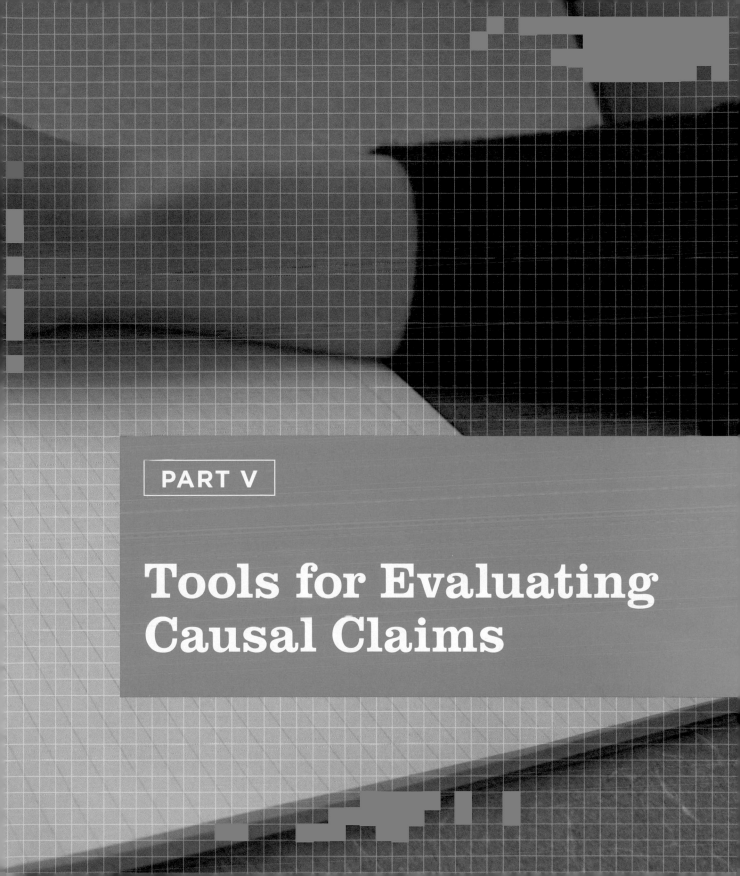

PART V

Tools for Evaluating Causal Claims

Serving Food on a Larger Plate "Makes People Eat More"

Independent, 2015

10

Introduction to Simple Experiments

A CAUSAL CLAIM IS the boldest kind of claim a scientist can make. A causal claim replaces verb phrases such as *related to, is associated with,* or *linked to* with powerful verbs such as *makes, influences,* or *affects.* Causal claims are special: When researchers make a causal claim, they are also stating something about interventions and treatments. The advice to not take notes with a laptop is based on a causal inference: Taking notes on a laptop causes something negative. Similarly, if serving food in a larger bowl makes people eat more, then dieters can be advised to serve foods in smaller bowls or use smaller individual plates. Interventions are often the ultimate goal of scientific studies, and they must be based on sound experimental research. Experiments are the only way to investigate such causal issues.

TWO EXAMPLES OF SIMPLE EXPERIMENTS

Let's begin with two examples of experiments that supported valid causal claims. As you read the two studies, consider how each one differs from the bivariate correlational studies in Chapter 8. What makes each of these studies an experiment? How does the experimental design allow the researchers to support a causal claim rather than an association claim?

Example 1: Taking Notes

Do you bring a pen to class for taking notes on what your professor is saying? Or do you open your laptop and type? If you're like most students, you use the note-taking habit you think works for you. But should you trust your own experience? Maybe one way of taking notes is actually better than the other (**Figure 10.1**).

Researchers Pam Mueller and Daniel Oppenheimer (2014) decided to conduct an experiment that compared the two practices. When they considered the processes involved, both approaches seemed to have advantages. When typing on a laptop, they reasoned, students can easily transcribe the exact words and phrases a professor is saying, resulting in seemingly more complete notes. However, students might not have to think about the material when they're typing. When taking handwritten notes, in contrast, students can summarize, paraphrase, or make drawings to connect ideas—even if fewer words are used than on a computer. Longhand notes could result in deeper processing of the material and more effective comprehension. Which way would be better?

Sixty-seven college students were recruited to come a laboratory classroom, usually in pairs. The classroom was prepared in advance: Half the time it contained laptops; the other half, notebooks and pens. Having selected five different TED talks on interesting topics, the researchers showed one of the lectures on a video screen. They told the students to take notes on the lectures using their assigned method (Mueller & Oppenheimer, 2014). After the lecture, students spent 30 minutes doing another activity meant to distract them from thinking about the lecture. Then they were tested on what they had learned from the TED talk.

FIGURE 10.1
Take note.

Which form of notetaking would lead to better learning?

The essay questions asked about straightforward factual information (e.g., "Approximately how many years ago did the Indus civilization exist?") as well as conceptual information (e.g., "How do Japan and Sweden differ in their approaches to equality in their societies?"). Their answers were scored by a research assistant who did not know which form of taking notes each participant had used.

The results Mueller and Oppenheimer obtained are shown in **Figure 10.2**. Students in both the laptop and the longhand groups scored about equally on the factual questions, but the longhand group scored higher on the conceptual questions.

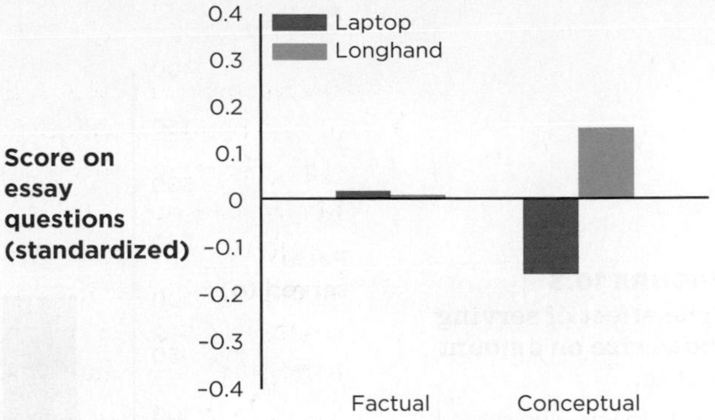

Mueller and Oppenheimer didn't stop at just one study. They wanted to demonstrate that the original result could happen again. Their journal article reports two other studies, each of which compared longhand to laptop notetaking, and each of which showed the same effect: The longhand group performed better on conceptual test questions. (The two other studies, unlike the first, showed that longhand notetakers did better on factual questions, too.) The authors made a causal claim: Taking notes in longhand *causes* students to do better. Do you think their study supports the causal claim?

FIGURE 10.2
The effect of laptop and longhand notetaking on test performance.

In this study, performance on factual questions was the same in the laptop and longhand groups, but performance on conceptual questions was better for those who took handwritten notes. (Source: Adapted from Mueller & Oppenheimer, 2014.)

Example 2: Eating Pasta

An article with this headline—"Serving food on a larger plate makes people eat more"—summarized studies on plate size and eating patterns. One such study was conducted at Cornell University's Food and Brand Lab, by researchers Ellen van Kleef, Mitsuru Shimizu, and Brian Wansink (2012). They invited 68 college students to come to a kitchen laboratory during the lunch hour, where they participated in smaller groups.

Behind the scenes, the researchers had assigned the students to one of two experimental sessions by flipping a coin. Half were assigned to a "large bowl" session and half were assigned to a "medium bowl" session. They were invited to serve themselves pasta from a bowl at the buffet. The bowl was continually refilled when about half the pasta was gone, so nobody felt the food was getting scarce. After they filled their plates, a research assistant weighed the plates to measure the amount they took. Participants were allowed to eat their pasta lunches at a comfortable pace. When they were finished, the assistants weighed each plate again, to determine how much food each person had actually eaten.

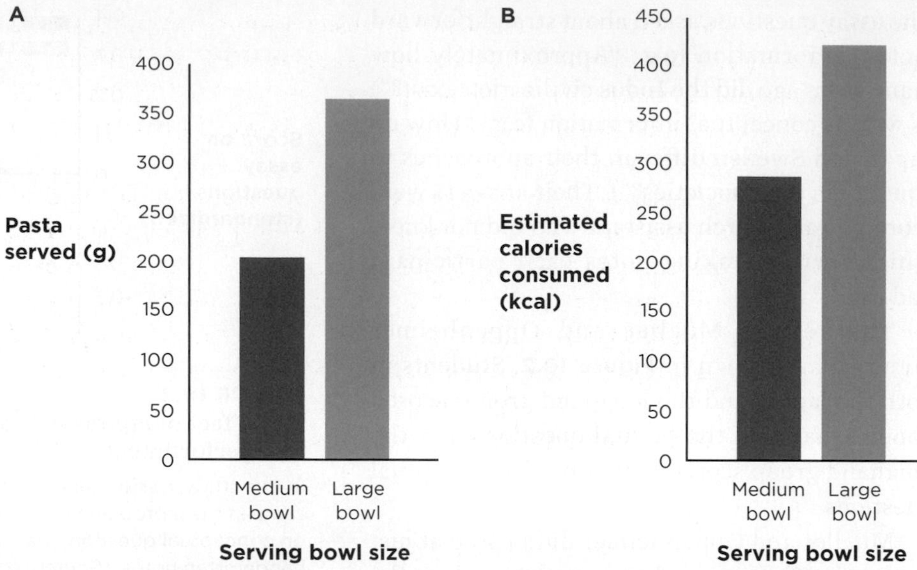

FIGURE 10.3
The effect of serving bowl size on amount eaten.

Participants who served themselves from a large bowl took more and ate more, compared to those who served themselves from a medium bowl. (Source: Adapted from van Kleef et al., 2012.)

The results are shown in **Figure 10.3**. On average, the participants took more pasta from the large serving bowl than the medium one (Figure 10.3A). When the researchers converted the amount of consumed pasta into calories, it was clear that the large-bowl participants had eaten about 140 calories more than the medium-bowl ones (Figure 10.3B). The researchers used causal language in their article's conclusion: "The size of the serving bowl had a substantial influence" on the amount of food people ate (van Kleef et al., 2012, p. 70).

EXPERIMENTAL VARIABLES

The word *experiment* is common in everyday use. Colloquially, "to experiment" means to try something out. A cook might say he experimented with a recipe by replacing the eggs with applesauce. A friend might say she experimented with a different driving route to the beach. In psychological science, the term **experiment** specifically means that the researchers manipulated at least one variable and measured another (as you learned in Chapter 3). Experiments can take place in a laboratory and just about anywhere else: movie theaters, conference halls, zoos, daycare centers, and even online environments—anywhere a researcher can manipulate one variable and measure another.

A **manipulated variable** is a variable that is controlled, such as when the researchers assign participants to a particular level (value) of the variable. For example, Mueller and Oppenheimer (2014) manipulated notetaking by flipping a coin to determine whether a person would take notes with a laptop or in longhand. (In other words, the participants did not get to choose which form they would use.) Notetaking method was a variable because it had more than one level (laptop and longhand), and it was a manipulated variable because the experimenter assigned each participant to a particular level. The van Kleef team (2012) similarly manipulated the size of the pasta serving bowl by flipping a coin ahead of time to decide which session participants were in. (Participants did not choose the bowl size from which they would serve themselves.)

Measured variables take the form of records of behavior or attitudes, such as self-reports, behavioral observations, or physiological measures (see Chapter 5). After an experimental situation is set up, the researchers simply record what happens. In their first study, Mueller and Oppenheimer measured student performance on the essay questions. After manipulating the notetaking method, they watched and recorded—that is, they measured—how well people answered the factual and conceptual questions. The van Kleef team manipulated the serving bowl size, and then measured two variables: how much pasta people took and how much they ate.

Independent and Dependent Variables

In an experiment, the manipulated (causal) variable is the **independent variable**. The name comes from the fact that the researcher has some "independence" in assigning people to different levels of this variable. A study's independent variable should not be confused with its levels, which are also referred to as **conditions**. The independent variable in the van Kleef study was serving bowl size, which had two conditions: medium and large.

The measured variable is the **dependent variable**, or *outcome variable*. How a participant acts on the measured variable *depends* on the level of the independent variable. Researchers have less control over the dependent variable; they manipulate the independent variable and then watch what happens to people's self-reports, behaviors, or physiological responses. A dependent variable is not the same as its levels, either. The dependent variable in the van Kleef study was the amount of pasta eaten (not "200 calories").

Experiments must have at least one independent variable and one dependent variable, but they often have more than one dependent variable. For example, the notetaking study had two dependent variables: performance on factual questions and performance on conceptual questions. Similarly, the pasta bowl study's dependent variables were the grams of pasta taken from the bowl and the calories of pasta consumed. When the dependent variables are measured on different scales (e.g., grams and calories), they are usually presented on separate graphs (see Figure 10.3). (Chapter 12 introduces experiments that have more than one independent variable.)

Here's a way to tell the two kinds of variables apart. When researchers graph their results, the independent variable is almost always on the x-axis, and the dependent variable is almost always on the y-axis (see Figures 10.2 and 10.3 for examples). A mnemonic for remembering the two types of variables is that the independent variable comes first in time (and the letter I looks like the number 1), and the dependent variable is measured afterward (or second).

Control Variables

When researchers are manipulating an independent variable, they need to make sure they are varying only one thing at a time—the potential causal force or proposed "active ingredient" (e.g., only the form of notetaking, or only the size of the serving bowl). Therefore, besides the independent variable, researchers also control potential third variables (or nuisance variables) in their studies by holding all other factors constant between the levels of the independent variable. For example, Mueller and Oppenheimer (2014) manipulated the method people used to take notes, but they held constant a number of other potential variables: People in both groups watched lectures in the same room and had the same experimenter. They watched the same videos and answered the same questions about them, and so on. Any variable that an experimenter holds constant on purpose is called a **control variable**.

In the van Kleef et al. study (2012), one control variable was the quality of the food: It was always the same kind of pasta. The researchers also controlled the size of the serving spoon and the size of the plates (each participant served pasta onto a 9-inch plate).

Control variables are not really variables at all because they do not vary; experimenters keep the levels the same for all participants. Clearly, control variables are essential in experiments. They allow researchers to separate one potential cause from another and thus eliminate alternative explanations for results. Control variables are therefore important for establishing internal validity.

CHECK YOUR UNDERSTANDING

1. What are the minimum requirements for a study to be an experiment?

2. Define independent variable, dependent variable, and control variable, using your own words.

1. A manipulated variable and a measured variable; see p. 276. 2. See pp. 276–278.

WHY EXPERIMENTS SUPPORT CAUSAL CLAIMS

In both of the examples above, the researchers manipulated one variable and measured another, so both studies can be considered experiments. But are these researchers really justified in making causal claims on the basis of these experiments? Yes. To understand how experiments support causal claims, you can first apply the three rules for causation to the pasta bowl study. The three rules should be familiar to you by now:

1. *Covariance.* Do the results show that the causal variable is related to the effect variable? Are distinct levels of the independent variable associated with different levels of the dependent variable?
2. *Temporal precedence.* Does the study design ensure that the causal variable comes before the outcome variable in time?
3. *Internal validity.* Does the study design rule out alternative explanations for the results?

Experiments Establish Covariance

The results of the experiment by van Kleef and her colleagues did show covariance between the causal (independent) variable (size of bowl) and the outcome (dependent) variable (amount of pasta eaten). On average, students who were in the large-bowl condition ate 425 calories worth of pasta, and students in the medium-bowl condition ate 283 calories (see Figure 10.3). In this case, covariance is indicated by a *difference* in the group means: The large-bowl calories were different from the medium-bowl calories. The notetaking study's results also showed covariance, at least for conceptual questions: Longhand notetakers had higher scores on conceptual questions than laptop notetakers.

INDEPENDENT VARIABLES ANSWER "COMPARED TO WHAT?"

The covariance criterion might seem obvious. In our everyday reasoning, though, we tend to ignore its importance because most of our personal experiences do not have the benefit of a **comparison group**, or *comparison condition*. For instance, you might suspect that your mom's giant pasta bowl is making you eat too much, but without a comparison bowl, you cannot know for sure. An experiment, in contrast, provides the comparison group you need. Therefore, an experiment is a better source of information than your own experience because an experiment allows you to ask and answer: Compared to what? (For a review of experience versus empiricism, see Chapter 2.)

If independent variables did not vary, a study could not establish covariance. For example, in Chapter 1, you read about a non-peer-reviewed study that concluded dogs don't like being hugged (Coren, 2016). Having collected Internet photos of people hugging their dogs, the researchers reported that 82% of the dogs showed signs of stress. However, this study did not have a comparison group: There were no photos of dogs *not* being hugged. Therefore, we cannot know, based on this study, if signs of stress are actually higher in hugged dogs than not-hugged dogs. In contrast, true experiments manipulate an independent variable. Because every independent variable has at least two levels, true experiments are always set up to look for covariance.

COVARIANCE: IT'S ALSO ABOUT THE RESULTS

Manipulating the independent (causal) variable is necessary for establishing covariance, but the results matter, too. Suppose the van Kleef researchers had found no difference in how much pasta people consumed in the two groups. In that case, the study would have found no covariance, and the experimenters would have had to conclude that serving bowl size does not cause people to eat more pasta. After all, if pasta consumption does not vary with serving bowl size, there is no causal impact to explain.

CONTROL GROUPS, TREATMENT GROUPS, AND COMPARISON GROUPS

There are a couple of ways an independent variable might be designed to show covariance. Your early science classes may have emphasized the importance of a control group in an experiment. A **control group** is a level of an independent variable that is intended to represent "no treatment" or a neutral condition. When a study has a control group, the other level or levels of the independent variable are usually called the **treatment group(s)**. For example, if an experiment is testing the effectiveness of a new medication, the researchers might assign some participants to take the medication (the treatment group) and other participants to take an inert sugar pill (the control group). When the control group is exposed to an inert treatment such as a sugar pill, it is called a **placebo group**, or a *placebo control group*.

» For more details on the placebo effect and how researchers control for it, see Chapter 11, pp. 323–325.

Not every experiment has—or needs—a control group, and often, a clear control group does not even exist. The Mueller and Oppenheimer notetaking study (2014) had two comparison groups—laptop and longhand—but neither was a control group, in the sense that neither of them clearly established a "no notetaking" condition. The van Kleef pasta eating study (2012) did not have a true control group either; the researchers simply used two different serving bowl sizes.

Also consider the experiment by Harry Harlow (1958), discussed in Chapter 1, in which baby monkeys were put in cages with artificial "mothers" made of either cold wire or warm cloth. There was no control group, just a carefully designed comparison condition. When a study uses comparison groups, the levels of the independent variable differ in some intended and meaningful way. All experiments need a comparison group so the researchers can compare one condition to another, but the comparison group does not need to be a control group.

Experiments Establish Temporal Precedence

The experiment by van Kleef's team also established temporal precedence. The experimenters manipulated the causal (independent) variable (serving bowl size) to ensure that it came first in time. Then the students picked up the spoon to serve their own pasta. The causal variable clearly did come before the outcome (dependent) variable. This ability to establish temporal precedence, by controlling which variable comes first, is a strong advantage of experimental designs. By manipulating the independent variable, the experimenter virtually ensures that the cause comes before the effect (or outcome).

The ability to establish temporal precedence is a feature that makes experiments superior to correlational designs. A simple correlational study is a snapshot—all variables are measured at the same time, so when two variables covary (such as multitasking frequency and multitasking ability, or deep conversations and well-being), it's impossible to tell which variable came first. In contrast, experiments unfold over time, and the experimenter makes sure the independent variable comes first.

Well-Designed Experiments Establish Internal Validity

Did the van Kleef study establish internal validity? Are there any alternative explanations for why people in the large-bowl condition took more pasta than people in the medium-bowl condition?

A well-designed experiment establishes internal validity, which is one of the most important validities to interrogate when you encounter causal claims. To be internally valid, a study must ensure that the causal variable (the active ingredient), and not other factors, is responsible for the change in the outcome variable. You can interrogate internal validity by exploring potential alternative explanations. For example, you might ask whether the participants in the large-bowl group were served tastier-looking pasta than those in the medium-bowl group. If so, the quality of the pasta would be an alternative explanation for why people took more. However, the researchers put the same type of pasta in both serving bowls (**Figure 10.4**). In fact, the quality of the pasta was a control variable: It was held constant for all participants, for just this reason.

You might be wondering whether the experimenters treated the large-bowl group differently than the other group. Maybe the research assistants acted in a more generous or welcoming fashion with participants in the large-bowl group than the medium-bowl group. That would have been another threat to internal validity, so it's important to know whether the assistants knew the hypothesis of the study.

For any given research question, there can be several possible alternative explanations, which are known as **confounds**, or potential threats to internal validity. The word *confound* can mean "confuse": When a study has a confound, you are confused about what is causing the change in the dependent variable. Is it the intended causal variable (such as bowl size)? Or is there some alternative explanation (such as the generous attitude of the research assistants)? Internal validity is subject to a number of distinct threats, three of which

»
For a discussion about how researchers use blind and double-blind designs to control internal validity, see Chapter 11, p. 323.

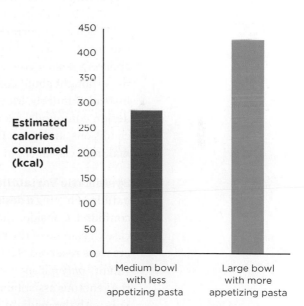

FIGURE 10.4

A threat to internal validity.

If the pasta in the large bowl had been more appetizing than the pasta in the medium bowl, that would have been an internal validity problem in this study. (Study design is fabricated for illustration purposes.)

are discussed in this chapter. Design confounds and selection effects are described next, and order effects are described in a later section. The rest are covered in Chapter 11. As experimenters design and interpret studies, they keep these threats to internal validity in mind and try to avoid them.

DESIGN CONFOUNDS

A **design confound** is an experimenter's mistake in designing the independent variable; it is a second variable that happens to vary systematically along with the intended independent variable and therefore is an alternative explanation for the results. As such, a design confound is a classic threat to internal validity. If the van Kleef team had accidentally served a more appetizing pasta in the large bowl than the medium bowl, the study would have a design confound because the second variable (pasta quality) would have systematically varied along with the independent variable. If the research assistants had treated the large-bowl group with a more generous attitude, the treatment of each participant would have been a design confound, too.

Consider the study on notetaking. If all of the students in the laptop group had to answer more difficult essay questions than the longhand group, that would be a design confound. We would not know whether the difference in conceptual performance was caused by the question difficulty or the notetaking method. However, the researchers did not make this error; they gave the same questions to all participants, no matter what notetaking condition they were in, so there would be no systematic differences between the groups.

When an experiment has a design confound, it has poor internal validity and cannot support a causal claim. Because the van Kleef study did not have any apparent design confounds, its internal validity is sound. The researchers carefully thought about confounds in advance and turned them into control variables instead. Similarly, Mueller and Oppenheimer controlled for a number of potential design confounds, such as question difficulty, experimenter expectations, room conditions, and so on. In both cases, the researchers took steps to help them justify making a causal claim.

Systematic Variability Is the Problem. You need to be careful before accusing a study of having a design confound. Not every potentially problematic variable is a confound. Consider the example of the pasta bowl experimenters. It might be the case that some of the research assistants were generous and welcoming, and others were reserved. The attitude of the research assistants is a problem for internal validity *only if* it shows **systematic variability** with the independent variable. Did the generous assistants work only with the large-bowl group and the reserved ones only with the medium-bowl group? Then it would be a design confound. However, if the research assistants' demeanor showed **unsystematic variability** (random or haphazard) across both groups, then their attitude would not be a confound.

Here's another example. Perhaps some of the participants in the notetaking study were interested in the video lectures and others were not. This variability in interest would not be a design confound unless it varied systematically with the notetaking condition to which they were assigned. If those in the longhand group all happened to be very interested in the lectures and those in the laptop group were all uninterested, that would vary systematically with the notetaking condition—and would be a confound. But if some participants in each condition were interested and some were not, that would be unsystematic variability and would not be a confound.

Unsystematic variability can lead to other problems in an experiment. Specifically, it can obscure, or make it difficult to detect differences in, the dependent variable, as discussed fully in Chapter 11. However, unsystematic variability should not be called a design confound (**Figure 10.5**).

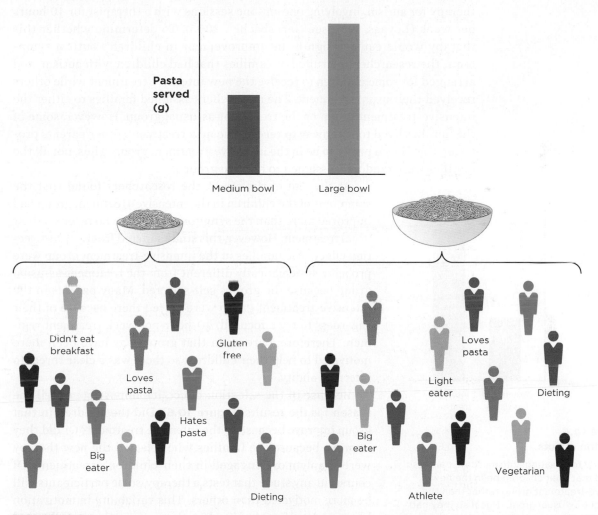

FIGURE 10.5
Unsystematic variability is not the same as a confound.

Some people eat more than others, some like pasta more than others, and some eat breakfast while others do not. But individual differences don't become a confound unless one type of people end up in one group systematically more than another group. If individual differences are distributed evenly in both groups, they are not a confound.

SELECTION EFFECTS

In an experiment, when the kinds of participants in one level of the independent variable are systematically different from those in the other, **selection effects** can result. They can also happen when the experimenters let participants choose (select) which group they want to be in. A selection effect may result if the experimenters assign one type of person (e.g., all the women, or all who sign up early in the semester) to one condition, and another type of person (e.g., all the men, or all those who wait until later in the semester) to another condition.

Here's a real-world example. A study was designed to test a new intensive therapy for autism, involving one-on-one sessions with a therapist for 40 hours per week (Lovaas, 1987; see Gernsbacher, 2003). To determine whether this therapy would cause a significant improvement in children's autism symptoms, the researchers recruited 38 families that had children with autism, and arranged for some children to receive the new intensive treatment while others received their usual treatment. The researchers assigned families to either the intensive-treatment group or the treatment-as-usual group. However, some of the families lived too far away to receive the new treatment; other parents protested that they'd prefer to be in the intensive-treatment group. Thus, not all the families were randomly assigned to the two groups.

At the end of the study, the researchers found that the symptoms of the children in the intensive-treatment group had improved more than the symptoms of those who received their usual treatment. However, this study suffered from a clear selection effect: The families in the intensive-treatment group were probably systematically different from the treatment-as-usual group because the groups self-selected. Many parents in the intensive-treatment group were placed there because of their eagerness to try a focused, 40-hour-per-week treatment regimen. Therefore, parents in that group may have been more motivated to help their children, so there was a clear threat to internal validity.

Because of the selection effect, it's impossible to tell the reason for the results (**Figure 10.6**). Did the children in that group improve because of the intensive treatment? Or did they improve because the families who selected the new therapy were simply more engaged in their children's treatment? Of course, in any study that tests a therapy, some participants will be more motivated than others. This variability in motivation becomes a confound only when the more motivated folks tend to be in one group—that is, when the variability is systematic.

Avoiding Selection Effects with Random Assignment. Well-designed experiments often use **random assignment** to

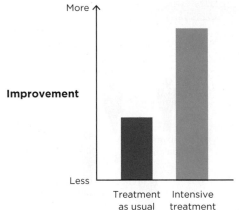

FIGURE 10.6
Selection effects.

In a study for treating autism, some parents insisted that their children be in the new intensive-treatment group rather than the treatment-as-usual group. Because they had this choice, it's not possible to determine whether the improvement in the intensive group was caused by the treatment itself or by the fact that the more motivated parents chose it. (Data are fabricated for illustration purposes.)

avoid selection effects. In the pasta bowl study, an experimenter flipped a coin to decide which participants would be in each group, so each one had an *equal chance* of being in the large-bowl or medium-bowl condition. What does this mean? Suppose that, of the 68 participants who volunteered for the study, 20 were exceptionally hungry that day. Probabilistically speaking, the rolls of the die would have placed about 10 of the hungry people in the medium-bowl condition and about 10 in the large-bowl condition. Similarly, if 12 of the participants were dieting, random assignment would place about 6 of them in each group. In other words, since the researchers used random assignment, it's very unlikely, given the random (deliberately unsystematic) way people were assigned to each group, that all the hungry people, dieters, and so on would have been clustered in the same group.

Assigning participants at random to different levels of the independent variable—by flipping a coin, rolling a die, or using a random number generator—controls for all sorts of potential selection effects (**Figure 10.7**). Of course in practice, random assignment may not usually create numbers that are perfectly even. The 20 exceptionally hungry people may be distributed as 9 and 11, or 12 and 8, rather than exactly 10 and 10. However, random assignment almost always works. In fact, simulations have shown that random assignment creates similar groups up to 98% of the time, even when there are as few as 4 people in each group (Sawilowsky, 2005; Strube, 1991).

Random assignment is a way of desystematizing the types of participants who end up in each level of the independent variable. Of course, some people are more motivated than others; some are hungrier than others; some are more extroverted. Successful random assignment spreads these differences out more evenly. It creates a situation in which the experimental groups will become virtually equal, on average, before the independent variable is applied. After random assignment (and before manipulating the independent variable), researchers should be able

« To review the difference between random assignment and random sampling, see Chapter 7, pp. 190–191.

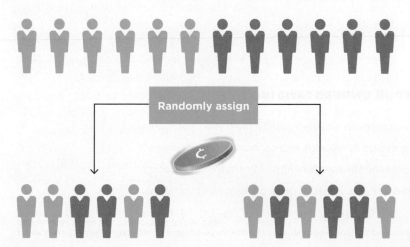

FIGURE 10.7
Random assignment.
Random assignment ensures that every participant in an experiment has an equal chance to be in each group.

Randomly assign

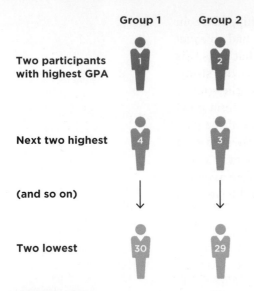

Group 1 **Group 2**

Two participants
with highest GPA

Next two highest

(and so on)

Two lowest

FIGURE 10.8
**Matching groups to eliminate
selection effects.**

To create matched groups, participants are
sorted from lowest to highest on some variable
and grouped into sets of two. Individuals within
each set are then assigned at random to the
two experimental groups.

to test the experimental groups for intelligence, extroversion, motivation, and so on, and averages of each group should be comparable on these traits.

Avoiding Selection Effects with Matched Groups. In the simplest type of random assignment, researchers assign participants at random to one condition or another in the experiment. In certain situations, researchers may wish to be absolutely sure the experimental groups are as equal as possible before they administer the independent variable. In these cases, they may choose to use **matched groups**, or *matching*.

To create matched groups from a sample of 30, the researchers would first measure the participants on a particular variable that might matter to the dependent variable. Student ability, operationalized by GPA, for instance, might matter in a study of notetaking. They would next match participants up in pairs, starting with the two having the highest GPAs, and *within that matched set*, randomly assign one of them to each of the two notetaking conditions. They would then take the pair with the next-highest GPAs and within that set again assign randomly to the two groups. They would continue this process until they reach the participants with the lowest GPAs and assign them at random, too (**Figure 10.8**).

Matching has the advantage of randomness. Because each member of the matched pair is randomly assigned, the technique prevents selection effects. This method also ensures that the groups are equal on some important variable, such as GPA, before the manipulation of the independent variable. The disadvantage is that the matching process requires an extra step—in this case, finding out people's GPA before assigning to groups. Matching, therefore, requires more time and often more resources than random assignment.

CHECK YOUR UNDERSTANDING

1. Why do experiments usually satisfy the three causal criteria?

2. How are design confounds and control variables related?

3. How does random assignment prevent selection effects?

4. How does using matched groups prevent selection effects?

INDEPENDENT-GROUPS DESIGNS

Although the minimum requirement for an experiment is that researchers manipulate one variable and measure another, experiments can take many forms. One of the most basic distinctions is between independent-groups designs and within-groups designs.

Independent-Groups vs. Within-Groups Designs

In the notetaking and pasta bowl studies, there were different participants at each level of the independent variable. In the notetaking study, some participants took notes on laptops and others took notes in longhand. In the pasta bowl study, some participants were in the large-bowl condition and others were in the medium-bowl condition. Both of these studies used an **independent-groups design**, in which different groups of participants are placed into different levels of the independent variable. This type of design is also called a *between-subjects design* or *between-groups design*.

In a **within-groups design**, or *within-subjects design*, there is only one group of participants, and each person is presented with *all* levels of the independent variable. For example, Mueller and Oppenheimer (2014) might have run their study as a within-groups design if they had asked each participant to take notes twice—once using a laptop and another time handwritten.

Two basic forms of independent-groups designs are the posttest-only design and the pretest/posttest design. The two types of designs are used in different situations.

Posttest-Only Design

The posttest-only design is one of the simplest independent-groups experimental designs. In the **posttest-only design**, also known as an *equivalent groups, posttest-only design*, participants are randomly assigned to independent variable groups and are tested on the dependent variable once (**Figure 10.9**).

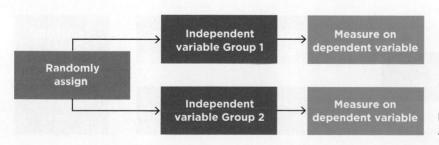

FIGURE 10.9
A posttest-only design.

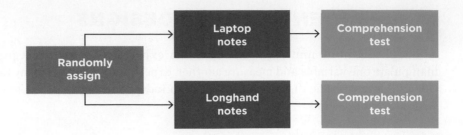

FIGURE 10.10
Studying notetaking:
a posttest-only design.

The notetaking study is an example of a posttest-only design, with two independent variable levels (Mueller & Oppenheimer, 2014). Participants were randomly assigned to a laptop condition or a longhand condition (**Figure 10.10**).

Posttest-only designs satisfy all three criteria for causation. They allow researchers to test for covariance by detecting differences in the dependent variable. (Having at least two groups makes it possible to do so.) They establish temporal precedence because the independent variable comes first in time. And when they are conducted well, they establish internal validity. When researchers use appropriate control variables, there should be no design confounds, and random assignment takes care of selection effects.

Pretest/Posttest Design

In a **pretest/posttest design**, or *equivalent groups, pretest/posttest design*, participants are randomly assigned to at least two different groups and are tested on the key dependent variable twice—once before and once after exposure to the independent variable (**Figure 10.11**).

A study on the effects of mindfulness training, introduced in Chapter 1, is an example of a pretest/posttest design. In this study, 48 students were randomly assigned to participate in either a 2-week mindfulness class or a 2-week nutrition class (Mrazek, Franklin, Phillips, Baird, & Schooler, 2013). One week before starting their respective classes, all students completed a verbal-reasoning section of a GRE test. One week after their classes ended, all students completed another verbal-reasoning GRE test of the same difficulty. The results, shown in

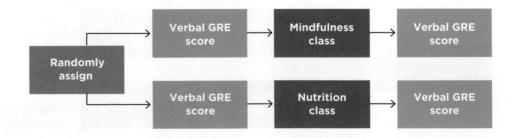

FIGURE 10.11
A pretest/posttest
design.

Figure 10.12, revealed that, while the nutrition group did not improve significantly from pretest to posttest, the mindfulness group scored significantly higher at posttest than at pretest.

Researchers might use a pretest/posttest design when they want to demonstrate that random assignment made groups equal. In this case, a pretest/posttest design means researchers can be absolutely sure there is no selection effect in a study. If you examine the white pretest bars in Figure 10.12, you'll see the nutrition and mindfulness groups had almost identical pretest scores, indicating that random assignment worked as expected.

In addition, pretest/posttest designs can enable researchers to track people's change in performance over time. Although the two groups started out, as expected, with about the same GRE ability, only the mindfulness group improved their GRE scores.

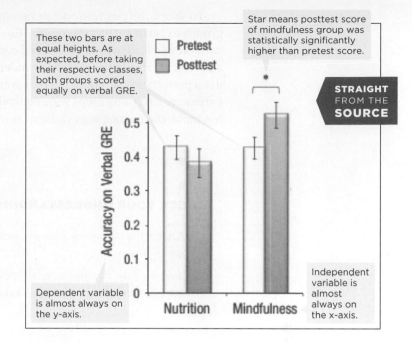

FIGURE 10.12
Results using a pretest/posttest design.

In this study, mindfulness training caused students to improve their GRE verbal scores. (Source: Mrazek et al., 2013, Fig. 1A.)

Which Design Is Better?

Why might researchers choose to do a posttest-only experiment rather than use a pretest/posttest design? Shouldn't they always make sure groups are equal on GRE ability or pasta appetite *before* they experience a manipulation? Not necessarily.

In some situations, it is problematic to use a pretest/posttest design. Imagine how the van Kleef team might have done this. Maybe they would want to pretest participants to see how much pasta they usually eat. But if they did that, people would have felt too full to participate in the rest of the study. Instead, the researchers trusted in random assignment to create equivalent groups. Big eaters and light eaters all had an equal chance of being in either one of the serving bowl groups, and if they were distributed evenly across both groups, their effects would cancel each other out. Therefore, any observed difference in overall eating behavior between these two groups should be attributable only to the two different bowl sizes. In other words, "being a big eater" could have been a selection effect, but random assignment helped avoid it.

In contrast, a pretest/posttest design made sense for the Mrazek team's study. They could justify giving their sample of students the GRE test two times because they had told participants they were studying ways of "improving cognitive performance."

In short, the posttest-only design may be the most basic type of independent-groups experiment, but its combination of random assignment plus a manipulated variable can lead to powerful causal conclusions. The pretest/posttest design adds a pretesting step to the most basic independent-groups design. Researchers might use a pretest/posttest design if they want to study improvement over time, or to be extra sure that two groups were equivalent at the start—as long as the pretest does not make the participants change their more spontaneous behavior.

CHECK YOUR UNDERSTANDING

1. What is the difference between independent-groups and within-groups designs?

2. Describe how posttest-only and pretest/posttest designs are both independent-groups designs. Explain how they differ.

1. See p. 287. 2. See pp. 287-289.

WITHIN-GROUPS DESIGNS

There are two basic types of within-groups design. When researchers expose participants to all levels of the independent variable, they might do so by repeated exposures, over time, to different levels, or they might do so concurrently.

Repeated-Measures Design

A **repeated-measures design** is a type of within-groups design in which participants are measured on a dependent variable more than once, after exposure to each level of the independent variable. Here's an example. Humans are social animals, and we know that many of our thoughts and behaviors are influenced by the presence of other people. Happy times may be happier, and sad times sadder, when experienced with others. Researchers Erica Boothby and her colleagues used a repeated-measures design to investigate whether a shared experience would be intensified even when people do not interact with the other person (Boothby, Clark, & Bargh, 2014). They hypothesized that sharing a good experience with another person makes it even better than it would have been if experienced alone.

They recruited 23 college women to a laboratory. Each participant was joined by a female confederate. The two sat side-by-side, facing forward, and never spoke to each other. The experimenter explained that each person in the pair

A

B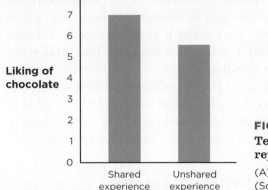

FIGURE 10.13

Testing the effect of sharing an experience using a repeated-measures design.

(A) The design of the study. (B) The results of the study. (Source: Adapted from Boothby et al., 2014.)

would do a variety of activities, including tasting some dark chocolates and viewing some paintings. During the experiment, the order of activities was determined by drawing cards. The drawings were rigged so that the real participant's first two activities were always tasting chocolates. In addition, the real participant tasted the first chocolate at the same time the confederate was also tasting it, but tasted the second chocolate while the confederate was viewing a painting. The participant was told that the two chocolates were different, but in fact they were exactly the same. After tasting each chocolate, participants rated how much they liked it. The results showed that people liked the chocolate more when the confederate was also tasting it (**Figure 10.13**).

In this study, the independent variable had two levels: Sharing and not sharing an experience. Participants experienced both levels, making it a within-groups design. The dependent variable was rating of the chocolate. It was a repeated-measures design because people rated the chocolate twice (i.e., repeatedly).

Concurrent-Measures Design

In a **concurrent-measures design**, participants are exposed to all the levels of an independent variable at roughly the same time, and a single attitudinal or behavioral preference is the dependent variable. An example is a study investigating infant cognition, in which infants were shown two faces at the same time, a male face and a female face; an experimenter recorded which face they looked at the longest (Quinn, Yahr, Kuhn, Slater, & Pascalis, 2002). The independent variable is the gender of the face, and babies experience both levels

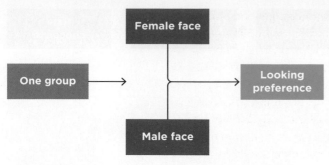

FIGURE 10.14
A concurrent-measures design for an infant cognition study.

Babies saw two faces simultaneously, and the experimenters recorded which face they looked at the most.

(male and female) at the same time. The baby's looking preference is the dependent variable (**Figure 10.14**). This study found that babies show a preference for looking at female faces, unless their primary caretaker is male.

Harlow also used a concurrent-measures design when he presented baby monkeys with both a wire and a cloth "mother" (Harlow, 1958). The monkeys indicated their preference by spending more time with one mother than the other. In Harlow's study, the type of mother was the independent variable (manipulated as within-groups), and each baby monkey's clinging behavior was the dependent variable.

Advantages of Within-Groups Designs

The main advantage of a within-groups design is that it ensures the participants in the two groups will be equivalent. After all, they are the same participants! For example, some people really like dark chocolate, and others do not. But in a repeated measures design, people bring their same level of chocolate affection to both conditions, so their individual liking for the chocolate stays the same. The only difference between the two conditions will be attributable to the independent variable (whether people were sharing the experience with the confederate or not). In a within-groups design such as the chocolate study, researchers say that each woman "acted as her own control" because individual or personal variables are kept constant.

Similarly, when the Quinn team (2002) studied whether infants prefer to look at male or female faces as a within-groups design, they did not have to worry (for instance) that all the girl babies would be in one group or the other, or that babies with older siblings or who go to daycare would be in one group or the other. Every baby saw both types of faces, which kept any extraneous personal variables constant across the two facial gender conditions.

» To review matched-groups design, see p. 286.

The idea of "treating each participant as his or her own control" also means matched-groups designs can be treated as within-groups designs. As discussed earlier, in a matched-groups design, researchers carefully match sets of participants on some key control variable (such as GPA) and assign each member of a set to a different group. The matched participants in the groups are assumed to be more similar to each other than in a more traditional independent-groups design, which uses random assignment.

Besides providing the ability to use each participant as his or her own control, within-groups designs also give researchers more power to notice differences between conditions. Statistically speaking, when extraneous differences (unsystematic variability) in personality, food preferences, gender, ability, and so on are held constant across all conditions, researchers will be more likely to detect an effect of the independent variable manipulation if there is one. In this context, the term **power** refers to the probability that a study will show a statistically significant result when an independent variable truly has an effect in the population. For example, if mindfulness training really does improve GRE scores, will the study's results find a difference? Maybe not. If extraneous differences exist between two groups, too much unsystematic variability may be obscuring a true difference. It's like being at a noisy party—your ability to detect somebody's words is hampered when many other conversations are going on around you.

«
For more on power, see Chapter 11, pp. 340–341, and Statistics Review: Inferential Statistics, pp. 487–490.

A within-groups design can also be attractive because it generally requires fewer participants overall. Suppose a team of researchers is running a study with two conditions. If they want 20 participants in each condition, they will need a total of 40 people for an independent-groups design. However, if they run the same study as a within-groups design, they will need only 20 participants because each participant experiences all levels of the independent variable (**Figure 10.15**). In this way, a repeated-measures design can be much more efficient.

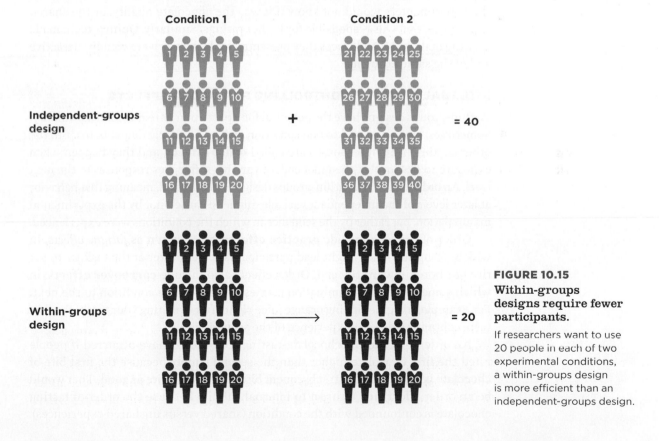

FIGURE 10.15
Within-groups designs require fewer participants.

If researchers want to use 20 people in each of two experimental conditions, a within-groups design is more efficient than an independent-groups design.

Covariance, Temporal Precedence, and Internal Validity in Within-Groups Designs

Do within-groups designs allow researchers to make causal claims? In other words, do they stand up to the three criteria for causation?

Because within-groups designs enable researchers to manipulate an independent variable and incorporate comparison conditions, they provide an opportunity for establishing covariance. The Boothby team (2014) observed, for example, that the chocolate ratings covaried with whether people shared the tasting experience or not.

A repeated-measures design also establishes temporal precedence. The experimenter controls the independent variable and can ensure that it comes first. In the chocolate study, each person tasted chocolate as either a shared or an unshared experience, *and then* rated the chocolate. In the infant cognition study, the researchers presented the faces first, *and then* measured looking time.

What about internal validity? With a within-groups design, researchers don't have to worry about selection effects because participants are exactly the same in the two conditions. They might be concerned about design confounds. For example, Boothby's team made sure both chocolates were exactly the same. If the chocolate that people tasted in the shared condition was of better quality, the experimenters would not know if it was the chocolate quality, or the shared experience, that was responsible for higher ratings. Similarly, Quinn's team made sure the male and female faces they presented to the babies were equally attractive and of the same ethnicity.

INTERNAL VALIDITY: CONTROLLING FOR ORDER EFFECTS

Within-groups designs have the potential for a particular threat to internal validity: Sometimes, being exposed to one condition changes how participants react to the other condition. Such responses are called **order effects**, and they happen when exposure to one level of the independent variable influences responses to the next level. An order effect in a within-groups design is a confound, meaning that behavior at later levels of the independent variable might be caused not by the experimental manipulation, but rather by the sequence in which the conditions were experienced.

Order effects can include **practice effects**, also known as *fatigue effects*, in which a long sequence might lead participants to get better at the task, or to get tired or bored toward the end. Order effects also include **carryover effects**, in which some form of contamination carries over from one condition to the next. For example, imagine sipping orange juice right after brushing your teeth; the first taste contaminates your experience of the second one.

An order effect in the chocolate-tasting study could have occurred if people rated the first chocolate higher than the second simply because the first bite of chocolate is always the best; subsequent bites are never quite as good. That would be an order effect, and a threat to internal validity because the order of tasting chocolate is confounded with the condition (shared versus unshared experiences).

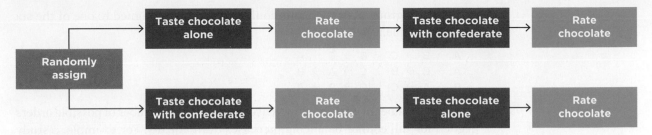

FIGURE 10.16
Counterbalanced design.

Using counterbalancing in an experiment will cancel out any order effects in a repeated-measures design.

AVOIDING ORDER EFFECTS BY COUNTERBALANCING

Because order effects are potential internal validity problems in a within-groups design, experimenters want to avoid them. When researchers use **counterbalancing**, they present the levels of the independent variable to participants in different sequences. With counterbalancing, any order effects should cancel each other out when all the data are collected.

Boothby and her colleagues (2014) used counterbalancing in their experiment (**Figure 10.16**). Half the participants tasted the first chocolate in the shared condition, followed by a second chocolate in the unshared condition. The other half tasted chocolate in the unshared followed by the shared condition. Therefore, the effect of "first taste of chocolate" was present for half of the people in each condition. When the data were combined from these two sequences, any order effect dropped out of the comparison between the shared and unshared conditions. As a result, the researchers knew that the difference they noticed was attributable only to the shared (versus unshared) experiences, and not to practice, carryover, or some other order effect.

Procedures Behind Counterbalancing. When researchers counterbalance conditions (or levels) in a within-groups design, they have to split their participants into groups; each group receives one of the condition sequences. How do the experimenters decide which participants receive the first order of presentation and which ones receive the second? Through random assignment, of course! They might recruit, say, 30 participants to a study and randomly assign 15 of them to receive the order A then B, and assign 15 of them to the order B then A.

There are two methods for counterbalancing an experiment: full and partial. When a within-groups experiment has only two or three levels of an independent variable, researchers can use **full counterbalancing**, in which all possible condition orders are represented. For example, a repeated-measures design with two conditions is easy to counterbalance because there are only two orders (A → B and B → A). In a repeated-measures design with three conditions—A, B, and C—each group of participants could be randomly assigned to one of the six following sequences:

$$A \rightarrow B \rightarrow C \qquad B \rightarrow C \rightarrow A$$
$$A \rightarrow C \rightarrow B \qquad C \rightarrow A \rightarrow B$$
$$B \rightarrow A \rightarrow C \qquad C \rightarrow B \rightarrow A$$

As the number of conditions increases, however, the number of possible orders needed for full counterbalancing increases dramatically. For example, a study with four conditions requires 24 possible sequences! If experimenters want to put at least a few participants in each order, the need for participants can quickly increase, counteracting the typical efficiency of a repeated-measures design. Therefore, they might use **partial counterbalancing**, in which only some of the possible condition orders are represented. One way to partially counterbalance is to present the conditions in a randomized order for every subject. (This is easy to do when an experiment is administered by a computer; the computer delivers conditions in a new random order for each participant.)

Another technique for partial counterbalancing is to use a **Latin square**, a formal system to ensure that every condition appears in each position at least once. A Latin square for six conditions (conditions 1 through 6) looks like this:

1	2	6	3	5	4
2	3	1	4	6	5
3	4	2	5	1	6
4	5	3	6	2	1
5	6	4	1	3	2
6	1	5	2	4	3

The first row is set up according to a formula, and then the conditions simply go in numerical order down each column. Latin squares work differently for odd and even numbers of conditions. If you wish to create your own, you can find formulas for setting up the first rows of a Latin square online.

Disadvantages of Within-Groups Designs

Within-groups designs are true experiments because they involve a manipulated variable and a measured variable. They potentially establish covariance, they ensure temporal precedence, and when experimenters control for order effects and design confounds, they can establish internal validity, too. So why wouldn't a researcher choose a within-groups design all the time?

Within-groups designs have three main disadvantages. First, as noted earlier, repeated-measures designs have the potential for order effects, which can threaten internal validity. But a researcher can usually control for order effects by using counterbalancing, so they may not be much of a concern.

A second possible disadvantage is that a within-groups design might not be possible or practical. Suppose someone has devised a new way of teaching children how to ride a bike, called Method A. She wants to compare Method A with the older method, Method B. Obviously, she cannot teach a group of children to ride a bike with

Method A and then return them to baseline and teach them again with Method B. Once taught, the children are permanently changed. In such a case, a within-groups design, with or without counterbalancing, would make no sense. The study on mindfulness training on GRE scores fits in this category. Once people had participated in mindfulness training, they presumably could apply their new skill indefinitely.

A third problem occurs when people see all levels of the independent variable and then change the way they would normally act. If participants in the van Kleef pasta bowl study had seen both the medium and large serving bowls (instead of just one or the other), they might have thought, "I know I'm participating in a study at the moment; seeing these two bowls makes me wonder whether it has something to do with serving bowl size." As a result, they might have changed their spontaneous behavior. A cue that can lead participants to guess an experiment's hypothesis is known as a **demand characteristic**, or an *experimental demand*. Demand characteristics create an alternative explanation for a study's results. You would have to ask: Did the manipulation really work, or did the participants simply guess what the researchers expected them to do, and act accordingly?

Is Pretest/Posttest a Repeated-Measures Design?

You might wonder whether pretest/posttest independent-groups design should be considered a repeated-measures design. After all, in both designs, participants are tested on the dependent variable twice.

In a true repeated-measures design, however, participants are exposed to all levels of a meaningful independent variable, such as a shared or unshared experience, or the gender of the face they're looking at. The levels of such independent variables can also be counterbalanced. In contrast, in a pretest/posttest design, participants see only one level of the independent variable, not all levels (**Figure 10.17**).

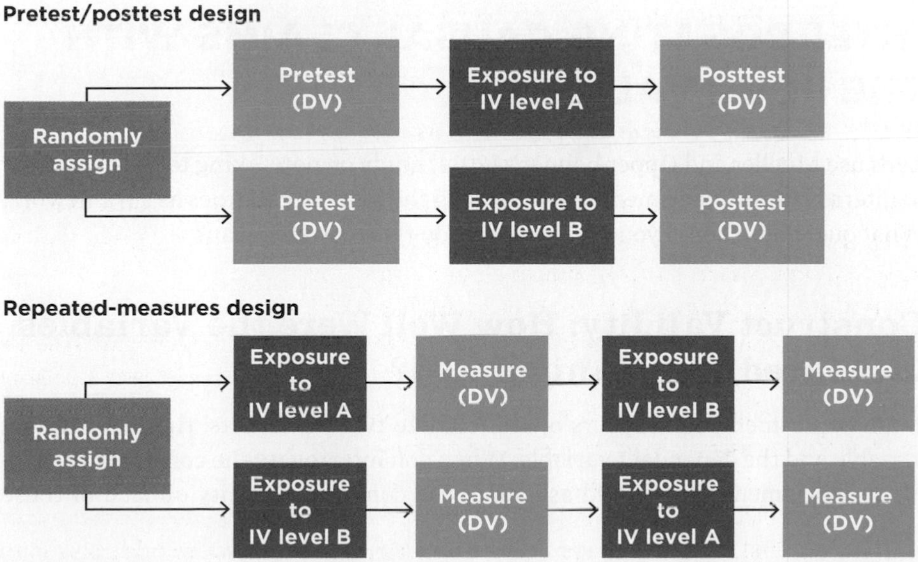

FIGURE 10.17
Pretest/posttest design versus repeated-measures design.

In a pretest/posttest design, participants see only one level of the independent variable, but in a repeated-measures design, they see all the levels.
(DV = dependent variable. IV = independent variable.)

Table 10.1 summarizes the four types of experimental designs covered in this chapter.

TABLE 10.1

Two Independent-Groups Designs and Two Within-Groups Designs

INDEPENDENT-GROUPS DESIGNS		WITHIN-GROUPS DESIGNS	
DIFFERENT PARTICIPANTS AT EACH LEVEL OF INDEPENDENT VARIABLE		SAME PARTICIPANTS SEE ALL LEVELS OF INDEPENDENT VARIABLE	
Posttest-only design	Pretest/posttest design	Concurrent-measures design	Repeated-measures design

CHECK YOUR UNDERSTANDING

1. What are the two basic types of within-groups design?

2. Describe how counterbalancing improves the internal validity of a within-groups design.

3. Summarize the three advantages and the three potential disadvantages of within-groups designs.

1. Concurrent measures and repeated measures; see pp. 290–292. 2. See pp. 295–296. 3. See pp. 292–293 and pp. 296–297.

INTERROGATING CAUSAL CLAIMS WITH THE FOUR VALIDITIES

Let's use Mueller and Oppenheimer's (2014) study on notetaking to illustrate how to interrogate an experimental design using the four big validities as a framework. What questions should you ask, and what do the answers mean?

Construct Validity: How Well Were the Variables Measured and Manipulated?

In an experiment, researchers operationalize two constructs: the independent variable and the dependent variable. When you interrogate the construct validity of an experiment, you should ask about the construct validity of each of these variables.

DEPENDENT VARIABLES: HOW WELL WERE THEY MEASURED?

Chapters 5 and 6 explained in detail how to interrogate the construct validity of a dependent (measured) variable. To interrogate construct validity in the notetaking study, you would start by asking how well the researchers measured their dependent variables: factual knowledge and conceptual knowledge.

One aspect of good measurement is face validity. Mueller and Oppenheim (2014) provided examples of the factual and conceptual questions they used, so you could examine these and evaluate if they actually do constitute good measures of factual learning (e.g., "What is the purpose of adding calcium propionate to bread?") and conceptual learning (e.g., "If a person's epiglottis was not working properly, what would be likely to happen?"). These two examples do seem to be appropriate types of questions because the first asks for direct recall of a lecture's factual information, and the second requires people to understand the epiglottis and make an inference. The researchers also noted that each of these open-ended questions was graded by two coders. The two sets of scores, they reported, showed good interrater reliability (.89). In this study, the strong interrater reliability indicates that the two coders agreed about which participants got the right answers and which ones did not. (To review interrater reliability, see Chapter 5.)

INDEPENDENT VARIABLES: HOW WELL WERE THEY MANIPULATED?

To interrogate the construct validity of the independent variables, you would ask how well the researchers manipulated (or operationalized) them. In the Mueller and Oppenheimer study, this was straightforward: People were given either a pen or a laptop. This operationalization clearly manipulated the intended independent variable.

Manipulation Checks and Pilot Studies. In other studies, researchers need to use manipulation checks to collect empirical data on the construct validity of their independent variables. A **manipulation check** is an extra dependent variable that researchers can insert into an experiment to convince them that their experimental manipulation worked.

A manipulation check was not necessary in the notetaking study because research assistants could simply observe participants to make sure they were actually using the laptops or pens they had been assigned. Manipulation checks are more likely to be used when the intention is to make participants think or feel certain ways. For example, researchers may want to manipulate feelings of anxiety by telling some students they have to give a public speech. Or they may wish to manipulate people's empathy by showing a poignant film. They may manipulate amusement by telling jokes. In these cases, a manipulation check can help researchers determine whether the operationalization worked as intended.

Here's an example. Researchers were interested in investigating whether humor would improve students' memory of a college lecture (Kaplan & Pascoe, 1977). Students were randomly assigned to listen to a serious lecture or one punctuated by humorous examples. To ensure they actually found the humorous lecture funnier than the serious one, students rated the lecture on how "funny" and "light" it was. These items were in addition to the key dependent variable, which was their memory for the material. As expected, the students in the humorous lecture condition rated the speaker as funnier and lighter than students in the serious lecture condition. The researchers concluded that the manipulation worked as expected.

The same procedure might also be used in a pilot study. A **pilot study** is a simple study, using a separate group of participants, that is completed before (or sometimes after) conducting the study of primary interest. Kaplan and Pascoe (1977) might have exposed a separate group of students to either a serious or a humorous lecture, and then asked them how amusing they found it. Researchers may use pilot study data to confirm the effectiveness of their manipulations before using them in a target study.

CONSTRUCT VALIDITY AND THEORY TESTING

Experiments are designed to test theories. Therefore, interrogating the construct validity of an experiment requires you to evaluate how well the measures and manipulations researchers used in their study capture the conceptual variables in their theory.

Recall that Mueller and Oppenheimer (2014) originally proposed that laptop notetaking would let students more easily take notes verbatim, compared to taking handwritten notes. In fact, their study included measures of "verbatim overlap" so they could test their theory about why laptop notetakers might perform worse. After transcribing each person's notes, they measured how closely the notes overlapped verbatim with the video lecture narration. It turned out that people in the laptop condition had, in fact, written more verbatim notes than people in the longhand condition. In addition, the more people wrote verbatim notes, the worse they did on the essay test. The researchers supported their theory by measuring key constructs that their theory proposed.

Here's another example of how theory guides the variables researchers manipulate and measure in an experiment. Recall that the chocolate-tasting study was designed to test the theory that sharing an experience makes it more intense (Boothby et al., 2014). In addition to showing that good-tasting chocolate tastes better when another person is tasting it, the researchers also needed to demonstrate the same effect in response to a negative experience. Using the same repeated-measures design, in a second study they used squares of 90% dark chocolate, containing almost no sugar, so it was bitter as opposed to the sweeter chocolate in the first study. People rated their liking for the bitter chocolate lower when the experience was shared, compared to unshared (**Figure 10.18**).

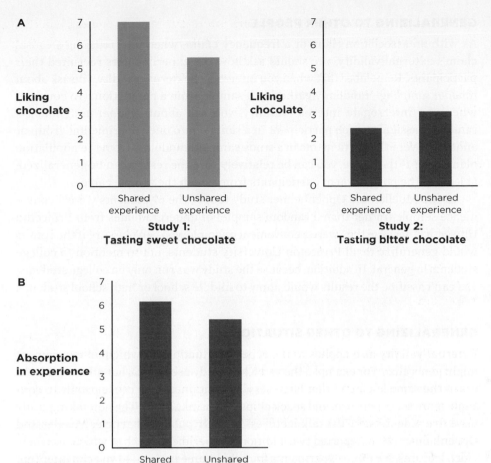

A

Liking chocolate

Study 1:
Tasting sweet chocolate

Shared experience | Unshared experience

Liking chocolate

Study 2:
Tasting bitter chocolate

Shared experience | Unshared experience

B

Absorption in experience

Study 2:
Tasting bitter chocolate

Shared experience | Unshared experience

FIGURE 10.18
Construct validity is theory-driven.
(A) When people tasted bitter chocolate in this study, they rated it more negatively when the experience was shared, compared to unshared. They also rated both of the bitter chocolates lower than the sweet chocolates in the first study, providing construct validity evidence that the experience in the second study was negative.
(B) People were more absorbed in the shared experience, evidence that the shared versus unshared experience was manipulated as intended. (Source: Adapted from Boothby et al., 2014.)

Two main results of the chocolate studies support their construct validity. (1) People in the first study rated the chocolate higher overall than those in the second study, which is what you'd expect if one was supposed to represent a positive experience and the other a negative experience. (2) People reported being more absorbed in the shared experience than the unshared one. This result supports the theory that shared experiences should be more intense (absorbing) than unshared ones.

External Validity: To Whom or What Can the Causal Claim Generalize?

Chapters 7 and 8 discussed external validity in the context of frequency claims and association claims. Interrogating external validity in the context of causal claims is similar. You ask whether the causal relationship can generalize to other people, places, and times. (Chapter 14 goes into even more detail about external validity questions.)

GENERALIZING TO OTHER PEOPLE

As with an association claim or a frequency claim, when interrogating a causal claim's external validity, you should ask how the experimenters recruited their participants. Remember that when you interrogate external validity, you ask about *random sampling*—randomly gathering a sample from a population. (In contrast, when you interrogate internal validity, you ask about *random assignment*— randomly assigning each participant in a sample into one experimental group or another.) Were the participants in a study sampled randomly from the population of interest? If they were, you can be relatively sure the results can be generalized, at least to the population of participants from which the sample came.

In the Mueller and Oppenheimer study (2014), the 67 students were a convenience sample (rather than a random sample) of undergraduates from Princeton University. Because they were a convenience sample, you can't be sure if the results would generalize to all Princeton University students, not to mention to college students in general. In addition, because the study was run only on college students, you can't assume the results would apply to middle school or high school students.

GENERALIZING TO OTHER SITUATIONS

External validity also applies to the types of situations to which an experiment might generalize. For example, the van Kleef study used pasta, but other researchers in the same lab found that large serving containers also cause people to consume more soup, popcorn, and snack chips (Wansink, 2006). The notetaking study used five videotaped TED talk lectures. In their published article, Mueller and Oppenheimer (2014) reported two additional experiments, each of which used new video lectures. All three experiments found the same pattern, so you can infer that the effect of laptop notetaking does generalize to other TED talks. However, you can't be sure from this study if laptop notetaking would generalize to a live lecture class. You also don't know if the effect of laptop notetaking would generalize to other kinds of college teaching, such as team-based learning or lab courses.

To decide whether an experiment's results can generalize to other situations, it is sometimes necessary to consider the results of other research. One experiment, conducted after Mueller and Oppenheimer's three studies, helped demonstrate that the laptop notetaking effect can generalize to live lecture classes (Carter, Greenberg, & Walker, 2016). College students at West Point were randomly assigned to their real, semester-long economics classes. There were 30 sections of the class, which all followed the same syllabus, used the same textbook, and gave almost the same exams. In 10 of the sections, students were not allowed to use laptops or tablets, and in another 10 sections, they were allowed to use them. In the last 10 sections, students could use tablets as long as they were kept flat on their desk during the class. The results indicated that students in the two computerized sections scored lower on exams than students in the computer-free classrooms. This study helps us generalize from Mueller and Oppenheimer's short-term lecture situation to a real, semester-long college class. Similarly, you might ask if

FIGURE 10.19
Generalizing to other situations.

The chocolate-tasting study showed that flavors are more intense when the experience is shared. A future study might explore whether the shared experiences effect generalizes to other situations, such as watching a happy or sad movie.

the hypothesis about shared experiences might generalize to other experiences besides tasting chocolate (**Figure 10.19**).

WHAT IF EXTERNAL VALIDITY IS POOR?

Should you be concerned that Mueller and Oppenheimer did not select their participants at random from the population of college students? Should you be concerned that all three of their studies used TED talks instead of other kinds of classroom material?

Remember from Chapter 3 that in an experiment, researchers usually prioritize experimental control—that is, internal validity. To get a clean, confound-free manipulation, they may have to conduct their study in an artificial environment like a university laboratory. Such locations may not represent situations in the real world. Although it's possible to achieve both internal and external validity in a single study, doing so can be difficult. Therefore, many experimenters decide to sacrifice real-world representativeness for internal validity.

«
For more discussion on prioritizing validities, see Chapter 14, pp. 438–452.

Testing their theory and teasing out the causal variable from potential confounds were the steps Mueller and Oppenheimer, like most experimenters, took care of first. In addition, running an experiment on a relatively homogenous sample (such as college students) meant that the unsystematic variability was less likely to obscure the effect of the independent variable (see Chapter 11). Replicating the study using several samples in a variety of contexts is a step saved for later. Although Mueller and Oppenheimer sampled only college students and ran their studies in a laboratory, at least one other study demonstrated that taking notes by computer can cause lower grades even in real, semester-long courses. Future researchers might also be interested in testing the effect of using laptops in younger students or for other subjects (such as psychology or literature courses). Such studies would demonstrate whether longhand notetaking is more effective than laptop notetaking for all subjects and for all types of students.

Statistical Validity: How Well Do the Data Support the Causal Claim?

For the present context, interrogating the statistical validity of an experiment involves two basic concerns: statistical significance and effect size. In your statistics class, you will learn how to ask other questions about experimental designs, such as whether the researchers conducted the right statistical tests.

IS THE DIFFERENCE STATISTICALLY SIGNIFICANT?

The first question to ask is whether the difference between means obtained in the study is statistically significant. Recall from Chapter 8 that when a result is statistically significant, it is unlikely to have been obtained by chance from a population in which nothing is happening. When the difference (say, between a laptop group and a longhand group) in a study is statistically significant, you can be more confident the difference is not a fluke result. In other words, a statistically significant result suggests covariance exists between the variables in the population from which the sample was drawn.

When the difference between conditions is not statistically significant, you cannot conclude there is covariance—that the independent variable had a detectable effect on the dependent variable. Any observed difference between the groups found in the study is similar to the kinds of differences you would find just by chance when there is no covariance. And if there is no covariance, the study does not support a causal claim.

HOW LARGE IS THE EFFECT?

Knowing a result is statistically significant tells you the result probably was not drawn by chance from a population in which there is no difference between groups. However, if a study used a very large sample, even tiny differences might be statistically significant. Therefore, asking about effect size can help you evaluate the strength of the covariance (i.e., the difference). In general, the larger the effect size, the more important, and the stronger, the causal effect. When a study's result is statistically significant, it is not necessarily the same as having a large effect size.

As discussed in Chapter 8, the correlation coefficient r can help researchers evaluate the effect size of an association. In experiments, they often use a different indicator of standardized effect size, called d. This measure represents how far apart two experimental groups are on the dependent variable. It indicates not only the distance between the means, but also how much the scores within the groups overlap. The standardized effect size, d, takes into account both the difference between means and the spread of scores within each group (the standard deviation). When d is larger, it usually means the independent variable caused the dependent variable to change for more of the participants in the study. When d is smaller, it usually means the scores of participants in the two experimental

» For more detail on standard deviation and effect size, see Statistics Review: Descriptive Statistics, pp. 462–465 and pp. 472–477.

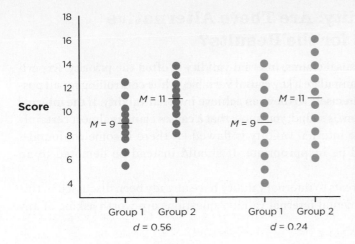

FIGURE 10.20
Effect size and overlap between groups.

Effect sizes are larger when the scores in the two experimental groups overlap less. Overlap is a function of how far apart the group means are, as well as how variable the scores are within each group. On both sides of the graph, the two group means (*M*) are the same distance apart (about 2 units), but the overlap of the scores between groups is greater in the blue scores on the right. Because there is more overlap between groups, the effect size is smaller.

groups overlap more. **Figure 10.20** shows what two *d* values might look like when a study's results are graphed showing all participants. Even though the difference between means is exactly the same in the two graphs, the effect sizes reflect the different degrees of overlap between the group participants.

In Mueller and Oppenheimer's first study (2014), the effect size for the difference in conceptual test question performance between the longhand and laptop groups was *d* = 0.77. **Table 10.2** shows how the conventions apply to *d* as well as *r*. According to these guidelines, a *d* of 0.77 would be considered fairly strong. It means the laptop group scored about 0.77 of a standard deviation higher than the longhand group. Therefore, if you were interrogating the statistical validity of Mueller and Oppenheimer's causal claim, you would conclude that the effect of the notetaking method on essay performance was strong, and you may be more convinced of the study's importance. By comparison, the effect size for the difference between the shared and unshared experience in the second, bitter chocolate study was *d* = 0.31. According to Cohen's guidelines, a *d* of 0.31 represents a small to moderate effect of shared experience on people's rating of a negative experience.

« For more questions to ask when interrogating statistical validity, such as whether the researchers used the appropriate tests or whether they made any inferential errors, see Statistics Review: Inferential Statistics, pp. 479–503.

TABLE 10.2

Cohen's Guidelines for Effect Size Strength

AN EFFECT SIZE IN WHICH *d* =	CAN BE DESCRIBED AS	AND IS COMPARABLE TO AN *r* OF
0.20	Small, or weak	.10
0.50	Medium, or moderate	.30
0.80	Large, or strong	.50

Internal Validity: Are There Alternative Explanations for the Results?

When interrogating causal claims, internal validity is often the priority. Experimenters isolate and manipulate a key causal variable, while controlling for all possible other variables, precisely so they can achieve internal validity. If the internal validity of an experiment is sound, you know that a causal claim is almost certainly appropriate. But if the internal validity is flawed—if there is some confound—a causal claim would be inappropriate. It should instead be demoted to an association claim.

Three potential threats to internal validity have already been discussed in this chapter. These fundamental internal validity questions are worth asking of any experiment:

1. Did the experimental design ensure that there were no design confounds, or did some other variable accidentally covary along with the intended independent variable? (Mueller and Oppenheimer made sure people in both groups saw the same video lectures, in the same room, and so on.)
2. If the experimenters used an independent-groups design, did they control for selection effects by using random assignment or matching? (Random assignment controlled for selection effects in the notetaking study.)
3. If the experimenters used a within-groups design, did they control for order effects by counterbalancing? (Counterbalancing is not relevant in Mueller and Oppenheimer's design because it was an independent-groups design.)

Chapter 11 goes into further detail on these threats to internal validity. In addition, nine more threats are covered.

CHECK YOUR UNDERSTANDING

1. How do manipulation checks provide evidence for the construct validity of an experiment's independent variable? Why does theory matter in evaluating construct validity?
2. Besides generalization to other people, what other aspect of generalization does external validity address?
3. What does it mean when an effect size is large (as opposed to small) in an experiment?
4. Summarize the three threats to internal validity discussed in this chapter.

1. See pp. 299–301. 2. Generalization to other situations; see pp. 302–303. 3. See pp. 304–305. 4. See p. 306.

CHAPTER REVIEW

Summary

Causal claims are special because they can lead to advice, treatments, and interventions. The only way to support a causal claim is to conduct a well-designed experiment.

Two Examples of Simple Experiments

- An experiment showed that taking notes on a laptop rather than in longhand caused students to do worse on a conceptual test of lecture material.
- An experiment showed that providing a large serving bowl caused people to serve themselves more pasta, and to eat more of it, than a medium serving bowl.

Experimental Variables

- Experiments study the effect of an independent (manipulated) variable on a dependent (measured) variable.
- Experiments deliberately keep all extraneous variables constant as control variables.

Why Experiments Support Causal Claims

- Experiments support causal claims because they potentially allow researchers to establish covariance, temporal precedence, and internal validity.
- The three potential internal validity threats covered in this chapter that researchers work to avoid are design confounds, selection effects, and order effects.

Independent-Groups Designs

- In an independent-groups design, different participants are exposed to each level of the independent variable.

- In a posttest-only design, participants are randomly assigned to one of at least two levels of an independent variable and then measured once on the dependent variable.
- In a pretest/posttest design, participants are randomly assigned to one of at least two levels of an independent variable, and are then measured on a dependent variable twice—once before and once after they experience the independent variable.
- Random assignment or matched groups can help establish internal validity in independent-groups designs by minimizing selection effects.

Within-Groups Designs

- In a within-groups design, the same participants are exposed to all levels of the independent variable.
- In a repeated-measures design, participants are tested on the dependent variable after each exposure to an independent variable condition.
- In a concurrent-measures design, participants are exposed to at least two levels of an independent variable at the same time, and then indicate a preference for one level (the dependent variable).
- Within-groups designs allow researchers to treat each participant as his or her own control, and require fewer participants than independent-groups designs. Within-groups designs also present the potential for order effects and demand characteristics.

Interrogating Causal Claims with the Four Validities

- Interrogating construct validity involves evaluating whether the variables were manipulated and measured in ways consistent with the theory behind the experiment.

- Interrogating external validity involves asking whether the experiment's results can be generalized to other people or to other situations and settings.

- Interrogating statistical validity starts by asking how strongly the independent variable covaries with the dependent variable (effect size), and whether the effect is statistically significant.

- Interrogating internal validity involves looking for design confounds and seeing whether the researchers used techniques such as random assignment and counterbalancing.

Key Terms

experiment, p. 276
manipulated variable, p. 276
measured variable, p. 277
independent variable, p. 277
condition, p. 277
dependent variable, p. 277
control variable, p. 278
comparison group, p. 279
control group, p. 280
treatment group, p. 280
placebo group, p. 280
confound, p. 281

design confound, p. 282
systematic variability, p. 282
unsystematic variability, p. 282
selection effect, p. 284
random assignment, p. 284
matched groups, p. 286
independent-groups design, p. 287
within-groups design, p. 287
posttest-only design, p. 287
pretest/posttest design, p. 288
repeated-measures design, p. 290
concurrent-measures design, p. 291

power, p. 293
order effect, p. 294
practice effect, p. 294
carryover effect, p. 294
counterbalancing, p. 295
full counterbalancing, p. 295
partial counterbalancing, p. 296
Latin square, p. 296
demand characteristic, p. 297
manipulation check, p. 299
pilot study, p. 300

 To see samples of chapter concepts in the popular media, visit www.everydayresearchmethods.com and click the box for Chapter 10.

Review Questions

Max ran an experiment in which he asked people to shake hands with an experimenter (played by a female friend) and rate the experimenter's friendliness using a self-report measure. The experimenter was always the same person, and used the same standard greeting for all participants. People were randomly assigned to shake hands with her either after she had cooled her hands under cold water or after she had warmed her hands under warm water. Max's results found that people rated the experimenter as more friendly when her hands were warm than when they were cold.

1. Why does Max's experiment satisfy the causal criterion of temporal precedence?

   a. Because Max found a difference in rated friendliness between the two conditions, cold hands and warm hands.

   b. Because the participants shook the experimenter's hand before rating her friendliness.

   c. Because the experimenter acted the same in all conditions, except having cold or warm hands.

   d. Because Max randomly assigned people to the warm hands or cold hands condition.

2. In Max's experiment, what was a control variable?

   a. The participants' rating of the friendliness of the experimenter.

   b. The temperature of the experimenter's hands (warm or cold).

   c. The gender of the students in the study.

   d. The standard greeting the experimenter used while shaking hands.

3. What type of design is Max's experiment?

    a. Posttest-only design

    b. Pretest/posttest design

    c. Concurrent-measures design

    d. Repeated-measures design

4. Max randomly assigned people to shake hands either with the "warm hands" experimenter or the "cold hands" experimenter. Why did he randomly assign participants?

    a. Because he had a within-groups design.

    b. Because he wanted to avoid selection effects.

    c. Because he wanted to avoid an order effect.

    d. Because he wanted to generalize the results to the population of students at his university.

5. Which of the following questions would be interrogating the construct validity of Max's experiment?

    a. How large is the effect size comparing the rated friendliness of the warm hands and cold hands conditions?

    b. How well did Max's "experimenter friendliness" rating capture participants' actual impressions of the experimenter?

    c. Were there any confounds in the experiment?

    d. Can we generalize the results from Max's friend to other experimenters with whom people might shake hands?

Learning Actively

1. Design a posttest-only experiment that would test each of the following causal claims. For each one, identify the study's independent variable(s), identify its dependent variable(s), and suggest some important control variables. Then, sketch a bar graph of the results you would predict (remember to put the dependent variable on the y-axis). Finally, apply the three causal criteria to each study.

    a. Having a friendly (versus a stern) teacher for a brief lesson causes children to score better on a test of material for that lesson.

    b. Practicing the piano for 30 minutes a day (compared with 10 minutes a day) causes new neural connections in the temporal region of the brain.

    c. Drinking sugared lemonade (compared to sugar-free lemonade) makes people better able to perform well on a task that requires self-control.

2. For each of the following independent variables, how would you design a manipulation that used an independent-groups design? How would you design a manipulation that used a within-groups design? Explain the advantages and disadvantages of manipulating each independent variable as independent-groups versus within-groups.

    a. Listening to a lesson from a friendly teacher versus a stern teacher.

    b. Practicing the piano for 30 minutes a day versus 10 minutes a day.

    c. Drinking sugared versus sugar-free lemonade.

3. To study people's willingness to help others, social psychologists Latané and Darley (1969) invited people to complete questionnaires in a lab room. After handing out the questionnaires, the female experimenter went next door and staged a loud accident: She pretended to fall off a chair and get hurt (she actually played an audio recording of this accident). Then the experimenters observed whether each participant stopped filling out the questionnaire and went to try to help the "victim."

    Behind the scenes, the experimenters had flipped a coin to assign participants randomly to either an "alone" group, in which they were in the questionnaire room by themselves, or a "passive confederate" group, in which they were in the questionnaire room with a confederate (an actor) who sat impassively during the "accident" and did not attempt to help the "victim."

    In the end, Latané and Darley found that when participants were alone, 70% reacted, but when participants were with a passive confederate, only 7% reacted. This experiment supported the researchers' theory that during an accident, people take cues from others, looking to others to decide how to interpret the situation.

    a. What are the independent, dependent, and control variables in this study?

    b. Sketch a graph of the results of this study.

    c. Is the independent variable in this study manipulated as independent-groups or as repeated-measures? How do you know?

    d. For this study, ask at least one question for each of the four validities.

"Was it really the therapy, or something else, that caused symptoms to improve?"

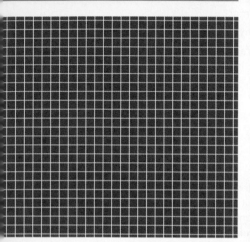

"How should we interpret a null result?"

11

More on Experiments: Confounding and Obscuring Variables

CHAPTER 10 COVERED THE basic structure of an experiment, and this chapter addresses a number of questions about experimental design. Why is it so important to use a comparison group? Why do many experimenters create a standardized, controlled, seemingly artificial environment? Why do they use so many (or so few) participants? Why do researchers often use computers to measure their variables? Why do they insist on double-blind study designs? For the clearest possible results, responsible researchers specifically design their experiments with many factors in mind. They want to detect differences that are really there, and they want to determine conclusively when their predictions are wrong.

The first main section describes potential internal validity problems and how researchers usually avoid them. The second main section discusses some of the reasons experiments may yield null results.

LEARNING OBJECTIVES

A year from now, you should still be able to:

1.
Interrogate a study and decide whether it rules out twelve potential threats to internal validity.

2.
Describe how researchers can design studies to prevent internal validity threats.

3.
Interrogate an experiment with a null result to decide whether the study design obscured an effect or whether there is truly no effect to find.

4.
Describe how researchers can design studies to minimize possible obscuring factors.

THREATS TO INTERNAL VALIDITY: DID THE INDEPENDENT VARIABLE REALLY CAUSE THE DIFFERENCE?

When you interrogate an experiment, internal validity is the priority. As discussed in Chapter 10, three possible threats to internal validity include design confounds, selection effects, and order effects. All three of these threats involve an alternative explanation for the results.

With a design confound, there is an alternative explanation because the experiment was poorly designed; another variable happened to vary systematically along with the intended independent variable. Chapter 10 presented the study on pasta serving bowl size and amount of pasta eaten. If the pasta served to the large-bowl group had looked more appetizing than the pasta served to the medium-bowl group, that would have been a design confound (see Figure 10.4). It would not be clear whether the bowl size or the appearance of the pasta caused the large-bowl group to take more.

With a selection effect, a confound exists because the different independent variable groups have systematically different types of participants. In Chapter 10, the example was a study of an intensive therapy for autism, in which children who received the intensive treatment did improve over time. However, we are not sure if their improvement was caused by the therapy or by greater overall involvement on the part of the parents who elected to be in the intensive-treatment group. Those parents' greater motivation could have been an alternative explanation for the improvement of children in the intensive-treatment group.

With an order effect (in a within-groups design), there is an alternative explanation because the outcome might be caused by the independent variable, but it also might be caused by the order in which the levels of the variable are presented. When there is an order effect, we do not know whether the independent variable is really having an effect, or whether the participants are just getting tired, bored, or well-practiced.

These types of threats are just the beginning. There are other ways—about twelve in total—in which a study might be at risk for a confound. Experimenters think about all of them, and they plan studies to avoid them. Normally, a well-designed experiment can prevent these threats and make strong causal statements.

The Really Bad Experiment (A Cautionary Tale)

Previous chapters have used examples of published studies to illustrate the material. In contrast, this chapter presents three fictional experiments. You will rarely encounter published studies like these because, unlike the designs in Chapter 10, the basic design behind these examples has so many internal validity problems.

Nikhil, a summer camp counselor and psychology major, has noticed that his current cabin of 15 boys is an especially rowdy bunch. He's heard a change in diet might help them calm down, so he eliminates the sugary snacks and desserts from their meals for 2 days. As he expected, the boys are much quieter and calmer by the end of the week, after refined sugar has been eliminated from their diets.

Dr. Yuki has recruited a sample of 40 depressed women, all of whom are interested in receiving psychotherapy to treat their depression. She measures their level of depression using a standard depression inventory at the start of therapy. For 12 weeks, all the women participate in Dr. Yuki's style of cognitive therapy. At the end of the 12-week session, she measures the women again and finds that on the whole, their levels of depression have significantly decreased.

A dormitory on a university campus has started a Go Green Facebook campaign, focused on persuading students to turn out the lights in their rooms when they're not needed. Dorm residents receive e-mails and messages on Facebook that encourage energy-saving behaviors. At the start of the campaign, the head resident noted how many kilowatt hours the dorm was using by checking the electric meters on the building. At the end of the 2-month campaign, the head resident checks the meters again and finds that the usage has dropped. He compares the two measures (pretest and posttest) and finds they are significantly different.

Notice that all three of these examples fit the same template, as shown in **Figure 11.1**. If you graphed the data of the first two studies, they would look something like the two graphs in **Figure 11.2**. Consider the three examples: What alternative explanations can you think of for the results of each one?

The formal name for this kind of design is the **one-group, pretest/posttest design**. A researcher recruits one group of participants, measures them on a pretest, exposes them to a treatment, intervention, or change, and then measures them on a posttest. This design differs from the true pretest/posttest design you learned in Chapter 10, because it has only one group, not two. There is no comparison group. Therefore, a better name for this design might be "the really bad experiment." Understanding why this design is problematic can help you learn about threats to internal validity and how to avoid them with better designs.

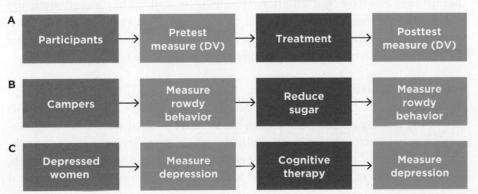

FIGURE 11.1
The really bad experiment.

(A) A general diagram of the really bad experiment, or the one-group, pretest/posttest design. Unlike the pretest/posttest design, it has only one group: no comparison condition. (B, C) Possible ways to diagram two of the examples given in the text. Using these as a model, try sketching a diagram of the Go Green example.

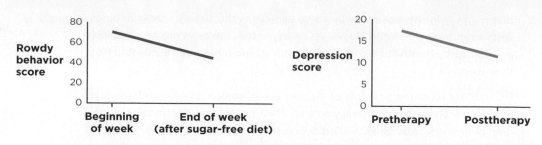

FIGURE 11.2
Graphing the really bad experiment.

The first two examples can be graphed this way. Using these as a model, try sketching a graph of the Go Green example.

Six Potential Internal Validity Threats in One-Group, Pretest/Posttest Designs

By the end of this chapter, you will have learned a total of twelve internal validity threats. Three of them we just reviewed: design confounds, selection effects, and order effects. Several of the internal validity threats apply especially to the really bad experiment, but are prevented with a good experimental design. These include maturation threats, history threats, regression threats, attrition threats, testing threats, and instrumentation threats. And the final three threats (observer bias, demand characteristics, and placebo effects) potentially apply to any study.

MATURATION THREATS TO INTERNAL VALIDITY

Why did the boys in Nikhil's cabin start behaving better? Was it because they had eaten less sugar? Perhaps. An alternative explanation, however, is that most of them simply settled in, or "matured into," the camp setting after they got used to the place. The boys' behavior improved on its own; the low-sugar diet may have had nothing to do with it. Such an effect is called a **maturation threat**, a change in behavior that emerges more or less spontaneously over time. People adapt to changed environments; children get better at walking and talking; plants grow taller—but not because of any outside intervention. It just happens.

Similarly, the depressed women may have improved because the cognitive therapy was effective, but an alternative explanation is that a systematically high portion of them simply improved on their own. Sometimes the symptoms of depression or other disorders disappear, for no known reason, with time. This phenomenon, known as *spontaneous remission*, is a specific type of maturation.

Preventing Maturation Threats. Because the studies both Nikhil and Dr. Yuki conducted followed the model of the really bad experiment, there is no way of knowing whether the improvements they noticed were caused by maturation or by the treatments they administered. In contrast, if the two researchers had conducted true experiments (such as a pretest/posttest design, which, as you learned in Chapter 10, has at least two groups, not one), they would also have included an appropriate comparison group. Nikhil would have observed a comparison group of equally lively campers who did not switch to a low-sugar diet. Dr. Yuki would have studied a comparison group of women who started out equally depressed but did not receive the cognitive therapy. If the treatment groups improved significantly more than the comparison groups did, each researcher could essentially subtract out the effect of maturation when they interpret their results. **Figure 11.3** illustrates the benefits of a comparison group in preventing a maturation threat for the depression study.

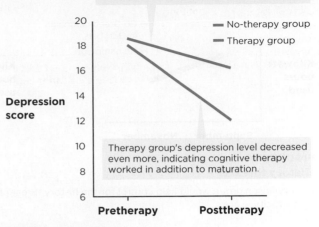

No-therapy comparison group's depression level decreased over time, suggesting simple maturation or spontaneous improvement.

Therapy group's depression level decreased even more, indicating cognitive therapy worked in addition to maturation.

FIGURE 11.3
Maturation threats.

A pretest/posttest design would help control for the maturation threat in Dr. Yuki's depression study.

HISTORY THREATS TO INTERNAL VALIDITY

Sometimes a threat to internal validity occurs not just because time has passed, but because something specific has happened between the pretest and posttest. In the third example, why did the dorm residents use less electricity? Was it the Go Green campaign? Perhaps. But a plausible alternative explanation is that the weather got cooler and most residents did not use air conditioning as much.

Why did the campers' behavior improve? It could have been the low-sugar diet, but maybe they all started a difficult swimming course in the middle of the week and the exercise tired most of them out.

These alternative explanations are examples of **history threats**, which result from a "historical" or external factor that systematically affects *most members* of the treatment group at the same time as the treatment itself, making it unclear whether the change is caused by the treatment received. To be a history threat, the external factor must affect most people in the group in the same direction (systematically), not just a few people (unsystematically).

Preventing History Threats. As with maturation threats, a comparison group can help control for history threats. In the Go Green study, the students would need to measure the kilowatt usage in another, comparable dormitory during the same 2 months, but not give the students in the second dorm the Go Green campaign materials. (This would be a pretest/posttest design rather than a one-group prettest/posttest design.) If both groups decreased their electricity usage about the same over time (**Figure 11.4A**), the decrease probably resulted from the change of seasons, not from the Go Green campaign. However, if the treatment group decreased its usage more than the

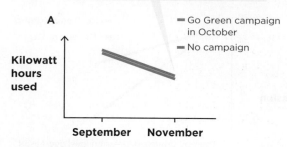

This result indicates Go Green campaign did not work, as all dorms reduced energy usage by same amount during fall.

A

Kilowatt hours used

— Go Green campaign in October
— No campaign

September   November

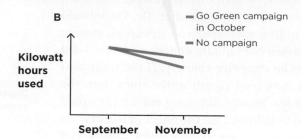

Decreased energy usage for both groups, but Go Green dorm's usage decreased even more, indicating campaign worked in addition to weather.

B

Kilowatt hours used

— Go Green campaign in October
— No campaign

September   November

FIGURE 11.4
History threats.

A comparison group would help control for the history threat of seasonal differences in electricity usage.

»

For more on pretest/posttest design, see Chapter 10, pp. 288–289.

»

For more detail on arithmetic mean, see Statistics Review: Descriptive Statistics, p. 461.

comparison group did (**Figure 11.4B**), you can rule out the history threat. Both the comparison group and the treatment group should experience the same seasonal "historical" changes, so including the comparison group controls for this threat.

REGRESSION THREATS TO INTERNAL VALIDITY

A **regression threat** refers to a statistical concept called **regression to the mean**. When a group average (mean) is unusually extreme at Time 1, the next time that group is measured (Time 2), it is likely to be less extreme—closer to its typical or average performance.

Everyday Regression to the Mean. Real-world situations can help illustrate regression to the mean. For example, during the 2014 World Cup semifinal, the men's team from Germany outscored the team from Brazil 7–1. That's a huge score; soccer (football) teams hardly ever score 7 points in a game. Without being familiar with either team, people who know about soccer would predict that in their next game, Germany would score fewer than 7 goals. Why? Simply because most people have an intuitive understanding of regression to the mean.

Here's the statistical explanation. Germany's score in the semifinal was exceptionally high partly because of the team's talent, and partly because of a unique combination of random factors that happened to come out in Germany's favor. The German team's injury level was, just by chance, much lower than usual, while Brazil had one star player out with an injury and their captain had been benched for yellow cards in previous games. The weather may have favored Germany as well, and Brazil may have felt unusual pressure on their home field. Therefore, despite Germany's legitimate talent as a team, they also benefited from randomness—a chance combination of lucky events that would probably never happen in the same combination again. Overall, the team's score in the subsequent game would almost necessarily be worse than in this game. Indeed, the team did regress; they beat Argentina in the final, but the score was only 1–0. In other words, Germany finished closer to their average level of performance.

Here's another example. Suppose you're normally cheerful and happy. On any given day, though, your usual upbeat mood can be affected by random factors, such as the weather, your friends' moods, and even parking problems. Every once in a while, just by chance, several of these random factors will affect you negatively: It will pour rain, your friends will be grumpy, and you won't be able to find a parking space. Your day is terrible! The good news is that tomorrow will almost certainly be better because those random factors are unlikely to occur in that same, unlucky combination again. It might still be raining, but your friends won't be grumpy, and you'll quickly find a good parking space. If even one of these factors is different, your day will go better and you will regress toward your average, happy mean.

Regression works at both extremes. An unusually good performance or outcome is likely to regress downward (toward its mean) the next time. And an unusually bad performance or outcome is likely to regress upward (toward its mean) the next time. Either extreme is explainable by an unusually lucky, or an unusually unlucky, combination of random events.

Regression and Internal Validity. Regression threats occur only when a group is measured twice, and only when the group has an extreme score at pretest. If the group has been selected because of its unusually high or low group mean at pretest, you can expect them to regress toward the mean somewhat when it comes time for the posttest.

You might suspect that the 40 depressed women Dr. Yuki studied were, as a group, quite depressed. Their group average at pretest may have been partly due to their true, baseline level of depression. The group was selected because they were extreme on the pretest. In a group of people who are seeking treatment for depression, a large proportion are feeling especially depressed at that moment, partly because of random events (e.g., the winter blues, a recent illness, family or relationship problems, job loss, divorce). At the posttest, the same unlucky combination of random effects on the group mean probably would not be the same as they were at pretest (maybe some saw their relationships get better, or the job situation improved for a few), so the posttest depression average would go down. The group's change would not occur because of the treatment, but simply because of regression to the mean, so in this case there would be an internal validity threat.

Preventing Regression Threats. Once again, comparison groups can help researchers prevent regression threats, along with a careful inspection of the pattern of results. If the comparison group and the experimental group are equally extreme at pretest, the researchers can account for any regression effects in their results.

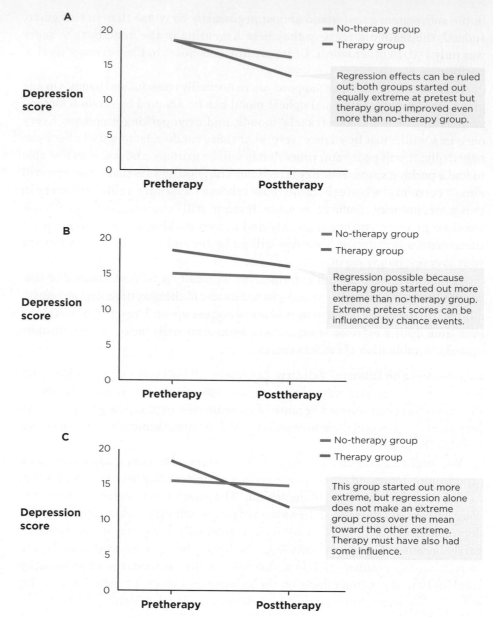

A

Depression score

Regression effects can be ruled out; both groups started out equally extreme at pretest but therapy group improved even more than no-therapy group.

— No-therapy group
— Therapy group

Pretherapy   Posttherapy

B

Depression score

Regression possible because therapy group started out more extreme than no-therapy group. Extreme pretest scores can be influenced by chance events.

— No-therapy group
— Therapy group

Pretherapy   Posttherapy

C

Depression score

This group started out more extreme, but regression alone does not make an extreme group cross over the mean toward the other extreme. Therapy must have also had some influence.

— No-therapy group
— Therapy group

Pretherapy   Posttherapy

FIGURE 11.5
Regression threats to internal validity.

Regression to the mean can be analyzed by inspecting different patterns of results.

In **Figure 11.5A**, you can rule out regression and conclude that the therapy really does work: If regression played a role, it would have done so for both groups because they were equally at risk for regression at the start. In contrast, if you saw the pattern of results shown in **Figure 11.5B**, you would suspect that regression had occurred. Regression is a particular threat in exactly this situation—when one group has been selected for its extreme mean. In **Figure 11.5C**, in contrast, the therapy group started out more extreme on depression, and therefore probably regressed to the mean. However, regression probably can't make a group cross over the comparison group, so the pattern shows an effect of therapy, in addition to a little help from regression effects.

ATTRITION THREATS TO INTERNAL VALIDITY

Why did the average level of rowdy behavior in Nikhil's campers decrease over the course of the week? It could have been because of the low-sugar diet, but maybe it was because the most unruly camper had to leave camp early.

Similarly, the level of depression among Dr. Yuki's patients might have decreased because of the cognitive therapy, but it might have been because three of the most depressed women in the study could not maintain the treatment regimen and dropped out of the study. The posttest average is lower only because these extra-high scores are not included.

In studies that have a pretest and a posttest, attrition (sometimes referred to as mortality) is a reduction in participant numbers that occurs when people drop out before the end. Attrition can happen when a pretest and posttest are administered on separate days and some participants are not available on the second day. An **attrition threat** becomes a problem for internal validity when attrition is systematic; that is, when only a certain kind of participant drops out. If any random camper leaves midweek, it might not be a problem for Nikhil's research, but it is a problem when the rowdiest camper leaves early. His departure creates an alternative explanation for Nikhil's results: Was the posttest average lower because the low-sugar diet worked, or because one extreme score is gone?

Similarly, as shown in **Figure 11.6**, it would not be unusual if two of 40 women in the depression therapy study dropped out over time. However, if the two most depressed women *systematically* drop out, the mean for the posttest is going to be lower, only because it does not include these two extreme scores (not because of the therapy). Therefore, if the depression score goes down from pretest to posttest, you wouldn't know whether the decrease occurred because

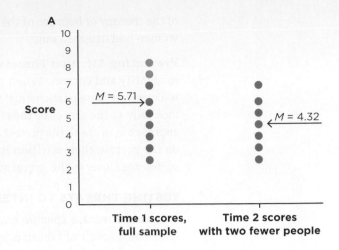

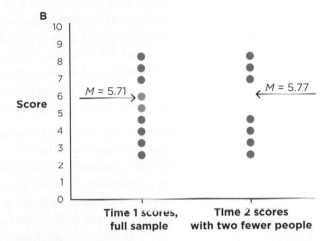

FIGURE 11.6
Attrition threats.

(A) If two people (noted by blue dots) drop out of a study, both of whom scored at the high end of the distribution on the pretest, the group mean changes substantially when their scores are omitted, even if all other scores stay the same. (B) If the dropouts' scores on the pretest are close to the group mean, removing their scores does not change the group mean as much.

of the therapy or because of the alternative explanation—that the highest-scoring women had dropped out.

Preventing Attrition Threats. An attrition threat is fairly easy for researchers to identify and correct. When participants drop out of a study, most researchers will remove those participants' scores from the pretest average too. That way, they look only at the scores of those who completed both parts of the study. Another approach is to check the pretest scores of the dropouts. If they have extreme scores on the pretest, their attrition is more of a threat to internal validity than if their scores are closer to the group average.

TESTING THREATS TO INTERNAL VALIDITY

A **testing threat**, a specific kind of order effect, refers to a change in the participants as a result of taking a test (dependent measure) more than once. People might have become more practiced at taking the test, leading to improved scores, or they may become fatigued or bored, which could lead to worse scores over time. Therefore, testing threats include practice effects (see Chapter 10).

In an educational setting, for example, students might perform better on a posttest than on a pretest, but not because of any educational intervention. Instead, perhaps they were inexperienced the first time they took the test, and they did better on the posttest simply because they had more practice the second time around.

Preventing Testing Threats. To avoid testing threats, researchers might abandon a pretest altogether and use a posttest-only design (see Chapter 10). If they do use a pretest, they might opt to use alternative forms of the test for the two measurements. The two forms might both measure depression, for example, but use different items to do so. A comparison group can also help. If the comparison group takes the same pretest and posttest but the treatment group shows an even larger change, testing threats can be ruled out (**Figure 11.7**).

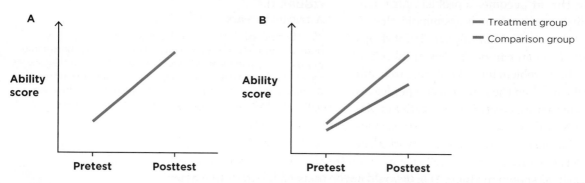

FIGURE 11.7
Testing threats.

(A) If there is no comparison group, it's hard to know whether the improvement from pretest to posttest is caused by the treatment or simply by practice. (B) The results from a comparison group can help rule out testing threats. Both groups might improve, but the treatment group improves even more, suggesting that both practice *and* a true effect of the treatment are causing the improvement.

INSTRUMENTATION THREATS TO INTERNAL VALIDITY

An **instrumentation threat** occurs when a measuring instrument changes over time. In observational research, the people who are coding behaviors are the measuring instrument, and over a period of time, they might change their standards for judging behavior by becoming more strict or more lenient. Thus, maybe Nikhil's campers did not really become less disruptive; instead, the people judging the campers' behavior became more tolerant of shoving and hitting.

Another case of an instrumentation threat would be when a researcher uses different forms for the pretest and posttest, but the two forms are not sufficiently equivalent. Dr. Yuki might have used a measure of depression at pretest on which people tend to score a little higher, and another measure of depression at posttest that tends to yield lower scores. As a result, the pattern she observed was not a sign of how good the cognitive therapy is, but merely reflected the way the alternative forms of the test are calibrated.

Preventing Instrumentation Threats. To prevent instrumentation threats, researchers could switch to a posttest-only design, or should take steps to ensure that the pretest and posttest measures are equivalent. To do so, they might collect data from each instrument to be sure the two are calibrated the same. To avoid shifting standards of behavioral coders, researchers might retrain their coders throughout the experiment, establishing their reliability and validity at both pretest and posttest. Using clear coding manuals would be an important part of this process. Another simple way to prevent an instrumentation threat is to use a posttest-only design (in which behavior is measured only once).

Finally, to control for the problem of different forms, Dr. Yuki could also counterbalance the versions of the test, giving some participants version A at pretest and version B at posttest, and giving other participants version B, and then version A.

Instrumentation vs. Testing Threats. Because these two threats are pretty similar, here's a way to remember the difference. An instrumentation threat means the *measuring instrument* has changed from Time 1 to Time 2. A testing threat means the *participants* change over time from having been tested before.

COMBINED THREATS

You have learned throughout this discussion that true pretest/posttest designs (those with two or more groups) normally take care of many internal validity threats. However, in some cases, a study with a pretest/posttest design might combine selection threats with history or attrition threats. In a **selection-history threat**, an outside event or factor affects only those at one level of the independent variable. For example, perhaps the dorm that was used as a comparison group was undergoing construction, and the construction crew used electric tools that drew on only that dorm's power supply. Therefore, the researcher won't be sure: Was it because the Go Green campaign reduced student energy usage? Or was it only because the comparison group dorm used so many power tools?

Similarly, in a **selection-attrition threat**, only one of the experimental groups experiences attrition. If Dr. Yuki conducted her depression therapy experiment as a pretest/posttest design, it might be the case that the most severely depressed people dropped out—but only from the treatment group, not the control group. The treatment might have been especially arduous for the most depressed people, so they drop out of the study. Because the control group was not undergoing treatment, they are not susceptible to the same level of attrition. Therefore, selection and attrition can combine to make Dr. Yuki unsure: Did the cognitive therapy really work, compared to the control group? Or is it just that the most severely depressed people dropped out of the treatment group?

Three Potential Internal Validity Threats in Any Study

Many internal validity threats are likely to occur in the one-group prettest/posttest design, and these threats can often be examined simply by adding a comparison group. Doing so would result in a pretest/posttest design. The posttest-only design is another option (see Chapter 10). However, three more threats to internal validity—observer bias, demand characteristics, and placebo effects—might apply even for designs with a clear comparison group.

OBSERVER BIAS

Observer bias can be a threat to internal validity in almost any study in which there is a behavioral dependent variable. **Observer bias** occurs when researchers' expectations influence their interpretation of the results. For example, Dr. Yuki might be a biased observer of her patients' depression: She expects to see her patients improve, whether they do or do not. Nikhil may be a biased observer of his campers: He may expect the low-sugar diet to work, so he views the boys' posttest behavior more positively.

Although comparison groups can prevent many threats to internal validity, they do not necessarily control for observer bias. Even if Dr. Yuki used a no-therapy comparison group, observer bias could still occur: If she knew which participants were in which group, her biases could lead her to see more improvement in the therapy group than in the comparison group.

» For more on observer bias, see Chapter 6, p. 169.

Observer bias can threaten two kinds of validity in an experiment. It threatens internal validity because an alternative explanation exists for the results. Did the therapy work, or was Dr. Yuki biased? It can also threaten the construct validity of the dependent variable because it means the depression ratings given by Dr. Yuki do not represent the true levels of depression of her participants.

DEMAND CHARACTERISTICS

Demand characteristics are a problem when participants guess what the study is supposed to be about and change their behavior in the expected direction.

For example, Dr. Yuki's patients know they are getting therapy. If they think Dr. Yuki expects them to get better, they might change their self-reports of symptoms in the expected direction. Nikhil's campers, too, might realize something fishy is going on when they're not given their usual snacks. Their awareness of a menu change could certainly change the way they behave.

«

For more on demand characteristics, see Chapter 10, p. 297.

Controlling for Observer Bias and Demand Characteristics. To avoid observer bias and demand characteristics, researchers must do more than add a comparison group to their studies. The most appropriate way to avoid such problems is to conduct a **double-blind study**, in which neither the participants nor the researchers who evaluate them know who is in the treatment group and who is in the comparison group.

Suppose Nikhil decides to test his hypothesis as a double-blind study. He could arrange to have two cabins of equally lively campers and for only one group, replace their sugary snacks with good-tasting low-sugar versions. The boys would not know which kind of snacks they were eating, and the people observing their behavior would also be blind to which boys were in which group.

When a double-blind study is not possible, a variation might be an acceptable alternative. In some studies, participants know which group they are in, but the observers do not; this is called a **masked design**, or *blind design* (see Chapter 6). The students exposed to the Go Green campaign would certainly be aware that someone was trying to influence their behavior. Ideally, however, the raters who were recording their electrical energy usage should not know which dorm was exposed to the campaign and which was not. Of course, keeping observers unaware is even more important when they are rating behaviors that are more difficult to code, such as symptoms of depression or behavior problems at camp.

Recall the Chapter 10 study by Mueller and Oppenheimer (2014) in which people took notes in longhand or on laptops. The research assistants in that study were blind to the condition each participant was in when they graded their tests on the lectures. The participants themselves were not blind to their notetaking method. However, since the test-takers participated in only one condition (an independent-groups design), they were not aware that the form of notetaking was an important feature of the experiment. Therefore, they were blind to the *reason* they were taking notes in longhand or on a laptop.

PLACEBO EFFECTS

The women who received Dr. Yuki's cognitive therapy may have improved because her therapeutic approach really works. An alternative explanation is that there was a placebo effect: The women improved simply because they *believed* that they were receiving an effective treatment.

A **placebo effect** occurs when people receive a treatment and really improve—but only because the recipients believe they are receiving a valid treatment. In most studies on the effectiveness of medications, for example, one group receives a pill or an injection with the real drug, while another group receives a

FIGURE 11.8
Are herbal remedies placebos?

It is possible that perceived improvements in mood, joint pain, or wellness promised by herbal supplements are simply due to the belief that they will work, not because of the specific ingredients they contain.

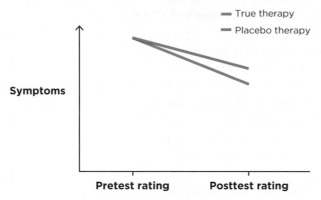

FIGURE 11.9
A double-blind placebo control study.

Adding a placebo comparison group can help researchers separate a potential placebo effect from the true effect of a particular therapy.

pill or an injection with no active ingredients—a sugar pill or a saline solution. People can even receive placebo psychotherapy, in which they simply talk to a friendly listener about their problems; these placebo conversations have no therapeutic structure. The inert pill, injection, or therapy is the placebo. Often people who receive the placebo see their symptoms improve because they believe the treatment they are receiving is supposed to be effective. In fact, the placebo effect can occur whenever any kind of treatment is used to control symptoms, such as an herbal remedy to enhance wellness (**Figure 11.8**).

Placebo effects are not imaginary. Placebos have been shown to reduce real symptoms, both psychological and physical, including depression (Kirsch & Sapirstein, 1998); postoperative pain or anxiety (Benedetti, Amanzio, Vighetti, & Asteggiano, 2006); terminal cancer pain; and epilepsy (Beecher, 1955). They are not always beneficial or harmless; physical side effects, including skin rashes and headaches, can be caused by placebos, too. People's symptoms appear to respond not just to the active ingredients in medications or to psychotherapy, but also to their belief in what the treatment can do to improve their situation.

A placebo can be strong medicine. Kirsch and Sapirstein (1998) reviewed studies that gave either antidepressant medication, such as Prozac, or a placebo to depressed patients, and concluded that the placebo groups improved almost as much as groups that received real medicine. In fact, up to 75% of the depression improvement in the Prozac groups was also achieved in placebo groups.

Designing Studies to Rule Out the Placebo Effect. To determine whether an effect is caused by a therapeutic treatment or by placebo effects, the standard approach is to include a special kind of comparison group. As usual, one group receives the real drug or real therapy, and the second group receives the placebo drug or placebo therapy. Crucially, however, neither the people treating the patients nor the patients themselves know whether they are in the real group or the placebo group. This experimental design is called a **double-blind placebo control study**.

The results of such a study might look like the graph in **Figure 11.9**. Notice that both groups improved, but the group receiving the real drug improved even more, showing placebo effects *plus* the effects of the real drug. If the results turn out like this, the researchers can conclude that the treatment they are testing does cause improvement above and beyond a placebo effect. Once again, an internal validity threat—a placebo effect—can be avoided with a careful research design.

Is That Really a Placebo Effect? If you thought about it carefully, you probably noticed that the results in Figure 11.9 do not definitively show a placebo effect pattern. Both the group receiving the real drug and the group receiving the placebo improved over time. However, some of the improvement in both groups could have been caused by maturation, history, regression, testing, or instrumentation threats (Kienle & Kiene, 1997). If you were interested in showing a placebo effect specifically, you would have to include a no-treatment comparison group—one that receives neither drug nor placebo.

Suppose your results looked something like those in **Figure 11.10**. Because the placebo group improved over time, even more than the no-therapy/no-placebo group, you can attribute the improvement to placebo and not just to maturation, history, regression, testing, or instrumentation.

With So Many Threats, Are Experiments Still Useful?

After reading about a dozen ways a good experiment can go wrong, you might be tempted to assume that most experiments you read about are faulty. However, responsible researchers consciously avoid internal validity threats when they design and interpret their work. Many of the threats discussed in this chapter are a problem only in one-group pretest/posttest studies—those with no comparison group. As shown in the Working It Through section (p. 328), a carefully designed comparison group will correct for many of these threats. The section analyzes the study on mindfulness (Mrazek, Franklin, Phillips, Baird, & Schooler, 2013), discussed in Chapter 10 and presented again here in **Figure 11.11**.

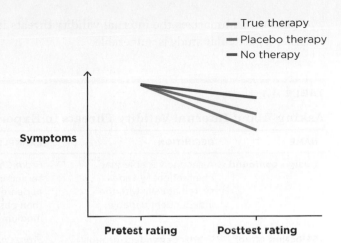

FIGURE 11.10
Identifying a placebo effect.

Definitively showing a placebo effect requires three groups: one receiving the true therapy, one receiving the placebo, and one receiving no therapy. If there is a placebo effect, the pattern of results will show that the no-therapy group does not improve as much as the placebo group.

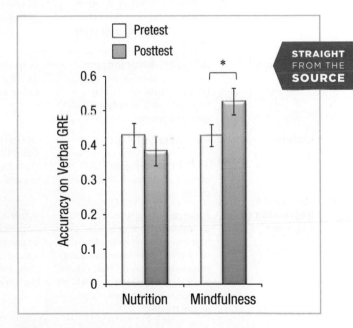

FIGURE 11.11
Mindfulness study results.

This study showed that mindfulness classes, but not nutrition classes, were associated with an increase in GRE scores. Can the study rule out all twelve internal validity threats and support a causal claim? (Source: Mrazek et al., 2013, Fig. 1A.)

Table 11.1 summarizes the internal validity threats in Chapters 10 and 11, and suggests ways to find out whether a particular study is vulnerable.

TABLE 11.1

Asking About Internal Validity Threats in Experiments

NAME	DEFINITION	EXAMPLE	QUESTIONS TO ASK
Design confound	A second variable that unintentionally varies systematically with the independent variable.	*From Chapter 10*: If pasta served in a large bowl appeared more appetizing than pasta served in a medium bowl.	Did the researchers turn potential third variables into control variables, for example, keeping the pasta recipe constant?
Selection effect	In an independent-groups design, when the two independent variable groups have systematically different kinds of participants in them.	*From Chapter 10*: In the autism study, some parents insisted they wanted their children to be in the intensive-treatment group rather than the control group.	Did the researchers use random assignment or matched groups to equalize groups?
Order effect	In a repeated-measures design, when the effect of the independent variable is confounded with carryover from one level to the other, or with practice, fatigue, or boredom.	*From Chapter 10*: People rated the shared chocolate higher only because the first taste of chocolate is always more delicious than the second one.	Did the researchers counterbalance the orders of presentation of the levels of the independent variable?
Maturation	An experimental group improves over time only because of natural development or spontaneous improvement.	Disruptive boys settle down as they get used to the camp setting.	Did the researchers use a comparison group of boys who had an equal amount of time to mature but who did not receive the treatment?
History	An experimental group changes over time because of an external factor that affects all or most members of the group.	Dorm residents use less air conditioning in November than September because the weather is cooler.	Did the researchers include a comparison group that had an equal exposure to the external factor but did not receive the treatment?
Regression to the mean	An experimental group whose average is extremely low (or high) at pretest will get better (or worse) over time because the random events that caused the extreme pretest scores do not recur the same way at posttest.	A group's average is extremely depressed at pretest, in part because some members volunteered for therapy when they were feeling much more depressed than usual.	Did the researchers include a comparison group that was equally extreme at pretest but did not receive the therapy?
Attrition	An experimental group changes over time, but only because the most extreme cases have systematically dropped out and their scores are not included in the posttest.	Because the rowdiest boy in the cabin leaves camp early, his unruly behavior affects the pretest mean but not the posttest mean.	Did the researchers compute the pretest and posttest scores with only the final sample included, removing any dropouts' data from the pretest group average?

NAME	DEFINITION	EXAMPLE	QUESTIONS TO ASK
Testing	A type of order effect: An experimental group changes over time because repeated testing has affected the participants. Practice effects (fatigue effects) are one subtype.	GRE verbal scores improve only because students take the same version of the test both times and therefore are more practiced at posttest.	Did the researchers have a comparison group take the same two tests? Did they use a posttest-only design, or did they use alternative forms of the measure for the pretest and posttest?
Instrumentation	An experimental group changes over time, but only because the measurement instrument has changed.	Coders get more lenient over time, so the same behavior is coded as less disruptive at posttest than at pretest.	Did the researchers train coders to use the same standards when coding? Are pretest and posttest measures demonstrably equivalent?
Observer bias	An experimental group's ratings differ from a comparison group's, but only because the researcher expects the groups' ratings to differ.	The researcher expects a low-sugar diet to decrease the campers' unruly behavior, so he notices only calm behavior and ignores wild behavior.	Were the observers of the dependent variable unaware of which condition participants were in?
Demand characteristic	Participants guess what the study's purpose is and change their behavior in the expected direction.	Campers guess that the low-sugar diet is supposed to make them calmer, so they change their behavior accordingly.	Were the participants kept unaware of the purpose of the study? Was it an independent-groups design, which makes participants less able to guess the study's purpose?
Placebo effect	Participants in an experimental group improve only because they believe in the efficacy of the therapy or drug they receive.	Women receiving cognitive therapy improve simply because they believe the therapy will work for them.	Did a comparison group receive a placebo (inert) drug or a placebo therapy?

CHECK YOUR UNDERSTANDING

1. How does a one-group pretest/posttest design differ from a pretest/posttest design, and which threats to internal validity are especially applicable to this design?

2. Using Table 11.1 as a guide, indicate which of the internal validity threats would be relevant even to a (two-group) posttest-only design.

1. See pp. 312–322. 2. See pp. 326–327.

WORKING IT THROUGH

Did Mindfulness Training Really Cause GRE Scores to Improve?

In Chapter 10, you read about a pretest/posttest design in which students were randomly assigned to a mindfulness training course or to a nutrition course (Mrazek et al., 2013). Students took GRE verbal tests both before and after their assigned training course. Those assigned to the mindfulness course scored significantly higher on the GRE posttest than pretest. The authors would like to claim that the mindfulness course caused the improvement in GRE scores. Does this study rule out internal validity threats?

QUESTIONS TO ASK	CLAIMS, QUOTES, OR DATA	INTERPRETATION AND EVALUATION
Is the study susceptible to any of these internal validity threats?		
Design confound	The paper reports that classes met for 45 minutes four times a week for 2 weeks and were taught by professionals with extensive teaching experience in their respective fields."Both classes were taught by expert instructors, were composed of similar numbers of students, were held in comparable classrooms during the late afternoon, and used a similar class format, including both lectures and group discussions" (p. 778).	These passages indicate that the classes were equal in their time commitment, the quality of the instructors used, and other factors, so these are not design confounds. It appears the two classes did not accidentally vary on anything besides their mindfulness or nutrition content.
Selection effect	The article reports that "students . . . were randomly assigned to either a mindfulness class . . . or a nutrition class" (p. 777).	Random assignment controls for selection effects, so selection is not a threat in the study.

QUESTIONS TO ASK	CLAIMS, QUOTES, OR DATA	INTERPRETATION AND EVALUATION
Order effect		Order effects are relevant only for repeated-measures designs, not independent-groups designs like this one.
Maturation threat		While it's possible that people could simply get better at the GRE over time, maturation would have happened to the nutrition group as well (but it did not). We can rule out maturation.
History threat		Could some outside event, such as a free GRE prep course on campus, have improved people's GRE scores? We can rule out such a history threat because of the comparison group: It's unlikely a campus GRE program would just happen to be offered only to students in the mindfulness group.
Regression threat		A regression threat is unlikely here. First, the students were randomly assigned to the mindfulness group, not selected on the basis of extremely low GRE scores. Second, the mindfulness group and the nutrition group had the same pretest means. They were equally extreme, so if regression had affected one group, it would also have affected the other.
Attrition threat	There's no indication in the paper that any participants dropped out between pretest and posttest.	Because all participants apparently completed the study, attrition is not a threat.
Testing threat		Participants did take the verbal GRE two times, but if their improvement was simply due to practice, we would see a similar increase in the nutrition group, and we do not.
Instrumentation threat	The study reports, "We used two versions of the verbal GRE measure that were matched for difficulty and counterbalanced within each condition" (p. 777).	The described procedure controls for any difference in test difficulty from pretest to posttest.
Observer bias	"We minimized experimenter expectancy effects by testing participants in mixed-condition groups in which nearly all task instructions were provided by computers" (p. 778).	Experimenter expectancy is another name for observer bias. These procedures seem to be reasonable ways to prevent an experimenter from leading participants in one group to be more motivated to do well on the dependent measure.
Demand characteristics or placebo effects	"All participants were recruited under the pretense that the study was a direct comparison of two equally viable programs for improving cognitive performance, which minimized motivation and placebo effects" (p. 778).	This statement argues that all students expected their assigned program to be effective. If true, then placebo effects and demand characteristics were equal in both conditions.

This study's design and results have controlled for virtually all the internal validity threats in Table 11.1, so we can conclude its internal validity is strong and the study supports the claim that mindfulness training improved students' GRE verbal scores. (Next you could interrogate this study's construct, statistical, and external validity!)

INTERROGATING NULL EFFECTS: WHAT IF THE INDEPENDENT VARIABLE DOES NOT MAKE A DIFFERENCE?

So far, this chapter has discussed cases in which a researcher works to ensure that any covariance found in an experiment was caused by the independent variable, not by a threat to internal validity. What if the independent variable did not make a difference in the dependent variable; there is no significant covariance between the two? That outcome is known as a **null effect**, also referred to as a *null result*.

You might not read about null effects very often. Journals, newspapers, and websites are much more likely to report the results of a study in which the independent variable does have an effect. However, research that finds null effects are surprisingly common—something many students learn when they start to conduct their own studies. Often, researchers who get a null result will say their study "didn't work." What might null effects mean?

Here are three hypothetical examples:

Many people believe having more money will make them happy. But will it? A researcher designed an experiment in which he randomly assigned people to three groups. He gave one group nothing, gave the second group a little money, and gave the third group a lot of money. The next day, he asked each group to report their happiness on a mood scale. The group who received cash (either a little or a lot) was not significantly happier, or in a better mood, than the group who received nothing.

Do online reading games make kids better readers? An educational psychologist recruited a sample of 5-year-olds, all of whom did not yet know how to read. She randomly assigned the children to two groups. One group played with a commercially available online reading game for 1 week (about 30 minutes per day), and the other group continued "treatment as usual," attending their normal kindergarten classes. Afterward, the children were tested on their reading ability. The reading game group's scores were a little higher than those of the kindergarten-as-usual group, but the difference was not statistically significant.

Researchers have hypothesized that feeling anxious can cause people to reason less carefully and logically. To test this hypothesis, a research team randomly assigned people to three groups: low, medium, and high anxiety. After a few minutes of being exposed to the anxiety manipulation, the participants solved problems requiring logic, rather than emotional reasoning. Although the researchers had predicted the anxious people would do worse on the problems, participants in the three groups scored roughly the same.

These three examples of null effects, shown as graphs in **Figure 11.12**, are all posttest-only designs. However, a null effect can happen in a within-groups design or a pretest/posttest design, too (and even in a correlational study). In all three of these cases, the independent variable manipulated by the experimenters did not result in a change in the dependent variable. Why didn't these experiments show covariance between the independent and dependent variables?

Any time an experiment gives a null result, it might be the case that the independent variable really does not affect the dependent variable. In the real world, perhaps money does not make people happier, online reading games do not improve kids' reading skill, and being anxious does not affect logical reasoning. In other words, the experiment gave an accurate result, showing that the manipulation the researchers used did not cause a change in the dependent variable. Importantly, therefore, when we obtain a null result, it can mean our theory is incorrect.

Another possible reason for a null effect is that the study was not designed or conducted carefully enough. The independent variable actually does cause a change in the dependent variable, but some obscuring factor in the study prevented the researchers from detecting the true difference. Such obscuring factors can take two general forms: There might not have been enough between-groups difference, or there might have been too much within-groups variability.

To illustrate these two types of problems, suppose you prepared two bowls of salsa: one containing two shakes of hot sauce and the other containing four shakes

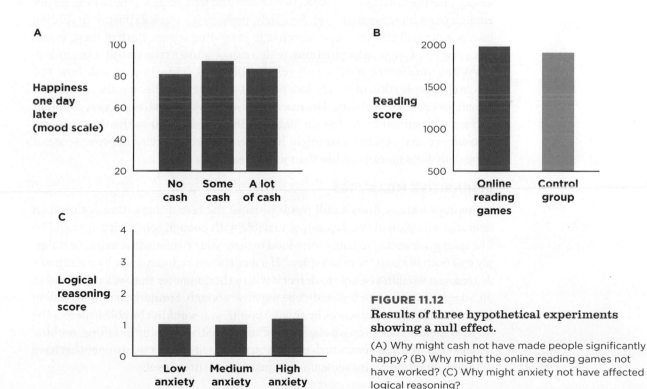

FIGURE 11.12
Results of three hypothetical experiments showing a null effect.

(A) Why might cash not have made people significantly happy? (B) Why might the online reading games not have worked? (C) Why might anxiety not have affected logical reasoning?

of hot sauce. People might not taste any difference between the two bowls. One reason is that four shakes is not different enough from two; there's not enough between-groups difference. A second reason is that each bowl contains many other ingredients (tomatoes, onions, jalapeños, cilantro, lime juice), so it's hard to detect any change in hot sauce intensity, with all those other flavors getting in the way. This is a problem of too much within-groups variability. Now let's see how this analogy plays out in psychological research.

Perhaps There Is Not Enough Between-Groups Difference

When a study returns a null result, sometimes the culprit is not enough between-groups difference. Weak manipulations, insensitive measures, ceiling and floor effects, and reverse design confounds might prevent study results from revealing a true difference that exists between two or more experimental groups.

WEAK MANIPULATIONS

Why did the study show that money did not affect people's moods? You might ask how much money the researcher gave each group. What if the amounts were $0.00, $0.25, and $1.00? In that case, it would be no surprise that the manipulation didn't work; a dollar doesn't seem like enough money to affect most people's mood. Like the difference between two shakes and four shakes of hot sauce, it's not enough of an increase to matter. Similarly, perhaps a 1-week exposure to reading games is not sufficient to cause any change in reading scores. Both of these would be examples of weak manipulations, which can obscure a true causal relationship.

When you interrogate a null result, then, it's important to ask how the researchers operationalized the independent variable. In other words, you have to ask about construct validity. The researcher might have obtained a very different pattern of results if he had given $0.00, $5.00, and $150.00 to the three groups. The educational psychologist might have found reading games improve scores if done daily for 3 months rather than just a week.

INSENSITIVE MEASURES

Sometimes a study finds a null result because the researchers have not used an operationalization of the dependent variable with enough sensitivity. It would be like asking a friend who hates spicy food to taste your two bowls of salsa; he'd simply call both of them "way too spicy." If a medication reduces fever by a tenth of a degree, you wouldn't be able to detect it with a thermometer that was calibrated in one-degree increments; it wouldn't be sensitive enough. Similarly, if online reading games improve reading scores by about 2 points, you wouldn't be able to detect the improvement with a simple pass/fail reading test (either passing or failing, nothing in between). When it comes to dependent measures, it's smart to use ones that have detailed, quantitative increments—not just two or three levels.

» For more on scales of measurement, see Chapter 5, pp. 122–124.

CEILING AND FLOOR EFFECTS

In a **ceiling effect**, all the scores are squeezed together at the high end. In a **floor effect**, all the scores cluster at the low end. As special cases of weak manipulations and insensitive measures, ceiling and floor effects can cause independent variable groups to score almost the same on the dependent variable.

Ceilings, Floors, and Independent Variables. Ceiling and floor effects can be the result of a problematic independent variable. For example, if the researcher really did manipulate his independent variable by giving people $0.00, $0.25, or $1.00, that would be a floor effect because these three amounts are all low—they're squeezed close to a floor of $0.00.

Consider the example of the anxiety and reasoning study. Suppose the researcher manipulated anxiety by telling the groups they were about to receive an electric shock. The low-anxiety group was told to expect a 10-volt shock, the medium-anxiety group a 50-volt shock, and the high-anxiety group a 100-volt shock. This manipulation would probably result in a ceiling effect because expecting *any* amount of shock would cause anxiety, regardless of the shock's intensity. As a result, the various levels of the independent variable would appear to make no difference.

Ceilings, Floors, and Dependent Variables. Poorly designed dependent variables can also lead to ceiling and floor effects. Imagine if the logical reasoning test in the anxiety study was so difficult that nobody could solve the problems. That would cause a floor effect: The three anxiety groups would score the same, but only because the measure for the dependent variable results in low scores in all groups. Similarly, your friend has a ceiling effect on spiciness; he rates both bowls as extremely spicy.

In the money and mood study, participants rated their happiness on the following scale:

1 = I feel horrible.
2 = I feel awful.
3 = I feel bad.
4 = I feel fine.

Because there is only one option on this measure to indicate feeling good (and people generally tend to feel good, rather than bad), the majority would report the maximum, 4. Money would appear to have no effect on their mood, but only because the dependent measure of happiness used was subject to a ceiling effect.

Or suppose the reading test used in the online game study asked the children to point to the first letter of their own name. Almost all 5-year-olds can do this, so the measure would result in a ceiling effect. All children would get a perfect

« Ceiling and floor effects are examples of restriction of range; see Chapter 8, pp. 218–220.

score; there would be no room for between-group variability on this measure. Similarly, if the reading test asked children to analyze a passage of Tolstoy, almost all children would fail, creating a floor effect (**Figure 11.13**).

MANIPULATION CHECKS HELP DETECT WEAK MANIPULATIONS, CEILINGS, AND FLOORS

When you interrogate a study with a null effect, it is important to ask how the independent and dependent variables were operationalized. Was the independent variable manipulation strong enough to cause a difference between groups? And was the dependent variable measure sensitive enough to detect that difference?

Recall from Chapter 10 that a **manipulation check** is a separate dependent variable that experimenters include in a study, specifically to make sure the manipulation worked. For example, in the anxiety study, after telling people they were going to receive a 10-volt, 50-volt, or 100-volt shock, the researchers might have asked: How anxious are you right now, on a scale of 1 to 10? If the manipulation check showed that participants in all three groups felt nearly the same level of anxiety (**Figure 11.14A**), you'd know the researchers did not effectively manipulate what they intended to manipulate. If the manipulation check showed that the independent variable levels differed in an expected way—participants in the high-anxiety group really felt more anxious than those in the other two groups (**Figure 11.14B**)—then you'd know the researchers did effectively manipulate anxiety, the independent variable. If the manipulation check worked, the researchers would have to look for another reason for the null effect of anxiety on logical reasoning. Perhaps the dependent measure has a floor effect; that is, the logical reasoning test might be too difficult, so everyone scores low (see Figure 11.13). Or perhaps there really is no effect of anxiety on logical reasoning.

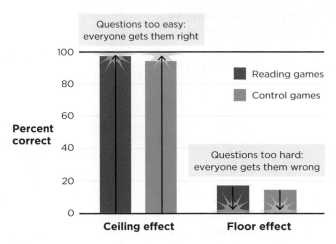

FIGURE 11.13
Ceiling and floor effects.

A ceiling or floor effect on the dependent variable can obscure a true difference between groups. If all the questions on a test are too easy, everyone will get a perfect score. If the questions are too hard, everyone will score low.

DESIGN CONFOUNDS ACTING IN REVERSE

Confounds are usually considered to be internal validity threats—alternative explanations for some observed difference in a study. However, they can apply to null effects, too. A study might be designed in such a way that a design confound actually counteracts, or reverses, some true effect of an independent variable.

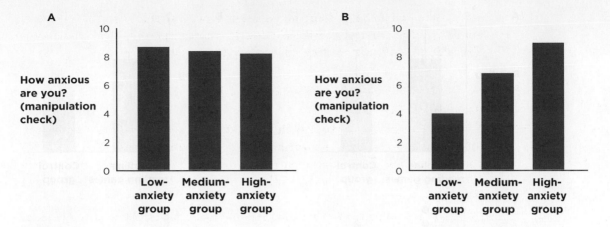

FIGURE 11.14
Possible results of a manipulation check.
(A) These results suggest the anxiety manipulation did not work because people at all three levels of the independent variable reported being equally anxious. (B) These results suggest the manipulation did work because the anxiety of people in the three independent variable groups did vary in the expected way.

In the money and happiness study, for example, perhaps the students who received the most money happened to be given the money by a grumpy experimenter, while those who received the least money were exposed to a more cheerful person; this confound would have worked against any true effect of money on mood.

Perhaps Within-Groups Variability Obscured the Group Differences

Another reason a study might return a null effect is that there is too much unsystematic variability within each group. This is referred to as **noise** (also known as *error variance* or *unsystematic variance*). In the salsa example, noise refers to the great number of the other flavors in the two bowls. Noisy within-group variability can get in the way of detecting a true difference between groups.

Consider the sets of scores in **Figure 11.15**. The bar graphs and scatterplots depict the same data, but in two graphing formats. In each case, the mean difference *between* the two groups is the same. However, the variability *within* each group is much larger in part A than part B. You can see that when there is more variability within groups, it obscures the differences between the groups because more overlap exists between the members of the two groups. It's a statistical

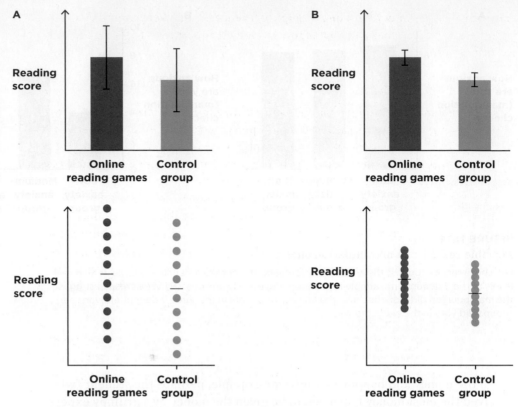

FIGURE 11.15
Within-group variability can obscure group differences.
Notice that the group averages are the same in both versions, but the variability within each group is greater in part A than part B. Part B is the situation researchers prefer because it enables them to better detect true differences in the independent variable.

validity problem: The greater the overlap, the smaller the effect size, and the less likely the two group means will be statistically significant; that is, the less likely the study will detect covariance.

» For more on statistical significance, see Chapter 10, p. 304; and Statistics Review: Inferential Statistics.

When the data show less variability within the groups (see Figure 11.15B), the effect size will be larger, and it's more likely the mean difference will be statistically significant. The less within-group variability, the less likely it is to obscure a true group difference. If the two bowls of salsa contained nothing but tomatoes, the difference between two and four shakes of hot sauce would be more easily detectable because there would be fewer competing, "noisy" flavors within bowls.

In sum, the more unsystematic variability there is within each group, the more the scores in the two groups overlap with each other. The greater the overlap, the less apparent the average difference. As described next, most researchers prefer to keep within-group variability to a minimum, so they can more easily detect between-group differences. They keep in mind a few common culprits: measurement error, irrelevant individual differences, and situation noise.

MEASUREMENT ERROR

One reason for high within-group variability is **measurement error**, a human or instrument factor that can inflate or deflate a person's true score on the dependent variable. For example, a man who is 160 centimeters tall might be measured at 160.5 cm because of the angle of vision of the person using the meter stick, or he might be recorded as 159.5 cm because he slouched a bit.

All dependent variables involve a certain amount of measurement error, and researchers try to keep those errors as small as possible. For example, the reading test used as a dependent variable in the educational psychologist's study is not perfect. Indeed, a group's score on the reading test represents the group's "true" reading ability—that is, the actual level of the construct in a group—plus or minus some random measurement error. Maybe one child's batch of questions happened to be more difficult than average. Perhaps another student just happened to be exposed to the tested words at home. Maybe one child was especially distracted during the test, and another was especially focused. When these distortions of measurement are random, they cancel each other out across a sample of people and will not affect the group's average, or mean. Nevertheless, an operationalization with a lot of measurement error will result in a set of scores that are more spread out around the group mean (see Figure 11.15A).

A child's score on the reading measure can be represented with the following formula:

child's reading score =
    child's true reading ability +/– random error of measurement

Or, more generally:

dependent variable score =
    participant's true score +/– random error of measurement

The more sources of random error there are in a dependent variable's measurement, the more variability there will be within each group in an experiment (see Figure 11.15A). In contrast, the more precisely and carefully a dependent variable is measured, the less variability there will be within each group (see Figure 11.15B). And lower within-groups variability is better, making it easier to detect a difference (if one exists) between the different independent variable groups.

Solution 1: Use Reliable, Precise Tools. When researchers use measurement tools that have excellent reliability (internal, interrater, and test-retest), they can reduce measurement error (see Chapter 5). When such tools also have good construct validity, there will be a lower error rate as well. More precise and accurate measurements have less error.

Solution 2: Measure More Instances. A precise, reliable measurement tool is sometimes impossible to find. What then? In this case, the best alternative is to use a larger sample (e.g., more people, more animals). In other words, one solution to measuring badly is to take more measurements. When a tool potentially causes a great deal of random error, the researcher can cancel out many errors simply by including more people in the sample.

Is one person's score 10 points too high because of a random measurement error? If so, it's not a problem, as long as another participant's score is 10 points too low because of a random measurement error. The more participants there are, the better the chances of having a full representation of all the possible errors. The errors cancel each other out, and the result is a better estimate of the "true" average for that group. The reverse applies as well: When a measurement tool is known to have a very low error rate, the researcher might be able to use fewer participants in the study.

INDIVIDUAL DIFFERENCES

Individual differences can be another source of within-group variability. They can be a problem in independent-groups designs. In the experiment on money and mood, for example, the normal mood of the participants must have varied. Some people are naturally more cheerful than others, and these individual differences have the effect of spreading out the scores of the students within each group, as **Figure 11.16** shows. In the $1.00 condition is Candace, who is typically unhappy. The $1.00 gift might have made her happier, but her mood would still be relatively low because of her normal level of grumpiness. Michael, a cheerful guy, was in the no-money control condition, but he still scored high on the mood measure.

Looking over the data, you'll notice that, on average, the participants in the experimental condition did score a little higher than those in the control condition. But the data are mixed and far from consistent; there's a lot of overlap between the scores in the money group and the control group. Because of this overlap, the effect of a money gift might not reach statistical significance. It is hard to detect the effect of money above and beyond these individual differences in mood. The effect of the gift would be small compared to the variability within each group.

Solution 1: Change the Design. One way to accommodate individual differences is to use a within-groups

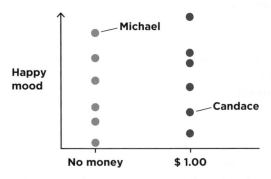

FIGURE 11.16
Individual differences.

Overall, students who received money were slightly more cheerful than students in the control group, but the scores in the two groups overlapped a great deal.

design instead of an independent-groups design. In **Figure 11.17**, each pair of points, connected by a line, represents a single person whose mood was measured under both conditions. The top pair of points represents Michael's mood after a money gift and after no gift. Another pair of points represents Candace's mood after a money gift and after no gift. Do you see what happens? The individual data points are exactly where they were in Figure 11.16, but the pairing process has turned a scrambled set of data into a clear and very consistent finding: Every participant was happier after receiving a money gift than after no gift. This included Michael, who is always cheerful, and Candace, who is usually unhappy, as well as others in between.

A within-groups design, which compares each participant with himself or herself, controls for irrelevant individual differences. Finally, notice that the study required only half as many participants as the original independent-groups experiment. You can see again the two strengths of within-groups designs (introduced in Chapter 10): They control for irrelevant individual differences, and they require fewer participants than independent-groups designs.

Solution 2: Add More Participants. If within-groups or matched-groups designs are inappropriate (and sometimes they are, because of order effects, demand characteristics, or other practical concerns), another solution to individual difference variability is to measure more people. The principle is the same as it is for measurement error: When a great deal of variability exists because of individual differences, a simple solution is to increase the sample size. The more people you measure, the less impact any single person will have on the group's average. Adding more participants reduces the influence of individual differences *within* groups, thereby enhancing the study's ability to detect differences *between* groups.

Another reason larger samples reduce the impact of irrelevant individual differences is mathematical. The number of people in a sample goes in the denominator of the statistical formula for a *t* test—used for detecting a difference between two related means. As you will learn in your statistics class, the formula for a *t* test for dependent groups (one possible *t* test) is:

$$\frac{\text{mean difference}}{\left(\dfrac{\text{standard deviation of the difference}}{\sqrt{n}}\right)}$$

The larger the number of participants (*n*), the smaller the denominator of *t*. And the smaller that denominator is, the larger *t* can get, and the easier it is to find a significant *t*. A significant *t* means you do not have a null result.

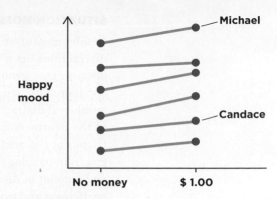

FIGURE 11.17
Within-groups designs control for individual differences.

When each person participates in both levels of the independent variable, the individual differences are controlled for, and it is easier to see the effect of the independent variable.

« For more on *t* tests, see Statistics Review: Inferential Statistics, pp. 491–495.

SITUATION NOISE

Besides measurement error and individual differences, **situation noise**—external distractions—is a third factor that could cause variability within groups and obscure true group differences. Suppose the money and mood researcher had conducted his study in the middle of the student union on campus. The sheer number of distractions in this setting would make a mess of the data. The smell of the nearby coffee shop might make some participants feel peaceful, seeing friends at the next table might make some feel extra happy, and seeing the cute guy from sociology class might make some feel nervous or self-conscious. The kind and amount of distractions in the student union would vary from participant to participant and from moment to moment. The result, once again, would be unsystematic variability within each group.

Situation noise, therefore, can add unsystematic variability to each group in an experiment. Unsystematic variability, like that caused by random measurement error or irrelevant individual differences, will obscure true differences between groups.

Researchers often attempt to minimize situation noise by carefully controlling the surroundings of an experiment. The investigator might choose to distribute money and measure people's moods in a consistently undistracting laboratory room, far from coffee shops and classmates. Similarly, the researcher studying anxiety and logical reasoning might reduce situation noise by administering the logical reasoning test on a computer in a standardized classroom environment.

Sometimes the controls for situation noise have to be extreme. Consider one study on smell (cited in Mook, 2001), in which the researchers had to control *all* extraneous odors that might reach the participants' noses. The researchers dressed the participants in steam-cleaned plastic parkas fastened tightly under the chin to trap odors from their clothes, and placed them in a steam-cleaned plastic enclosure. A layer of petroleum jelly over the face trapped odors from the skin. Only then did the researchers introduce the odors being studied by means of tubes placed directly in the participants' nostrils.

Obviously, researchers do not usually go to such extremes. But they do typically try to control the potential distractions that might affect the dependent variable. To control the situation so it doesn't induce unsystematic variability in mood (his dependent variable), the researcher would not have a TV turned on in the lab. To control the situation to avoid unsystematic variability in her dependent variable, reading performance, the educational psychologist may limit children's exposure to alternative reading activities. The researchers in the anxiety and reasoning study would want to control any kind of unsystematic situational factor that might add variability to people's scores on the logical reasoning test.

ANOTHER NAME FOR THESE SOLUTIONS: POWER

When researchers use a within-groups design, employ a strong manipulation, carefully control the experimental situation, or add more participants to a study, they are increasing the power of their study. Recall from Chapter 10 that **power**, an aspect of statistical validity, is the likelihood that a study will return a statistically significant result when the independent variable really has an effect. If online reading games really do make a difference, even a small one, will the experiment reveal it? If anxiety really affects problem solving, will the study find a significant result? A within-groups design, a strong manipulation, a larger number of participants, and less situation noise are all things that will increase the power of an experiment. Of these, the easiest way to increase power is to add more participants.

When researchers design a study with a lot of power, they are more likely to detect true patterns—even small ones. Consider the analogy of looking for an object in a dark room. If you go into the room with a big, powerful flashlight, you have a better chance of finding what you're looking for—even if it's something small, like an earring. But if you have just a candle, you'll probably miss finding smaller objects. A study with a lot of participants is like having a strong flashlight: It can detect even small differences in reading scores or happiness. Importantly, a study with a lot of participants is also desirable because it prevents a few extreme ones from having undue influence on the group averages, which could cause misleading results.

Similarly, a study with a strong manipulation is analogous to increasing the size of the object you're looking for; you'll be able to find a skateboard in the room more easily than an earring—even if you have only a candle for light (**Figure 11.18**). Good experimenters try to maximize the power of their experimental designs by strengthening their "light source" (i.e., their sample size) or increasing the size of their effects.

«
For more on power, see Statistics Review: Inferential Statistics, pp. 487–490.

Studies with low power can find only large effects

Studies with high power can find both large and small effects

FIGURE 11.18
Studies with more power can detect small effects.

Experimenters can increase a study's power by strengthening the "light source" (through large samples or accurate measurements), or by increasing the size of the effects (through strong manipulations). If a study has high power, you can be more confident it has detected any result worth finding. If a study has low power, it might return a null result inconclusively.

Sometimes There Really Is No Effect to Find

When an experiment reveals that the independent variable conditions are not significantly different, what should you conclude? The study might be flawed in some way, so you might first ask whether it was designed to elicit and detect between-group differences. Was the manipulation strong? Was the dependent measure sensitive enough? Could either variable be limited to a ceiling or floor effect? Are any design confounds working against the independent variable?

You would also ask about the study's ability to minimize within-group differences. Was the dependent variable measured as precisely as possible, to reduce measurement error? Could individual differences be obscuring the effect of the independent variable? Did the study include enough participants to detect an effect? Was the study conducted with appropriate situational controls? Any of these factors, if problematic, could explain why an experiment showed a null effect. **Table 11.2** summarizes the possible reasons for a null result in an experiment.

If, after interrogating these possible obscuring factors, you find the experiment was conducted in ways that maximized its power and yet still yielded a nonsignificant result, you can probably conclude the independent variable truly does not

TABLE 11.2

Reasons for a Null Result

OBSCURING FACTOR	EXAMPLE	QUESTIONS TO ASK
NOT ENOUGH VARIABILITY BETWEEN LEVELS **(E.G., NOT ENOUGH DIFFERENCE BETWEEN TWO AND FOUR SHAKES OF HOT SAUCE)**		
Ineffective manipulation of independent variable	One week of reading games might not improve reading skill (compared with a control group), but 3 months might improve scores.	How did the researchers manipulate the independent variable? Was the manipulation strong? Do manipulation checks suggest the manipulation did what it was intended to do?
Insufficiently sensitive measurement of dependent variable	Researchers used a pass/fail measure, when the improvement was detectable only by using a finer-grained measurement scale.	How did the researchers measure the dependent variable? Was the measure sensitive enough to detect group differences?
Ceiling or floor effects on independent variable	Researchers manipulated three levels of anxiety by threatening people with 10-volt, 50-volt, or 100-volt shocks (all of which make people very anxious).	Are there meaningful differences between the levels of the independent variable? Do manipulation checks suggest the manipulation did what it was intended to do?
Ceiling or floor effects on dependent variable	Researchers measured logical reasoning ability with a very hard test (a floor effect on logical reasoning ability).	How did the researchers measure the dependent variable? Do participants cluster near the top or near the bottom of the distribution?

OBSCURING FACTOR	EXAMPLE	QUESTIONS TO ASK
TOO MUCH VARIABILITY WITHIN LEVELS **(E.G., TOO MANY OTHER INGREDIENTS IN THE SALSA BOWLS)**		
Measurement error	Logical reasoning test scores are affected by multiple sources of random error, such as item selection, participant's mood, fatigue, etc.	Is the dependent variable measured precisely and reliably? Does the measure have good construct validity? If measurements are imprecise, did the experiment include enough participants to counteract this obscuring effect?
Individual differences	Reading scores are affected by irrelevant individual differences in motivation and ability.	Did the researchers use a within-groups design to better control for individual differences? If an independent-groups design is used, larger sample size can reduce the impact of individual differences.
Situation noise	The money and happiness study was run in a distracting location, which introduced several external influences on the participants' mood.	Did the researchers attempt to control any situational influences on the dependent variable? Did they run the study in a standardized setting?
IT'S ALSO POSSIBLE THAT . . .		
The independent variable, in truth, has no effect on the dependent variable		Did the researchers take precautions to maximize between-group variability and minimize within-group variability? In other words, does the study have adequate power? If so, and they still don't find a group difference, it's reasonable to conclude that the independent variable does not affect the dependent variable.

affect the dependent variable. Perhaps money really doesn't buy happiness. Maybe online reading games just don't help students score higher. Or perhaps anxiety really doesn't affect logical reasoning. In other words, if you read about a study that used a really strong flashlight, and yet still didn't find anything—that's a sign there's probably no effect to be found. And if their theory had predicted a difference between groups but found none, then the theory is incorrect. The Working It Through section provides an example.

There are many occurrences of true null effects in psychological science. An analysis of 1.2 million children concluded that vaccinating children does not cause autism (Taylor, Swerdfeger, & Eslick, 2014). Certain therapeutic programs apparently do not have the intended effect (such as the Scared Straight program, discussed in Chapter 1). After a certain level of income, money does not appear to be related to happiness (Diener, Horwitz, & Emmons, 1985; Lyubomirsky, King, & Diener, 2005; Lucas & Schimmack, 2009; Myers, 2000). And despite stereotypes to the contrary, women and men apparently do not differ in how much they talk (Mehl, Vazire, Ramirez-Esparza, Slatcher, & Pennebaker, 2007).

Will People Get More Involved in Local Government If They Know They'll Be Publicly Honored?

A group of researchers tested ways to get citizens more involved in local government (Arceneaux & Butler, 2016). They sent a survey to citizens of a small town, 340 of whom replied. Near the end of the survey, residents were invited to volunteer for local city committees. They were randomly assigned to read one of two messages embedded in the survey—a baseline message simply asking people to volunteer, or another promising to "publicly honor" volunteers on the city website. The dependent variable was whether people signed up to volunteer at the end of the survey. The results showed that 18.4% of people in the baseline message group expressed interest in volunteering, while 17.8% of people in the "publicly honor" message group expressed interest. The difference was not statistically significant. Can the researchers conclude that publicly honoring people doesn't make them volunteer? We'll work through the questions in Table 11.2 to find out.

QUESTIONS TO ASK	CLAIMS, QUOTES, OR DATA	INTERPRETATION AND EVALUATION
Was there enough variability between levels?		
Were the baseline message and the experimental message different enough from each other?	The title used in the baseline message was "Serve on a City Committee!" while the title used in the experimental message added, "Be a Hero to Your Community!"	These titles seem clearly different, but it's possible people did not read the text of the appeal very carefully, weakening the manipulation.
Could there have been a floor effect on the dependent variable?	The dependent variable was a simple "yes" or "no" to volunteering.	Perhaps measure the dependent variable with a finer scale, such as interest from 1 to 9.
Could there be a confound acting in reverse?	The experimental group not only read about being thanked, they also were told volunteering was heroic. This "may have reinforced the notion that participation in this context is special rather than a common expectation of democratic citizens" (p. 137).	A true effect of being publicly honored could have been counteracted by the impression that volunteering is too difficult.

QUESTIONS TO ASK	CLAIMS, QUOTES, OR DATA	INTERPRETATION AND EVALUATION
Was there too much variability within levels?		
Was there situation noise or individual differences?	People completed surveys online, so there could be a lot of distracting situation noise. In addition, individuals may differ wildly in their civic engagement and their ability to volunteer.	There was likely some within-group variability due to situation noise and irrelevant individual differences.
Was the sample size large enough to counteract situation noise and individual differences?	The sample sizes in the two groups were fairly large (more than 100 in each group).	The sample size was probably large enough to counteract these influences.
Could there be no effect of the message on volunteering?		An improved study (with a more sensitive dependent measure and a cleaner manipulation of public gratitude) might show an effect of gratitude on volunteering.
		However, we have learned that if a town uses the exact experimental message tested here, it will not increase volunteering.

Null Effects May Be Published Less Often

When studies are conducted with adequate power, null results can be just as interesting and just as informative as experiments that show group differences. However, if you're looking for studies that yielded null effects, you won't find many. There is a publication bias about what gets published in scientific journals and which stories are picked up by magazines and newspapers. Most readers are more interested in independent variables that matter than in those that do not. It's more interesting to learn dark chocolate has health benefits rather than that it doesn't, and that women and men differ on a particular trait, as opposed to being the same. Differences seem more interesting than null effects, so a publication bias, in both journals and journalism, favors differences. (For more on this publication bias, see Chapter 14.)

CHECK YOUR UNDERSTANDING

1. How can a study maximize variability between independent variable groups? (There are four ways.)

2. How can a study minimize variability within groups? (There are three ways.)

3. In your own words, describe how within-groups designs minimize unsystematic variability.

1. See pp. 332–335 and Table 11.2. 2. See pp. 335–341 and Table 11.2. 3. See pp. 338–339.

CHAPTER REVIEW

Summary

Responsible experimenters may conduct double-blind studies, measure variables precisely, or put people in controlled environments to eliminate internal validity threats and increase a study's power to avoid false null effects.

Threats to Internal Validity: Did the Independent Variable Really Cause the Difference?

- When an experiment finds that an independent variable affected a dependent variable, you can interrogate the study for twelve possible internal validity threats.

- The first three threats to internal validity to consider are design confounds, selection effects, and order effects (introduced in Chapter 10).

- Six threats to internal validity are especially relevant to the one-group, pretest/posttest design: maturation, history, regression, attrition, testing, and instrumentation threats. All of them can usually be ruled out if an experimenter conducts the study using a comparison group (either a posttest-only design or a pretest/posttest design).

- Three more internal validity threats could potentially apply to any experiment: observer bias, demand characteristics, and placebo effects.

- By interrogating a study's design and results, you can decide whether the study has ruled out all twelve threats. If it passes all your internal validity queries, you can conclude with confidence that the study was a strong one: You can trust the result and make a causal claim.

Interrogating Null Effects: What If the Independent Variable Does Not Make a Difference?

- If you encounter a study in which the independent variable had no effect on the dependent variable (a null effect), you can review the possible obscuring factors.

- Obscuring factors can be sorted into two categories of problems. One is the problem of not enough between-groups difference, which results from weak manipulations, insensitive measures, ceiling or floor effects, or a design confound acting in reverse.

- The second problem is too much within-groups variability, caused by measurement error, irrelevant individual differences, or situation noise. These problems can be counteracted by using multiple measurements, more precise measurements, within-groups designs, large samples, and very controlled experimental environments.

- If you can be reasonably sure a study avoided all the obscuring factors, then you can probably trust the result and conclude that the independent variable really does not cause a change in the dependent variable.

Key Terms

To see samples of chapter concepts in the popular media, visit www.everydayresearchmethods.com and click the box for Chapter 11.

Review Questions

1. Dr. Weber conducted a long-term study in which people were tested on happiness, asked to make two new friends, and then tested on happiness 1 month later. He noticed that six of the most introverted people dropped out by the last session. Therefore, his study might have which of the following internal validity threats?

   a. Attrition

   b. Maturation

   c. Selection

   d. Regression

2. How is a testing threat to internal validity different from an instrumentation threat?

   a. A testing threat can be prevented with random assignment; an instrumentation threat cannot.

   b. A testing threat applies only to within-groups designs; an instrumentation threat applies to any type of study design.

   c. A testing threat can be prevented with a double-blind study; an instrumentation threat can be prevented with a placebo control.

   d. A testing threat refers to a change in the participants over time; an instrumentation threat refers to a change in the measuring instrument over time.

3. A regression threat applies especially:

   a. When there are two groups in the study: an experimental group and a control group.

   b. When the researcher recruits a sample whose average is extremely low or high at pretest.

   c. In a posttest-only design.

   d. When there is a small sample in the study.

4. Dr. Banks tests to see how many training sessions it takes for dogs to learn to "Sit and stay." She randomly assigns 60 dogs to two reward conditions: one is miniature hot dogs, the other is small pieces of steak. Surprisingly, she finds the dogs in each group learn "Sit and stay" in about the same number of sessions. Given the design of her study, what is the *most likely* explanation for this null effect?

   a. The dogs loved both treats (her reward manipulation has a ceiling effect).

   b. She used too many dogs.

   c. She didn't use a manipulation check.

   d. There were too many individual differences among the dogs.

5. Dr. Banks modifies her design and conducts a second study. She uses the same number of dogs and the same design, except now she rewards one group of dogs with miniature hot dogs and another group with pieces of apple. She finds a big difference, with the hot-dogs group learning the command faster. Dr. Banks avoided a null result this time because her design:

   a. Increased the between-groups variability.

   b. Decreased the within-groups variability.

   c. Improved the study's internal validity.

6. When a study has a large number of participants and a small amount of unsystematic variability (low measurement error, low levels of situation noise), then it has a lot of:

   a. Internal validity

   b. Manipulation checks

   c. Dependent variables

   d. Power

Learning Actively

The scenarios described in items 1–3 below contain threats to internal validity. For each scenario:

   a. Identify the independent variable (IV) and dependent variable (DV).

   b. Identify the design (posttest-only, pretest/posttest, repeated measures, one-group pretest/posttest).

   c. Sketch a graph of the results. (Reminder: Put the dependent variable on the y-axis.)

   d. Decide whether the study is subject to any of the internal validity threats listed in Table 11.1.

   e. Indicate whether you could redesign the study to correct or prevent any of the internal validity threats.

1. For his senior thesis, Jack was interested in whether viewing alcohol advertising would cause college students to drink more alcohol. He recruited 25 seniors for a week-long study. On Monday and Tuesday, he had them use a secure website and record how many alcoholic beverages they had consumed the day before. On Wednesday, he invited them to the lab, where he showed them a 30-minute TV show interspersed with entertaining ads for alcoholic products. Thursday and Friday were the follow-up measures: Students logged in to the website and recorded their alcoholic beverage consumption again. Jack found that students reported increased drinking after seeing the alcohol advertising, and he concluded the advertising caused them to drink more.

2. In a cognitive psychology class, a group of student presenters wanted to demonstrate the power of retrieval cues. First, the presenters had the class memorize a list of 20 words that were read aloud to them in a random order. One minute later, the class members wrote down as many words as they could remember. On average, the class recalled 6 words. Second, the presenters told the class to try sorting the words into categories as the words were read (color words, vehicle words, and sports words). The presenters read the same words again, in a different random order. On the second test of recall, the class remembered, on average, 14 words. The presenters told the class this experiment demonstrated that categorizing helps people remember words because of the connections they can develop between various words.

3. A group of researchers investigated the effect of mindfulness meditation on mental health workers, 10 weeks after a major hurricane. A sample of 15 mental health workers were pretested on their depression and anxiety symptoms. Then they engaged in meditation training for 8 weeks. After the training was completed, they were tested on their symptoms again, using the same test. The study found that anxiety and depression symptoms were significantly lower at posttest. The researchers concluded the meditation training helped the participants (based on Waelde et al., 2008).

4. Dr. Dove was interested in the effects of eating chocolate on well-being. She randomly assigned 20 participants to two groups. Both groups ate as they normally would, but one group was instructed to eat a 1-ounce square of dark chocolate after lunch. After 4 weeks on this diet, they completed a questionnaire measuring their level of well-being (happiness, contentment). Dr. Dove was surprised to find the chocolate had no effect: Both groups, on average, scored the same on the well-being measure. Help Dr. Dove troubleshoot her study. What should she do next time to improve her chances of finding a significant effect for the chocolate-enhanced diet, if eating chocolate really does improve well-being?

The Reason Why You're an Angry Drunk

Men's Health, 2012

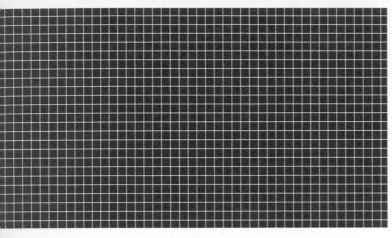

New California Law Prohibits All Cell Phone Use While Driving

KSBW8 News, 2016

12

Experiments with More Than One Independent Variable

SO FAR, YOU HAVE read two chapters about evaluating causal claims. Chapters 10 and 11 introduced experiments with one independent variable and one dependent variable. Now you're ready for experiments with more than one independent variable. What happens when more independent variables are added to the mix?

REVIEW: EXPERIMENTS WITH ONE INDEPENDENT VARIABLE

Let's start with the first headline on the opposite page: Is it true that certain people can be angry drunks? According to research, there's almost no doubt that drunk people are more aggressive than sober folks. In several studies, psychologists have brought participants into comfortable laboratory settings, had them drink various amounts of alcohol, and then placed them in different settings to measure their aggressive tendencies. For example, a team of researchers led by Aaron Duke invited community members into their lab (Duke, Giancola, Morris, Holt, & Gunn, 2011). After screening out volunteers who had problem drinking behaviors, were pregnant, or had other risky health conditions, they randomly assigned them to drink a glass of orange juice that contained different amounts of alcohol. The "active placebo" group drank orange juice with a very small amount of vodka—enough

LEARNING OBJECTIVES

A year from now, you should still be able to:

1.
Explain why researchers combine independent variables in a factorial design.

2.
Describe an interaction effect in both everyday terms and arithmetic terms.

3.
Identify and interpret the main effects and interactions from a factorial design.

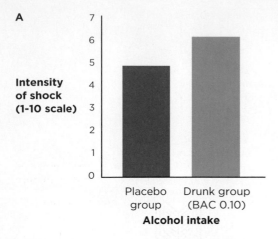

A

Intensity
of shock
(1-10 scale)

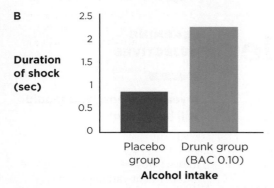

B

Duration
of shock
(sec)

FIGURE 12.1

Alcohol intake and aggressive tendencies.

Compared to a placebo group in this study, drunk participants delivered (A) higher-intensity shocks and (B) shocks for longer duration. These results demonstrated that alcohol causes people to behave aggressively (Source: Adapted from Duke et al., 2011.)

» To review counterbalancing, see Chapter 10, pp. 295–296.

to smell and to taste, but not enough to make them drunk. Another group was assigned to drink enough vodka to get drunk, by reaching a blood alcohol concentration (BAC) of 0.10% (legally impaired is BAC 0.08% or higher).

After confirming the two groups' intoxication levels with a breathalyzer test, the researchers had the volunteers play a computer game with an opponent who was supposedly in another room (the opponent was actually a computer programmed in advance). The players took turns, and when one made a mistake, the opponent was allowed to deliver a shock as punishment. Players chose the intensity of the shock their opponents would receive for each mistake (on a scale of 1 to 10), and they could hold the shock delivery button down for different lengths of time. The researchers measured the intensity and duration of the shocks each participant delivered. The more intense the shocks and the longer their duration, the more aggressive the participants were said to be. Results showed a difference: drunk participants were more aggressive (**Figure 12.1**).

The new California law in the second headline responds to research showing that using a cell phone while behind the wheel impairs a person's ability to drive. Some of the evidence comes from experiments by David Strayer and his colleagues (Strayer & Drews, 2004), who asked people to talk on hands-free cell phones in a driving simulator that looked almost exactly like a real car. As the participants drove, the researchers recorded several dependent variables, including driving speed, braking time, and following distance. In a repeated-measures (within-groups) design, they had participants drive on several 10-mile segments of highway in the simulator. For two of the segments, the drivers carried on a conversation on a hands-free cell phone. For the other two segments, drivers were not on the phone (of course, the order of the different segments was counterbalanced). The results showed that when drivers were simply talking on cell phones (not even texting or using apps), their reactions to road hazards were 18% slower. Drivers on cell phones also took longer to regain their speed after slowing down and got into more (virtual) accidents (**Figure 12.2**).

The Strayer and Drews study, like the Duke team's study, had one independent variable (cell phone use, manipulated as a within-groups variable) and one dependent variable (driving quality). Their study also showed a *difference*: People drove more poorly while using cell phones. Studies with one independent variable can demonstrate a difference between conditions. These two studies were analyzed with a simple difference score: placebo minus drunk conditions, or cell phone minus control.

Experiments with Two Independent Variables Can Show Interactions

The Strayer and Drews study found that hands-free cell phones cause people to drive badly. These researchers also wondered whether that overall difference would apply in all situations and to all people. For example, might younger drivers be less distracted by using cell phones than older drivers? On the one hand, they might, because they grew up using cell phones and are more accustomed to them. On the other hand, older drivers might be less distracted because they have more years of driving experience. By asking these questions, the researchers were thinking about adding another independent variable to the original study: driver age, and the levels could be old and young. Would the effect of driving while using a cell phone depend on age?

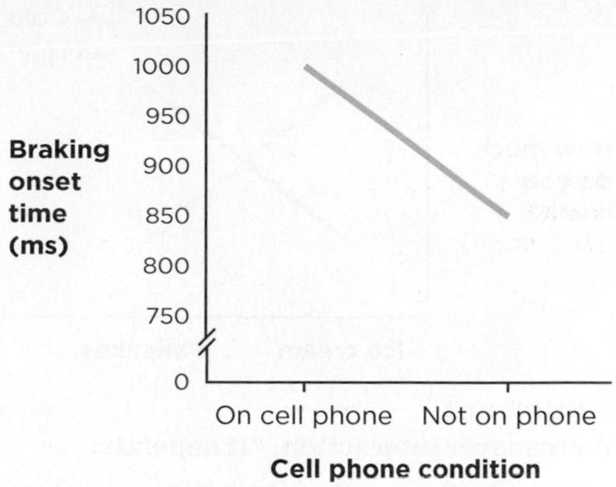

Adding an additional independent variable allows researchers to look for an **interaction effect** (or *interaction*)— whether the effect of the original independent variable (cell phone use) *depends on* the level of another independent variable (driver age). Therefore, an interaction of two independent variables allows researchers to establish whether or not "it depends." They can now ask: Does the effect of cell phones depend on age?

The mathematical way to describe an interaction of two independent variables is to say that there is a "difference in differences." In the driving example, the *difference* between the cell phone and control conditions (cell phone minus control) might be *different* for older drivers than younger drivers.

FIGURE 12.2
Cell phone use and driver reaction time.
In this study, drivers using hands-free cell phones were slower to hit the brakes in response to a road hazard. (Source: Adapted from Strayer & Drews, 2004.)

$$\text{Interaction} = \begin{array}{c} \text{a difference} \\ \text{in differences} \end{array} = \begin{array}{l} \text{the effect of one independent} \\ \text{variable depends on the level of} \\ \text{the other independent variable} \end{array}$$

Intuitive Interactions

Behaviors, thoughts, motivations, and emotions are rarely simple; they usually involve interactions between two or more influences. Therefore, much of the most important research in psychology explores interactions among multiple independent variables. What's the best way to understand what an interaction means?

Here's one example of an interaction: Do you like hot foods or cold foods? It probably depends on the food. You probably like your ice cream cold, but you like your pancakes hot. In this example, there are two independent variables: the food you are judging (ice cream or pancakes) and the temperature of the food (cold or hot).

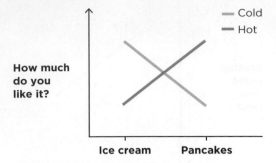

FIGURE 12.3
A crossover interaction: "It depends."

How much you like certain foods depends on the temperature at which they are served. It's equally correct to say that the temperature you prefer depends on which food you're eating.

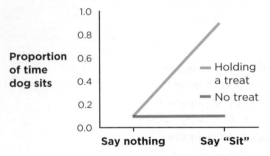

FIGURE 12.4
A spreading interaction: "Only when…"

My dog sits when I say "Sit," but only when I'm holding a treat.

The dependent variable is how much you like the food. A graph of the interaction is shown in **Figure 12.3**. Notice that the lines cross each other; this kind of interaction is sometimes called a *crossover interaction,* and the results can be described with the phrase "it depends." People's preferred food temperature depends on the type of food.

To describe this interaction, you could say that when people eat ice cream, they like their food cold more than hot; when people eat pancakes, they like their food hot more than cold. You could also apply the mathematical definition by saying that there is a *difference in differences.* You like ice cream cold more than you like it hot (cold minus hot is a positive value), but you like pancakes cold less than you like them hot (cold minus hot is a negative value).

Here's another example: the behavior of my dog, Fig. Does he sit down? It depends on whether I say "Sit," and on whether I have a treat in my hand. When I don't have a treat, Fig will not sit, even if I tell him to sit. If I do hold a treat, he will sit, but only when I say "Sit." (In other words, my stubborn dog has to be bribed.) In this example, the probability that my dog will sit is the dependent variable, and the two independent variables are what I say ("Sit" or nothing) and what I am holding (a treat or nothing). **Figure 12.4** shows a graph of this interaction. Notice that the lines are not parallel, and they do not cross over each other. This kind of interaction is sometimes called a *spreading interaction,* and the pattern can be described with the phrase "only when." My dog sits when I say "Sit," but only when I'm holding a treat.

Here is the mathematical description of this interaction: When I say nothing, there is *zero* difference between the treat and no-treat conditions (treat minus no treat equals zero). When I say "Sit," there is a *large* difference between the treat and no-treat conditions (treat minus no treat equals a positive value). There is a difference in differences.

You can graph the interaction accurately either way—by putting the "What I say" independent variable on the x-axis, as in Figure 12.4, or by putting the "What I'm holding" independent variable on the x-axis, as shown in **Figure 12.5**. Although the two graphs may look a little different, each one is an accurate representation of the data.

When psychological scientists think about behavior, they might start with a simple link between an independent and a dependent variable, but often they find they need a second independent variable to tell the full story. For example, in a romantic relationship, are positive attitudes, such as forgiveness, healthy? (In other words, does the independent variable of positive versus negative attitudes affect the dependent variable, relationship health?) The answer depends on how serious the disagreements are. Research shows that when difficulties are minor, positive attitudes are healthy for the relationship, but when the issues are major (e.g., one partner is abusive to the other or is drug-dependent), positive attitudes seem to prevent a couple from addressing their problems (McNulty, 2010). Thus, the degree of severity of the problems (minor versus major) is the second independent variable.

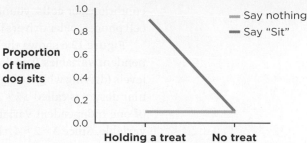

FIGURE 12.5
The same interaction, graphed the other way.
The data in Figure 12.4 can be graphed equally accurately with the other independent variable on the x-axis.

Does going to daycare hurt children's social and intellectual development? It seems to depend on the quality of care. According to one study, high-quality daycare can benefit the social and intellectual development of kids (compared to children who have only parental care); when the quality of daycare is poor, development might be impaired (Vandell, Henderson, & Wilson, 1988). Reflect for a moment: What would the dependent and independent variables be in this example?

Factorial Designs Study Two Independent Variables

When researchers want to test for interactions, they do so with factorial designs. A **factorial design** is one in which there are two or more independent variables (also referred to as *factors*). In the most common factorial design, researchers *cross* the two independent variables; that is, they study *each possible combination* of the independent variables. Strayer and Drews (2004) created a factorial design to test whether the effect of driving while talking on a cell phone depended on the driver's age. They used two independent variables (cell phone use and driver age), creating a condition representing each possible combination of the two. As shown in **Figure 12.6**, to cross the two independent variables, they essentially overlaid one independent variable on top of another. This overlay process created four unique

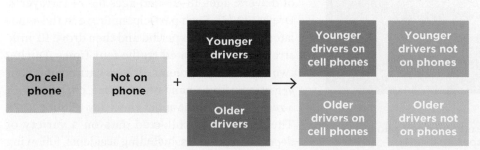

FIGURE 12.6
Factorial designs cross two independent variables.

A second independent variable was overlaid on top of a first independent variable, creating (in this case) four new experimental conditions, or cells.

conditions, or **cells**: younger drivers using cell phones, younger drivers not using cell phones, older drivers using cell phones, and older drivers not using cell phones.

Figure 12.6 shows the simplest possible factorial design. There are two independent variables (two factors)—cell phone use and age—and each one has two levels (driving while using a cell phone or not; younger or older driver). This particular design is called a 2 × 2 (two-by-two) factorial design, meaning that two levels of one independent variable are crossed with two levels of another independent variable. Since 2 × 2 = 4, there are four cells in this design.

USING FACTORIAL DESIGNS TO STUDY MANIPULATED VARIABLES OR PARTICIPANT VARIABLES

You might have noticed that one of the variables, cell phone use, was truly manipulated; the researchers had participants either talk or not talk on cell phones while driving (Strayer & Drews, 2004). The other variable, age, was not manipulated; it was a measured variable. The researchers did not assign people to be older or younger; they simply selected participants who fit those levels. Age is an example of a **participant variable**—a variable whose levels are selected (i.e., measured), not manipulated. Because the levels are not manipulated, variables such as age, gender, and ethnicity are not truly "independent" variables. However, when they are studied in a factorial design, researchers often call them independent variables, for the sake of simplicity.

Factorial Designs Can Test Limits

One reason researchers conduct studies with factorial designs is to test whether an independent variable affects different kinds of people, or people in different situations, in the same way. The study on cell phone use while driving is a good example of this purpose. By crossing age and cell phone use, the researchers were asking whether the effect of using a cell phone was limited to one age group only, or whether it would have the same effect on people of different ages.

This research team observed two samples of drivers: ages 18–25 and ages 65–74 (Strayer & Drews, 2004). Each participant drove in the simulator for a warm-up period and then drove 10-mile stretches in simulated traffic four times. During two of the four segments, drivers carried on a conversation using a hands-free phone, chatting with a research assistant about their day (**Figure 12.7**). The researchers collected data on a variety of dependent variables, including accidents, following

FIGURE 12.7
A young driver using a hands-free cell phone while driving in a simulator.

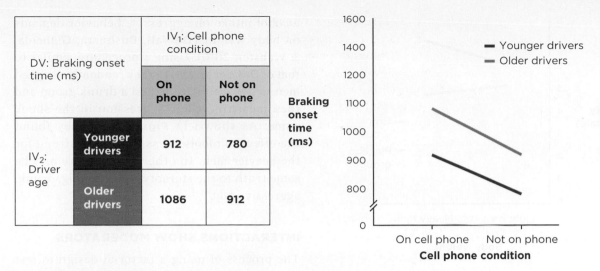

DV: Braking onset time (ms)		IV₁: Cell phone condition	
		On phone	**Not on phone**
IV₂: Driver age	**Younger drivers**	912	780
	Older drivers	1086	912

FIGURE 12.8
Factorial design results in table and graph formats. Table values depict group means.

(Source: Adapted from Strayer & Drews, 2004.)

distance, and braking onset time (how long it takes, in milliseconds, for a driver to brake for an upcoming road hazard). **Figure 12.8** shows the results for braking onset time. Notice that the same results are presented in two ways: as a table and as a graph.

The results might surprise you. The primary conclusion from this study is that the effect of talking on a cell phone did not depend on age. Older drivers did tend to brake more slowly than younger ones, overall; that finding is consistent with past research on aging drivers. However, Strayer and Drews wanted to know whether the *difference* between the cell phone and control conditions would be *different* for older drivers. The answer was no. The effect of using a cell phone (i.e., the simple difference between the cell phone condition and the control condition) was about the same in both age groups. In other words, cell phone use *did not interact with* (did not *depend on*) age. At least for these two age groups, the harmful effect of cell phone use was the same.

A FORM OF EXTERNAL VALIDITY

You might have recognized this goal of testing limits as being related to external validity. When researchers test an independent variable in more than one group at once, they are testing whether the effect generalizes. Sometimes, as in the example of age and cell phone use while driving, the independent variable affects the groups in the same way, suggesting that the effect of cell phone use generalizes to drivers of all ages.

In other cases, groups might respond differently to an independent variable. In one study, for instance, researchers tested whether the effect of

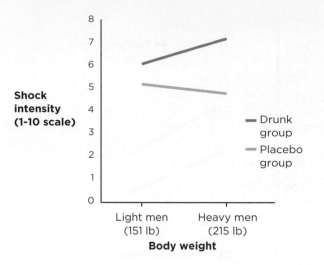

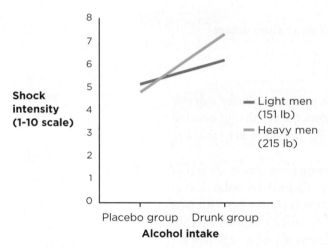

FIGURE 12.9
Testing limits with factorial design.

According to this study, the effect of alcohol on aggression is stronger in heavier men than lighter men. The same results are graphed two ways, with different independent variables on the x-axis. (Source: Adapted from DeWall et al., 2010.)

»
To review how moderators work in correlational designs, see Chapter 8, pp. 228–230.

»
To review the theory-data cycle, see Chapter 1, pp. 11–15.

alcohol intake on aggressive behavior depends on body weight (DeWall, Bushman, Giancola, & Webster, 2010). Using a procedure similar to that of Duke et al. (2011), they randomly assigned men to a placebo group and a drunk group and then measured their aggression in the shock game. As shown in **Figure 12.9**, they found the effect of alcohol was especially strong for the heavier men. In other words, there may be some truth to the stereotype of the "big, drunk, aggressive guy."

INTERACTIONS SHOW MODERATORS

The process of using a factorial design to test limits is sometimes called testing for moderators. Recall from Chapter 8 that a moderator is a variable that changes the relationship between two other variables (Kenny, 2009). In factorial design language, a moderator is an independent variable that changes the relationship between another independent variable and a dependent variable. In other words, a moderator results in an interaction; the effect of one independent variable depends on (is moderated by) the level of another independent variable. When Strayer and Drews studied whether driver age would interact with cell phone use, they found that driver age did not moderate the impact of cell phone use on braking onset time. However, DeWall and his colleagues showed that body weight moderates the effect of alcohol on aggression.

Factorial Designs Can Test Theories

Researchers can use factorial designs not only to test the generalizability of a causal variable but also to test theories. The goal of most experiments in psychological science is to test hypotheses derived from theories. Indeed, many theories make statements about how variables interact with one another. The best way to study how variables interact is to combine them in a factorial design and measure whether the results are consistent with the theory.

USING A FACTORIAL DESIGN TO TEST A THEORY OF ALCOHOL CUES

Once studies established that alcohol intake can lead to aggressive behavior, researchers wanted to dig deeper. They theorized about *why* drinking alcohol causes aggression. One idea is that alcohol impairs the brain's executive functioning; it interferes with a person's ability to consider the consequences of his or her actions (Giancola, 2000). In addition to pharmacological effects, another theory suggests that through exposure to cultural messages and stereotypes about drinking behavior, people learn to cognitively associate alcohol with aggression. Merely *thinking* about alcohol might prime people to think about aggression. Researchers Bruce Bartholow and Adrienne Heinz (2006) sought to test the theory that alcohol can become cognitively associated with thoughts of aggression. They didn't get anybody drunk in their research; they simply exposed them to pictures of alcohol.

In the lab, participants viewed a series of images and words on a computer screen. Their task was to indicate whether a string of letters was a word or a nonword. For example, the letter string EDVIAN would be classified as a nonword, and the letter string INVADE would be classified as a word. Some of the words were aggression-related (e.g., *hit*, *combat*, or *fight*) and others were neutral (e.g., *sit*, *wonder*, or *caught*).

Before seeing each of the word strings, participants viewed a photograph on the computer screen for a brief period (300 ms). Sometimes the photograph was related to alcohol, perhaps a beer bottle or a martini glass. Other times the photograph was not related to alcohol; it was a photo of a plant. The researchers hypothesized that people would be faster to identify aggression-related words after seeing the photos of alcohol. They used the computer to measure how quickly people responded to the words.

As shown in **Figure 12.10**, Bartholow and Heinz were interested in the interaction of two independent variables: photo type (alcohol or plant) and word type (aggressive or neutral). The results told the story they hypothesized: When people

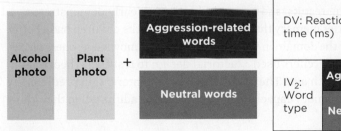

FIGURE 12.10

Theory testing by crossing two independent variables.

This type of design creates all possible combinations of the independent variables. Here, one independent variable (photo type) is crossed with another independent variable (word type) to create all four possible combinations.

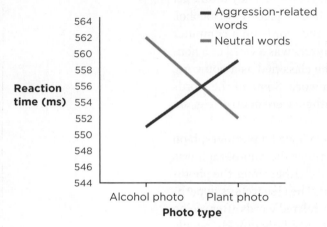

DV: Reaction time (ms)	IV₁: Photo type	
	Alcohol	**Plant**
IV₂: Word type — **Aggressive**	551	559
Neutral	562	552

FIGURE 12.11
Factorial study results in table and graph formats.
(Source: Adapted from Bartholow & Heinz, 2006.)

had just seen a photo of alcohol, they were quicker to identify an aggressive word. When people had just seen a photo of a plant, they were slower to identify an aggressive word (**Figure 12.11**).

This study is a good example of how a researcher can test a theory using a factorial design. The resulting interaction supported one theory of why alcohol intake causes aggressive behavior: People cognitively associate alcohol cues with aggressive concepts.

USING AN INTERACTION TO TEST A MEMORY THEORY

Another study used a factorial design to test why memory capacity develops as children get older. One theory stated that adults remember more than children do simply because of accumulated knowledge. A richer knowledge structure enables adults to make more mental connections for storing new information. One researcher tested this theory by comparing the memory abilities of two groups: Children who were chess experts (recruited from a chess tournament) and adults who were chess novices (Chi, 1978). Both groups performed two memory tasks: recalling digits (numbers) read in random order, and recalling the placement of pieces on a chessboard during a game in progress. Over a series of trials, participants were asked to remember more and more numbers and more and more chess pieces.

This study had a 2 × 2 design, with a participant variable (child experts or adult novices) and an independent variable (digits versus chess pieces). The number of items recalled was the dependent variable. The results, shown in **Figure 12.12**, clearly demonstrate that while the adults had better memory than children for digits, the children had a better memory than adults for the domain in which they had more knowledge: chess pieces.

In this study, the researchers used a factorial design to test their theory about why memory develops with age. The results showed the interaction predicted by the theory: Children's memory capacity can be better than adults when they know a lot about the topic.

Interpreting Factorial Results: Main Effects and Interactions

After running a study with a factorial design with two independent variables, researchers, of course, want to analyze the results. In a design with two

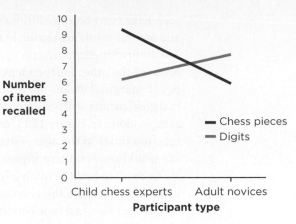

DV: Items recalled		IV₁: Participant type	
		Child chess experts	**Adult novices**
IV₂: Type of item	**Chess pieces**	9.3	5.9
	Digits	6.1	7.8

FIGURE 12.12
A factorial study of memory development.

Do children have less memory capacity than adults? It depends on the type of memory task.
(Source: Adapted from Chi, 1978.)

independent variables, there will be three results to inspect: two main effects
and one interaction effect.

MAIN EFFECTS: IS THERE AN OVERALL DIFFERENCE?

In a factorial design, researchers test each independent variable to look for a **main
effect** the overall effect of one independent variable on the dependent variable,
averaging over the levels of the other independent variable. In other words, a main
effect is a simple difference. In a factorial design with two independent variables,
there are two main effects.

Figure 12.13 shows the data from the Bartholow and Heinz (2006) study on
word association. One independent variable, word type, is highlighted in blue;
the other, photo type, is highlighted in yellow. First, to look for a main effect of
word type, you would compute the reaction time to aggressive words (averaging
across the two photo conditions), and the reaction time to neutral words (averaging

FIGURE 12.13
**Using marginal means
to look for main effects.**

Looking for the main effect
of an independent variable
(IV) involves computing the
overall score for each level
of that IV, averaging over the
levels of the other IV. Neither
main effect in this study
is statistically significant.
(DV = dependent variable.)
(Source: Adapted from
Bartholow & Heinz, 2006.)

DV: Reaction time (ms)		IV₁: Photo type		**Main effect for IV₂:** Word type
		Alcohol	**Plant**	
IV₂: Word type	**Aggressive**	551	559	**555 (average of 551 and 559)**
	Neutral	562	552	**557 (average of 562 and 552)**
Main effect for IV₁: Photo type		**556.5 (average of 551 and 562)**	**555.5 (average of 559 and 552)**	

across the two photo conditions). The resulting two marginal means for aggressive and neutral words are shown in the far-right column of the table. **Marginal means** are the arithmetic means for each level of an independent variable, averaging over levels of the other independent variable. If the sample size in each cell is exactly equal, marginal means are a simple average. If the sample sizes are unequal, the marginal means will be computed using the weighted average, counting the larger sample more. In Figure 12.13, notice there's not much difference overall between reaction times to the aggressive words (555 ms) and the neutral words (557 ms). We would say that there appears to be no main effect of word type.

Second, to find the main effect of photo type, the other independent variable, you would compute the reaction time after seeing the alcohol photos, averaged across the two word type conditions, and the reaction time after seeing the plant photos, also averaged across the two word type conditions. These two marginal means are shown in the bottom row of the table. Here again, there is not much overall difference: On average, people are about as fast to respond after an alcohol photo (556.5 ms) as they are after a plant photo (555.5 ms). There appears to be no main effect of photo type.

» For more on statistical significance, see Chapter 10, p. 304, and Statistics Review: Inferential Statistics, pp. 499–500.

Main Effects May or May Not Be Statistically Significant. Researchers look at the marginal means to inspect the main effects in a factorial design, and they use statistics to find out whether the difference in the marginal means is statistically significant. Recall from Chapter 10 that Mueller and Oppenheimer (2014) asked whether the observed differences between laptop and longhand notetaking were statistically significant. Similarly, Bartholow and Heinz explored whether the overall difference in reaction times to the two word types was statistically significant. They also investigated whether the overall difference in reaction times after the two types of photos was statistically significant. In their study, neither of these main effects was statistically significant. The observed difference in marginal means is about what you would expect to see by chance if there were no difference in the population.

Sometimes statistical significance tests indicate that a main effect is, in fact, statistically significant. For example, **Figure 12.14** shows results from the study

FIGURE 12.14
A study with two main effects.
The marginal means on the right show a statistically significant main effect of alcohol intake (such that drunk men are more aggressive than sober men). The marginal means in the bottom row show a statistically significant main effect of body weight (heavy men are more aggressive than light men). (Source: Adapted from DeWall et al., 2010.)

DV: Shock intensity (1-10 scale)		IV$_1$: Body weight		
		Light men (151 lb)	**Heavy men (215 lb)**	Main effect for IV$_2$: Drinking condition
IV$_2$: Drinking condition	**Placebo group**	**5.09**	**4.72**	**4.91 (average of 5.09 and 4.72)**
	Drunk group	**6.00**	**7.19**	**6.60 (average of 6.00 and 7.19)**
Main effect for IV$_1$: Body weight		**5.55 (average of 5.09 and 6.00)**	**5.96 (average of 4.72 and 7.19)**	

DV: Reaction time (ms)		IV₁: Photo type	
		Alcohol	**Plant**
IV₂: Word type	**Aggressive**	551	559
	Neutral	562	552

Difference is –11 (551 – 562 = –11)   Difference is 7 (559 – 552 = 7)

Differences are statistically significantly different (–11 < 7). There is an interaction.

FIGURE 12.15
Estimating interactions from a table (the difference in differences): option 1.

This format focuses on row differences. (Source: Adapted from Bartholow & Heinz, 2006.)

that measured aggression in drunk and sober men (DeWall et al., 2010). The analysis of the marginal means revealed a statistically significant main effect for the drinking condition, such that drunk men were more aggressive than sober men. It also revealed a statistically significant main effect for body weight, such that heavy men were more aggressive than light men.

Main Effect = Overall Effect. The term *main effect* is usually misleading because it seems to suggest that it is the most important effect in a study. It is not. In fact, when a study's results show an interaction, the interaction itself is the most important effect. Think of a main effect instead as an *overall effect*—the overall effect of one independent variable at a time.

INTERACTIONS: IS THERE A DIFFERENCE IN DIFFERENCES?

In a factorial design with two independent variables, the first two results obtained are the main effects for each independent variable. The third result is the interaction effect. Whereas the main effects are simple differences, the interaction effect is the difference in differences.

Estimating Interactions from a Table. You can use a table to estimate whether a study's results show an interaction. Because an interaction is a difference in differences, you start by computing two differences. **Figure 12.15** shows the process using the Bartholow and Heinz (2006) study. Begin with one level of the first independent variable: the alcohol photos. The difference in reaction time between the aggressive and neutral words for the alcohol photos is 551 – 562 = –11 ms. Then go to the second level of the first independent variable: the plant photos. The difference in reaction time between the aggressive and neutral words for the plant photos is 559 – 552 = 7 ms. (Be sure to compute the difference in the same direction both times; in this case, always subtracting the results for the neutral words from those for the aggressive words.) There are two differences: –11 ms and 7 ms. These differences are different: One is negative and one is positive. Indeed, statistical tests told the researchers that the difference of 18 ms is statistically significant. Therefore, you can conclude that there is an interaction in this factorial study.

This format focuses on column differences, whereas the table format in Figure 12.15 focused on row differences. Interactions can be computed either way. (Source: Adapted from Strayer & Drews, 2004.)

DV: Braking onset time (ms)		IV$_1$: Cell phone condition		
		On cell phone		**Not on phone**
IV$_2$: Driver age	**Younger drivers**	912	Difference is 132 (912 – 780 = 132)	780
	Older drivers	1086	Difference is 174 (1086 – 912 = 174)	912

These differences are not significantly different (174 is not significantly larger than 132). There is no interaction.

You could estimate the difference in differences the other way instead, by computing the difference in reaction times to the alcohol and plant photos, first for aggressive words (551 – 559 = –8 ms) and then for neutral words (562 – 552 = 10 ms). Although the values will be slightly different this time, you will reach the same conclusion: There is an interaction. The differences are different (–8 is different from 10).

Similarly, **Figure 12.16** shows how to compute the interaction for the Strayer and Drews (2004) study on using cell phones while driving. Again, if you start with one level of one independent variable, the younger drivers, the difference in braking onset time between drivers using cell phones and drivers who are not using cell phones is 912 – 780 = 132 ms. Next, among the older drivers, the difference in braking onset time between drivers using cell phones and drivers not using cell phones is 1086 – 912 = 174 ms. Are the two differences, 132 and 174, different? They may look a little different, but this is where statistics come in. Just as with main effects, researchers use significance tests to tell them whether a difference in differences is significantly different from zero. Strayer and Drews's statistical significance tests told them that the two differences are *not* significantly different. So, in this case, there is not a significant difference in differences. In fact, at each age level, there is a 15% drop in braking onset time.

Detecting Interactions from a Graph. While it's possible to compute interactions from a table, it is sometimes easier to notice them on a graph. When results from a factorial design are plotted as a line graph and the lines are not parallel, there may be an interaction, something you would confirm with a significance test. In **Figure 12.17A**, you would suspect an interaction because the lines cross (indeed, the researchers report that the interaction is significant). If the lines are parallel, as in **Figure 12.17B**, there probably is *no* interaction (these researchers reported that the interaction was not significant). Notice that lines don't have to cross to indicate an interaction; they simply have to be nonparallel. For example, look back at the first graph in Figure 12.9, and see nonparallel lines indicating an interaction between aggression and body weight.

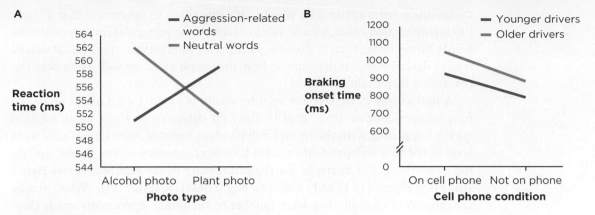

FIGURE 12.17
Detecting interactions from a line graph.

(A) An interaction in the Bartholow and Heinz (2006) study—the lines are not parallel.
(B) No interaction in the Strayer and Drews (2004) study—the lines are almost
perfectly parallel.

You can also estimate interactions from a bar graph. As you inspect the bar
graphs in **Figure 12.18** (parts A and B), imagine drawing a line to connect the tops
of the two orange bars and a line to connect the tops of the two pink bars. Would
those lines be parallel or not? Or you might notice if the differences between the
bar heights change as you go across the x-axis. Are the differences different, or are
they the same? Remember that statistical tests must confirm that any apparent
difference in differences is significant.

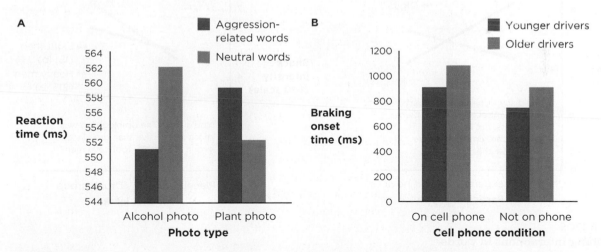

FIGURE 12.18
Detecting interactions from a bar graph.

(A) Results of the Bartholow and Heinz (2006) study. (B) Results of the Strayer and
Drews (2004) study. Is it easier to detect interactions in this format or in the line graphs
in Figure 12.17?

Describing Interactions in Words. It's one thing to determine that a study has an interaction effect; it's another to describe the pattern of the interaction in words. Since there are many possible patterns for interactions, there's no standard way to describe one: It depends on how the graph looks, as well as on how the researcher frames the results.

A foolproof way to describe an interaction is to start with one level of the first independent variable (that is, the first category on the x-axis), explain what's happening with the second independent variable, then move to the next level of the first independent variable (the next category on the x-axis) and do the same thing. For example, for the interaction in the Bartholow and Heinz study (see Figures 12.17 and 12.18), you might describe it like this: "When people saw photos of alcohol, they were quicker to recognize aggression words than neutral words, but when people saw photos of plants, they were slower to recognize aggression words than neutral words." As you move across the x-axis, you make it clear that the effect of the other independent variable (word type) is changing.

Another way to describe interactions involves key phrases. Some interactions, like the crossover interaction in **Figure 12.19A**, can be described using the phrase "it depends," as in: "The memory capacity of children depends on their level of expertise." Other interactions, like those in **Figure 12.19B**, can be described using the phrase "especially for," as in: "Alcohol leads to aggression, especially for heavy guys."

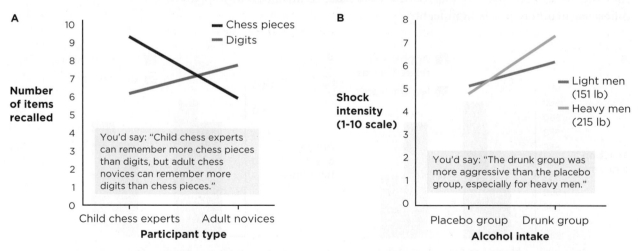

FIGURE 12.19
Describing interactions in words.
Method 1: Start with the first level of the independent variable (IV) on the x-axis, and describe what's happening with the other IV. Then move to the second level of the IV on the y-axis, and describe what's happening with the other IV. Method 2: Describe the difference in differences, using phrases like "especially for" and "depends on."

INTERACTIONS ARE MORE IMPORTANT THAN MAIN EFFECTS

When researchers analyze the results of a factorial design, they look at main effects for each independent variable and they look for interactions. When a study shows both a main effect and an interaction, *the interaction is almost always more important*.

The study on alcohol, aggression, and body weight provides an example of this principle (DeWall et al., 2010). This factorial design resulted in a main effect for body weight (heavy men were more aggressive than light men), a main effect for alcohol intake (alcohol made people more aggressive than the placebo), and a significant interaction. However, the overall difference (main effect) for body weight actually hides the fact that body weight influences aggressive behavior only when men are drunk. And the overall difference (main effect) for alcohol intake actually hides the fact that alcohol intake makes a difference *especially* for heavy men. So there may be real differences in the marginal means, but the exciting—and most accurate—story in this study is the interaction.

POSSIBLE MAIN EFFECTS AND INTERACTIONS IN A 2 × 2 FACTORIAL DESIGN

Figure 12.20 shows a variety of hypothetical outcomes from a single study. In all the examples, the independent variables are the same: a cell phone condition and an age condition. The dependent variable is the average number of accidents. This figure presents a variety of outcomes, all of which were invented in order to show different possible combinations of main effects and interactions in a 2 × 2 factorial design. Note, too, how each main effect and interaction can be described in words.

CHECK YOUR UNDERSTANDING

1. Describe why Bartholow and Heinz's word association study on alcohol and thoughts of aggression was a factorial design.

2. What are two common reasons to use a factorial design?

3. How can you detect an interaction from a table of means? From a line graph?

4. Why might it be better to call a main effect an "overall effect"?

1. It's factorial because they used all possible combinations of two independent variables. See p. 359.
2. See pp. 358–360. 3. See pp. 363–365. 4. See pp. 361–363.

Summary of effects	Cell means and marginal means	Line graph of the results
Main effect for cell phone: **No** Main effect for age: **No** Age × cell phone interaction: **Yes**—younger drivers on a cell phone cause more accidents; older drivers on a cell phone cause fewer accidents	**DV: Number of accidents** — On cell phone / Not on phone Younger drivers: 10 / 4 → 7 Older drivers: 4 / 10 → 7 7 / 7	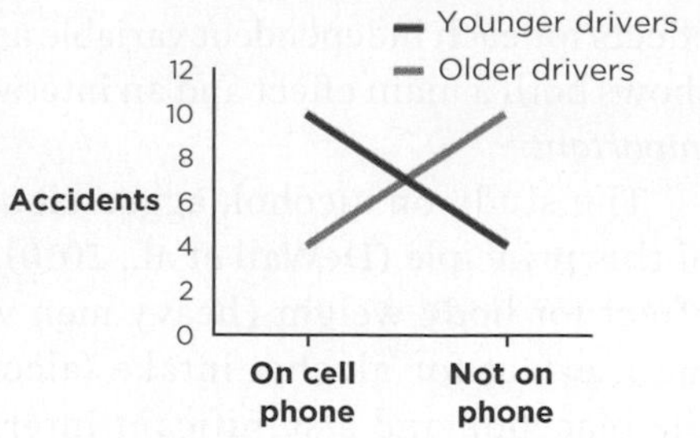
Main effect for cell phone: **No** Main effect for age: **Yes**—younger drivers have more accidents Age × cell phone interaction: **No**	**DV: Number of accidents** — On cell phone / Not on phone Younger drivers: 10 / 10 → 10 Older drivers: 4 / 4 → 4 7 / 7	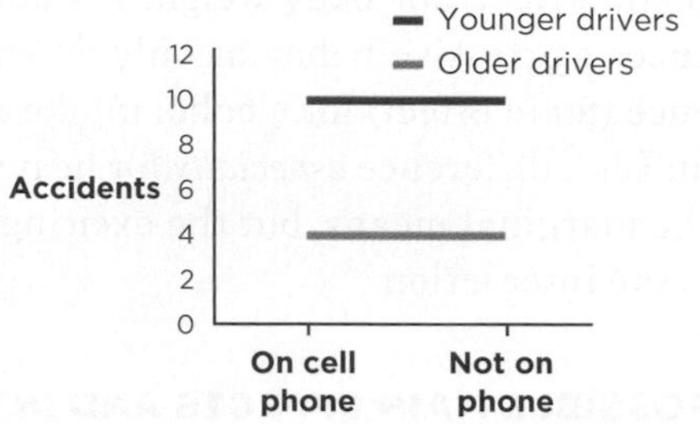
Main effect for cell phone: **Yes**—cell phones cause more accidents Main effect for age: **No** Age × cell phone interaction: **No**	**DV: Number of accidents** — On cell phone / Not on phone Younger drivers: 10 / 4 → 7 Older drivers: 10 / 4 → 7 10 / 4	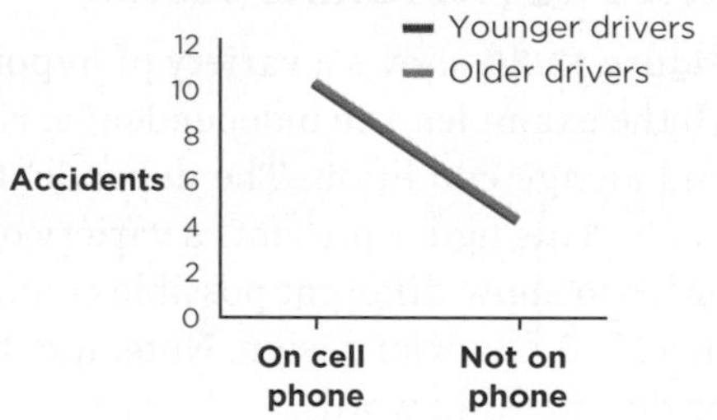
Main effect for cell phone: **Yes**—cell phones cause more accidents Main effect for age: **Yes**—younger drivers have more accidents Age × cell phone interaction: **Yes**—for younger drivers, cell phones do not make a difference, but for older drivers, cell phones cause more accidents	**DV: Number of accidents** — On cell phone / Not on phone Younger drivers: 10 / 10 → 10 Older drivers: 10 / 4 → 7 10 / 7	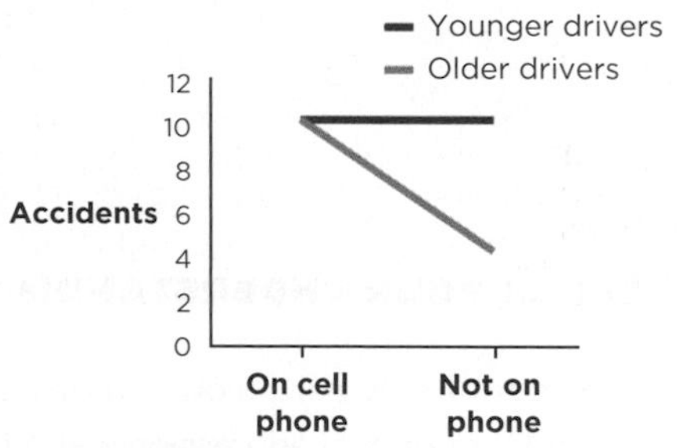

FIGURE 12.20

A range of possible outcomes from a single 2 × 2 factorial design.

Use this chart to study how various outcomes result in different patterns of main effects and interactions. (All data are fabricated for illustration purposes.)

Summary of effects	Cell means and marginal means	Line graph of the results
Main effect for cell phone: **Yes**—cell phones cause more accidents Main effect for age: **Yes**—older drivers have more accidents Age × cell phone interaction: **Yes**—impact of a cell phone is larger for older than for younger drivers	DV: Number of accidents — On cell phone / Not on phone Younger drivers: 8, 2, 5 Older drivers: 12, 3, 7.5 10, 2.5	
Main effect for cell phone: **No** Main effect for age: **No** Age × cell phone interaction: **No**	DV: Number of accidents — On cell phone / Not on phone Younger drivers: 5, 5, 5 Older drivers: 5, 5, 5 5, 5	
Main effect for cell phone: **Yes**—cell phones cause more accidents Main effect for age: **No** Age × cell phone interaction: **Yes**—for younger drivers, cell phones make no difference, but for older drivers, cell phones cause more accidents	DV: Number of accidents — On cell phone / Not on phone Younger drivers: 5, 5, 5 Older drivers: 8, 2, 5 6.5, 3.5	
Main effect for cell phone: **No** Main effect for age: **Yes**—younger drivers have more accidents Age × cell phone interaction: **Yes**—for younger drivers, cell phones cause more accidents, but for older drivers, cell phones cause fewer accidents	DV: Number of accidents — On cell phone / Not on phone Younger drivers: 8, 5, 6.5 Older drivers: 2, 5, 3.5 5, 5	

FACTORIAL VARIATIONS

Now you're ready to explore some advanced variations on the basic 2 × 2 factorial design. What happens when one of the independent variables is manipulated within groups? What happens when an independent variable has more than two levels? What if there's a third independent variable?

Recall from Chapter 10 that in a simple experiment, the independent variable can be manipulated as either an independent-groups variable (different people participate at each level) or a within-groups variable (the same people participate at each level, as in a repeated-measures design). The same is true for factorial designs. Researchers can choose whether to manipulate *each* independent variable as independent-groups or within-groups.

Independent-Groups Factorial Designs

In an independent-groups factorial design (also known as a between-subjects factorial), both independent variables are studied as independent-groups. Therefore, if the design is a 2 × 2, there are four different groups of participants in the experiment. The DeWall team's study on alcohol, aggression, and body weight was an independent-groups factorial: Some lighter-weight men drank a placebo beverage, other light men drank an alcoholic one, some heavier men drank a placebo beverage, and other heavy men drank an alcoholic one. In other words, there were different men in each cell. If the researchers decided to use 50 participants in each cell of the design, they would have needed a full 200 participants: 50 in each of the four groups.

Within-Groups Factorial Designs

In a within-groups factorial design (also called a repeated-measures factorial), both independent variables are manipulated as within-groups. If the design is 2 × 2, there is only one group of participants, but they participate in all four combinations, or cells, of the design. The Bartholow and Heinz study was a within-groups factorial design. All participants saw both alcohol photos and plant photos, which alternated over successive trials. In addition, all participants responded to both aggression-related words and neutral words.

A within-groups factorial design requires fewer participants. If Bartholow and Heinz had decided to use 50 people in each cell of their study, they would need a total of only 50 people because every person participates in each of the four cells. Therefore, within-groups designs make efficient use of participants (**Figure 12.21**). Because it was a within-groups design, the researchers counterbalanced the order of presentation of photos and words by having the computer present the photos and their subsequent words in a different random order for each participant.

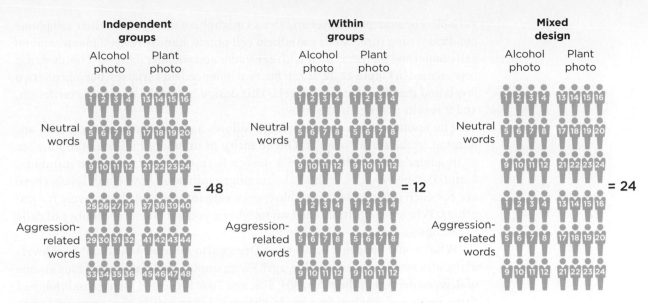

FIGURE 12.21
Within-groups designs are more efficient.
To achieve a goal of 12 observations per cell, an independent-groups factorial design would need 48 participants. A within-groups factorial design would require 12 participants, and a mixed design would require 24 participants.

Mixed Factorial Designs

In a mixed factorial design, one independent variable is manipulated as independent-groups and the other is manipulated as within-groups. The Strayer and Drews study on cell phone use while driving for two different age groups is an example of a mixed factorial design. Age was an independent-groups participant variable: Participants in one group were younger and those in the other group were older. But the cell phone condition independent variable was manipulated as within-groups. Each participant drove in both the cell phone and the control conditions of the study. If Strayer and Drews had wanted 50 people in each cell of their 2 × 2 mixed design, they would have needed a total of 100 people: 50 younger drivers and 50 older drivers, each participating at both levels of the cell phone condition.

Increasing the Number of Levels of an Independent Variable

The discussion so far has focused on the simplest factorial design, the 2 × 2. This design has two independent variables, each with two levels, creating four conditions (2 × 2 = 4). However, researchers can add more levels to each independent variable. For example, Strayer and Drews might have manipulated their cell phone condition using three levels (handheld cell phone, hands-free cell phone, and no cell phone) and then crossed it with age (older and younger drivers). This design is represented in **Figure 12.22**. It still has two independent variables, but one has two levels and the other has three levels. This design is called a 2 × 3 factorial design, and it results in six cells (2 × 3 = 6).

The notation for factorial designs follows a simple pattern. Factorials are notated in the form "— × —." The quantity of numbers indicates the number of independent variables (a 2 × 3 design is represented with two numbers, 2 and 3). The value of each of the numbers indicates how many levels there are for each independent variable (two levels for one and three levels for the other). When you multiply the two numbers, you get the total number of cells in the design.

What would happen if Strayer and Drews also increased the number of levels of the other independent variable, age? For example, what if they used four groups of drivers: drivers in their 20s, 30s, 50s, and 70s? If the cell phone condition had three levels and age had four levels, the new design would be represented as in **Figure 12.23**. There are still two independent variables, but one of them has three levels and the other has four levels. The new design is called a 3 × 4 factorial design, and it results in 12 cells (3 × 4 = 12).

When independent variables have more than two levels, researchers can still investigate main effects and interactions by computing the marginal means and seeing whether they are different. The easiest way to detect interactions is to plot the results on a line graph and see whether the lines run parallel. As in a 2 × 2 factorial design, statistical tests would confirm whether any of the main effects or interactions are statistically significant.

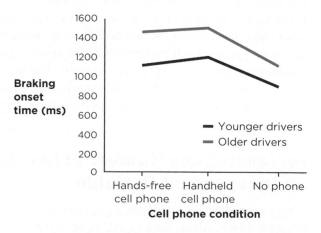

DV: Braking onset time (ms)		IV$_1$: Cell phone condition		
		Hands-free cell phone	**Handheld cell phone**	**No phone**
IV$_2$: Driver age	**Younger drivers**	1100	1200	850
	Older drivers	1450	1500	1050

FIGURE 12.22
A 2 × 3 factorial design.

(Data are fabricated for illustration purposes.)

DV: Braking onset time (ms)		IV$_1$: Cell phone condition		
		Hands-free cell phone	Handheld cell phone	No phone
IV$_2$: Driver age	Age 20-29	1100	1200	850
	Age 30-49	1120	1225	820
	Age 50-69	1300	1400	900
	Age 70+	1600	1500	1050

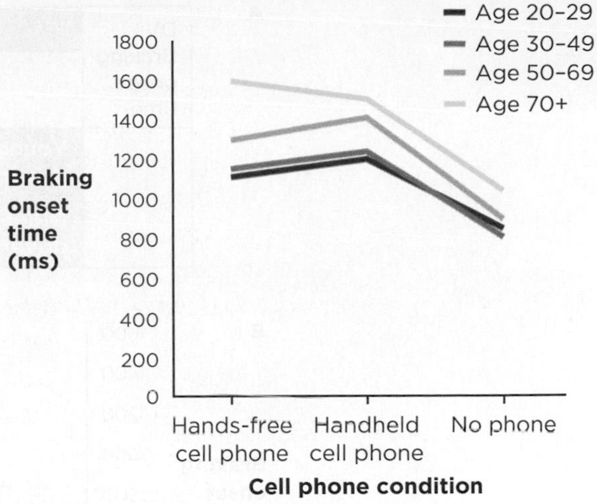

FIGURE 12.23
A 3 × 4 factorial design.
(Data are fabricated for illustration purposes.)

Increasing the Number of Independent Variables

For some research questions, researchers find it necessary to have more than two independent variables in a crossed factorial design. For instance, suppose Strayer and Drews decided to study not only the cell phone independent variable and the age independent variable, but also two kinds of traffic conditions: dense traffic and light traffic. Would this third independent variable make a difference?

Such a design is called a 2 × 2 × 2 factorial, or a three-way design. There are two levels of the first independent variable, two levels of the second, and two levels of the third. This design would create eight cells, or conditions, in the experiment (2 × 2 × 2 = 8). The best way to depict a three-way design is to construct the original 2 × 2 table twice, once for each level of the third independent variable, as shown in **Figure 12.24A**. To graph a three-way design, you create two side-by-side line graphs, as shown in **Figure 12.24B**.

To make this study a three-way design, Strayer and Drews might manipulate the new variable as independent-groups, having some participants drive in light traffic only and others drive in heavy traffic only. Or they might manipulate the new variable as within-groups, having all participants drive in both light and heavy traffic. Either way, the design is considered a three-way factorial design.

MAIN EFFECTS AND INTERACTIONS FROM A THREE-WAY DESIGN

When a factorial design has three independent variables, the number of differences to be investigated increases dramatically. In a three-way design, you are concerned with three main effects (one for each independent variable), plus three separate two-way interactions and a three-way interaction.

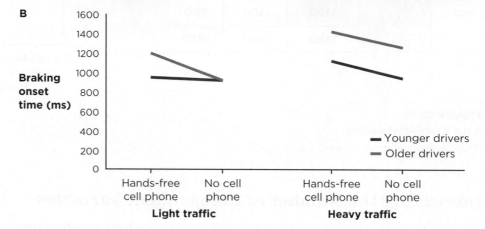

DV: Braking onset time	Light traffic			Heavy traffic		
		Hands-free cell phone	No cell phone		Hands-free cell phone	No cell phone
	Younger drivers	957	928	Younger drivers	1112	933
	Older drivers	1200	929	Older drivers	1412	1250

FIGURE 12.24

A 2 × 2 × 2 factorial design.

(A) Two side-by-side tables. (B) Two side-by-side line graphs. (Data are fabricated for illustration purposes.)

TABLE 12.1

Main Effects in a Three-Way Factorial Design

MAIN EFFECT FOR CELL PHONE VS. CONTROL

Cell phone (mean of 957, 1200, 1112, 1412)	1170.25
No cell phone (mean of 928, 929, 933, 1250)	1010.00

MAIN EFFECT FOR DRIVER AGE

Younger drivers (mean of 957, 928, 1112, 933)	982.50
Older drivers (mean of 1200, 929, 1412, 1250)	1197.75

MAIN EFFECT FOR TRAFFIC CONDITIONS

Light traffic (mean of 957, 1200, 928, 929)	1003.50
Heavy traffic (mean of 1112, 1412, 933, 1250)	1176.75

Note: To estimate each main effect in a three-way factorial design, you average the means for braking onset time for each level of each independent variable, ignoring the levels of the other two independent variables. The means come from Figure 12.2. (These estimates assume there are equal numbers of participants in each cell.)

Main Effects: Is There a Difference? Because there are three independent variables in a 2 × 2 × 2 design, there will be three main effects to test. Each main effect represents a simple, overall difference: the effect of one independent variable, averaged across the other two independent variables. **Table 12.1** shows how the three main effects were computed. Overall, drivers brake more slowly in the cell phone condition than in the control condition. Overall, older drivers brake more slowly than younger drivers. And overall, drivers are slower to brake in heavy traffic than in light traffic. Remember that main effects test only one independent variable at a time. When describing each main effect, you don't mention the other two independent variables because you averaged across them.

Two-Way Interactions: Is There a Difference in Differences? In a three-way design, there are three possible two-way interactions. In the driving with cell phone example, these would be:

1. Age × traffic condition (a two-way interaction averaging over the cell phone condition variable).
2. Age × cell phone condition (a two-way interaction averaging over the traffic conditions variable).
3. Cell phone condition × traffic condition (a two-way interaction averaging over the age variable).

To inspect each of these two-way interactions, you construct three 2 × 2 tables, as in **Figure 12.25**. After computing the means, you can investigate the difference

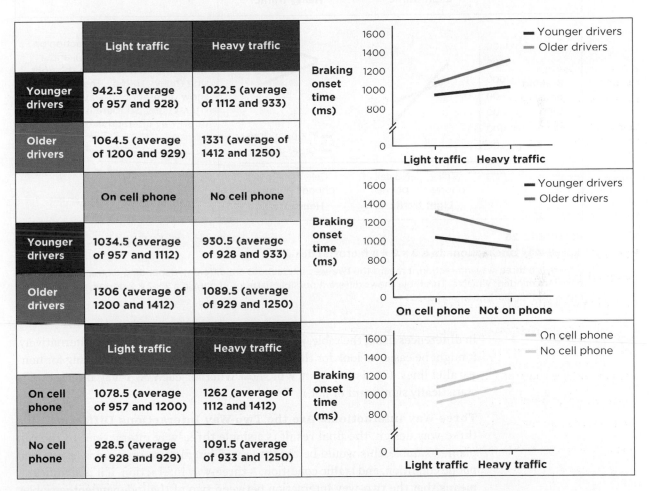

FIGURE 12.25

Two-way interactions in a 2 × 2 × 2 factorial design.

Data are recombined to estimate the three two-way interactions in this study. The means come from Figure 12.24.

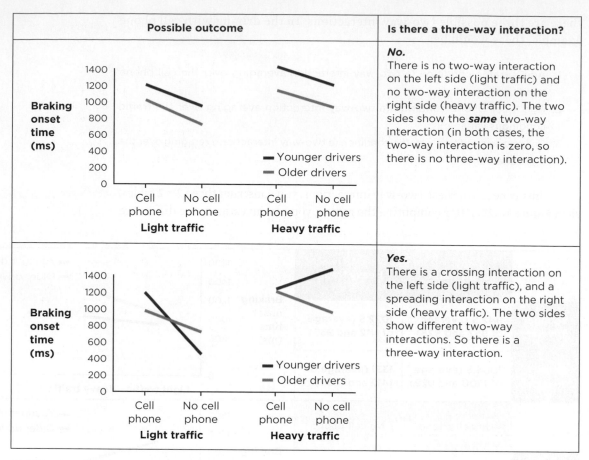

Possible outcome	Is there a three-way interaction?
	No. There is no two-way interaction on the left side (light traffic) and no two-way interaction on the right side (heavy traffic). The two sides show the **same** two-way interaction (in both cases, the two-way interaction is zero, so there is no three-way interaction).
	Yes. There is a crossing interaction on the left side (light traffic), and a spreading interaction on the right side (heavy traffic). The two sides show different two-way interactions. So there is a three-way interaction.

FIGURE 12.26

Three-way interactions in a 2 × 2 × 2 factorial design.

If there is a three-way interaction, it means the two-way interactions are different, depending on the level of a third independent variable. This table shows different possible patterns of data in a 2 × 2 × 2 design. (Data are fabricated for illustration purposes.)

in differences using the table, just as you did for a two-way design. Alternatively, it might be easier to look for the interaction by graphing it and checking for non-parallel lines. (Statistical tests will show whether each two-way interaction is statistically significant or not.)

Three-Way Interactions: Are the Two-Way Interactions Different? In a three-way design, the final result is a single three-way interaction. In the cell phone example, this would be the three-way interaction among driver age, cell phone condition, and traffic condition. A three-way interaction, if it is significant, means that the two-way interaction between two of the independent variables *depends on* the level of the third independent variable. In mathematical terms, a significant three-way interaction means that the "difference in differences . . . is different." (You are allowed to smile when you say this.)

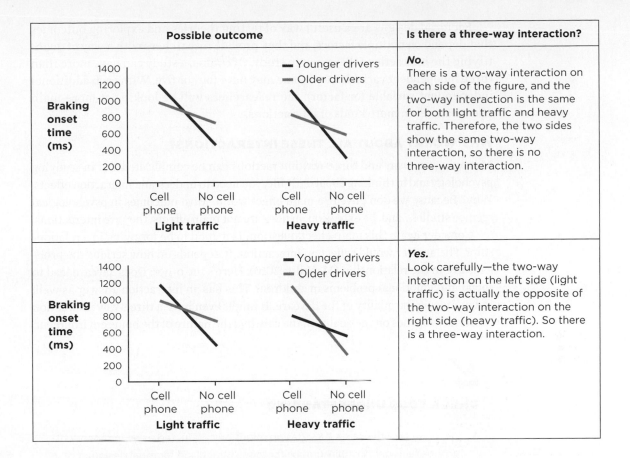

Possible outcome	Is there a three-way interaction?
Braking onset time (ms) — Younger drivers / Older drivers. Light traffic (Cell phone / No cell phone), Heavy traffic (Cell phone / No cell phone)	**No.** There is a two-way interaction on each side of the figure, and the two-way interaction is the same for both light traffic and heavy traffic. Therefore, the two sides show the same two-way interaction, so there is no three-way interaction.
Braking onset time (ms) — Younger drivers / Older drivers. Light traffic (Cell phone / No cell phone), Heavy traffic (Cell phone / No cell phone)	**Yes.** Look carefully—the two-way interaction on the left side (light traffic) is actually the opposite of the two-way interaction on the right side (heavy traffic). So there is a three-way interaction.

A three-way interaction is easiest to detect by looking at line graphs of the data. Look again at Figure 12.24B. Notice that in light traffic, there's a two-way interaction between driver age and cell phone condition, but in heavy traffic, there is no two-way interaction between these two independent variables. The two-way interaction of driver age × cell phone condition therefore depends on the level of traffic conditions. The interaction of driver age and cell phone is not the same on both sides of the graph. In other words, there is a difference in differences for the light traffic side of the graph, but there is no difference in differences for the heavy traffic side of the graph.

You would find a three-way interaction whenever there is a two-way interaction for one level of a third independent variable but not for the other (because the two-way interactions are different—there is a two-way interaction on one side but not on the other). You will also find a three-way interaction if a graph shows one pattern of two-way interaction on one side but a different pattern of two-way interaction on the other side—in other words, if there are different two-way interactions. However, if you found the same kind of two-way interaction for both levels of the third independent variable, there would not be a three-way interaction. **Figure 12.26** shows some of the possible outcomes of a three-way design.

Factorial designs are a useful way of testing theories and exploring outcomes that depend on multiple factors, and they provide researchers with a way of quantifying the interactions they want to study. Of course, a study can have more than three independent variables, and some may have four or five. With each additional independent variable (or factor), the researchers will be looking at more main effects and even more kinds of interactions.

WHY WORRY ABOUT ALL THESE INTERACTIONS?

Managing two-way and three-way interactions can be complicated, but in studying psychology and in thinking about daily life, you need to understand interaction effects. Why? Because we don't live in a main effect world. Most outcomes in psychological science studies—and, by extension, in life—are not main effects; they are interactions.

Consider again this main effect question: Is it good to be forgiving in a relationship? The answer would reflect an interaction: It depends on how serious the problems are in the relationship (McNulty, 2010). Here's the other: Does daycare lead to social and emotional problems in children? This has an interaction answer as well: It depends on the quality of the daycare. It might even have a three-way interaction answer: It depends on the quality of the care *and* the nature of the home environment.

CHECK YOUR UNDERSTANDING

1. Describe how the same 2 × 2 design might be conducted as an independent-groups factorial, a within-groups factorial, or a mixed factorial design. Explain how different designs change the number of participants required: Which design requires the most? Which requires the fewest?

2. What does the notation (e.g., 2 × 2, 3 × 4, 2 × 2 × 3) indicate about the number of independent variables in a study? How does it convey the number of cells?

3. In a 2 × 2 × 2 design, what is the number of main effects and interactions?

4. Describe how you can tell whether a study has a three-way interaction.

1. See pp. 370–371; an independent-groups factorial requires the most participants, and a within-groups factorial requires the fewest. 2. A 3 × 4 design has two independent variables, one with three levels and one with four levels. See pp. 371–373. 3. See pp. 373–377; three main effects, three two-way interactions, and one three-way interaction. 4. See pp. 376–378 and Table 12.26.

IDENTIFYING FACTORIAL DESIGNS IN YOUR READING

Whether you're reading original research published in a journal or secondhand reports of research published in the popular media, certain clues will alert you that the study had a factorial design.

Identifying Factorial Designs in Empirical Journal Articles

In an empirical journal article, researchers almost always describe the design they used in the Method section. You can tell the researchers used a factorial design if they refer to their study as a 2 × 2 design, a 3 × 2 design, a 2 × 2 × 2 design, or the like. Such descriptions indicate the number of independent variables in the study as well as how many levels there were for each independent variable.

In the study on using a cell phone while driving, for example, the researchers describe their experimental design as follows:

> The design was a 2 (Age: Younger vs. Older adults) × 2 (Task: Single- vs. Dual-task) factorial. Age was a between-subjects factor and the single- vs. dual-task condition was a within-subjects factor. (Strayer & Drews, 2004, p. 643)

In their article, they use "dual-task" for driving while using a cell phone and "single-task" for driving without a cell phone. Notice that Strayer and Drews use the notation 2 × 2, labeling each independent variable in parentheses. They also specify that the design was factorial. You can also infer they used a mixed factorial design because they mentioned that one independent variable was independent-groups ("between-subjects") and one was within-groups ("within-subjects").

Whereas the Method section outlines the study's design, independent variables, and dependent variables, the Results section of an empirical journal article discusses whether the main effects and interactions are significant. Authors may use the term *significant*, the notation $p < 0.05$, or even an asterisk in a table to indicate that a main effect or interaction is statistically significant. Here is how Strayer and Drews described the main effects and interactions in their study:

> The MANOVA indicated significant main effects of age, $F(4, 35) = 8.74$, $p < 0.01$, and single- vs. dual-task, $F(4, 35) = 11.44$, $p < 0.01$. However, the Age × Single vs. Dual-Task interaction was not significant, $F(4, 35) = 1.46$, $p = 0.23$. This latter finding suggests that older adults do not suffer a significantly greater penalty for talking on a cell phone while driving than do their younger counterparts. (Strayer & Drews, 2004, p. 644)

Your statistics course will teach you what MANOVA and F mean in the quoted text above, but you should now be able to recognize the terms *main effect, interaction,* and *significant*.

Identifying Factorial Designs in Popular Media Articles

Whereas empirical journal articles must specify what kind of design was used in a study, popular media articles usually do not. Media outlets probably assume most of their readers would not know what a 2 × 2 factorial design means. Indeed, most journalists gloss over the details of an experimental design to make their articles simpler. However, you can detect a factorial design from a report if you know what to look for.

Here's an example of how a journalist described the DeWall study on alcohol use, aggressive behavior, and body weight in the online news outlet, *Pacific Standard*. After explaining the study in some detail, the journalist described the interaction like this: "The researchers found that alcohol, compared to placebo, increased aggression among the heavier men but had little effect on the lighter men" (Best, 2010).

In other cases, you may need to read between the lines in order to know that a study had a factorial design. There are certain clues you can look for to identify factorial designs in the popular media.

LOOK FOR "IT DEPENDS" OR "ONLY WHEN"

Journalists might gloss over the details of a factorial design, but sometimes they will use a phrase like "it depends" or "only when" to highlight an interaction in a report of a factorial design. This example uses "it depends" to describe gender differences in talking:

> In her own and others' work, La France noted, "the research is consistently showing either no sex differences in the amount that men and women talk, or if there *is* a difference, then it depends on the context. For example, in a professional context, men actually outspeak women by a long shot." (Mundell, 2007)

The example started with the dependent variable of how much people talk. It mentioned one factor (gender) and then used "it depends" to add a second factor (the context: work, nonwork) to describe the interaction. The relationship between gender and how much people talk *depends on* the context in which they are talking.

The passage below describes a 2 × 2 within-groups factorial design in which dogs were trained to willingly lie still in an MRI machine (Andics, Gábor, Gácsi, Faragó, Szabó, & Miklósi, 2016). The dogs' brains were scanned while the researchers played different words through dog-size headphones (**Figure 12.27**). The researchers were investigating whether dogs' brains process only the intonation of speech, only the lexical content (the words), or both. The CNN reporter uses "only when" to describe the interaction effect:

> . . . positive or meaningful words such as "well done," "good boy" and "clever" were said in both a praising intonation and a neutral intonation. Neutral or meaningless words, such as "even if," "although" and "however," also were said in both intonations. Only when a praise word was spoken to the dogs in a praising tone of voice did the brain's reward center light up like a Christmas tree in the brain scans. The reward center is the part of the brain that responds to pleasurable stimuli, like food treats or being petted. (Howard, 2016)

FIGURE 12.27
Dogs as subjects in a factorial design.
According to a study covered in the popular media, researchers learned that, like the human brain, a dog's brain processes both the emotional tone and the lexical content of speech.

This description introduces all four conditions of the factorial first. Then it uses "only when" to explain how one independent variable (type of word: praise words or meaningless words) interacted with the other independent variable (tone of voice: praising tone or neutral tone). The dependent variable was activity in the brain's reward center. Could you sketch a graph of the result described in the dog MRI study?

LOOK FOR PARTICIPANT VARIABLES

You can sometimes detect factorial designs when journalists discuss a participant variable such as age, personality, gender, or ethnicity. In such stories, the participant variable often moderates another independent variable. And when there is a moderator, there is an interaction (as well as a factorial design to test it).

The following example describes a factorial design with a participant variable (self-esteem). The journalist does not mention the study's factors or design. But you can tell there's an interaction because the author describes different responses to the intervention for participants with high and low self-esteem:

> Joanne Wood of the University of Waterloo in Ontario and two colleagues conducted experiments in which they asked students to repeat statements to themselves such as "I am a lovable person"—then measured how it affected their mood. But in one of their studies involving 32 male and 36 female psychology students, the researchers found that repeating the phrase did not improve the mood of those who had low self-esteem, as measured by a standard test. They actually ended up feeling worse, and the gap between those with high and low self-esteem widened. (Stein, 2009)

The statement "the gap between those with high and low self-esteem widened" is a sign that there was a difference in differences—an interaction (probably a spreading interaction). Because the journalist mentions that mood improved, you can infer the dependent variable was mood. One factor in this design was self-esteem (high or low); the other was whether or not the participants repeated the statement "I am a lovable person." You can work more with this study in the Review Questions and Learning Actively sections at the end of the chapter.

CHECK YOUR UNDERSTANDING

1. In an empirical journal article, in what section will you find the independent and dependent variables of the study's design? In what section will you find whether the main effects and interactions are statistically significant?

2. Describe at least two cues indicating that a story in the popular media is probably describing a factorial design.

1. The Method section lists the variables and design; the Results section reports the significance of main effects and interactions. See p. 379. 2. You can look for phrases such as "it depends" or for participant variables. See pp. 379–380.

CHAPTER REVIEW

Summary

Simple experiments involve one independent variable and one dependent variable. Many hypotheses in psychological science are more complex; they involve studying two or more independent variables.

Review: Experiments with One Independent Variable

- In a study with one independent variable, researchers look for a simple difference, such as the difference between being drunk or sober or the difference between being on a cell phone or not.

Experiments with Two Independent Variables Can Show Interactions

- When testing more than one variable, researchers are testing for interactions, asking whether the effect of one independent variable depends on the level of the other one. An interaction is a "difference in differences."

- Factorial designs cross two or more independent variables, creating conditions (cells) that represent every possible combination of the levels of each independent variable.

- Factorial designs can describe multiple influences on behavior; they enable researchers to test their theories and determine whether some manipulation affects one type of person more than another.

- Analyzing the data from a factorial design involves looking for main effects for each independent variable by estimating the marginal means, then looking for interaction effects by checking for a difference in differences (in a line graph, interactions appear as nonparallel lines).

- When there is an interaction effect, it is more important than any main effects found.

Factorial Variations

- The factors can be independent-groups or within-groups variables; the factors can be manipulated (independent) variables or measured, participant variables.

- When a factorial design has three or more independent variables, the number of interactions increases to include all possible combinations of the independent variables.

- In a design with three independent variables, the three-way interaction tests whether two-way interactions are the same at the levels of the third independent variable.

Identifying Factorial Designs in Your Reading

- In empirical journal articles, the type of design is given in the Method section.

- In popular media stories, factorial designs may be indicated by language such as "it depends" and "only when," or descriptions of both participant variables and independent variables.

Key Terms

interaction effect, p. 353
factorial design, p. 355

cell, p. 356
participant variable, p. 356

main effect, p. 361
marginal means, p. 362

To see samples of chapter concepts in the popular media, visit www.everydayresearchmethods.com and click the box for Chapter 12.

Review Questions

Psychologist Joanne Wood and her colleagues recruited people with different levels of self-esteem to investigate the effect of positive self-statements on mood (Wood, Perunovic, & Lee, 2009). Participants wrote their thoughts and feelings down for 4 minutes. The researchers randomly assigned half the participants to repeat to themselves a positive self-statement, "I am a lovable person," at 15-second intervals (cued by a bell sound). The other half did not repeat this statement. After the 4-minute session, all participants rated their mood on a questionnaire. Here are the results:

DV: POSITIVE MOOD	LOW SELF-ESTEEM PARTICIPANTS	HIGH SELF-ESTEEM PARTICIPANTS
"I am a lovable person"	11.18	30.47
No statement	16.94	24.59

1. Why might the Wood team have conducted their study as a factorial design?

   a. To test how well positive self-statements work, compared to no statements.

   b. To compare the moods of high self-esteem and low self-esteem people.

   c. To test whether the effect of positive self-statements would depend on a person's level of self-esteem.

2. What are the factors in this study?

   a. Self-esteem level: high versus low

   b. Self-statement instructions: positive versus none

   c. Self-esteem level: high versus low; and self-statement instructions: positive versus none

   d. Positive mood

3. There is an interaction in the results. How do you know?

   a. When the cell means are graphed, the lines are not parallel.

   b. The difference between low and high self-esteem is large for the positive self-statement condition, and smaller for the "no statement" condition.

   c. Positive self-statements raised the mood of high self-esteem people and lowered the mood of low self-esteem people.

   d. All of the above.

4. Which of the following sentences describes the *main effect for self-esteem* in the Wood study?

   a. Overall, the moods of high self-esteem people are more positive than the moods of low self-esteem people.

   b. Mood depended on both the participants' level of self-esteem and what self-statement condition they were in.

   c. Overall, the moods of people in the "I am a lovable person" condition are about the same as the moods of people in the "no statement" condition.

   d. Positive self-statements raised the moods of high self-esteem people and lowered the moods of low self-esteem people.

5. This study is an example of a(n):

   a. Independent-groups factorial design

   b. Within-groups factorial design

   c. Mixed factorial design

6. Suppose these researchers ran their study again, but this time they compared how high or low self-esteem people responded to three kinds of statements: Positive self-statements, negative self-statements, and no statements. What kind of design would this be?

   a. 2 × 2

   b. 2 × 3

   c. 2 × 2 × 2

   d. 6 × 1

Learning Actively

1. Create a line graph from the data in the review questions above (the study by Wood et al., 2009). Create the graph both ways: *Self-statement type* on the x-axis (representing the two levels of self-statement with two different lines); *Self-esteem level* on the x-axis (with the two self-esteem levels as the two lines). Describe the interaction you see.

2. For practice, compute the marginal means in the two studies shown in the figures below. (Assume each cell has an equal number of participants.) You would need significance tests to be sure, but does it look as if there will be significant main effects for both the cell phone condition and the driver age? Why or why not? Does it look as if there are main effects for participant type and and the type of item to remember? Why or why not?

DV: Braking onset time (ms)	IV$_1$: Cell phone condition		
	Cell phone	**Not on phone**	Main effect for IV$_2$: Driver age
IV$_2$: Driver age — **Younger drivers**	912	780	
Older drivers	1086	912	
Main effect for IV$_1$: Cell phone condition			

DV: Items recalled	IV$_1$: Participant type		
	Child chess experts	**Adult novices**	Main effect for IV$_2$: Type of item
IV$_2$: Type of item — **Chess pieces**	9.3	5.9	
Digits	6.1	7.8	
Main effect for IV$_1$: Participant type			

3. In one of their studies, Strayer and his students tested whether people would get better at driving while talking on a cell phone if they practiced doing so (Cooper & Strayer, 2008). They had participants drive in a simulator while talking on a hands-free cell phone and while not talking on a phone. The same people participated over several days so they had a chance to practice this multitasking. On the first day, they were considered to be least experienced; on the last day, the most experienced. On the last day, they were tested in both a familiar environment and a slightly different driving environment, to see if the first days of practice would transfer to a new context. The researchers collected data on how many collisions (accidents) the drivers got into on the simulator (trained in the "city" condition). Here are their data:

	NUMBER OF COLLISIONS		
	DAY 1	DAY 4 (DRIVING IN A FAMILIAR CONTEXT)	DAY 4 (DRIVING IN A NEW CONTEXT)
Single-task (not using cell phone)	15	6	10
Dual-task (using cell phone)	20	7.5	24

a. What kind of design is this? (Put your answer in the form "_____ × _____.")

b. What are the independent and dependent variables?

c. Indicate whether each independent variable was manipulated as independent-groups or within-groups.

d. Create a line graph depicting these results.

e. Estimate and describe any main effects and interactions in this study. (Of course, you would need statistics to determine if the observed effects are statistically significant.)

f. What might you conclude from the results of this study? Does experience affect cell phone use while driving?

4. Are participant variables independent-groups variables or within-groups variables? Why?

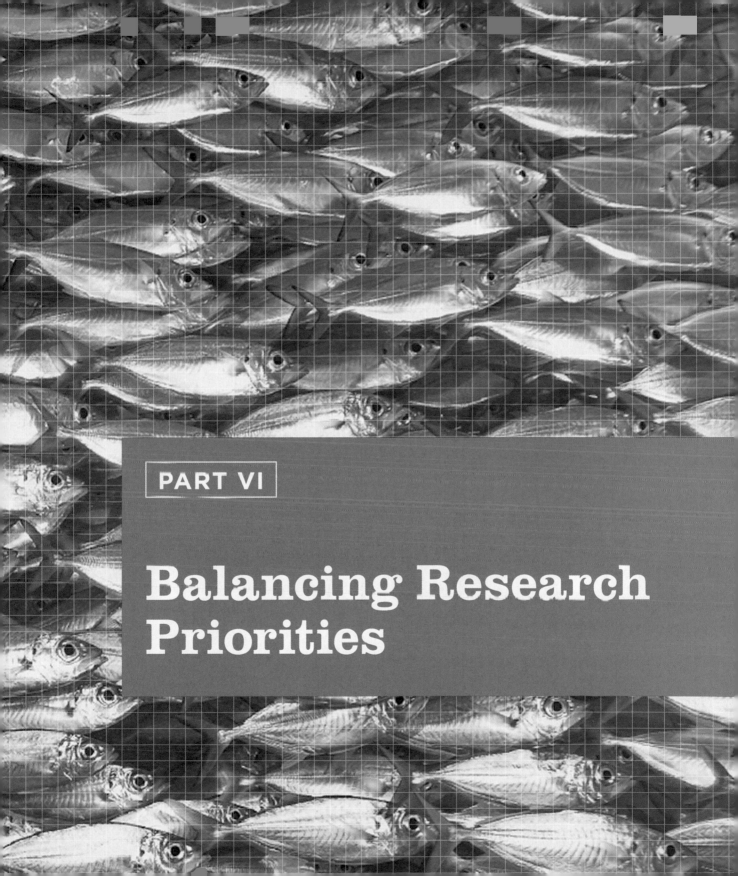

PART VI

Balancing Research Priorities

"What if you can't randomly assign participants to the independent variable levels?"

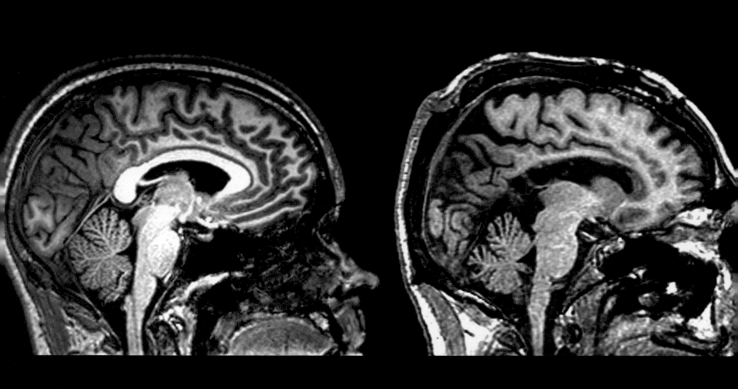

"What is the value of an experiment with just one participant?"

13

Quasi-Experiments and Small-*N* Designs

PREVIOUS CHAPTERS HAVE EXPLAINED how to interrogate frequency claims (Chapters 6 and 7), association claims (Chapters 8 and 9), and causal claims (Chapters 10–12). The last two chapters focus on a more general issue: how researchers balance priorities while conducting their studies. Of course, psychological scientists always want to carry out the best studies possible, but they are constrained by practical issues, and they must perform their work ethically. How do they balance their research goals with practical realities?

This chapter discusses situations in which conducting a true experiment is not feasible. For example, a researcher might not be able to randomly assign participants to different groups or counterbalance conditions in a within-groups experiment. What are the trade-offs? How do they establish internal validity when full experimental control is impossible? Sometimes researchers may be able to collect data from only one case, such as a single child or a person with an unusual behavioral problem. How can they balance priorities for internal and external validity when they're studying just a single instance?

QUASI-EXPERIMENTS

A **quasi-experiment** differs from a true experiment in that the researchers do not have full experimental control. They start by selecting an independent variable and a dependent variable.

LEARNING OBJECTIVES

A year from now, you should still be able to:

1.
Articulate how quasi-experiments differ from true experiments.

2.
Analyze the design and results of quasi-experiments to evaluate the support they provide for causal claims.

3.
Explain the major differences between small-*N* designs and large-*N* designs.

4.
Analyze the design and results of small-*N* experiments to evaluate the support they provide for causal claims.

Then they study participants who are exposed to each level of the independent variable. However, in a quasi-experiment, the researchers might not be able to randomly assign participants to one level or the other; they are assigned by teachers, political regulations, acts of nature—or even by their own choice.

Two Examples of Independent-Groups Quasi-Experiments

The following two examples of quasi-experiments use an independent-groups design, in which there are different participants at each level of the independent variable. This type of quasi-experimental design is typically called a **nonequivalent control group design**. It has at least one treatment group and one comparison group, but unlike in a true experiment, participants have not been randomly assigned to the two groups.

THE PSYCHOLOGICAL EFFECTS OF WALKING BY A CHURCH

Can walking by a church affect how you think and feel about others? One set of researchers tested the idea in neighborhoods in London, England, and Maastricht, the Netherlands. They compared the attitudes of people who were passing by churches, such as Westminster Abbey, to those passing by government buildings, such as Parliament (LaBouff, Rowatt, Johnson, & Finkle, 2012).

The researchers hypothesized that walking past a religious landmark would make people biased against social groups that are different from their own. You might be surprised by this hypothesis because most of the world's religious organizations encourage followers to treat others with love and generosity. However, correlational research has shown that more religious people tend to be more negative toward outgroups (members of a social group they don't identify with). And when people are primed in a lab with religious words compared to neutral words, they report more prejudiced feelings toward an outgroup. LaBouff and his colleagues sought to test these findings in real-world settings.

Researchers approached 99 people who were passing by either a religious or a nonreligious landmark in the two cities. They selected people from each setting using systematic sampling and approached only people who were passing by—not entering or leaving the buildings. They had each person complete a short questionnaire asking about their religiosity, political views, and attitudes toward a variety of social groups.

In this study, there is an independent variable (the type of building), and several dependent variables (the attitude measures). But people were not randomly assigned to walk by one of the buildings, so it's a quasi-experiment. It is an example of a nonequivalent control group posttest-only design because the participants were not randomly assigned to groups, and were tested only after exposure to one level of the independent variable or the other.

TABLE 13.1

Selected Results from a Quasi-Experiment

VARIABLE	WALKING BY RELIGIOUS BUILDING OR LANDMARK	WALKING BY NONRELIGIOUS BUILDING OR LANDMARK
Belief in God	54%	46%
Religiosity (1 = *not at all* to 7 = *very much*)	3.85	3.07*
Political conservatism (1 = *extremely conservative* to 7 = *extremely liberal*)	3.91	4.62*
Warmth toward Christians (1 = *very cold* to 10 = *very warm*)	6.62	7.27
Warmth toward foreigners (1 = *very cold* to 10 = *very warm*)	6.81	7.62*
Warmth toward Arabic people (1 = *very cold* to 10 = *very warm*)	5.67	7.24*
Warmth toward African people (1 = *very cold* to 10 = *very warm*)	6.12	7.75*

Note: Means are shown for each variable.
*Difference between religious building and nonreligious building is statistically significant.
Source: Adapted from LaBouff et al., 2012.

The results supported the hypothesis (**Table 13.1**). People walking by churches reported being more religious and politically conservative than those passing by nonreligious buildings. They also reported cooler feelings for almost all social groups (including African, Arabic, and Asian people, Jewish and Muslim people, rich and poor people, and gay people). Only Christians were evaluated equally warmly by people walking by a church compared to those walking by a nonreligious building. The authors concluded that being primed by a religious landmark can increase bias toward outgroups. As you read the rest of this chapter, consider what these results mean: Do you think the study supports their conclusion?

THE PSYCHOLOGICAL EFFECTS OF COSMETIC SURGERY

Around the world, plastic surgeons perform about 8.5 million cosmetic surgeries each year (International Society of Aesthetic Plastic Surgery, 2011). Anecdotal evidence indicates that people who undergo such procedures think they'll improve their body image, self-esteem, and overall sense of well-being. But does cosmetic surgery really achieve these results? One approach would be to randomly assign people to have plastic surgery or not. In normal circumstances, though, this would not be ethically or practically feasible because researchers cannot assign people to undergo an unnecessary and possibly risky surgery.

A team of psychological scientists found a way to study the effects of cosmetic surgery (Margraf, Meyer, & Lavallee, 2013). They recruited a sample of about 600 patients at a clinic in Germany who had already elected to undergo plastic surgery.

The researchers measured this group's self-esteem, life satisfaction, self-rated general attractiveness, and other variables at four time periods: before surgery, and then 3 months, 6 months, and 1 year after surgery. As a comparison group, the researchers found a sample of about 250 people who had registered at the same plastic surgery clinic, having indicated their interest in receiving surgery, but who had not yet undergone any procedures. This comparison group filled out the self-esteem, life satisfaction, and attractiveness measures at the same times as the surgery group.

This study looks like an experiment. There is an independent variable (having cosmetic surgery or not), and there are dependent variables (measures of self-esteem, life satisfaction, and attractiveness). However, the participants were not randomly assigned to the two conditions, and the lack of random assignment made this a quasi-experiment. People were self-assigned to the two independent variable groups according to whether they had actually had cosmetic surgery or not. The Margraf team's study is an example of a **nonequivalent control group pretest/posttest design** because the participants were not randomly assigned to groups, and were tested both before and after some intervention.

The results of the study are shown in **Figure 13.1**. Although both groups started out the same on a standard measure of self-esteem, the two groups had diverged a year later. Similarly, the surgery group started out with slightly higher life satisfaction and general attractiveness than the comparison group, and the surgery group had increased on these measures 1 year later. Does this study allow us to say that the cosmetic surgery *caused* people's self-image and life satisfaction to improve?

Two Examples of Repeated-Measures Quasi-Experiments

Quasi-experiments can be repeated-measures designs, too, in which participants experience all levels of an independent variable. In a quasi-experimental version of this design, as opposed to a true repeated-measures experiment, the researcher relies on an already-scheduled event, a new policy or regulation, or a chance occurrence that manipulates the independent variable. The following two studies are examples of repeated-measures quasi-experiments.

FOOD BREAKS AND PAROLE DECISIONS

» To review reasoning biases, see Chapter 2, pp. 32–38.

Legal decisions, such as whether or not a prison inmate should be granted parole, are made by judges who presumably consider the facts of each case objectively. However, research on human biases in reasoning raises the possibility that even judicial decisions might be distorted by irrelevant, extraneous factors.

A team of researchers set out to investigate the effect of one particular extraneous factor on judicial decision making: a food break (Danziger, Levav, & Avnaim-Pesso, 2011). They collected data on more than 1,100 parole rulings that took place on 50 different days for inmates of one of four prisons in Israel. Judges had to decide whether each prisoner should be granted parole or not. They were both Israeli and Arab, male and female, and had committed crimes such as assault, theft, embezzlement,

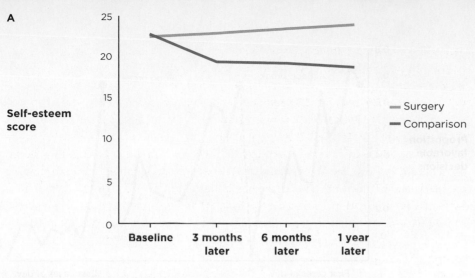

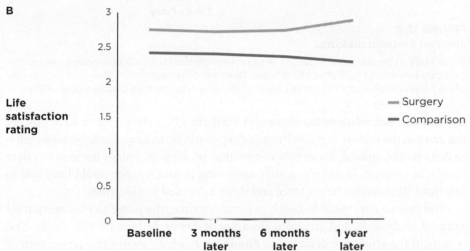

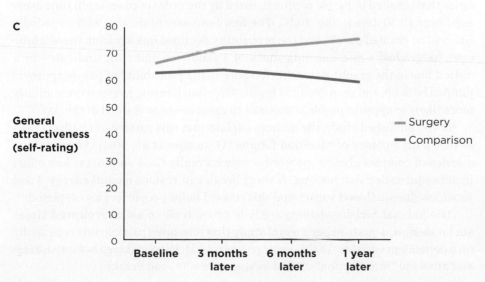

FIGURE 13.1
Cosmetic surgery and well-being.

Compared to a group of people who had expressed interest in, but had not undergone, cosmetic surgery, people who had the surgery showed an increase in (A) self-esteem, (B) life satisfaction, and (C) general attractiveness. According to the results of this quasi-experiment, does cosmetic surgery work? Does it cause people to feel better about themselves? (Source: Adapted from Margraf et al., 2013.)

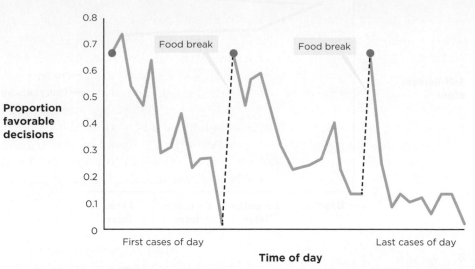

FIGURE 13.2
Judicial decision making.

In this study, as the day went on, judges were increasingly less likely to approve parole, unless the case they heard came right after a food break. Does this quasi-experiment show that food breaks cause judges to consider a case more carefully? (Source: Adapted from Danziger et al., 2011.)

and murder. According to Danziger and his team, given the seriousness of most of the crimes, the easiest decision in each case would be to keep the prisoner in jail—to deny parole. Indeed, about 65% of the time, on average, judges decided to reject parole. In contrast, in order to justify approving parole, a judge would have had to pay close attention to the evidence and write a detailed justification.

The researchers recorded each prisoner's crime, the judge's decision (parole granted or denied), and crucially, the time of day each decision was made. The results of the study are depicted in **Figure 13.2**, which shows the proportion of cases that resulted in parole approval, listed by the order of cases (each time averaged over all 50 days in the study). The first few cases of the day were especially likely to be granted parole, and the probability declined quickly from there. However, judges had a mid-morning snack of a sandwich and fruit (indicated by a dotted line in the graph). After this food break the probability of parole approval jumped back up, and then declined again. After lunch break, judges were similarly more likely to approve parole, compared to cases heard at the end of the day.

In the published study, the authors explain that this pattern of results is consistent with a theory of "decision fatigue" (Danziger et al., 2011). After making a series of complex choices, people become mentally tired and invest less effort in subsequent decision making. A short break can restore mental energy. Food provides glucose (blood sugar), and this reward helps people feel less depleted.

The judicial decision-making study is an example of an **interrupted time-series design**, a quasi-experimental study that measures participants repeatedly on a dependent variable (in this example, parole decision making) before, during, and after the "interruption" caused by some event (a food break).

ASSESSING THE IMPACT OF HEALTH CARE LAWS

Another quasi-experiment took advantage of variability in state laws in the United States. In 2010, the federal government enacted the Affordable Care Act, requiring all citizens to acquire health insurance or face fines. Four years earlier, a similar policy had been implemented in only one state: Massachusetts. A team of public health researchers decided to evaluate whether the Massachusetts law made any difference in people's access to health care (Pande, Ross-Degnan, Zaslavsky, & Salomon, 2011).

Specifically, the researchers acquired data from a sample of over 178,000 non-elderly adults. Some of them lived in Massachusetts (the target state), and others lived in neighboring states in New England without health insurance requirements. The researchers used data from a national yearly survey that asks people whether they have insurance, have a personal doctor, or if they have ever gone without medical care because they couldn't afford it.

The research team acquired the survey results for the years before the Massachusetts law took effect (2002–2005), comparing them to the years after the law (2007–2009). Thus, in this study, one independent variable was the time period before, compared to after, the law changed. Another independent variable was state of residence (Massachusetts or a neighboring state). The dependent variables were the survey questions about insurance coverage, having a doctor, and foregoing medical care because of cost. The independent variables were not controlled by researchers—people were not randomly assigned to states that had health insurance laws and those that did not. The lack of full experimenter control is what made the study a quasi-experiment.

Let's focus on the results for just one dependent variable: foregoing medical care because of cost. As **Figure 13.3** shows, in the years before the law, the overall rate was fairly stable in both Massachusetts and neighboring states. After 2006, however, rates in Massachusetts and neighboring states start to diverge. Do these results show that the law in Massachusetts *caused* an improvement in people's ability to pay for medical care?

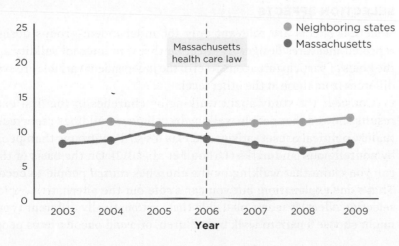

Percentage unable to see doctor due to cost

Massachusetts health care law

● Neighboring states
● Massachusetts

Year

FIGURE 13.3

State laws and access to health care.

Among states without health care laws, foregoing medical care increased slightly over the years. After 2006, residents of Massachusetts were less likely to report they had gone without care. Does this quasi-experiment demonstrate that the new Massachusetts law caused people to afford health care? (Source: Adapted from Pande et al., 2011.)

The design used in the Pande study is called a **nonequivalent control group interrupted time-series design**. It combines two of the previous designs (the nonequivalent control group design and the interrupted time-series design). In this example, the independent variable was studied as both a repeated-measures variable (interrupted time-series) and an independent-groups variable (nonequivalent control group). In both cases, however, the researchers did not have experimental control over either independent variable.

Internal Validity in Quasi-Experiments

Each of the four previous examples *looks* like a true experiment: Each one has an independent variable and a dependent variable. What is missing in every case is full experimenter control over the independent variable.

What did the researchers give up when they conducted studies in which they didn't have full experimenter control? The main concern is internal validity—the ability to draw causal conclusions from the results. The degree to which a quasi-experiment supports a causal claim depends on two things: its design and its results. To interrogate internal validity, you ask about alternative explanations for an observed pattern of results. The internal validity threats for experiments discussed in Chapters 10 and 11 also apply to quasi-experiments. How well do the four examples of quasi-experiments hold up to an internal validity interrogation? Are they susceptible to the internal validity threats?

As you read this section, keep in mind that quasi-experiments can have a variety of designs, and the support that a quasi-experiment provides for a causal claim depends partly on its design and partly on the results a researcher obtains. Researchers do not have full control of the independent variable in a quasi-experiment (as they do in a true experiment), but they can choose better designs, and they can use the pattern of results to rule out some internal validity threats.

SELECTION EFFECTS

Selection effects are relevant only for independent-groups designs, not for repeated-measures designs. A selection threat to internal validity applies when the kinds of participants at one level of the independent variable are systematically different from those at the other level.

Consider the study about walking by churches in the first example. The results showed that people walking by religious buildings reported more spirituality, political conservatism, and bias toward outgroups than people walking by nonreligious landmarks (LaBouff et al., 2012). On the basis of these results, can you claim that walking by the churches *caused* people to become biased? That's one explanation, but you can't rule out the alternative explanation of a selection effect. It seems plausible that systematically different types of people might choose a path to walk by a church, or avoid one. Perhaps people who are

FIGURE 13.4
Selection effects in the religious landmarks study.
Because people were not randomly assigned which path to take, we can't be sure that people had been spiritual, conservative, or biased first, and then chose to walk by the religious (rather than the nonreligious) landmarks.

more spiritual, conservative, or biased are more likely to choose a path near a religious landmark (**Figure 13.4**).

Similarly, in the cosmetic surgery study, the people who actually had the surgery may have been different from those who simply expressed interest in it. When the researchers asked, a full 61% of the comparison group reported they had not gone through with surgery because they couldn't afford it (Margraf et al., 2013). Therefore, there may have been a selection effect in this study; people who had cosmetic surgery might have been more financially well-off than people who did not have the procedure. On the other hand, the pretest/posttest nature of the study helps rule out selection effects, too. Financial stability might explain why one group started out higher in life satisfaction, but it does not seem to be a reasonable explanation for why the surgery group increased in self-esteem and general attractiveness over time (see Figure 13.1).

The Margraf team took steps to help counteract selection effects in their study. For some of their analyses, they used information on age, gender, body mass index, income, and several other variables to create matched groups, matching 179 people from the surgery group with 179 people from the comparison group. They compared the results from the matched-groups data to the results from the full samples (about 500 people in the surgery group and 264 in the comparison group), and found similar results both times. The matched-groups version of the data gave these researchers confidence that selection effects were not responsible for the differences they observed.

Some researchers control for selection effects by using a **wait-list design**, in which all the participants plan to receive treatment but are randomly assigned to do so at different times. The Margraf team could have studied a group of people, all of whom were scheduled for cosmetic surgery, instructing half to receive their surgery right away and placing others on a waiting list for surgery at a later time. They could then measure the patterns of self-esteem, life satisfaction, and general attractiveness in both groups over several months, when only one of the groups would have had surgery. The wait-list design, unlike the original, is a true experiment because it ensures that the same kinds of people are in each group.

DESIGN CONFOUNDS

In certain quasi-experiments, design confounds can be a problem. Recall that in a design confound, some outside variable accidentally and systematically varies with the levels of the targeted independent variable. In the study on food breaks and parole decision making, you might question whether the judicial cases scheduled right after the food breaks were systematically different from those that occurred later (Danziger et al., 2011). For example, were the prisoners the judges saw right after they'd had a food break guilty of less serious crimes? Had they been in prison a shorter time? Did they have fewer previous incarcerations? If the early cases were not as serious as the later ones, that would be an alternative explanation for why they were more likely to have been granted parole.

Danziger and his team, however, were able to use additional data from the study to rule out this design confound. When they tracked the seriousness of each case across its position during the day, they found absolutely no relationship. Earlier cases and those heard right after a food break involved prisoners who, on average, had the same number of previous incarcerations, had just as serious offenses, and had served the same amount of time. Therefore, by inspecting the data carefully, the researchers were able to rule out potential design confounds.

MATURATION THREAT

Maturation threats occur when, in an experimental or quasi-experimental design with a pretest and posttest, an observed change could have emerged more or less spontaneously over time. The cosmetic surgery study had a pretest and posttest, so it was potentially susceptible to a maturation threat. Because the participants who had surgery did improve over time in self-esteem, life satisfaction, and general attractiveness (see Figure 13.1), you might ask whether the surgery was the reason, or whether it was maturation. Perhaps everybody simply improves in these qualities over time. Fortunately, the design of this quasi-experiment included a comparison group, and the results indicated that the comparison group did not improve over time; in fact, they got slightly worse on the same variables. Because of the design and the pattern of results, you can probably rule out maturation as an internal validity threat in this study.

In the fourth study, did the Massachusetts health insurance law cause the use of medical services to improve, or did rates simply increase on their own? The overall

trend in Figure 13.3, across all years, indicates that not being able to afford a doctor fluctuated a bit, showing a slight upward trend consistent with maturation (Pande et al., 2011). But because this study used a comparison group, you can compare the patterns in the two types of states (those with health insurance laws and those without). Foregoing medical care because of cost began to decrease in Massachusetts, but not in the neighboring states, and only from the year 2007 on. In short, the design and results of the study let you conclude that ability to afford medical care increased over time, but primarily in states neighboring Massachusetts. You can rule out the maturation threat to internal validity (**Figure 13.5**).

HISTORY THREAT

A history threat occurs when an external, historical event happens for everyone in a study at the same time as the treatment. With a history threat, it is unclear whether the outcome is caused by the treatment or by the external event or factor. In the Massachusetts health insurance study, residents' ability to afford medical care between 2007 and 2009 may have improved, for instance, not because of the state law but because of an economic upturn or a presidential election. As you might imagine, history threats can be especially relevant when a quasi-experiment relies on external factors to manipulate its key variable. However, because this particular study included a comparison group, the researchers could rule out most history threats. Economic conditions and political climate would likely have affected *all* neighboring states, but according to the study results, only Massachusetts showed a decline in the variable of affording care (Pande et al., 2011).

Of course, it is possible that Massachusetts also implemented some other laws (perhaps a new cap on medical fees) that would explain the pattern in only Massachusetts. Such a threat would be a selection-history threat because the history threat applies to only one group, not the other. In a selection-history threat, the historical event systematically affects participants only in the treatment group

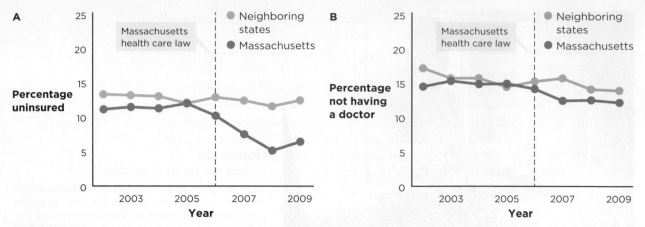

FIGURE 13.6
Does history threat explain the change in ability to afford a doctor?

Perhaps improved affordability of medical care was caused not by the Massachusetts health care law, but by an economic upturn or by a different state law. Such criticisms would have to explain why neighboring states did not improve, and why two other outcomes—(A) uninsured percentage and (B) percentage having a doctor—also improved. Most proposed historical events are not a parsimonious alternative explanation for the complete set of results. (Source: Adapted from Pande et al., 2011.)

or only in the comparison group—not both. This kind of threat is a possibility in the Pande analysis because states do pass different laws and regulations. Arguing against a history threat, however, is the fact that Massachusetts residents improved not only in rates of affording medical care, but also in the number of uninsured and the number of people with a regular doctor (**Figure 13.6**). Any proposed history threat would have to parsimoniously explain these outcomes as well.

Similarly, perhaps the participants in the cosmetic surgery study experienced increased life satisfaction over time because the economy in Germany (where the study took place) was improving during the same time period (Margraf et al., 2013). Economic events like recessions can be potential history threats for any longitudinal study, but there are two reasons for ruling that out in this case. First, the study design included a comparison group, and results showed that this group did not increase in life satisfaction over the same time periods. When quasi-experiments include a comparison group, history threats to internal validity can usually be ruled out. Second, while good economic conditions provide an alternative explanation for increased life satisfaction, they are unlikely to explain an increase in the other dependent variables, such as self-esteem and general attractiveness.

REGRESSION TO THE MEAN

Regression to the mean occurs when an extreme finding is caused by a combination of random factors that are unlikely to happen in the same combination again, so the extreme finding gets less extreme over time. Chapter 11 gave the example of Germany's 7–1 win in a World Cup soccer game. That extreme score was a lucky combination of random factors that did not repeat itself in the next game, so the next game's score regressed back toward the average, or mean.

Remember that regression to the mean can threaten internal validity only for pretest/posttest designs, and even then, only when a group is selected because of its initially very high or very low scores. The initial group means are extreme, in part, because of a combination of random factors that will not happen the same way twice.

Could regression to the mean be at play in the cosmetic surgery study? We might suspect that many of the people in the group who elected to have surgery were feeling exceptionally bad about themselves at the time, meaning that their subsequent increase in self-esteem was only a regression effect. Although this is possible, we can rule it out for two reasons. Most obviously, the researchers did not select the surgery group because of unusually low scores at pretest; they simply followed everyone who visited their targeted clinics. Regression is mainly a problem when a group is purposefully selected for its unusually low (or high) mean at pretest. Second, if regression to the mean was the explanation, the surgery group would have started out lower than the comparison group, but they started out the same on self-esteem, and started out even a little higher than the comparison group on life satisfaction and general attractiveness (see Figure 13.1).

Regression to the mean has been an alternative explanation for certain other quasi-experiments (e.g., Shadish & Luellen, 2006). However, the study designs described in this chapter are generally not susceptible to it. Either the results do not fit the regression pattern, or the researchers do not use pretest/posttest designs. Recall, as well, that true experiments use random assignment to place participants into groups, a practice that eliminates regression to the mean as an internal validity threat.

ATTRITION THREAT

In designs with pretests and posttests, attrition occurs when people drop out of a study over time. Attrition becomes an internal validity threat when *systematic* kinds of people drop out of a study. In the cosmetic surgery study, for example, you might wonder whether people's self-image improved only because individuals who were disappointed with their surgery outcomes stopped responding to the study over time. If only the happiest, most satisfied participants completed the study, that would explain the apparent increase in self-esteem, life satisfaction, and general attractiveness over time. In this case, it would not be the surgery, but the attrition of the most dissatisfied participants, that caused the decrease.

Fortunately, attrition is easy to check for, and the researchers in the Margraf team made sure it was not an explanation for their results. Here is an excerpt from the Method section of the published study:

Missing Values Analysis. Completers were defined as having available data at all four time points, as opposed to dropouts who did not. The comparison group contained more dropouts than the surgery group. . . . Completers did not differ from dropouts with respect to any analyzed outcome variable at baseline,

3- and 6-month follow-up, and neither with respect to the following eight features at baseline: clinic, occupation, treatment type, gender, age, body mass index, income. . . . (Margraf et al., 2013, pp. 7–8)

The statement above indicates that although some people—especially those in the comparison group—dropped out of the study, the dropouts were not systematically different from completers. Because the attrition was unsystematic, the researchers concluded that attrition was not a threat to internal validity.

TESTING AND INSTRUMENTATION THREATS

Whenever researchers measure participants more than once, they need to be concerned about testing threats to internal validity. A testing threat is a kind of order effect in which participants tend to change as a result of having been tested before. Repeated testing might cause people to improve, regardless of the treatment they received. Repeated testing might also cause performance to decline because of fatigue or boredom.

Instrumentation, too, can be an internal validity threat when participants are tested or observed twice. A measuring instrument could change over repeated uses, and this change would threaten internal validity. If a study uses two versions of a test with different standards (e.g., one test is more difficult) or if a study uses coders who change their standards over time, then participants might appear to change, when in reality there is no change between one observation and the next.

You can use a study's results and design to interrogate testing and instrumentation threats to internal validity. Consider the design and results of the cosmetic surgery study. Participants in both the surgery group and the comparison group were tested multiple times on their self-esteem, life satisfaction, and body image. A simple testing effect or instrumentation effect would have caused both groups to improve or both to worsen, but the surgery group improved over time while the comparison group declined. A comparison group like the one in this study almost always helps rule out a testing threat to internal validity.

The judicial decision-making study provides a unique instance of an instrumentation effect. The measuring instrument in this case was the judge's assessment of a prisoner's readiness for parole. This study illustrated how the judge's objectivity changed over time with fatigue. Although you might call this an instrumentation effect, rather than being a threat to internal validity, the effect is actually the study's central result!

OBSERVER BIAS, DEMAND CHARACTERISTICS, AND PLACEBO EFFECTS

Three final threats to internal validity are related to human subjectivity. Observer bias, in addition to being a threat to construct validity, can also threaten internal validity when the experimenters' expectations influence their interpretation of the results. Other threats include demand characteristics, when participants guess what the study is about and change their behavior in the expected direction, and placebo effects, when participants improve, but only because they believe they are receiving an effective treatment. Fortunately, these three threats are easy to interrogate. For observer bias, you simply ask who measured the behaviors. Was the design blind (masked) or double-blind? For experimental demand, you can think about whether the participants were able to detect the study's goals and respond accordingly. For placebo effects, you can ask whether the design of a study included a comparison group that received an inert, or placebo, treatment.

Consider the study that evaluated the psychological effects of cosmetic surgery (Margraf et al., 2013). Even though this study was not double-blind (participants obviously knew whether or not they had had surgery), the chance of observer bias was low because the experimenters asked participants to self-report their own self-esteem and other variables. However, the study might have been susceptible to a placebo effect. People who have cosmetic surgery are usually aware that they chose to undergo such a procedure in order to feel better about themselves. Perhaps it's not surprising, then, that they increased their self-reported self-esteem and life satisfaction! A better way to study the question might be to disguise the fact that the longitudinal study was investigating cosmetic surgery and instead simply present a series of questionnaires. Although this approach might be difficult in terms of practicality, it might reduce the chance for participants in either group to consciously increase or decrease their scores (**Figure 13.7**).

In the parole decision study, judges probably value being objective, and would almost certainly not have intentionally changed their behavior in the observed direction (Danziger et al., 2011). In fact, the judges' decisions were simply analyzed through public records; they did not know they were part of a study, thereby eliminating demand characteristics as an internal validity threat. Thinking about

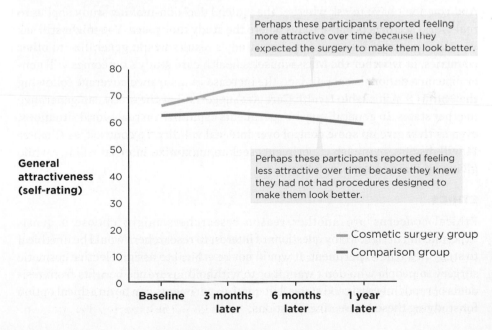

FIGURE 13.7
Interrogating placebo effects in the cosmetic surgery study.

(Source: Adapted from Margraf et al., 2013.)

the other examples in this chapter, to what extent can you rule out observer bias, demand characteristics, or placebo effects?

Balancing Priorities in Quasi-Experiments

What does a researcher gain by conducting a quasi-experiment? If quasi-experimental studies can be vulnerable to internal validity threats, why would a researcher use one?

REAL-WORLD OPPORTUNITIES

One reason is that quasi-experimental designs, such as those in the Massachusetts health care study, the cosmetic surgery study, and the judicial-decision making study, present real-world opportunities for studying interesting phenomena and important events. The Pande team would never have been able to randomly assign states to require health insurance (or not) but they took advantage of the research opportunity Massachusetts provided. Similarly, Margraf and his colleagues did not manipulate cosmetic surgery and the Danziger team did not manipulate the timing of food breaks. However, both research teams took advantage of the next-best thing—events that occurred in real-world settings.

EXTERNAL VALIDITY

The real-world settings of many quasi-experiments can enhance external validity because of the likelihood that the patterns observed will generalize to other circumstances and other individuals. In the religious landmarks study, the main goal was to show that laboratory manipulations of religious imagery (typically true experimental designs conducted on computers) generalize to the real world. And you don't have to ask whether the judicial decision-making study applies to real-world settings because that's where the study took place. You might still ask whether the judicial decision-making study's results would generalize to other countries, or whether the Massachusetts health care study's outcomes will generalize on a national scale. In fact, the increase in insurance coverage following the 2010 U.S. Affordable Health Care Act suggests that the study can generalize to other states. In general, quasi-experiments capitalize on real-world situations, even as they give up some control over internal validity. In contrast, as Chapter 14 will discuss, many lab experiments seek to maximize internal validity while giving up some external validity.

ETHICS

Ethical concerns are another reason researchers might choose a quasi-experimental design. Many questions of interest to researchers would be unethical to study in a true experiment. It would not be ethical to assign elective cosmetic surgery to people who don't want it or to withhold insurance benefits from residents of randomly assigned states, but quasi-experiments can be an ethical option for studying these interesting questions.

CONSTRUCT VALIDITY AND STATISTICAL VALIDITY IN QUASI-EXPERIMENTS

Thus far, this chapter has focused on internal validity because researchers usually conduct quasi-experiments in order to make causal statements. External validity—the ability to generalize to real-world situations—was also mentioned as an advantage of many quasi-experimental designs. The other two validities should be interrogated as well.

For construct validity, you would interrogate how successfully the study manipulated or measured its variables. Usually, quasi-experiments show excellent construct validity for the independent variable (as the preceding examples have shown). In the religious landmarks study, people really did or did not walk by a church. In the judicial decision-making study, judges really did or did not get a food break. You also have to ask how successfully the dependent variables were measured in these studies: How well did the landmarks study measure religious and political attitudes? How well did the cosmetic surgery researchers measure self-esteem, life satisfaction, and general attractiveness? Did the researchers use measures that were reliable and that measured what they were intended to measure?

Finally, to assess a quasi-experimental study's statistical validity, you could ask how large the group differences were (the effect size), and whether the results were statistically significant.

Are Quasi-Experiments the Same as Correlational Studies?

Some quasi-experiments seem similar in design to correlational studies (see Chapters 8 and 9). When a quasi-experiment uses an independent-groups design—that is, when it compares two groups without using random assignment—the groups in the study can look similar to categorical variables in correlational studies.

Consider, for example, the Cacioppo et al. (2013) study about meeting one's spouse online and marital satisfaction (from Chapter 8). The categorical variable in that study—whether people met online or in person—looks like a quasi-experimental independent variable. There are two categories (meeting online or not), and couples were not randomly assigned to one or the other category. It seems like a correlational study because there were two measured variables, but it also seems like a quasi-experiment because it studied two groups of people who were not randomly assigned. Quasi-experiments and correlational designs also have similar internal validity concerns: Just as you might ask about third variables or unmeasured "lurking" variables in a correlational study, you might ask about selection effects in a quasi-experimental study.

Although the two are similar, in quasi-experiments the researchers tend to do a little more meddling than they do in most correlational designs. In correlational studies, researchers simply select some people (such as a large survey sample, as in the Cacioppo study), measure two variables, and test the relationship between them. In quasi-experiments, however, the researchers might obtain groups by targeting key locations (as in the religious landmarks study) or seeking out comparison groups provided by nature or by public policy (as in the judicial decision-making and Massachusetts health care studies). Therefore, whereas correlational researchers primarily measure variables in a sample and analyze their relationships, quasi-experimental researchers more actively select groups for an independent variable.

Ultimately, the distinction between quasi-experiments and correlational studies can be a blurry one, and some studies may be difficult to categorize. Rather than becoming too concerned about how to categorize a particular study as either quasi-experimental or correlational, focus instead on applying what you know about threats to internal validity and evaluating causal claims. These critical thinking tools apply regardless of how you classify the study's design.

CHECK YOUR UNDERSTANDING

1. How is a nonequivalent control group design different from a true independent-groups experiment?

2. How are interrupted time-series designs and nonequivalent control group interrupted time-series designs different from true within-groups experiments?

3. Describe why both the design and the results of a study are important for assessing a quasi-experiment's internal validity.

4. What are three reasons a researcher might conduct a quasi-experiment, rather than a true experiment, to study a research question?

1. See p. 390; only a true independent-groups experiment randomly assigns participants to the groups. 2. See pp. 392-396; only a true within-groups experiment can control the order of presentation of the levels of the independent variable. 3. See pp. 396-404. 4. See pp. 404-405.

SMALL-*N* DESIGNS: STUDYING ONLY A FEW INDIVIDUALS

Sometimes researchers conduct experiments and studies with just a few participants. As discussed in earlier chapters, having a very large sample (a large *N*) is not always necessary. For the purpose of external validity, how a sample is selected is more important than the sample's size (see Chapter 7). When a researcher expects a large effect size, a small sample can be sufficient to detect it (see Chapter 11), meaning that statistical validity is not necessarily undermined by a small sample. If small samples are sometimes appropriate in research, how small can they be? Is

TABLE 13.2

Differences Between Large-*N* and Small-*N* Designs

LARGE-*N* DESIGNS	SMALL-*N* DESIGNS
1. *Participants are grouped.* The data from an individual participant are not of interest in themselves; data from all participants in each group are combined and studied together.	1. *Each participant is treated separately.* Small-*N* designs are almost always repeated-measures designs, in which researchers observe how the person or animal responds to several systematically designed conditions.
2. Data are represented as *group averages*.	2. Data for *each individual* are presented.

it possible to draw conclusions from a study that uses just one or two participants? What priorities are researchers balancing when they study only a few people or animals at a time?

When researchers use a **small-*N* design**, instead of gathering a little information from a larger sample, they obtain a lot of information from just a few cases. They may even restrict their study to a single animal or one person, using a **single-*N* design**. Large-*N* designs and small-*N* designs differ in two key ways, summarized in **Table 13.2.**

Research on Human Memory

The famous case of Henry Molaison (1926–2008), who was known by his initials H.M., is one of the most important in the field of neuroscience and human memory. As a young adult, Henry suffered from repeated, debilitating epileptic seizures. Medication helped, but after several years, it no longer controlled the seizures and the large doses had started to destroy his cerebellum (the brain structure that controls movement and balance). In 1953, at the age of 27, he had a surgical operation to remove the area of his brain thought to be the origin of his seizures. A surgeon excised the front half of his hippocampus on both the right and left sides (bilaterally), along with other brain areas, including portions of his hippocampal gyrus, amygdala, and medial temporal lobes.

The surgery was successful in that it dramatically reduced Henry's seizures. But as he was recovering, his family and medical staff noticed he didn't recognize the nurses and doctors caring for him. He remembered his parents and could recall memories from before his surgery with varying levels of detail. Yet he'd seemingly lost the ability to learn anything new, including how to find the bathroom in the hospital.

Surgeons at the time did not know that the hippocampus and surrounding brain areas are responsible for memory formation. H.M.'s tragic case filled this gap in their knowledge (Corkin, 2013). After the outcome became clear, surgeon William Scoville expressed deep regret at the memory difficulties he'd inadvertently caused his patient and cautioned other neurosurgeons against removing both sides of the hippocampus in future procedures (Scoville & Milner, 1957).

Henry Molaison's grave memory loss provided neuropsychologists such as Brenda Milner, then a graduate student in psychology, an unprecedented opportunity to study the neuroanatomy of human memory. By studying Henry and patients with similar surgeries, Scoville and Milner learned that bilateral hippocampal lesions do not affect intelligence or personality, only the ability to form new memories (Scoville & Milner, 1957).

Milner, and later Suzanne Corkin and her colleagues, studied H.M. extensively over more than 40 years. The tasks they developed, along with the patient's gracious participation, helped document the biological separation between declarative memory, or *knowing that* something happened, and nondeclarative memory, *knowing how* to do something. For instance, Corkin's group taught Henry to trace a star pattern with a pencil while seeing his hand only in a mirror (Corkin, 2013). Over repeated trials, his mirror-tracing skill improved just as quickly as that of a control participant with an intact brain (this was his nondeclarative, "knowing how" memory). But each day when he saw the task, he'd claim he'd never tried it before (his declarative, "knowing that" memory) (**Figure 13.8**).

In another task, researchers showed Henry a series of complex pictures from magazines. A few hours later, they showed him two pictures, only one of which he had seen earlier. Although his declarative memory was impaired (he claimed never to have seen either image), he could almost always guess the correct picture (apparently, he used feelings of familiarity to select one). The same separation was present in his spatial memory. When told there was a secret buzzer hidden under the carpet in a testing room, Henry eagerly walked around looking for it. On the

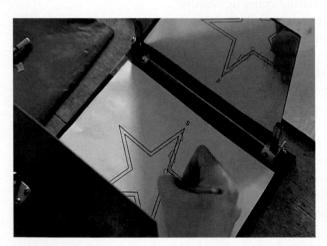 

FIGURE 13.8
Case studies show separate memory systems.
Henry Molaison (right) got better every day at a mirror-tracing task (nondeclarative memory), even though he claimed each day that he'd never seen the task before (declarative memory).

first day, it took him several minutes to find it. On subsequent days, he expressed surprise each time he was told about the secret, but then walked directly to the buzzer, having no trouble locating where it was (Corkin, 2013).

Studies showed that Henry's short-term (working) memory was fairly intact. He could remember a set of numbers (such as "5, 8, 4") for a short period of time, reciting a span he'd heard up to 30 seconds earlier. And if he continually rehearsed a number, he could accurately recite it even an hour later. But if he was distracted for a minute (talking to a nurse, for instance), it was lost. When asked to recall it, he'd say, "What number?"

The contributions this case made to the study of memory and neuroscience were significant. Research on H.M. (and on a few people with similar lesions) helped neuroscientists and psychologists learn the role of hippocampal and medial-temporal brain regions in memory storage. They were able to test hypotheses about the separation of declarative and nondeclarative memory, the difference between feelings of familiarity and feelings of knowing, and even how the brain processes odors (interestingly, Henry smelled odors but could not identify them accurately). From 1957 until a few years before his death, he willingly participated in hundreds of hours of research. Though he didn't always remember hearing he was famous, he enjoyed the attention, and once said, "You just live and learn. I'm living, and you're learning" (Corkin, 2013, p. 113).

BALANCING PRIORITIES IN CASE STUDY RESEARCH

How convinced should we be by the results of research on special cases such as H.M.? These studies, after all, were conducted with only a small number of participants. (Fortunately, this kind of brain damage is rare.) Can we really conclude anything from research conducted on so few people?

Experimental Control. Case studies can effectively advance our knowledge when researchers use careful research designs. Because of the empirical strengths of these studies, we can, in fact, make some conclusions. First, Corkin and her colleagues used the power of experimental control. In some cases, such as testing Henry's ability to remember numbers or recognize magazine photos, researchers compared his performance to age-matched control participants who had no brain damage. Second, researchers deliberately designed tasks meant to isolate different elements of memory, such as declarative from nondeclarative memory. And they worked hard to present a range of activities, including visual, spatial, and auditory learning tasks, which helped them distinguish Henry's perceptual processes from memory processes.

Some of what researchers learned about H.M. was obtained spontaneously. For example, a coffee cup from McDonald's on the dashboard of a car he was riding in prompted Henry to tell the driver a story about a childhood friend with the last name McDonald. He repeated the story verbatim three separate times, not realizing he'd already told it (Corkin, 2013). In contrast to these anecdotes, the laboratory studies in which Henry participated were experimentally controlled.

Studying Special Cases. Just as quasi-experiments can take advantage of natural accidents, laws, or historical events, small-*N* studies often take advantage of special medical cases. Studying people like Henry Moliason gave researchers the opportunity to test which kinds of tasks require hippocampal regions and which do not, under controlled conditions.

Disadvantages of Small-*N* Studies

Brain damage usually affects more than one discrete region, creating an internal validity problem in small-*N* brain damage studies like H.M.'s. The surgeon removed not only the hippocampus, but also some areas around it (**Figure 13.9**). Henry's cerebellum was also damaged from antiseizure medications. The multiple types of damage make it more difficult to narrow down the specific region responsible for each behavioral deficit—an internal validity issue.

FIGURE 13.9
The brain of Henry Molaison.

H.M. and his guardians gave written permission for his brain to be studied after his death. After he died in 2008, scientists carried out a plan to study his brain through imaging and surgery. Areas outlined as *a* and *b* show where some of the temporal lobes had been surgically lesioned in 1957. The *c* area shows another lesion in the frontal lobe.

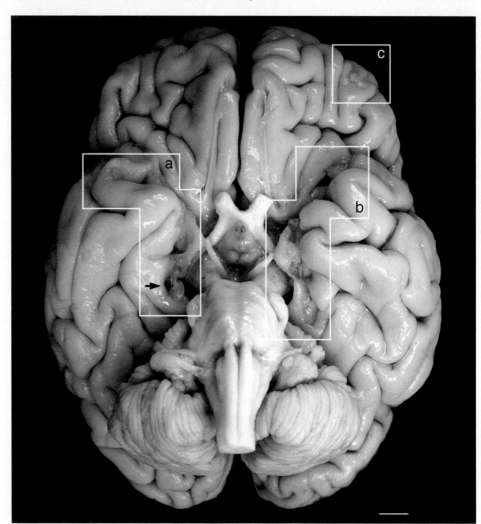

Another disadvantage involves external validity: Participants in small-N studies may not represent the general population very well. Therefore, it's important that researchers found similar memory deficits in several patients with bilateral hippocampal lesions (Scoville & Milner, 1957). However, any patient who undergoes such surgery usually has health problems not found in the general population. Some, like H.M., had a history of severe epilepsy, and others underwent surgery in the 1950s for the treatment of mental illnesses such as schizophrenia. Still others lost their hippocampus through encephalitis (Wilson & Wearing, 1995).

Therefore, we cannot be sure whether results from studies on surgery patients would apply to people with no history of epilepsy or schizophrenia. Furthermore, it clearly would be unethical to remove regions of a nonepileptic person's brain to create the necessary comparison. What could a researcher do to explore the generalizability of the findings from such patients? One option would be to triangulate, meaning to compare a case study's results to research using other methods. For example, the Corkin team's results are consistent with contemporary research using functional brain imagery on nonepileptic adults (e.g., Kensinger, Clarke, & Corkin, 2003). The findings from these studies confirm what has been observed behaviorally in individuals with surgical lesions. In sum, this is another example of how the weight of a variety of evidence supports a parsimonious theory about how the human brain is organized.

« For more on pattern and parsimony, see Chapter 9, pp. 256–258.

Behavior-Change Studies in Applied Settings: Three Small-N Designs

Research on people with brain damage is only one example of the power of a small-N design. In educational, clinical, and work settings, practitioners can use small-N designs to learn whether their interventions work. Small-N designs are frequently used in behavior analysis, a technique in which practitioners use reinforcement principles to improve a client's behavior. In the examples that follow, an occupational therapist might teach an elderly Alzheimer's patient a new memory strategy and then observe whether the patient's memory has improved. A therapist might try to help a child with autism become less afraid of dogs, or teach a developmentally delayed adult to stop a self-harming behavior. In such applied settings, practitioners, like researchers, need to think empirically: They develop theories about people's behaviors; make predictions about what treatments should help; and then implement changes, observe the results, and modify their theories or treatments in response to these observations.

« For a review of the theory-data cycle, see Chapter 1, pp. 11–15.

When practitioners notice improvement after using some treatment, they might wonder whether the improvement was caused by the intervention or by something else. Would the memory of a person with Alzheimer's have improved anyway, or could the improvement have been caused by, say, a change in medication? Did the therapy decrease a child's fear of dogs, or did her fear subside simply because she got attention from the therapist? Notice that these questions are internal validity questions—questions about alternative explanations for the result.

Carefully designed small-*N* or single-*N* studies can help practitioners decide whether changes are caused by their interventions or by some other influence.

STABLE-BASELINE DESIGNS

A **stable-baseline design** is a study in which a practitioner or researcher observes behavior for an extended baseline period before beginning a treatment or other intervention. If behavior during the baseline is stable, the researcher is more certain of the treatment's effectiveness. One example comes from a study of a memory technique known as *expanded rehearsal*, which was used with a real Alzheimer's patient, Ms. S (Moffat, 1989). Before teaching her the new strategy, the practitioners spent several weeks recording baseline information, such as how many words Ms. S could recall after hearing them only once. It was important that the baseline data were stable: Ms. S remembered very few words, and there was no upward trend. Then she was taught the new technique, as researchers continued to monitor how many words she could remember. The researchers noticed a sudden improvement in her memory ability (**Figure 13.10**).

Why should these results convince you that the patient's improvement was caused by the new expanded rehearsal technique? One reason is that the baseline was stable. If the researchers had collected a single baseline measure before the new treatment and a single test afterward (a before-and-after comparison), the improvement could be explained by any number of factors, such as maturation (spontaneous change), regression to the mean, or a history effect. (In fact, a single baseline record followed by a single posttreatment measure would have been a small-*N* version of the "really bad experiment"; see Chapter 11.) Instead, the researchers recorded an extended, stable baseline, which made it unlikely that some sudden, spontaneous change just happened to occur right at the time the new therapy began. Furthermore, the stable baseline meant there was not a single, extreme low point from which improvement would almost definitely occur (a regression effect). Performance began low and stayed low until the experimental technique was introduced.

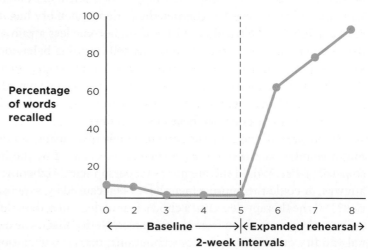

FIGURE 13.10

Using a stable-baseline design.

In this study, the patient's memory was consistently poor until the new expanded rehearsal technique was introduced; then it dramatically improved. (Source: Adapted from Moffat, 1989.)

The stable baseline gave this study internal validity, enabling the researcher to rule out some alternative explanations. In addition, the study was later repeated with a few other Alzheimer's clients (**Figure 13.11**). This replication provided further evidence that expanded rehearsal can help people with Alzheimer's.

MULTIPLE-BASELINE DESIGNS

In a **multiple-baseline design**, researchers stagger their introduction of an intervention across a variety of individuals, times, or situations to rule out alternative explanations. Here's an example. Up to 30% of children with autism express a fear of dogs, and one study attempted to help three such children (Tyner et al., 2016). Participants were John, Sally, and Bob, ages 5–10 (not their real names). At first, they would all shake their heads, plug their ears, or refuse to enter a room containing a dog. Before starting therapy, the researchers recorded each child's initial behavior several times. They introduced each child to a gym where a therapy dog sat with a handler about 98 feet away. Children were told to "go as close as you can to the dog," and observers recorded how close, in feet, each child could approach.

After recording baseline behaviors for several days, therapists began a treatment called *contact desensitization plus reinforcement*. During daily training sessions, each child was accompanied into the gym with a therapy dog at the far end. The child sat with the therapist, playing on a laptop until he or she appeared calm (that was the contact desensitization). Then the therapist would move 5 feet, saying, "Let's come closer." If the child moved ahead, he or she got a favorite snack and praise from the therapist (the reinforcement). (Children were allowed to back away 1 foot at a time if they appeared anxious.) Then the cycle was repeated. Each training session lasted 30 minutes or until the child actually touched the dog. Each child received seven to twelve therapy sessions. About 2 weeks after the training ended, children were shown different dogs in different situations (such as a parking lot), and their distance to the dog was recorded.

The results for John, Sally, and Bob are shown in **Figure 13.12**. Notice how each child's baseline distance to the dog was fairly stable, indicating that simply being tested in the gym did not improve his or her fear. Notice also that each child's treatment began at different times—illustrating the multiple-baseline aspect of this small-*N* design. And notice that each child's distance to the dog reduced dramatically as treatment sessions began.

Should these results convince you that the children's fear was reduced by the contact desensitization plus reinforcement therapy? Probably. First, each child's baseline distance to the dog showed no improvement until the therapy started. Second, the same pattern was observed in three children, which helps rule out alternative explanations, such as an outside event that could have affected only one child. This multiple-baseline design has the internal validity to support a causal conclusion.

In this example, multiple baselines were represented by three children, starting at different times. In other studies, multiple baselines might be represented by different situations or behaviors. One such study was conducted in the notoriously dangerous mining industry. After collecting baseline data on accident rates, managers used tokens to encourage employees of a strip mine to enact safety rules, prevent accidents, or be a member of an injury-free workgroup (Fox, Hopkins, & Anger, 1987). Managers tested the token system in 1972 at one mining location and in 1974 at another. They found that injury-related absences (the key outcome behavior) decreased only after the system began in each location. The multiple baselines at the two mining locations helped the researchers conclude that the token system, not other factors, was responsible for reducing injuries.

REVERSAL DESIGNS

In a **reversal design**, as in the other two small-*N* designs (stable baseline and multiple baseline), a researcher observes a problem behavior both with and without treatment, but takes the treatment away for a while (the reversal period) to see whether the problem behavior returns (reverses). They subsequently reintroduce the treatment to see if the behavior improves again. By observing how the behavior changes as the treatment is removed and reintroduced, the researcher can test for internal validity and make a causal statement: If the treatment is really working, behavior should improve only when the treatment is applied.

An example concerns a man who had autism and severe language deficits. Darnell (not his real name), age 18, lived in a residential treatment center. His therapists wanted to change his behavioral habit of rumination—bringing up food he had previously swallowed. The consequences were serious: Darnell had been hospitalized for weight loss because of this recurring behavior.

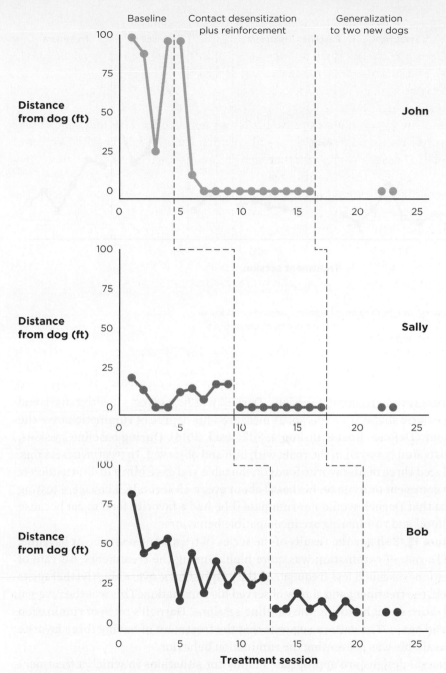

FIGURE 13.12
Using a multiple-baseline design.

In this study, three different children with autism who feared dogs initially stayed a long distance from a dog on the far side of a gym. After several sessions of therapy in which they were praised for moving closer and closer, all three children showed dramatic improvements in their willingness to approach the training dog, and then later, two new dogs. (Source: Adapted from Tyner et al., 2016.)

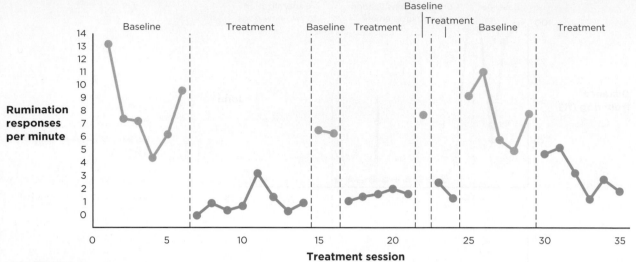

FIGURE 13.13
Using a reversal design.

In this study, the client's rumination behavior was high during baseline sessions and lower during treatment sessions. This pattern supports the idea that the treatment caused his rumination to decrease. (Source: Adapted from DeRosa et al., 2016.)

Across several treatment sessions, Darnell was first given a healthy snack and a high-calorie shake, then therapists measured his degree of rumination over the next hour (DeRosa, Roane, Bishop, & Silkowski, 2016). During baseline sessions, therapists simply stayed in the room with him and observed. In treatment sessions, they placed three of his favorite foods on the table and gave him a little attention (a simple comment or a rub on his head) about every 45 seconds. They were testing the idea that Darnell would not ruminate if he had a favorite food to eat because eating food and ruminating are incompatible behaviors.

Figure 13.13 shows the results of the series of treatment sessions. At baseline, Darnell's rate of rumination was quite high. During the treatments, his rate of rumination was much less frequent. As the graph shows, over time, the therapists withheld the treatment and simply observed his rumination: This was the reversal period. Sure enough, during the baseline sessions, Darnell's rates of rumination increased again. The pattern suggests that the treatment of having three favorite foods available was preventing the rumination behavior.

Reversal designs are appropriate mainly for situations in which a treatment may not cause lasting change. Perhaps because of his disabilities, Darnell's rumination seemed to be automatically reinforcing to him, which is probably why the behavior returned during baseline sessions. In contrast, reversal designs would not make sense to use for an educational intervention. Once a student has learned a new skill (such as Ms. S's expanded rehearsal technique), it's unlikely the skill would simply reverse, or go away.

While a reversal design enables a practitioner to evaluate the effectiveness of a treatment, some might question the ethics of withdrawing a treatment that appears to be working. In fact, two ethical priorities come into play here: On the one hand, it may be considered harmful to withdraw effective treatment from a patient or client; on the other hand, it also may be unethical to use a treatment that is not empirically demonstrated to be effective. (To review a full discussion of ethics in psychology research, see Chapter 4.)

Other Examples of Small-*N* Studies

Research in psychological science boasts several influential small-*N* and single-*N* studies. The Swiss clinical psychologist Jean Piaget worked out a theory of cognitive development in children through careful, systematic observations of his own three children (Piaget, 1923). He found, for example, that as children get older, they learn that when a short glass of liquid is poured into a taller glass, the amount of liquid does not change (**Figure 13.14**). Younger kids, in contrast, tend to respond that there is more liquid in the taller glass because the level appears higher. Although Piaget observed only a few children, he designed systematic questions, made careful observations, and replicated his extensive interviews with each of them.

The German psychologist Hermann Ebbinghaus was a pioneer in the experimental study of memory. In a series of studies conducted over many years, he made himself memorize long lists of nonsense syllables, such as *pon* and *mip*. He systematically varied the frequency and duration of studying each list, and carefully recorded how many syllables he remembered at different time intervals (Ebbinghaus, 1913). He was the first to document several fundamental memory

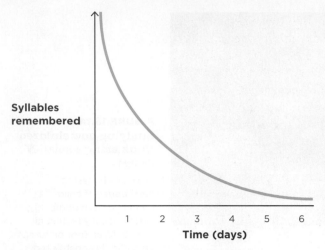

FIGURE 13.15
A single-*N* design: the forgetting curve.

Ebbinghaus' carefully designed experiments on memory processes contributed to psychology, even though he used only one person—himself—as a subject.

2	7	1	2	5	8	2	3
7	0	8	7	5	0	9	9
9	2	5	4	1	6	1	8
7	9	6	1	0	0	5	6
7	8	0	0	1	1	5	6
6	2	6	2	5	3	4	8
2	1	1	9	1	8	4	3
1	1	3	9	5	4	9	2
3	9	9	9	5	6	5	8
7	8	0	5	6	8	5	5

FIGURE 13.16
Remembering random numbers.

Do you think you could recall up to 80 random digits like these after hearing them only once? A college student known as S.F. learned to do so by practicing short-term memory skills for a year and a half.

phenomena, one of which is called the forgetting curve, shown in **Figure 13.15**. It depicts how memory for a newly learned list of nonsense syllables declines most dramatically over the first hour, but then declines more slowly after that. Although he studied only himself—a single-*N* design—Ebbinghaus created testing situations with experimental precision and, eventually, replicability.

In another example of a single-*N* study, memory researchers recruited an average college student (known as S.F.) and asked him to come to their laboratory three to five times a week for a year and a half (Ericsson, Chase, & Faloon, 1980). Each day, they read S.F. random numbers—one digit per second. Later, S.F. would try to recall the numbers in the correct order. Ordinarily, the average memory span for retaining numbers is about seven (Miller, 1956). After regularly practicing in the lab, S.F. developed the ability to recite back 79 random numbers at a time (**Figure 13.16**).

S.F.'s remarkable performance resulted, in part, from his strategy of grouping clusters of numbers according to track and field times (e.g., a string of 3392 might become 3:39.2, "a great time for the mile"). In fact, the researchers tested whether the "running time" strategy *caused* his improved performance by generating some number strings that purposefully did not correspond well to running times. S.F.'s memory span for those special strings dropped down to his beginning level. His incredible memory skill demonstrates what can happen with extensive training and motivation. And the researchers' clever manipulation also showed *why* S.F. got so good at learning strings of numbers—supporting a causal conclusion.

Evaluating the Four Validities in Small-*N* Designs

So far we've focused on how studies using small-*N* designs can eliminate alternative explanations, thereby enhancing internal validity. In all the examples described in this chapter, researchers designed careful, within-subject experiments that allowed them to draw causal conclusions. Even if there was only one participant, the researchers usually measured behaviors repeatedly, both before and after some intervention or manipulation. Therefore, the internal validity of these single-*N* studies is high.

It may seem easy to criticize the external validity of a small-*N* design. How can one person represent a population of interest? Even when researchers can demonstrate that their manipulation, intervention, or procedure replicates in a second or third case, the question of generalizability remains. Remember, though, that researchers can take steps to maximize the external validity of their findings. First, they can triangulate by combining the results of single-N studies with other studies on animals or other groups, as the team did when comparing H.M.'s results with subsequent research on people without brain damage. Second, researchers can specify the population to which they want to generalize, and they rarely intend to generalize to everyone. They may not care, for example, if a memory strategy for Alzheimer's clients applies to everybody in the world, but they do care whether it generalizes to other people with Alzheimer's. Understandably, researchers sometimes limit a study's population of interest to a particular subset of possible participants. Third, sometimes researchers are not concerned about generalizing at all. It may be sufficient to Darnell's caregivers to learn about the one technique that helps him keep down nutritious food. In such cases, even if the causal statement applies only to one person, it is still useful.

When interrogating a small-N design, you should also evaluate construct validity. Of course, researchers want to be sure their measurements are reliable and valid. The researchers in the previous examples recorded how well H.M. drew a pattern, how close children got to a dog, and whether Darnell ruminated or not. Construct validity is fairly straightforward when researchers are recording whether a person with a brain lesion reports seeing this picture or that one, and for objective measures such as memory for a string of numbers. But when researchers are recording the distance a child gets to a dog or whether a person is ruminating, they should use multiple observers and check for interrater reliability, in case one observer is biased or the behavior is difficult to identify.

Regarding statistical validity, in single-N designs, researchers do not typically use traditional statistics. However, they still draw conclusions from data and they should treat data appropriately. In many cases graphs (such as those in Figures 13.10, 13.12, and 13.13) provide enough quantitative evidence. In addition, you might think about effect sizes more simply in small-N cases, by asking: By what margin did the client's behavior improve?

CHECK YOUR UNDERSTANDING

1. What are three small-N designs used in applied settings?
2. Are small-N designs within-groups or between-groups designs?
3. How is a multiple-baseline design similar to a nonequivalent control group interrupted time-series design?
4. How do small-N researchers approach the question of external validity?

1. See pp. 411–417. 2. Within-groups designs, see p. 418. 3. See pp. 413–414; compare Figures 13.3 and 13.12. 4. See pp. 418–419.

CHAPTER REVIEW

Summary

Experiments do not always take place in ideal conditions with clean manipulations, large samples of participants, and random assignment. Quasi-experiments and small-*N* designs use strategies that optimize naturally occurring groups or single individuals.

Quasi-Experiments

- Quasi-experiments can use independent-groups designs such as a nonequivalent control group design and a nonequivalent control group pretest/posttest design. They can also follow within-groups designs, as in an interrupted time-series design or a nonequivalent control group interrupted time-series design.

- When a quasi-experiment includes a comparison group and the right pattern of results, researchers can often support a causal claim, even when participants cannot be randomly assigned to conditions and the researchers do not have complete experimental control of the independent variable.

- Examining the results and design of a quasi-experiment reveals its vulnerablity to alternative explanations, such as selection, maturation, history, regression, attrition, testing, and instrumentation effects; observer biases, demand characteristics, and placebo effects—the same kinds of internal validity threats that can occur in true experiments.

- In quasi-experiments, researchers balance confidence in internal validity with other priorities, such as opportunities to ethically study in a real-world situation or to take advantage of a political event.

Small-*N* Designs: Studying Only a Few Individuals

- Small-*N* studies balance an intense, systematic investigation of one or a few people against the usual approach of studying groups of people. The internal validity of small-*N* studies can be just as high as that of repeated-measures experiments conducted on larger samples.

- Three small-*N* designs used in applied settings are the stable-baseline design, the multiple-baseline design, and the reversal design.

- Small-*N* designs can establish excellent construct and internal validity. They can achieve external validity by replicating the results in other settings, but in applied settings, researchers might prioritize the ability to establish a treatment's effectiveness for a single individual over broad generalizability.

- Researchers must be aware of the trade-offs of each research decision, making conscious choices about which validities are most important—and most possible—to prioritize as they study a particular issue in psychological science.

Key Terms

quasi-experiment, p. 389
nonequivalent control group design, p. 390
nonequivalent control group pretest/posttest design, p. 392

interrupted time-series design, p. 394
nonequivalent control group interrupted time-series design, p. 396
wait-list design, p. 398

small-N design, p. 407
single-N design, p. 407
stable-baseline design, p. 412
multiple-baseline design, p. 413
reversal design, p. 414

 To see samples of chapter concepts in the popular media, visit www.everydayresearchmethods.com and click the box for Chapter 13.

Review Questions

1. What is the term for a quasi-experimental design with at least one treatment group and one comparison group, in which the participants are measured once and have not been randomly assigned to the groups?

   a. Nonequivalent control group design

   b. Independent-groups design

   c. Factorial design

   d. Reversal design

2. Which of these is not a reason for a researcher to select a quasi-experimental design?

   a. To enhance external validity.

   b. To avoid the ethical issues a true experiment would cause.

   c. To ensure internal validity.

   d. To take advantage of real-world opportunities to study phenomena and events.

3. Researchers studied preteens at an outdoor education camp that prevented kids from using devices with screens, such as cell phones (Uhls et al., 2014). They predicted the camp would improve children's nonverbal communication skills. One group of sixth graders attended the camp in the spring. They were compared to a group of sixth graders from the same school the following fall,

who had not attended the camp. The kids were given a test of how well they could read emotions in faces. The camp group took the emotion test on both Monday and Friday of their camp week; the control group took the emotion test on Monday and Friday of a regular school week. What type of design was this?

   a. Interrupted time-series design

   b. Nonequivalent control group interrupted time-series design

   c. Nonequivalent control group design

   d. Nonequivalent control group pretest/posttest design

4. In the kids' camp study, you could ask: Did the researchers use a reliable and valid test of nonverbal communication skills? You would be asking about which kind of validity?

   a. Construct validity

   b. Statistical validity

   c. Internal validity

   d. External validity

5. The researchers found that the ability to read emotions in faces improved significantly in the kids who'd been to the camp, but not in the control kids. Which of the following would be a threat to internal validity in this study?

   a. If the kids who went to camp were selected for their low levels of emotional communication skills, but the control children were not.

   b. If the kids in the two groups were representative of children from their local school district.

   c. If there was no significant difference between the children in the camp group and the control group.

6. A psychologist is working with the parents of four children, all of whom exhibit violent behavior toward one another. The parents were instructed to record the number of violent behaviors each child exhibits in the pre-dinner hour for 1 week. The parents then begin using a positive reinforcement technique to shape the behavior of the youngest child, while continuing to record the behavior of all children. The recording continues and the technique is used on one additional child each week. By the end of 6 weeks, there is a significant decrease in violent behaviors for each of the children. What type of design did the psychologist use?

   a. Stable-baseline design

   b. Multiple-baseline design

   c. Reversal design

   d. Interrupted time-series design

7. Which of these is not a method for addressing the external validity of the conclusions of a small-N study?

   a. Triangulate by comparing results with other research.

   b. Specify a limited population to which to generalize.

   c. Randomly assign people to the treatment and control conditions.

   d. Specify that the result applies only to the participant studied.

Learning Actively

1. Researchers Owens, Belon, & Moss (2010) wanted to investigate the impact of school start time on the sleep patterns of adolescents. They studied teenagers who were enrolled in an American high school, both before (fall semester) and after (spring semester) the entire school had decided to shift its start time from 8:00 A.M. to 8:30 A.M. Students completed a survey asking what time they went to bed the night before, how many hours of sleep they'd gotten, and their daytime sleepiness and level of depressed mood. The researchers found that after the 8:30 start time was implemented, students reported getting 45 minutes more sleep each night, and the percentage of students who reported more than 8 hours per night jumped from 16.4% to 54.7%. In addition, students' level of daytime sleepiness and depressed mood decreased after the 8:30 start time began.

   a. Is this study a nonequivalent control group design, a nonequivalent control group pretest/posttest design, an interrupted time-series design, or a nonequivalent control group interrupted time-series design?

   b. Graph the results of the study, according to the results in the description. (There are multiple dependent variables; choose only one to graph.)

   c. What causal statement might the researchers be trying to make, if any? Is it appropriate? Use the results and design to interrogate the study's internal validity.

   d. If you notice any internal validity flaws, can you redesign the study to remove the flaw?

   e. Ask one question to address construct validity and one to address external validity.

2. Suppose you're a dog owner and are working with your 3-year-old Labrador retriever. When the dog goes for walks, he growls fiercely at other dogs. You want to reduce your dog's growling behavior, so you decide to try a technique you learned on television: pressing firmly on the dog's neck and saying a forceful, quick "Shhhhh!" sound when the dog begins to growl at other dogs. You decide to apply a small-N design to investigate the effectiveness of your training regimen.

a. Which small-N design(s) would be appropriate for this situation?

b. Choose one small-N design and describe how you would conduct your study.

c. Sketch a graph of the results you would predict from your design if your treatment worked. Use Figures 13.10, 13.12, and 13.13 as models.

d. Explain whether you could conclude from your study's results that the treatment caused your dog's aggressive behavior to decrease.

"Is there a replication crisis in psychology?"

"Would we find these same results in other cultural contexts?"

"Does this study need a random sample of participants?"

14

Replication, Generalization, and the Real World

WHAT MAKES A STUDY important? Evaluating this question will be one of your goals as a consumer of research. As you read about a research finding, either in the popular media or in your classes, you will want to know not only whether the study was conducted well but also whether it is important. This chapter outlines several dimensions to consider as you judge a study's importance. The first topic reminds you that a study must be replicated to be important. Other topics, such as a study's applicability to real-world contexts, might challenge what you already think. Deciding about a study's importance requires a nuanced consideration of the researcher's priorities and the study's purpose.

TO BE IMPORTANT, A STUDY MUST BE REPLICATED

Responsible researchers always consider whether the results of an investigation could be a fluke or whether they will get the same results if they conduct the same study again—in other words, whether it is **replicable** (or *reproducible*). "Replicable" means the same results have actually been reproduced.

It makes sense that a finding should be replicated in order to be considered important. If a scientist claimed to have discovered evidence of life on Mars, but other scientists could not find similar evidence, nobody would believe there is life on Mars. If research found that playing violent video games increased aggressive behavior but other studies did not yield the same result, the first result cannot be considered accurate. Replication gives a study credibility, and it is a crucial part of the scientific process.

Replication Studies

When a researcher performs a study again, it is known as a replication study. Even when the original investigation has a statistically significant result, researchers still have to conduct a replication study. There are three major types: direct replication, conceptual replication, and replication-plus-extension.

DIRECT REPLICATION

In **direct replication**, researchers repeat an original study as closely as they can to see whether the effect is the same in the newly collected data. An example follows.

Researchers have theorized that because most people like themselves, they implicitly associate positive feelings with the letters in their own name and the numbers in their birthday. Because of these implicit associations, one team of researchers hypothesized that people might become more attracted to others who share their birthday, name, or initials (Jones, Pelham, Carvallo, & Mirenberg, 2004). In fact, a set of correlational studies showed that people are slightly more likely to marry people who have similar first names than would be predicted just by chance (e.g., Frank is more likely to marry Frances, and Charles is more likely to marry Charlotte).

To test this theory experimentally, researcher John Jones and his team invited people to participate in a study that was ostensibly about "how much people can figure out about another person using only a limited amount of information" (Jones et al., 2004, p. 672). After completing a short self-report survey, each person was given the responses of a randomly selected partner. The page of responses had the partner's ID number printed in large type at the top, such as 12–27. In half the cases, the ID number had been matched to the participant's own birthday (i.e., if the participant's birthday was September 25, the number was 9–25). In the other half, it was not. Besides the ID number, all other information provided by the (invented) partner was exactly the same. A few minutes later, the experimenters asked each person to rate their anonymous partner on a variety of dimensions. They found that when the partner's ID number matched their own birthday, participants reported liking the partner more. Most importantly, they replicated the study almost exactly and found virtually the same results (**Figure 14.1**).

Of course, a direct replication can never replicate the initial study in every detail. In the Jones experiments, the two samples contained distinct sets of participants, and the authors noted that the chairs in the room were set up differently.

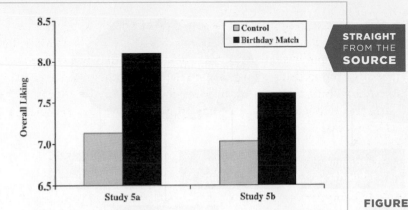

Figure 1. Liking of bogus partner as a function of experimental condition in Studies 5a and 5b. Liking scores are a composite of two liking measures: "How much do you look forward to getting to know this person during the upcoming conversation?" and "How much do you think you would like this person if you got to know her?"

FIGURE 14.1
Direct replication of the birthday similarity effect.

This graph shows the results for the first study (Study 5a) and the direct replication study (Study 5b), as they appeared in the original journal article. (Source: Jones et al., 2004.)

In addition, the two studies may have been conducted at different times of the year. Despite these small variations, however, in a direct replication the researchers try to reproduce the original experiment as closely as possible.

Direct replication makes good sense. However, if there were any threats to internal validity or flaws in construct validity in the original study, such threats would be repeated in the direct replication too. In addition, when successful, a direct replication confirms what we already learned, but it doesn't test the theory in a new context (Crandall & Sherman, 2016). For this reason, researchers value other types of replication as a supplement to direct replication.

CONCEPTUAL REPLICATION

In a **conceptual replication**, researchers explore the same research question but use different procedures. The conceptual variables in the study are the same, but the procedures for operationalizing the variables are different.

Consider the theory of implicit egotism, in which people's implicit self-associations predict their social behaviors (Pelham et al., 2005). In addition to the ID number study, researchers have tested the constructs in other ways. They have operationalized "implicit self-associations" through first name, last name, and birthday similarity, and operationalized "social behaviors" through liking for a person, marriage patterns, residence location, and career choice. For example, using professional membership lists, they found that people named Denise or Dennis are more likely to become dentists than lawyers, but people named Laura or Lawrence are more likely to become lawyers than dentists. People born on February 2 are more likely to live in a town called Two Harbors than Three Forks, but people born on March 3 show the opposite pattern (Pelham, Mirenberg, & Jones, 2002). Because many factors influence our

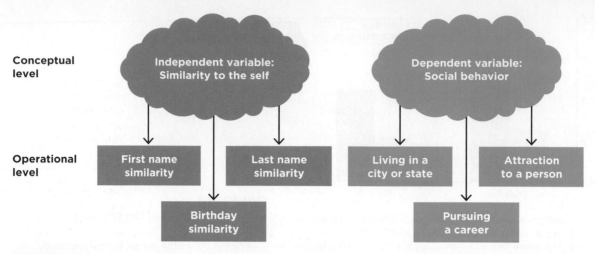

FIGURE 14.2

Conceptual replication: manipulating and measuring the same variables with different operationalizations.

The abstract (conceptual) level of the variables is the same, but the operational level of the variables changes.

social behaviors, implicit egotism effects are very small. However, they appear in almost all instances tested by the researchers (**Figure 14.2**).

REPLICATION-PLUS-EXTENSION

In a **replication-plus-extension** study, researchers replicate their original experiment and add variables to test additional questions.

One example is the research on notetaking, discussed in Chapter 10 (Mueller & Oppenheimer, 2014). In the original posttest-only design, students taking notes with a laptop performed worse on subsequent exams than those taking notes by hand. In follow-up analyses of the original study, the researchers noticed that when people used laptops, their notes had more verbatim overlap with the lectures compared to longhand notetakers. The researchers suspected that the laptop users were merely transcribing directly, so they were processing the information superficially rather than thinking about it and making deep connections. Thus, they performed poorly when tested.

Researchers tested this hypothesis in a second study with three conditions: a longhand condition, a laptop condition, and a new laptop condition in which people were warned not to copy the lecturer's words exactly. This was a replication-plus-extension study because it replicated the original study and included one new condition.

To the researchers' surprise, the notes of the "warned laptop" users contained the same level of verbatim overlap as laptop users with the original instructions. In addition, both laptop groups performed worse on the test questions compared to the longhand notetakers (**Figure 14.3**). This study replicated the original finding

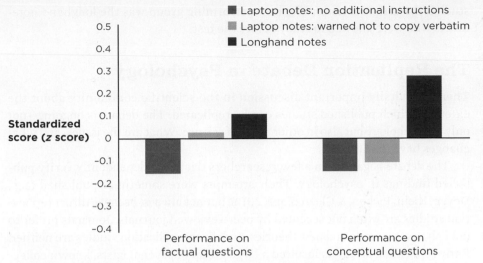

FIGURE 14.3
A replication-plus-extension with an added condition.

This study replicated the original research demonstrating that people do worse on tests when they take notes on a laptop, and extended the initial finding to see if laptop users could resist taking verbatim notes. (Source: Adapted from Mueller & Oppenheimer, 2014.)

and extended it to show that laptop notetakers cannot resist the temptation of taking verbatim notes.

Another way to conduct a replication-plus-extension study is to introduce a new independent variable. Mueller and Oppenheimer's third study illustrates this approach. They speculated that the verbatim notes of the laptop participants might be valuable if the students were allowed to study the notes before the test. The researchers assigned people to take notes using laptops or longhand, as before. But this time, their recall test occurred 1 week after the lectures—as in a real college class. Upon returning to the lab the following week, students were either allowed to study the notes they'd taken the week before, or not. Therefore, this was a 2 × 2 factorial design, with notetaking type as one independent variable and study time as the second independent variable. The results, shown in **Figure 14.4**, indicated that laptop notetakers did poorly on the delayed recall test whether or not they'd

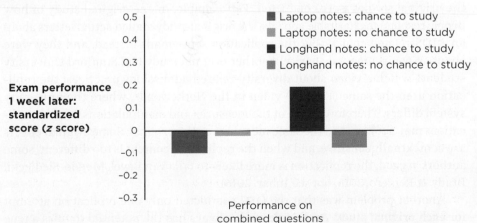

FIGURE 14.4
Replication-plus-extension with a factorial design.

This study replicated the laptop notetaking effect, extending the research by allowing half the students to study their notes a week later. (Source: Adapted from Mueller & Oppenheimer, 2014.)

studied the verbatim notes. The best-performing group was the longhand note-takers who were allowed to study before the test.

The Replication Debate in Psychology

There is a vitally important discussion in the scientific community about the extent to which published studies can be replicated. The debate is ongoing—not only in psychology but also in other areas of science. What are the issues, and what changes have they led to?

The debate began when a few researchers tried to independently verify published findings in psychology. Their attempts were sometimes published (e.g., Doyen, Klein, Pichon, & Cleeremans, 2012), but not always, because direct replication studies are often not accepted by peer-reviewed journals. Journals prefer to publish new methods and new theories, and direct replication studies are neither. Early replication attempts inspired a large group of psychologists, known collectively as the Open Science Collaboration (OSC), to attempt replication on a larger, systematic scale (Open Science Collaboration, 2015). The OSC selected 100 studies from three major psychology journals and recruited researchers around the world to conduct direct replications. They used different metrics to judge whether a study was a successful replication. By one metric, only 39% of the studies had clearly replicated the original effects. (Other measures yielded better rates of replication, but the media usually reported the lowest—the 39% figure.)

The announcement was alarming. Science writers dubbed the problem a "replication crisis," and in the months that followed, scientists began to analyze the situation. The replication crisis has been scrutinized in terms of problems with the replication attempt, with the original study, and with publication practices. The issues are summarized in **Table 14.1**.

WHY MIGHT REPLICATION STUDIES FAIL?

Right away, certain writers took issue with the OSC's 39% replicability estimate because some of the replication attempts were insensitive to the context in which the original studies were conducted. For example, in one original study of how people respond to charitable appeals, the original study mailed actual letters about an AIDS-related charity, but the replication sent emails instead, and they were about an environmental charity. Another original study had Stanford University students watch a video about diversity-related admissions practices; the replication used the same (English) video in the Netherlands, where the university system differs. Therefore, some of the measures and manipulations used in replications may not have had the same meanings as the original. Some original effects are contextually sensitive, and when the replication context is too different, some authors argued, the replication is more likely to fail (Van Bavel, Mende-Siedlecki, Brady, & Reinero, 2016; but see Inbar, 2016).

Another problem was that the OSC conducted only one replication attempt for each original study. Any single study always has the potential to miss a true

TABLE 14.1

Themes in the "Replication Crisis" and Potential Solutions

POTENTIAL PROBLEM	PROBLEM CAN MEAN	PROPOSED CHANGES IN SCIENTIFIC PRACTICE
PROBLEMS WITH THE REPLICATION ATTEMPT		
Replication used exact operationalizations from the original study, but these were not relevant in the replication setting.	Replication study fails, but only because it was not a true test of the original effect.	Permit conceptual replications, which use operationalizations that make sense in new contexts.
Replication did not use a large enough sample to detect the original effect.	Replication studies obtain inconclusive results.	Conduct replication studies with appropriate sample size (Simonsohn, 2015).
PROBLEMS WITH THE ORIGINAL STUDY		
Original study's sample size was very small.	A few chance values could have influenced the data set, so the study's outcome was a fluke.	Use large sample sizes so that unusual cases have less chance of influencing a study's pattern (Fraley & Vazire, 2014).
Original study used questionable research practices, such as trying multiple statistical analyses until an effect is found, hypothesizing after the results were known, or failing to report study variables that showed no effect.	Reported result is more likely to be a fluke, rather than a true, replicable pattern.	Make all data available for review and analysis by other scientists (open science). Require the Method section to report all variables used in the study and report all statistical practices that were used. Preregister studies by making public (online) the hypothesis and study design before data collection and analysis.
PROBLEMS WITH PUBLICATION PRACTICES		
Scientific journals prefer to publish new findings over replication studies.	Scientists don't conduct enough replication studies. Reviews of the literature reach incorrect conclusions about the weight of the evidence.	Devote sections of high-status journals to publishing replication attempts.
Publication bias in psychology: Scientific journals prefer to publish significant differences over null effects.	Hypotheses that are reasonable, but not supported by the data, are not allowed to become known in the literature.	Journals can prioritize preregistered studies. They can peer-review preregistered designs and promise publication regardless of the study's outcome.

finding (leading to a failed replication). To counter this problem, some researchers obtained data from another large-scale effort, the Many Labs Project (MLP), which had conducted up to 36 replications of each study, combining the results of them all. Using this more powerful approach, the replication rate rose to 85% (Gilbert, King, Pettigrew, & Wilson, 2016; see, e.g., Klein et al., 2014).

A different set of arguments pointed out problems with the *original* studies rather than the replications. In certain cases, the original study's sample size was too small, so a few extreme individuals could have had a disproportionate influence on means

FIGURE 14.5
Hypothesizing after the results are known (HARKing).

One problematic research practice involves creating a hypothesis *after* seeing surprising results. Such findings may be due to chance and cannot be replicated. Careful scientists must replicate surprising findings in a new, independent study. The practice of preregistration aims to prevent HARKing because researchers publish their target (the hypothesis) before they start to collect data.

and patterns. In large samples, extreme cases will almost certainly be cancelled out by individuals at other extremes. But in small samples, this is less likely to happen. Small samples can accidentally lead to significant findings that can't be replicated because there probably wasn't a real effect in the first place (Fraley & Vazire, 2014; Simonsohn, 2015).

In other cases, authors of the original study may have engaged in questionable research practices that led to fluke effects. Researchers include multiple dependent variables in an experiment, and perhaps only one out of seven or eight variables show a significant difference. A researcher might report the significant effect, dismissing all the variables that didn't work. Scientists might craft an after-the-fact hypothesis about a surprising result, making it appear as if they predicted it all along, a practice called HARKing, for "hypothesizing after the results are known" (**Figure 14.5**). Or a researcher might peek at the study's results, and if they are not quite significant, run a few more individuals, decide to remove certain outliers from the data, or run a different type of analysis. This last set of practices has been dubbed **p-hacking**, in part because the goal is to find a *p* value of just under .05, the traditional value for significance testing (Simmons, Nelson, & Simonsohn, 2011). Researchers may not intentionally analyze their data in a biased way, but cognitive biases can creep in (Nuzzo, 2015). The result is that a reported effect is not really there, and therefore cannot be replicated.

IMPROVEMENTS TO SCIENTIFIC PRACTICE

In response to these critiques, psychologists and other scientists have introduced changes. One is for research journals to require much larger sample sizes, both for original studies (Fraley & Vazire, 2014) and for replication studies (Simonsohn, 2015). Researchers are also urged to report all of the variables and analyses they tested (Simmons, Nelson, & Simonsohn, 2011).

Another development is **open science**, the practice of sharing one's data and materials freely so others can collaborate, use, and verify the results. When *data* are open, psychologists provide their full data set, so other researchers can conduct new analyses on it (increasing its usefulness) or simply reproduce the published results. When *materials* are open, psychologists provide their full set of measures and manipulations, so others can conduct replication studies more easily. With open materials, all variables are reported—not just the ones that worked. As you learned in Chapter 1, making research public and transparent is a fundamental feature of science.

A third change is **preregistration**; scientists can preregister their study's method, hypotheses, or statistical analyses online, in advance of data collection. Certain journals treat preregistered studies more favorably than others; some even peer-review the proposals and promise to publish the results regardless of the outcome. Preregistration gives researchers credit for their predictions and study designs—not just for the results (Chambers, 2017). This process could discourage p-hacking because it values the full, honest theory-data cycle rather than only the significant findings.

Finally, while the majority of a journal's content is reserved for new studies, some journals now devote a section to replication attempts. It's a new incentive to engage in the important practice of replication while still publishing papers—the basis of any scientist's research career.

The replication debate has been scientifically driven. The proposed solutions are intended to prevent cognitive biases from sneaking into psychologists' thinking and to promote the rigorous, unbiased pursuit of knowledge.

Meta-Analysis: What Does the Literature Say?

Progress in psychological science occurs incrementally, as researchers successfully conduct systematic sets of direct replications, conceptual replications, and replication-plus-extension studies. The most important conclusions are those based on a body of evidence. A **scientific literature** (or simply *literature*) consists of a series of related studies conducted by various researchers that have tested similar variables. Thus, literatures are composed of several studies on a particular topic, often carried out by many different researchers. For example, you might hear your instructors talk about the literature on the effects of cell phone use while driving, or the literature on which notetaking form or studying technique is most effective.

Sometimes researchers collect all the studies on a topic and consider them together—generating what is known as a review article, or a literature review (see Chapter 2). One approach is simply to summarize the literature in a narrative way, describing what the studies typically show and explaining how the body of evidence supports a theory.

Researchers can also use the quantitative technique of meta-analysis to create a mathematical summary of a scientific literature. A **meta-analysis**, as you learned in Chapter 2, is a way of mathematically averaging the results of all the studies (both published and unpublished) that have tested the same variables to see what conclusion that whole body of evidence supports. The following example will help you understand the basic process involved in a meta-analysis.

EXAMPLE: LYING TAKES TIME

A common scene in crime dramas shows lie detection equipment hooked up to a suspect. The theory is that liars experience stress: They display agitated heart rate and sweatier palms when lying compared to answering truthfully. However, empirical evidence does not support that stress-based lie detection instruments work (Saxe, 1991). In fact, they're not permitted in court.

An alternative theory proposes cognitive (rather than emotional) burdens of lying. Liars have to fabricate a story, avoid contradicting themselves, and keep

TABLE 14.2

Cohen's Guidelines for Effect Sizes

EFFECT SIZE d	STRENGTH OF RELATIONSHIP	EFFECT SIZE r
0.20	Small, or weak	.10
0.50	Medium, or moderate	.30
0.80	Large, or strong	.50

Source: Cohen, 1992.

the truth under wraps. As a result, people should take more time to respond to questions when they are lying compared to telling the truth. A number of laboratory studies have tested this theory. In one such study, experimenters gave students an envelope containing a jack of spades playing card and a 20-euro bank note, telling them to lie throughout the experiment by saying they'd never seen them (Gamer, Bauerman, Stoeter, & Vossel, 2007). Later, during a timed computer task, the students were shown a variety of playing cards and bank notes and were asked if they'd seen them before (**Figure 14.6**). Their reaction times were slower when they denied seeing the jack of spades or 20-euro note compared to when they denied seeing innocent items ($d = 1.34$).

A group of researchers conducted a meta-analysis on studies like these (Suchotzki, Vershuere, Van Bockstaele, Ben-Shakhar, & Crombez, 2017). By searching databases, contacting online groups, and emailing colleagues, they collected 114 experiments. They computed the effect size d of each study, such that the larger the effect size, the greater the reaction time difference between lies and truths. Then they calculated the average of all effect sizes. Although they used d, a meta-analysis can also compute the average of effect sizes as measured by r. Cohen's (1992) conventions for effect sizes describe the average effect size as small, medium, or large (**Table 14.2**). The average effect size in the 114 studies was 1.26—a very large effect size supporting the cognitive cost of lying.

In follow-up analyses, the team separated the studies into different categories. For example, some studies told participants to go as fast as possible; others did not. The theory predicts that the reaction time difference will be especially noticeable when people are trying to go fast. As expected, the average effect size for the "fast as possible" studies was larger (**Table 14.3**). In other words, speed

» To review moderators, see Chapter 8, pp. 228–230.

TABLE 14.3

Results for the Reaction Time Difference Between Lying and Truthful Conditions, Categorized by Type of Instructions to Participants

TYPE OF STUDY	NUMBER OF STUDIES	TOTAL NUMBER OF PARTICIPANTS	AVERAGE EFFECT SIZE d (LYING CONDITION MINUS TRUTHFUL CONDITION)
Participants instructed to go as fast as possible	100	2,866	1.29
Participants not instructed to go fast	11	354	0.97

Note: Three studies were not able to be categorized.
Source: Adapted from Suchotzki et al., 2017, Table 2.

instructions moderated the relationship between lying and reaction time.

The researchers also separately analyzed studies in which participants had an incentive to avoid being caught—a situation similar to a criminal interrogation. Motivation to avoid getting caught moderated the influence of lying on reaction time (**Table 14.4**), such that when people were motivated, the reaction time difference was smaller.

STRENGTHS AND LIMITATIONS OF META-ANALYSIS

The example illustrates several important features of meta-analysis. In a meta-analysis, researchers collect all possible examples of a particular kind of study. They then average all the effect sizes to find an overall effect size. Using meta-analysis, researchers can also sort a group of studies into categories (i.e., moderators), computing separate effect size averages for each category. From these follow-up analyses, researchers can detect new patterns in the literature as well as test new questions.

Because meta-analyses usually contain data that have been published in empirical journals, you can be more certain that the data have been peer-reviewed, providing one check on their quality. However, as you have learned, there is a publication bias in psychology: Significant relationships are more likely to be published

FIGURE 14.6
Laboratory studies of lying.

Some studies showed people cards or notes and asked them to lie about what they had seen. Why is a meta-analysis more valuable than a single study?

TABLE 14.4

Results for the Reaction Time Difference Between Lying and Truthful Conditions Categorized by Participants' Motivation to Avoid Detection

TYPE OF STUDY	NUMBER OF STUDIES	TOTAL NUMBER OF PARTICIPANTS	AVERAGE EFFECT SIZE d (LYING CONDITION MINUS TRUTHFUL CONDITION)
No motivation	85	2,552	1.33
Instructed to avoid detection	23	626	1.00
Incentive to avoid detection	6	129	1.13

Source: Adapted from Suchotzki et al., 2017, Table 2.

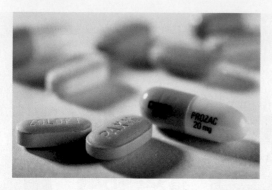

FIGURE 14.7
Selective publication rates.

About 51% of FDA-registered studies found that antidepressant medications are effective, yet the studies with positive effects are more likely to actually be published in medical journals.

than null effects. This tendency leads to the **file drawer problem**, the idea that a meta-analysis might be overestimating the true size of an effect because null effects, or even opposite effects, have not been included in the collection process. (The name comes from the notion that instead of being published, these studies sit forgotten in the researchers' filing cabinets.) To combat the problem, researchers who are conducting a meta-analysis should follow the practice of contacting their colleagues (via social media groups and subscription lists), requesting both published and unpublished data for their project.

Here's an illustration of the potential seriousness of the file drawer problem. A group of medical researchers analyzed data from a set of 74 studies in the U.S. on the effectiveness of antidepressant medications, such as Paxil and Zoloft (Turner, Matthews, Linardatos, Tell, & Rosenthal, 2008). All the studies had been registered in advance, as required by law, with the U.S. Food and Drug Administration (FDA), which oversees pharmaceutical research. Of the 74 studies, only 38 had shown positive results for these drugs (i.e., they alleviated symptoms of depression). Of the rest, 24 studies showed negative and 12 showed "questionable" effects of antidepressants. However, all but one of the positive studies had been published in medical journals, whereas the studies with null findings were much less likely to ever be published (**Figure 14.7**). In fact, only 3 of the 36 negative or questionable outcomes were ultimately published. Therefore, if you read only published studies, you'd conclude that 94% of them demonstrate antidepressants are effective, when in fact, only 51% of all registered studies have shown that they work!

Literature reviews and meta-analyses are considered valuable by many psychologists because they assess the weight of the evidence in a scientific literature. They tell you whether, across a number of studies, there is a relationship between two variables—and if so, how strong it is. However, a meta-analysis is only as powerful as the data that go into it. If researchers don't work hard to include unpublished results or if studies they do include have followed questionable research practices, the meta-analysis will reach a biased conclusion. New methods try to ensure the studies included in a meta-analysis were well-conducted.

Replicability, Importance, and Popular Media

Can you count on the media to tell you which scientific studies are most important? Not always. For one, journalists do not always consider replicability when they report on science stories. Sometimes journalists will report on a single, hot-off-the-press study because it makes a splashy headline. Responsible journalists, however, not only report on the *latest* studies; they also give readers a sense of what the *entire literature* says on a particular topic. For example, rather than merely announcing the results of a recent study on coffee and depression, a responsible journalist should talk about the context, too: How well does this latest study fit in with the larger body of evidence on the same subject? If journalists do not provide the context of the entire literature surrounding a study, then you would be right to reserve judgment about the study's importance.

You also can't be sure journalists have critically evaluated the original research. Some simply summarize press releases and don't question the study's quality. A science journalist exposed this practice in an online article (Bohannon, 2015). He'd worked with colleagues to conduct and publish a flawed research study. They randomly assigned only 16 dieters to a diet that included 1.5 ounces of daily chocolate or to a control condition. After a few weeks, dieters who ate chocolate had lost weight 10% faster than the control group. One problem with the study was its small sample size, meaning its results were more likely to be biased by one or two extreme cases. Another problem was that the study measured 18 variables (weight, sleep quality, mood, etc.). Only one variable worked, so the result is probably due simply to chance. Nevertheless, Bohannon and his collaborators sent the data to a for-profit online journal, which published the findings—without peer review—for a large fee. Then Bohannon wrote a press release about his study and tracked the story: It was picked up uncritically by at least a dozen popular outlets (**Figure 14.8**).

Has the world gone coco? Eating chocolate can help you LOSE weight

GOOD news slimmers! New research claims that eating chocolate can actually help you beat the bulge.

By Laura Mitchell / Published 30th March 2015

FIGURE 14.8
Journalists don't always check the original research.

The UK's *Daily Star* ran this story about a deeply flawed study, created by a science journalist and published in an online journal without peer review. The journalist probably did not read the original study or question its design. (Source: Mitchell, 2015.)

CHECK YOUR UNDERSTANDING

1. Describe how the three types of replication studies are similar and different.

2. Describe at least three reasons why a replication attempt might fail, using Table 14.1 as a guide.

3. Compare the value of a single study to that of a body of evidence, or a scientific literature.

4. In your own words, describe the steps a researcher follows in a meta-analysis. What can a meta-analysis tell you?

1. See pp. 426–430. 2. See pp. 430–432. 3. See p. 433. 4. See pp. 433–436.

TO BE IMPORTANT, MUST A STUDY HAVE EXTERNAL VALIDITY?

Asking about replicability is one way to judge a study's importance. Reproducing a study's results is an essential step that allows researchers to be far more confident in the accuracy of their results and more convinced of their importance.

Replicability also helps you interrogate one of the four big validities: external validity—the degree to which a study's results are generalizable, to other participants and other settings. Although direct replication studies do not support external validity, conceptual replications and replication-plus-extension studies can. When researchers test their questions using slightly different methods, different kinds of participants, or different situations, or when they extend their research to study new variables, they are demonstrating how their results generalize to other populations and settings. The more settings and populations in which a study is conducted, the better you can assess the generalizability of the findings.

Generalizing to Other Participants

Recall that to assess a study's generalizability to other people, you would ask *how* the participants were obtained. If a study is intended to generalize to some population, the researchers must draw a probability sample from that population. If a study uses a convenience sample (such as a haphazard sample of whoever is close by), you can't be sure of the study's generalizability to the population the researcher intends. For example, if a group of researchers wanted to generalize a study's results from a sample of U.S. soldiers to the population of all U.S. soldiers, they would have to use random sampling techniques to draw the sample from the total population of American soldiers.

IT'S *A* POPULATION, NOT *THE* POPULATION

Bear in mind that you learned how the population to which researchers want to generalize usually is not the population of every living person. Instead, when researchers are generalizing from a sample to a population, they will specify what the population of interest is. It might be all U.S. soldiers. It might be all the college students in Manitoba. It might be all the third graders in a Beijing elementary school. It might be a group of lab-reared rhesus monkeys. Researchers are at liberty to specify what their population of interest is based on the variables they are interested in and the theories they are testing.

EXTERNAL VALIDITY COMES FROM *HOW*, NOT *HOW MANY*

Recall that when you are assessing the generalizability of a sample to a population, "how" matters more than "how many." In other words, a randomly selected sample of 200 participants has external validity; a haphazardly selected sample of 2,000 participants does not.

« For a review of sample size and generalizability, see Chapter 7, pp. 179–192.

JUST BECAUSE A SAMPLE COMES FROM A POPULATION DOESN'T MEAN IT GENERALIZES TO THAT POPULATION

Some students assume that if a convenience sample simply includes some members of a population (perhaps dog owners, or Asian men, or Methodist ministers), the sample can therefore generalize to those populations (of all dog owners, Asian men, or Methodist ministers). Instead, the same rules apply. In order to generalize to any population, you would need a probability sample of dog owners, or of Asian men, or Methodist ministers. If you had only a convenience sample, it might primarily contain the dog owners whom the researcher could contact and who were willing to participate in the study.

Generalizing to Other Settings

The other aspect of external validity is a study's generalizability to different settings. Conceptual replications illustrate this aspect of external validity very well. When researchers extended the studies of implicit egotism to occupations, marriages, and housing choices, it showed that the results could generalize from one setting to another setting.

Sometimes you want to know whether a lab situation created for a study generalizes to real-world settings. For example, you might ask whether the studies on lying about playing cards, which took place in the laboratory on a computer, would generalize meaningfully to real-world lies. A study's similarity to real-world contexts is sometimes called its **ecological validity**, or *mundane realism* (explained in detail later in this chapter). Many psychologists consider ecological validity to be one aspect of external validity (Brewer, 2000).

Does a Study Have to Be Generalizable to Many People?

How is external validity related to a study's importance? Read the following two statements, and decide whether you agree with each one:

1. The best research uses random samples from the population.
2. The best research uses people of all genders, ages, and ethnicities, and from all socioeconomic classes, regions, countries, and so on.

Of course, both of these statements address the external validity of a particular study. When the sample for a study has been selected from a population *at random* (using a probability sample), the results from that sample can be generalized to the population it was drawn from. It also makes sense that if a study's sample includes only men, you may not generalize its results to women; if a study's sample includes only college students from Manitoba, you may not generalize its results to elderly residents of Florida. Because most people have a strong intuitive understanding of external validity, they will agree with the two statements above.

However, the two statements are only *sometimes* right. Evaluating the importance of external validity requires a nuanced approach that considers the researcher's priorities. Whether a researcher strives for external validity in a study depends on what research mode he or she is operating in: theory-testing mode or generalization mode.

THEORY-TESTING MODE

When researchers work in **theory-testing mode**, they are usually designing correlational or experimental research to investigate support for a theory. As discussed in Chapter 1, the theory-data cycle is the process of designing studies to test a theory and using the data from the studies to reject, refine, or support the theory. In theory-testing mode, external validity often matters less than internal validity.

Example: The Contact Comfort Theory. Harlow's classic study of attachment in infant monkeys (described in Chapters 1 and 10) is a good example of theory-testing mode (Harlow, 1958). Harlow created two artificial monkey "mothers" in order to test two competing theories of infant attachment: the cupboard theory (babies are attached to their mothers because their mothers feed them) and the contact comfort theory (babies are attached to their mothers because their mothers are soft and cozy). In a real monkey mother, of course, the features of food and coziness are confounded. So Harlow separated the two features by creating one cloth mother that was soft and cozy but did not provide food and one wire mother that was cold and uncomfortable but did provide food. By separating the two confounded variables, Harlow was prioritizing internal validity.

Harlow was clearly in theory-testing mode here, wondering which theory, the cupboard theory or the contact comfort theory, was right. And the results from his study could not have been clearer: The baby monkeys in this study spent almost all of their time cuddling with the soft, cozy mother. The contact comfort theory was overwhelmingly supported.

The monkeys in Harlow's study were hardly representative of monkeys in the wild. He didn't even use a random sample of monkeys from his laboratory. But Harlow didn't care because he was in theory-testing mode: He created the artificial situation to test his *theory*—not to test the truth in some population of monkeys. In fact, according to the cupboard theory, *any* sample of monkeys—no matter how representative—should have been equally or more interested in the wire mother than they were in the cloth mother. The data, however, did not support the cupboard theory of attachment.

Example: The "Parent-as-Grammar-Coach" Theory. Another example of a study conducted in theory-testing mode comes from research on how children learn grammar. Some psychologists used to believe that children learn correct grammar through reinforcement; they believed parents praise a child's grammatically correct sentences and correct the ungrammatical ones. They thought children learned grammar through this constant correction process.

The reinforcement theory predicted that parents would praise their kids for grammatical sentences and correct the ungrammatical sentences. But read the following interaction, audiotaped by Brown and Hanlon in a study that observed parents interacting with their children (1970, cited in Mook, 1989, p. 27):

Child: Mama isn't boy, he girl.
Parent: That's right.
Child: There's the animal farmhouse.
Parent: No, that's a lighthouse.

What Brown and Hanlon noticed—and you probably did, too—is that the parent accepted the child's first sentence, which was ungrammatical but factually true. (*That's right—he girl!*) But the parent corrected the child's second sentence, which was grammatically correct but factually wrong. (*Not a farmhouse—a lighthouse!*) This one incident illustrates the overall trend in the data. After coding hours of conversations between parents and children, Brown and Hanlon found that most of the time, parents corrected their children's sentences for factual accuracy but not for grammar. Furthermore, the reinforcement theory predicted that the children in this study would not learn to speak properly without having their grammar corrected. But even though the parents didn't point out errors, the children did learn to speak grammatically. The reinforcement theory of speech development therefore was not supported.

This study included only upper-middle-class Boston families, so the children and parents were not representative of all children, even of all Boston children (Brown & Hanlon, 1970). Moreover, the parents in the study were willing to let a researcher record their interactions with their children on tape; they might have been especially eager to be involved in research or were more educated than

FIGURE 14.9
When is external validity crucial?

In the "parent-as-grammar-coach" study, the sample included only upper-middle-class Boston families (Brown & Hanlon, 1970). Why was it acceptable to use a nonrandom sample in this research?

average (**Figure 14.9**). Yet the bias of this sample didn't matter because the researchers were testing a theory: If the reinforcement theory of grammar were true, *any* sample of parents would have corrected ungrammatical sentences, but the parents in this study did not.

Of course, the reinforcement theory of grammar might apply to some other population in the world, and if Brown and Hanlon had studied a wider sample of people, they might have found evidence that some parents, somewhere, do correct their children's grammar. Keep two things in mind. First, the researchers chose a strong test of their theory. If the reinforcement theory of grammar should apply anywhere, it would be among precisely the kinds of parents who volunteered for the study: upper-middle class, well-educated, and interested in research. Such parents presumably use standard grammar themselves and are willing to explain grammar rules to their children. Second, if the researchers had found some other cultural group of parents who did correct their children's grammar, they would have to modify the reinforcement theory to fit these new data. They'd have to change the theory to explain why reinforcement applies only in this population but not in others. In either case, the data from Brown and Hanlon's study mean that the "parent-as-grammar-coach" theory must be rejected or at least modified.

Other Examples. The overwhelming majority of studies in psychology are of the theory-testing type (Mook, 1989). Most researchers design variables that enable them to test competing explanations and confirm or disconfirm their hypotheses. For example, Pelham and his colleagues were testing the theory that implicit egotism influences important social behaviors. Research on people's reaction times while lying tested the theory that lying entails a cognitive cost. Strayer's research on cell phone use while driving tested the theory that cell phones are cognitively distracting to drivers. When researchers are in theory-testing mode, they are not very concerned (at least not yet) with the external validity of their samples or procedures (Berkowitz & Donnerstein, 1982).

GENERALIZATION MODE

Although much of the research in psychology is conducted in theory-testing mode, at certain times theory-testing takes place in **generalization mode**, when researchers want to generalize the findings from the sample in a previous study to a larger population. They are careful, therefore, to use probability samples with appropriate diversity of gender, age, ethnicity, and so on. In other words, researchers in generalization mode are concerned about external validity.

In addition, you'll probably notice that some studies have aspects of both modes, such as when researchers test an established theory to see if it applies in a new culture or for a different age group. For example, as covered in Chapter 12, Strayer and Drews (2004) were testing their theory about cognitive distractions of phone conversations, but they also were attempting to see if their original findings would generalize to an older group of drivers.

Frequency Claims: Always in Generalization Mode. Survey research that is intended to support frequency claims is done in generalization mode. A researcher must have a representative sample in order to answer such questions as: "How many U.S. teenagers text while driving?" "What percentage of voters support the health care law?" "At what age do American children learn to read?" It would not be acceptable to estimate U.S. teenage texting-while-driving rates from a haphazard sample of youths in an upper-middle-class high school in New York City. Estimating the percentage of voters who support a national health care law by interviewing only people living in Dallas, Texas, wouldn't be okay either. And it wouldn't be acceptable to estimate the age at which children learn to read by asking a self-selected sample on a web page dedicated to gifted children. All these samples would be biased.

As you have learned, representative samples are essential for supporting frequency claims. (For a review, see Chapters 3 and 7.) Therefore, when researchers are testing frequency claims, they are always in generalization mode.

Association and Causal Claims: Sometimes in Generalization Mode. Most of the time, association and causal claims are conducted in theory-testing mode. But researchers sometimes conduct them in generalization mode, too.

Suppose a researcher tries out a new therapeutic technique on a limited sample of clients (such as a sample of American women of European descent) and finds that it works. If the therapy is effective in this sample, the researcher would then want to learn whether it will also be effective more generally, in other samples. Will it work on African-American women? Will it work on men? To learn whether the therapy's effectiveness generalizes to other populations, the researcher has to collect data on samples from those populations. In this case, the researcher cares about generalizability from one cultural group to another.

Consider a marketing researcher who learns a sample of local teenagers prefers an advertising campaign featuring tattoo artists over an ad campaign featuring a professional skateboarder. The researcher would hope to generalize the pattern from this particular sample to the teenagers around the country who will eventually view the ads. Therefore, the marketing researcher would care very much that the sample used in the study represents teenagers nationwide. Are they the same age? Are they of the same social class? Do they show the same distribution of ethnicities? Was the focus group sample unusually interested in

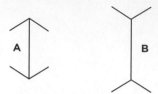

FIGURE 14.10
The Müller-Lyer illusion.

The vertical lines labeled A and B are the same length, but North Americans and Europeans usually perceive line B to be longer than line A. That perception is not true for all people worldwide.

tattoos, compared with the rest of the U.S. teenage population? Only if the external validity were sound would the preferences of this sample be generalizable to the preferences of the nation's teens.

CULTURAL PSYCHOLOGY: A SPECIAL CASE OF GENERALIZATION MODE

Cultural psychology is a subdiscipline of psychology focusing on how cultural contexts shape the way a person thinks, feels, and behaves (Heine, 2016; Markus & Hamedani, 2007; Shweder, 1989). In conducting their studies, cultural psychologists work in generalization mode. They have challenged researchers who work exclusively in theory-testing mode by identifying several theories that were supported by data in one cultural context but not in any other. Two examples follow.

The Müller-Lyer Illusion. You may already be familiar with the Müller-Lyer illusion, illustrated in **Figure 14.10**. Does the vertical line B appear longer than the vertical line A? If you take out a ruler and measure the two vertical lines, you'll find they are exactly the same length.

Almost all North Americans and Europeans fall for this illusion, but not all *people* do. Indeed, one team of researchers found that many people around the world, when tested, do not see line B as being longer than line A (Segall, Campbell, & Herskovits, 1966). **Figure 14.11** shows the cross-cultural results of this study.

Suppose a group of researchers in theory-testing mode used the Müller-Lyer data from a single North American sample to test a theory about human visual perception. Though they might not think culture would affect such a basic cognitive process—the illusion feels so natural!—they would be wrong.

FIGURE 14.11
Cross-cultural results for the Müller-Lyer illusion.

Segall et al. (1966) tested the Müller-Lyer illusion on adults in 16 societies and found that North Americans are most likely to perceive the illusion. The y-axis shows how much longer line B appears to participants compared with line A. The higher the value, the greater the degree of the illusion. (Source: Adapted from Henrich, Heine, & Norenzayan, 2010.)

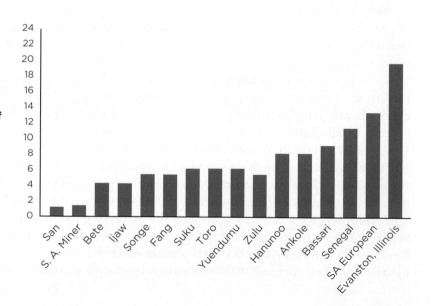

FIGURE 14.12
Figure and ground: testing visual attention.

This is the original image in the Masuda and Nisbett (2001) study.

In fact, the Segall team used their global data to conclude that people who grow up in a "carpentered world" have more visual experience with right angles as cues for depth perception than people who grow up in other societies. (Look at the corner of the room you're in right now. Do you see the angles of line B in the Müller-Lyer illusion?) In environments with few square buildings, a child's developing visual system doesn't perceive the end-lines of walls angling in as indicating a corner is near, or end-lines angling out suggesting a corner is farther away. Such culturally learned cues are the proposed explanation for the Müller-Lyer illusion.

Cultural studies like these remind other researchers they cannot take generalization for granted. Even basic psychological or cognitive processes can be affected by cultural environments and influences.

Figure and Ground. Research conducted by Masuda and Nisbett (2001) provides another example of cultural psychology in action. In describing the scene in **Figure 14.12**, what would you mention first? In the study, North Americans tended to comment on one of the three large fish swimming in the middle of the frame—the focal objects. Later, they tended to mention the background objects—the plants, water, and smaller fish. This makes sense, right? Of course people focus on what seems to be the most important—the big things in front.

When the researchers showed this image to a sample of Japanese college students, however, more students commented on the background first. Apparently,

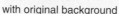

Previously Seen Objects

FIGURE 14.13

Figure and ground: altering the background.

To investigate how well people could remember the fish they saw, the researchers manipulated the background, presenting a large fish against the original background, no background, and a novel (new) background.

with original background   with no background   with novel background

these participants paid attention to the background as much as, or even more than, what the North Americans perceived as the focal objects—the large fish. Later, the researchers quizzed participants from both groups on what they had seen. Sometimes they showed one of the original large fish but changed the background (**Figure 14.13**). When the background was changed, North Americans could still recognize the fish, suggesting that they had processed the focal fish separately from the surrounding scene. In contrast, the Japanese students were less able to identify the fish when it was removed from the surrounding scene. (The graph in **Figure 14.14** shows the results; you can see it's a 2 × 3 factorial design.) Their errors suggested, in fact, that the Japanese participants had processed the fish in context, and when the context changed, their memories were less accurate.

If a study had tested only the North American sample, researchers might have concluded that visual attention is drawn to focal objects first and foremost, whereas background objects receive much less attention. However, because Masuda and Nisbett were working in generalization mode, they found visual attention worked differently in different cultures. This study is another

FIGURE 14.14

Figure and ground: context-sensitivity study results.

North Americans were more accurate than Japanese at recognizing the large fish when it was presented without the original background. Japanese participants were more accurate when the fish was presented in the original background. These results suggest that the way North Americans pay attention to "focal" and "ground" aspects of a scene does not generalize to a Japanese sample. (Source: Adapted from Masuda & Nisbett, 2001.)

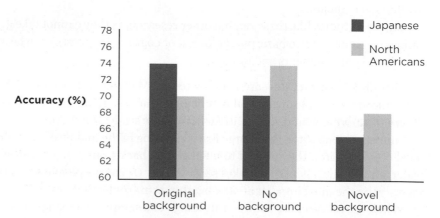

good example of how cultural psychologists challenge other researchers to combine generalization mode with theory-testing mode—to test a theory in multiple cultures before assuming it applies to all people.

THEORY TESTING USING WEIRD PARTICIPANTS

To understand the importance of cultural psychologists' work, consider that most research in psychological science has been conducted on North American college students. One researcher recorded the samples used in the top six journals in psychology for the year 2007. In these core journals, 68% of the participants were American and 96% of the participants were from North America, Europe, Australia, or Israel (Arnett, 2008). Participants from these countries are from a unique subset of the world's population, which researchers refer to as WEIRD: Western, educated, industrialized, rich, and democratic (Henrich, Heine, & Norenzayan, 2010). Obviously, WEIRD samples are not very representative of all the world's people. The two examples above—the Müller-Lyer illusion and the figure and ground study—both demonstrate how seemingly basic human processes can work differently in different cultural contexts.

When researchers in psychology operate in theory-testing mode, they do not prioritize external validity, and they may even test their theories only on WEIRD participants. However, cultural psychologists raise the alarm, reminding researchers that their theories, when tested only on WEIRD subjects, may not apply to everyone (Arnett, 2008; Henrich et al., 2010; Sears, 1986).

Does a Study Have to Take Place in a Real-World Setting?

People sometimes assume that studies conducted in real-world settings are more important than those held in artificial laboratory settings. Read the following descriptions and ask yourself whether each study is important:

1. To investigate recognizing the human form, a researcher dressed a student model in black and taped small lights to her head, shoulders, elbows, wrists, hips, knees, and ankles (Johansson, 1973). The model was videotaped while walking in the dark in the lab. Later, the researcher showed either the video or a still photograph to a group of college students, asking them what they saw. Observers of the photo saw a meaningless jumble of lights and observers of the movie reported seeing a person walking (**Figure 14.15**).
2. Memory researcher Suzanne Corkin and her colleagues asked the famous patient H.M. to trace a star shape with a pencil while seeing his hand only in a mirror (see Chapter 13). Although his performance improved every day, he had to be reintroduced to the task daily because he claimed he'd never seen it before (Corkin, 2013).

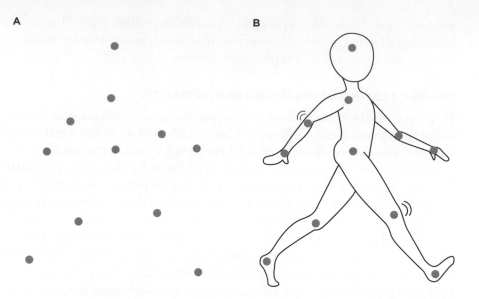

FIGURE 14.15
Recognizing a human form.

In this study, a model wore lights on several body parts. Participants viewed either (A) a still photo of the model or (B) a video of the model walking in a dark room. The results demonstrated that people cannot recognize the human form from points of light alone; the figure has to be moving. In the real world, you never observe people walking around in the dark with small lights illuminating their joints. (Source: Adapted from Johansson, 1973.)

3. Researcher Elizabeth Paluck investigated the positive impact of a radio show in post-genocide Rwanda in Africa. After the mass slaughter of Tutsis by Hutus in the 1990s, Rwanda faced a crisis of intergroup trust as returned refugees, victims, and accused perpetrators tried to live together within a single community. One hope for healing came from a radio soap opera called *New Dawn* (*Musekeweya*), about a fictional multiethnic community facing shortages and intergroup violence. The characters later reconcile and the radio show delivered messages about cooperation and communication. Paluck and her team randomly assigned groups of Rwandan community members to listen to either *New Dawn* or a control program about healthy behavior (Paluck, 2009). Participants listened to the radio in small groups (a common practice in Rwanda) once a month over the course of a year (**Figure 14.16**). At the end of the year, the researchers interviewed each participant. The results showed that people who had listened to the *New Dawn* program (compared to controls) endorsed more trusting, cooperative social norms. They were also more likely to express their opinions in a situation that required making a cooperative group decision. The researchers concluded that media programming can improve people's perceptions of cooperation.

   Are these three studies important? You might argue, for instance, that the lights study does not tell you anything about the real world; after all, how often do you see someone walking around in a dark room with lights taped to his or her knees? You might say that most people do not have lesions in their hippocampus, so the mirror-tracing memory study doesn't apply to the majority of people. Finally, you might conclude the radio study is the most important because it took place in a real-world setting and addressed a serious

FIGURE 14.16
The power of radio in Rwanda.
Listening to radio programs in small groups is common in the African country of Rwanda. Divisive radio propaganda played a role in inciting violence in Rwanda in 1994. As the country recovered from genocide, a field experiment tested the power of a healing-oriented radio soap opera to improve social norms of cooperation.

problem. If so, you were probably guided by the assumption that a study should be similar to real-world contexts and daily life in order to be important. But is this always true?

EXTERNAL VALIDITY AND THE REAL WORLD

When interrogating a study's external validity, you ask whether the results can generalize not only to other populations but also to other settings. When research takes place in the real world, sometimes referred to as a **field setting**, it has a built-in advantage for external validity because it clearly applies to real-world contexts. As mentioned previously, ecological validity is one aspect of external validity referring to the extent to which a study's tasks and manipulations are similar to the kinds of situations participants might encounter in their everyday lives. Paluck's study in Rwanda has excellent ecological validity because of its field setting. However, ecological validity is just one factor in generalizability; a study's setting may not represent all possible environments. Would the results of the radio study apply to a different social problem? Would it also apply in a cultural context that doesn't have a tradition of radio dramas?

The situation a researcher creates in a lab can be just as real as one that occurs in a restaurant or workplace. Although it may be easy to dismiss a study that does not seem realistic, remember that in daily life people find themselves in many different settings, all of which are real, including community centers, shops, and theaters, as well as classrooms and research labs. Indeed, the emotions and behaviors generated by a laboratory manipulation (e.g., an ID number matching your birthday or having a real cell phone conversation during a driving simulator task) can also be quite real, visible, and meaningful. Many lab experiments are high in what's known as **experimental realism**: They create situations in which people experience authentic emotions, motivations, and behaviors. People in lab studies have interacted with actual people, drunk real alcoholic beverages, and played games with other participants. Many of these situations are truly engaging and emotionally evocative.

To what extent does the real-world similarity—the ecological validity—of a study affect your ideas about a study's importance? A nuanced answer will consider the mode in which it is conducted: generalization mode or theory-testing mode.

GENERALIZATION MODE AND THE REAL WORLD

Because external validity is of primary importance when researchers are in generalization mode, they might strive for a representative sample of a population. But they might also try to enhance the ecological validity of a study in order to ensure its generalizability to nonlaboratory settings. By the time Paluck (2009) studied the impact of radio programs in Rwanda, people had already tested the short-term impact of media messages in the lab. For example, one study established that when people feel empathy with others, they feel less prejudice (Batson et al., 1997). Studies had also tested how social norms can affect biased behavior (Crandall & Stangor, 2005). But no one had explored the impact of an engaging radio soap opera over the long term with adults in a field setting.

THEORY-TESTING MODE AND THE REAL WORLD

When a researcher is working in theory-testing mode, external validity and real-world applicability may be lower priorities. Take, for instance, the Johansson (1973) study, in which the model had lights attached to her head and her joints. Of course, no one is going to encounter these circumstances in the real world, but the ecological validity of the situation didn't matter to the researcher. He was testing a research question: How much information do people need before they can conclude they're looking at a human? By keeping the room dark and having lights only on the model's head and joints, the researcher was able to cut out all other visual information. He was concerned with internal validity—eliminating alternative explanations for an interpretation. To narrow down exactly what visual information was necessary to recognize a human form, Johansson had to create an extremely artificial situation.

Was the Johansson study important? In terms of the theory he was testing, it was invaluable because he was able to show that both joint location and movement are necessary and sufficient to recognize a human form. What about generalizability and real-world applicability? On the one hand, both the model and the study's participants were drawn haphazardly, not randomly, from a small group of North American college students. The situation created in the lab would never occur in the real world. On the other hand, the ability to recognize human gestures, postures, and moods is undoubtedly essential for many aspects of social life. The theoretical understanding gained from this seemingly artificial study contributes to our understanding of a perceptual process involved in basic social cognition.

Let's consider the study design that many people (quite correctly) respect as a pinnacle of behavioral research: the randomized, double-blind, placebo-controlled study, introduced in Chapter 11. In such a study, an experimenter goes to extreme artificial lengths to assign people at random to carefully constructed experimental conditions that control for placebo effects, experimenter bias, and experimental demand. Such studies have virtually no equivalent in everyday, real-world settings, yet their results can be among the most valuable in psychological science.

In short, theory-testing mode often demands that experimenters create artificial situations that allow them to minimize distractions, eliminate alternative explanations, and isolate individual features of some situation. Theory-testing mode prioritizes internal validity at the expense of all other considerations, including ecological validity. Nonetheless, such studies make valuable contributions to the field of psychology.

Table 14.5 summarizes the approach to external validity that has been emphasized in this chapter.

TABLE 14.5

Responding Appropriately to the "Latest Scientific Breakthrough"

SAY THIS	NOT THAT
"Was that finding replicated?" "That is a single study. How does the study fit in with the entire literature?"	"Look at this single, interesting result!"
"How well do the methods of this study get at the theory they were testing?"	"I don't think this study is important because the methods had nothing to do with the real world."
"Was the study conducted in generalization mode? If so, were the participants representative of the population of interest?"	"I reject this study because they didn't use a random sample." "This is a bad study because they used only North Americans as participants."
"The study had thousands of participants, but were they selected in such a way to allow generalization to the population of interest?"	"They used thousands of participants. It must have great external validity."
"Would the result hold up in another cultural context?" "Would that result apply in other settings?"	"That psychological principle seems so basic, I'm sure it's universal."

CHECK YOUR UNDERSTANDING

1. Describe the difference between generalization mode and theory-testing mode.

2. Which of the three types of claims (frequency, association, causal) is/are almost always conducted in generalization mode? Which of the three types of claims is/are usually conducted in theory-testing mode?

3. Explain why researchers who are operating in theory-testing mode might not use a random sample in their study. What validity are they prioritizing? What aspects of their research are they emphasizing (for now)?

4. Summarize the goal of cultural psychology. What does this field suggest about working in theory-testing and generalization modes?

5. When an experiment tests hypotheses in an artificial laboratory setting, it does not necessarily mean the study does not apply to the real world. Explain why not.

1. See pp. 440–447. 2. See p. 443. 3. See pp. 440–442. 4. See p. 444. 5. See pp. 447–451.

CHAPTER REVIEW

Summary

A nuanced approach can be used to evaluate a study's importance. A study must be replicated to be important, but it might not need to be generalizable or have immediate real-world applicability.

To Be Important, a Study Must Be Replicated

- Replication studies determine whether the findings of an original study are reproducible.

- A direct replication repeats the original study exactly. A conceptual replication has the same conceptual variables as the original study but operationalizes the variables differently. A replication-plus-extension study repeats the original study and introduces new participant variables, situations, or independent variable levels.

- Psychologists are currently concerned about the extent to which published findings can be directly replicated. Original studies might have had fluke results because of small sample sizes or questionable research practices, but sometimes the replication attempts were not powerful or were too different from the original study.

- Many psychology journals now promote open science and preregistration to strengthen the verifiability and replicability of studies.

- A meta-analysis collects and mathematically averages the effect sizes from all studies that have tested the same variables. It helps quantify whether an effect exists in the literature and, if so, its size and what moderates it.

To Be Important, Must a Study Have External Validity?

- The importance of external validity depends on whether researchers are operating in generalization mode or theory-testing mode.

- In generalization mode, researchers focus on whether their samples are representative, whether the data from their sample apply to the population of interest, and even whether the data might apply to a new population of interest.

- In theory-testing mode, researchers design studies that test a theory, leaving the generalization step for later studies, which will test whether the theory holds in a sample that is representative of another population.

- In contrast to what many casual observers assume, important research might not (1) use random samples from populations or (2) study people of all genders, ethnicities, social classes, geographical location, and so on. Diverse, representative samples are primarily important when researchers are in generalization mode. In theory-testing mode, researchers do not (yet) consider whether their samples are representative of some population, so external validity is less important than theory testing.

- Researchers who make frequency claims are always in generalization mode, but they are also in generalization mode when asking whether an association or causal claim can be generalized to a different group of people.
- Cultural psychologists have documented how psychological discoveries, including basic cognitive or visual processes, are not always applicable cross-culturally.
- When researchers collect data only from WEIRD (Western, educated, industrialized, rich, and democratic) samples, they cannot assume the theories

they develop in theory-testing mode will apply to all people.
- Research does not necessarily have to be conducted in a field setting to have ecological validity. Laboratory studies conducted in theory-testing mode might have strong experimental realism even if they do not resemble real-world situations outside the lab. Yet the data from such artificial settings help researchers test theories in the most internally valid way possible, and the results may still be important and apply to real-world circumstances.

Key Terms

replicable, p. 425
direct replication, p. 426
conceptual replication, p. 427
replication-plus-extension, p. 428
p-hacking, p. 432
open science, p. 432

preregistration, p. 432
scientific literature, p. 433
meta-analysis, p. 433
file drawer problem, p. 436
ecological validity, p. 439
theory-testing mode, p. 440

generalization mode, p. 442
cultural psychology, p. 444
field setting, p. 449
experimental realism, p. 449

 To see samples of chapter concepts in the popular media,
visit www.everydayresearchmethods.com and click the box for Chapter 14.

Review Questions

1. If you repeat a study and find the same results as the first time, what can you say about the original study?

   a. It is replicable.

   b. It is statistically significant.

   c. It is valid.

   d. It is consistent.

2. When a researcher conducts a replication study in which she has the same variables at an abstract level, but uses different operationalizations of each variable, what type of study is it?

   a. Direct replication

   b. Meta-analysis

   c. Conceptual replication

   d. Replication-plus-extension

3. _____ is a technique in which the researcher mathematically averages the results of all studies that have been completed with the same conceptual variables.

   a. Meta-analysis

   b. Correlation

   c. Literature review

   d. Analysis of variance

4. Which of the following claims is most likely to have been tested in generalization mode?

   a. Four out of ten teenagers can't identify fake news when they see it.

   b. Reading stressful news makes adults anxious.

   c. People who walk faster live longer.

5. Which of these is a field setting?

   a. A psychology lab with a hidden camera

   b. A neuropsychology lab with an MRI machine

   c. A preschool playground with video cameras

   d. A biology lab with galvanic skin response detectors

6. Which of these statements is true of external validity?

   a. Psychologists usually strive to generalize to all people.

   b. For generalization to a population, the larger the sample the better.

   c. External validity comes from how the sample is obtained, rather than sample size.

   d. A sample that contains female college students can generalize to all female college students.

Learning Actively

1. Consider the study that recorded people's substantive conversations and their well-being, from Chapter 8 (Mehl et al., 2010). How would you conduct a direct replication of this study? A conceptual replication? A replication-plus-extension?

2. A study with a sample of 28 participants per condition showed that people reported being less satisfied with their lives when asked on a rainy day compared to a sunny day (Schwarz & Clore, 1983). Later, a replication study using polling data from 1 million people found almost no effect of weather on mood (Lucas & Lawless, 2013). Which of the issues in Table 14.1 could account for this failure to replicate?

3. For each short study description below, indicate whether you think it would have been conducted in theory-testing mode or generalization mode or whether it could be done in either mode. Explain your answer. For which of these studies would a random sample of participants be the most important? For which would external validity be the least important?

   a. A study found that most Holocaust survivors struggle with depression, sleep disorders, and emotional distress. The conclusion was based on a government data set that has tracked 220,000 Holocaust survivors ("Most Holocaust Survivors Battle Depression," 2010).

   b. A team of neuropsychologists tested memory in mice, using a pretest/posttest design. The mice cages were exposed to a typical cell phone's electromagnetic field for 1 hour a day, for 9 months. Later, the researchers tested each mouse's memory and found the mice had better memory after exposure to the electromagnetic fields than before and better memory compared with the no-exposure control group (Hamzelou, 2010).

   c. A group of researchers studied three people in India who were born blind. At ages 7, 12, and 29, each one received surgery and treatment to correct his vision. (In all three cases, their families couldn't afford treatment for the blindness.) After the patients regained their sight, the researchers studied how they'd developed their newly acquired abilities to decode the visual world. At first, each patient thought that a two-dimensional picture, such as the one labeled B in the figure, depicted three objects instead of two. With several months of experience, however, they all learned to interpret the images correctly. By moving the objects apart from each other on some of the trials, the researchers discovered that all three men could use motion cues to decode what lines belonged to which object (similar to how people in Johansson's study could identify that a lighted model was a walking human only when the model was moving). The researchers concluded that as the brain learns about the visual world, it uses motion cues to decide which lines belong to which objects (Ostrovsky, Meyers, Ganesh, Mathur, & Sinha, 2009).

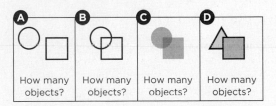

Statistics Review

DESCRIPTIVE STATISTICS

In everyday language, the word *statistics* is used to describe quantitative records, such as a baseball player's batting average or the average life span of a country's citizens. In science, the word refers to the set of tools researchers use to make sense of data that they have collected in a study. This supplementary chapter provides a very brief overview of one set of such statistical tools: **descriptive statistics**, used for organizing and summarizing the properties of a set of data. The other set of statistical tools, inferential statistics, is covered in the supplementary chapter that follows this one.

DESCRIBING DATA

Recall that when a researcher collects data from a group of people or animals, the group is often a sample from a larger population. If we tested 5 rhesus monkeys on their ability to discriminate blue from green, and the 5 came from a larger population of 25 monkeys in the lab, then the 5 monkeys would be the sample. If we tested 50 students on their anagram skills, the 50 students might be a sample from a larger population of students who could have signed up for the research. However, researchers don't always study a sample from a larger population.

If a midterm exam is given to 31 students, the 31 students are a complete set of cases; they are not a sample because they are the whole population of interest. Or we might collect data on the average air temperature and teen pregnancy rates in all 50 states in the U.S. These 50 states are not a sample, either; they are a population. We might simply have a batch of scores—perhaps a set of prices from the local supermarket, or some data on reading speed from a group of third graders. Regardless of whether our data are best described as a sample, a population, or a simple set of scores, we can still apply the descriptive techniques explained here.

Variables are what researchers measure or manipulate in a study. If we study 31 students' grades on a midterm exam, then exam score is the variable. In other studies, variables might be the ability to discriminate blue from green, the average air temperature, or the pregnancy rate among teenagers. Variables vary: They take on different levels, or values, for the different members of a sample. Thus, the values for an exam score might range from 16 to 33 on a 35-point scale. Ability to

«
For a review of categorical and quantitative variables, see Chapter 5, pp. 122–123.

Student name	Exam score
Henry	17
Emma	29
Caitlyn	19
Lonnie	27
Lalia	22
Alek	27
Rohan	22
Max	20
Shane	29
Yukiko	29
Alexi	18
Marianna	30
Mira	21
Cristina	27
Emmanuel	26
Raul	30
Ian	19
Sena	29
Jordan	27
Ayase	32
Luke	25
Miguel	32
Jon	30
Gabriel	31
Rhianna	32
Juniper	24
Malika	25
Shawn	30
Adhya	24
Harriet	33
Lucio	25

FIGURE S1.1

A data matrix of exam scores.

A data matrix is the starting point for computing most statistics.

discriminate blue from green might have the categorical values of "yes" or "no." Average air temperature might have quantitative values ranging from 50 to 81 degrees Fahrenheit and anything in between.

Data Matrices

After we collect a set of data, we usually enter the data in a grid format, called a **data matrix**, using a computer program. Programs such as Excel, SPSS, R, SAS, or JASP can not only calculate formulas, they can also facilitate making graphs and organizing data in various ways. **Figure S1.1** shows a data matrix with the scores of 31 students who took a short-answer exam consisting of 35 items. The first column identifies each person by name (this column might contain simple ID numbers instead). The second column shows the person's score on the exam. In a data matrix, each column represents a variable, and each row represents a case (such as a person, an animal, a state, a product, or any other case under study).

Frequency Distributions and Stemplots

Frequency distributions and stemplots are techniques for organizing a column of data in a data matrix. At first glance, the data matrix shows a disorganized list of scores. However, we can quickly bring some order to the scores by making a **frequency distribution**, a table that gives a visual picture of the observations on a particular variable. It clearly shows how many of the cases scored each possible value on the variable.

To make a frequency distribution, we list possible values for the variable from lowest to highest and tally how many people obtained each score, as in **Figure S1.2A**. Normally, we do not leave the tally marks there; we count them and enter the value in the table, as in **Figure S1.2B**. Based on the data from a frequency distribution, it is a fairly simple step to create a graph called a **frequency histogram** (often called simply a *histogram*), as in **Figure S1.3A**. Note that the possible exam scores are on the x-axis, while the frequency of each score is on the y-axis. We could also draw the histogram the other way, as in **Figure S1.3B**.

Instead of giving individual numerical scores, we could group the exam score values. For example, if we call any score between 30 and 33 an A, any score between 25 and 29 a B, and so on, the frequency histogram looks simpler, as in **Figure S1.4**.

Another option for organizing data visually is a graphical representation called a **stemplot**, also known as a *stem-and-leaf plot*. **Figure S1.5** shows the data from the midterm exam in stemplot form. The values on the left of the line are called *stems*, and the values on the right are called *leaves*. To make a stemplot, we would first decide the units for the stems—tens, hundreds, thousands—using the most appropriate level for the data. In this example, tens are used as the unit for the stems because the possible scores on the exam could range from 0 to 35. After listing the stems (in this case, 10, 20, 30), we would enter the leaves, which represent each individual score. For example, there is one score of 17, so on the stem 10

A	Possible value	Number of cases		B	Possible value	Number of cases
	17	I			17	1
	18	I			18	1
	19	II			19	2
	20	I			20	1
	21	I			21	1
	22	II			22	2
	23				23	0
	24	II			24	2
	25	III			25	3
	26	I			26	1
	27	IIII			27	4
	28				28	0
	29	IIII			29	4
	30	IIII			30	4
	31	I			31	1
	32	III			32	3
	33	I			33	1

FIGURE S1.2

A frequency distribution for exam scores.

(A) List the possible values in one column and tally the number of times each value occurs in the data set in the next column. Then convert the tallies to numerals. (B) The final frequency distribution.

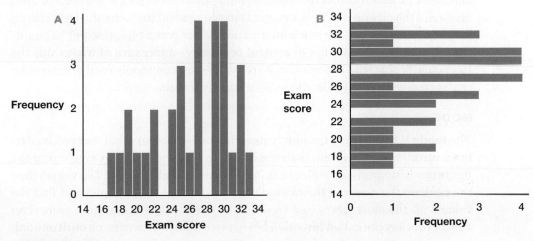

FIGURE S1.3

Frequency histogram of the scores in Figure S1.1.

(A) Exam scores are on the x-axis. (B) Exam scores are on the y-axis.

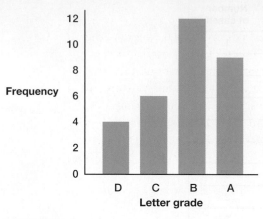

FIGURE S1.4
Grouped frequency histogram of the scores in Figure S1.1.

Stem	Leaves
10	7 8 9 9
20	0 1 2 2 4 4 5 5 5 6 7 7 7 7 9 9 9 9
30	0 0 0 0 1 2 2 2 3

FIGURE S1.5
Stemplot of the 31 short-answer test scores.

A stemplot serves as both a table and a graph, making it easy to see all the scores in a batch and how they are distributed.

there is one leaf marked with "7." There are two scores of 19, so on the stem 10 there are two leaves marked "9." The stemplot is useful because it is a table and a graph at the same time. It is simple to see all the scores in a stemplot. A grouped frequency distribution might tell us that nine students got an A in the class, but we would not know what the students' exact scores were. In contrast, a stemplot reveals this information.

Compared with a disorganized list of scores, a frequency distribution, frequency histogram, or stemplot makes it easier to visualize the scores collected.

Describing Central Tendencies (Mode, Median, and Mean)

Suppose a professor comes to class carrying a bundle of exams, and a student asks, "How did the class do?" The instructor starts to read off the individual test scores, but the student says, "Too much information. What was a *typical* score?" The student is asking for a measure of **central tendency**—a measure of what value the individual scores tend to center on. Three values are commonly used to determine central tendency: the mode, the median, and the mean.

MODE

The **mode** is the value of the most common score—the score that was received by more members of the group than any other. To find the mode, we can look at the frequency histogram (as in Figure S1.3) and find the highest peak. The value below the peak on the x-axis is the mode. Or we can look at the stemplot and find the value with the most leaves (see Figure S1.5). Some distributions have more than one mode; they are called **bimodal**, having two modes or scores, or **multimodal**, having more than two modes or scores. For an example, see the distribution in Figure S1.3, which has three modes: 27, 29, and 30.

MEDIAN

The **median** is the value at the middlemost score of a distribution of scores—the score that divides a frequency distribution into halves. The median is a typical score in the sense that if we were to guess that every student in the class received the median score, we would be too high or too low equally often. To find the median of 31 scores, we would line up the scores in order from smallest to largest and find the value of the 16th, or middlemost, score. A stemplot makes it easy to find the median. In the stemplot in Figure S1.5, the median is a score of 27 because if we count the leaves starting from the lowest score, the 16th leaf is the score of 27.

MEAN

The **mean**, also called the *average*, is found by adding all the scores in the batch and then dividing by the number of scores. The mean is abbreviated with the symbol M. Here is the formula for determining the mean:

$$M = \frac{\Sigma X}{N}$$

The X in this formula stands for each student's score on the test. The sigma (Σ) means "the sum of." Therefore, ΣX means we must sum all the values of X—all the scores. The N stands for the number of scores. In our example, we would find the mean by adding up 33, 32, 32, 32, 31, 30, 30, 30, 30, 29, 29, 29, 29, 27, and so on (down to 17), and then we would divide by 31, the number of people who took the exam. We would find that the mean exam value in this class is 26.16.

MODE, MEDIAN, MEAN: WHICH TO USE?

The mean is by far the most common measure of central tendency. However, when a set of scores contains a few extreme scores on one end (outliers; see Chapter 8), the median or mode may be a more accurate measure of central tendency. Suppose we want to know the typical annual income in a community of only five families: four with modest incomes and a fifth that is very wealthy. Let's say the five incomes are as follows:

$20,000
$30,000
$40,000
$50,000
$1,000,000

The mean (average) would be $228,000—a very misleading idea of the community's income. In such a case, the median income—$40,000—would be a better estimate of what is typical for the community as a whole. In short, the mean is usually the most appropriate measure of central tendency, but when a set of data has outliers, the median (or sometimes the mode) may provide a better description.

When a distribution has a clear mode, the mode can be a good choice for describing central tendency. For example, a class's evaluations of a professor's teaching performance might be distributed as follows:

Overall, this professor's teaching was:	Number of respondents
1 = poor	0
2 = average	0
3 = good	1
4 = very good	4
5 = excellent	10

The professor's mean rating would be 4.60, but she might also wish to report the modal response—that the overwhelming majority of the students rated her "excellent," or 5.

Describing Variability (Variance and Standard Deviation)

Besides describing the central tendency of a set of scores, we can also describe how spread out the scores are. In **Figure S1.6**, compare the top set of scores to the bottom set. Notice that both sets have the same number of scores, and both have the same mean as well. However, the top set has less variability than the bottom one. In the top set, scores are, on average, closer to the mean. In the bottom set, scores are, on average, farther from the mean.

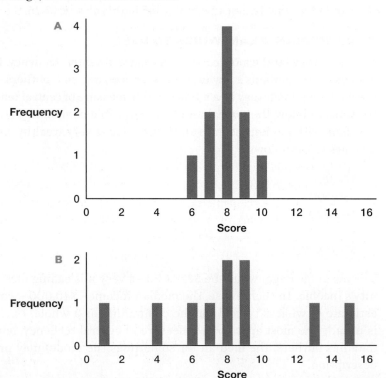

FIGURE S1.6

Two sets of scores with the same mean but different variability.

(A) The top set has less variability than (B) the bottom set, but they both have the same mean and the same number of scores.

Variance and Standard Deviation Computations for the Set of Scores in Figure S1.6A

PARTICIPANT	SCORE	DEVIATION (SCORE – MEAN)	DEVIATION SQUARED
A	6	6 – 8.0 = –2	4
B	7	7 – 8.0 = –1	1
C	7	7 – 8.0 = –1	1
D	8	8 – 8.0 = 0	0
E	8	8 – 8.0 = 0	0
F	8	8 – 8.0 = 0	0
G	8	8 – 8.0 = 0	0
H	9	9 – 8.0 = 1	1
I	9	9 – 8.0 = 1	1
J	10	10 – 8.0 = 2	4
	Sum = 80		Sum = 12
	Mean = 80/10 = **8.00**		Variance = 12/10 = 1.20
			$SD = \sqrt{1.20} = 1.10$

The two most common descriptive techniques that capture the relative spread of scores are the variance (sometimes abbreviated as SD^2) and the standard deviation (abbreviated SD). **Variance** is a computation that quantifies how spread out the scores of a sample are around their mean; it is the square of the standard deviation. **Standard deviation** is a computation that captures how far, on average, each score in a data set is from the mean. It's important to fully understand the logic behind these computations because the logic applies to some other statistics.

When computing the variance of a set of scores, we start by calculating how far each score is from the mean. The first two columns of **Table S1.1** present the set of scores that goes with Figure S1.6A.

The first step is to calculate the mean of this set of 10 scores. We add up all the scores in the second column, divide by 10, and get the mean: 8.0. Next, we create a deviation score for each participant. We subtract the mean, 8.0, from each score. The deviation scores are in the third column. One possible way to figure out the "average" deviation score would be simply to add up all the deviation scores in the third column and divide by 10. However, because some of the deviation scores are positive and some are negative, they would cancel each other out when added up. They would add up to zero for any distribution of scores, so merely summing them would not give us any sense of the variability in the scores.

To eliminate this problem, we square each deviation score, since the square of either a positive or a negative number is a positive number. The squared deviations are given in the fourth column of Table S1.1. We now compute the average of the squared deviations by summing them (to get 12) and dividing by the number of scores (10). The result is the variance. Finally, to reverse the step in which we squared the scores, we take the square root of the variance to find the standard deviation, or *SD* (1.10).

Here is the mathematical formula for the variance when you are interested in describing only your current batch of scores:

$$SD^2 = \frac{\Sigma(X - M)^2}{N}$$

This formula can be explained as follows:

1. From each score X, we subtract the mean: $(X - M)$
2. We square each of the resulting deviation scores: $(X - M)^2$
3. We add up all the squared deviation scores: $\Sigma(X - M)^2$ (This quantity is called the "sum of squares" because we *sum* all of the *squared* deviation scores.)
4. We divide the sum of squares by the number of scores to get the mean squared deviation, called the variance:

$$SD^2 = \frac{\Sigma(X - M)^2}{N}$$

Finally, if we take the positive square root of the variance, we get the standard deviation:

$$SD = \sqrt{SD^2}$$

The standard deviation is more commonly reported than the variance because it better captures how far, on average, each score is from the mean. When the standard deviation is large, there is a great deal of variability in the set; the scores are spread out far from the mean, either above or below. When the standard deviation is small, there is less variability in the set; most of the scores are closer to the mean, above or below. Indeed, the standard deviation for Figure S1.6A is 1.10, but the *SD* for Figure S1.6B is 3.82. The standard deviation computations for the scores are shown in **Table S1.2**. The more spread out the scores are, the higher the standard deviation value will be.

When you are computing the standard deviation from a batch of scores and your goal is to estimate the population's standard deviation, you should know that the formula for *SD* changes a bit. Instead of using N in the denominator, you use $N - 1$. This small adjustment makes the *SD* from your sample a more accurate estimate of the true *SD* in the population from which your sample was drawn. Here are the formulas to use in that case:

$$SD^2 = \frac{\Sigma(X - M)^2}{N - 1}$$

$$SD = \sqrt{SD^2}$$

HOW MEAN AND STANDARD DEVIATION ARE REPRESENTED IN JOURNAL ARTICLES

In an empirical journal article, the mean and standard deviation information is usually presented either within the text of the Results section or as part of a table.

Variance and Standard Deviation Computations for the Set of Scores in Figure S1.6B

PARTICIPANT	SCORE	DEVIATION (SCORE – MEAN)	DEVIATION SQUARED
A	1	1 – 8.0 = –7	49
B	4	4 – 8.0 = –4	16
C	6	6 – 8.0 = –2	4
D	7	7 – 8.0 = –1	1
E	8	8 – 8.0 = 0	0
F	8	8 – 8.0 = 0	0
G	9	9 – 8.0 = 1	1
H	9	9 – 8.0 = 1	1
I	13	13 – 8.0 = 5	25
J	15	15 – 8.0 = 7	49
	Sum = 80		Sum = 146
	Mean = 80/10 = **8.00**		Variance = 146/10 = 14.60
			$SD = \sqrt{14.6} = 3.82$

Following are two examples of mean and standard deviation data that appeared in actual journal articles.

First is an example of how mean and standard deviation information can be presented in a text. Read the following excerpt from an article (discussed in Chapter 2) on using a punching bag to express anger (Bushman, 2002, p. 728):

> *How hard the punching bag was hit.* . . . Overall, men hit the punching bag harder than did women, $M = 6.69$, $SD = 2.05$, and $M = 4.73$, $SD = 1.88$, $F(1, 396) = 99.14$, $p < .0001$, $d = 1.00$. No other effects were significant ($ps > .05$).
>
> *Number of times punching bag was hit.* Participants who thought about becoming physically fit hit the punching bag more times than did participants who thought about the person who insulted them, $M = 127.5$, $SD = 63.5$, and $M = 112.2$, $SD = 57.5$, $F(1, 396) = 6.31$, $p < .05$, $d = 0.25$. In other words, participants in the rumination group vented less than did participants in the distraction group. No other effects were significant ($ps > .05$).

Even if all of the statistical symbols are not familiar to you, look for the mean (M) and standard deviation (SD).

TEST YOURSELF 1

In the excerpt above, can you find the average force with which men hit the punching bag? Can you find the average force with which women hit the punching bag? Which group, males or females, has the higher variability? How can you tell?

Descriptive statistics for consumption volume and quality ratings of popcorn. Table shows *M* (*SD*) values.

| | Medium Container (120 g) n = 77 | | Large Container (240 g) n = 80 | |
	Fresh Popcorn	Stale Popcorn	Fresh Popcorn	Stale Popcorn
Popcorn eaten, *g*	58.9 (16.7)	38.0 (16.1)	85.6 (19.8)	50.8 (14.1)
"This popcorn tasted good"[1]	7.7 (1.4)	3.9 (2.4)	6.8 (1.5)	2.2 (1.7)
"This popcorn was of high quality"[1]	7.3 (2.1)	3.1 (1.5)	6.8 (1.9)	2.1 (2.1)

[1]Ratings were made on a 9-point scale (1 = *strongly disagree*; 9 = *strongly agree*).

FIGURE S1.7
How mean and standard deviation information might be presented as a table in an empirical journal article.

(Source: Wansink & Kim, 2005.)

The second example comes from a study that offered people popcorn to eat during a movie (Wansink & Kim, 2005). The popcorn was served in medium or large containers, and it was either fresh or stale (14 days old). **Figure S1.7** shows how mean and standard deviation information might be presented in a table. Depending on the article and the journal, tables will differ, but you can use the column labels or table captions to locate the means and standard deviations of particular cells.

TEST YOURSELF 2

According to Figure S1.7, how much stale popcorn, on average, did people eat from a large container? What was the mean and standard deviation of how much fresh popcorn people ate from a medium container?

Describing Relative Standing (*z* Scores)

Thus far we have covered, among other tools, frequency distributions, means, and standard deviations. If we combine some of these techniques, we can also describe where an individual score stands in relation to the whole batch of scores. A **z score** describes whether an individual's score is above or below the mean and how far it is from the mean in standard deviation units.

DESCRIBING RELATIVE STANDING IN STANDARD DEVIATION UNITS

Let's start with the exam scores we used to illustrate frequency distributions, in Figure S1.1. Suppose Max, who has a score of 20, wants to know how good his exam score was in relation to the scores of the rest of the class. Because we already know that the mean score was 26.16, we can tell Max that his score, 20, was 6.16 points below the mean.

Perhaps Max also wants to know whether 6.16 points was far below the mean or just a little below the mean. We might answer Max's question by using standard deviation units of distance.

The standard deviation for this group of test scores was 4.52—meaning that on average, scores were 4.52 points away from the mean. We can tell Max his score was 6.16 points below the mean, and that the standard deviation was 4.52. Therefore, Max's score was 1.36 standard deviation units below the mean. Now Max has learned that he did worse than average, by a fairly large margin. His score was more than one standard deviation below the mean.

COMPUTING Z SCORES

To describe people's relative standing in standard deviation units, we compute z scores using the following formula:

$$z = \frac{(X - M)}{SD}$$

We start with the individual score, X, and subtract the mean from that score. Then we divide the difference by the standard deviation. When we follow the z score formula, any score below the mean (like Max's) will have a negative z score. Any score above the mean will have a positive z score. Any score that is directly at the mean will have a z score of zero.

TEST YOURSELF 3

Can you compute the z score for Emma, who got a 29 on the same exam Max took?

USING Z SCORES

One of the useful qualities of a z score is that it lets us compare the relative standing of individual cases on variables that might have been measured in different units. (For this reason, the z score is sometimes referred to as a *standardized score*.) Suppose, for example, the first exam was a midterm exam with only 35 questions on it, and Max's score was 20. Now imagine the final exam has 100 questions, and Max's score was 65. Was Max's score on the final, relative to those of his classmates, better than his relative score on the midterm? We could use z scores to find out.

If the mean score on the final was 80, with a standard deviation of 14 points, we can use this information to compute Max's z score on the final exam:

$$z = \frac{(65 - 80)}{14} = -1.07$$

Max's z score for the first exam was −1.34, and for the final it was −1.07. Both scores are below average, but his final exam score was closer to the mean than his midterm score. Therefore, Max's performance on the final was a little better, relatively, than his performance on the midterm.

TEST YOURSELF 4

Emma's score on the final exam was 94. Which test did she perform better on (the first exam or the final), relative to her classmates?

In this way, to describe the relative standing of the scores in a set, we can convert each score to a z score. The z score lets us describe how far any individual's score on a variable is from the mean, in standard deviation units. In addition, if we convert each person's scores on two or more variables to z scores, we can meaningfully compare the relative standings of each person on those variables, even when the variables are measured in different units.

One variable, for instance, might be height, measured in centimeters, and the other variable might be weight, measured in kilograms. If a person's z score for height is $z = 0.58$ and his z score for weight is $z = 0.00$, for example, we could conclude he is above average in height but at the mean in weight (and thus probably a rather thin person). Or perhaps one variable, such as a state's air temperature, is measured in degrees Fahrenheit, and the other variable, teen pregnancy rate, is measured as the number of pregnancies per 100,000 teens. The z scores can tell us whether a state is relatively warm or cool and whether its teen pregnancy rate is higher or lower than average.

Describing Associations Using Scatterplots or the Correlation Coefficient r

Three chapters in the main text introduced the logic of scatterplots and the correlation coefficient r (see Chapters 3, 5, and 8). We use scatterplots and r to describe the association between two variables that are measured in the same set of cases. For example, we might want to describe the association between 2-year-old height and adult height (see Figure 8.7). Or we might want to describe the association between how often people multitask and their ability to do so (see Figure 8.2).

SCATTERPLOTS

As discussed previously, one way to describe associations between two variables is to draw a scatterplot. With one variable on the x-axis and another variable on the y-axis, we plot each case as a dot on the graph so that it represents the person's score on both variables.

Figure S1.8 shows a hypothetical scatterplot for the association between 2-year-old height and adult height. The marked dot represents Eliana, one member of the group. The scatterplot shows that Eliana was fairly short at age 2 and is also fairly short as an adult. Other dots on the scatterplot represent other members of the group, showing their height at the two different ages.

Similarly, **Figure S1.9** shows a scatterplot of the association between frequency of media multitasking and ability to multitask, based on a study by David Sanbonmatsu and his colleagues (2013). The black dot represents Rhoslyn, a person who is not very good at media multitasking, and who engages in media multitasking a bit more than average. The other dots on that scatterplot represent other members of the batch, showing how much they engage in multitasking and how well they performed on the multitasking ability task (their OSPAN score).

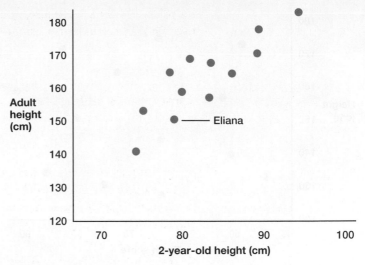

FIGURE S1.8
Scatterplot of adult height and 2-year-old height.

By inspecting a scatterplot, we can describe two important aspects of an association: the *direction* of the relationship between two variables (positive, negative, or zero) and the *strength* of the positive or negative relationship (strong or weak).

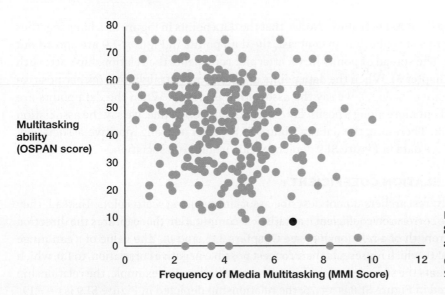

FIGURE S1.9
Scatterplot of multitasking ability and frequency.

(Source: Adapted from Sanbonmatsu et al., 2013.)

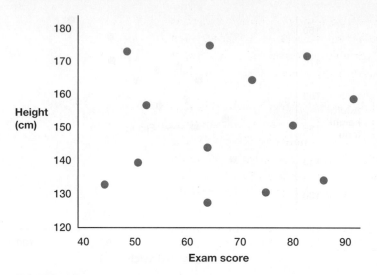

FIGURE S1.10
Hypothetical scatterplot of exam score and height.

Direction of Association: Positive, Negative, or Zero. In Figure S1.8, notice that the cloud of points on the scatterplot slopes upward from left to right. The slope of the dots is positive; mathematically speaking, a line drawn through the center of that cloud of points would have a positive slope. Because the slope is positive, we call the association between the two variables positive. High scores on one variable go with high scores on the other variable, and low scores on one variable go with low scores on the other variable. In a positive association, "high goes with high and low goes with low."

In contrast, in Figure S1.9 notice that the cloud of points on the scatterplot slopes downward from left to right. Because the slope of the dots is negative—mathematically speaking, a line drawn through the center of that cloud of points would have a negative slope—the association between the two variables is referred to as negative (or an inverse association). High scores on one variable go with low scores on the other variable. In a negative association, "high goes with low and low goes with high."

Finally, we might draw a scatterplot like the one in **Figure S1.10.** Here, the cloud of points does not slope clearly upward or downward. The slope of the dots is zero; mathematically speaking, a line drawn through the center of that cloud of points would be flat, or have a zero slope; there is no association, or zero association.

Strength of Association. Notice that the data points in Figure S1.8 hang together closer to a straight line; in contrast, the data points in Figure S1.9 are spread out wider. The spread of points in a scatterplot represents the relationship's strength (see Chapter 5). When the data points are closer to a straight line (either positive or negative in slope), we say the association is strong. When the data points are spread out more along a positively or negatively sloped line, we say the association is weak. Therefore, the data in Figure S1.8 depict a strong, positive association, while the data in Figure S1.9 depict a weak, negative association.

CORRELATION COEFFICIENT *r*

Usually, researchers do not describe associations using scatterplots. Instead, they use the correlation coefficient *r*, a statistical computation that captures the direction and strength of a relationship (see Chapters 3, 5, and 8). The value of *r* can range from –1.0, which represents the strongest possible negative correlation, to 1.0, which represents the strongest possible positive correlation. For example, the relationship depicted in Figure S1.8 is *r* = .75; the relationship depicted in Figure S1.9 is *r* = –.19.

The sign of r indicates the direction of the relationship. If r is positive (such as $r = .75$), the relationship between the two variables is positive. If r is negative (such as $r = -.19$), the relationship between the two variables is negative. If r is zero, or very close to zero (such as $r = .02$), then the relationship between the two variables is essentially zero.

The magnitude of the absolute value of r indicates the strength of the relationship. If r is large (such as .75), the relationship between two variables is strong (the dots on the scatterplot would be closer together). If r is smaller (such as −.19), the relationship between two variables is weaker (the dots on the scatterplot would be more spread out). The strength of a correlation is independent of its sign, so an r of −.85 would represent a stronger correlation than an r of .35.

Computing r. The formula for computing the correlation coefficient r can be represented in many ways. Here is the formula used by most statistical software packages:

$$r = \frac{\Sigma z_x z_y}{N - 1}$$

Let's break it down step by step. First, we have two variables per case (often that means two variables per person). **Table S1.3** shows how to carry out the steps in calculating r for a set of seven people. Notice that the first three columns of the

TABLE S1.3

Computing the Correlation Coefficient r

(1) PERSON	(2) SCORE ON X (2-YEAR-OLD HEIGHT, IN CM)	(3) SCORE ON Y (ADULT HEIGHT, IN CM)	(4) z_x (Z SCORE FOR 2-YEAR-OLD HEIGHT)	(5) z_y (Z SCORE FOR ADULT HEIGHT)	(6) $z_x z_y$
Eliana	78	150	−1.00, or (78 − 83.28) / 5.28	−1.88, or (150 − 165.29) / 8.16	1.88, or (−1.00 × −1.88)
Ella	00	160	−0.62	−0.65	0.40
Eshaan	91	170	1.45	0.58	0.84
Ava	84	168	0.13	0.33	0.04
Annamaria	79	165	−0.81	−0.04	0.03
Oscar	90	175	1.26	1.19	1.50
Oliver	81	169	−0.43	0.45	−0.19
	$M = 83.28$	$M = 165.29$			$\Sigma z_x z_y = 4.50$
	$SD = 5.28$	$SD = 8.16$			$\Sigma z_x z_y / N - 1 = 0.75$
					$r = .75$

table represent a data matrix for this data set, including one column for each variable (X and Y) and one row for each person. The three right-hand columns show the computations for r. In the formula, the variables are labeled X and Y. If we are computing the correlation between 2-year-old height and adult height, for example, 2-year-old height would be variable X (column 2), and adult height would be variable Y (column 3).

The second step is converting each person's scores on X and Y to z scores, z_X and z_Y, using the formula for computing z given earlier. If someone's 2-year-old height was above the mean, his or her z score (z_X) would be positive; if someone's 2-year-old height was below the mean, his or her z score (z_X) would be negative (columns 4 and 5 of Table S1.3). The third step is to multiply these two z scores, z_X and z_Y, for each person (column 6). Finally, we sum the products of the z scores and divide by the number of cases—in this example, seven people—to get r.

The Logic of the r Formula. It is worth reflecting on two aspects of the formula for r. First, notice that r can easily capture the association between adult height and 2-year-old height, even though the two variables have very different ranges of scores. The height for 2-year-olds ranges from 78 to 91 cm; adult height ranges from 150 to 175 cm. However, the formula for r converts each height value to its z score first. That way, it does not matter that the two heights fall within very different ranges.

Second, think about what it means that r multiplies the two z scores for each person. Take Eliana, for example. Her height is below average at age 2 and below average at adulthood, so both of her z scores are negative. When we multiply them together, we get a positive number. Now consider Oscar, whose height is above average at age 2 and above average at adulthood. Both of his z scores are positive, so when we multiply them, we also get a positive number. In Table S1.3, most of the products are positive, though some are negative. After summing all these products and dividing by $N - 1$, we get an r value of .75—a positive r, meaning that "high goes with high and low goes with low." This makes sense; people with high 2-year-old height tend to have high adult height, and people with low 2-year-old height tend to have low adult height.

In contrast, if the relationship between two variables is negative, high goes with low and low goes with high. In this situation, when we compute the r, positive z scores for one variable will tend to be multiplied with negative z scores for the other variable, so the products will be mostly negative. When we sum these negative products and divide by $N-1$, the result will be a negative number, or a negative r, meaning that "high goes with low and low goes with high." Normally we use computers to calculate r values. However, knowing the mathematics behind the formula for r can help us understand what r values represent.

Describing Effect Size

Because the value of r indicates the strength of the relationship between two variables, many researchers use r as a measure of effect size, a computation that describes the magnitude of a study's result (see Chapters 8 and 14). There are several measures of effect size, and all of them are used for the same purpose:

to describe the strength of the relationship between two variables. For example, when a study's outcome demonstrates a difference between two groups, the effect size describes how large or small that difference is.

Let's revisit the study that found that people ate more popcorn out of large containers than they did out of medium containers (Wansink & Kim, 2005; see Figure S1.7). If we were to ask about this study's effect size, we would ask how *much* more popcorn people ate from the large containers. Was it just a little more or a lot more? We are asking: Is the effect size large or small?

DESCRIBING EFFECT SIZE WITH COHEN'S *d*

When a study involves group or condition means (such as the mean amount of popcorn eaten from a large container compared with the mean amount from a medium container), we can describe the effect size in terms of how far apart the two means are, in standard deviation units. This will also tell us how much overlap there is between the two sets of scores. This commonly used effect size measure is called *d*, also known as **Cohen's *d***.

For simplicity, let's focus on the results for the *fresh* popcorn condition in Wansink and Kim's study (see Figure S1.7):

- From the medium container, people ate a mean of 58.9 grams of popcorn, with a standard deviation of 16.7 grams.
- From the large container, people ate a mean of 85.6 grams of popcorn, with a standard deviation of 19.8 grams.

To determine how far apart these two means are in standard deviation units, we use the following formula for *d*:

$$d = \frac{M_1 - M_2}{SD_{(pooled)}}$$

The numerator is the mean of one group minus the mean of the other group. The denominator is the *SD* of these two groups, "pooled." The pooled *SD* is an average of the two standard deviations for the two groups. If the two groups are the same size, we can take a simple mean of the two standard deviations, but when the two groups are different sizes, we need to compute a weighted mean of the two standard deviations; that is, we weight the *SD* of the larger group more.[1]

If we apply this formula to Wansink and Kim's data, the numerator is simply the mean difference between the two groups (the large container group and the medium container group), or 58.9 – 85.6. The denominator is the pooled *SD*, which is 18.3. So, for the fresh popcorn condition, we would compute the effect size for bucket size as follows:

$$d = \frac{58.9 - 85.6}{18.3} = \frac{-26.7}{18.3} = -1.46$$

---

[1] The general formula for a pooled *SD* is as follows, where n_1 and n_2 are the number of observations in the two groups, and SD_1^2 and SD_2^2 are the variances of each group.

$$SD_{(pooled)} = \sqrt{\frac{(n_1 - 1)SD_1^2 + (n_2 - 1)SD_2^2}{n_1 + n_2 - 2}}$$

Cohen's Guidelines for Effect Size

d	STRENGTH OF RELATIONSHIP
0.20	Small, or weak
0.50	Medium, or moderate
0.80	Large, or strong

In other words, the effect size of the container manipulation is $d = 1.46$. (We can omit the negative sign when it is clear which group is higher than the other.)

Effect Size Conventions for Cohen's d. What does a d of 1.46 mean? It means that the average of the large container group is 1.46 standard deviations higher than the average of the medium container group. But is that large or small? One way to tell is to consult Cohen's conventions for interpreting effect size (**Table S1.4**).

According to this table, the effect size in Wansink and Kim's study was very large, well above $d = 0.80$. Therefore, we can conclude that container size makes a large difference in the amount of popcorn people eat.

Or suppose we conduct an experiment in which we praise the appearance of one group of people and say something neutral to members of another group. Later we ask each group to take a self-esteem test that uses a 5-point scale. We compute the two group means and find a mean of 4.10 ($SD = 1.46$) for the people whose appearance was praised, and a mean of 3.58 ($SD = 1.50$) for those who were not praised. When we compute the effect size, d, we come up with $d = 0.35$. Therefore the groups are about 0.35 of a standard deviation unit apart on self-esteem. According to Cohen's conventions, this could be described as a small to medium effect of appearance praise on self-esteem.

Effect Size d and Group Overlap. Another way of looking at group-difference effect sizes such as d is to know that d represents the amount of overlap between two groups or conditions. Parts A and B of **Figure S1.11** show how two groups might overlap at different effect sizes in our examples. The larger the effect size, the less overlap between the two experimental groups; the smaller the effect size, the more overlap. If the effect size is zero, there is full overlap between the two groups (Figure S1.11C).

WHICH EFFECT SIZE MEASURE TO USE?

Researchers often use the effect size r to determine the strength of the relationship between two quantitative variables. The effect size d is more often used when one variable is categorical. These two measures of effect size are based on different scales: r can only range between 1 and −1, but d can be higher than 1 or lower than −1. Therefore, the size conventions for r are different from those for d (**Table S1.5**). In psychological science research, if a study finds an r of .50 or higher, that relationship (that effect size) is considered to be large, or strong. If the r is .10 or lower, that effect is considered small, or weak.

OTHER EFFECT SIZE MEASURES

As you read empirical journal articles, you may notice other indicators of effect size, such as Hedge's g. Hedge's g is very similar to d. Like d, it gives the distance

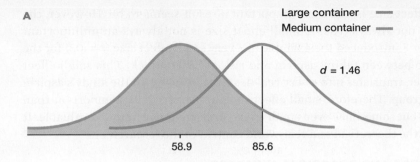

A

Large container —
Medium container —

d = 1.46

58.9   85.6

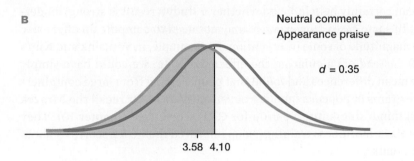

B

Neutral comment —
Appearance praise —

d = 0.35

3.58 4.10

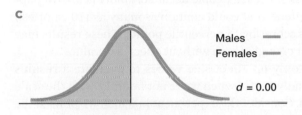

C

Males —
Females —

d = 0.00

FIGURE S1.11

The larger the effect size, the less overlap between the two experimental groups.

(A) At an effect size of 1.46, 92% of the medium container group members in the Wansink and Kim study (2005) ate less popcorn than the average member of the large container group. (B) At an effect size of 0.35, 64% of people hearing a neutral phrase had lower self-esteem than the average member of the group hearing praise for their appearance. (C) An effect size of d = 0.00 represents full overlap between the two groups, the greatest possible overlap, with 50% of Group 1 members (males) falling below the average member of Group 2 (females).

between two means in standard deviation units, but it is computed with a different formula. The conventions for small, medium, and large for Hedge's g are the same as they are for Cohen's d.

Another effect size measure you might encounter is η^2, or eta squared. This effect size may be used when researchers describe differences among several groups (i.e., more than two means), or when they describe the effect sizes of interaction effects. Size conventions for η^2 have not been published in peer-reviewed sources; some Internet sources write that η^2 of .14 to .26 would be considered large, and .01 to .02 would be small.

EFFECT SIZE AND IMPORTANCE

Chapters 8 and 10 explored the relationship between effect size and importance. Generally speaking, the

TABLE S1.5

Cohen's Guidelines for Two Measures of Effect Size: d and r

d	STRENGTH OF RELATIONSHIP	r
0.20	Small, or weak	.10
0.50	Medium, or moderate	.30
0.80	Large, or strong	.50

larger an effect size is, the more important a result seems to be. However, the converse is not always true: A small effect size is not always an unimportant one. Chapter 8 introduced the example of a very small effect size ($r = .03$) for the relationship between taking aspirin and risk of heart attack. This small effect size, however, translates into a very real decrease in deaths in the study's aspirin treatment group. Therefore, small effect sizes are generally less important than large ones—but sometimes even small effect sizes are important and valuable. It depends on the theoretical and real-world context of the research.

EFFECT SIZES AND PRACTICAL NUMBERS

Effect sizes can certainly help indicate whether a study's result is strong, moderate, or weak. In some cases, however, we may not need to compute an effect size to assess the magnitude of some intervention. For example, in Wansink and Kim's study (2005), instead of calculating the effect size, 1.46, we could have simply looked at the mean differences and found that people eating from large containers ate 26.7 more grams of popcorn (about 4 cups), on average. Or recall the Mrazek team's (2013) mindfulness intervention for GRE scores (see Chapter 10). They reported that the mindfulness training group improved their GRE scores by about 16 percentile points.

In these examples, it is relatively easy to evaluate the strength of the manipulation's impact: The large container caused people to eat 26.7 more grams of popcorn. (Depending on the fat content, that could contain as many as 140 calories.) Mindfulness training improves scores by 16 percentile points. These results may seem substantial and important enough—even without effect size values.

Other times we must rely only on effect size values to evaluate a result's strength. Effect sizes are especially useful when we're not familiar with the scale on which a variable is measured. Consider the experiment in which we praised the appearance of one group and said something neutral to members of another group. Because self-esteem was measured on an arbitrary self-report scale, it would be hard to put the difference between the two means into practical terms. Praising people's appearance made their scores on self-esteem increase about half of a point (0.52) on the 5-point scale, so we might say the two group means were about one-half of a "self-esteem unit" apart. Is half a point a large difference or a small one? Indeed, it is difficult to translate this into a practical difference; it's not the same as GRE percentile points or grams of popcorn.

However, knowing the effect size in the self-esteem study was $d = 0.35$ provides a somewhat better understanding of its magnitude, especially if we compare the effect size to something else we know. For example, we might say the effect size of praising someone's appearance on self-esteem is $d = 0.35$, but the effect size of praising someone's personal qualities on self-esteem is larger, say $d = 0.45$.

In addition, the effect size from one study can be compared to the effect size from another study—even a study using different variables. In one article, Brad Bushman and Craig Anderson (2001) were summarizing the evidence that violent media can cause aggressive behavior. They compared the average magnitude of

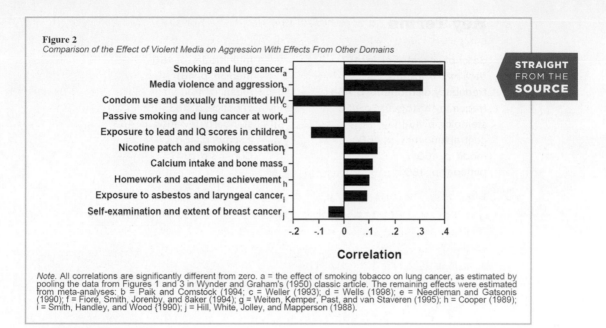

Figure 2
Comparison of the Effect of Violent Media on Aggression With Effects From Other Domains

STRAIGHT
FROM THE
SOURCE

Note. All correlations are significantly different from zero. a = the effect of smoking tobacco on lung cancer, as estimated by pooling the data from Figures 1 and 3 in Wynder and Graham's (1950) classic article. The remaining effects were estimated from meta-analyses: b = Paik and Comstock (1994; c = Weller (1993); d = Wells (1998); e = Needleman and Gatsonis (1990); f = Fiore, Smith, Jorenby, and Baker (1994); g = Weiten, Kemper, Past, and van Staveren (1995); h = Cooper (1989); i = Smith, Handley, and Wood (1990); j = Hill, White, Jolley, and Mapperson (1988).

FIGURE S1.12

Comparing effect sizes.

Effect sizes enable comparisons of the magnitudes of different studies, even ones that do not investigate the same interventions or risk factors. (Source: Bushman & Anderson, 2001.)

the effect size for studies of the relationship between these two variables, which is about $r = .31$ (obtained from a meta-analysis), to studies of the impact of smoking on lung cancer, the effect of exposure to lead on IQ, and other effects whose scientific acceptance is more widely known among the general public (**Figure S1.12**). With the studies lined up in such a way, the authors were able to make a more convincing argument that violent media constitute a public health risk. (Meta-analysis is covered in Chapter 14.)

ANSWERS TO TEST YOURSELF

TEST YOURSELF 1 The average force for men was 6.69. The average force for women was 4.73. Men had a slightly higher *SD* on this variable (2.05) than women (1.88).

TEST YOURSELF 2 On average, people ate 50.8 grams stale popcorn from a large container. The mean amount of fresh popcorn from a medium container was 58.9 grams, with a standard deviation of 16.7 grams.

TEST YOURSELF 3 Emma's *z* score on the midterm exam was 0.63. Her score is less than one standard deviation above the mean.

TEST YOURSELF 4 Emma's *z* score on the final was 1.0, so she did better on the final than she did on the midterm—relative to the rest of the class, at least.

Key Terms

Statistics Review

INFERENTIAL STATISTICS

The preceding discussion reviewed descriptive statistics, a set of tools for organizing and summarizing certain characteristics of a sample. Here we cover **inferential statistics**, a set of techniques that uses the laws of chance and probability to help researchers make decisions about the meaning of their data and the inferences they can make from that information.

THE GOALS OF STATISTICAL INFERENCE

Inferential statistical techniques are performed with the goal of *estimation*. Based on some result in a sample, the aim of statistical inference is to estimate the result—Does it exist? How large is it?—in a larger population of interest.

Inferential statistics are not so much a process of mathematics (although some basic algebra is involved) as a way of thinking through a logical set of steps. Inferential statistical thinking involves theories about how chance operates: What kinds of results can happen just by chance? For example, suppose we conduct a study in which we test a new medication for schizophrenia. Our randomized, controlled study finds that the group taking the drug experienced reduced symptoms. Inferential statistics are used to estimate whether, and how well, the drug works in the full population of interest or if the results might just be the result of chance variation.

Similarly, when researchers investigate a phenomenon (such as whether talking on a cell phone while driving affects accident rates or whether gratitude is related to relationship quality in couples), they do not test every possible individual to whom the behavior might apply. Instead, they conduct the study on a sample of people. Based on the results in that sample, they make an inference about what would happen if they tested the whole population.

This discussion is organized around the traditional inferential statistical technique called **null hypothesis significance testing (NHST)**. NHST follows a set of steps to determine whether the result from a study is statistically significant. For example, we can estimate the probability that we would get a similar result just by chance, even if the schizophrenia drug doesn't work. There are several statistical tests, and four are covered here: the t test, the F test, and tests of the significance of a correlation and beta. All of them share the same underlying logical steps.

It's important to note that NHST is not always appropriate; furthermore, your instructor may emphasize different techniques. Instead of NHST, many instructors prefer to simply estimate how large some effect is in a population and estimate the level of confidence in that estimate.

In sum, inferential statistics is the process of using data from a sample whose characteristics are known, to make inferences about some population whose characteristics are often unknown. Although we may never be able to study every person in a population, we can use the tools of inferential statistics to estimate what the population's values are.

An Example

Here's a fictional scenario to illustrate the process of null hypothesis significance testing. Suppose we encounter a woman named Sarah, who claims that in any crowd, she can pick out smart people—that is, she can identify people with high IQs. Her claim might seem a bit preposterous, so at first we're skeptical and assume she doesn't have this power. However, we're open to testing Sarah's claim. Across a large sample of people, IQ, as it is usually measured, has a mean of 100, with a standard deviation of 15, as shown in **Figure S2.1**. In addition, IQ is *normally distributed*, meaning that if we plot the IQ scores of a very large random sample on a frequency histogram, about 68% of people fall between one standard deviation above and one standard deviation below the mean. About 14% of people fall between one and two standard deviations above the mean, and 14% of people fall between one and two standard deviations below the mean. Furthermore, 2% fall higher or lower than two standard deviations. Armed with this basic knowledge, let's put Sarah to the test.

We take her to a local professional basketball stadium. It is full of people from all walks of life, both smart and dull, and their IQs span the usual range—with an average of 100 and an *SD* of 15. We ask Sarah to pick out a smart person. She looks around and chooses a woman in the 18th row. After obtaining the woman's permission, we take her to a private room and administer an IQ test with the help of a school psychologist. The woman's IQ is 115.

Are we convinced by this datum that Sarah has a special ability to detect smart people? Intuitively, we might think: 115 is a higher-than-average IQ, but it is not *that* much higher than average. So we might not be convinced that Sarah has special talents.

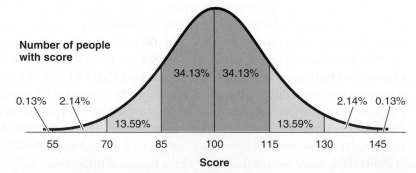

FIGURE S2.1
A normal distribution of IQ scores, where
M = 100 and SD = 15.

If we were to unpack this (correct) intuition, we would reason like this: Even if Sarah does not have special abilities, she could have selected a person with an IQ of 115 or higher just by chance about 16% of the time. According to the normal distribution in Figure S2.1, 16% of the people in the stadium should have an IQ score of 115 or higher. Sarah could have selected a person at random with an IQ that high or higher 16% of the time, even if she does not have a special ability to pick out smart people. And 16% seems too high to rule out the possibility that she just happened to choose a smarter-than-average person by chance.

Now suppose the scenario has produced a different result. Suppose we take Sarah to the stadium and ask her to identify a smart person. This time, however, she identifies a person who, when tested, has an IQ of 130. Are we convinced now?

If we're thinking probabilistically, then we should find this second outcome much more convincing because now there is a much smaller probability that Sarah could have guessed correctly just by chance. As Figure S2.1 shows, only 2% of the people in the stadium are likely to have an IQ of 130 or higher. We can interpret this 2% as follows: If Sarah does not have special powers, she would have to be extremely lucky to have picked a person with an IQ that high or higher—only 2% of the time would she be so lucky. Of course, it could happen. But because the chance of her getting lucky is very low, we feel confident that she does, in fact, have a special ability to detect smart people. In other words, the assumption you started with—the skeptical assumption that Sarah cannot identify smart people—is probably wrong. (This example is adapted from Aron, 2009.)

Incidentally, Sarah's ability to identify intelligent people is actually not uncommon. An entire line of research on this phenomenon finds that most people are fairly accurate at judging traits such as extroversion, agreeableness, and intelligence just by looking at other people for a few seconds. This phenomenon is known as *zero-acquaintance accuracy* (Borkenau & Liebler, 1993; Kenny & West, 2008).

The Steps of Null Hypothesis Significance Testing

The steps described in the example above illustrate those taken by researchers when they use NHST. To apply them to the scenario in which Sarah chose a person with an IQ of 130, we would proceed as follows.

STEP 1: ASSUME THERE IS NO EFFECT (THE NULL HYPOTHESIS)

When we tested Sarah's abilities, we started with the skeptical assumption that she was not able to identify smart people. In statistical hypothesis testing, this kind of starting assumption is known as a **null hypothesis**. *Null* means "nothing," and colloquially, a null hypothesis means "assume that nothing is going on." Depending on the research question, the null hypothesis can mean that a person does not have special abilities, that an independent variable does not have an effect on the dependent variable, or that two variables are not correlated with each other.

STEP 2: COLLECT DATA

To test Sarah's ability to identify smart people, we asked her to demonstrate it by locating a smart person in the crowd. We then gave the person she chose an IQ test to see whether she was correct. That was the datum: She correctly identified a person with an IQ of 130.

STEP 3: CALCULATE THE PROBABILITY OF GETTING SUCH DATA, OR EVEN MORE EXTREME DATA, IF THE NULL HYPOTHESIS IS TRUE

In this step, we calculated a probability: We used our knowledge of the normal distribution to compute the probability that Sarah could have chosen a person with an IQ of 130 or greater, just by chance, if the null hypothesis is true. What is the probability that Sarah could have chosen a person this smart or smarter by chance if she is not in fact able to identify smart people?

In making the calculations, we used what we know about IQ—that it is normally distributed with a mean of 100 and a standard deviation of 15—to estimate what percentage of people in the stadium would have each range of IQ scores. We also used our understanding of chance. Combined, these two pieces of knowledge directed us to predict that if Sarah had chosen a person at random, she would have chosen a person with an IQ of 130 or higher about 2% of the time.

STEP 4: DECIDE WHETHER TO REJECT OR RETAIN THE NULL HYPOTHESIS

In the fourth step, we made a decision based on the probability we obtained in Step 3. Since the probability of choosing a person with an IQ of 130 or higher just by chance is so small, we rejected our original assumption. That is, we rejected the null hypothesis that Sarah is not able to identify smart people.

The Decision to Reject the Null Hypothesis. The probability we obtained in Step 3 was so small that we rejected the null hypothesis assumption. In other words, we concluded that our data on Sarah's abilities were statistically significant. When we reject the null hypothesis, we are essentially saying that:

Data like these could have come about by chance,

but

data like these happen very rarely by chance;

therefore

we are pretty sure the data were not the result of chance.

The Decision to Retain the Null Hypothesis. To clarify this decision, consider a situation in which we would retain the null hypothesis: the first scenario, in which Sarah identified a person with a score of 115. The probability that Sarah would identify a person who is at least that smart just by chance even if she is not special is 16%, or .16. That probability seemed high enough that we would not reject our initial assumption that she is not able to detect smart people (the null hypothesis).

The Decision to Reject or Retain the Null Hypothesis

THIS TERM	MEANS THE SAME AS:	IN OTHER WORDS:	YOU MAY SEE, IN PUBLISHED WORK:	IN A RESEARCH CONTEXT, MAY MEAN:
Rejecting the null hypothesis	The result is statistically significant.	The probability of getting a result this extreme, or more extreme, by chance, if the null hypothesis is true, is less than 5%.	$p < .05$ * (asterisk)	The difference is significantly larger than zero. The association is significantly stronger than zero.
Retaining the null hypothesis	A result of this magnitude is not statistically significant.	The probability of getting a result of this magnitude or more extreme, by chance, if the null hypothesis is true, is greater than or equal to 5%.	$p \geq .05$ n.s.	We cannot conclude that the difference is larger than zero. We cannot conclude that the relationship is stronger than zero.

When we retain the null hypothesis, we are saying that:

Data like these could have happened just by chance;

in fact

data like these are likely to happen by chance 16% of the time;

therefore

we conclude that we are not confident enough, based on these data,

to reject the null hypothesis.

Finally, at what probability level should we decide to reject the null hypothesis? Why did we reject the null hypothesis at $p = .02$ but not at $p = .16$? In psychological science, the level researchers typically use is 5% or less, or $p < .05$ (**Table S2.1**). This decision point is called the **alpha level**—the point at which researchers will decide whether the p is too high (and therefore will retain the null hypothesis) or very low (and therefore will reject the null hypothesis).

Samples, Populations, and Inference

The previous section outlined the four basic NHST steps for drawing a conclusion. The process involves using data from a sample (one of Sarah's guesses) to make an inference about the nature of a population (the population of all possible guesses Sarah could have made). In other words, we did not ask Sarah to demonstrate that she could classify every person in the basketball stadium as smart or not smart; we did not collect data on the entire *population* of possible guesses in the stadium. Instead, we measured a *sample* of the population of guesses.

« For details on sampling techniques, see Chapter 7, pp. 179–192.

Almost all research studies a sample of some population. For example, when researchers conduct a political poll, they do not attempt to telephone every member of the voting population; instead, they select a sample of the voting population and make inferences about the voting population based on what the sample tells them. In the average experiment, researchers draw samples from populations such as monkeys, college students, or children in third grade. Often these samples are not selected randomly, but they are still drawn from a population.

UNDERSTANDING INFERENCE: TYPE I AND TYPE II ERRORS

Recall that the process of statistical hypothesis testing requires us, in Step 4, to make a decision. We decide whether to reject or retain the null hypothesis. In the example of Sarah, if we reject the null hypothesis, we would conclude, based on this sample of data, that Sarah really is able to identify smart people. If we retain the null hypothesis, we would decide that we have insufficient evidence, based on this sample of data, to conclude that Sarah is able to identify smart people.

Because we are studying only a sample of Sarah's behavior, not the full population of her behavior, the decision we make about her abilities could be right, or it could be wrong. Therefore, when we follow the process of inferential statistics, there are two possible ways to be right and two possible ways to be wrong. These four possibilities come from the two decisions we might make, based on the sample, and the two possible states of affairs in the population.

Two Possible Correct Conclusions. There are two ways to make a correct decision. (1) We could conclude from the sample of behavior that Sarah has a special ability to identify smart people (reject the null hypothesis), and in truth, Sarah really does—so our conclusion is correct. (2) We could decide that we cannot confidently conclude that Sarah can identify smart people (retain the null hypothesis), and in truth, she really cannot. Again, our conclusion would be correct.

Two Possible Errors. There are also two ways to make an incorrect decision. (1) We could conclude that Sarah probably has special abilities, when she really does not. This kind of mistake is known as a **Type I error**, a "false positive." (2) We could conclude that Sarah probably does not have special abilities, when she really does. This kind of mistake is known as a **Type II error**, or a "miss." (These two types of errors were introduced in Chapter 3.)

   Table S2.2 shows the four possibilities.

Which Error Is Worse? In the research context, the two types of errors can lead to different types of problems. On the one hand, if we make a Type I error, we may conclude that we have found something interesting in our study, which could encourage other researchers or practitioners to follow a false lead. Other researchers would not be able to replicate the result. For example, we might conclude from a study that a particular medication is effective for schizophrenia symptoms when it is not (a Type I error). This Type I error might be a costly mistake in terms of false hopes, unnecessary side effects, or fruitless follow-up research.

TABLE S2.2

Two Possible Correct Decisions and Two Possible Errors from the Process of Statistical Inference

DECISION BASED ON THE SAMPLE:	TRUE NATURE OF THE POPULATION	
	THERE IS REALLY NO EFFECT IN THE POPULATION	THERE IS REALLY AN EFFECT IN THE POPULATION
Reject the null hypothesis (conclude there is an effect).	Type I error	Correct conclusion
Retain the null hypothesis (conclude there is not enough evidence of an effect).	Correct conclusion	Type II error

DECISION BASED ON THE SAMPLE:	TRUE NATURE OF SARAH'S ABILITIES	
	SARAH REALLY CANNOT IDENTIFY SMART PEOPLE	SARAH REALLY CAN IDENTIFY SMART PEOPLE
Reject the null hypothesis (conclude Sarah can identify smart people).	Type I error: We conclude Sarah can identify smart people, but she really cannot.	Correct conclusion: We conclude Sarah can identify smart people, and she really can.
Retain the null hypothesis (conclude there is not enough evidence that Sarah can identify smart people).	Correct conclusion: We have not shown that Sarah can identify smart people, and she really does not have this ability.	Type II error: Sarah really can identify smart people, but we have failed to show it.

DECISION BASED ON THE SAMPLE:	TRUE NATURE OF THE MEDICATION	
	DRUG DOES NOT IMPROVE SCHIZOPHRENIA SYMPTOMS	DRUG DOES IMPROVE SCHIZOPHRENIA SYMPTOMS
Reject the null hypothesis (conclude the drug does work).	Type I error: We conclude the drug works, but it really does not.	Correct conclusion: We conclude the drug works, and it really does.
Retain the null hypothesis (conclude there is not sufficient evidence that the drug works).	Correct conclusion: We cannot conclude that the drug works, and it really does not work.	Type II error: The drug really does work, but we have failed to show it.

NOTE: The top section of this table shows the general case; the middle and bottom sections repeat the information in terms of two examples.

On the other hand, we might conclude that a drug is not effective when it really is (a Type II error). This might be a costly mistake, too. Suppose the new schizophrenia drug is, in fact, effective, but an early study incorrectly finds that it is not effective. These results could delay the availability of the medication for people who could benefit from it—or even prevent it from ever becoming available.

Deciding which error is more costly depends on the context. We might decide it's important to be conservative, in which case avoiding Type I errors might be our priority. Especially if the schizophrenia drug is expensive or has troublesome side effects, we may not want to conclude that it works when it actually does not (i.e., we don't want to make a Type I error). We may not want to spend the money or make people endure side effects by prescribing a drug that is ineffective. To be conservative in this way, we would design our study to minimize the probability of making a Type I error.

In other situations, we might decide we don't want to overlook an effect that is really there, so our priority would be to avoid Type II errors (i.e., being sure to reject the null hypothesis if in fact it is false). We might decide that if the drug for schizophrenia really does work, we want to be able to detect that. Perhaps the disease being treated is particularly serious and there are no other cures. Or maybe we are running the first study on a research question and we want to find the effect if it is really there; if there is an effect, we don't want to miss it because we are thinking about investing time in a promising research direction. In such cases, we want to reduce the chances of missing something important, so we design our study to reduce the probability of making a Type II error.

Finally, no matter how we design our study, there is always the possibility that no matter what we conclude, we might make an error because the true relationship, true difference, or true state of affairs in the population is often unknowable. The schizophrenia medication either has an effect or does not—but because we cannot evaluate the entire population of people who might use this drug, we will never know. However, we can choose the probability that we will make a Type I error and we can estimate the probability of making a Type II error. We can design studies in order to minimize these probabilities.

PREVENTING TYPE I ERRORS

Theoretically, only one aspect of a study affects the likelihood of making a Type I error: the level of probability (or p) at which we decide whether or not to reject the null hypothesis. As mentioned earlier, that decision point is called the alpha level. Researchers set the alpha level for a study in advance. They decide ahead of time that if the probability of their result happening just by chance (assuming the null hypothesis is true) is *less* than alpha, they will reject the null hypothesis. If the probability of their result happening just by chance (assuming the null hypothesis is true) is *greater* than alpha, they will retain the null hypothesis. In psychological science research, the convention is to set the alpha level at 5%, or alpha = .05.

To understand alpha level better, recall how we evaluated Sarah's abilities. In doing so, we used the conventional alpha level of alpha = .05. When Sarah identified a person with a 115 IQ, we knew the probability of her doing so by chance was $p = .16$ even if she didn't have any special ability to identify smart people. Because that probability was "high"—higher than .05—we thought it was possible that Sarah made a lucky guess this time. In other words, because the probability of the result turned out to be higher than .05, we retained the null hypothesis. In contrast, when Sarah identified someone with an IQ of 130, we knew the probability of her doing so by chance, even if she had no particular skill, was .02. Because that probability was "low"—less than .05—we assumed she probably didn't identify that person by chance, and therefore we rejected the null hypothesis.

Alpha Is the Type I Error Rate. The alpha we set in advance is also the probability of making a Type I error if the null hypothesis is true. Returning to our example, when we computed that the probability of Sarah choosing someone with a 130 IQ by chance was .02 (if the null hypothesis is really true), we rejected the null hypothesis. However, it's still possible that Sarah did not have special abilities and that she simply got lucky this time. In this case, we would have drawn the wrong conclusion.

When we set alpha in advance at alpha = .05, we are admitting that 5% of the time, when the null hypothesis is true, we will end up rejecting the null hypothesis anyway. Because we know how chance works, we know that if we asked someone who has no special abilities to select 100 people in the stadium at random, 5% of them will have an IQ of 125 or higher (the IQ score associated with the top 5% of people). However, we are admitting that we are comfortable with the possibility that we will make this particular mistake—a Type I error—5% of the time when the null hypothesis is true.

Alpha Conventions. Even though the alpha level is conventionally set at .05, researchers can set it at whatever they want it to be, depending on the priorities of their research. If they prioritize being conservative, they might set alpha lower than 5%—perhaps at 1%, or .01. By setting alpha lower, they are trying to minimize the chances of making a Type I error—of accidentally concluding there is a true effect or relationship when there actually is none.

In contrast, there may be situations in which researchers choose to set alpha higher—say, .10. In this case, they would be comfortable making false conclusions 10% of the time if, in truth, there is no effect. By setting alpha higher, they are also increasing the probability of making a Type I error. Researchers may wish to set alpha higher as one of the strategies to avoid missing an effect of a drug or intervention—that is, to avoid a Type II error.

PREVENTING TYPE II ERRORS (POWER, EFFECT SIZE, AND ALPHA)

Whereas preventing a Type I error involves only one factor (alpha level), preventing a Type II error depends on a set of factors, collectively known as power. Formally defined, **power** is the likelihood of not making a Type II error when the null hypothesis is false. In positive terms, it is the probability that a researcher will be able to reject the null hypothesis if it should be rejected (i.e., if there is really some effect in the population). If we are testing a schizophrenia drug that, in truth, does reduce the symptoms of schizophrenia, then power refers to how likely a study is to detect that effect by finding a significant result (see Chapters 10 and 11).

The following analogy will further clarify Type II errors. Suppose the electricity goes out in your house and all the rooms are dark. You think you left a book somewhere in the bedroom, so you go upstairs with a flashlight and shine the light around the room. Assuming the book is really there, can you find it?

If, in truth, the book is in the room, two things could happen. First, you might find it with your flashlight. Finding the book is analogous to making a correct research decision: You have rejected the null hypothesis (so in effect, you have decided, "The book is in this room") and indeed, it is there. Second, you might *not* find the book with your flashlight. Failing to find the book is analogous to making a Type II error: You have retained the null hypothesis (you retained the assumption that the book is not in the room, implying "The book is not here"). Power is about the first case: being able to detect the book when it is really there.

In this example, one factor that will help you detect the missing book is to have a good, strong flashlight. If the flashlight puts out a lot of light, you will be able to find the book in the room much more easily. But if the flashlight's batteries are running low and its beam is weak, you might not see the book and you might erroneously conclude it's not in the room when in fact it is there. That would be a Type II error.

Another factor that influences the Type II error rate is the size of what you are looking for. If you are looking for something large (your skateboard, perhaps), you will probably find it, even if the flashlight is very weak. However, if you are looking for something very small (a lost earring), you may not detect it, even with a bright flashlight.

Similarly, when researchers predict the chance of making a Type II error, they consider several factors simultaneously. The alpha level, the sample size, the effect size, the degree of variability in the sample, and the choice of statistical test all have an impact on the power of a study, and thus they all influence the Type II error rate.

Alpha Level. The alpha level is the first factor that influences power. Usually set at .05, alpha is the point at which researchers decide whether or not to reject the null hypothesis. When researchers set alpha lower in a study (say, at .01), it will be more difficult for them to reject the null hypothesis. But if it is harder to reject the null hypothesis, it is also more likely that they will *retain* the null hypothesis even if it deserves to be rejected. Therefore, when researchers set the alpha level low (usually to avoid Type I errors), they increase the chances of making a Type II error. In this one sense, Type I and Type II errors compete: As the chance of Type I errors goes down, the chance of Type II errors goes up.

Because of this competition between Type I and Type II errors, alpha levels are conventionally set at .05. According to most researchers, this level is low enough to keep Type I error rates in control but high enough that they can still find a significant result (keeping Type II error rates down).

Sample Size. A second factor that influences power is the sample size used in a study. All else being equal, a study that has a larger sample will have more power to reject the null hypothesis if there really is an effect in the population. A large sample is analogous to carrying a big, bright flashlight and a small sample is analogous to carrying a candle, or a weak flashlight. The bright, powerful flashlight will enable you to find what you are looking for more easily. If you carry a candle, you might mistakenly conclude that your missing object is not in the dark room when it really is (a Type II error). Similarly, if a drug really reduces the symptoms of schizophrenia in the population, we are more likely to detect that effect in a study with a larger sample than with a smaller sample.

Besides being less powerful, another problem with small samples is replicability. In a small sample, one or two unusual scores might occur simply by chance (see Chapter 14), leading to a fluke result that cannot be replicated. In contrast, in a large sample, extreme scores are more likely to be cancelled out by scores in the other direction, making such one-time results less likely.

Effect Size. A third factor that influences power is the size of the effect in the population. All else being equal, when there is a large effect size in the population, there is a greater chance of conducting a study that rejects the null hypothesis. As an analogy, no matter what kind of light you use, you are much more likely to find a skateboard than an earring. Skateboards are just easier to see. Similarly, if, in the population, a drug has a large effect on schizophrenia symptoms, we would be likely to detect that effect easily, even if we used a small sample and a low alpha level. But if the drug has a small effect on schizophrenia symptoms in the population, we are less likely to find it easily and we might miss it in our sample. When there is a small effect size in the population, Type II errors are more likely to occur.

Sample Size and Effect Size. How large does a study's sample size need to be? Suppose we come across a study that found a statistically significant result but had a very small sample size—only 20 participants. Should the researchers conducting this study have used more participants—say 100 or 200 more?

There are two issues to consider. First, large samples are necessary when researchers are trying to detect a *small* effect size. In contrast, if researchers are confident in advance that they are trying to detect a *large* effect size, a small sample may be all that is necessary. Think again about the lost object analogy. If, on the one hand, you are looking for a lost skateboard, you can find it easily even if you only have a small candle in the dark room. If the skateboard is there (like a large effect size), your candle (like a small sample) is all you need to detect it. (Of course, you would also find it with a powerful flashlight, but all you need is the candle.) On the other hand, if you are looking for a lost earring, you may not be able to find it with the small candle, which is not powerful enough to illuminate the darkest corners. You need a big flashlight (like a large sample) to be sure to find the earring (like a small effect size) that is there. Therefore, the smaller the effect size in the population, the larger the sample needed to reject the null hypothesis (and therefore to avoid a Type II error).

The second issue is that a small sample is more likely to return a fluke result that cannot be replicated. Therefore, when a researcher is unsure how large an effect is in the population, a large sample is more likely to (1) prevent a Type II error and (2) produce results that can be replicated.

Degree of Unsystematic Variability. A fourth factor that influences power is the amount of unsystematic variability in a sample's data. All else being equal, when a study's design introduces more unsystematic variability into the results, researchers have less power to detect effects that are really there. Unsystematic variability, like having too many different flavors in two bowls of salsa (see Chapter 11), prevents researchers from seeing a clear effect resulting from their experimental manipulation.

Three sources of unsystematic variability are measurement error, irrelevant individual differences, and situation noise. Measurement error occurs when the variables are measured with a less precise instrument or with less careful coding. Irrelevant individual differences among study participants can obscure the difference between two groups and thus weaken power. Using a repeated-measures design in an experiment reduces the impact of individual differences and strengthens the study's power. Situation noise can weaken power by adding extraneous sources of variability into the results. Researchers can conduct studies in controlled conditions to avoid such situation noise.

Statistical Choices. A fifth factor that influences power involves the statistical choices the researcher makes. A researcher selects a statistical test (e.g., a sign test, a chi-square test, a *t* test, an *F* test, analysis of covariance, or multiple regression) to compute the results from a sample of data. Some of these tests make it more difficult to find significant results and thus increase the chance of Type II errors. Researchers must carefully decide which statistical test is appropriate. (Some of the commonly used statistical tests are explained below.)

Another statistical choice that affects power is the decision to use a "one-tailed" or a "two-tailed" test. The choice is related to the researcher's hypothesis. For example, if we are only interested in finding out whether the schizophrenia drug significantly *reduces* symptoms, we use a one-tailed test. If we are interested in finding out whether the schizophrenia drug significantly reduces symptoms *or* significantly increases them, we use a two-tailed test. When we have a good idea about the direction in which the effect will occur, a one-tailed test is more powerful than a two-tailed test.

In summary, power is the probability of not making a Type II error. It is the probability that a researcher will be able to reject the null hypothesis if it deserves to be rejected. Researchers have more power to detect an effect in a population if:

1. They select a larger (less stringent) alpha level.
2. The effect size in the population is large rather than small.
3. The sample size is large rather than small.
4. The data have lower levels of unsystematic variability.
5. They use the most appropriate statistical test.

COMMON INFERENTIAL STATISTICAL TESTS

There are dozens of statistical tests used in psychological science. Researchers use different tests depending on whether they are testing frequency, association, or causal claims. They also use different tests depending on whether the variables are categorical (such as gender or political party affiliation), numeric (such as test grade or height), or a combination of the two.

This section describes four of the inferential tests commonly used in psychology research, all of which follow the same set of four logical steps outlined earlier. (A full-length statistics book will provide more detail on these and other statistical tests.)

Is That Difference Significant? The *t* Test

The *t* test (introduced in Chapter 8) allows researchers to test whether the difference between two group means in an independent-groups design is statistically significant. Let's recall the study from Chapter 14, in which 52 students were told they would be evaluating a person based on just a single information sheet about their partner (Jones, Pelham, Carvallo, & Mirenberg, 2004). The partner's ID number, printed on the information sheet, either matched the student's own birthday (the birthday match group), or it did not (the control group). The researchers were investigating whether participants would like the partner more if the person was similar to them in this superficial way. After the students read the person's description (and saw their ID number), the researchers had the students rate how much they liked the person on a scale of 1 to 9.

The researchers obtained the following results:

- Mean liking rating in the birthday match group: 8.10
- Mean liking rating in the control group: 7.15

To conduct inferential statistics for this study, we ask whether these two means, 8.10 and 7.15, are significantly different from each other. In other words, what is the probability that this difference, or an even larger one, could have been obtained by chance alone, even if there's no mean difference in the population?

STEP 1: STATING THE NULL HYPOTHESIS

We begin by stating the null hypothesis for the Jones study. Here, the null hypothesis would be that there is no difference between the mean of the birthday match group and the mean of the control group.

STEP 2: COMPUTING THE *t* TEST FOR INDEPENDENT GROUPS

The next step is to organize the data and decide which statistical test to use. The appropriate inferential test in this case is the *t* test for independent groups. The *t* test helps us estimate whether the difference in scores between two samples is significantly greater than zero.

Two features of the data influence the distance between two means. One is the difference *between* the two means themselves, and the other is how much variability there is *within* each group. The *t* test is a ratio of these two values. The numerator of the *t* test is the simple difference between the means of the two groups: Mean 1 minus Mean 2. The denominator of the *t* test contains information about the variance within each of the two means, as well as the number of cases (n) that make up each of the means. Here is the formula:

$$t = \frac{M_1 - M_2}{\sqrt{\left(\dfrac{SD^2_{\text{pooled}}}{n_1} + \dfrac{SD^2_{\text{pooled}}}{n_2}\right)}}$$

As you can see, t will be larger if the difference between M_1 and M_2 is larger. The value of t will also be larger if the SD^2 (variance) for each mean is smaller. (The SD^2_{pooled} in the formula means that we take a weighted average of the two samples' SD^2 estimates.) The less the two groups overlap—either because their means are farther apart or because there is less variability within each group—the larger the value of t will be. Sample size (n) also influences t. All else being equal, if n is larger, then the denominator of the t formula becomes smaller, making t larger.

The Jones team obtained a t value from their study of 2.57. Once we know this t value, we must decide whether it is statistically significant.

STEP 3: CALCULATING THE PROBABILITY OF THE RESULT, OR ONE EVEN MORE EXTREME, IF THE NULL HYPOTHESIS IS TRUE

Next we calculate the probability of getting this result, or a result even more extreme, if the null hypothesis is true. To do so, we compare the t value from our sample of data to the types of t values we are likely to get if the null hypothesis is true.

By far the most common way to estimate this probability is to use a **sampling distribution** of t. This method estimates the probability of obtaining the t we got, just by chance, from a null hypothesis population.

Sampling Distribution of t. To start, it helps to know that we never actually create a sampling distribution; instead, we estimate what its properties will be. To do so, we theorize about what values of t we would get if the null hypothesis is true in the population. If we were to run the study many, many times, drawing different random samples from this same null hypothesis population, what values of t would we get? Most of the time, we should find only a small difference in the means, so t would be close to zero most of the time (i.e., the numerator of the t test would be close to zero, making t close to zero). Therefore, the average of the t values should be around 0.00. Half the time, just by chance, t might be a little higher than 0.00. And just by chance, half the time, t might be a little lower than 0.00. Sometimes, we might even get a t that is *much* higher or lower than 0.00. Thus, when the null hypothesis is true, we will still get a variety of values of t, but they will average around zero.

In null hypothesis significance testing, sampling distributions of t are always centered at zero because they are always created based on the assumption that the null hypothesis is true. But the width of the sampling distribution

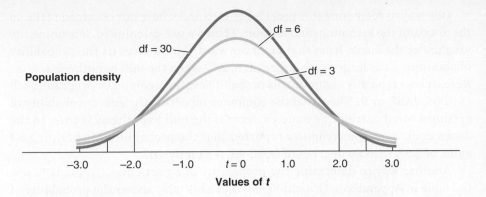

FIGURE S2.2

Sampling distributions of *t* for small samples (degrees of freedom = 3 and 6) and large samples (degrees of freedom = 30 or larger).

As the sample size increases, the *t* distribution gets thinner and approximates a normal distribution.

of *t* will depend on the sample size (i.e., the sample size of the study that we hypothetically run many times). As shown in **Figure S2.2**, when the sample size in our study is small, the sampling distribution will be wider and will result in more values at the extremes. This occurs because a small sample is more likely, just by chance, to obtain *t* values that are far from the mean because of sampling error. In contrast, in a large sample, the sampling distribution will be thinner.

Sampling distributions are created based on sample size, but they do not use sample sizes directly; instead, they use a slightly smaller number called *degrees of freedom*. A full-length statistics book will tell you more about this value. In the present example, the degrees of freedom are computed from the number of people in the first group, minus 1, plus the number of people in the second group, minus 1: (26 − 1) + (26 − 1) = 50. The sampling distribution of *t* for the example from Jones et al. (2004) would look like **Figure S2.3**.

This sampling distribution of *t* tells us what values of *t* we would be likely to get if the null hypothesis is true. In addition, this figure tells us that occasionally it is possible (but very rare) to get *t* values of 1.8, 2.0, or even larger, just by chance.

Using the Sampling Distribution to Evaluate Significance, or *p*. Why did we go to the trouble of estimating that sampling distribution anyway? Doing so helps us complete Step 3 of the null hypothesis testing process: Now that we have derived the sampling distribution, we can use it to evaluate the probability of getting the *t* obtained in the Jones study (2.57), or an even more extreme value of *t*, if the null hypothesis is true in the population.

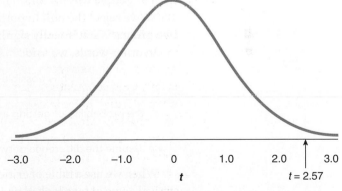

FIGURE S2.3

The sampling distribution of *t* for degrees of freedom of 50.

If the null hypothesis is true and we ran a study many times with a same number of people, these are the values of *t* we would expect. The average is zero; half of the *t* values are above zero, and half of them are below zero. The *t* obtained in the Jones study, 2.57, is marked with the small black arrow.

One way to determine this probability is to find where our obtained *t* falls on the x-axis of the sampling distribution. Then we use calculus to determine the area under the curve from that point outward, which gives us the probability of obtaining a *t* as large as, or larger than, 2.57 when the null hypothesis is true. Researchers typically compute this probability using a computer program, such as SPSS, JASP, or R. The *p* that the computer reports is the exact probability of getting a *t* that extreme or more extreme if the null hypothesis is true. In the Jones et al. case, the computer reported that the probability of obtaining a *t* value of 2.57, with 50 degrees of freedom, is exactly .013.

Another way to determine the probability of a particular *t* value is to use the table in Appendix B, Critical Values of *t*. This table shows the probability of obtaining different values of *t* for different degrees of freedom. Such a table does not give the exact area under the curve, as the computer can do. However, using that table, we can look up the **critical value** of *t*—the *t* value that is associated with our alpha level. For example, we can look up the critical *t* value associated with a .05 alpha level and 50 degrees of freedom: 2.009. (As an analogy, this is like establishing that the IQ score associated with the .05 alpha level was 125.) The critical value of *t* means that in a sampling distribution of *t* based on 50 degrees of freedom, we would get a *t* of 2.009 or more extreme 5% of the time, just by chance. In Step 4, we will compare the critical value of *t* to the *t* we actually obtained, 2.57.

STEP 4: DECIDING WHETHER TO REJECT OR RETAIN THE NULL HYPOTHESIS

Now we are ready for Step 4 of the hypothesis-testing process. Again, according to the computer, the probability of the Jones team obtaining the *t* of 2.57 in a study with 52 people was $p = .013$. This *p* is smaller than the conventional alpha level of .05, so we reject the null hypothesis and conclude that the difference between the two groups is statistically significant.

In other words, we said:

It is possible to get a *t* of 2.57 just by chance,

but

the probability of getting a *t* of that size (or larger) is very small—only .013;

therefore

we assume the difference between the two means did not happen just by chance.

When we use a table of critical values of *t*, we compare the *t* we obtained to the critical value of *t* we looked up (see Appendix B). Because the *t* we obtained (2.57) is greater than the critical *t* associated with the alpha level of .05 (2.009), we conclude that the result is statistically significant. Because our *t* is even more extreme than the *t* associated with the .05 alpha level, we can reject the null hypothesis. This means the probability of getting the *t* we got is something less than .05 if the null hypothesis is true.

Notice that the two methods—the computer-derived probability and the critical value method—lead to the same conclusion from different directions. When using the computer's estimate of probability, we decide whether or not that estimate of *p* is *smaller* than our alpha level of .05. In contrast, when we use the critical values table, we are assessing whether our obtained *t* is *larger* than the critical value of *t*. *Larger* values of *t* are associated with *smaller* probabilities.

COMPUTING CONFIDENCE INTERVALS

It's becoming more common for researchers to present the confidence intervals for their results. A **confidence interval** provides a range which is likely to include the true population value (e.g., the mean of a population or a difference between two means in the population). By convention, confidence intervals correspond to the traditional alpha level of .05 and provide us with 95% confidence that our interval contains the true population value.

In the case of the Jones et al. study, we might have been interested in estimating the population difference between the birthday match group and the control group. To create a confidence interval, we start with the observed difference in the sample. The difference was 8.10 (birthday match group) minus 7.15 (control group), which gives us 0.95 (difference between means). (Note: It's only a coincidence that this difference is 0.95 and we are creating a 95% confidence interval!)

Next, we add a distance to each side of this 0.95 estimate. To compute the correct distance, we multiply the standard error of the mean difference (the denominator of the *t* formula) by the critical value of *t*. In this example, we multiply 0.36 (the standard error of the difference between the two means obtained in the Jones study) by the critical value for *t* with 50 degrees of freedom, which is 2.009. This gives us 0.36 × 2.009, or 0.74. Then we add the distance of 0.74 to each side of our initial estimate: 0.95 + 0.74 and 0.95 − 0.74. Our resulting confidence interval for this example is 0.21 to 1.69, which is presented like this: [0.21, 1.69].

The interpretation of our confidence interval is as follows: There is a 95% probability that the interval represented by [0.21, 1.69] contains the *true* population difference between the birthday match group and the control group.

It's possible to use confidence intervals to decide whether or not to reject the null hypothesis. If the confidence interval does not include zero, we can reject the null hypothesis. If the confidence interval does contain zero, then we cannot reject the null hypothesis. Since Jones et al.'s range [0.21, 1.69] does not include zero, we can reject the null hypothesis—the same conclusion we drew before.

A confidence interval can be simple to understand and it offers more information than simply rejecting the null hypothesis or not. A confidence interval gives a clear picture about the precision with which some study has estimated a population value (Cumming & Finch, 2005). When a confidence interval is narrow, we have more precision, and when it is wide, we have less.

Is That Difference Significant?
The *F* Test (ANOVA)

The *t* test for independent groups is the appropriate test for evaluating whether two group means are significantly different. When a study compares two *or more* groups to each other, the appropriate test is the **F test**, obtained from an analysis of variance, also referred to as ANOVA.

A study conducted by Bushman (2002), introduced in Chapter 2, illustrates research for which the *F* test is appropriate. As you may recall, Bushman was testing the hypothesis that venting one's anger (by punching a punching bag) would reduce a person's subsequent anger and aggression. The study had three stages. In the first stage, a student wrote an essay, which was subsequently criticized by another student, who called it "one of the worst essays I have ever read!" In the second stage, Bushman divided the insulted (and angry) participants into groups. One group sat quietly in the lab room. Another group had the chance to punch a punching bag and was told to imagine the insulting student's face on it (this was the venting group). A third group had the chance to punch a punching bag, but they were told they were doing so for exercise. Finally, in the third stage, all three groups of participants rated their anger on a scale of mood and they had a chance to punish the insulting student by playing a very loud noise blast.

The researchers obtained three group means. Here we present the means representing how angry each group reported feeling:

- Mean of group who sat quietly: 26.25
- Mean of venting group: 29.78
- Mean of exercise group: 27.32

To conduct inferential statistics for this study, we need to ask whether the three means—26.25, 29.78, and 27.32—are significantly different from one another. Could differences between means of this size plausibly have been obtained just by chance? The authors used an *F* test, or ANOVA, to find out.

The *F* test helps determine whether the differences among the three groups are statistically significant. Just as with the *t* test, two sources of variability will influence the distances between these three groups. One is the variability *between* the three means themselves. The other is how much variability there is *within* each of the groups. Like *t*, the *F* test is a ratio of these two values. The numerator contains the value representing the variability between the means, and the denominator contains the value representing the variability within the groups.

The computations of the *F* ratio are not that complicated, but they are also beyond the scope of this discussion. In brief, when the *F* ratio is large, it means there is more variability between the groups than there is within the groups: The groups' scores are far apart and do not overlap much. When the *F* ratio is small, it means there is about the same (or even less) variability between the groups than there is within the groups; the groups overlap more.

Let's walk through how we would use an ANOVA in the example.

STEP 1: STATING THE NULL HYPOTHESIS

To go through the hypothesis-testing steps for the Bushman study, which compared groups who sat quietly, vented their anger, or exercised, we start by assuming the null hypothesis. In this case, we assume there is no difference among the three groups. In other words, the null hypothesis is that all possible differences among the three means result in zero.

STEP 2: COMPUTING THE F RATIO

Next, we calculate the F ratio for the study. In their article, the researchers reported that they obtained an F value of 5.23 for their results. We won't discuss the computations here, but this means the variability between the three means was 5.23 times larger than the variability within the three means. That sounds like a large ratio, but is it statistically significant?

STEP 3: CALCULATING THE PROBABILITY OF THE F VALUE WE OBTAINED, OR AN EVEN LARGER VALUE, IF THE NULL HYPOTHESIS IS TRUE

Next, we compare the F we obtained in Step 2 to a sampling distribution of F values, similar to what we did for the t value. We derive the sampling distribution of F by assuming that the null hypothesis is true in the population and then imagining that we run the study many more times, drawing different samples from that null hypothesis population. If we use the same design and run the study again and again, what values of F would we expect from such a population if the null hypothesis is true?

If there is no difference between means in the population, then most of the time the variance between the groups will be about the same as the variance within the groups. When these two variances are about the same, the F ratio will be close to 1 most of the time. Therefore, most of the F values we get from the null hypothesis population will be close to 1.0.

The sampling distribution of F is not symmetrical (**Figure S2.4**). While it is possible to get an F that is lower than 1 (e.g., when the between-groups variance is smaller than the within-groups variance), it is not possible to get an F that is less than zero. Zero is the lowest

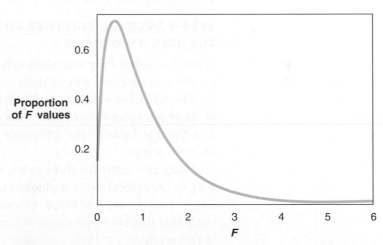

FIGURE S2.4
A sampling distribution of F.

The sampling distribution of F is not symmetrical. If the null hypothesis is true, most of the F values would be close to 1.0. The F value cannot be lower than zero, but it can be infinitely large. The exact shape of the F distribution will differ slightly depending on the degrees of freedom.

that F can be. However, F can be very large sometimes, such as when the between-groups variance is much larger than the within-groups variance.

Just like t, the sampling distribution of F will take on slightly different shapes, depending on the degrees of freedom for F. The degrees of freedom for the sampling distribution of F contain two values. For the numerator (the between-groups variance), it is the number of groups minus 1 (in this example, 3 − 1, or 2). The degrees of freedom value for the denominator (the within-groups variance) is computed from the number of participants in the study, minus the number of groups. (There were 602 students in Bushman's study, about 200 in each group, so the degrees of freedom would be 602 − 3 = 599.)

By deriving the sampling distribution, a computer program will calculate the probability of getting the F we got, or one more extreme, if the null hypothesis is true. The larger the F we obtained, the less likely it is to have happened just by chance if the null hypothesis is true. In the case of the Bushman study, the computer reported that value as $p = .0056$. This means that if the null hypothesis is true, we could get an F value of 5.23 only 0.56% of the time, just by chance.

Usually we use the computer to tell us the exact probability of getting the F we got if the null hypothesis is true. If a computer is not available, we can use a table like the one in Appendix B, Critical Values of F. The critical value of F is the F value associated with our alpha level. According to that table, the critical value of F at 2 and 599 degrees of freedom is 3.10. This means that if we ran the study many times, we would get an F of 3.10 or higher 5% of the time when the null hypothesis is true.

In Step 4, we will compare this critical value (3.10) to the one we obtained in our study (5.23).

STEP 4: DECIDING WHETHER TO REJECT OR RETAIN THE NULL HYPOTHESIS

When we use the computer, we simply compare the computer's estimated p value, $p = .0056$, to the conventional alpha level of .05. In this case, we will reject the null hypothesis and conclude that there is a significant difference among the means of the three groups in the Bushman study. In other words, we have concluded that there is a significant difference in anger among the control, venting, and exercise groups.

Using the critical values table, we can compare the value we obtained, 5.23, to the critical value we looked up, 3.10. Because the F we obtained is even *larger* than the critical value, we can also reject the null hypothesis and conclude that there is a significant difference among the means of the three groups in this study.

Just as with the t test, the two decision techniques lead to the same conclusion from different directions. When we use the computer's estimate of exact probability, we are assessing whether the computer's estimate of p is *smaller* than our alpha level of .05. But when we use the critical values table, we are assessing whether our obtained F is *larger* than the critical value of F. Larger F values are associated with smaller probabilities under the null hypothesis assumption.

A statistically significant F means that there is some difference, somewhere, among the groups in your study. The next step is to conduct a set of post-hoc comparisons to identify which of the group means is significantly different from the others. A full-length statistics text will explain the procedure for these post-hoc comparisons.

Is That Correlation Significant? Inferential Statistics with r

Two chapters (Chapter 8 and Statistics Review: Descriptive Statistics) discussed the correlation coefficient r in detail. The correlation coefficient is considered a descriptive statistic because it describes the direction and strength of a relationship between two numeric variables.

In addition to using r to describe an association, we can also evaluate the statistical significance of a correlation coefficient. As with t and F, we follow the four steps of null hypothesis testing. Step 1: We assume that there is no relationship in the population. Step 2: We collect some data and calculate r. Step 3: We estimate the probability of getting the r we got, or one more extreme, if the null hypothesis is true. Step 4: We decide whether to reject or retain the null hypothesis. When we reject the null hypothesis, we are concluding that the relationship (the r) we observed in our sample is statistically significant—in other words, that r we obtained is unlikely to occur just by chance in a null hypothesis population.

SAMPLING DISTRIBUTION OF r

Just as t and F had sampling distributions, so does the correlation coefficient. The sampling distribution of r is developed based on the probable values of r we would get if we ran the study many times on random samples from a population in which the null hypothesis is true. If the null hypothesis is true, most of the values of r would be around .00. Some would be greater than .00, and some would be less than .00, but they would average near .00. If the null hypothesis is true and there is a large sample (greater than 30), then the sampling distribution of r is shaped very much like the t distribution. It is centered on zero and it varies in width depending on degrees of freedom—that is, the number of cases in the sample.

The larger our study's r is (the closer it gets to 1.0 or –1.0), the less likely it becomes that we would get that value, just by chance, if the null hypothesis is true. (Therefore, the larger the r, the more likely that r is statistically significant.)

When we use a computer program to calculate r, the computer usually reports the value of r in the sample, along with an exact p value. That exact p tells us the probability of obtaining the *r* we got or a more extreme *r* if the null hypothesis is true. As in most statistical tests, when the *p* value is below alpha (usually, below a *p* of .05), we conclude that the result is statistically significant.

SAMPLE SIZE AND *r*

A larger *r* (a stronger *r*) is more likely to be statistically significant. However, the statistical significance of a value of *r* depends heavily on the sample size. When a study has a very small sample—fewer than 15 participants—it requires a large value of *r* to be statistically significant. In contrast, when a study has a very large sample—more than 1,000 participants—a small *r* (e.g., even an *r* of only .09 or −.09) will be statistically significant. Therefore, it is important to remember that *r* can also be used as a measure of effect size. In other words, an *r* of .09 may be statistically significant, but it still represents a very weak, or small, effect size (see Table S1.5).

» For more on statistical significance, see Chapter 8, pp. 214–217.

As you evaluate the meaning of a correlation coefficient, recall what you have learned in this book about statistical significance, effect size, and practical importance. As you consider these three elements, you will be interrogating statistical validity in a nuanced way.

Is That Regression Coefficient Significant? Inferential Statistics for Beta

Chapter 9 introduced beta, a value obtained from the multiple-regression process. Beta is similar to *r* in that both are used to estimate the association between two variables. However, beta goes further than *r* because it usually represents the relationship between a predictor (independent) variable and a dependent variable, *controlling for* other variables. Chapter 9 presented a study that estimated the relationship between viewing sexual content on TV and teen pregnancy rates, controlling for other variables such as age, grades in school, and peer characteristics.

We can evaluate the statistical significance of beta by following a series of mathematical steps leading to a *t* value. After finding the *t* value associated with a beta, we use the sampling distribution of *t* to evaluate the statistical significance of that beta. The sampling distributions of the *t* that are used to evaluate beta are the same as those for evaluating the difference between two samples. (Recall that these sampling distributions vary in width depending on their degrees of freedom.)

Other than that, the steps are the same as for all other statistical tests. We assume there is no relationship in the population (Step 1). We collect some data and calculate beta (Step 2). We estimate the probability of getting the beta we got or one more extreme, if the null hypothesis is true (Step 3). We decide whether to reject or retain the null hypothesis (Step 4).

A multiple-regression table in an empirical journal article will usually have a column indicating whether each beta is statistically significant. As discussed in

Chapter 9, sometimes the significance column will contain the actual t value associated with that beta along with the p value associated with that t. Alternatively, it might contain only the p value associated with the beta and its t. Or this column may simply contain an asterisk (*), indicating the beta is statistically significant, or the letters n.s., indicating the beta is not significant.

Other Statistical Tests: Same Process, Different Letters

We have discussed four statistical tests: the t test, the F test, and tests of the significance of r and beta. These four tests were developed for different research designs. The t test is for evaluating the difference between two group means. The F test is for evaluating the differences between two or more group means. The correlation coefficient r and its sampling distribution are used for evaluating whether an association between two variables is statistically significant. And beta, evaluated with a t test, indicates whether an association between two variables, controlling for some other variable(s), is statistically significant. **Table S2.3** presents a more comprehensive list of inferential statistical tests.

Although these tests are used for different research situations, they all follow the same general steps in null hypothesis significance testing:

Step 1: We assume the null hypothesis.

Step 2: We collect data and calculate a statistical test (a t, F, or r).

Step 3: We create a sampling distribution of that statistic: the distribution of the values of t, F, or r we would get if we ran the study using many samples from a null hypothesis population. We then use the sampling distribution to evaluate the probability of getting the t, F, or r that we got in our data, or one even more extreme, if the null hypothesis is true.

Step 4: We decide whether to reject or retain the null hypothesis based on this probability.

No matter what the test is, the inferential process is the same. In the future, you may see a statistical test you haven't seen before. If it is an inferential statistic, you can assume it will follow the same logic—the same null hypothesis testing process. For example, suppose a researcher reports a test that's unfamiliar, called Q. If the test is accompanied by a p value, you are safe to assume the researcher derived a sampling distribution of Q and then used the sampling distribution to evaluate the probability (p) of getting the Q she obtained in her sample if the null hypothesis is true.

As you continue reading about psychological research in empirical journal articles, you will encounter a variety of statistical tests developed for different kinds of data and for different research designs. However, no matter what the test is, it will probably be accompanied by a p value, and in most cases, the p value will tell you whether or not the results are statistically significant.

Which Statistical Test to Use?

	ONE VARIABLE IS:	THE OTHER VARIABLE IS:	SAMPLE RESEARCH QUESTIONS	USE THIS TEST:
Testing the significance of a difference between two independent groups (comparing two group means)	Categorical/nominal e.g., gender	Quantitative e.g., exam score	Did girls score significantly higher than boys?	t test for independent groups (returns a t value)
	e.g., experimental vs. control group	e.g., severity of symptoms	Did the experimental group show a significant reduction in symptom severity?	
Testing the significance of a difference between two groups (comparing group percentages)	Categorical e.g., gender	Categorical (2 levels) e.g., pass/fail rate	Are girls more likely to pass than boys?	Most common: chi-square test of goodness of fit (returns a $\chi2$ value)
Testing the significance of a difference between two or more groups (comparing group means)	Categorical e.g., major (chemistry, psychology, or biology)	Quantitative e.g., exam score	Is there a significant difference in exam score among the three groups?	One-way ANOVA (returns an F value)
Testing the significance of a difference between two or more groups (comparing group percentages)	Categorical e.g., grade level (grade 1, 3, or 5)	Categorical (2 levels) e.g., pass/fail rate	Is there a significant difference in the passing rate among the three groups?	Most common: chi-square test of goodness of fit (returns a $\chi2$ value)
Testing a difference between two means, measured in the same sample	Categorical e.g., kind of cola (regular or diet; people taste both kinds of cola)	Quantitative e.g., rating of cola flavor on a scale of 1 to 10	Which of the two colas do people rate the highest?	Paired-samples t test (also known as t test for dependent groups). Also used: sign test
Testing a difference between two or more means, all measured in the same sample	Categorical e.g., kind of cola (regular, diet, caffeine-free, or vitamin-fortified; people taste all kinds)	Quantitative e.g., rating of flavor on a scale of 1 to 10	Which of the four colas do people rate the highest?	Repeated-measures ANOVA (returns an F value)

	ONE VARIABLE IS:		THE OTHER VARIABLE IS:	SAMPLE RESEARCH QUESTIONS	USE THIS TEST:
Testing two or more independent variables at a time and their interaction (see Chapter 12)	First independent variable is categorical e.g., type of drink (alcohol or placebo)	Second independent variable is categorical e.g., weight category (heavy or light)	Dependent variable is quantitative e.g., degree of shock delivered to partner	Do drunk people deliver more shock? Do heavy people deliver more shock? Does the effect of alcohol depend on body weight?	Factorial analysis of variance (returns F values for each main effect and each interaction)
Testing an association between two variables	Quantitative e.g., hours of study for exam		Quantitative e.g., grade on exam	Do people who study longer get better grades?	Correlation coefficient (returns an r value)
Testing an association between two variables, controlling for a third variable	Quantitative e.g., hours of study for exam		Quantitative e.g., grade on exam	Do people who study longer get better grades, even when their preference for the material is controlled for?	Multiple regression (returns beta values or b values). Sampling distribution of beta and b is the t distribution.
Testing an association between two variables	Categorical e.g., class year: freshman, sophomore, junior, senior		Categorical e.g., form of transportation to campus: bike, bus, car	Do people in different class years differ systematically in what form of transportation they use?	Chi-square test of independence (returns a χ2)

NOTE: Not all of the statistical tests in this table are included in this supplementary chapter.

Key Terms

Presenting Results

APA-STYLE REPORTS AND CONFERENCE POSTERS

Scientists make the results of their research public in order to tell others about the advances they have made or the phenomena they have documented. The dissemination of research results can involve key aspects of scientific practice discussed in Chapter 1.

Publication contributes to the theory-data cycle because researchers write about the results in terms of how well they support a theory. Published data also become the basis for theory development and theory revision. Through the peer-review process, methods and results are scrutinized by peers who evaluate the quality of the research and the importance of the findings. Published data can contribute to either basic or applied research. Basic research findings can be adapted to applied settings and when applied research is made public, basic researchers may be inspired to refine or develop new theories. Finally, data published in scientific journals or presented at a conference may also be transmitted to the public if a journalist decides the results would be interesting to a general audience. A well-written report can help ensure that journalists interpret and present scientific findings accurately.

This supplementary chapter covers two forms in which psychological scientists present their data: the written research report and the conference poster.

WRITING RESEARCH REPORTS IN APA STYLE

As part of your psychology courses, you will probably be required to prepare a research report. The most common format for report writing is APA style, outlined in the *Publication Manual of the American Psychological Association* (6th edition, 2009). In the classroom, your research reports will be read only by your professors and fellow students. However, psychological scientists use the same APA style to write research reports that may become empirical journal articles.

APA Style Overview

A scientific research report is different from other kinds of nonfiction writing you may have tried so far. All APA-style research reports contain the same sections, which present particular kinds of information (see Chapter 2). When you write an APA-style report, you will be expected to include certain information in each section for your readers to find easily. An APA-style report includes the following elements:

Title

Abstract

Introduction

Method

Results

Discussion

References

APA style prescribes not only the content that belongs in each section, but also the format, including margin specifications, heading styles, and the presentation of statistical tests.

TITLE

By reading the title alone, readers should understand the main idea of the article. The *APA Manual* recommends that the title be no more than 12 words long.

Table S3.1 presents examples of titles of research papers cited in this textbook. You can see that, overall, they are informative and concise. In some cases, they even communicate their message with style. Most of the titles in the table contain a colon and a subtitle. The main title, the words before the colon, are intended to attract readers' interest; the subtitle, the words after the colon, specify the article's content.

TABLE S3.1

Titles of Empirical Journal Articles

ARTICLE TITLE	AUTHORS
Well-being from the knife? Psychological effects of aesthetic surgery	Margraf, Meyer, & Lavallee, 2013
Profiles in driver distraction: Effects of cell phone conversations on younger and older drivers	Strayer & Drews, 2004
Eavesdropping on happiness: Well-being is related to having less small talk and more substantive conversations	Mehl et al., 2010
Extraneous factors in judicial decisions	Danziger, Levav, & Avnaim-Pesso, 2011

TITLE CHECKLIST

- A title should communicate the purpose of the research in about 12 words or less.
- A title does not typically contain abbreviations.
- A title does not use the words "method," "results," "a study of," or "an experimental investigation of."
- In an APA-style manuscript, the title is centered and presented in uppercase and lowercase letters; it is not boldfaced. It appears in two places in the typed manuscript: on the cover page, which is page 1, and on the first page of the introduction (see the sample paper, pp. 525 and 527).

ABSTRACT

The abstract is a summary of the article's content. It does not present the nuances and details of the research—for that, readers will consult the full report. However, the abstract should clearly communicate the report's main research question, the methods used to test it, the major results, and an indication of why the results are important—for example, how the results support or shape a theory.

The abstract is the first section of your paper that most readers will encounter, but it is often the last thing you will write. After you complete the other sections of the paper, you can easily create an abstract by writing one or two sentences each to capture the introduction and the Method, Results, and Discussion sections. Above all, the abstract should be concise, accurate, and clear. Readers should be able to get a good sense of your research question and the results you obtained by reading the abstract alone.

ABSTRACT CHECKLIST

- An abstract clearly and accurately summarizes the research question, methods used, primary results, and interpretation of the results in terms of some theory or application.
- An abstract should be about 150 words long. (Different journals have different word limits for abstracts, and the APA Manual does not specify abstract length; ask your professor how long he or she would like your abstract to be.)
- In an APA-style manuscript, the abstract is presented on its own page, page 2. The page is labeled with the word Abstract in plain text at the top center. The abstract itself should be typed as a single paragraph with no indentation (see the sample paper, p. 526).

INTRODUCTION

The first major section of your paper is the introduction. This is where the main narrative of the research report begins.

Components of an Introduction. The main body of the introduction introduces the problem you studied and explains why it is important—usually because it tests some element of a theory. Your study may also be important because your particular approach or method has not been used in past research. Therefore, the bulk of your introduction is an explanation of the theory or theories your study is testing as well as an explanation of any past research that is pertinent to the problem you studied. In the introduction, you describe what other researchers have found and explain why their research is relevant to yours.

In the last paragraph of the introduction, you briefly introduce the method you used. (Was it a correlational study? A single-N design? An experiment? Did you use a factorial design?) The introduction is not the place to explain all the methodological details, such as how many participants you used or what questionnaires or tasks they completed; that information belongs in the Method section. However, you do have to tell your readers whether your method was correlational or experimental and what your primary variables were. Then, usually in the same paragraph, you state your hypothesis or research question. If you had a clear prediction about what would happen in the study, that's your hypothesis. If you conducted a study to see which of several interesting outcomes might happen (Will A happen? Or will B?), that's your research question. The hypothesis or research question is stated in terms of the variables you mentioned when you briefly described the method.

Here's a paragraph from a study featured in Chapter 10 (Boothby, Clark, & Bargh, 2014) illustrating how to describe the method and hypotheses (predictions) in the introduction:

> In two laboratory studies, we investigated the difference between experiencing a stimulus simultaneously with someone else (i.e., shared experience) and experiencing a stimulus while that other person is present but not sharing the experience of the stimulus (i.e., unshared experience). We predicted that sharing an experience, even in the absence of communication with the coexperiencer, would render the experienced stimulus more intense. Thus, we expected that generally pleasant stimuli would be perceived more positively and generally unpleasant stimuli would be perceived more negatively when they were part of a shared experience. (p. 2)

Here's another example, from Chapter 12's study on cell phones while driving (Strayer & Drews, 2004). In this excerpt, "dual task" means talking on the phone while driving:

> In this article, we explore the extent to which older adults are penalized by this real-world dual-task activity. Based on the aging and dualtask literature, we predict that as the dual-task demands increase, the driving performance of older adults will deteriorate more rapidly than that of younger drivers. (p. 641)

Writing the Introduction. For many students, the introduction is the hardest section to write. Although you'll probably have read review articles or empirical journal articles that inspired your study, writing about these sources to create a coherent introduction is a challenge.

If you are writing an introduction for the first time, try writing the last paragraph of it first. Write about the method you used and the variables you studied. State your research question or hypothesis.

Next, try writing the first paragraph. Introduce the main area of research (perhaps it is stereotyping, eating preferences, cultural differences, or brain activity during reading). You may introduce your topic in a creative way to describe why this area of research is potentially interesting. However, the balance can be tricky. It might be appropriate to link your topic to contemporary events, but it is not appropriate to explain why you personally became interested in the research topic. For the sake of your readers, you should avoid being too broad in this opening paragraph, lest you sound trite or say things you cannot back up (such as "From the dawn of time, stereotypes have plagued humankind" or "Cultural differences are a common source of tension in our society today"). You also want to avoid jumping into technical waters too early. A good balance is to link your topic to a concrete story—but to do so briefly. Here's how Brad Bushman (2002) introduced his report of an experimental study on venting anger, described in Chapter 2:

> The belief in the value of venting anger has become widespread in our culture. In movies, magazine articles, and even on billboards, people are encouraged to vent their anger and "blow off steam." For example, in the movie *Analyze This*, a psychiatrist (played by Billy Crystal) tells his New York gangster client (played by Robert De Niro), "You know what I do when I'm angry? I hit a pillow. Try that." The client promptly pulls out his gun, points it at the couch, and fires several bullets into the pillow. "Feel better?" asks the psychiatrist. "Yeah, I do," says the gunman. (p. 724)

It can be particularly challenging to organize the middle portion of the introduction—the paragraphs after the opening paragraph and before those containing the statement of your hypothesis or research question. In general, it's not effective simply to summarize each empirical journal article in isolation, one after another. Instead, try using past studies to build an argument that leads to your hypothesis. This requires planning. Reread the background articles you have. Write each article's results and arguments on separate index cards, summarizing the main point, and move the index cards around on your desk as you explore the most logical way to arrange them. What order of presentation will let you explain the past research so it leads to your hypothesis? Then you can turn your index card arrangement into an outline and start writing.

When summarizing past research, keep in mind that psychologists do not generally use direct quotes when describing work by other researchers. They almost always paraphrase it, putting it into their own words.

As you write your introduction, alternate between summaries of past research, including brief paraphrased descriptions (e.g., "In one study, Strayer and Drews (2004) asked younger and older drivers to complete a driving simulator task either undistracted or while talking on a hands-free cell phone") and statements that reflect your own interpretations and arguments (e.g., "This study demonstrated that people drive much worse when they are talking on a cell phone; it does not test whether people will also drive worse if they are talking to the navigation app in their car"). It might help to think of the past research descriptions as the "bricks" of your introduction, and the interpretations, arguments, and transitions you provide as the "mortar." As you build your introduction, you arrange the bricks in a logical order and then provide the mortar that connects them. By the end, it should be very clear to the reader why you conducted your study the way you did and why you formed your hypothesis.

INTRODUCTION CHECKLIST

- Follow the typical introduction format:
  - The first paragraph of the introduction describes the general area of research.
  - The middle paragraphs summarize past research studies (the "bricks") and give your interpretation of their meaning and importance (the "mortar"), arranged in a way that logically leads to your hypothesis.
  - The last paragraphs briefly describe the method used and the primary variables studied, and they state the hypothesis or research question.
- Document the sources you are summarizing by listing the authors' last names and year of publication, using parentheses or a signal phrase, as described below (in Citing Sources in APA Style, pp. 522–524). You should not type the full titles of the articles you describe.
- Describe past research by paraphrasing or summarizing, not quoting. Be careful to avoid plagiarizing (see pp. 520–522), and be sure to cite each article you describe.
- Describe completed research in the past tense. In general, it is appropriate to write the entire introduction in the past tense.
- If needed for organizing a long introduction, use subheadings.
- In the opening paragraph, avoid phrases that are vague and undocumentable, such as "in our society today" and "since the beginning of time."
- In an APA-style manuscript, the introduction begins at the top of page 3. Retype the paper's title at the top of the introduction and begin the text on the next line. (The heading "Introduction" is not used.) Do not insert any extra line breaks or extra spacing throughout the introduction. If you use subheadings to organize a long introduction, they should be boldfaced, capitalized, and flush left.

METHOD

The Method section explains, in concise and accurate detail, the procedures you followed in conducting your study. When you write the Method section, your goal is to communicate the details of your study so completely that a reader who had only your report to go on could conduct an exact replication study.

A conventional Method section contains about four subsections. They will vary according to the study. Possible subsections include Design, Participants, Measures, Materials (or, alternatively, Apparatus), and Procedure.

Design. If you conducted a factorial experiment, it can be helpful to open the Method section with a statement of the study's design, naming its independent and dependent variables. You state whether the independent variables were manipulated as between-subjects or within-subjects. For example, you might write, "We conducted a 3 (distraction condition: none, cell phone, or navigation app) × 2 (type of driver: younger or older) between-subjects factorial experiment. The dependent variable was the delay in braking time in the driving simulator."

If your study is a simple experiment or if you conducted a correlational study, the Design subsection may not be necessary. But a complex study may require a section headed Overview, in which you describe the variables you measured and the procedure you followed.

Participants (or for Animals: Subjects). Here you describe the number, type, and characteristics of the people or animals you studied. Human participants are referred to as "participants," and animals are usually called "subjects" in psychological science writing. For human participants, you say how many people participated, and give relevant demographic information, such as gender identity, ethnicity, socioeconomic status, age range, immigrant status, and native language. In addition, other characteristics may be relevant to report. Participants' intellectual abilities or disabilities may be relevant for a study on educational techniques; participants' sexual orientation may be relevant for a study on dating behaviors. In describing human participants, you also indicate how the participants were selected (randomly? by convenience?), recruited (by e-mail? in a shopping mall? in psychology classes?), and compensated (Were they paid? Did they get course credit? Did they volunteer?).

When describing animal subjects, it is conventional to give the species' common name and taxonomic name (e.g., "We observed 10 piping plovers [*Charadrius melodus*] in their natural environment") and indicate for laboratory animals the strain and provider used.

Materials (or Apparatus). Here you describe in detail the instruments you used to measure or manipulate the variables in your study. If you presented information on a computer screen, indicate how large the screen was and how far participants sat from it. If you used a commercially available computer program, specify the program you used. If animals were exposed to a particular piece of equipment, give its dimensions, manufacturer, and model.

If you used questionnaires or published scales to measure well-being or self-esteem, you'd devote one paragraph to each measurement scale. Indicate who wrote the items by citing the authors who first published the scale. Give one or two sample items from the questionnaire and indicate what the response scale was (e.g., "a 5-point scale ranging from 1 [*strongly disagree*] to 5 [*strongly agree*]"). Explain how you combined items for the scales, for example, if you computed a mean or a sum. Indicate what higher and lower scores signify (e.g., "high scores indicated higher self-esteem"). Also indicate the scale's reliability and validity. For example, you might give the Cronbach's alpha value you obtained in your own study, and the extent to which past researchers have validated the measure.

« For types of reliability and validity that might be relevant, see Chapter 5, pp. 124-143.

Although the Materials section should be complete and detailed, you don't have to describe obvious features, such as what kind of paper a questionnaire was printed on (unless there was something special about it) or whether the participants used pens or pencils to record their answers.

Procedure. This is where you describe what happened in your study, in what order. Did participants come to a laboratory or classroom or did they participate online? What did participants do first, next, and last? If there was a series of trials, what happened in each trial? If there were counterbalanced orders of presentation, what were they, and how were participants assigned to each order? How were participants assigned to independent variable groups (randomly or not)? Were participants or experimenters blind to conditions in the study? If so, how was this achieved? If there was a confederate in the study, what did the confederate say (exactly), and when?

In writing the Procedure subsection, be careful not to repeat information you already described in other sections. In the Method section, each element is presented only once, in the most appropriate place and the most appropriate order. Often it makes sense to put Procedure last, but in some cases it may need to go earlier in the Method section for more clarity.

METHOD CHECKLIST

- The reader should be able to use the Method section to conduct an exact replication study, without asking any further questions.
- In APA style, the heading should be "Method," not "Methods."
- Use subsections such as Design, Participants, Materials, and Procedure, presented in the order that is most appropriate and clear.
- Do not put the same information in more than one section. If you describe a measure in the Materials subsection, do not describe it again or give more detail about it in the Procedure subsection.
- If you used published questionnaires, describe each one in its own short paragraph, citing its source, sample items, relevant computations, and response options. Indicate relevant reliability and validity results for each questionnaire.
- In an APA-style manuscript, the Method section is labeled Method in boldface, centered. The Method section does not start on a new page; it begins directly after the introduction with no extra line spacing. Subheadings for Participants, Materials, or Procedure should be typed flush left, boldfaced, and capitalized. Do not insert extra line spacing between subsections.

RESULTS

The Results section of a research report presents the study's numerical results, including any statistical tests and their significance, sometimes in the form of a table or figure. You don't report the values for individual participants; you present group means or overall associations. In the Results section, you type numerals for means, standard deviations, correlation coefficients, effect sizes, or other descriptive statistics. You also enter the results and symbols for any statistical tests you calculated. The *APA Manual* provides precise guidelines for presenting these values. Generally, the symbols for statistical computations and means (such as M for mean, SD for standard deviation, t for t test, and F for ANOVA) are presented in italics, but the numerals themselves are not (e.g., $M = 3.25$).

A well-organized Results section is systematic and its sentence structure may even be a little repetitive. The priority is to be crystal clear. It is often best to begin with simple results and then move to more complicated ones. For example, if you included a manipulation check in an experiment, begin with its results. Then move to group means, followed by tests of significance. If your study was correlational, begin by presenting the simple bivariate correlations and then present multiple-regression results. If your study was a factorial design, present main effects first and then interactions. If your study included multiple dependent variables, present the results for each one in turn, but try to keep the sentence structure the same for each dependent variable, so the reader can follow a predictable pattern.

It might also be appropriate to refer to your study's hypothesis and expectations as you write your Results section. For example, you might write, "As predicted, people were less affected by bowl size when eating healthy food than when eating unhealthy food."

Tables and Figures. It is good practice to present certain results in a table or figure. While a sentence is appropriate for presenting one to three numerical values, a table can summarize a larger set of descriptive statistics, such as four or more means and standard deviations, much more clearly and easily than you could do in a sentence. Tables are also appropriate for presenting multiple-regression results.

Tables must follow APA style guidelines. They may be single- or double-spaced, but they must include only horizontal lines as spacers, not vertical lines. You should never simply copy and paste tables of output from a statistical program into your manuscript. Instead, you must reformat them in APA style, usually retyping the numbers and formatting them appropriately. Tables are not included within the main body of the text. They are placed near the end of the paper, after the References. If you have more than one table, number each one consecutively (Table 1, Table 2, and so on), and place each on its own page. A title for each table appears at the top of the page. The label (e.g., Table 1) is in plain text, and the title itself appears on the next line, italicized, in upper- and lowercase letters. In the text of the Results section, refer to each table you created (e.g., "Means and standard deviations for the main dependent variables are presented in Table 1"). An example of an APA-style table is provided in the sample paper (see p. 537).

A figure can often highlight your data's strongest result. For example, if your factorial design found a predicted interaction, you might want to present the result as a line graph or bar graph. Figures should be created using a computer program such as Excel. Each figure should have clearly labeled axes and should be presented in black and white rather than color, whenever feasible. Like tables, figures do not appear in the body of the Results section; they are placed at the end of the printed manuscript. If you have more than one figure, number each one consecutively (Figure 1, Figure 2, and so on), and place each on its own page. You must refer to each figure that you are including in the text of the Results section (e.g., "Figure 1 depicts the effect of distraction type on braking response time"). Provide a descriptive caption for each figure, typed on the same page as the figure, appearing below it. The label (e.g., *Figure 1*) appears in italics followed by a period. The caption follows on the same line, in plain text.

If you present results in a table or figure, do not repeat the same numerical values (such as the same group means) in the text of the Results section. Mention the general pattern in the text, and refer readers to the table or figure for the full story (e.g., "As Figure 2 depicts, people braked the fastest when they were distracted, regardless if they were older or younger").

The key guideline for the Results section is to state the numerical findings clearly, concisely, and accurately, and then stop writing. The Results section is likely to be the shortest section of a student research report.

RESULTS CHECKLIST

- A good Results section is well organized and crystal clear. Present simple results first, and use repetitive sentence structures when presenting multiple, related results.
- Use a table to present multiple values such as means, correlations, or multiple inferential tests.
- Figures are always called figures, not graphs. Use figures to present the strongest results in your study. Don't overdo it; most papers contain only one to three figures.
- Call out all tables and figures in the text of the Results section, but place the tables and figures themselves at the end of the manuscript.
- Do not present the same results twice. If you present a result in the text, do not repeat it in a table or figure.
- In an APA-style manuscript, the Results section begins right after the Method section, with no page break or extra line spacing. It is labeled with the word Results in boldface. You may insert additional subheadings to organize a long Results section; such subheads should be boldfaced, capitalized, and flush left.
- Check the APA Manual or the sample paper on pp. 525–539 for examples of how to present statistical results.

DISCUSSION

A well-written Discussion section achieves three goals. First, you summarize the results of your study and describe the extent to which the results support your hypothesis or answer your research question. You tell the reader how well the results fit with the theory or background literature that you described in the introduction. Second, you evaluate your study, advocating for its strengths and defending its weaknesses. Third, you suggest what the next step might be for the theory-data cycle.

Summarizing and Linking to the Theory-Data Cycle. The first paragraph or two of the Discussion section summarizes the hypotheses and major results of your study. Clearly indicate which results supported your hypothesis and which did not. Tie the results back to the literature and theories you mentioned in the introduction. In this sense, the Discussion section and introduction are like bookends to your paper—they both address the theory-data cycle. Describe how your results support the broader theory and why (or why not). If the results support the theory you were testing, you should explain how.

If the results do not support your theory, it will mean one of two things (as shown in **Figure 1.5**): Either the theory is incorrect (and therefore must be modified in some way), or your study was flawed (and therefore a better study should be conducted). The Discussion is the place to explore these options and explain what you think is going on. For example, if you conducted an experiment that found a null result, what factors might be responsible?

« For some common resons for a null result, see Table 11.2, pp. 342–343.

Evaluating Your Study. In the next paragraphs of the Discussion section, you evaluate the choices you made in conducting your study. Generally speaking, authors advocate for the strengths of their own studies and anticipate criticisms others might make so they can deflect them in advance. An excellent strategy is to write about the four big validities one by one.

Start by addressing the construct validity of your study, explaining whether your variables were manipulated or measured well, and how you know (review the evidence). Then, if you conducted an experiment, assess how well your study addressed potential internal validity threats. If your study was correlational, you might remind your readers that your data do not allow you to make a causal statement, and explain why. Address the statistical validity of your study by discussing the statistical choices you made. Finally, you might address the study's external validity. Because many student papers are not based on random samples of participants, however, you need to consider how much this matters in your case. Maybe it does not—if you were in theory-testing mode, for example. Reviewing your study in terms of the four big validities is an excellent way to make sure you have thoroughly evaluated and defended your study. The average student paper can probably include about one paragraph for each of the four big validities. (To review balancing research priorities, see Chapters 13 and 14.)

Specifying the Next Step. In the last paragraph or two, you write about some directions for further research. It's not sufficient to conclude with a vague statement, such as "Future research is needed." Suggest a specific, theory-driven direction for the next study to take. If your study was flawed in some way, could specific steps be taken to correct the flaws, and what results would you expect? If your study was conducted well, what part of the theory should be tested next? How could you test it, what results would you expect, and what would such results mean? If your study was correlational, could you conduct an experiment next? If so, how would you do so, what results would you expect, and what would those results mean? Could the next study be a conceptual replication? If so, what new contexts might you test, what results would you expect, and what would those results mean?

Push yourself to answer these questions so you can write thoughtful suggestions about the next step. Who knows—you might even inspire yourself to conduct another study.

- The Discussion section has three components.
- The first one or two paragraphs summarize the results and interpret how the results fit with the theory and literature discussed in the introduction.
- The middle paragraphs evaluate your study. Work through each of the four big validities in turn, explaining the extent to which your study has fulfilled each one.
- The last one or two paragraphs give suggestions for future research. For each suggestion, explain four things: Why you would study that question, how you would study it, what your results might be, and what those results would mean.
- Do not report new statistical findings in the Discussion section; numerals and statistics belong in the Results section.
- The Discussion section and introduction are bookends; they both describe how your particular study fits in with the larger body of literature on a topic. If you opened your paper with a real-world example or story, you might consider closing it by reflecting on how your findings can help interpret that same example.
- In an APA-style manuscript, the Discussion section starts directly after the Results section with no page break or extra line spacing. Head the section with the word Discussion, boldfaced and centered. You may insert additional subheadings to organize a long Discussion section; such subheads should be boldfaced, capitalized, and flush left.

REFERENCES

In the course of writing the introduction and the Discussion section, you consulted and summarized articles written by other authors. You cited these papers within the text using the authors' last names and the year of publication. Near the end of your paper, in a section titled References, you provide the full bibliographic information for each of the sources you cited, in an alphabetized list. The format is shown on p. 535.

Formatting an APA-Style Manuscript

When you prepare a research report in APA style, you'll follow a number of specific guidelines. It can be hard to assimilate all the rules the first time. A good strategy is to use the sample paper on pp. 525–539. Pay attention to every detail, such as line spacing, font size and style, and the use of boldface and italic terms. Here's an overview of APA format rules that apply to all sections of the research report:

- In an APA-style paper, everything is double-spaced with the exception of tables and figures, which may contain single-spaced text.
- All text is in the same-sized font (usually 12-point) and printed in black. Section headings are the same font size and color as the main text.
- Margins on all sides should be 1 inch (2.54 centimeters). Do not right-justify the text. This means to leave the right side ragged.

- The paper's title is not boldfaced but is centered and capitalized, both on the first page and at the top of page 3.
- Headings are boldfaced. The first-level heading—used for section headings such as Method, Results, and Discussion—is centered and capitalized. The second-level heading is boldfaced and flush left, and the first letters of major words are capitalized; the text following the heading begins on the next line. The third-level heading, if any, is boldfaced and indented and is followed by a period; only the first letter of the heading and any proper nouns are capitalized, and the text following the heading begins on the same line.
- The title page of the paper contains the title, the authors' names, the authors' institutional affiliations, an author note with contact information, and a running head, which is a shortened version of the title that appears at the top of each page.
- The following sections start on a new page: abstract, introduction, and References. (The Method, Results, and Discussion sections do not start on new pages.)
- The order of pages is as follows: title page, abstract, main body of paper (including introduction and Method, Results, and Discussion sections), References, footnotes (if any), appendices (if any), tables, figures. Tables and figures should be presented one per page.
- The top of each page includes the three- to four-word shortened title (running head), printed in all capitals and flush left, as well as the page number, which goes on the same line but flush right. In word processing programs, you might "insert header" or "view header" to add this information.

Writing Style: Five Suggestions

An APA-style research report should be written in clear, concise language. This is not the place to use long, complex sentences or show off a large vocabulary. In general, research writing is straightforward, not fancy.

Such writing is easier said than done: It takes practice, feedback, and attention. Here are five suggestions that can go a long way toward making your research report writing more sophisticated and clear. Your course instructor may have further suggestions to help you improve your writing.

WRITE IN THE FIRST PERSON

In APA style, the first person ("I" or "we") is permitted because it can make a sentence more readable. First-person writing sounds especially natural and clear when there are two or more authors on a paper. Compare the following sentences:

The authors presented participants with three distraction conditions: none, cell phone conversation, and navigation app. It was expected that participants would brake slower in the two distraction conditions.

We presented participants with three distraction conditions: none, cell phone conversation, and navigation app. We expected that participants would brake more slowly in the two distraction conditions.

Whereas the first-person singular pronoun "I" is acceptable in report writing, it can sound awkward, so use it sparingly. In addition, the second person ("you") is considered too casual for report writing; in a research report, do not refer to the reader directly.

CHOOSE THE MOST APPROPRIATE SUBJECT FOR EACH SENTENCE

Sometimes when you are comparing competing theories or briefly describing past research, it makes sense to use the author names as the subject of the sentence, as in the following example:

> Darley and Latané's (1968) laboratory studies supported a theory of bystander intervention known as diffusion of responsibility, but Shaffer and colleagues (1975) wanted to test the theory in a real-world context.

Often, however, when you are primarily describing the behavior of people, children, students, or animals, it is better to start a sentence with them, not with the researchers who studied them. Compare the following two sentences:

> Latané and Darley (1970) have found that in an emergency, people are less likely to help others when there are other people around who might also offer help.

> In an emergency, people are less likely to help others when there are other people around who might also offer help (Latané & Darley, 1970).

The first sentence emphasizes the *names* of the researchers, whereas the second sentence more appropriately emphasizes the *findings*: what people do in an emergency. Emphasizing the findings will make your descriptions of past research more vivid and interesting. Notice that in the second sentence above, the citation in parentheses makes it clear that the preceding statement is a research finding by Latané and Darley.

PREFER THE ACTIVE VOICE

The subject you use for a sentence can also determine whether the sentence is written in the active voice or the passive voice. Sentences in the active voice are more direct and usually easier to read, so you should strive to write in the active voice as much as possible. Compare the following examples:

> **Passive:** The target actions were never seen by the children.

> **Active:** The children never saw the target actions.

> **Passive:** Some of the action sequences were verbally commented upon by the adults.

> **Active:** The adults verbally commented on some of the action sequences.

In these examples, both options are grammatically correct, but the active sentences are clearer, shorter, and easier to read.

Sometimes, however, the passive voice makes the most sense. For example:

The rats were injected with ethanol 2 hours before each trial.

This sentence is written in the passive voice, but it appropriately places the focus of the sentence on the rats, not the people who injected them.

USE STRONG VERBS

A precise verb can improve a sentence's clarity and style. Search your paragraphs for linking verbs such as *is, are,* and *be.* Try to replace them with stronger verbs, as in the following examples:

Our results are consistent with past research on eating behavior.

Our results replicate past research on eating behavior.

Cell phones are an important influence on how people drive.

Cell phones distract people when they drive.

The manual was the guide for how to conduct the study.

The manual explained how to conduct the study.

CUT CLUTTER

Concise writing is more readable. You can often write clearer sentences simply by cutting needless words. For example, the following sentence originally appeared in an early draft of this material:

A precise verb can improve a sentence's clarity and make your writing easier to read. (15 words)

This shorter sentence conveys the same meaning without being repetitive:

A precise verb can improve a sentence's clarity. (8 words)

In the next example, the writer streamlined a long sentence by trimming unnecessary words:

When challenged to do so by their professors, most students find that they can cut out 20% of their manuscript's length simply by taking out a few extra words from each sentence. (32 words)

Most students can shorten their manuscript by 20% by removing unnecessary words from each sentence. (15 words)

Your writing becomes more readable when you cut redundant phrases and replace strings of short words with a single, effective one.

Avoiding Plagiarism[1]

When you use the words or ideas of others, you must acknowledge that by crediting the original published source. If you don't credit your sources, you are guilty of plagiarism. Plagiarism is often unintentional, such as when a writer paraphrases someone else's ideas in language that is close to the original. It is essential, therefore, to know what constitutes plagiarism: (1) using another writer's words or ideas without in-text citation and documentation, (2) using another writer's exact words without quotation marks, and (3) paraphrasing or summarizing someone else's ideas using language or sentence structures that are too close to the original, even if you cited the source in parentheses. The following practices will help you avoid plagiarizing:

- **Take careful notes,** clearly labeling quotations and using your own phrasing and sentence structure in paraphrases and summaries.
- **Know what sources you must document,** and credit them both in the text and in the reference list.
- **Be especially careful with online material;** copying material from a website directly into a document you are writing is all too easy. Like other sources, information from the web must be acknowledged.
- **Check all paraphrases and summaries** to be sure they are in your words and your style of sentence structure, and that you put quotation marks around any of the source's original phrasing.
- **Check to see that all quotations are documented;** it is not enough just to include quotation marks or indent a block quotation. (Remember, however, that in APA style it is not conventional to quote; you should paraphrase instead.)

Whether deliberate or accidental, plagiarism has consequences. Students who plagiarize may automatically fail a course or even be expelled from school. If you are having trouble completing an assignment, ask your instructor for help, or seek assistance at your school's writing center.

Using Appropriate Paraphrasing[2]

When you paraphrase, you restate information from a source in your own words, using your own sentence structures. (APA style requires paraphrasing and restricts direct quotes to very special circumstances.) Paraphrase when the source material is important but the original wording is not. Because it includes

---

[1] This section is adapted from "Avoiding Plagiarism" in *The Norton Field Guide to Writing, 3rd Edition* by Richard Bullock.

[2] This section is from "Using Appropriate Paraphrasing" in *The Norton Field Guide to Writing, 3rd Edition* by Richard Bullock. Copyright © 2013, 2009, 2006 by W. W. Norton & Company, Inc. Used by permission of W. W. Norton & Company, Inc. This selection may not be reproduced, stored in a retrieval system, or transmitted in any form or by any means without the prior written permission of the publisher.

all the main points of the source, a paraphrase is usually about the same length as the original.

Here is an excerpt from a source, followed by three paraphrased versions. The first two demonstrate some of the challenges of paraphrasing:

Original Source

In 1938, in a series of now-classic experiments, exposure to synthetic dyes derived from coal and belonging to a class of chemicals called aromatic amines was shown to cause bladder cancer in dogs. These results helped explain why bladder cancers had become so prevalent among dyestuffs workers. With the invention of mauve in 1854, synthetic dyes began replacing natural plant-based dyes in the coloring of cloth and leather. By the beginning of the twentieth century, bladder cancer rates among this group of workers had skyrocketed, and the dog experiments helped unravel this mystery.

—Sandra Steingraber, 2008, p. 976

Unacceptable Paraphrase: Wording Too Close to Original

Now-classic experiments in 1938 showed that when dogs were exposed to aromatic amines, chemicals used in synthetic dyes derived from coal, they developed bladder cancer. Similar cancers were prevalent among dyestuffs workers, and these experiments helped to explain why. Mauve, a synthetic dye, was invented in 1854, after which cloth and leather manufacturers replaced most of the natural plant-based dyes with synthetic dyes. By the early twentieth century, this group of workers had skyrocketing rates of bladder cancer, a mystery the dog experiments helped to unravel (Steingraber, 2000).

This paraphrase borrows too much of the language of the original or changes it only slightly, as the underlined words and phrases show.

Unacceptable Paraphrase: Sentence Structure Too Close to Original

In 1938, several path-breaking experiments showed that being exposed to synthetic dyes that are made from coal and belong to a type of chemicals called aromatic amines caused dogs to get bladder cancer. These results helped researchers identify why cancers of the bladder had become so common among textile workers who worked with dyes. With the development of mauve in 1854, synthetic dyes began to be used instead of dyes based on plants in the dyeing of leather and cloth. By the end of the nineteenth century, rates of bladder cancer among these workers had increased dramatically, and the experiments using dogs helped clear up this oddity (Steingraber, 2008).

This paraphrase uses different language but follows the sentence structure of Steingraber's text too closely.

Acceptable Paraphrase

Biologist Sandra Steingraber (2008) explains that path-breaking experiments in 1938 demonstrated that dogs exposed to aromatic amines (chemicals used in coal-derived synthetic dyes) developed cancers of the bladder that were similar to cancers common among dyers in the textile industry. After mauve, the first synthetic dye, was invented in 1854, leather and cloth manufacturers replaced most natural dyes made from plants with synthetic dyes, and by the early 1900s textile workers had very high rates of bladder cancer. The experiments with dogs proved the connection.

Use your own words and sentence structure. If you use a few words from the original, put them in quotation marks.

Citing Sources in APA Style

As you write, you must briefly document the sources you use within the text. You must also include the full documentation of every cited source in the References.

BRIEF DOCUMENTATION IN TEXT

When you are describing another researcher's ideas, words, methods, instruments, or research findings in your research report, you cite the source by indicating the author's last name and the year of publication. There are two ways to provide in-text documentation: by using a signal phrase or by placing the entire citation in parentheses.

When using a signal phrase, you present the last names as part of the sentence and place only the year of publication in parentheses:

Results by Strayer and Drews (2004) indicate . . .

According to Brummelman and his colleagues (2015), . . .

Alternatively, you can provide in-text documentation by putting both the author name(s) and the date in parentheses:

One study showed that both older and younger drivers brake more slowly when talking on the phone (Strayer & Drews, 2004).

With the second method, remember to use an ampersand (&) and to place the sentence's period outside the closing parenthesis.

As mentioned earlier, in APA-style papers, you will not usually quote directly; instead, you paraphrase the research descriptions in your own words. However, if you do quote directly from another author, use quotation marks and indicate the page number:

"It is also important to note that performance decrements for cell phone drivers were obtained even when there was no possible contribution from the manual manipulation of the cell phone" (Strayer & Drews, 2004, p. 648).

When a source is written by either one or two authors, cite their names and the date every time you refer to that source, as in the previous example. When a source is written by three or more authors, cite all the names and the date the first time. The next time you cite the source, use the first author's name followed by "et al." and the date:

> Parental overvaluation predicted higher levels of child narcissism over time (Brummelman, Thomaes, Nelemans, de Castro, Overbeek, & Bushman, 2015). However, parental warmth predicted higher levels of child self-esteem (Brummelman et al., 2015).

These are the rules for sources with obvious authors—the most common types of sources used by psychology students. You might need to cite other sources, such as websites with no author or government agency reports. In those cases, consult the *APA Manual* for the correct documentation style.

FULL DOCUMENTATION IN THE REFERENCES

The References section contains an alphabetized list of all the sources you cited in your paper—and only those sources. If you did not cite an article, chapter, or book in the main body of your text, it does not belong in the References. Do not list the sources in the order in which you cited them in the text; alphabetize them by the first author's last name.

In the following examples, notice the capitalization patterns for the titles of different types of publications—articles, journals, books, and book chapters—and whether they are italicized or formatted as plain text. Notice that while the journal's name is capitalized, only the first word of the article title is capitalized. Pay attention to the placement of periods and commas. Finally, note that if the journal article includes a digital object identifier (doi), it is included at the end.

Journal Articles with One Author. Here and in the next set of examples, notice that only the volume number of a journal, not the issue, is included, and that the volume number is italicized along with the journal title. Only the second example had an available doi to report.

> Gernsbacher, M. A. (2003). Is one style of autism early intervention "scientifically proven"? *Journal of Developmental and Learning Disorders, 7,* 19–25.

> McNulty, J. K. (2010). When positive processes hurt relationships. *Current Directions in Psychological Science, 19*, 167–171. doi: 10.1177/0963721410370298

Journal Articles with Two or More Authors. These examples follow the same pattern as a single-authored article. Notice how a list of authors is separated with commas in APA style.

> Brummelman, E., Thomaes, S., Nelemans, S. A., Orobio de Castro, B., Overbeek, G., & Bushman, B. J. (2015). Origins of narcissism in children. *Proceedings of the National Academy of Sciences of the United States of America, 112*, 3659–3662. doi:10.1073/pnas.1420870112

Mueller, C. M., & Dweck, C. S. (1998). Intelligence praise can undermine motivation and performance. *Journal of Personality and Social Psychology, 75*, 33–52. doi: 10.1037/0022-3514.75.1.33

Books. In the next two sets of examples, pay attention to how the publisher and its location are listed.

Tomasello, M. (1999). *The cultural origins of human cognition.* Cambridge, MA: Harvard University Press.

Heine, S. J. (2017). *DNA is not destiny: The remarkable, completely misunderstood relationship between you and your genes.* New York: W. W. Norton.

Chapters in Edited Books. Here, compare the way the chapter authors' names and those of the book editors are given, and notice how and where the page numbers appear.

Geen, R. G., & Bushman, B. J. (1989). The arousing effects of social presence. In H. Wagner & A. Manstead (Eds.), *Handbook of psychophysiology* (pp. 261–281). New York, NY: John Wiley.

Kitayama, S., & Bowman, N. A. (2010). Cultural consequences of voluntary settlement in the frontier: Evidence and implications. In M. Schaller, A. Norenzayan, S. J. Heine, T. Yamagishi, & T. Kameda (Eds.), *Evolution, culture, and the human mind* (pp. 205–227). New York, NY: Psychology Press.

CHECKLIST FOR DOCUMENTING SOURCES

- In the References, entries are listed in alphabetical order by the author's last name. They are not listed in the order in which you mentioned them in the paper.
- Within a source entry, the order of the authors matters; often the first author contributed the most to the paper, and the last author contributed the least. Therefore, if an article or book chapter has multiple authors, list them all in the same order that they appeared in the publication.
- The entry for each source starts on a new line, using a hanging indent format (see the examples and the sample paper). Do not insert extra line spacing between entries.
- The list is double-spaced and starts on a new page, after the Discussion section. The heading References appears at the top of the page, in plain text and centered. (Do not label this section Bibliography or Works Cited.)

Running head: NEGATIVE "CHILD OF DIVORCE" STEREOTYPES   1

A short version of the title appears on the top of every page, in all caps. To edit this, view the "headers" area in your word processor. On the title page, the shortened title is preceded by "Running head" with a colon. On subsequent pages, only the shortened title appears.

Page numbers start with 1 on the title page and appear on the right corner of each page.

The Effect of Negative "Child of Divorce" Stereotypes on

Thinking About Future Romantic Relationships

Kristina Ciarlo

Muhlenberg College

Provide a middle initial if you have one.

If there are multiple authors, list all their names, followed by their shared institution. If they are from different institutions, list name, institution, next name, next institution.

Author Note

Kristina Ciarlo, Psychology Department, Muhlenberg College.

This research was supported by an undergraduate research award from Muhlenberg College.

Correspondence concerning this article should be addressed to:

123 Main Street, Bloomville, NY, 12000; E-mail: ciarlo@college.edu.

The word Abstract is centered and not bold. The abstract begins on Page 2.

The abstract text is not indented.

It is appropriate to use the first person (I, we) in a research report. This student is presenting the results of a group project, so "we" is appropriate.

Avoid sexist language by using both "his" and "her" or by using plural rather than singular.

Abstract

This study investigated whether negative stereotypes about children with divorced parents extend to beliefs about their romantic relationships. Specifically, we looked at whether people would use information about the level of conflict of a child's parents, as well as information about the marital status of the child's parents, in predicting a child's future relationship success. Undergraduates (N = 38) read a vignette about a child and his or her family and then predicted the child's future romantic relationships. We found that participants predicted the future relationships of children from divorced families to be more negative than those from married parents (p = .02), and predicted that the relationships of children from high-conflict families would be more negative than those from low-conflict families (p < .001). The results suggest that people use both the marital status of a child's parents and the conflict level of the child's parents to predict the child's future success in romantic relationships.

Keywords: conflict, parental divorce, stereotyping

The abstract should be about 150 words long; some journals allow an abstract to be as long as 250 words.

Provide three to five keywords for your paper, centered under the abstract. Use the Thesaurus of Psychological Index Terms, available in psycINFO, for appropriate keywords.

The Effect of Negative "Child of Divorce" Stereotypes on

Thinking About Future Relationships

People use categories to simplify the task of processing the enormous amount of stimuli that confronts us (Gilovich, Keltner, & Nisbett, 2006). In social interactions, categorization may involve stereotypes, which are defined as "beliefs about attributes that are thought to be characteristic of particular groups" (Gilovich et al., 2006, p. 432). Even though stereotypes are not always accurate, we still knowingly or unknowingly use them as we interact with the social world. Stereotypes can apply to people from different ethnic populations, genders, or social classes, as well as other categories. The present study investigated the stereotype content and effects of one social category: children from divorced parents.

Past research has established that people hold stereotypes about children from divorced families, at least at the implicit level (Amato, 1991). In three studies, Amato (1991) assessed people's implicit beliefs about offspring of divorce. The first study demonstrated that people hold implicit negative stereotypes about individuals from divorced families, including the beliefs that they are distrustful, insecure, rebellious, prone to delinquency, shy, unpopular, have trouble relating to the opposite sex, and have nontraditional attitudes about marriage and family life. The results of the second study showed how these stereotypes work: Participants recalled fewer favorable facts about children from divorce than individuals from intact families. That is, participants implicitly ignored information that did not go along with the "child of divorce" stereotypes. However, when participants were explicitly asked if they thought that divorce caused negative effects for children, most responded that they thought divorce had few effects on children. Amato concluded that negative child of divorce stereotypes are widespread but implicit. They affect people's implicit beliefs even if they do not want them to.

> The introduction begins on Page 3.

> Repeat the title of the manuscript at the top of the introduction.

> There is no extra space or heading between the title and the introduction text.

> Citation format for a paper with three or more authors, first citation

> Citation format for a paper with three or more authors, second citation

> Citation format for a direct quotation; includes quotation marks and the page number

> Parenthetical citation format for a single-authored source

> Signal phrase citation format

One stereotype documented by Amato's study is that people perceive children of divorce as having trouble relating to the opposite sex. This particular stereotype is based upon some truth. Segrin, Taylor, and Altman (2005) found that children who come from divorced parents are more reluctant to enter into relationships because of the negative observations they made regarding their parents' committed relationship. The researchers also found that these children are less intimate even when they do enter into romantic relationships. The experimenters believe that this is the case because good communication skills were never modeled for them.

Although divorce may predict poor romantic relationships at an overall level, the context of the divorce seems to matter, too. The amount of parental conflict before the divorce moderates divorce's consequences for children (Kaslow & Schwartz, 1987). Some studies have shown that sometimes divorce has severe negative effects on children, and sometimes it has minimal effects or no consequences at all (Bartell, 2006). This discrepancy is partly due to the level of parental conflict that occurred prior to the divorce. Parental hostility and conflict have a stronger influence on children than the actual family structure does (Ensign, Scherman, & Clark, 1998). Furthermore, the cognitive-developmental model of the influence of parental divorce on romantic relationships explains that the level of parental conflict and proper modeling of relationships determines if children experience negative effects from the divorce or not (Bartell, 2006). Hence, the context surrounding the divorce matters more than the actual divorce does when considering the effects on future romantic relationships.

In the present study, we tested whether undergraduates' stereotypes about divorced children would be sensitive to the contextual factor of parental conflict. We predicted that although parental conflict matters in actual divorce cases, people's stereotypes would not be sensitive to this factor. Instead, we

Citation format for a two-author source

When possible, do not simply discuss past research articles one at a time; integrate them into an argument, as the student has done here.

The final paragraph of the introduction describes the method briefly and explains the hypotheses of the study in terms of this method.

hypothesized that people would ignore the context of the divorce and perceive overall negative effects of divorce across situations, because people fail to notice or tend to discard information that does not confirm their previous stereotypes (Amato, 1991). To test this prediction, we used a factorial design that manipulated both parental conflict and parental marital status in a set of vignettes. Participants read a high- or low-conflict vignette about parents who were married or divorced, and then responded to statements about the future romantic relationships of the couple's child.

Due to overall negative stereotypes about individuals whose parents are divorced, we predicted that participants would perceive more harmful outcomes for such individuals' romantic relationships than for those who came from intact families (a main effect for marital status). However, we predicted that participants would fail to consider the effect of conflict, predicting that participants would not make any distinction between the low- and high-parental conflict vignettes (no main effect for conflict). We hypothesized that these predictions will hold true for all the participants regardless of their own family situations because of how far-reaching negative child of divorce stereotypes are.

Method

Design

We conducted a 2 x 2 between-subjects factorial experiment. The independent variables were the level of parental conflict in the vignette, either low conflict or high conflict, and the marital status of the parents in the passage, either married or divorced. The dependent variable of the study was the participants' responses to the statements regarding the romantic relationships of the children.

Participants

Participants were nine male students and 29 female students from upper-level psychology classes at Muhlenberg College. Thirty-three participants came from parents who were married, three came from divorced parents, one came from parents who were separated, and one came from a single parent. In terms of class year, one was a first-year student, 20 were sophomores, 12 were juniors, and five were seniors. All the participants participated to fulfill a requirement in their psychology courses.

Materials

We randomly assigned each participant to read one of four vignettes and answer several dependent-variable questions.

Vignettes. We used four different vignettes representing each cell of the 2 × 2 design, specifically: high-conflict/divorced, high-conflict/married, low-conflict/divorced, and low-conflict/married (see Appendix). Each scenario described two parents, John and Elizabeth, who were involved in either a high-conflict or a low-conflict relationship. The last line of the passage stated either that the couple remain married or that they had gotten divorced.

We confirmed the effectiveness of the vignette manipulation by conducting a pilot test. Subjects answered questions pertaining to a passage thought to portray either high parental conflict or low parental conflict. Participants used a 5-point scale to rate the level of conflict that they felt the vignette represented (1 = *very low conflict* to 5 = *very high conflict*). In addition, students were asked to rate how realistic they thought the scenario was, using a 5-point scale (1 = *extremely unrealistic* to 5 = *extremely realistic*). We found a very large, significant effect for level of conflict, $t(9) = 6.43$, $p < .001$, $d = 4.29$. The students rated the high-conflict scenario as containing much more conflict than the low-conflict scenario (see Table 1 for the means). Hence, we determined that the parental conflict manipulation was effective. Furthermore, there was not a significant effect for realism, $t(9) = 0.98$, $p = .35$, $d = 0.65$. The participants did not

---

Format for a third-level heading: indented, boldfaced, sentence case, followed by a period; the text starts on the same line.

Refer to appendices in the main text. Place appendices after any figures or tables.

It is appropriate to present construct validity results, such as these pilot-tested manipulation checks, in the Method section.

Format for presenting a *t* test.

Call out all tables in the text. Do not repeat values presented in a table in the text.

rate the low-conflict scenario as being significantly more realistic than the high-conflict scenario. From these results, we concluded that the vignettes were equally realistic.

Dependent variables. The vignettes were followed by nine statements that addressed predictions about the future romantic relationships of John and Elizabeth's child. Each statement was assessed using a 5-point scale (1 = *strongly disagree* to 5 = *strongly agree*). We asked the students to circle the number that most appropriately corresponded with their feelings regarding the statements about the child from the previous passage. Examples of the statements include "This child will have difficulty sustaining a long term relationship" and "Their child will be able to effectively communicate with a significant other." After appropriate recoding, higher scores on the survey indicate a more negative view of the child's future romantic relationships. Possible scores could range from 9 to 45.

One survey question reassessed the construct validity of the vignettes, as we did in the pilot testing. Specifically, we asked, "What level of parental conflict does this vignette represent?" This statement was assessed using a different 5-point scale than the rest of the survey (1 = *very low conflict* to 5 = *very high conflict*).

The final four questions of the survey requested demographic information, including age, class year, sex, and parents' marital status.

Results

A factorial analysis of variance was calculated to determine if level of parental conflict or marital status had an effect on the students' perceptions of the children's future romantic relationships. Figure 1 presents the pattern of means. There was a significant main effect for level of conflict, $F(1, 34) = 55.88$, $p < .001$. The romantic relationships of children coming from high-conflict situations were rated more negatively than relationships of those

Indicate rating scales and anchors when describing self-report scales.

Use numerals for the point numbers and anchors of scales, and italicize scale anchors.

Give example items when describing self-report scales.

There is no extra space between the end of the Method section and the Results heading.

Call out all figures in the text. Do not repeat values in the text if they also appear in a figure.

Format for presenting an *F* statistic.

coming from low-conflict situations. There was also a significant main effect for parents' marital status, $F(1, 34) = 5.95$, $p = .02$. The romantic relationships of individuals coming from divorced parents were rated more negatively than children coming from married parents. Finally, there was not a significant interaction between level of conflict and marital status, $F(1, 34) = 0.09$, $p = .76$. Thus, the relationship ratings did not depend on the combined effects of parental conflict and marital status.

In addition, there was not a significant effect for the sex of the participant.[1] The female subjects rated the relationships ($M = 25.17$, $SD = 7.06$) slightly worse than the males ($M = 20.67$, $SD = 6.28$); however, this difference was not statistically significant, $t(36) = 1.71$, $p = .095$, $d = 0.67$.

To reassess construct validity, as was done in the pilot test, we computed another independent-samples t test to determine if the ratings of conflict level differed between the high- and low-conflict vignettes. The results replicated the findings from the pilot test: There was a very large, statistically significant difference between the two scenarios, $t(36) = 8.68$, $p < .001$, $d = 2.89$. Students rated the high-conflict vignette ($M = 4.53$, $SD = 0.61$) as containing much more conflict than the low-conflict vignette ($M = 2.37$, $SD = 0.90$).

Discussion

Due to globally negative child of divorce stereotypes, we hypothesized that people would ignore the context of divorce and perceive overall negative effects across situations. Our results supported this hypothesis; students rated the romantic relationships of the children from divorced parents more negatively than the relationships of those coming from married parents. This result replicates past research showing that negative child of divorce stereotypes include negative perceptions about their future romantic relationships (Amato, 1991). We had also hypothesized that participants' ratings would not be affected by the conflict

---

Report exact p values between .001 and .99. If p is less than .001, report $p < .001$.

Use a repetitive sentence structure when describing related results.

Use a zero before a decimal fraction when the statistic can be greater than 1 (e.g., F and t values). Do not use a zero before a decimal fraction when the statistic cannot be greater than 1 (e.g., correlations, proportions, and p values).

Footnotes should be used sparingly. They appear on a new page titled Footnotes after the References.

Some journals require confidence intervals as well as effect sizes.

There is no extra space between the end of the Results section and the Discussion heading.

The first paragraph of the Discussion section summarizes the hypotheses and major results.

level of the parents, but the results showed otherwise. Students rated the romantic relationships of children coming from high-conflict situations much more negatively than those coming from low-conflict circumstances. Hence, even though negative child of divorce stereotypes were activated, participants also took the context of the situation into account, contrary to predictions.

In our study, the contextual factor of conflict may have mattered because the vignettes were so extreme. The high-conflict passage contained an excessive amount of conflict, including verbal and physical violence, while the low-conflict vignette contained almost no conflict at all. The scenarios were made to represent opposite ends of a conflict spectrum in order to ensure that the manipulation was effective—it had good construct validity. However, this may also have increased demand characteristics. Participants may have realized what we were trying to study after reading such extreme situations. Thus, future studies should use vignettes that are more subtle in their differences and maybe even include a greater variety of conflict levels.

> When the results do not support the hypothesis, offer an explanation.

Our study was designed with good internal validity. We used a between-subjects design so that participants would not be easily aware of the comparisons we were making between divorced and married parents, or low- and high-conflict families. The vignette paradigm made it easy to keep extraneous variables controlled.

> The middle paragraphs of the Discussion section evaluate the study's strengths and weaknesses.

On the one hand, our external validity was not strong in this study; we recruited most of the participants from upper-level psychology classes, which means that they have all probably been taught a lot about stereotypes and biases. Additionally, all the subjects were college students and probably know someone whose parents are divorced. These individuals may realize that the effects of divorce depend on the context because of their personal experience. Such students may be better at controlling their implicit beliefs because they are aware of the automatic activation of certain stereotypes. Even so, they

> In a student paper, address how well the study meets the four big validities.

showed evidence of stereotypes that favor the children of married parents and low-conflict parents. Such stereotypes may, if anything, be even stronger among a non-student population.

We originally wanted to look at the difference between the relationship ratings of participants coming from married, divorced, separated, and single parents. However, the sample size was small and most of the students came from an intact family. Consequently, we could not run statistical tests to identify if there was a difference between the participants based on their family structure. However, we examined other sample characteristics, like participant sex, to look for discrepancies. Females rated the relationships more negatively than the males across all the conditions, but this difference was not statistically significant.

At the end of the Discussion, point to future research questions, explain what you would expect, and explain why they would be important.

A future study could examine the possible dissimilarities between the perceptions of people coming from married versus divorced parents. We predict that children of divorce would be even more sensitive to contextual factors because of their own personal experiences—that is, we would predict an interaction between the participant's own family status and the experimental factor of parental conflict.

References

Amato, P. R. (1991). The "child of divorce" as a person prototype: Bias in the recall of information about children in divorced families. *Journal of Marriage and the Family, 53,* 59–69. doi: 10.2307/353133

Bartell, D. (2006). Influence of parental divorce on romantic relationships in young adulthood: A cognitive-developmental perspective. In M. A. Fine & J. H. Harvey (Eds.), *Handbook of divorce and relationship dissolution* (pp. 339–360). London, England: Psychology Press.

Ensign, J., Scherman, A., & Clark, J. J. (1998). The relationship of family structure and conflict to levels of intimacy and parental attachment in college students. *Adolescence, 33,* 575–582.

Gilovich, T., Keltner, D., & Nisbett, R. E. (2006). *Social psychology.* New York, NY: W. W. Norton & Company.

Kaslow, F. W., & Schwartz, L. L. (1987). *The dynamics of divorce*: *A life cycle perspective.* Philadelphia, PA: Brunner/Mazel.

Segrin, C., Taylor, M. E., & Altman, J. (2005). Social cognitive mediators and relational outcomes associated with parental divorce. *Journal of Social and Personal Relationships, 22,* 361–377. doi: 10.1177/0265407505052441

The reference list begins on a new page. The heading is not boldfaced. Sources are listed in alphabetical order by first author.

Reference format for an empirical journal article with one author. Notice that the journal volume is italicized and the issue number is not included.

Reference format for a chapter in an edited book

Reference format for an empirical journal article with more than one author

Reference format for a book

Within a single source, preserve the order of authorship; do not list authors alphabetically unless they originally appeared that way.

When a DOI is available for a source, provide it at the end of the citation.

Footnotes

[1]We originally intended to test the effect of the participants' own family status, but we did not have enough participants in each category for this analysis.

Numbered footnotes begin on a new page. The heading is not boldfaced. The first line of each footnote is indented.

Table 1

Pilot Testing Data: Conflict and Realism Perceived for the Two Vignettes

Rating	High-conflict vignette M (SD)	Low-conflict vignette M (SD)
Conflict	4.40 (0.55)	2.33 (0.52)
Realism	3.50 (0.55)	3.20 (0.45)

Note. $n = 10$ for all values. Conflict ratings ranged from 1 (*very low conflict*) to 5 (*very high conflict*). Realism ratings ranged from 1 (*extremely unrealistic*) to 5 (*extremely realistic*).

Tables are numbered consecutively and placed one per page.

Table titles are presented in italics and are printed in title case.

Do not simply copy output from a statistical program into a table. Retype the data and its labels in the APA format.

Tables may be double- or single-spaced.

Table format can include horizontal separation lines, but no vertical lines.

Use the table note to describe any abbreviations used in the table or explain the nature of measures used in the table. The table note should be double-spaced.

Prepare figures in a computer program, not by hand.

Do not use gridlines (horizontal lines across the figure).

Label both the x-axis and the y-axis clearly.
Use shades of gray, not color, to represent levels of a variable.

Each figure goes on its own page and is numbered consecutively. Figure labels are italicized.

Figure captions are double-spaced and appear in plain text below each figure.

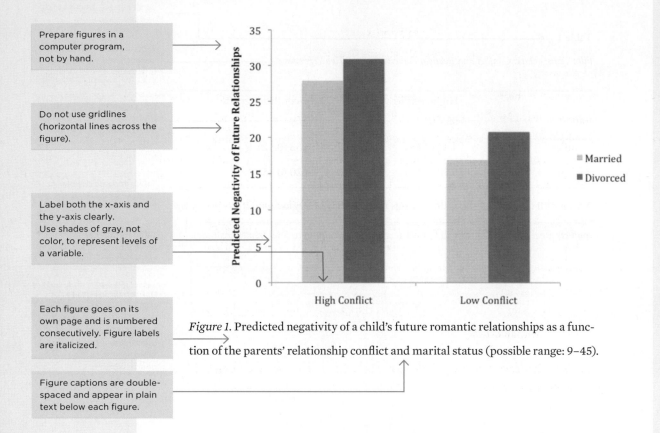

Figure 1. Predicted negativity of a child's future romantic relationships as a function of the parents' relationship conflict and marital status (possible range: 9–45).

Appendix

Vignettes Used in the Research

High Conflict:

John and Elizabeth have a child who just graduated from high school and is about to leave for college. Growing up, their child noticed that John and Elizabeth weren't always affectionate towards each other. They rarely hugged or held hands. The parents often fought over what was to be served for dinner, sometimes to the point that dinner was only served at 10:30 at night when they had finally settled on what to have. Their child had seen one parent or the other storm out of the house from time to time after a fight. Sometimes their verbal arguments turned violent, with either John hitting Elizabeth or Elizabeth hitting John. They would eventually apologize to each other only to get into another argument the next day. Their child often heard them yelling after going to bed, and it seemed that John and Elizabeth had more difficulties getting along than other parents.

Note. The vignette was followed by either of the following statements: "John and Elizabeth divorced about 1 year ago" or "John and Elizabeth remain married."

Low Conflict:

John and Elizabeth have a child who just graduated from high school and is about to leave for college. Growing up, their child noticed that John and Elizabeth were often affectionate toward each other. The parents sometimes had disagreements about what was to be served for dinner, but these problems were always resolved and dinner was served at 6:00 every evening. Their child had occasionally seen one parent or the other storm out of the room after a fight. However, they would apologize to each other soon after and the argument would be resolved. The child also noticed that John and Elizabeth could always make each other laugh and knew how to cheer each other up.

Note. The vignette was followed by either of the following statements: "John and Elizabeth divorced about 1 year ago" or "John and Elizabeth remain married."

An appendix is appropriate for presenting the full text of research materials, when such information is too long to present in the Method section.

If there is more than one appendix, they are called Appendix A, Appendix B, and so on.

PREPARING POSTERS FOR CONFERENCES

If you become involved in conducting original research—whether as part of a class project, for a student thesis, or as a research assistant for a professor—you may have the opportunity to present your research in a poster session. A poster is a brief summary of a research study, typed in a large, easy-to-read font and printed on a page as large as 4 to 5 feet wide. Poster sessions, in which several researchers present their posters simultaneously, are a common part of psychology conferences, both at undergraduate psychology conferences (where undergraduate research is the sole focus) and at regional and national psychology conferences (where faculty and graduate student research is the primary focus).

The Purpose of a Poster Session

A poster session is an informal way to share research results with the scientific community. At a typical poster session, dozens of researchers stand next to their posters in a large conference room (as in **Figure S3.1**). Other researchers mingle, stopping to read posters that attract their interest, and perhaps talking one-on-one with the poster authors about the research.

Besides sharing results with the scientific community, the other goal of a poster session is to enable researchers to talk informally. The one-on-one conversations and the nonthreatening context let people talk to potential collaborators, meet people they admire, or simply learn more about research conducted at other colleges and universities.

FIGURE S3.1
A poster session at a psychology conference.

Preparing the Poster

An APA-style research report will be the starting point for your poster, which should contain sections labeled Introduction, Method, Results, Discussion, and References. The poster format lends itself to less text and more images, as shown in the sample poster on pp. 542–543.

KEEP THE TEXT SHORT

A poster should give only a *brief* summary of the study you conducted. Many posters contain more text than most people are willing to read as they walk by, and it's best to keep the text short. Limit yourself to one or two paragraphs (perhaps even bulleted statements) for the introduction and the Discussion section. Keep the Method section focused on the bare minimum of information (such as the number of participants and the operationalizations of the primary variables). Let your tables and figures tell the story of your results.

SHOW, DON'T TELL

Present as much information as you can in tables, images, and figures. Visual art attracts an audience: People are more likely to stop by a poster that contains a large, interesting photo or a colorful figure. Tables and figures can also help you talk about your results in an interactive way. (For example, while pointing to your poster, you could explain, "Here are the two distraction groups we used. And you can see in this figure that the two distraction groups braked much more slowly than the undistracted group").

MAKE THE POSTER READABLE AND ATTRACTIVE

The typeface and formatting rules for a poster are flexible. Any text should be in a font that is large enough to read from a distance—at least 20-point. The title of your poster (printed across the top edge) should be even larger—at least 40-point. You can combine a variety of font sizes, colors, and backgrounds if you wish, as long as the poster is readable. (Be careful not to go overboard with too many visual effects.)

Attending a Poster Session

When you participate in a poster session, you will find your assigned space, hang up your poster with the pushpins provided, and stand next to it wearing your best outfit and a friendly expression. As people approach your poster, give them a moment to look it over, and then offer to explain your work. Some people prefer to read silently, but most of your audience will appreciate the chance to talk one-on-one.

It is a good idea to practice delivering a "poster talk," in which you describe your research in 1 minute or less. Using your poster's images as props, practice delivering the key points—the purpose of the study, the method, and the results—in this very short time period. After your brief description, a visitor can ask follow-up questions, and you can begin a conversation about the research. Congratulations—you are now participating in the scientific community!

In addition to preparing your poster, bring handouts to the session—regular-sized pages on which you have printed the text and images from the poster. You can offer handouts to interested people. Be sure to include your name and e-mail address, so people can contact you with questions.

Finally, during a poster session, it is perfectly appropriate to leave your poster for a few minutes to mingle and look at the other posters. This is especially important if your conference contains only one poster session. Don't miss this chance to learn about others' research as well as show off your own.

Effect of Negative "Child of Divorce" Stereotypes

KRISTINA CIARLO, MUHLENBERG COLLEGE

INTRODUCTION

People hold negative stereotypes about children from divorced families; for example, they make negative predictions about such children's future relationships (Amato, 1991). For real families, studies show that divorce on its own is not the main factor in actual outcomes. Family conflict moderates the outcomes of divorce for children (Bartell, 2006).

The present study investigated whether people would stereotype children of divorced families as having less positive romantic relationships, and whether people would stereotype differently depending on whether the relationship had been high or low in conflict. We predicted that parental marital status alone, not marriage conflict, would affect people's predictions about a child's future relationships.

METHOD

Participants were 38 college students (29 female).

We used a 2 (marital status: divorced or married) × 2 (relationship conflict: high or low) between-subjects factorial design. Each student read one version of the story and predicted the child's future relationship success (see the vignettes to the right).

Statements about future relationships included "This child will have difficulty sustaining a long term relationship" and "Their child will be able to effectively communicate with a significant other."

Each statement was assessed using a 5-point scale (1 = *strongly disagree* to 5 = *strongly agree*).

VIGNETTES

HIGH CONFLICT: John and Elizabeth have a child who just graduated from high school and is about to leave for college. Growing up, their child noticed that John and Elizabeth **weren't always affectionate towards** each other. **They rarely hugged or held hands.** The parents often fought over what was to be served for dinner, sometimes to the point that **dinner was only served at 10:30 at night** when they had finally settled on what to have. Their child had seen one parent or the other storm out of the house from time to time after a fight. Sometimes their **verbal arguments turned violent**, with either John hitting Elizabeth or Elizabeth hitting John. They would eventually apologize to each other **only to get into another argument the next day**.

NOTE. The vignette was followed by one of the following statements: "John and Elizabeth divorced about 1 year ago" or "John and Elizabeth remain married."

LOW CONFLICT: John and Elizabeth have a child who just graduated from high school and is about to leave for college. Growing up, their child noticed that John and Elizabeth were **often affectionate toward each other**. The parents sometimes had disagreements about what was to be served for dinner, but these problems **were always resolved and dinner was served at 6:00 every evening**. Their child had occasionally seen one parent or the other storm out of the room after a fight. However, they **would apologize to each other soon after and the argument would be resolved**. The child also noticed that John and Elizabeth **could always make each other laugh and knew how to cheer each other up**.

NOTE. The vignette was followed by one of the following statements: "John and Elizabeth divorced about 1 year ago" or "John and Elizabeth remain married."

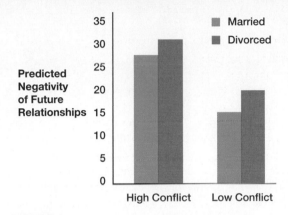

FIGURE 1

Predicted negativity of a child's future romantic relationships as a function of the parents' relationship conflict and marital status.

TABLE 1

Pretesting data on the vignettes

RATING	HIGH-CONFLICT VIGNETTE	LOW-CONFLICT VIGNETTE
Conflict	4.40 (0.55)	2.33 (0.52)
Realism	3.50 (0.55)	3.20 (0.45)

NOTE: Table presents *Ms* (*SDs*). The pretest was conducted on a sample of 10 undergraduates, using only the high- and low-conflict versions of the vignettes.

RESULTS

There were main effects for conflict, $F(1,34) = 55.88$, $p < .001$, and marital status, $F(1,34) = 5.95$, $p = .02$, but no interaction.

DISCUSSION

The results suggest that people used both marital status and marriage conflict when they predicted the future relationships of a child. As hypothesized, people predicted worse relationships for children of divorced parents than children of married parents. But counter to predictions, people also predicted worse relationships for children whose parents had high levels of conflict. These results suggest that people may, in fact, be sensitive to the level of conflict in a marriage, as well as marital status, when applying stereotypes to children of divorced parents.

REFERENCES

Amato, P. R. (1991). The "child of divorce" as a person prototype: Bias in the recall of information about children in divorced families. *Journal of Marriage and the Family, 53, 59–69.*

Bartell, D. (2006). Influence of parental divorce on romantic relationships in young adulthood: A cognitive-developmental perspective. In M. A. Fine & J. H. Harvey (Eds.), *Handbook of divorce and relationship dissolution* (pp. 339–360). London, England: Psychology Press.

Appendix A

RANDOM NUMBERS AND
HOW TO USE THEM

There are two uses of the term *randomization* in psychology, and it is important not to confuse them. Sometimes it refers to *probability sampling* (often called *random sampling*) from a population, and sometimes it refers to *random assignment* of participants to groups in a between-subjects experiment. Whereas random sampling (probability sampling) is a method for selecting participants from some population in an unbiased way, random assignment is a method for assigning participants to two or more experimental conditions in an unbiased way. Random sampling enhances a study's external validity, and random assignment enhances a study's internal validity. (For more on probability sampling, see Chapter 7; for more on random assignment, see Chapter 10.)

Table A.1 contains a random series of two-digit numbers, from 00 to 99. This kind of random number table is useful for both probability sampling and random assignment, but they are used differently in each case.

RANDOM SAMPLING (PROBABILITY SAMPLING)

Suppose we have a classroom with no more than 100 people in it; that's our population. We want to sample 20 cases from this population using *simple random sampling*. The first step is to assign a number to each member of the population, from 00 to 99. Using the random numbers table, we select a starting value haphazardly—by dropping a pen onto the page, perhaps. Starting with this value, we then read across the rows. For example, if the pen drops on the third entry in the first row, 78, person number 78 will be sampled in our study. Then we continue moving along the row from there—persons 71, 21, 28, and so on—until we sample 20 cases. If a number is duplicated, we simply ignore the duplicate and go to the next number. If the population has fewer than 100 people in it—say, only 60 people—we ignore any random numbers that are greater than 60.

The example assumes we have a population of no more than 100 cases. If the population is larger than 100, we take the numbers in pairs, making the first entry on the table 7917. By using two columns at a time, we can handle populations up to 10,000 members.

We can also use the random number table for *systematic sampling,* another variation of random sampling. We drop a pen on Table A.1 and choose a value—say, 98. We split this into two digits, 9 and 8. Then we count off. Starting with the ninth person in a group, we select every eighth person after that until we have a full sample.

RANDOM ASSIGNMENT

Now let's assume we have already selected some sample of people who are going to be subjects in an experiment, and we're ready to assign participants to each experimental condition.

We plan to have 90 participants in our study, which includes three groups (say, laptop, notebook, and no notes). Ninety participants have agreed to be in our study, and we decide that laptop will be Group 1, notebook will be Group 2, and no notes will be Group 3. We can start anywhere on the random number table (perhaps by dropping a pen on it) and read along the row, considering only the digits 1, 2, and 3; we ignore any other numbers.

We assign our participants in sets of three. If we had a prearranged list of participant names, we would start with the first three on the list. If we did not have names in advance, we could set up a schedule based on the order in which participants show up for the experiment and start with the first three participants who arrive. Suppose we drop the pen on a part of the table that starts with the following row of random numbers:

93   94   17   15   28   07   16   87   22   06

Starting with the 9 in 93 and reading across, the first value of 1, 2, or 3 we encounter is a 3. That means the first person in the first set of three people will be in Group 3—no notes. The next value we encounter is 1, so the second person will be in Group 1—laptop. Therefore, by elimination, the final person in this group of three will be in Group 2—notebook.

Now we start again with the next set of three people. The next appropriate value we encounter is a 1, so the fourth person is in Group 1. Next is a 2, so the fifth person will be in Group 2, and, by elimination, the sixth person will be in Group 3, and so on.

Of course, if we had four experimental groups, we would consider the numbers 1, 2, 3, and 4. If we had two experimental groups, we might consider numbers 1 and 2. Or we could consider odd and even numbers—any odd number would mean an assignment to Group 1, and any even number would mean an assignment to Group 2. (In the case of two groups, we can also flip a coin to assign people to conditions.)

Random Numbers

79	17	78	71	21	28	49	08	47	79
17	33	72	97	86	45	44	65	97	29
27	65	06	82	98	28	36	03	72	93
33	57	70	34	39	91	78	99	64	53
76	81	31	42	31	04	00	10	82	13
27	72	54	77	94	97	92	56	20	98
97	95	39	36	02	43	10	08	19	00
87	84	51	57	65	03	46	70	94	69
40	80	05	81	12	90	02	90	44	38
21	90	78	37	47	61	92	69	35	30
40	61	04	23	42	76	72	13	08	83
59	02	28	10	82	77	75	89	13	34
91	37	80	64	61	39	19	38	91	28
24	42	44	77	45	44	03	46	25	94
66	49	81	89	88	40	81	60	25	26
57	55	52	54	53	31	49	38	14	72
83	26	59	05	42	05	89	74	68	10
16	97	26	84	41	14	94	94	94	03
53	16	08	29	29	28	19	28	01	83
87	73	84	55	94	57	52	68	56	90
56	55	60	96	53	21	18	59	55	86
83	59	56	38	86	84	07	40	77	20
37	39	88	49	43	00	49	13	02	51
14	20	68	04	90	94	70	05	83	10
11	16	82	54	39	36	56	00	52	07
46	97	32	82	63	13	42	30	20	64
25	04	76	44	88	19	61	20	56	97
05	54	35	78	93	94	17	15	28	07
16	87	66	77	22	06	50	76	95	09
67	78	65	43	99	96	82	04	48	30
50	70	46	81	33	52	89	59	09	49
57	90	31	77	96	04	97	17	87	54
51	85	26	99	70	46	88	58	00	99
45	07	47	13	64	79	44	06	15	07
46	72	46	81	14	12	17	48	07	33
04	62	90	98	01	48	00	54	91	65

(continued)

Random Numbers (continued)

75	83	67	58	01	28	14	42	41	00
84	72	63	83	39	67	62	67	28	05
61	91	27	17	24	76	64	22	20	75
01	05	20	78	51	19	23	31	44	61
71	71	55	10	29	62	30	90	52	04
08	98	57	51	73	55	96	67	02	36
57	83	20	73	45	93	21	48	23	95
33	51	57	26	11	16	82	56	63	55
10	35	48	50	12	09	09	83	81	46
26	07	34	35	97	89	11	71	88	75
94	08	05	65	43	55	83	00	20	64
03	80	52	12	55	86	62	79	39	72
50	86	61	36	18	43	48	01	71	04
24	58	31	51	91	55	43	43	17	27
76	96	32	12	33	99	74	96	26	65
41	63	83	68	38	74	97	45	30	82
22	25	34	52	80	38	18	62	53	15
79	88	43	73	32	02	38	51	22	47
28	37	38	51	44	13	10	03	18	97
95	09	89	59	94	87	96	44	55	82
53	37	57	01	72	33	79	00	85	10
84	83	02	29	98	81	77	79	49	28
86	67	93	57	32	17	50	69	42	12
18	61	05	12	59	12	71	25	42	60
26	09	16	23	90	39	33	49	11	64
48	83	61	38	67	06	46	03	18	83
88	46	69	96	53	83	10	91	06	15
89	34	46	69	45	65	42	29	04	04
58	06	18	26	65	07	55	36	54	05
85	87	13	15	14	37	25	31	61	36
01	81	81	80	61	99	67	81	14	25
14	46	11	80	94	45	75	84	92	28
17	04	08	18	02	51	04	84	31	76
79	72	38	16	74	54	22	00	51	22
71	17	12	26	47	03	30	51	27	95
08	64	24	69	14	90	49	53	37	89
65	79	53	49	56	27	20	15	10	59

33	13	86	60	94	48	27	27	98	84
14	78	26	31	01	57	02	92	55	81
56	57	03	39	92	45	53	36	69	25
42	54	21	57	40	71	99	66	91	48
93	10	88	86	67	14	03	16	38	89
32	61	47	42	04	94	25	65	84	76
60	44	66	51	94	34	21	32	12	86
06	70	13	90	90	05	68	01	98	87
76	38	70	73	55	62	94	24	47	06
66	22	83	26	59	77	97	79	04	97
80	38	89	80	14	96	13	64	16	12
51	16	75	12	20	77	85	30	59	76
87	74	55	86	74	38	76	81	30	94
00	16	08	49	50	55	59	33	65	93
75	61	81	62	03	92	94	27	41	67
23	87	37	06	08	56	34	86	06	86
41	48	68	45	23	89	04	83	37	38
84	34	63	36	22	31	02	53	42	53
35	20	23	20	76	56	73	88	60	17
80	49	38	13	41	00	93	37	62	53
70	35	78	06	05	91	52	81	98	14
33	14	40	54	94	39	20	69	69	15
54	42	74	80	12	98	76	28	42	91
30	55	14	38	26	06	33	44	94	24
96	28	58	93	82	45	63	13	15	79
85	46	30	34	09	39	37	55	46	01
53	57	10	83	57	51	79	05	90	76
17	19	89	90	27	01	50	84	55	09
40	09	81	67	07	32	52	40	68	71
49	17	66	61	97	30	20	66	54	53
22	32	35	81	47	32	70	73	87	77
89	97	08	70	87	39	11	40	15	46
46	74	00	02	80	39	85	92	57	65
42	75	86	23	09	75	28	28	40	73
94	43	80	48	64	63	01	02	80	22
54	72	93	31	34	07	50	42	60	66
55	16	04	74	47	21	43	16	70	89
07	92	33	15	38	36	86	79	95	71
54	11	73	86	13	49	10	10	89	36

(continued)

Random Numbers *(continued)*

05	52	32	81	69	27	76	65	87	73
93	65	64	46	20	42	68	34	85	95
09	38	86	01	19	06	94	71	04	16
71	01	97	48	42	07	38	90	53	56
37	65	03	46	22	79	31	84	70	20
04	81	54	72	34	51	85	03	07	83
13	57	23	30	11	58	68	32	83	96
67	61	33	63	86	59	14	58	99	17
60	35	99	45	88	44	76	17	69	96
22	03	82	01	22	27	58	50	89	24
87	30	73	72	02	93	22	09	27	89
99	94	97	86	75	02	95	33	44	88
45	52	41	35	79	56	51	82	60	26
41	94	12	01	61	24	15	62	89	77
52	14	05	73	11	94	46	70	97	64
60	00	84	59	49	21	31	13	02	92
39	68	23	26	03	47	31	65	19	44

Appendix B
STATISTICAL TABLES

AREAS UNDER THE NORMAL CURVE (DISTRIBUTION OF z)

After computing a z score, we can use this table to look up the percentage of the scores between that z score and the mean in a normal distribution or the percentage of scores that lie beyond that z score in a normal distribution.

The percentage of scores in the entire normal distribution is 100%, or an area of 1.00. A score that is directly at the mean would have a z score of 0.00, in the exact center of the distribution. Therefore, 0% of the scores fall between a z score of 0.00 and the mean, and 50% (i.e., half) of them fall beyond that z score.

For a z score of 1.11, using the table we can see that 36.65% of the scores fall between that z score and the mean, and 13.35% fall beyond that z score.

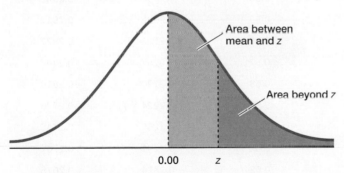

The normal distribution is symmetrical, so if our z score is negative, we use the absolute value of z to look up the relevant areas.

z SCORE	AREA BETWEEN MEAN AND z	AREA BEYOND z	z SCORE	AREA BETWEEN MEAN AND z	AREA BEYOND z
0.00	0.0000	0.5000	0.02	0.0080	0.4920
0.01	0.0040	0.4960	0.03	0.0120	0.4880

(continued)

z SCORE	AREA BETWEEN MEAN AND z	AREA BEYOND z	z SCORE	AREA BETWEEN MEAN AND z	AREA BEYOND z
0.04	0.0160	0.4840	0.37	0.1443	0.3557
0.05	0.0199	0.4801	0.38	0.1480	0.3520
0.06	0.0239	0.4761	0.39	0.1517	0.3483
0.07	0.0279	0.4721	0.40	0.1554	0.3446
0.08	0.0319	0.4681	0.41	0.1591	0.3409
0.09	0.0359	0.4641	0.42	0.1628	0.3372
0.10	0.0398	0.4602	0.43	0.1664	0.3336
0.11	0.0438	0.4562	0.44	0.1700	0.3300
0.12	0.0478	0.4522	0.45	0.1736	0.3264
0.13	0.0517	0.4483	0.46	0.1772	0.3228
0.14	0.0557	0.4443	0.47	0.1808	0.3192
0.15	0.0596	0.4404	0.48	0.1844	0.3156
0.16	0.0636	0.4364	0.49	0.1879	0.3121
0.17	0.0675	0.4325	0.50	0.1915	0.3085
0.18	0.0714	0.4286	0.51	0.1950	0.3050
0.19	0.0753	0.4247	0.52	0.1985	0.3015
0.20	0.0793	0.4207	0.53	0.2019	0.2981
0.21	0.0832	0.4168	0.54	0.2054	0.2946
0.22	0.0871	0.4129	0.55	0.2088	0.2912
0.23	0.0910	0.4090	0.56	0.2123	0.2877
0.24	0.0948	0.4052	0.57	0.2157	0.2843
0.25	0.0987	0.4013	0.58	0.2190	0.2810
0.26	0.1026	0.3974	0.59	0.2224	0.2776
0.27	0.1064	0.3936	0.60	0.2257	0.2743
0.28	0.1103	0.3897	0.61	0.2291	0.2709
0.29	0.1141	0.3859	0.62	0.2324	0.2676
0.30	0.1179	0.3821	0.63	0.2357	0.2643
0.31	0.1217	0.3783	0.64	0.2389	0.2611
0.32	0.1255	0.3745	0.65	0.2422	0.2578
0.33	0.1293	0.3707	0.66	0.2454	0.2546
0.34	0.1331	0.3669	0.67	0.2486	0.2514
0.35	0.1368	0.3632	0.68	0.2517	0.2483
0.36	0.1406	0.3594	0.69	0.2549	0.2451

z SCORE	AREA BETWEEN MEAN AND z	AREA BEYOND z	z SCORE	AREA BETWEEN MEAN AND z	AREA BEYOND z
0.70	0.2580	0.2420	1.03	0.3485	0.1515
0.71	0.2611	0.2389	1.04	0.3508	0.1492
0.72	0.2642	0.2358	1.05	0.3531	0.1469
0.73	0.2673	0.2327	1.06	0.3554	0.1446
0.74	0.2704	0.2296	1.07	0.3577	0.1423
0.75	0.2734	0.2266	1.08	0.3599	0.1401
0.76	0.2764	0.2236	1.09	0.3621	0.1379
0.77	0.2794	0.2206	1.10	0.3643	0.1357
0.78	0.2823	0.2177	1.11	0.3665	0.1335
0.79	0.2852	0.2148	1.12	0.3686	0.1314
0.80	0.2881	0.2119	1.13	0.3708	0.1292
0.81	0.2910	0.2090	1.14	0.3729	0.1271
0.82	0.2939	0.2061	1.15	0.3749	0.1251
0.83	0.2967	0.2033	1.16	0.3770	0.1230
0.84	0.2995	0.2005	1.17	0.3790	0.1210
0.85	0.3023	0.1977	1.18	0.3810	0.1190
0.86	0.3051	0.1949	1.19	0.3830	0.1170
0.87	0.3078	0.1922	1.20	0.3849	0.1151
0.88	0.3106	0.1894	1.21	0.3869	0.1131
0.89	0.3133	0.1867	1.22	0.3888	0.1112
0.90	0.3159	0.1841	1.23	0.3907	0.1093
0.91	0.3186	0.1814	1.24	0.3925	0.1075
0.92	0.3212	0.1788	1.25	0.3944	0.1056
0.93	0.3238	0.1762	1.26	0.3962	0.1038
0.94	0.3264	0.1736	1.27	0.3980	0.1020
0.95	0.3289	0.1711	1.28	0.3997	0.1003
0.96	0.3315	0.1685	1.29	0.4015	0.0985
0.97	0.3340	0.1660	1.30	0.4032	0.0968
0.98	0.3365	0.1635	1.31	0.4049	0.0951
0.99	0.3389	0.1611	1.32	0.4066	0.0934
1.00	0.3413	0.1587	1.33	0.4082	0.0918
1.01	0.3438	0.1562	1.34	0.4099	0.0901
1.02	0.3461	0.1539	1.35	0.4115	0.0885

(continued)

z SCORE	AREA BETWEEN MEAN AND z	AREA BEYOND z	z SCORE	AREA BETWEEN MEAN AND z	AREA BEYOND z
1.36	0.4131	0.0869	1.69	0.4545	0.0455
1.37	0.4147	0.0853	1.70	0.4554	0.0446
1.38	0.4162	0.0838	1.71	0.4564	0.0436
1.39	0.4177	0.0823	1.72	0.4573	0.0427
1.40	0.4192	0.0808	1.73	0.4582	0.0418
1.41	0.4207	0.0793	1.74	0.4591	0.0409
1.42	0.4222	0.0778	1.75	0.4599	0.0401
1.43	0.4236	0.0764	1.76	0.4608	0.0392
1.44	0.4251	0.0749	1.77	0.4616	0.0384
1.45	0.4265	0.0735	1.78	0.4625	0.0375
1.46	0.4279	0.0721	1.79	0.4633	0.0367
1.47	0.4292	0.0708	1.80	0.4641	0.0359
1.48	0.4306	0.0694	1.81	0.4649	0.0351
1.49	0.4319	0.0681	1.82	0.4656	0.0344
1.50	0.4332	0.0668	1.83	0.4664	0.0336
1.51	0.4345	0.0655	1.84	0.4671	0.0329
1.52	0.4357	0.0643	1.85	0.4678	0.0322
1.53	0.4370	0.0630	1.86	0.4686	0.0314
1.54	0.4382	0.0618	1.87	0.4693	0.0307
1.55	0.4394	0.0606	1.88	0.4699	0.0301
1.56	0.4406	0.0594	1.89	0.4706	0.0294
1.57	0.4418	0.0582	1.90	0.4713	0.0287
1.58	0.4429	0.0571	1.91	0.4719	0.0281
1.59	0.4441	0.0559	1.92	0.4726	0.0274
1.60	0.4452	0.0548	1.93	0.4732	0.0268
1.61	0.4463	0.0537	1.94	0.4738	0.0262
1.62	0.4474	0.0526	1.95	0.4744	0.0256
1.63	0.4484	0.0516	1.96	0.4750	0.0250
1.64	0.4495	0.0505	1.97	0.4756	0.0244
1.65	0.4505	0.0495	1.98	0.4761	0.0239
1.66	0.4515	0.0485	1.99	0.4767	0.0233
1.67	0.4525	0.0475	2.00	0.4772	0.0228
1.68	0.4535	0.0465	2.01	0.4778	0.0222

z SCORE	AREA BETWEEN MEAN AND z	AREA BEYOND z	z SCORE	AREA BETWEEN MEAN AND z	AREA BEYOND z
2.02	0.4783	0.0217	2.35	0.4906	0.0094
2.03	0.4788	0.0212	2.36	0.4909	0.0091
2.04	0.4793	0.0207	2.37	0.4911	0.0089
2.05	0.4798	0.0202	2.38	0.4913	0.0087
2.06	0.4803	0.0197	2.39	0.4916	0.0084
2.07	0.4808	0.0192	2.40	0.4918	0.0082
2.08	0.4812	0.0188	2.41	0.4920	0.0080
2.09	0.4817	0.0183	2.42	0.4922	0.0078
2.10	0.4821	0.0179	2.43	0.4925	0.0075
2.11	0.4826	0.0174	2.44	0.4927	0.0073
2.12	0.4830	0.0170	2.45	0.4929	0.0071
2.13	0.4834	0.0166	2.46	0.4931	0.0069
2.14	0.4838	0.0162	2.47	0.4932	0.0068
2.15	0.4842	0.0158	2.48	0.4934	0.0066
2.16	0.4846	0.0154	2.49	0.4936	0.0064
2.17	0.4850	0.0150	2.50	0.4938	0.0062
2.18	0.4854	0.0146	2.51	0.4940	0.0060
2.19	0.4857	0.0143	2.52	0.4941	0.0059
2.20	0.4861	0.0139	2.53	0.4943	0.0057
2.21	0.4864	0.0136	2.54	0.4945	0.0055
2.22	0.4868	0.0132	2.55	0.4946	0.0054
2.23	0.4871	0.0129	2.56	0.4948	0.0052
2.24	0.4875	0.0125	2.57	0.4949	0.0051
2.25	0.4878	0.0122	2.58	0.4950	0.0050
2.26	0.4881	0.0119	2.59	0.4952	0.0048
2.27	0.4884	0.0116	2.60	0.4953	0.0047
2.28	0.4887	0.0113	2.61	0.4955	0.0045
2.29	0.4890	0.0110	2.62	0.4956	0.0044
2.30	0.4893	0.0107	2.63	0.4957	0.0043
2.31	0.4896	0.0104	2.64	0.4959	0.0041
2.32	0.4898	0.0102	2.65	0.4960	0.0040
2.33	0.4901	0.0099	2.66	0.4961	0.0039
2.34	0.4904	0.0096	2.67	0.4962	0.0038

(continued)

z SCORE	AREA BETWEEN MEAN AND z	AREA BEYOND z	z SCORE	AREA BETWEEN MEAN AND z	AREA BEYOND z
2.68	0.4963	0.0037	3.02	0.4987	0.0013
2.69	0.4964	0.0036	3.03	0.4988	0.0012
2.70	0.4965	0.0035	3.04	0.4988	0.0012
2.71	0.4966	0.0034	3.05	0.4989	0.0011
2.72	0.4967	0.0033	3.06	0.4989	0.0011
2.73	0.4968	0.0032	3.07	0.4989	0.0011
2.74	0.4969	0.0031	3.08	0.4990	0.0010
2.75	0.4970	0.0030	3.09	0.4990	0.0010
2.76	0.4971	0.0029	3.10	0.4990	0.0010
2.77	0.4972	0.0028	3.11	0.4991	0.0009
2.78	0.4973	0.0027	3.12	0.4991	0.0009
2.79	0.4974	0.0026	3.13	0.4991	0.0009
2.80	0.4974	0.0026	3.14	0.4992	0.0008
2.81	0.4975	0.0025	3.15	0.4992	0.0008
2.82	0.4976	0.0024	3.16	0.4992	0.0008
2.83	0.4977	0.0023	3.17	0.4992	0.0008
2.84	0.4977	0.0023	3.18	0.4993	0.0007
2.85	0.4978	0.0022	3.19	0.4993	0.0007
2.86	0.4979	0.0021	3.20	0.4993	0.0007
2.87	0.4979	0.0021	3.21	0.4993	0.0007
2.88	0.4980	0.0020	3.22	0.4994	0.0006
2.89	0.4981	0.0019	3.23	0.4994	0.0006
2.90	0.4981	0.0019	3.24	0.4994	0.0006
2.91	0.4982	0.0018	3.25	0.4994	0.0006
2.92	0.4982	0.0018	3.26	0.4994	0.0006
2.93	0.4983	0.0017	3.27	0.4995	0.0005
2.94	0.4984	0.0016	3.28	0.4995	0.0005
2.95	0.4984	0.0016	3.29	0.4995	0.0005
2.96	0.4985	0.0015	3.30	0.4995	0.0005
2.97	0.4985	0.0015	3.31	0.4995	0.0005
2.98	0.4986	0.0014	3.32	0.4995	0.0005
2.99	0.4986	0.0014	3.33	0.4996	0.0004
3.00	0.4987	0.0013	3.34	0.4996	0.0004
3.01	0.4987	0.0013	3.35	0.4996	0.0004

z SCORE	AREA BETWEEN MEAN AND z	AREA BEYOND z	z SCORE	AREA BETWEEN MEAN AND z	AREA BEYOND z
3.36	0.4996	0.0004	3.51	0.4998	0.0002
3.37	0.4996	0.0004	3.52	0.4998	0.0002
3.38	0.4996	0.0004	3.53	0.4998	0.0002
3.39	0.4997	0.0003	3.54	0.4998	0.0002
3.40	0.4997	0.0003	3.55	0.4998	0.0002
3.41	0.4997	0.0003	3.56	0.4998	0.0002
3.42	0.4997	0.0003	3.57	0.4998	0.0002
3.43	0.4997	0.0003	3.58	0.4998	0.0002
3.44	0.4997	0.0003	3.59	0.4998	0.0002
3.45	0.4997	0.0003	3.60	0.4998	0.0002
3.46	0.4997	0.0003	3.70	0.4999	0.0001
3.47	0.4997	0.0003	3.80	0.4999	0.0001
3.48	0.4997	0.0003	3.90	0.49995	0.00005
3.49	0.4998	0.0002	4.00	0.49997	0.00003
3.50	0.4998	0.0002			

Note: This table is included for basic statistical reference. It is not discussed in detail in this book.

CRITICAL VALUES OF *t*

To use this table, we first decide whether a one- or a two-tailed test is appropriate. We decide the level of significance. Then we read down the corresponding column to the number of degrees of freedom. The tabled entry gives the value of *t* that must be *exceeded* in order to be significant. For example, if we do a two-tailed test with 20 degrees of freedom, our *t* must be greater than 2.086 to be significant at the 0.05 level.

df	ONE-TAILED TESTS			TWO-TAILED TESTS		
	.10	.05	.01	.10	.05	.01
1	3.078	6.314	31.821	6.314	12.706	63.657
2	1.886	2.920	6.965	2.920	4.303	9.925
3	1.638	2.353	4.541	2.353	3.182	5.841
4	1.533	2.132	3.747	2.132	2.776	4.604
5	1.476	2.015	3.365	2.015	2.571	4.032
6	1.440	1.943	3.143	1.943	2.447	3.708

(continued)

	ONE-TAILED TESTS			TWO-TAILED TESTS		
df	.10	.05	.01	.10	.05	.01
7	1.415	1.895	2.998	1.895	2.365	3.500
8	1.397	1.860	2.897	1.860	2.306	3.356
9	1.383	1.833	2.822	1.833	2.262	3.250
10	1.372	1.813	2.764	1.813	2.228	3.170
11	1.364	1.796	2.718	1.796	2.201	3.106
12	1.356	1.783	2.681	1.783	2.179	3.055
13	1.350	1.771	2.651	1.771	2.161	3.013
14	1.345	1.762	2.625	1.762	2.145	2.977
15	1.341	1.753	2.603	1.753	2.132	2.947
16	1.337	1.746	2.584	1.746	2.120	2.921
17	1.334	1.740	2.567	1.740	2.110	2.898
18	1.331	1.734	2.553	1.734	2.101	2.897
19	1.328	1.729	2.540	1.729	2.093	2.861
20	1.326	1.725	2.528	1.725	2.086	2.846
21	1.323	1.721	2.518	1.721	2.080	2.832
22	1.321	1.717	2.509	1.717	2.074	2.819
23	1.320	1.714	2.500	1.714	2.069	2.808
24	1.318	1.711	2.492	1.711	2.064	2.797
25	1.317	1.708	2.485	1.708	2.060	2.788
26	1.315	1.706	2.479	1.706	2.056	2.779
27	1.314	1.704	2.473	1.704	2.052	2.771
28	1.313	1.701	2.467	1.701	2.049	2.764
29	1.312	1.699	2.462	1.699	2.045	2.757
30	1.311	1.697	2.458	1.698	2.042	2.750
35	1.306	1.690	2.438	1.690	2.030	2.724
40	1.303	1.684	2.424	1.684	2.021	2.705
45	1.301	1.680	2.412	1.680	2.014	2.690
50	1.299	1.676	2.404	1.676	2.009	2.678

df	ONE-TAILED TESTS			TWO-TAILED TESTS		
	.10	.05	.01	.10	.05	.01
55	1.297	1.673	2.396	1.673	2.004	2.668
60	1.296	1.671	2.390	1.671	2.001	2.661
65	1.295	1.669	2.385	1.669	1.997	2.654
70	1.294	1.667	2.381	1.667	1.995	2.648
75	1.293	1.666	2.377	1.666	1.992	2.643
80	1.292	1.664	2.374	1.664	1.990	2.639
85	1.292	1.663	2.371	1.663	1.989	2.635
90	1.291	1.662	2.369	1.662	1.987	2.632
95	1.291	1.661	2.366	1.661	1.986	2.629
100	1.290	1.660	2.364	1.660	1.984	2.626
∞	1.282	1.645	2.327	1.645	1.960	2.576

CRITICAL VALUES OF F

This table can handle up to seven independent treatment groups. To use it, we decide our level of significance (.01, .05, or .10). We determine degrees of freedom for the numerator (number of conditions minus 1) and degrees of freedom for the denominator (sum of the number of subjects, minus 1 in each group). The table then gives the value of F that must be *exceeded* to be significant at the specified level.

Thus, if we have three treatment groups with 10 subjects each, we have 2 *df* for the numerator and 9 + 9 + 9 = 27 *df* for the denominator. If we set our significance criterion at .05, we need an F larger than 3.36 to reject the null hypothesis.

DENOMINATOR df	SIGNIFICANCE LEVEL	NUMERATOR DEGREES OF FREEDOM					
		1	2	3	4	5	6
1	.01	4,052	5,000	5,404	5,625	5,764	5,859
	.05	162	200	216	225	230	234
	.10	39.9	49.5	53.6	55.8	57.2	58.2
2	.01	98.50	99.00	99.17	99.25	99.30	99.33
	.05	18.51	19.00	19.17	19.25	19.30	19.33
	.10	8.53	9.00	9.16	9.24	9.29	9.33

(continued)

DENOMINATOR df	SIGNIFICANCE LEVEL	NUMERATOR DEGREES OF FREEDOM					
		1	2	3	4	5	6
3	.01	34.12	30.82	29.46	28.71	28.24	27.91
	.05	10.13	9.55	9.28	9.12	9.01	8.94
	.10	5.54	5.46	5.39	5.34	5.31	5.28
4	.01	21.20	18.00	16.70	15.98	15.52	15.21
	.05	7.71	6.95	6.59	6.39	6.26	6.16
	.10	4.55	4.33	4.19	4.11	4.05	4.01
5	.01	16.26	13.27	12.06	11.39	10.97	10.67
	.05	6.61	5.79	5.41	5.19	5.05	4.95
	.10	4.06	3.78	3.62	3.52	3.45	3.41
6	.01	13.75	10.93	9.78	9.15	8.75	8.47
	.05	5.99	5.14	4.76	4.53	4.39	4.28
	.10	3.78	3.46	3.29	3.18	3.11	3.06
7	.01	12.25	9.55	8.45	7.85	7.46	7.19
	.05	5.59	4.74	4.35	4.12	3.97	3.87
	.10	3.59	3.26	3.08	2.96	2.88	2.83
8	.01	11.26	8.65	7.59	7.01	6.63	6.37
	.05	5.32	4.46	4.07	3.84	3.69	3.58
	.10	3.46	3.11	2.92	2.81	2.73	2.67
9	.01	10.56	8.02	6.99	6.42	6.06	5.80
	.05	5.12	4.26	3.86	3.63	3.48	3.37
	.10	3.36	3.01	2.81	2.69	2.61	2.55
10	.01	10.05	7.56	6.55	6.00	5.64	5.39
	.05	4.97	4.10	3.71	3.48	3.33	3.22
	.10	3.29	2.93	2.73	2.61	2.52	2.46
11	.01	9.65	7.21	6.22	5.67	5.32	5.07
	.05	4.85	3.98	3.59	3.36	3.20	3.10
	.10	3.23	2.86	2.66	2.55	2.45	2.39
12	.01	9.33	6.93	5.95	5.41	5.07	4.82
	.05	4.75	3.89	3.49	3.26	3.11	3.00
	.10	3.18	2.81	2.61	2.48	2.40	2.33

DENOMINATOR df	SIGNIFICANCE LEVEL	NUMERATOR DEGREES OF FREEDOM					
		1	2	3	4	5	6
13	.01	9.07	6.70	5.74	5.21	4.86	4.62
	.05	4.67	3.81	3.41	3.18	3.03	2.92
	.10	3.14	2.76	2.56	2.43	2.35	2.28
14	.01	8.86	6.52	5.56	5.04	4.70	4.46
	.05	4.60	3.74	3.34	3.11	2.96	2.85
	.10	3.10	2.73	2.52	2.40	2.31	2.24
15	.01	8.68	6.36	5.42	4.89	4.56	4.32
	.05	4.54	3.68	3.29	3.06	2.90	2.79
	.10	3.07	2.70	2.49	2.36	2.27	2.21
16	.01	8.53	6.23	5.29	4.77	4.44	4.30
	.05	4.49	3.63	3.24	3.01	2.85	2.74
	.10	3.05	2.67	2.46	2.33	2.24	2.18
17	.01	8.40	6.11	5.19	4.67	4.34	4.10
	.05	4.45	3.59	3.20	2.97	2.81	2.70
	.10	3.03	2.65	2.44	2.31	2.22	2.15
18	.01	8.29	6.01	5.09	4.58	4.25	4.02
	.05	4.41	3.56	3.16	2.93	2.77	2.66
	.10	3.01	2.62	2.42	2.29	2.20	2.13
19	.01	8.19	5.93	5.01	4.50	4.17	3.94
	.05	4.38	3.52	3.13	2.90	2.74	2.63
	.10	2.91	2.61	2.40	2.27	2.18	2.11
20	.01	8.10	5.85	4.94	4.43	4.10	3.87
	.05	4.35	3.49	3.10	2.87	2.71	2.60
	.10	2.98	2.59	2.38	2.25	2.16	2.09
21	.01	8.02	5.78	4.88	4.37	4.04	3.81
	.05	4.33	3.47	3.07	2.84	2.69	2.57
	.10	2.96	2.58	2.37	2.23	2.14	2.08

(continued)

DENOMINATOR df	SIGNIFICANCE LEVEL	NUMERATOR DEGREES OF FREEDOM					
		1	2	3	4	5	6
22	.01	7.95	5.72	4.82	4.31	3.99	3.76
	.05	4.30	3.44	3.05	2.82	2.66	2.55
	.10	2.95	2.56	2.35	2.22	2.13	2.06
23	.01	7.88	5.66	4.77	4.26	3.94	3.71
	.05	4.28	3.42	3.03	2.80	2.64	2.53
	.10	2.94	2.55	2.34	2.21	2.12	2.05
24	.01	7.82	5.61	4.72	4.22	3.90	3.67
	.05	4.26	3.40	3.01	2.78	2.62	2.51
	.10	2.93	2.54	2.33	2.20	2.10	2.04
25	.01	7.77	5.57	4.68	4.18	3.86	3.63
	.05	4.24	3.39	2.99	2.76	2.60	2.49
	.10	2.92	2.53	2.32	2.19	2.09	2.03
26	.01	7.72	5.53	4.64	4.14	3.82	3.59
	.05	4.23	3.37	2.98	2.74	2.59	2.48
	.10	2.91	2.52	2.31	2.18	2.08	2.01
27	.01	7.68	5.49	4.60	4.11	3.79	3.56
	.05	4.21	3.36	2.96	2.73	2.57	2.46
	.10	2.90	2.51	2.30	2.17	2.07	2.01
28	.01	7.64	5.45	4.57	4.08	3.75	3.53
	.05	4.20	3.34	2.95	2.72	2.56	2.45
	.10	2.89	2.50	2.29	2.16	2.07	2.00
29	.01	7.60	5.42	4.54	4.05	3.73	3.50
	.05	4.18	3.33	2.94	2.70	2.55	2.43
	.10	2.89	2.50	2.28	2.15	2.06	1.99
30	.01	7.56	5.39	4.51	4.02	3.70	3.47
	.05	4.17	3.32	2.92	2.69	2.53	2.42
	.10	2.88	2.49	2.28	2.14	2.05	1.98
35	.01	7.42	5.27	4.40	3.91	3.59	3.37
	.05	4.12	3.27	2.88	2.64	2.49	2.37
	.10	2.86	2.46	2.25	2.11	2.02	1.95

DENOMINATOR df	SIGNIFICANCE LEVEL	NUMERATOR DEGREES OF FREEDOM					
		1	2	3	4	5	6
40	.01	7.32	5.18	4.31	3.83	3.51	3.29
	.05	4.09	3.23	2.84	2.61	2.45	2.34
	.10	2.84	2.44	2.23	2.09	2.00	1.93
45	.01	7.23	5.11	4.25	3.77	3.46	3.23
	.05	4.06	3.21	2.81	2.58	2.42	2.31
	.10	2.82	2.43	2.21	2.08	1.98	1.91
50	.01	7.17	5.06	4.20	3.72	3.41	3.19
	.05	4.04	3.18	2.79	2.56	2.40	2.29
	.10	2.81	2.41	2.20	2.06	1.97	1.90
55	.01	7.12	5.01	4.16	3.68	3.37	3.15
	.05	4.02	3.17	2.77	2.54	2.38	2.27
	.10	2.80	2.40	2.19	2.05	1.96	1.89
60	.01	7.08	4.98	4.13	3.65	3.34	3.12
	.05	4.00	3.15	2.76	2.53	2.37	2.26
	.10	2.79	2.39	2.18	2.04	1.95	1.88
65	.01	7.04	4.95	4.10	3.62	3.31	3.09
	.05	3.99	3.14	2.75	2.51	2.36	2.24
	.10	2.79	2.39	2.17	2.03	1.94	1.87
70	.01	7.01	4.92	4.08	3.60	3.29	3.07
	.05	3.98	3.13	2.74	2.50	2.35	2.23
	.10	2.78	2.38	2.16	2.03	1.93	1.86
75	.01	6.99	4.90	4.06	3.58	3.27	3.05
	.05	3.97	3.12	2.73	2.49	2.34	2.22
	.10	2.77	2.38	2.16	2.02	1.93	1.86
80	.01	6.96	4.88	4.04	3.56	3.26	3.04
	.05	3.96	3.11	2.72	2.49	2.33	2.22
	.10	2.77	2.37	2.15	2.02	1.92	1.85
85	.01	6.94	4.86	4.02	3.55	3.24	3.02
	.05	3.95	3.10	2.71	2.48	2.32	2.21

(continued)

DENOMINATOR df	SIGNIFICANCE LEVEL	NUMERATOR DEGREES OF FREEDOM					
		1	2	3	4	5	6
	.10	2.77	2.37	2.15	2.01	1.92	1.85
90	.01	6.93	4.85	4.01	3.54	3.23	3.01
	.05	3.95	3.10	2.71	2.47	2.32	2.20
	.10	2.76	2.36	2.15	2.01	1.91	1.84

r TO *z'* CONVERSION

r	z'	r	z'	r	z'
0.00	0.0000	0.21	0.2132	0.42	0.4477
0.01	0.0100	0.22	0.2237	0.43	0.4599
0.02	0.0200	0.23	0.2342	0.44	0.4722
0.03	0.0300	0.24	0.2448	0.45	0.4847
0.04	0.0400	0.25	0.2554	0.46	0.4973
0.05	0.0500	0.26	0.2661	0.47	0.5101
0.06	0.0601	0.27	0.2769	0.48	0.5230
0.07	0.0701	0.28	0.2877	0.49	0.5361
0.08	0.0802	0.29	0.2986	0.50	0.5493
0.09	0.0902	0.30	0.3095	0.51	0.5627
0.10	0.1003	0.31	0.3205	0.52	0.5763
0.11	0.1104	0.32	0.3316	0.53	0.5901
0.12	0.1206	0.33	0.3428	0.54	0.6042
0.13	0.1307	0.34	0.3541	0.55	0.6184
0.14	0.1409	0.35	0.3654	0.56	0.6328
0.15	0.1511	0.36	0.3769	0.57	0.6475
0.16	0.1614	0.37	0.3884	0.58	0.6625
0.17	0.1717	0.38	0.4001	0.59	0.6777
0.18	0.1820	0.39	0.4118	0.60	0.6931
0.19	0.1923	0.40	0.4236	0.61	0.7089
0.20	0.2027	0.41	0.4356	0.62	0.7250

r	z'	r	z'	r	z'
0.63	0.7414	0.76	0.9962	0.89	1.4219
0.64	0.7582	0.77	1.0203	0.90	1.4722
0.65	0.7753	0.78	1.0454	0.91	1.5275
0.66	0.7928	0.79	1.0714	0.92	1.5890
0.67	0.8107	0.80	1.0986	0.93	1.6584
0.68	0.8291	0.81	1.1270	0.94	1.7380
0.69	0.8480	0.82	1.1568	0.95	1.8318
0.70	0.8673	0.83	1.1881	0.96	1.9459
0.71	0.8872	0.84	1.2212	0.97	2.0923
0.72	0.9076	0.85	1.2562	0.98	2.2976
0.73	0.9287	0.86	1.2933	0.99	2.6467
0.74	0.9505	0.87	1.3331		
0.75	0.9730	0.88	1.3758		

Note: This table is included for basic statistical reference. Its use is not discussed in detail in this book.

CRITICAL VALUES OF r

To use this table, first decide whether a one- or a two-tailed test is appropriate. Then decide the level of significance. Read down the corresponding column to the row associated with the number of degrees of freedom in the correlation (the number of pairs of scores minus 2). The table entry gives the value of r that must be exceeded in order to be significant. If the obtained r is negative, use the absolute value of it. For example, if we do a two-tailed test with 40 degrees of freedom, our r must be more extreme than .304 (or −.304) to be significant at the .05 level.

	LEVEL OF SIGFINICANCE FOR A ONE-TAILED TEST				
	.10	.05	.025	.01	.0005
	LEVEL OF SIGFINICANCE FOR A TWO-TAILED TEST				
df	.20	.10	.05	.02	.001
1	.951	.988	.997	.9995	.99999
2	.800	.900	.950	.980	.999
3	.687	.805	.878	.934	.991
4	.608	.729	.811	.882	.974
5	.551	.669	.755	.833	.951

(continued)

	LEVEL OF SIGFINICANCE FOR A ONE-TAILED TEST				
	.10	.05	.025	.01	.0005
	LEVEL OF SIGFINICANCE FOR A TWO-TAILED TEST				
df	.20	.10	.05	.02	.001
6	.507	.621	.707	.789	.925
7	.472	.582	.666	.750	.898
8	.443	.549	.632	.715	.872
9	.419	.521	.602	.685	.847
10	.398	.497	.576	.658	.823
11	.380	.476	.553	.634	.801
12	.365	.457	.532	.612	.780
13	.351	.441	.514	.592	.760
14	.338	.426	.497	.574	.742
15	.327	.412	.482	.558	.725
16	.317	.400	.468	.542	.708
17	.308	.389	.456	.529	.693
18	.299	.378	.444	.515	.679
19	.291	.369	.433	.503	.665
20	.284	.360	.423	.492	.652
21	.277	.352	.413	.482	.640
22	.271	.344	.404	.472	.629
23	.265	.337	.396	.462	.618
24	.260	.330	.388	.453	.607
25	.255	.323	.381	.445	.597
26	.250	.317	.374	.437	.588
27	.245	.311	.367	.430	.579
28	.241	.306	.361	.423	.570
29	.237	.301	.355	.416	.562
30	.233	.296	.349	.409	.554
40	.202	.257	.304	.358	.490
60	.165	.211	.250	.295	.408
120	.117	.150	.178	.210	.294
500	.057	.073	.087	.103	.146

Note: This table is included for basic statistical reference. Its use is not discussed in detail in this book.

Glossary

A

acquiescence Answering "yes" or "strongly agree" to every item in a survey or interview. Also called *yea-saying*.

alpha level The value, determined in advance, at which researchers decide whether the *p* value obtained from a sample statistic is low enough to reject the null hypothesis or too high, and thus retain the null hypothesis.

anonymous study A research study in which identifying information is not collected, thereby completely protecting the identity of participants. *See also* confidential study.

applied research Research whose goal is to find a solution to a particular real-world problem. *See also* basic research, translational research.

association claim A claim about two variables, in which the value (level) of one variable is said to vary systematically with the value of another variable.

attrition threat In a pretest/posttest, repeated-measures, or quasi-experimental study, a threat to internal validity that occurs when a systematic type of participant drops out of the study before it ends.

autocorrelation In a longitudinal design, the correlation of one variable with itself, measured at two different times.

availability heuristic A bias in intuition, in which people incorrectly estimate the frequency of something, relying predominantly on instances that easily come to mind rather than using all possible evidence in evaluating a conclusion.

B

basic research Research whose goal is to enhance the general body of knowledge, without regard for direct application to practical problems. *See also* applied research, translational research.

beneficence *See* principle of beneficence.

bias blind spot The tendency for people to think that compared to others, they themselves are less likely to engage in biased reasoning.

biased sample A sample in which some members of the population of interest are systematically left out, and therefore the results cannot generalize to the population of interest. Also called *unrepresentative sample*. *See also* unbiased sample.

bimodal Having two modes, or most common scores.

bivariate correlation An association that involves exactly two variables. Also called *bivariate association*.

C

carryover effect A type of order effect, in which some form of contamination carries over from one condition to the next.

categorical variable A variable whose levels are categories (e.g., male and female). Also called *nominal variable*.

causal claim A claim arguing that a specific change in one variable is responsible for influencing the value of another variable.

ceiling effect An experimental design problem in which independent variable groups score almost the same on a dependent variable, such that all scores fall at the high end of their possible distribution. *See also* floor effect.

cell A condition in an experiment; in a simple experiment, a cell can represent the level of one independent variable; in a factorial design, a cell represents one of the possible combinations of two independent variables.

census A set of observations that contains all members of the population of interest.

central tendency A value that the individual scores in a data set tend to center on. *See also* mean, median, mode.

claim The argument a journalist, researcher, or scientist is trying to make.

cluster sampling A probability sampling technique in which clusters of participants within the population of interest are selected at random, followed by data collection from all individuals in each cluster.

Cohen's _d_ A measure of effect size indicating how far apart two group means are, in standard deviation units.

comparison group A group in an experiment whose levels on the independent variable differ from those of the treatment group in some intended and meaningful way. Also called _comparison condition_.

conceptual definition A researcher's definition of a variable at the theoretical level. Also called _construct_. _See also_ conceptual variable.

conceptual replication A replication study in which researchers examine the same research question (the same conceptual variables) but use different procedures for operationalizing the variables. _See also_ direct replication, replication-plus-extension.

conceptual variable A variable of interest, stated at an abstract, or conversational, level. Also called _construct_. _See also_ conceptual definition.

concurrent-measures design An experiment using a within-groups design in which participants are exposed to all the levels of an independent variable at roughly the same time, and a single attitudinal or behavioral preference is the dependent variable.

condition One of the levels of the independent variable in an experiment.

confederate An actor who is directed by the researcher to play a specific role in a research study.

confidence interval An inferential statistic, providing a range of values that has a high probability of containing the true population value.

confidential study A research study in which identifying information is collected, but protected from disclosure to people other than the researchers. _See also_ anonymous study.

confirmation bias The tendency to consider only the evidence that supports a hypothesis, including asking only the questions that will lead to the expected answer.

confound A general term for a potential alternative explanation for a research finding; a threat to internal validity.

constant An attribute that could potentially vary but that has only one level in the study in question.

construct A variable of interest, stated at an abstract level, usually defined as part of a formal statement of a psychological theory. _See also_ conceptual variable.

construct validity An indication of how well a variable was measured or manipulated in a study.

content validity The extent to which a measure captures all parts of a defined construct.

control for Holding a potential third variable at a constant level (statistically or experimentally) while investigating the association between two other variables. _See also_ control variable, multiple regression.

control group A level of an independent variable that is intended to represent "no treatment" or a neutral condition. _Also called_ control condition.

control variable In an experiment, a variable that a researcher holds constant on purpose.

convenience sampling Choosing a sample based on those who are easiest to access and readily available; a biased sampling technique.

convergent validity An empirical test of the extent to which a self-report measure correlates with other measures of a theoretically similar construct. _See also_ discriminant validity.

correlate To occur or vary together (covary) systematically, as in the case of two variables. _See also_ correlational study, covariance.

correlation coefficient _r_ A single number, ranging from –1.0 to 1.0, that indicates the strength and direction of an association between two variables.

correlational study A study that includes two or more variables, in which all of the variables are measured; can support an association claim.

counterbalancing In a repeated-measures experiment, presenting the levels of the independent variable to participants in different sequences to control for order effects. _See also_ full counterbalancing, partial counterbalancing.

covariance The degree to which two variables go together. Also one of three criteria for establishing a causal claim, which states that, in a study's results, the proposed causal variable must vary systematically with changes in the proposed outcome variable. _See also_ internal validity, temporal precedence.

criterion validity An empirical form of measurement validity that establishes the extent to which a measure is associated with a behavioral outcome with which it should be associated.

criterion variable The variable in a multiple-regression analysis that the researchers are most interested in understanding or predicting. Also called _dependent variable_.

critical value A value of a statistic that is associated with a desired alpha level.

Cronbach's alpha A correlation-based statistic that measures a scale's internal reliability. Also called _coefficient alpha_.

cross-lag correlation In a longitudinal design, a correlation between an earlier measure of one variable and a later measure of another variable.

cross-sectional correlation In a longitudinal design, a correlation between two variables that are measured at the same time.

cultural psychology A subdiscipline of psychology concerned with how cultural settings shape a person's thoughts, feelings, and behavior, and how these in turn shape cultural settings.

curvilinear association An association between two variables which is not a straight line; instead, as one variable increases, the level of the other variable increases and then decreases (or vice versa). *See also* positive association, negative association, zero association.

D

data (plural; singular **datum**) A set of observations representing the values of some variable, collected from one or more research studies.

data fabrication A form of research misconduct in which a researcher invents data that fit the hypothesis.

data falsification A form of research misconduct in which a researcher influences a study's results, perhaps by deleting observations from a data set or by influencing participants to act in the hypothesized way.

data matrix A grid presenting collected data.

debrief To inform participants afterward about a study's true nature, details, and hypotheses.

deception The withholding of some details of a study from participants (deception through omission) or the act of actively lying to them (deception through commission).

demand characteristic A cue that leads participants to guess a study's hypotheses or goals; a threat to internal validity. Also called *experimental demand*.

dependent variable In an experiment, the variable that is measured. In a multiple-regression analysis, the single outcome, or criterion variable, the researchers are most interested in understanding or predicting. Also called *outcome variable*. *See also* independent variable.

descriptive statistics A set of statistics used to organize and summarize the properties of a set of data.

design confound A threat to internal validity in an experiment in which a second variable happens to vary systematically along with the independent variable and therefore is an alternative explanation for the results.

direct replication A replication study in which researchers repeat the original study as closely as possible to see whether the original effect shows up in the newly collected data. *See also* conceptual replication, replication-plus-extension.

directionality problem In a correlational study, the occurrence of both variables being measured around the same time, making it unclear which variable in the association came first. *See also* temporal precedence.

discriminant validity An empirical test of the extent to which a self-report measure does not correlate strongly with measures of theoretically dissimilar constructs. Also called *divergent validity*. *See also* convergent validity.

double-barreled question A type of question in a survey or poll that is problematic because it asks two questions in one, thereby weakening its construct validity.

double-blind placebo control study A study that uses a treatment group and a placebo group and in which neither the researchers nor the participants know who is in which group.

double-blind study A study in which neither the participants nor the researchers who evaluate them know who is in the treatment group and who is in the comparison group.

E

ecological validity The extent to which the tasks and manipulations of a study are similar to real-world contexts; an aspect of external validity. Also called *mundane realism*.

effect size The magnitude, or strength, of a relationship between two or more variables.

empirical journal article A scholarly article that reports for the first time the results of a research study.

empiricism The use of verifiable evidence as the basis for conclusions; collecting data systematically and using it to develop, support, or challenge a theory. Also called *empirical method* or *empirical research*.

evidence-based treatment A psychotherapy technique whose effectiveness has been supported by empirical research.

experiment A study in which one variable is manipulated and the other is measured.

experimental realism The extent to which a laboratory experiment is designed so that participants experience authentic emotions, motivations, and behaviors.

external validity An indication of how well the results of a study generalize to, or represent, individuals or contexts besides those in the study itself. *See also* generalizability.

F

face validity The extent to which a measure is subjectively considered a plausible operationalization of the conceptual variable in question.

factorial design A study in which there are two or more independent variables, or factors.

faking bad Giving answers on a survey (or other self-report measure) that make one look worse than one really is.

faking good *See* socially desirable responding.

falsifiability A feature of a scientific theory, in which it is possible to collect data that will indicate that the theory is wrong.

fence sitting Playing it safe by answering in the middle of the scale for every question in a survey or interview.

field setting A real-world setting for a research study.

file drawer problem A problem relating to literature reviews and meta-analyses based only on published literature, which might overestimate the support for a theory because studies finding null effects are less likely to be published than studies finding significant results, and are thus less likely to be included in such reviews.

floor effect An experimental design problem in which independent variable groups score almost the same on a dependent variable, such that all scores fall at the low end of their possible distribution. *See also* ceiling effect.

forced-choice question A survey question format in which respondents give their opinion by picking the best of two or more options.

frequency claim A claim that describes a particular rate or degree of a single variable.

frequency distribution A table showing how many of the cases in a batch of data scored each possible value, or range of values, on the variable.

frequency histogram A graph showing how many of the cases in a batch of data scored each possible value, or range of values, on the variable.

F test A statistical test based on analysis of variance that determines the degree of difference among two or more group means.

full counterbalancing A method of counterbalancing in which all possible condition orders are represented. *See also* counterbalancing, partial counterbalancing.

G

generalizability The extent to which the subjects in a study represent the populations they are intended to represent; how well the settings in a study represent other settings or contexts.

generalization mode The intent of researchers to generalize the findings from the samples and procedures in their study to other populations or contexts. *See also* theory-testing mode.

H

history threat A threat to internal validity that occurs when it is unclear whether a change in the treatment group is caused by the treatment itself or by an external or historical factor that affects most members of the group.

hypothesis A statement of the specific result the researcher expects to observe from a particular study, if the theory is accurate. Also called *prediction*.

I

independent-groups design An experimental design in which different groups of participants are exposed to different levels of the independent variable, such that each participant experiences only one level of the independent variable. Also called *between-subjects design* or *between-groups design*.

independent variable In an experiment, a variable that is manipulated. In a multiple-regression analysis, a predictor variable used to explain variance in the criterion variable. *See also* dependent variable.

inferential statistics A set of techniques that uses the laws of chance and probability to help researchers make decisions about what their data mean and what inferences they can make from them.

informed consent The right of research participants to learn about a research project, know its risks and benefits, and decide whether to participate.

institutional review board (IRB) A committee responsible for ensuring that research using human participants is conducted ethically.

instrumentation threat A threat to internal validity that occurs when a measuring instrument changes over time.

interaction effect A result from a factorial design, in which the difference in the levels of one independent variable changes, depending on the level of the other independent variable; a difference in differences. Also called *interaction*.

internal reliability In a measure that contains several items, the consistency in a pattern of answers, no matter how a question is phrased. Also called *internal consistency*.

internal validity One of three criteria for establishing a causal claim; a study's ability to rule out alternative explanations for a causal relationship between two variables. Also called *third-variable criterion*. *See also* covariance, temporal precedence.

interrater reliability The degree to which two or more coders or observers give consistent ratings of a set of targets.

interrupted time-series design A quasi-experiment in which participants are measured repeatedly on a dependent variable before, during, and after the "interruption" caused by some event.

interval scale A quantitative measurement scale that has no "true zero," and in which the numerals represent equal intervals (distances) between levels (e.g., temperature in degrees). *See also* ordinal scale, ratio scale.

J

journal A monthly or quarterly periodical containing peer-reviewed articles on a specific academic discipline or subdiscipline, written for a scholarly audience.

journalism News and commentary published or broadcast in the popular media and produced for a general audience.

justice *See* principle of justice.

K

known-groups paradigm A method for establishing criterion validity, in which a researcher tests two or more groups who are known to differ on the variable of interest, to ensure that they score differently on a measure of that variable.

L

Latin square A formal system of partial counterbalancing to ensure that every condition in a within-groups design appears in each position at least once.

leading question A type of question in a survey or poll that is problematic because its wording encourages one response more than others, thereby weakening its construct validity.

level One of the possible variations, or values, of a variable. Also called *condition*.

Likert scale A survey question format using a rating scale containing multiple response options anchored by the specific terms *strongly agree, agree, neither agree nor disagree, disagree,* and *strongly disagree.* A scale that does not follow this format exactly is called a *Likert type scale*.

longitudinal design A study in which the same variables are measured in the same people at different points in time.

M

main effect In a factorial design, the overall effect of one independent variable on the dependent variable, averaging over the levels of the other independent variable.

manipulated variable A variable in an experiment that a researcher controls, such as by assigning participants to its different levels (values). *See also* measured variable.

manipulation check In an experiment, an extra dependent variable researchers can include to determine how well a manipulation worked.

margin of error of the estimate A statistic, based in part on sample size, indicating the probable true value of a percentage estimate in the population.

marginal means In a factorial design, the arithmetic means for each level of an independent variable, averaging over the levels of another independent variable.

masked design A study design in which the observers are unaware of the experimental conditions to which participants have been assigned. Also called *blind design*.

matched groups An experimental design technique in which participants who are similar on some measured variable are grouped into sets; the members of each matched set are then randomly assigned to different experimental conditions. Also called *matching*.

maturation threat A threat to internal validity that occurs when an observed change in an experimental group could have emerged more or less spontaneously over time.

mean An arithmethic average; a measure of central tendency computed from the sum of all the scores in a set of data, divided by the total number of scores.

measured variable A variable in a study whose levels (values) are observed and recorded. *See also* manipulated variable.

measurement error The degree to which the recorded measure for a participant on some variable differs from the true value of the variable for that participant. Measurement errors may be random, such that scores that are too high and too low cancel each other out; or they may be systematic, such that most scores are biased too high or too low.

median A measure of central tendency that is the value at the middlemost score of a distribution of scores, dividing the frequency distribution into halves.

mediator A variable that helps explain the relationship between two other variables. Also called *mediating variable*.

meta-analysis A way of mathematically averaging the effect sizes of all the studies that have tested the same variables to see what conclusion that whole body of evidence supports.

mode A measure of central tendency that is the most common score in a set of data.

moderator A variable that, depending on its level, changes the relationship between two other variables.

multimodal Having two or more modes, or most common scores.

multiple-baseline design A small-*N* design in which researchers stagger their introduction of an intervention across a variety of contexts, times, or situations.

multiple regression A statistical technique that computes the relationship between a predictor variable and a criterion variable, controlling for other predictor variables. Also called *multivariate regression*.

multistage sampling A probability sampling technique involving at least two stages: a random sample of clusters followed by a random sample of people within the selected clusters.

multivariate design A study designed to test an association involving more than two measured variables.

N

negative association An association in which high levels of one variable go with low levels of the other variable, and vice versa. Also called *inverse association*, *negative correlation*. *See also* curvilinear association, positive association, zero association.

negatively worded question A question in a survey or poll that contains negatively phrased statements, making its wording complicated or confusing and potentially weakening its construct validity.

noise Unsystematic variability among the members of a group in an experiment, which might be caused by situation noise, individual differences, or measurement error. Also called *error variance, unsystematic variance*.

nonequivalent control group design An independent-groups quasi-experiment that has at least one treatment group and one comparison group, but participants have not been randomly assigned to the two groups.

nonequivalent control group interrupted time-series design A quasi-experiment with two or more groups in which participants have not been randomly assigned to groups; participants are measured repeatedly on a dependent variable before, during, and after the "interruption" caused by some event, and the presence or timing of the interrupting event differs among the groups.

nonequivalent control group pretest/posttest design An independent-groups quasi-experiment that has at least one treatment group and one comparison group, in which participants have not been randomly assigned to the two groups, and in which at least one pretest and one posttest are administered.

nonprobability sampling A category name for nonrandom sampling techniques, such as convenience, purposive, and quota sampling, that result in a biased sample. *See also* biased sample, probability sampling.

null effect A finding that an independent variable did not make a difference in the dependent variable; there is no significant covariance between the two. Also called *null result*.

null hypothesis In a common form of statistical hypothesis testing, the assumption that there is no difference, no relationship, or no effect in a population.

null hypothesis significance testing A common form of statistical hypothesis testing in which researchers calculate the probability of obtaining their result if the null hypothesis is true; they then decide whether to reject or retain the null hypothesis based on their calculations.

O

observational measure A method of measuring a variable by recording observable behaviors or physical traces of behaviors. Also called *behavioral measure*.

observational research The process of watching people or animals and systematically recording how they behave or what they are doing.

observer bias A bias that occurs when observer expectations influence the interpretation of participant behaviors or the outcome of the study.

observer effect A change in behavior of study participants in the direction of observer expectations. Also called *expectancy effect*.

one-group, **pretest/posttest design** An experiment in which a researcher recruits one group of participants; measures them on a pretest; exposes them to a treatment, intervention, or change; and then measures them on a posttest.

open-ended question A survey question format that allows respondents to answer any way they like.

open science As part of a study's publication process, the practice of sharing one's data and materials freely so others can collaborate, use, and verify the results.

operational definition The specific way in which a concept of interest is measured or manipulated as a variable in a study. Also called *operationalization* or *operational variable*.

operational variable *See* operational definition.

operationalize To turn a conceptual definition of a variable into a specific measured variable or manipulated variable in order to conduct a research study.

order effect In a within-groups design, a threat to internal validity in which exposure to one condition changes participant responses to a later condition. *See also* carryover effect, practice effect, testing threat.

ordinal scale A quantitative measurement scale whose levels represent a ranked order, and in which distances between levels are not equal (e.g., order of finishers in a race). *See also* interval scale, ratio scale.

outlier A score that stands out as either much higher or much lower than most of the other scores in a sample.

oversampling A form of probability sampling; a variation of stratified random sampling in which the researcher intentionally overrepresents one or more groups.

P

parsimony The degree to which a theory provides the simplest explanation of some phenomenon. In the context of investigating a claim, the simplest explanation of a pattern of data; the best explanation that requires making the fewest exceptions or qualifications.

partial counterbalancing A method of counterbalancing in which some, but not all, of the possible condition orders are represented. *See also* counterbalancing, full counterbalancing.

participant variable A variable such as age, gender, or ethnicity whose levels are selected (i.e., measured), not manipulated.

p-hacking A family of questionable data analysis techniques, such as adding participants after the results are initially analyzed, looking for outliers, or trying new analyses in order to obtain a *p* value of just under .05, which can lead to nonreplicable results.

physiological measure A method of measuring a variable by recording biological data.

pilot study A study completed before (or sometimes after) the study of primary interest, usually to test the effectiveness or characteristics of the manipulations.

placebo effect A response or effect that occurs when people receiving an experimental treatment experience a change only because they believe they are receiving a valid treatment.

placebo group A control group in an experiment that is exposed to an inert treatment, such as a sugar pill. Also called *placebo control group*.

plagiarism Representing the ideas or words of others as one's own; a form of research misconduct.

poll A method of posing questions to people on the telephone, in personal interviews, on written questionnaires, or via the Internet. Also called *survey*.

population A larger group from which a sample is drawn; the group to which a study's conclusions are intended to be applied. Also called *population of interest*.

positive association An association in which high levels of one variable go with high levels of the other variable, and low levels of one variable go with low levels of the other variable. Also called *positive correlation*. *See also* curvilinear association, negative association, zero association.

posttest-only design An experiment using an independent-groups design in which participants are tested on the dependent variable only once. Also called *equivalent groups, posttest-only design*.

power The likelihood that a study will show a statistically significant result when an independent variable truly has an effect in the population; the probability of not making a Type II error.

practice effect A type of order effect in which participants' performance improves over time because they become practiced at the dependent measure (not because of the manipulation or treatment). *Also called* fatigue effect. *See also* order effect, testing threat.

predictor variable A variable in multiple-regression analysis that is used to explain variance in the criterion variable. Also called *independent variable*.

preregistration The practice of posting a study's method, hypotheses, or statistical analyses publicly, in advance of data collection.

present/present bias A bias in intuition, in which people incorrectly estimate the relationship between an event and its outcome, focusing on times the event and outcome are present, while failing to consider evidence that is absent and harder to notice.

pretest/posttest design An experiment using an independent-groups design in which participants are tested on the key dependent variable twice: once before and once after exposure to the independent variable.

principle of beneficence An ethical principle from the Belmont Report stating that researchers must take precautions to protect participants from harm and to promote their well-being. *See also* principle of justice, principle of respect for persons.

principle of justice An ethical principle from the Belmont Report calling for a fair balance between the kinds of people who participate in research and the kinds of people who benefit from it. *See also* principle of beneficence, principle of respect for persons.

principle of respect for persons An ethical principle from the Belmont Report stating that research participants should be treated as autonomous agents and that certain groups deserve special protection. *See also* principle of beneficence, principle of justice.

probabilistic Describing the empirical method, stating that science is intended to explain a certain proportion (but not necessarily all) of the possible cases.

probability sampling A category name for random sampling techniques, such as simple random sampling, stratified random sampling, and cluster sampling, in which a sample is drawn from a population of interest so each member has an equal and known chance of being included in the sample. Also called *random sampling*. *See also* nonprobability sampling, unbiased sample.

purposive sampling A biased sampling technique in which only certain kinds of people are included in a sample.

Q

quantitative variable A variable whose values can be recorded as meaningful numbers.

quasi-experiment A study similar to an experiment except that the researchers do not have full experimental control (e.g., they may not be able to randomly assign participants to the independent variable conditions).

quota sampling A biased sampling technique in which a researcher identifies subsets of the population of interest, sets a target number for each category in the sample, and nonrandomly selects individuals within each category until the quotas are filled.

R

r *See* correlation coefficient.

random assignment The use of a random method (e.g., flipping a coin) to assign participants into different experimental groups.

ratio scale A quantitative measurement scale in which the numerals have equal intervals and the value of zero truly means "none" of the variable being measured. *See also* interval scale, ordinal scale.

reactivity A change in behavior of study participants (such as acting less spontaneously) because they are aware they are being watched.

regression threat A threat to internal validity related to regression to the mean, a phenomenon in which any extreme finding is likely to be closer to its own typical, or mean, level the next time it is measured (with or without the experimental treatment or intervention). *See also* regression to the mean.

regression to the mean A phenomenon in which an extreme finding is likely to be closer to its own typical, or mean, level the next time it is measured, because the same combination of chance factors that made the finding extreme are not present the second time. *See also* regression threat.

reliability The consistency of the results of a measure.

repeated-measures design An experiment using a within-groups design in which participants respond to a dependent variable more than once, after exposure to each level of the independent variable.

replicable Describing a study whose results have been reproduced when the study was repeated, or replicated. Also called *reproducible*. See also conceptual replication, direct replication, replication-plus-extension.

replication-plus-extension A replication study in which researchers replicate their original study but add variables or conditions that test additional questions. *See also* conceptual replication, direct replication.

representative sample A sample in which all members of the population of interest are equally likely to be included (usually through some random method), and therefore the results can generalize to the population of interest. Also called *unbiased sample*.

respect for persons *See* principle of respect for persons.

response set A shortcut respondents may use to answer items in a long survey, rather than responding to the content of each item. Also called *nondifferentiation*.

restriction of range In a bivariate correlation, the absence of a full range of possible scores on one of the variables, so the relationship from the sample underestimates the true correlation.

reversal design A small-*N* design in which a researcher observes a problem behavior both before and during treatment, and then discontinues the treatment for a while to see if the problem behavior returns.

review journal article An article summarizing all the studies that have been published in one research area.

S

sample The group of people, animals, or cases used in a study; a subset of the population of interest.

sampling distribution A theoretical prediction about the kinds of statistical outcomes likely to be obtained if a study is run many times and the null hypothesis is true.

scatterplot A graphical representation of an association, in which each dot represents one participant in the study measured on two variables.

scientific literature A series of related studies, conducted by various researchers, that have tested similar variables. Also called *literature*.

selection-attrition threat A threat to internal validity in which participants are likely to drop out of either the treatment group or the comparison group, not both.

selection effect A threat to internal validity that occurs in an independent-groups design when the kinds of participants at one level of the independent variable are systematically different from those at the other level.

selection-history threat A threat to internal validity in which a historical or seasonal event systematically affects only the participants in the treatment group or only those in the comparison group, not both.

self-report measure A method of measuring a variable in which people answer questions about themselves in a questionnaire or interview.

self-selection A form of sampling bias that occurs when a sample contains only people who volunteer to participate.

semantic differential format A survey question format using a response scale whose numbers are anchored with contrasting adjectives.

simple random sampling The most basic form of probability sampling, in which the sample is chosen completely at random from the population of interest (e.g., drawing names out of a hat).

single-*N* design A study in which researchers gather information from only one animal or one person.

situation noise Unrelated events or distractions in the external environment that create unsystematic variability within groups in an experiment.

slope direction The upward, downward, or neutral slope of the cluster of data points in a scatterplot.

small-*N* design A study in which researchers gather information from just a few cases.

snowball sampling A variation on purposive sampling, a biased sampling technique in which participants are asked to recommend acquaintances for the study.

socially desirable responding Giving answers on a survey (or other self-report measure) that make one look better than one really is. Also called *faking good*.

spurious association A bivariate association that is attributable only to systematic mean differences on subgroups within the sample; the original association is not present within the subgroups.

stable-baseline design A small-*N* design in which a researcher observes behavior for an extended baseline period before beginning a treatment or other intervention, and continues observing behavior after the intervention.

standard deviation A computation that captures how far, on average, each score in a data set is from the mean.

statistical significance A researcher's assessment of whether a result from a sample (such as an association or a difference between groups) could have come from a population in which there is no association or no difference. When the sample's result is extreme, it would rarely be found in such a population and is said to be statistically significant.

statistical validity The extent to which statistical conclusions derived from a study are accurate and reasonable. Also called *statistical conclusion validity*.

stemplot A graphical representation of the values obtained on some variable in a sample of data. Also called *stem-and-leaf plot*.

stratified random sampling A form of probability sampling; a random sampling technique in which the researcher identifies particular demographic categories, or strata, and then randomly selects individuals within each category.

strength A description of an association indicating how closely the data points in a scatterplot cluster along a line of best fit drawn through them.

survey A method of posing questions to people on the telephone, in personal interviews, on written questionnaires, or via the Internet. Also called *poll*.

systematic sampling A probability sampling technique in which the researcher uses a randomly chosen number *N*, and counts off every *N*th member of a population to achieve a sample.

systematic variability In an experiment, a description of when the levels of a variable coincide in some predictable way with experimental group membership, creating a potential confound. *See also* unsystematic variability.

T

temporal precedence One of three criteria for establishing a causal claim, stating that the proposed causal variable comes first in time, before the proposed outcome variable. *See also* covariance, internal validity.

testing threat In a repeated-measures experiment or quasi-experiment, a kind of order effect in which scores change over time just because participants have taken the test more than once; includes practice effects.

test-retest reliability The consistency in results every time a measure is used.

theory A statement or set of statements that describes general principles about how variables relate to one another.

theory-testing mode A researcher's intent for a study, testing association claims or causal claims to investigate support for a theory. *See also* generalization mode.

third-variable problem In a correlational study, the existence of a plausible alternative explanation for the association between two variables. *See also* internal validity.

translational research Research that uses knowledge derived from basic research to develop and test solutions to real-world problems. *See also* applied research, basic research.

treatment group The participants in an experiment who are exposed to the level of the independent variable that involves a medication, therapy, or intervention.

***t* test** A statistical test used to evaluate the size and significance of the difference between two means.

Type I error A "false positive" result in the statistical inference process, in which researchers conclude that there is an effect in a population, when there really is none.

Type II error A "miss" in the statistical inference process, in which researchers conclude that their study has not detected an effect in a population, when there really is one.

U

unbiased sample A sample in which all members of the population of interest are equally likely to be included (usually through some random method), and therefore the results can generalize to the population of interest. Also called *representative sample*. *See also* biased sample.

unobtrusive observation An observation in a study made indirectly, through physical traces of behavior, or made by someone who is hidden or is posing as a bystander.

unsystematic variability In an experiment, a description of when the levels of a variable fluctuate independently of experimental group membership, contributing to variability within groups. *See also* systematic variability.

V

validity The appropriateness of a conclusion or decision. *See also* construct validity, external validity, internal validity, statistical validity.

variable An attribute that varies, having at least two levels, or values. *See also* dependent variable, independent variable, manipulated variable, measured variable.

variance A computation that quantifies how spread out the scores of a sample are around their mean; it is the square of the standard deviation.

W

wait-list design An experimental design for studying a therapeutic treatment, in which researchers randomly assign some participants to receive the therapy under investigation immediately, and others to receive it after a time delay.

weight of the evidence A conclusion drawn from reviewing scientific literature and considering the proportion of studies that is consistent with a theory.

within-groups design An experimental design in which each participant is presented with all levels of the independent variable. Also called *within-subjects design*.

Z

zero association A lack of systematic association between two variables. Also called *zero correlation*. *See also* curvilinear association, positive association, negative association.

z score A computation that describes how far an individual score is above or below the mean, in standard deviation units. Also called *standardized score*.

Answers to End-of-Chapter Questions

Review Questions

Chapter 1
1. b
2. a
3. d
4. b
5. d

Chapter 2
1. a
2. c
3. b
4. b
5. b
6. a

Chapter 3
1. c, c
2. c
3. b
4. a
5. a
6. c
7. a

Chapter 4
1. d
2. c
3. d
4. b
5. a
6. c

Chapter 5
1. a. Quantitative, ratio
   b. Quantitative, ratio
   c. Quantitative, ordinal
   d. Categorical
   e. Categorical
   f. Quantitative, interval
2. b
3. a. Test-retest
   b. Interrater reliability
   c. Internal reliability
4. a. Criterion validity
   b. Convergent and discriminant validity
   c. Face validity
   d. Content validity

Chapter 6
1. c
2. d
3. c
4. b
5. c
6. a

Chapter 7
1. d
2. c
3. c
4. a

Chapter 8
1. b
2. c
3. d
4. d
5. a

Chapter 9
1. a
2. a
3. b
4. c
5. c
6. b
7. b
8. a

Chapter 10
1. b
2. d
3. a
4. b
5. b

Chapter 11
1. a
2. d
3. b
4. a
5. a
6. d

Chapter 12
1. c
2. c
3. d
4. a
5. a
6. b

Chapter 13
1. a
2. c
3. d
4. a
5. a
6. b
7. c

Chapter 14
1. a
2. c
3. a
4. a
5. c
6. c

Guidelines for Selected Learning Actively Exercises

Chapter 1

Answers will vary.

Chapter 2

1. Example A.

   a. How well does the baby sleep when he doesn't have a bath? (No bath is the comparison.)

   b.

	Bath (treatment)	No bath (no treatment)
Sleeps well (outcome present)		
Doesn't sleep well (outcome absent)		

   c. Perhaps the baby is more likely to get a bath on days when he played outside. Playing outside made the baby dirtier (leading to the bath) and gave the baby extra fresh air (making him sleepier). Or perhaps the baby is more likely to get a bath on days when the family's schedule is relaxed; the relaxed atmosphere, not the bath, is responsible for the baby's improved sleep.

   Example C.

   a. Would your GRE score have improved without the course? (No course is the comparison group.)

   b.

	Taking the GRE course (treatment group)	No course (comparison group)
Improvement in scores (outcome present)		
No improvement in scores (outcome absent)		

   c. What might be confounded with taking a GRE course? Perhaps the math and science courses you were enrolled in at the same time were helping to improve your scores? Or perhaps you were simply more motivated to do well on the test the second time.

2. a. This statement reflects the availability heuristic. The speaker bases the conclusion on evidence that comes easily to mind (what he or she sees the cousin eating).

   b. The conclusion your friend is talking about seems to be supported by empirical evidence, so this is a good source of evidence. You might also want to ask whether the newspaper source reported the research findings accurately.

   c. This statement reflects confirmation bias: While watching the debate, the speaker was more motivated to notice the preferred candidate's successes and to ignore the candidate's lapses.

   d. This speaker is relying on authority; in this case, information from marketing and advertising. She should ask: How good is the science on which this advertisement's conclusions are based, and is the ad reporting the science accurately?

   e. This statement reflects intuitive reasoning, namely the availability heuristic (students who are drinking are more visible than those who are in their rooms, at work, or at the movies) or the present-present bias (it's easier to notice the students who are drinking and more difficult to factor in the many students on campus who are not drinking).

   f. This statement reflects faulty intuition and the availability heuristic. Because airplane crashes get so much attention in the media, the speaker erroneously concludes that they are frequent. (Statistically, driving a car is much more dangerous than flying.)

   g. This speaker is basing her conclusions on her own experience. Experience lacks a comparison group. (What would have happened if the speaker didn't declutter the closet?) Experience may have confounds. (Maybe decluttering the closet coincided with other positive changes, such as eating better or getting more sleep.)

   h. The Match.com advertisement is exploiting people's intuitive reasoning. By failing to show people who used Match.com but who are not happily married, the website leverages the present/present bias to convince you their site is successful.

3. Answers will vary.
4. Answers will vary.

Chapter 3

1.

VARIABLE IN CONTEXT	CONCEPTUAL LEVEL (BOLDFACED IN THE DESCRIPTION)	OPERATIONAL DEFINITION	LEVELS OF THIS VARIABLE	MEASURED OR MANIPULATED
A questionnaire study asks for various demographic information, including participants' **level of education**.	Level of education	Asking participants to circle their highest level of education from this list: High school diploma Some college College degree Graduate degree	High school diploma Some college College degree Graduate degree	Measured
A questionnaire study asks about **anxiety**, measured on a 20-item Spielberger Trait Anxiety Inventory.	Anxiety	Score on 20-item Spielberger Trait Anxiety Inventory	Anxiety from low to high, represented by a numerical score	Measured
A study of readability has people read a passage of text printed in one of two **fonts: sans-serif or serif.**	Font of text	Sans-serif font or serif font	Sans-serif, serif	Manipulated
A study of **school achievement** requests each participant to report his or her SAT score, as a measure of college readiness.	School achievement	SAT score	SAT score, from 600 to 2400	Measured
A researcher studying self-control and **blood sugar levels** gives participants one of two glasses of sweet-tasting lemonade: one has sugar, one is sugar-free.	Blood sugar (glucose) levels	Drinking sugared lemonade or sugar-free lemonade	High glucose and low glucose	Manipulated

2. a. This is a causal claim.

   Variables: chewing gum (or not), level of focus.

   - You might ask: How well did they measure level of focus? (Construct validity)
   - How well did they manipulate chewing gum or not? (Construct validity)
   - Did they conduct an experiment, randomly assigning people to chew gum or not? (Internal validity)
   - How did they get their sample? Did they use random sampling? (External validity)
   - How strong is the relationship between chewing gum and focus? Is it statistically significant? (Statistical validity)

   b. This is an association claim.

   Variables: Workaholism (workaholic or not), presence of psychiatric disorder.

   - How well did they measure workaholism? How carefully did they diagnose psychiatric disorders? (Construct validity)

   - How strong is the relationship between workaholism and psychiatric disorders? (Statistical validity)
   - How did they get their sample? Is the sample representative? (External validity)

   c. This is a frequency claim.

   Variable: Feeling dissatisfied with one's body

   - How well did they measure people's body satisfaction? (Construct validity)
   - How did they get their sample? Is the sample representative of women? (External validity)

3. You would randomly assign a sample of people to either chew gum or not, then have everyone participate in a task that requires careful focus (in a separate study, you could also measure mood). The two variables would be gum chewing (or not) and degree of focus.

The results may be graphed as follows:

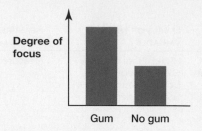

The experiment would fulfill covariance if the results turned out as depicted in the graph, because the causal variable (gum chewing) is covarying with the outcome (degree of focus). The method ensured temporal precedence: Because gum chewing was manipulated, it came before task focus was measured. There would be internal validity as long as participants were randomly assigned and all other aspects were kept the same (the two groups performed the same task under the same conditions).

Chapter 4

1. The IRB members might consider that publicly observable behavior is usually exempt from informed consent requirements, but children are considered a "vulnerable population." Children may not be able to give informed consent, and they may not monitor their public behavior to the same extent as adults do. Depending on the case, the IRB may require the researcher to request informed consent from parents in the play area before proceeding. In addition, the researcher has not yet explained what the purpose of the study will be. The IRB, in its evaluation of the research proposal, should consider the benefits of the knowledge to be gained from the study.

2. Normally, researchers using anonymous, low-risk questionnaires may be exempted from informed consent procedures, but a review board might be concerned about the risk of coercion in this situation. The IRB might wonder if students in the professor's class will feel coerced into completing the questionnaire, even if they do not wish to. (However, if there is truly no way to link responses back to the participants, then a student who does not wish to participate might be instructed to turn in a blank questionnaire.) In a small class, the students' handwriting might be recognized by the professor, so the surveys may not be truly anonymous. The IRB would probably evaluate this proposal more negatively if the questions on the survey were about personal values or private behaviors rather than study habits.

3. You might have listed some of the following costs and benefits: Deception might harm participants by making them feel tricked or embarrassed. Such negative feelings may make participants less likely to participate in future research and may make them less willing to accept or read research findings in the future. On the one hand, people might become aware of negative information about themselves, such as what kinds of actions they will perform—knowledge that may not be welcome or comfortable (e.g., in the Milgram studies, delivering shocks to the "learner"). On the other hand, deceived research participants may gain some valuable self-knowledge from their participation, thereby feeling they are contributing to the enterprise of science.

   Deception studies can be valuable to society because, as noted in the chapter, the results of such studies may provide important lessons about obedience, helping behavior, persuasion, or other research topics. In addition, human welfare might be improved when scientists or practitioners apply the knowledge from a deception study. However, when members of society read or hear about deceptive research studies, they may begin to mistrust scientists. They may also become more suspicious of others around them. (Text from this question and answer is based on an analysis by Dunn, 2009.)

4. Answers will vary.

5. Answers will vary.

Chapter 5

1. a. Coders will need to be tested on their interrater reliability. A scatterplot should have "Coder 1" on the x-axis and "Coder 2" on the y-axis; there would be a tight, upward-sloping cloud of points to show strong interrater reliability.

      Test-retest reliability may also be relevant. If you assume people's cell phone habits are stable over time, you should observe a positive relationship on a scatterplot, or a strong, positive correlation coefficient. The labels on the scatterplot should be "Rate of cell phone use at first recording" on one axis and "Rate of cell phone use at second recording" on the other axis.

   b. Because this scale has seven items that are likely to be averaged together, it will be important to establish internal reliability (through a high value on Cronbach's alpha), to make sure all seven items are answered consistently by most people. In addition, since risk for panic disorder is something that should be fairly stable over time, you should assess test-retest reliability. For test-retest reliability, a scatterplot should have "Time 1 test" on the x-axis and "Time 2 test" on the y-axis. There would be a tight, upward-sloping cloud of points to show strong interrater reliability.

c. Since observers are coding the eyeblink response, coders will need to be tested on their interrater reliability. A scatterplot should have "Coder 1" on the x-axis and "Coder 2" on the y-axis; there would be a tight, upward-sloping cloud of points to show strong interrater reliability.

d. Interrater (interteacher) reliability is relevant here. Test-retest reliability is also relevant because you can assume that shyness is stable over time.

2. To measure criterion validity, you would see whether the teacher ratings correlated with some behavioral measure of classroom shyness. For example, you might see if the shyness ratings correlated (negatively) with the number of times the student was seen to raise his hand in a classroom setting during the day.

For convergent validity, you would want to show that the classroom shyness rating is correlated with other ratings of shyness, perhaps parent ratings of shyness in the children or therapist ratings of shyness. To show convergent and discriminant validity, the ratings of shyness should be more strongly correlated with a measure of shyness than they are with a measure of autism or a measure of anxiety, for example.

3. Answers will vary.

Chapter 6

1. Answers will vary.

2. This is a forced-choice item. This question does not seem to be leading, negatively worded, or double-barreled. However, it seems possible that people would overrepresent their frequency of exercising because they believe they should exercise.

3. Your decisions will depend on where you are planning to code, but the one thing to attend carefully to is interrater reliability. To establish interrater reliability, you will need to have two coders each rate each driver, yielding two ratings per observation. The association between the two coders' ratings is the interrater reliability.

4. You could ask about the interrater reliability of the coders' rating of each face's gender and race, as well as the reliability of their coding of how long faces were in the babies' visual field. To ask about possible observer bias, you could find out if the coders knew the race of the babies from which each recording came. (If the coders knew the race of the babies, that might affect their judgment of the race of the faces in the video.)

Chapter 7

1. Many people are frustrated that opinion pollsters never call them, and they may even volunteer to contribute polling data for opinion polls during an election. Of course, the polling organizations cannot accept volunteer respondents. If they did, their polls would have poor external validity—or at least, they would be able to generalize only to other people who voluntarily call pollsters to share their opinions.

One reason this woman has not been called by pollsters is that each poll needs to sample only about 1,000 to 2,000 voters. With millions of voters in the population, the chance of being selected by a poll is extremely small.

2. a. The sample is the 200 titles you select and the population is the entire set of 13,000 titles.

b. To collect a simple random sample, use the database of all 13,000 titles. In that list, assign each book a random number, use the computer to sort the books into a list with the smallest numbers on top, and select the first 200 books on the sorted list. For each of the 200 books in the sample, you would record the price and take the average. That sample average would be a good estimate of the average price of the full book population in the store.

c. To collect a stratified random sample, you would first choose some categories, or strata, that might be important to you. For example, you might stratify the sample into textbooks and trade books. If the population includes 60% textbooks and 40% trade books, you could select a random sample of 120 textbooks and 80 trade books (in stratified random sampling, the sample size in each stratum is proportional to that in the population). Alternatively, you could categorize according to whether the books are paperback or hardback, fiction or nonfiction, or you might even stratify by topic (literature, foreign language, self-help, etc.). After identifying the categories, you would select at random the number of books you need in each stratum, according to the proportion they represent in the full list of titles.

d. A convenience sample would involve recording the price of the first 200 books you can pick up in the store, simply walking around and choosing books. (This would bias your sample toward books on the most reachable shelves.) Or you could stand by the cash register and record the price of the next 200 books sold at that store. (This convenience sample might bias your sample to include mainly the cheaper books, or mainly the sale books, or mainly the popular books.)

e. To conduct a systematic random sample, you would select two random numbers (say, 15 and 33). You would list the 13,000 books in the store, start with the 15th book, and then count off, selecting every 33rd book in the list until you get 200 books. Record the prices and take the average of the 200 books in the sample.

f. To conduct a cluster sample, you would first decide on some arbitrary clusters you could use; for example, you might use the last initial of the author as the cluster, creating 26 possible clusters. Of the 26 possible last initials, you could randomly select 6 letters, and then record the price of all the books in those 6 clusters. Alternatively, you could randomly sample 50 books from each of the 6 selected letters (this would be multistage sampling).

g. To conduct a quota sample, you would first choose some categories that might be important to you. For example, you might decide to study textbooks and trade books. If the population includes 60% textbooks and 40% trade books, you would decide to study 120 textbooks and 80 trade books. However, you would choose these books nonrandomly—perhaps by choosing the first 120 textbooks and the first 80 trade books you encounter.

Chapter 8

1. a. Measured variables: degree of stomach pain in childhood (present or absent) and level of anxiety disorders as adults. This should be plotted with a bar graph, since stomach pain was a categorical, yes or no variable. The x-axis should have "Stomach pain in childhood" or "No stomach pain" and the y-axis should have "Level of anxiety disorders in adulthood." The bar for "Stomach pain in childhood" should be higher.

   Construct validity: How accurately can they measure the degree of stomach pain in childhood? (The measures are probably good because they were medically diagnosed.) How well did they measure anxiety disorders as adults? Are self-reports appropriate here?

   Statistical validity: As for effect size, the rate of 51% is more than twice as high as the rate of 20%, so the effect size seems large. You could ask if this difference is statistically significant.

   External validity: This was probably a purposive sample; they started by identifying kids who had stomach pain. Because purposive sampling is not a representative sampling technique, you do not know if the results will generalize to a population.

   Internal validity: Can you make the claim that "Stomach pain in childhood causes anxiety disorders later on?" Clearly there is covariance: Stomach pain goes with anxiety. There is also temporal precedence: The stomach pain is measured before the anxiety disorder. However, there may be third variables that provide alternative explanations. For example, perhaps family stress is associated with both stomach pain and anxiety disorders.

   b. Measured variables: diagnosis of ADHD and likelihood of bullying. If ADHD is considered categorical (ADHD diagnosis or not), it could be plotted as a bar graph, but if it is considered quantitative (level of ADHD), then a scatterplot is appropriate.

   To interrogate construct validity, you could ask how well the researchers measured each of the two variables in this association: level of ADHD and level of bullying. You could first ask how the ADHD diagnosis was made. If a professional psychologist diagnosed each child, you could feel more confident in the construct validity of this measure. You would then ask about the measure of bullying. How well was this variable measured? The article mentions only that the researchers asked the children about bullying. You might wonder how valid a child's report of his or her own bullying behavior would be. Would a child's self-ratings correlate with teachers' ratings?

   For statistical validity, you could ask about effect size first. The article reports that children with ADHD are "four times more likely to bully" than non-ADHD children, which seems like a strong effect size. You might ask, as well, about subgroups—perhaps children from one socioeconomic group are more likely both to bully and to have an ADHD diagnosis. Finally, when the variables are categorical, as they seem to be in this study (children either have ADHD or they don't, and they are either bullies or not), outliers are typically not a problem, because a person cannot have an extreme score on a categorical variable.

   For external validity, the article reports that all the children in one grade level were studied. This study used a census, not a sample, so the findings clearly generalize to children in this Swedish town.

2. a. This strong correlation means that scientists who drank more beer published fewer articles.

   b. This means that the correlation is statistically significant—it is unlikely to have occurred by chance if there is really no relationship.

   c. The correlation would become stronger with this outlier.

d. No, the result establishes covariance, but it does not establish temporal precedence. (It could also be the case that the scientists drank beer to cope with a lower publication rate.) It does not establish internal validity, either: A third variable might be institution type; scientists working at universities might publish more and socialize less with beer, while scientists working at companies might publish less and socialize more with beer.

e. One possible table:

	Correlation between beer consumption and publication rate
Female scientists	−.63
Male scientists	−.14

Chapter 9

1. a. The autocorrelations are those in the top row: .489, .430, .446, as well as those in the bottom row: .466, .486, .471.

   b. There are no cross-sectional correlations in this figure. The authors chose to omit them, perhaps because they were not the focus of the article.

   c. The cross-lag correlations are similar in strength. The correlations between parental warmth at one time period and child self-esteem at the next time period are about as strong as the correlations between child self-esteem at one time period and parental warmth at a later time period. The pattern of results is consistent with the conclusion that parental warmth and child self-esteem are mutually reinforcing over time.

2. a. Education is a third variable problem.

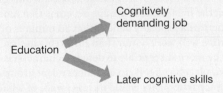

   b. Gender is a moderator.

Gender	Relationship between having a cognitively demanding job and later cognitive skills
Male	Significant r
Female	Nonsignificant r

c. "Building lasting connections in the brain" is the mediator.

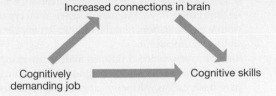

d. Birth order is a moderator (data below are fabricated).

Birth order	Relationship between sibling aggression and mental health symptoms
Firstborn	.10
Later-born	.18

e. Loneliness is a mediator.

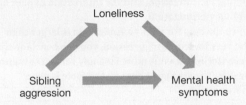

f. Parental conflict is a third variable problem.

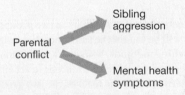

3. a. The criterion variable is mental health, measured by the Trauma Symptom Checklist. It is at the top of the table and in the table title.

   b. There are 17 predictors in this table (you don't count R^2 as a predictor).

   c. Kids who experience more total types of sibling victimization experience more mental health symptoms, controlling for parent education, ethnicity, language, age, gender, child maltreatment, sexual victimization, school victimization, Internet victimization, witnessing family or community violence, total types of peer victimization, and the interaction of peer and sibling victimization.

   d. Kids who experience more total types of peer victimization experience more mental health symptoms, controlling for parent education, ethnicity, language,

age, gender, child maltreatment, sexual victimization, school victimization, Internet victimization, witnessing family or community violence, total types of sibling victimization, and the interaction of peer and sibling victimization.

e. Kids who experience childhood maltreatment experience more mental health symptoms, controlling for parent education, ethnicity, language, age, gender, sexual victimization, school victimization, Internet victimization, witnessing family or community violence, total peer victimization, total types of sibling victimization, and the interaction of peer and sibling victimization.

f. Kids who experience Internet victimization do not experience significantly more mental health symptoms, at least when controlling for parent education, ethnicity, language, age, gender, sexual victimization, school victimization, witnessing family or community violence, total peer victimization, total types of sibling victimization, and the interaction of peer and sibling victimization.

g. Since the beta for peer victimization is larger than the beta for sibling aggression, you can conclude that peer victimization is more strongly related to mental health. The strongest beta on the table is peer victimization.

Chapter 10

1. (*Sample answer*)

a. You could randomly assign students to two groups. Both groups will be taught the same material, using the same teaching methods, homework, and examples. However, you would train a teacher to act either friendly or stern as he or she teaches the two groups of students. After the teaching unit, students would take the same school achievement test.

The bar graph should look something like this:

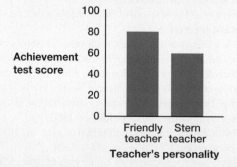

The independent (manipulated) variable is teacher's personality, with two levels (friendly and stern). The dependent (measured) variable is the achievement

test score. The control variables might include the teacher's appearance, the content of the material taught, the teaching method, the examples used, and the homework used.

Your assessment of covariance will depend on how your graph is prepared; however, this study would show covariance if the results came out as depicted in the graph shown above, in which the achievement test scores covary with the teacher's personality. This study also shows temporal precedence: The teacher's personality was manipulated, so it came first in time, followed by the achievement test. This study would also have internal validity if the researchers controlled for potential alternative explanations—for example, by keeping the teaching methods and homework the same. If the study has met all three causal rules, you can make a causal statement that a friendlier teacher causes students to score higher on school achievement tests.

2. (*Sample answer*)

b. If you manipulated the piano practice independent variable as independent-groups, you would have some participants practice the piano for 10 minutes per day and other participants practice for 30 minutes per day. You would randomly assign people to the two groups.

If you manipulated the piano practice variable as within-groups, you could have participants alternate blocks of practice months—some months practicing 10 minutes per day, and other months practicing 30 minutes per day. You would measure piano performance at the end of each monthly block. To control for order effects, you would counterbalance the months, so that some participants practice 10 minutes a day first, and others practice 30 minutes a day first.

For this independent variable, the advantage to using the independent-groups design is that most participants probably believe that 30 minutes of practice will work better than 10, so this design may be more susceptible to demand characteristics or placebo effects. In an independent groups design, participants would be less aware of what the experiment is testing. The within-groups design has the advantage that each participant will be serving as his or her own control for the two experimental conditions; their original piano playing ability will be constant for all conditions. In addition, the within-groups design has the advantage of needing fewer participants.

3. a. The independent variable is whether participants were doing their questionnaires alone or with a passive confederate. The dependent variable was

whether people stopped filling out their questionnaires to investigate the "accident" or help the "victim." The control variables were the tape recording of
the accident (always the same), the room in which the
study was held, the appearance and behavior of the
female experimenter, and the questionnaires participants completed.

b.

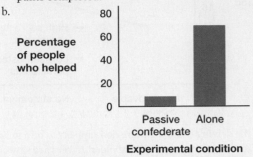

c. This was an independent-groups manipulation. People
were in either the alone group or the passive confederate group, not both.

d. For construct validity, you would ask whether getting
up to help is a good measure of helping behavior (it
seems to be). You would also ask whether participating alone or with a passive confederate is a reasonable manipulation of the presence of bystanders.
For internal validity, you would make sure that the
experimenters used random assignment (they did)
and appropriate control variables to avoid confounds.
Are any other control variables unaccounted for? For
external validity, you would ask how the experimenters gathered their sample: Was it a random sample of
some population of interest? You can also ask if this
situation—helping a woman falling from a chair in another room—would generalize to other emergencies,
such as helping a man bleeding on the street, helping
somebody who fainted, or helping in other kinds of
situations.

For statistical validity, you could ask how large
the effect size was. Indeed, the difference was 7%
versus 70%, and this is an extremely large effect size.
You would make sure it was statistically significant,
too. (An effect size that large probably is.)

Chapter 11

1. a. IV: Exposure to alcohol advertising or not.
DV: Reported level of drinking.
b. Design: One-group, pretest/posttest design (a within-
groups design).

c.

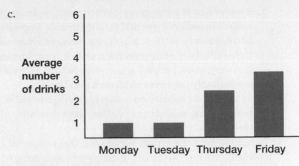

d. IV threats: Because this is a one-group, pretest/posttest
design, it is subject to multiple internal validity threats.
Perhaps the most obvious is history: It is plausible that
students drank more after exposure to the advertising
simply because the posttest was on a weekend.

e. To redesign the study, Jack could add a comparison
group that is also tested on the same days but does not
see the alcohol advertising.

2. a. IV: The use of the categorization strategy. DV: The
memory rate.
b. Design: one-group, pretest/posttest (a within-groups
design).
c.

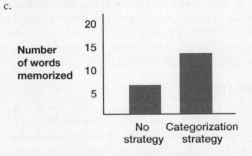

d. Because this is a one-group, pretest/posttest design, it
is subject to multiple internal validity threats. Perhaps
the most obvious here is testing: The students probably recalled more words the second time because they
had a second chance to learn the same list of words.

e. To fix this problem, the student presenters should use a
new word list the second time—when categorization is
used as a mnemonic. To control for the possibility that
one word list might be more difficult than the other
(which would be a design confound), the presenters
should also counterbalance the use of the two word lists.

3. a. IV: The meditation training. DV: Symptoms of anxiety
and depression.
b. Design: One-group, pretest/posttest design.
c. The x-axis should have "Before training" and "After
training," and the y-axis should read "Anxiety and
depression symptoms." The line or bar graph should
show a decline in symptoms.

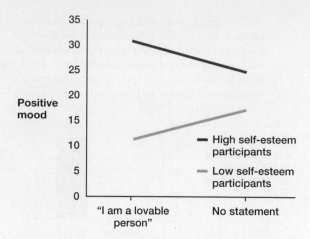

d. Because this is a one-group, pretest/posttest design, it is subject to multiple internal validity threats. Regression to the mean could be at play (if the workers' symptoms were especially keen at pretest), as well as maturation (in many cases, people's ability to cope with a stressful event simply improves on its own over time).

e. As always, a comparison group receiving no meditation training would improve the internal validity of this design.

4. *Increasing between-groups variability:* Was 1 ounce of chocolate enough to cause a difference in well-being? Was the well-being questionnaire sensitive enough to detect differences in this variable?

   Reducing within-group differences: With such a small sample, Dr. Dove might need to use a within-groups design, because there are likely to be individual differences in well-being. Otherwise, she might try using a larger number of participants (50 in each group might be better), thus reducing the impact of measurement errors or irrelevant individual differences. The participants in this study also seemed to be going about their normal routines in real-world settings. There may have been innumerable sources of situation noise in their lives over this 4-week period. In a future study, Dr. Dove might consider quarantining participants for some period of time. Of course, it's also possible that eating chocolate truly does not affect well-being, so Dr. Dove's study returned an appropriate result.

Chapter 12

1. Below are two possible line graphs that represent the Wood et al. (2009) data. You can describe this interaction in words as follows: People with low self-esteem feel worse after telling themselves "I am a lovable person," but people with high self-esteem feel better after telling themselves "I am a lovable person."

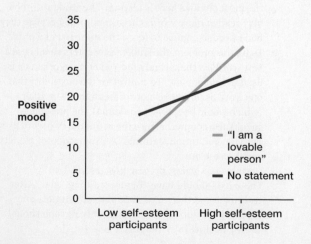

2. In the driving example, there does appear to be a main effect for driver age, such that older drivers are slower to brake. And there does appear to be a main effect for the cell phone condition, such that drivers using cell phones are slower to brake. Although you would need statistics to confirm that these differences are significant, you know that in the actual study, both main effects were statistically significant (see p. 379).

DV: Brake onset time (ms)		IV_1: Cell phone condition		
		On cell phone	Not on phone	Main effect for IV_2: Driver age
IV_2: Driver age	Younger drivers	912	780	846
	Older drivers	1086	912	989
Main effect for IV_1: Cell phone condition		989	846	

In the chess pieces example, there does not appear to be a main effect for type of item, since the two marginal means are fairly close to each other. There also does not appear to be a large main effect for participant type, since the two marginal means are almost the same here, too. You would need inferential statistics to determine whether the differences between the marginal means are statistically significant.

DV: Items recalled		IV_1: Participant type		
		Child chess experts	Adult novices	Main effect for IV_2: Type of item
IV_2: Type of item	Chess pieces	9.3	5.9	7.6
	Digits	6.1	7.8	7.0
Main effect for IV_1: Participant type		7.7	6.9	

3. a. This is a 3 × 2 within-groups factorial design.
   b. The independent variables are cell phone condition (two levels) and testing condition (three levels). The dependent variable is the number of collisions.
   c. Both independent variables are within-groups variables.
   d. Notice that you could put either independent variable on the x-axis; either would be correct, and you can detect interactions equally well from either graph.

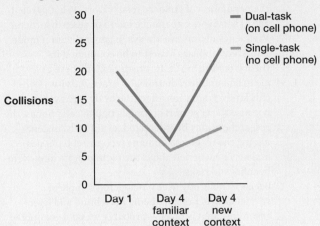

   e. There is a main effect for cell phone condition, such that talking on a cell phone causes more collisions. (You can say "cause" here because this was an experimental design with no confounds.) There is also a main effect for testing day: People had the fewest collisions on Day 4, familiar context, and the most collisions on Day 4, new context. There appears to be an interaction: The difference between single and dual task is about the same on Day 1 and Day 4, familiar context, but the difference is greater on Day 4, new context.
   f. The results of this study seem to show that regardless of experience level, using cell phones impairs people's driving skill.
4. Participant variables are usually independent-groups variables. In the case of gender, participants usually identify as one or the other. Ethnicity, too, is an independent-groups variable. Sometimes personality traits (such as high self-esteem versus low self-esteem or introversion versus extroversion) are used as participant variables; these, too, are independent-groups variables. Age, however, could go either way. Strayer and his colleagues recruited some people in their 20s and other people in their 70s, so age was an independent-groups variable in this design. However, if a researcher recruits one sample of people and tests them in their 20s, 30s, 40s, and 50s, age becomes a participant variable that is studied as a repeated-measures variable. (This kind of study is called a longitudinal design; see Chapter 9.)

Chapter 13

1. a. This is an interrupted time-series design.
   b. Your graph could have "Hours of sleep per night" on the y-axis and "Before change" and "After change" on the x-axis. The line should be increasing from left to right.
   c. The causal claim would be that starting school later caused students to get more sleep. This result shows covariance (students got more sleep when the school time started later) and temporal precedence (the school's change in start time preceded the measurement of how much sleep they were getting). However, in this quasi-experimental design, it is possible there are threats to internal validity. Increases in sleep could have been caused by seasonal changes from fall to spring, or by systematic changes in the school's activities or curriculum (if school events in the fall are more numerous or intense compared to spring).
   d. One alternative design would be a nonequivalent control groups interrupted time-series design, where you could study sleep patterns in two high schools, only one of which changed its school start time at mid-year. Another option would be to measure the students on the dependent variable, sleep, more frequently and for a longer time. The study could measure sleep patterns for multiple semesters first, then implement the start time change, and then continue to measure sleep patterns. By inspecting the results, you could tease apart seasonal changes in sleep from start time changes.
   e. Construct validity of the dependent variable: How well does a survey operationalize the amount of sleep students are getting? External validity: To what extent does the result from this one school generalize to other schools? Does it generalize to younger children?
2. a. Either the stable-baseline design or the reversal design is appropriate here. Since there is only one context for the growling behavior, the multiple-baseline design would not be appropriate.
   b. Using a stable-baseline design, you would observe and record your dog's growling behavior daily in the presence of other dogs for a long period of time (2–3 weeks). Then you would continue to observe and record your dog's growling behavior daily as you began to implement the behavioral technique.

c. The graph would look similar to Figure 13.10, except the growling behavior would be consistently high (rather than low) during the baseline period and would then decrease after the intervention starts.

d. If the results were as depicted in the graph you drew, you could rule out maturation and regression explanations for the dog's behavior, because the stable-baseline period shows that the dog's behavior has not changed on its own. A history threat might still apply to your data if some other change (such as a change in diet) happened to occur in the dog's life at the same time you started using the behavioral technique. However, in the absence of some other explanation, you could infer the causal success of the therapy if the dog's growling behavior began to decrease at the time you started the therapy.

Chapter 14

1. Answers will vary.
2. It's possible that the second study used different operationalizations of weather and mood, so that the second study was not a direct replication of the original. A second possibility is that because the original study's sample was small ($N = 28$), a few chance values could have influenced the data. In contrast, because the replication study had over a million cases, a few chance values will have been cancelled out. Finally, without having access to the original study's data and materials, we can't know if they had implemented any questionable research practices. New policies for open science

are aimed at making it easier to detect and prevent questionable research practices. In this particular case we cannot know why the weather effect on mood differs in the two studies.

3. a. This study could be conducted in theory-testing mode, because it may test a theory that exposure to a very stressful event is a potential cause of mental suffering and emotional problems. However, this study is also being conducted in generalization mode, since it appears to be testing a frequency claim about the population of Holocaust survivors: What percentage of survivors experience mood or sleep disorders? Frequency claims are always in generalization mode.

b. This study appears at first to be conducted in theory-testing mode. It is testing a link between electromagnetic radiation and brain activity. (Does this kind of radiation affect the brain?) However, because the type of radiation is tied to cell phones, the researchers may be interested, eventually, in generalizing the results to humans who use cell phones and may be worried about the technology's long-term benefits and risks.

c. Because this study used a restricted sample of a special kind of person—being born blind and later regaining sight is rare—it probably was not conducted in generalization mode. It is a good example of theory-testing mode because the results from this special sample allowed the researchers to learn that the brain uses motion (more than color or lines) to decode the visual world.

References

A Learning Secret: Don't Take Notes with a Laptop. *Chapter 10 opening headline.* May, D. (2014, June 3). A learning secret: Don't take notes with a laptop. *Scientific American* (online). Retrieved from http://www.scientificamerican.com/article/a-learning-secret-don-t-take-notes-with-a-laptop

Abelson, R. P. (1995). *Statistics as principled argument.* Hillsdale, NJ: Erlbaum.

American Psychological Association. (2002, with 2010 amendments). *Ethical principles of psychologists and code of conduct.* Retrieved from http://www.apa.org/ethics/code/index.aspx

American Psychological Association. (2010). *Publication manual of the American Psychological Association* (6th ed). Washington, DC: American Psychological Association.

Anderson, C. A., Berkowitz, L., Donnerstein, E., Huesmann, L. R., Johnson, J., Linz, D., . . . Wartella, E. (2003). The influence of media violence on youth. *Psychological Science in the Public Interest, 4*, 81–110. doi:10.1111/j.1529-1006.2003.pspi_1433.x

Anderson, C. A., Shibuya, A., Ihori, N., Swing, E. L., Bushman, B. J., Sakamoto, A., . . . Barlett, C. P. (2010). Violent video game effects on aggression, empathy, and prosocial behavior in Eastern and Western countries: A meta-analytic review. *Psychological Bulletin, 136*, 151–173. doi:10.1037/a0018251

Andics, A., Gábor, A., Gácsi, M., Faragó, T., Szabó, D., & Miklósi, A. (2016). Neural mechanisms for lexical processing in dogs. *Science, 353*, 1–4. doi:10.1126/science.aaf3777

Animal Welfare Act. (1966). Title 9 Code of Federal Regulations (CF), Chapter 1, Subchapter A: Animal Welfare. Retrieved from http://www.gpo.gov/fdsys/pkg/CFR-2009-title9-vol1/xml/CFR-2009-title9-vol1-chapI-subchapA.xml

Arceneaux, K., & Butler, D. M. (2016). How not to increase participation in local government: The advantages of experiments when testing policy interventions. *Public Administration Review, 76*, 131–139. doi:10.1111/puar.12387

Arnett, J. (2008). The neglected 95%: Why American psychology needs to become less American. *American Psychologist, 63*, 602–614. doi:10.1037/0003-066x.63.7.602

Aron, A. (2009). *Instructor's manual with tests for statistics for psychology* (5th ed.). New York: Pearson.

Association for Psychological Science (n.d.). APS Wikipedia initiative. Retrieved from http://www.psychologicalscience.org/index.php/members/aps-wikipedia-initiative

Baird, B., Mrazek, M. D., Phillips, D. T., & Schooler, J. W. (2014). Domain-specific enhancement of metacognitive ability following meditation training. *Journal of Experimental Psychology, 143*, 1972–1979. doi:10.1037/a0036882

Baird, B., Smallwood, J., Mrazek, M. D., Kam, J. W. Y., Franklin, M. S., & Schooler, J. W. (2012). Inspired by distraction mind wandering facilitates creative incubation. *Psychological Science, 23*, 1117–1122. doi:10.1177/0956797612446024

Barnett, W. S. (1998). Long-term effects on cognitive development and school success. In W. S. Barnett & S. S. Boocock (Eds.), *Early care and education for children in poverty: Promises, programs, and long-term outcomes* (pp. 11–44). Buffalo, NY: SUNY Press.

Baron, R. M., & Kenny, D. A. (1986). The moderator-mediator variable distinction in social psychological research: Conceptual, strategic and statistical considerations. *Journal of Personality and Social Psychology, 51*, 1173–1182. doi:10.1037//0022-3514.51.6.1173

Bartholow, B. D., & Heinz, A. (2006). Alcohol and aggression without consumption: Alcohol cues, aggressive thoughts, and hostile perception bias. *Psychological Science, 17*, 30–37. doi:10.1111/j.1467-9280.2005.01661.x

Batson, C. D., Polycarpou, M. P., Harmon-Jones, E., Imhoff, H. J., Mitchener, E. C., Bednar, L. L., . . . Highberger, L. (1997). Empathy and attitudes: Can feeling for a member of a stigmatized group improve feelings toward the group? *Journal of Personality and Social Psychology, 72*, 105–118. doi:10.1037//0022-3514.72.1.105

Baumrind, D. (1964). Some thoughts on the ethics of research: After reading Milgram's "Behavioral Study of Obedience." *American Psychologist, 19*, 421–423. doi:10.1037/h0040128

Beck, A. T., Ward, C., & Mendelson, M. (1961). Beck Depression Inventory (BDI). *Archives of General Psychiatry, 4*, 561–571.

Beck, A. T., Ward, C. H., Mendelson, M., Mock, J., & Erbaugh, J. (1961). An inventory for measuring depression. *Archives of General Psychiatry, 4*, 53–63. doi:10.1001/archpsyc.1961.01710120031004

Beecher, H. K. (1955). The powerful placebo. *Journal of the American Medical Association, 159*, 1601–1606. doi:10.1001/jama.1955.02960340022006

Benedetti, F., Amanzio, M., Vighetti, S., & Asteggiano, G. (2006). The biochemical and neuroendocrine bases of the hyperalgesic nocebo effect. *Journal of Neuroscience, 26*, 12014–12022. doi:10.1523/jneurosci.2947-06.2006

Berkowitz, L. (1973, July). The case for bottling up rage. *Psychology Today, 7*, 24–31.

Berkowitz, L., & Donnerstein, E. (1982). External validity is more than skin deep: Some answers to criticisms of laboratory experiments. *American Psychologist, 37*, 245–257. doi:10.1037//0003-066X.37.3.245

Best, E. (2010). Alcohol makes bigger guys more aggressive. *Pacific Standard*. http://www.psmag.com/culture-society/alcohol-makes-bigger-guys-more-aggressive-15485/

Bianchi, E. C., & Vohs, K. D. (2016). Social class and social worlds: Income predicts the frequency and nature of social contact. *Social Psychological and Personality Science, 7*, 479–486. doi:10.1177/1948550616641472

Blackman, A. (2014, November 10). Can money buy you happiness? *Wall Street Journal* (online). Retrieved from http://www.wsj.com/articles/can-money-buy-happiness-heres-what-science-has-to-say-1415569538

Blass, T. (2002). The man who shocked the world. *Psychology Today, 35*, 68–74.

Blumberg, S.F., & Luke J.V. (2015). Wireless substitution: Early release estimates from the National Health Interview Survey, July–December 2015. http://www.cdc.gov/nchs/data/nhis/earlyrelease/wireless201605.pdf

Bogg, T., & Roberts, B. W. (2004). Conscientiousness and health-related behaviors: A meta-analysis of the leading behavioral contributors to mortality. *Psychological Bulletin, 130*, 887–919. doi:10.1037/0033-2909.130.6.887

Bohannon, J. (2015, May 27). I fooled millions into thinking chocolate helps weight loss: Here's how. I09.com. Retrieved from http://io9.gizmodo.com/i-fooled-millions-into-thinking-chocolate-helps-weight-1707251800

Boothby, E., J., Clark, M. S., & Bargh, J. A. (2014). Shared experiences are amplified. *Psychological Science, 25*, 2209–2217. doi:10.1177/0956797614551162

Borkenau, P., & Liebler, A. (1993). Convergence of stranger ratings of personality and intelligence with self-ratings, partner ratings, and measured intelligence. *Journal of Personality and Social Psychology, 65*, 546–553. doi:10.1037//0022-3514.65.3.546

Borsboom, D., & Wagenmakers, E. J. (2013). Derailed: The rise and fall of Diederik Stapel (Book review). *APS Observer*. Retrieved from http://www.psychologicalscience.org/index.php/publications/observer/2013/january-13/derailed-the-rise-and-fall-of-diederik-stapel.html

Bothwell, R. K., Deffenbacher, K. A., & Brigham, J. C. (1987). Correlations of eyewitness accuracy and confidence: Optimality hypothesis revisited. *Journal of Applied Psychology, 72*, 691–695. doi:10.1037/0021-9010.72.4.691

Bowker, A., Boekhoven, B., Nolan, A., Bauhaus, S., Glover, P., Powell, T., & Taylor, S. (2009). Naturalistic observations of spectator behavior at youth hockey games. *Sport Psychologist, 23*, 301–316. doi:10.1123/tsp.23.3.301

Brewer, M. (2000). Research design and issues of validity. In H. Reis & C. Judd (Eds.), *Handbook of research methods in social and personality psychology*. Cambridge, UK: Cambridge University Press.

Brewer, N., & Wells, G. L. (2006). The confidence-accuracy relationship in eyewitness identification: Effects of lineup instructions, foil similarity, and target-absent base rates. *Journal of Experimental Psychology: Applied, 12*, 11–30. doi:10.1037/1076-898x.12.1.11

Bröder, A. (1998). Deception can be acceptable. *American Psychologist, 53*, 805–806. doi:10.1037/0003-066X.53.7.805.b

Brown, R., & Hanlon, C. (1970). Derivational complexity and order of acquisition in child speech. In J. R. Hayes (Ed.), *Cognition and the development of language* (pp. 11–54). New York: Wiley.

Brummelman, E., Crocker, J., & Bushman, B. J. (2016). The praise paradox: When and why praise backfires in children with low self-esteem. *Child Development Perspectives, 10*, 111–115. doi:10.1111/cdep.12171

Brummelman, E., Thomaes, S., Nelemans, S. A., Orobio de Castro, B. Overbeek, G., & Bushman, B. J. (2015). Origins of narcissism in children. *Proceedings of the National Academy of Sciences, 112*, 3659–3662. doi:10.1073/pnas.1420870112

Bushman, B. J., & Anderson, C. A. (2001). Media violence and the American public: Scientific facts versus media misinformation. *American Psychologist, 56*, 477–489. doi:10.1037/0003-066x.56.6-7.477

Bushman, B. J., Baumeister, R. F., & Phillips, C. M. (2001). Do people aggress to improve their mood? Catharsis beliefs, affect regulation opportunity, and aggressive responding. *Journal of Personality and Social Psychology, 81*, 17–32. doi:10.1037//0022-3514.81.1.17

Cacioppo, J., Cacioppo, S., Gonzaga, G. C., Ogburn, E. L., & VanderWeele, T. J. (2013). Marital satisfaction and break-ups differ across on-line and off-line meeting venues. *Proceedings of the National Academy of Sciences, 110,* 10135–10140. doi:10.1073/pnas.1222447110

Camara, W. J., & Echternacht, G. (2000). The SAT I and high school grades: Utility in predicting success in college. Research Notes, College Entrance Examination Board, New York, NY. http://files.eric.ed.gov/fulltext/ED446592.pdf

Campos, B., Wang, S., Plaksina, T., Repetti, R. L., Schoebi, D., Ochs, E., & Beck, M. E. (2013). Positive and negative emotion in the daily life of dual-earner couples with children. *Journal of Family Psychology, 27,* 76–85. doi:10.1037/a0031413

Can Money Buy You Happiness? *Chapter 5 opening headline.* Blackman, A. (2014, November 10). Can money buy you happiness? *Wall Street Journal* (online). Retrieved from http://www.wsj.com/articles/can-money-buy-happiness-heres-what-science-has-to-say-1415569538

Cantril, H. (1965). *The pattern of human concerns.* New Brunswick, NJ: Rutgers University Press.

Carlson, N. (2009). *Physiology of behavior* (10th ed.). New York: Allyn & Bacon.

Carroll, L. (2008, January 29). Kids with ADHD may be more likely to bully. NBC News (online). Retrieved from http://www.nbcnews.com/id/22813400/ns/health-childrens_health/t/kids-adhd-may-be-more-likely-bully/#.U1bKavldV8E

Carroll, L. (2013, August 12). Chronic stomach pain in kids linked to later anxiety. NBC News (Health). Retrieved from http://www.nbcnews.com/health/chronic-stomach-pain-kids-linked-later-anxiety-6C10887554

Carter, S.P., Greenberg, K., & Walker, M. (2016). The impact of computer usage on academic performance: Evidence from a randomized trial at the United States Military Academy. Working paper for the MIT School Effectiveness and Inequality Initiative. Retrieved from https://seii.mit.edu/wp-content/uploads/2016/05/SEII-Discussion-Paper-2016.02-Payne-Carter-Greenberg-and-Walker-2.pdf

CBS Local (2016). 8 out of 10 drivers say they experience road rage. http://newyork.cbslocal.com/2016/07/14/aaa-road-rage-survey/

CBSNews (2008, November 3). Study links sex on TV to teen pregnancy. CBSnews (online). Retrieved from http://www.cbsnews.com/news/study-links-sex-on-tv-to-teen-pregnancy/

Centers for Disease Control and Prevention. (2000). Clinical growth charts. Retrieved from http://www.cdc.gov/growthcharts/clinical_charts.htm

Centers for Disease Control and Prevention. (2008). Youth risk behavior surveillance—United States 2007. Retrieved from http://www.cdc.gov/mmwr/preview/mmwrhtml/ss5704a1.htm

Centers for Disease Control and Prevention (CDC) (2016). The Tuskeegee Timeline. Retrieved from http://www.cdc.gov/tuskegee/timeline.htm

Centers for Disease Control and Prevention (CDC) (n.d.). Distracted driving. Retrieved from http://www.cdc.gov/motorvehiclesafety/Distracted_Driving/index.html

Chambers, C. D. (2017). *The seven deadly sins of psychology: A manifesto for Open Science.* Princeton, NJ: Princeton University Press.

Chandra, A., Martino, S. C., Collins, R. L., Elliott , M. N., Berry, S. H., Kanouse, D. E., & Miu, A. (2008). Does watching sex on television predict teen pregnancy? Findings from a National Longitudinal Survey of Youth. *Pediatrics, 122,* 1047–1054. :doi:10.1542/peds.2007-3066

Chi, M. T. H. (1978). Knowledge structures and memory development. In R. Siegler (Ed.), *Children's thinking: What develops?* (pp. 73–96). Hillsdale, NJ: Erlbaum.

Childress, J. F., Meslin, E. M., & Shapiro, H. T. (2005). *Belmont revisited: Ethical principles for research with human subjects.* Washington, DC: Georgetown University Press.

Christian, L., Keeter, S., Purcell, K., & Smith, A. (2010). Assessing the cell phone challenge. Pew Research Center. Retrieved from http://pewresearch.org/pubs/1601/assessing-cell-phone-challenge-in-public-opinion-surveys

Clifford, S., Jewell, R. M., & Waggoner, P. D. (2015). Are samples drawn from Mechanical Turk valid for research on political ideology? *Research and Politics, 2,* 1–9. doi: 10.1177/2053168015622072

Clifton, J. (2016, March 16). The happiest people in the world? Retrieved from http://www.gallup.com/opinion/gallup/189989/happiest-people-world.aspx

Cohen, J. (1992). A power primer. *Psychological Bulletin, 112,* 155–159.

Cohen, S., Kamarck, T., & Mermelstein, R. (1983). A global measure of perceived stress. *Journal of Health and Social Behavior, 24,* 385–396. doi:10.2307/2136404

Coile, D. C., & Miller, N. E. (1984). How radical animal activists try to mislead humane people. *American Psychologist, 45,* 1304–1312. doi:10.1037//0003-066x.39.6.700

Collins, R. L., Martino, S. C., Elliott, M. N., & Miu, A. (2011). Relationships between adolescent sexual outcomes and exposure to sex in media: Robustness to propensity-based analysis. *Developmental Psychology, 47,* 585–591. doi:10.1037/a0022563

Conner Snibbe, A., & Markus, H. R. (2005). You can't always get what you want: Educational attainment, agency, and choice. *Journal of Personality and Social Psychology, 88,* 703–720. doi:10.1037/0022-3514.88.4.703

Cooper, C. (2015, September 14). Serving food on a larger plate "makes people eat more." *Independent* (online). Retrieved from http://www.independent.co.uk/life-style/health-and-families/health-news/serving-food-on-a-larger-plate-makes-people-eat-more-10500767.html

Copeland, J., & Snyder, M. (1995). When counselors confirm: A functional analysis. *Personality and Social Psychology Bulletin, 21*, 1210–1220. doi:10.1177/01461672952111009

Coren, S. (2016, April 13). The data says, "Don't hug the dog!" *Psychology Today* (Canine Corner Blog). Retrieved from https://www.psychologytoday.com/blog/canine-corner/201604/the-data-says-dont-hug-the-dog

Corkin, S. (2013). *Permanent present tense: The unforgettable life of the amnesic patient, H.M.* New York: Basic Books.

Couples Who Meet Online Have Better Marriages. *Chapter 8 opening headline.* Freakonomics, 2013. http://freakonomics.com/2013/06/21/couples-who-meet-online-have-better-marriages/

Cozby, P. C. (2007). *Methods in behavioral research* (9th ed.). New York: McGraw-Hill.

Crandall, C. S., & Sherman, J. W. (2016). On the scientific superiority of conceptual replications for scientific progress. *Journal of Experimental Social Psychology, 66*, 93–99. doi:10.1016/j.jesp.2015.10.002

Crandall, C. S., & Stangor, C. (2005). Conformity and prejudice. In J. F. Dovidio, P. Glick, & L. A. Rudman (Eds.), *On the nature of prejudice: Fifty years after allport* (pp. 295–309). Malden, MA: Wiley-Blackwell.

Cronbach, L. J., & Meehl, P. E. (1955). Construct validity in psychological tests. *Psychological Bulletin, 52*, 281–302. doi:10.1037/h0040957

Crowne, D. P., & Marlowe, D. (1960). A new scale of social desirability independent of psychopathology. *Journal of Consulting Psychology, 24*, 349–354. doi:10.1037/h0047358

Crume, D. M. (n.d.). Six great ways to vent your frustrations. Lifehack.org. Retrieved from http://www.lifehack.org/articles/featured/six-great-ways-to-vent-your-frustrations.html

Cumming, G., & Finch, S. (2005). Inference by eye: Confidence intervals and how to read pictures of data. *American Psychologist, 60*, 170–180. doi:10.1037/0003-066x.60.2.170

Dahl, M. (20016, April 25). Your dog hates hugs. NYMag.com. Retrieved from http://nymag.com/scienceofus/2016/04/your-dog-hates-hugs.html

Danziger, S., Levav, J., & Avnaim-Pesso, L. (2011). Extraneous factors in judicial decisions. *Proceedings of the National Academy of Sciences, 108*, 6889–6892. doi:10.1073/pnas.1018033108

Dart, T. (2016). "They're here for therapy": Houston's "rage room" a smash as economy struggles. *Guardian* (online). Retrieved from https://www.theguardian.com/us-news/2016/may/24/rage-room-anger-management-unemployment-houston-texas

Deary, I. J., Penke, J., & Johnson, W. (2010). The neuroscience of human intelligence differences. *Nature Reviews: Neuroscience, 11*, 201–212. doi:10.1038/nrn2793

De Langhe, B., Fernbach, P. M., & Lichtenstein, D. R. (2016). Navigating by the stars: Investigating the actual and perceived validity of online user ratings. *Journal of Consumer Research, 42*, 817–833. doi:10.1093/jcr/ucv047

DeNoon, D. J. (2008, May 7). Perk of a good job: Aging mind is sharp. Retrieved from http://www.webmd.com/brain/news/20080507/perk-of-good-job-aging-mind-is-sharp

DeRosa, N. M, Roane, H. S., Bishop, J. R., & Silkowski, E. L. (2016). The combined effects of noncontingent reinforcement and punishment on the reduction of rumination. *Journal of Applied Behavior Analysis, 49,* 680, 685. doi:10.1002/jaba.304

DeWall, C. N., Bushman, B. J., Giancola, P. R., & Webster, G. D. (2010). The big, the bad, and the boozed-up: Weight moderates the effect of alcohol on aggression. *Journal of Experimental Social Psychology, 46*, 619–623. doi:10.1016/j.jesp.2010.02.008

Diener, E., & Diener, C. (1996). Most people are happy. *Psychological Science, 7*, 181–185.

Diener, E., Emmons, R. A., Larsen, R. J., & Griffin, S. (1985). The satisfaction with life scale. *Journal of Personality Assessment, 49*, 71–75. doi:10.1097/HTR.0000000000000004

Diener, E., Horwitz, J., & Emmons, R. A. (1985). Happiness of the very wealthy. *Social Indicators, 16*, 263–274. doi:10.1007/BF00415126

Doyen, S., Klein, O., Pichon, C., & Cleeremans, A. (2012). Behavioral priming: It's all in the mind, but whose mind? *PLOS ONE, 7*, 7. doi:10.1371/journal.pone.0029081

Doyle, A. C. (1892/2002). Silver blaze. In *The complete Sherlock Holmes*. New York: Gramercy.

Duke, A. A., Giancola, P. R., Morris, D. H., Holt, J. C. D., & Gunn, R. L. (2011). Alcohol dose and aggression: Another reason why drinking more is a bad idea. *Journal of Studies on Alcohol and Drugs, 72*, 34–43. doi:10.15288/jsad.2011.72.34

Dunn, D. (2009). *Research methods for social psychology.* New York: Wiley-Blackwell.

Dunn, L. M., & Dunn, L. M. (1981). *PPVT: Revised manual.* Circle Pines, MN: American Guidance Service.

Ebbinghaus, H. (1913). *Memory: A contribution to experimental psychology.* New York: Columbia University Press. (Originally published 1885.)

8 Out of 10 Drivers Say They Experience Road Rage. *Chapter 7 opening headline.* CBS Local, 2016. http://newyork.cbslocal.com/2016/07/14/aaa-road-rage-survey/

Eisenberg, L. (1977). The social imperatives of medical research. *Science, 198*, 1105–1110. doi:10.1126/science.337491

Ericsson, K. A., Chase, W. G., & Faloon, S. (1980). Acquisition of a memory skill. *Science, 208*, 1181–1182. doi:10.1126/science.7375930

Family Dinner Benefits: Do Meals Together Really Make a Difference for Children? (POLL) (2012, September 26). *Huffington Post*. Retrieved from http://www.huffingtonpost.com/2012/09/26/family-dinner-benefits-make-a-difference-poll_n_1916602.html

Federal Register. (2000, December 6). FR Doc 06de00-72. Federal Research Misconduct Policy. Washington, DC: Department of Health and Human Services.

Federal Register. (2001). FR Doc 01-30627. Washington, DC: Department of Health and Human Services.

Feshbach, S. (1956). The catharsis hypothesis and some consequences of interaction with aggression and neutral play objects. *Journal of Personality, 24*, 449–462. doi:10.1111/j.1467-6494.1956.tb01281.x

Final Report of the Tuskegee Syphilis Study Ad Hoc Advisory Panel. Washington, DC: U.S. Department of Health, Education, and Welfare; Public Health Service, 1–3, 6–15, 23–24, 47.

Foa, E. B., Gillihan, S. J., & Bryant, R. A. (2013). Challenges and successes in dissemination of evidence-based treatments for posttraumatic stress: Lessons learned from prolonged exposure therapy for PTSD. *Psychological Science in the Public Interest, 14*, 65–111. doi:10.1177/1529100612468841

Fox, D. K., Hopkins, B. L., & Anger, W. K. (1987). The long-term effects of a token economy on safety performance in open-pit mining. *Journal of Applied Behavior Analysis, 201*, 215–224. doi:10.1901/jaba.1987.20-215

Fraley, R. C., & Vazire, S. (2014). The N-pact factor: Evaluating the quality of empirical journals with respect to sample size and statistical power. *PLOS ONE, 9*, 12. doi:10.1371/journal.pone.0109019

Frey, D., & Stahlberg, D. (1986). Selection of information after receiving more or less reliable self-threatening information. *Personality and Social Psychology Bulletin, 12*, 434–441. doi:10.1177/0146167286124006

Gallup. (2015). Three in four women worldwide rate their lives as "struggling" or "suffering." http://www.gallup.com/poll/181790/nearly-billion-women-worldwide-struggling-suffering.aspx

Gallup.com (2016). Gallup 2016 Global Emotions Report. Retrieved from http://www.gallup.com/services/189968/gallup-2016-global-emotions-report.aspx

Gallup. (n.d.). Gallup Daily: Frequent exercise. Retrieved from http://www.gallup.com/poll/182252/gallup-daily-frequent-exercise.aspx

Gallup. (n.d.). The Well-Being 5: Development and validation of a diagnostic instrument to improve population well-being (trends). Retrieved from http://www.gallup.com/services/178469/development-validation-diagnostic-instrument-improve-population-trends.aspx

Gamer, M., Bauermann, T., Stoeter, P., & Vessel, G. (2007). Covariations among fMRI, skin conductance, and behavioral data during processing of concealed information. *Human Brain Mapping, 28*, 1287–1301. doi:http://dx.doi.org/10.1002/hbm.20343

Gay, P. (Ed.). (1989). *A Freud reader.* New York: Norton.

Geen, R. G., & Quanty, M. B. (1977). The catharsis of aggression: An evaluation of a hypothesis. *Advances in Experimental Social Psychology, 10*, 2–39. doi:10.1016/s0065-2601(08)60353-6

Gernsbacher, M. A. (2003). Is one style of autism early intervention "scientifically proven"? *Journal of Developmental and Learning Disorders, 7*, 19–25.

Giancola, P. R. (2000). Executive functioning: A conceptual framework for alcohol-related aggression. *Experimental and Clinical Psychopharmacology, 8*, 576–597. doi:10.1037//1064-1297.8.4.576

Gidus, T. (2008, June 19). Mindless eating. (Blog post.) Retrieved from http://www.healthline.com/blogs/diet_nutrition/2008/06/mindless-eating.html

Gilbert, D. (2005). *Stumbling on happiness.* New York: Vintage.

Gilbert, D. T., King, G., Pettigrew, S., & Wilson, T. D. (2016). Comment on "Estimating the reproducibility of psychological science." *Science, 351*, 1037. doi:10.1126/science.aad7243

Goldacre, B. (2008, September 6). Cheer up, it's all down to random variation [Web log post]. Retrieved from http://www.guardian.co.uk/commentisfree/2008/sep/06/medicalresearch

Goldacre, B. (2011, August 19). Unemployment is rising—or is that statistical noise? *Guardian* [Online]. Retrieved from http://www.guardian.co.uk/commentisfree/2011/aug/19/bad-science-unemployment-statistical-noise

Goodman, J. K., Cryder, C. E., & Cheema, A. (2013). Data collection in a flat world: The strengths and weaknesses of Mechanical Turk samples. *Journal of Behavioral Decision Making, 26*, 213–224. doi: 10.1002/bdm.1753

Gordon, A. M. (2013, February 5). Gratitude is for lovers. Greater good: The science of a meaningful life. Retrieved from http://greatergood.berkeley.edu/article/item/gratitude_is_for_lovers

Gordon, A. M., Impett, E. A., Kogan, A., Oveis, C., & Keltner, D. (2012). To have and to hold: Gratitude promotes relationship maintenance in intimate bonds. *Journal of Personality and Social Psychology, 103*, 257–274. doi:10.1037/a0028723

Gottfredson, L. S. (Ed.). (1997). Foreword to special issue: Intelligence and social policy. *Intelligence, 24*. doi: 10.1016/S0160-2896(97)90010-6

Gould, S. J. (1996). *The mismeasure of man* (revised and expanded). New York: Norton.

Gratitude Is for Lovers. *Chapter 5 opening headline*. Gordon, A. M. (2013, February 5). Gratitude is for lovers. Greater good: The science of a meaningful life. Retrieved from http://greatergood.berkeley.edu/article/item/gratitude_is_for_lovers

Gray, F. D. (1998). *The Tuskegee syphilis study: The real story and beyond*. Montgomery, AL: River City Publishers.

Greenwald, A. G., Nosek, B. A., & Banaji, M. R. (2003). Understanding and using the Implicit Association Test: I. An improved scoring algorithm. *Journal of Personality and Social Psychology, 85*, 197–216. doi:10.1037/0022-3514.85.2.197

Grim, T. (2008). A possible role of social activity to explain differences in publication output among ecologists. *Oikos, 117*, 484–487. doi:10.1111/j.2008.0030-1299.16551.x

Gross, J. J. (2014). *The handbook of emotion regulation* (2nd ed.). New York: Guilford Press.

Gross, J. J., & John, O. P. (2002). Wise emotion regulation. In L. F. Barrett & P. Salovey (Eds.), *The wisdom in feeling: Psychological processes in emotional intelligence* (pp. 297–319). New York: Guilford Press.

Halavis, A. (2004, August 29). The Isuzu experiment. Retrieved from http://alex.halavais.net/the-isuzu-experiment

Haller, M. (2012, January). The reason why you're an angry drunk. *Men's Health* (online). Retrieved from http://news.menshealth.com/the-reason-why-you%E2%80%99re-an-angry-drunk/2012/01/06/

Hamzelou, J. (2010, January). Cell phone radiation is good for Alzheimer's mice. *New Scientist Health*. Retrieved from http://www.newscientist.com/article/ dn18351-cellphone-radiation-is-good-for-alzheimers-mice.html

Harlow, H. (1958). The nature of love. *American Psychologist, 13*, 673–685.

Harms, W. (2013, June 3). Meeting online leads to happier, more enduring marriages. University of Chicago News. Retrieved from https://news.uchicago.edu/article/2013/06/03/meeting-online-leads-happier-more-enduring-marriages

Hastorf, A., & Cantril, H. (1954). They saw a game: A case study. *Journal of Abnormal and Social Psychology, 49*, 129–134. doi:10.1037/h0057880

Heine, S. J. (2016). *Cultural psychology* (3rd ed.). New York: Norton.

Heinzen, T., Lillienfeld, S., & Nolan, S. A. (2015). *The horse that won't go away: Clever Hans, facilitated communication, and the need for clear thinking*. New York: Worth.

Heller, J. (1972, July 26). Syphilis victims went untreated for 40 years. *New York Times*. Retrieved from www.nytimes.com.

Henrich, J., Heine, S. J., & Norenzayan, A. (2010). The weirdest people in the world? (Target article, commentaries, and response.). *Behavioral and Brain Sciences, 33*, 61–83. doi:10.1017/S0140525X0999152X

Herzog, H. A., Jr. (1993). "The movement is my life": The psychology of animal rights activism. *Journal of Social Issues, 49*, 103–119. doi:10.1111/j.1540-4560.1993.tb00911.x

Hill, P. L., & Roberts, B. W. (2011). The role of adherence in the relationship between conscientiousness and perceived health. *Health Psychology, 30*, 797–804. doi:10.1037/a0023860

Hirst, W., Phelps, E. A., Buckner, R. L., Budson, A. E., Cuc, A., Gabrieli, J. D. E., . . . Chandan J. (2009). Long-term memory for the terrorist attack of September 11: Flashbulb memories, event memories, and the factors that influence their retention. *Journal of Experimental Psychology*: General, 138, 161–176. doi:10.1037/a0015527

Holmes, T. H., & Rahe, R. H. (1967). The social readjustment rating scale. *Journal of Psychosomatic Research, 11*, 213–218. doi:10.1016/0022-3999(67)90010-4

Houston's "Rage Room" a Smash as Economy Struggles. *Chapter 2 opening headline*. Dart, T. (2016). "They're here for therapy": Houston's "rage room" a smash as economy struggles. *Guardian* (online). Retrieved from https://www.theguardian.com/us-news/2016/may/24/rage-room-anger-management-unemployment-houston-texas

Howard, J. (2016, August 31). Your dog understands what you are saying, sort of. CNN online. Retrieved from http://www.cnn.com/2016/08/31/health/dogs-words-mri-study/

Hsu, J. (2009, April 12). Facebook users get worse grades in college. Retrieved from http://www.livescience.com/culture/090413-facebook-grades.html

Hubbard, F. O. A., & van Ijzendoorn, M. H. (1991). Maternal unresponsiveness and infant crying across the first 9 months: A naturalistic longitudinal study. *Infant Behavior and Development, 14*, 299–312. doi:10.1016/0163-6383(91)90024-M

Inbar, Y. (2016). Association between contextual dependence and replicability in psychology may be spurious. *Proceedings of the National Academy of Sciences, 113*, E4933–E4934. doi: 10.1073/pnas.1608676113

International Society of Aesthetic Plastic Surgery. (2011). *ISAPS International Survey on Aesthetic/Cosmetic Procedures Performed in 2010*. Retrieved from http://www.isaps.org/isaps-global-statistics-2011.html

Johansson, G. (1973). Visual perception of biological motion and a model for its analysis. *Perception and Psychophysics, 14*, 201–211. doi:10.3758/BF03212378

Johnson, J. G., Cohen, P., Smailes, E. M., Kasen, S., & Brook, J. S. (2002). Television viewing and aggressive behavior during adolescence and adulthood. *Science, 295*, 2468–2471. doi:10.1126/science.1062929

Jones, J. H. (1993). *Bad blood: The Tuskegee syphilis experiment* (Rev. ed.). New York: Free Press.

Jones, J. T., Pelham, B. W., Carvallo, M., & Mirenberg, M. C. (2004). How do I love thee? Let me count the J's: Implicit egotism and interpersonal attraction. *Journal of Personality and Social Psychology, 87*, 665–683. doi:10.1037/0022-3514.87.5.665

Jonsen, A. R. (2005). On the origins and future of the Belmont Report. In J. F. Childress, E. M. Meslin, & H. T. Shapiro (Eds.), *Belmont revisited: Ethical principles for research with human subjects* (pp. 3–11). Washington, DC: Georgetown University Press.

Kabat-Zinn, J. (2013). *Full catastrophe living: Using the wisdom of your body and mind to face stress, pain, and illness* (2nd ed.). New York: Bantam/Random House.

Kagay, M. (1994, July 8). Poll on doubt of Holocaust is corrected. *New York Times.* Retrieved from www.nytimes.com.

Kaplan, R. M., & Pascoe, G. C. (1977). Humorous lectures and humorous examples: Some effects upon comprehension and retention. *Journal of Educational Psychology, 89*, 61–66. doi:10.1037/0022-0663.69.1.61

Keeter, S., Christian, L., & Dimock, M. (2010). The growing gap between landline and dual-frame election polls. Retrieved from http://www.pewresearch.org/2010/11/22/the-growing-gap-between-landline-and-dual-frame-election-polls

Kenny, D. A. (2008). Mediation. Retrieved from http://davidakenny.net/cm/mediate.htm

Kenny, D. A. (2009). Modcrator variables. Retrieved from http://davidakenny.net/cm/moderation.htm

Kenny, D. A., & West, T. V. (2008). Zero acquaintance: Definitions, statistical model, findings, and process. In J. Skowronski & N. Ambady (Eds.), *First impressions* (pp. 129–146). New York: Guilford Press.

Kensinger, E. A., Clarke, R. J., & Corkin, S. (2003). What neural correlates underlie successful encoding and retrieval? A functional magnetic resonance imaging study using a divided attention paradigm. *Journal of Neuroscience, 23*, 2407–2415.

Kienle, G. S., & Kiene, H. (1997). The powerful placebo effect: Fact or fiction? *Journal of Clinical Epidemiology, 50*, 1311–1318. doi:10.1016/S0895-4356(97)00203-5

Kimmel, A. J. (1998). In defense of deception. *American Psychologist, 53*, 803–805. doi:10.1037//0003-066x.53.7.803

Kimmel, A. J. (2007). *Ethical issues in behavioral research* (2nd ed.). Malden, MA: Blackwell.

Kirsch, I., & Sapirstein, G. (1998). Listening to Prozac and hearing placebo: A meta-analysis of antidepressant medication. *Prevention & Treatment, 1.* doi:10.1037/1522-3736.1.1.12a

Klayman, J., & Ha, Y. W. (1987). Confirmation, disconfirmation, and information in hypothesis testing. *Psychological Review, 94*, 211–228. doi:10.1037//0033-295x.94.2.211

Klein, R. A., Ratliff, K. A., Vianello, M., Adams, R. B., Jr., Bahník, Š., Bernstein, M. J., . . . Nosek, B. A. (2014). Investigating variation in replicability: A "many labs" replication project. *Social Psychology, 45*, 142-152. doi:http://dx.doi.org/10.1027/1864-9335/a000178

Kramer, A.D. I., Guillory, J. E., & Hancock, J. T. (2014). Experimental evidence of massive-scale emotional contagion through social networks. *Proceedings of the National Academy of Sciences, 111*, 8788–8790. doi:10.1073/pnas.1320040111

Kringelbach, M. L., & Berridge, K. C. (2009). Towards a functional neuroanatomy of pleasure and happiness. *Trends in Cognitive Sciences, 13*, 479–487. doi:10.1016/j.tics.2009.08.006

Krosnick, J. (1999). Survey research. *Annual Review of Psychology, 50*, 537–567. doi:10.1146/annurev.psych.50.1.537

Kubicek, L. F., & Emde, R. N. (2012). Emotional expression and language: A longitudinal study of typically developing earlier and later talkers from 15 to 30 months. *Infant Mental Health Journal, 33*, 553–584. doi:10.1002/imhj.21364

LaBouff, J. P., Rowatt, W. C., Johnson, M. K., & Finkle, C. (2012). Differences in attitudes toward outgroups in religious and nonreligious contexts in a multinational sample: A situational context priming study. *International Journal for the Psychology of Religion, 22*, 1–9. doi:10.1080/10508619.2012.634778

Langer, E. J., & Abelson, R. P. (1974). A patient by any other name . . .: Clinician group differences in labeling bias. *Journal of Consulting and Clinical Psychology, 42*, 4–9. doi:10.1037/h0036054

Latané, B., & Darley, J. M. (1969). Bystander "apathy." *American Scientist, 57*, 244–268.

Lee, J. (1993). *Facing the fire: Experiencing and expressing anger appropriately.* New York: Bantam.

Lelkes, Y., Krosnick, J. A., Marx, D. M., Judd, C. M., & Park, B. (2012). Complete anonymity compromises the accuracy of self-reports. *Journal of Experimental Social Psychology, 48*, 1291-1299. doi:10.1016/j.jesp.2012.07.002

Leonhardt, D. (2007, May 2). Your plate is bigger than your stomach. *New York Times.* Retrieved from http://www.nytimes.com/2007/05/02/business/02leonhardt.html?pagewanted=all

Leppik, P. (2005, December 1). How authoritative is Wikipedia? Retrieved from http://66.49.144.193/C2011481421/E652809545/index.html

Likert, R. (1932). A technique for the measurement of attitudes. *Archives of Psychology, 22*, 1–55.

Lin-Siegler, X., Ahn, J. N., Chen, J., Fang, F.A., & Luna-Lucero, M. (2016). Even Einstein struggled: Effects of learning about great scientists' struggles on high school students' motivation to learn science. *Journal of Educational Psychology, 108*, 314–328. doi:10.1037/edu0000092

Lohr, J. M., Olatunji, B. O., Baumeister, R. F., & Bushman, B. J. (2007). The psychology of anger venting and empirically supported alternatives that do no harm. *Scientific Review of Mental Health Practice, 5*, 54–65.

Lovaas, O. I. (1987). Behavioral treatment and normal educational and intellectual functioning in young autistic children. *Journal of Consulting and Clinical Psychology, 55*, 3–9. doi:10.1037//0022-006x.55.1.3

Lucas, R. E., & Lawless, N. M. (2013). Does life seem better on a sunny day? Examining the association between daily weather conditions and life satisfaction judgments. *Journal of Personality and Social Psychology, 104*, 872–884. doi:10.1037/a0032124

Lucas, R. E., & Schimmack, U. (2009). Income and well-being: How big is the gap between the rich and the poor? *Journal of Research in Personality, 43*, 75–78. doi:http://dx.doi.org/10.1016/j.jrp.2008.09.004

Lutsky, N. (2008). Arguing with numbers: A rationale and suggestions for teaching quantitative reasoning through argument and writing. In B. L. Madison & L. A. Steen (Eds.), *Calculation vs. context: Quantitative literacy and its implications for teacher education* (pp. 59–74). Washington, DC: Mathematical Association of America.

Lyubomirsky, S., King, L. A., & Diener, E. (2005). The benefits of frequent positive affect: Does happiness lead to success? *Psychological Bulletin, 131*, 803–855. doi:10.1037/0033-2909.131.6.803

Margraf, J., Meyer, A. H., & Lavallee, K. L. (2013). Well-being from the knife? Psychological effects of aesthetic surgery. *Clinical Psychological Science, 3*, 1–14. doi:10.1177/2167702612471660

Markus, H. R., & Hamedani, M. G. (2007). Sociocultural psychology: The dynamic interdependence among self systems and social systems. In S. Kitayama & D. Cohen (Eds.), *Handbook of cultural psychology* (pp. 3–39). New York: Guilford Press.

Markus, H. R., & Kitayama, S. (1991). Culture and the self: Implications for cognition, emotion, and motivation. *Psychological Review, 98*, 224–253. doi:10.1037//0033-295x.98.2.224

Marshall, B. J., & Warren, J. R. (1983). Unidentified curved bacillus on gastric epithelium in active chronic gastritis. *Lancet, 1*(8336), 1273–1275. doi:10.1016/s0140-6736(83)92719-8

Marshall, B. J., & Warren, J. R. (1984). Unidentified curved bacilli in the stomach patients with gastritis and peptic ulceration. *Lancet, 1*(8390), 1311–1315. doi:10.1016/S0140-6736(84)91816-6

Masuda, T., & Nisbett, R. E. (2001). Attending holistically vs. analytically: Comparing the context sensitivity of Japanese and Americans. *Journal of Personality and Social Psychology, 81*, 922–934. doi:10.1037//0022-3514.81.5.922

May, D. (2014, June 3). A learning secret: Don't take notes with a laptop. *Scientific American* (online). Retrieved from http://www.scientificamerican.com/article/a-learning-secret-don-t-take-notes-with-a-laptop

McCallum, J. M., Arekere, D. M., Green, B. L., Katz, R. V., & Rivers, B. M. (2006). Awareness and knowledge of the U.S. Public Health Service syphilis study at Tuskegee: Implications for biomedical research. *Journal of Health Care for the Poor and Underserved, 17*, 716–733. doi:10.1353/hpu.2006.0130

McCartney, K., & Rosenthal, R. (2000). Effect size, practical importance, and social policy for children. *Child Development, 71*, 173–180. doi:10.1111/1467-8624.00131

McKey, R., Condelli, L., Ganson, H., Barrett, B., McConkey, C., & Plantz, M. (1985). *The impact of Head Start on children, families, and communities.* (Final report of the Head Start Evaluation, Synthesis, and Utilization Project.) Washington, DC: U.S. Department of Health and Human Services.

McNulty, J. K. (2010). When positive processes hurt relationships. *Current Directions in Psychological Science, 19*, 167–171. doi:10.1177/0963721410370298

Meaningful Conversations Linked to Happier People. *Chapter 8 opening headline. Scientific American*, 2010. http://www.scientificamerican.com/article/skip-the-small-talk/

Mehl, M. R., Gosling, S. D., & Pennebaker, J. W. (2006). Personality in its natural habitat: Manifestations and implicit folk theories of personality in daily life. *Journal of Personality and Social Psychology, 90*, 862–877. doi:10.1037/0022-3514.90.5.862

Mehl, M. R., & Pennebaker, J. W. (2003). The sounds of social life: A psychometric analysis of students' daily social environments and natural conversations. *Journal of Personality and Social Psychology, 84*(4), 857–870. doi:10.1037/0022-3514.84.4.857

Mehl, M. R., Vazire, S., Holleran, S. E., & Clark, C. S. (2010). Eavesdropping on happiness: Well-being is related to having less small talk and more substantive conversations. *Psychological Science, 21*, 539–541. doi:10.1177/0956797610362675

Mehl, M. R., Vazire, S., Ramirez-Esparza, N., Slatcher, R. B., & Pennebaker, J. W. (2007). Are women really more talkative than men? *Science, 317*, 82. doi:10.1126/science.1139940

Metzger, M. M. (2015). Knowledge of the Animal Welfare Act and Animal Welfare Regulations Influences Attitudes Toward Animal Research. http://www.ncbi.nlm.nih.gov/pmc/articles/PMC4311745/

Milgram, S. (1963). Behavioral study of obedience. *Journal of Abnormal and Social Psychology, 67*, 371–378. doi:10.1037/h0040525

Milgram, S. (1974). *Obedience to authority.* New York: Harper & Row.

Miller, D. P., Waldfogel, J., & Han, W. J. (2012). Family meals and child academic and behavioral outcomes. *Child Development, 83*, 2104–2120. doi:10.1111/j.1467-8624.2012.01825.x

Miller, G. E. (1956). The magic number seven plus or minus two: Some limits on our capacity for processing information. *Psychological Review, 63*, 81–97. doi:10.1037/h0043158

Mindfulness May Improve Test Scores (*Scientific American*, 2013): *Chapter 1 opening headline*. Nicholson, C. (2006, March 28). Mindfulness may improve test scores. *Scientific American* (online). Retrieved from http://www.scientificamerican.com/podcast/episode/mindfulness-may-improve-test-scores-13-03-28/

Mitchell, L. (2015, March 30). Has the world gone coco? Eating chocolate can help you LOSE weight. *Daily Star*. Retrieved from http://www.dailystar.co.uk/diet-fitness/433688/Chocolate-diet-how-to-lose-weight

Moffat, N. J. (1989). Home-based cognitive rehabilitation with the elderly. In L. W. Poon, D. C. Rubin, & B. A. Wilson (Eds.), *Everyday cognition in adulthood and late life* (pp. 659–680). Cambridge, UK: Cambridge University Press.

Mook, D. (1989). The myth of external validity. In L. W. Poon, D. C. Rubin, & B. A. Wilson (Eds.), *Everyday cognition in adulthood and late life* (pp. 25–43). Cambridge, UK: Cambridge University Press.

Mook, D. (2001). *Psychological research*. New York: Norton.

Most Holocaust survivors battle depression. (2010, January 26). NBC News (online). Retrieved from http://www.nbcnews.com/id/35082451/ns/health-mental_health/t/most-holocaust-survivors-battle-depression/#.U1bHs_ldV8E

Mrazek, M. D., Franklin, M. S., Phillips, D. T., Baird, B., & Schooler, J. W. (2013). Mindfulness training improves working memory capacity and GRE performance while reducing mind wandering. *Psychological Science, 24*, 776–781. doi:10.1177/0956797612459659

Mueller, C. M., & Dweck, C. S. (1998). Praise for intelligence can undermine children's motivation and performance. *Journal of Personality and Social Psychology, 75*, 33–52. doi.10.1037//0022-3514.75.1.33

Mueller, P. A., & Oppenheimer, D. M. (2014). The pen is mightier than the keyboard: Advantages of longhand over laptop note taking. *Psychological Science, 25*, 1–10. doi:10.1177/0956797614524581

Mundell, E. J. (2007, July 5). Science quiets myth of "chatterbox" females. Sexualhealth.com. Retrieved from http://sexualhealth.e-healtsource.com/index.php?p=news1&id=606134

Myers, D. (2000). The funds, friends, and faith of happy people. *American Psychologist, 55*, 56–67. doi:10.1037//0003-066x.55.1.56

Nasaw, D. (2012, July 24). Meet the "bots" that edit Wikipedia. BBC News Magazine [Online]. Retrieved from http://www.bbc.co.uk/news/magazine-18892510

National Institutes of Health, Office of Human Subjects Research. (1979). *Belmont Report*. Retrieved from http://ohsr.od.nih.gov/guidelines/belmont.html

National Research Council. (2011). *Guide for the care and use of laboratory animals* (8th ed.). Washington, DC: National Academies Press.

Neisser, U., & Harsch, N. (1992). Phantom flashbulbs: False recollections of hearing the news about Challenger. In E. Winograd and U. Neisser (Eds.), *Affect and accuracy in recall*. New York: Cambridge University Press.

Nelson, S. K., Kushlev, K., English, T., Dunn, E. W., & Lyubomirsky, S. (2013). In defense of parenthood: Children are associated with more joy than misery. *Psychological Science, 24*, 3–10. doi:10.1177/0956797612447798

New California Law Prohibits All Cell Phone Use While Driving. *Chapter 12 opening headline*. Whittaker, B. (2016, September 29). New California law prohibits all cell phone use while driving. KSBW8 News. Retrieved from http://www.ksbw.com/article/new-california-law-prohibits-all-cellphone-use-while-driving/4096079

New York Times (2009, July 18). Should cell phone use by drivers be illegal? *New York Times* (online). Retrieved from http://roomfordebate.blogs.nytimes.com/2009/07/18/should-cellphone-use-by-drivers-be-illegal/

Nicholson, C. (2006, March 28). Mindfulness may improve test scores. *Scientific American* (online). Retrieved from http://www.scientificamerican.com/podcast/episode/mindfulness-may-improve-test-scores-13-03-28/

Nisbett, R. E., & Wilson, T. (1977). Telling more than we can know: Verbal reports on mental processes. *Psychological Review, 84*, 231–259. doi:10.1037//0033-295X.84.3.231

Nuzzo, R. (2015). Fooling ourselves. *Nature, 526*, 182–185.

O'Connor, A. (2012). The chocolate diet? *New York Times Well Blog*. Retrieved from http://well.blogs.nytimes.com/2012/03/26/the-chocolate-diet/?src=me&ref=general

Oettingen, G. (2014). *Rethinking positive thinking: Inside the new science of motivation*. New York: Penguin/Current.

Oishi, S., Rothman, A. J., Snyder, M., Su, J., Zehm, K., Hertel, A. W., Gonzales, M. H., & Sherman, G. D. (2007). The socioecological model of procommunity action: The benefits of residential stability. *Journal of Personality and Social Psychology, 93*, 831–844. doi:10.1037/0022-3514.93.5.831

Open Science Collaboration (2015). Estimating the reproducibility of psychological science. (2015). *Science, 349*(6251), 1–8. doi:10.1126/science.aac4716

Ortmann, A., & Hertwig, R. (1997). Is deception acceptable? *American Psychologist, 52*, 746–747. doi:10.1037//0003-066x.52.7.746

Ostrovsky, Y., Meyers, E., Ganesh, S., Mathur, U., & Sinha, P. (2009). Visual parsing after recovery from blindness.

Psychological Science, 20, 1484–1491. doi:10.1111/j.1467-9280.2009.02471.x

Otway, L. J., & Vignoles, V. L. (2006). Narcissism and childhood recollections: A quantitative test of psychoanalytic predictions. *Personality and Social Psychology Bulletin, 22,* 104–116. doi:10.1177/0146167205279907

Owens, J. A., Belon, K., & Moss, P. (2010). Impact of delaying school start time on adolescent sleep, mood, and behavior. *Archives of Pediatric Adolescent Medicine, 164,* 608–614. doi:10.1001/archpediatrics.2010.96

Paik, H., & Comstock, G. (1994). The effects of television violence on antisocial behavior: A meta-analysis. *Communication Research, 21,* 516–546. doi:10.1177/009365094021004004

Paluck, E. L. (2009). Reducing intergroup prejudice and conflict using the media: A field experiment in Rwanda. *Journal of Personality and Social Psychology, 96,* 574–587. doi:10.1037/a0011989

Pande, A. H., Ross-Degnan, D. Zaslavsky, A. M., & Salomon, J. A. (2011). Effects of healthcare reforms on coverage, access, and disparities: Quasi-experimental analysis of evidence from Massachusetts. *American Journal of Preventive Medicine, 41,* 1–8. doi:10.1016/j.amepre.2011.03.010

Paulhus, D. L., & Vazire, S. (2007). The self-report method. In R. W. Robins, R. C. Fraley, & R. Krueger (Eds.), *Handbook of research methods in personality psychology* (pp. 224–239). New York: Guilford Press.

Pavot, W., & Diener, E. (1993). Review of the Satisfaction with Life Scale. *Psychological Assessment, 5,* 164–172. doi:10.1037/1040-3590.5.2.164

Pearson, C. (2015, August 6). Science proves reading to kids really does change their brains. *Huffington Post.* Retrieved from http://www.huffingtonpost.com/entry/science-proves-reading-to-kids-changes-their-brains_us_55c26bf4e4b0f1cbf1e38740

Pelham, B. W., Carvallo, M., & Jones, J. T. (2005). Implicit egotism. *Current Directions in Psychological Science, 14,* 106–110. doi:http://dx.doi.org/10.1111/j.0963-7214.2005.00344.x

Pelham, B. W., Mirenberg, M. C., & Jones, J. T. (2002). Why Susie sells seashells by the seashore: Implicit egotism and major life decisions. *Journal of Personality and Social Psychology, 82,* 469–487. doi:http://dx.doi.org/10.1037/0022-3514.82.4.469

People with Higher Incomes Spend Less Time Socializing. *Chapter 3 opening headline.* Simon-Thomas, E.R. (2016, June 4). Are the rich more lonely? *Huffington Post.* Retrieved from http://www.huffingtonpost.com/greater-good-science-center/are-the-rich-more-lonely_b_10296990.html

Perry, G. (2013). *Behind the shock machine: The untold story of the notorious Milgram psychology experiments.* New York: New Press.

Petrosino, A., Turpin-Petrosino, C., & Finckenauer, J. O. (2000). Well-meaning programs can have harmful effects! Lessons from experiments of programs such as Scared Straight. *Crime and Delinquency, 46,* 354–379. doi:10.1177/0011128700046003006

Pew Research Center. (2015, May 12). "America's Changing Religious Landscape." RLS-08-26-full-report.pdf

Pew Research Center (2015). Americans, Politics, and Science Issues. http://www.pewinternet.org/2015/07/01/chapter-7-opinion-about-the-use-of-animals-in-research/

Pew Research Center. (n.d.). Cell phone surveys. Retrieved from http://www.people-press.org/methodology/collecting-survey-data/cell-phone-surveys/

Pew Research Center. (n.d.). Random digit dialing—Our standard method. Retrieved from http://people-press.org/methodology/sampling/#1

Pezdek, K. (2003). Event memory and autobiographical memory for the events of September 11, 2001. *Applied Cognitive Psychology, 17,* 1033–1045. doi:10.1002/acp.984

Pfungst, O. (1911). *Clever Hans (The horse of Mr. Von Osten): A contribution to experimental animal and human psychology.* New York: Henry Holt.

Piaget, J. (1923). *The language and thought of the child* (M. Worden, trans.). New York: Harcourt, Brace, & World.

Piff, P. K., Stancato, D. M., Côté, S., Mendoza-Denton, R., & Keltner, D. (2012). Higher social class predicts increased unethical behavior. *Proceedings of the National Academy of Sciences, 109,* 4086–4091. doi:10.1073/pnas.1118373109

Pittenger, D. J. (2002). Deception in research: Distinctions and solutions from the perspective of utilitarianism. *Ethics and Behavior, 12,* 117–142. doi:10.1207/s15327019eb1202_1

Plous, S. (1996a). Attitudes toward the use of animals in psychological research and education: Results from a national survey of psychologists. *American Psychologist, 51,* 1167–1180. doi:10.1037//0003-066x.51.11.1167

Plous, S. (1996b). Attitudes toward the use of animals in psychological research and education: Results from a national survey of psychology majors. *Psychological Science, 7,* 352–358. doi:10.1111/j.1467-9280.1996.tb00388.x

Plous, S. (1998). Signs of change within the animal rights movement: Results from a follow-up survey of activists. *Journal of Comparative Psychology, 112,* 48–54. doi:10.1037//0735-7036.112.1.48

Plous, S., & Herzog, H. A., Jr. (2000). Poll shows researchers favor lab animal protection. *Science, 290,* 711. doi:10.1126/science.290.5492.711b

Pronin, E., Gilovich, T., & Ross, L. (2004). Objectivity in the eye of the beholder: Divergent perceptions of bias in self versus others. *Psychological Review, 111,* 781–799. doi:10.1037/0033-295x.111.3.781

Pronin, E., Lin, D. Y., & Ross, L. (2002). The bias blind spot: Perceptions of bias in self versus others. *Personality and Social Psychology Bulletin, 28,* 369–381. doi:10.1177/0146167202286008

Quinn, P. C., Yahr, J., Kuhn, A., Slater, A. M., & Pascalis, O. (2002). Representation of the gender of human faces by infants: A preference for female. *Perception, 31,* 1109–1121. doi:10.1068/p3331

Rampell, C. (2010, April 19). Want a higher GPA? Go to a private college. (Blog post.) Retrieved from http://economix.blogs.nytimes.com/2010/04/19/want-a-higher-g-p-a-go-to-a-private-college/

Raskin, R., & Terry, H. (1988). A principal components analysis of the Narcissistic Personality Inventory and further evidence of its construct validity. *Journal of Personality and Social Psychology, 54,* 890–902. doi:10.1037//0022-3514.54.5.890

Rauscher, F. H., Shaw, G. L., & Ky, K. N. (1993). Music and spatial task performance. *Nature, 365,* 520.

Raven, J. C. (1976). *Standard progressive matrices.* Oxford: Oxford Psychologists Press.

Rayner, K., Schotter, E. R., Masson, M. E. J., Potter, M. C., & Treiman, R. (2016). So much to read, so little time: How do we read, and can speed reading help? *Psychological Science in the Public Interest, 17,* 4–34. doi:10.1177/1529100615623267

Reiss, J. E., & Hoffman, J. E. (2006). Object substitution masking interferes with semantic processing: Evidence from event-related potentials. *Psychological Science, 17,* 1015–1020. doi:10.1111/j.1467-9280.2006.01820.x

Religion can spur goodness (2008, April 28). World-science .net. Retrieved from http://www.world-science.net/othernews/081002_religion

Rentfrow, P. J., & Gosling, S. D. (2003). The do-re-mi's of everyday life: The structure and personality correlates of music preferences. *Journal of Personality and Social Psychology, 84,* 1236–1256. doi:10.1037/0022-3514.84.6.1236

Reproducibility Project: Psychology [Website]. Retrieved from https://osf.io/project/EZcUj/wiki/home/

Reverby, S. (2009). *Examining Tuskegee: The infamous syphilis study and its legacy.* Chapel Hill: University of North Carolina Press.

Riedeger, M., & Klipker, K. (2014). Emotional regulation in adolescence. In J. J. Gross (Ed.) *The handbook of emotion regulation* (2nd ed., pp. 187–202). New York: Guilford Press.

Roberts, B. W., & Robins, R. W. (2000). Broad dispositions, broad aspirations: The intersection of personality traits and major life goals. *Personality and Social Psychology Bulletin, 26,* 1284–1296. doi:10.1177/0146167200262009

Ropeik, D. (2010). *How risky is it, really?: Why our fears don't always match the facts.* New York: McGraw-Hill Education.

Ropeik, D., & Gray, G. (2002). *Risk: A practical guide for deciding what's really safe and what's really dangerous in the world around you.* New York: Houghton Mifflin.

Rosenberg, M. (1965). *Society and the adolescent self-image.* Princeton, NJ: Princeton University Press.

Rosenthal, R., & Fode, K. (1963). The effect of experimenter bias on the performance of the albino rat. *Behavioral Science, 8,* 183–189. doi:10.1002/bs.3830080302

Sabin, L. (2015, March 10). The origins of narcissism: Children more likely to be self-centered if they are praised too much (Independent, 2015). *Independent* (online). Retrieved from http://ind.pn/2d10Zk7

Sanbonmatsu, D. M., Strayer, D. L., Medeiros-Ward, N., & Watson, J. M. (2013). Who multitasks and why? Multitasking ability, perceived multi-tasking ability, impulsivity, and sensation-seeking. *PLOS ONE, 8,* e54402. doi:10.1371/journal.pone.0054402

Sasaki, J., & Kim, H. (2011). At the intersection of culture and religion: A cultural analysis of religion's implications for secondary control and social affiliation. *Journal of Personality and Social Psychology, 101,* 401–414. doi:10.1037/a0021849a

Sathyanarayana Rao, T. S., & Andrade, C. (2011). The MMR vaccine and autism: Sensation, refutation, retraction, and fraud. *Indian Journal of Psychiatry, 53,* 95–96. doi:10.4103/0019-5545.82529

Sawilowsky, S. (2005). Teaching random assignment: Do you believe it works? Theoretical and behavioral foundations of education. Wayne State University Digital Commons. Retrieved from http://digitalcommons.wayne.edu/cgi/viewcontent.cgi?article=1015&context=coe_tbf

Saxe, L. (1991). Lying: Thoughts of an applied social psychologist. *American Psychologist, 46,* 409–415. doi:10.1037//0003-066X.46.4.409

Schellenberg, G. (2004). Music lessons enhance IQ. *Psychological Science, 15,* 511–514. doi:10.1111/j.0956-7976.2004.00711.x

Schwarz, N., & Clore, G. L. (1983). Mood, misattribution, and judgments of well-being: Informative and directive functions of affective states. *Journal of Personality and Social Psychology, 45,* 513. doi:10.1037/0022-3514.45.3.513

Schwarz, N., & Oyserman, D. (2001). Asking questions about behavior: Cognition, communication, and questionnaire construction. *American Journal of Evaluation, 22,* 127–160. doi:10.1016/s1098-2140(01)00133-3

ScienceDaily (2015, September 11). Pressure to be available 24/7 on social media causes teen anxiety, depression. Retrieved from https://www.sciencedaily.com/releases/2015/09/150911094917.htm

Scoville, W. B., & Milner, B. (1957). Loss of recent memory after bilateral hippocampal lesions. *Journal of Neurology, Neurosurgery, and Psychiatry, 20*, 11–21. doi:10.1136/jnnp.20.1.11

Sears, D. O. (1986). College sophomores in the laboratory: Influences of a narrow data base on social psychology's view of human nature. *Journal of Personality and Social Psychology, 51*, 515–539. doi:10.1037//0022-3514.51.3.515

Segal, D. L., Coolidge, F. L., Cahill, B. S., & O'Riley, A. A. (2008). Psychometric properties of the Beck Depression Inventory-II (BDI-II) among community-dwelling older adults. *Behavior Modification, 32*, 3–20. doi:10.1177/0145445507303833

Segall, M. H., Campbell, D. T., & Herskovits, M. J. (1966). *The influence of culture on visual perception.* Indianapolis, IN: Bobbs-Merrill.

Serving Food on a Larger Plate "Makes People Eat More." *Chapter 10 opening headline.* Cooper, C. (2015, September 14). Serving food on a larger plate "makes people eat more." *Independent* (online). Retrieved from http://www.independent.co.uk/life-style/health-and-families/health-news/serving-food-on-a-larger-plate-makes-people-eat-more-10500767.html

7 Secrets of Low-Stress Families. *Chapter 6 opening headline.* Yorio, N. (2010). Seven secrets of low-stress families. WebMD.com. Retrieved from http://www.webmd.com/parenting/features/seven-secrets-of-low-stress-families#1

72% of the World Smiled Yesterday. *Chapter 3 opening headline.* Gallup.com, 2016. Gallup 2016 Global Emotions Report. Retrieved from http://www.gallup.com/services/189968/gallup-2016-global-emotions-report.aspx

Shadish, W. R., & Luellen, J. K. (2006). Quasi-experimental design. In J. L. Green, G. Camilli, & P. B. Elmore (Eds.), *Handbook of complementary methods in education research* (pp. 539–550). Mahwah, NJ: Erlbaum.

Sharpe, D., Adair, J. G., & Roese, N. J. (1992). Twenty years of deception research: A decline in subjects' trust? *Personality and Social Psychology Bulletin, 18*, 585–590. doi:10.1177/0146167292185009

Shuster, E. (1997). Fifty years later: The significance of the Nuremberg Code. *New England Journal of Medicine, 337*, 1436–1440. doi:10.1056/nejm199711133372006

Shweder, R. (1989). Cultural psychology: What is it? In J. Stigler, R. Shweder, & G. Herdt (Eds.), *Cultural psychology: The Chicago symposia on culture and development* (pp. 1–46). New York: Cambridge University Press.

Silver, N. (2012). Fivethirtyeight: Nate Silver's political calculus. Retrieved from http://fivethirtyeight.blogs.nytimes.com

Simmons, J. P., Nelson, L. D., & Simonsohn, U. (2011). False-positive psychology: Undisclosed flexibility in data collection and analysis allows presenting anything as significant. *Psychological Science, 22*(11), 1359–1366. doi:10.1177/0956797611417632

Simon-Thomas, E.R. (2016, June 4). Are the rich more lonely? *Huffington Post.* Retrieved from http://www.huffingtonpost.com/greater-good-science-center/are-the-rich-more-lonely_b_10296990.html

Simonsohn, U. (2011). Spurious? Name similarity effects (implicit egotism) in marriage, job, and moving decisions. *Journal of Personality and Social Psychology, 101*, 1–24. doi:http://dx.doi.org/10.1037/a0021990

Simonsohn, U. (2015). Small telescopes: Detectability and the evaluation of replication results. *Psychological Science, 26*, 559–569. doi:10.1177/0956797614567341

Six Great Ways to Vent Your Frustrations. *Chapter 2 opening headline.* Crume, D. M. (n.d.). Six great ways to vent your frustrations. Lifehack.org. Retrieved from http://www.lifehack.org/articles/featured/six-great-ways-to-vent-your-frustrations.html

61% Said This Shoe "Felt True to Size." *Chapter 7 opening headline.* Zappos.com.

Smith, G. T. (2005a). On construct validity: Issues of method and measurement. *Psychological Assessment, 17*, 396–408. doi:10.1037/1040-3590.17.4.396

Smith, G. T. (2005b). On the complexity of quantifying construct validity. *Psychological Assessment, 17*, 413–414. doi:10.1037/1040-3590.17.4.413

Smith, S. S., & Richardson, D. (1983). Amelioriation of deception and harm in psychological research: The important role of debriefing. *Journal of Personality and Social Psychology, 44*, 1075–1082. doi:10.1037//0022-3514.44.5.1075

Snyder, M., & Campbell, B. (1980). Testing hypotheses about other people: The role of the hypothesis. *Personality and Social Psychology Bulletin, 6*, 421–426. doi:10.1177/014616728063015

Snyder, M., & Swann, W. B. (1978). Hypothesis-testing processes in social interaction. *Journal of Personality and Social Psychology, 36*, 1202–1212. doi:10.1037//0022-3514.36.11.1202

Snyder, M., & White, M. (1981). Testing hypotheses about other people: Strategies of verification and falsification. *Personality and Social Psychology Bulletin, 7*, 39–43. doi:10.1177/014616728171007

Spiegel, A. (2010, June 28). "Mozart effect" was just what we wanted to hear. National Public Radio transcript. Retrieved from http://www.npr.org/templates/ story/story.php?storyId=128104580

Stapel Investigation (2012). Flawed science: The fraudulent research practices of social psychologist Diederik Stapel. Retrieved from https://www.commissielevelt.nl

Steenhuysen, J. (2010, April 26). Depressed? You must like chocolate. MSNBC mental health. Retrieved from http://www.msnbc.msn.com/id/36786824/ns/health-mental_health

Stein, R. (2009, June 22). Positive is negative. *Washington Post*. Retrieved from www.washingtonpost.com.

Steinberg, L., & Monahan, K. (2011). Adolescents' exposure to sexy media does not hasten the initiation of sexual intercourse. *Developmental Psychology*, 47, 562–576. doi:10.1037/a0020613

Steingraber, S. (2008). Pesticides, animals, and humans. In L. H. Peterson & J. C. Brereton (Eds.), *The Norton Reader* (11th ed., pp. 971–982). New York: Norton. (Reprinted from *Living downstream: An ecologist looks at cancer and the environment*, by S. Steingraber, 1997, New York: Perseus Books.)

Stories Told of Brilliant Scientists Affect Kids' Interest in the Field. *Chapter 3 opening headline*. Vedantam, S. (2016, June 7). How Stories Told of Brilliant Scientists Affect Kids' Interest in the Field. Transcript from *Morning Edition, National Public Radio*. Retrieved from http://www.npr.org/2016/06/07/481058613/how-the-stories-told-of-brilliant-scientists-affect-kids-interest-in-the-field

Strayer, D. L., & Drews, F. A. (2004). Profiles in distraction: Effects of cell phone conversations on younger and older drivers. *Human Factors*, 46, 640–650. doi:10.1518/hfes.46.4.640.56806

Strayer, D. L., Drews, F. A., & Johnston, W. A. (2003). Cell phone induced failures in visual attention during simulated driving. *Journal of Experimental Psychology: Applied*, 9, 23–52. doi:10.1037/1076-898X.9.1.23

Stroebe, W., Postmes, T., & Spears, R. (2012). Scientific misconduct and the myth of self-correction in science. *Psychological Science, 7*, 670–688. doi:10.1177/1745691612460687

Strube, M. J. (1991). Small sample failure of random assignment: A further examination. *Journal of Consulting and Clinical Psychology, 59*, 346–350. doi:10.1037//0022-006x.59.2.346

Study Links Teen Pregnancy to Sex on TV Shows. *Chapter 9 opening headline*. Tighe, M. (2008, Nov 3). Study links teen pregnancy to sex on TV shows. Newsmax.com. Retrieved from http://www.newsmax.com/Newsfront/sex-tv-abstinence-teen/2008/11/03/id/326321/

Suchotzki, K., Verschuere, B., Van Bockstaele, B., Ben-Shakhar, G., & Crombez, G. (2017). Lying takes time: A meta-analysis on reaction time measures of deception. *Psychological Bulletin, 143*, 428–453. doi:http://dx.doi.org/10.1037/bul0000087

Suds seem to skew scientific success. (2008, March 18). UT San Diego. Retrieved from http://www.utsandiego.com/uniontrib/20080318/news_1n18science.html

Sugden, N. A., Mohamed-Ali, M. I., & Moulson, M. C. (2013). I spy with my little eye: Typical, daily exposure to faces documented from a first-person infant perspective.

Developmental Psychobiology, 56, 249–261. doi:10.1002/dev.21183

Tavris, C. (1989). *Anger: The misunderstood emotion*. New York: Simon & Schuster.

Taylor, L. E., Swerdfeger, A. L., Eslick, G. D.(2014). Vaccines are not associated with autism: An evidence-based meta-analysis of case-control and cohort studies. *Vaccine, 32*, 3623–3629. doi:10.1016/j.vaccine.2014.04.085

The Origins of Narcissism: Children More Likely to Be Self-Centered If They Are Praised Too Much. *Chapter 9 opening headline*. Sabin, L. (2015, March 10). The origins of narcissism: Children more likely to be self-centered if they are praised too much (Independent, 2015). *Independent* (online). Retrieved from http://ind.pn/2d1OZk7

The Reason Why You're an Angry Drunk: *Chapter 12 opening headline*. Haller, M. (2012, January). The reason why you're an angry drunk. *Men's Health* (online). Retrieved from http://news.menshealth.com/the-reason-why-you%E2%80%99re-an-angry-drunk/2012/01/06

Three in Four Women Worldwide Rate Their Lives as "Struggling" or "Suffering." *Chapter 7 opening headline*. Gallup, 2015. http://www.gallup.com/poll/181790/nearly-billion-women-worldwide-struggling-suffering.aspx

Tighe, M. (2008, Nov 3). Study Links Teen Pregnancy to Sex on TV Shows. Newsmax.com. Retrieved from http://www.newsmax.com/Newsfront/sex-tv-abstinence-teen/2008/11/03/id/326321/

Tucker, C. J., Finkelhor, D., Turner, H., & Shattuck, A. (2013). Association of sibling aggression with child and adolescent mental health. *Pediatrics, 132*, 79–84. doi:10.1542/peds.2012-3801

Turner, E. H., Matthews, A .M., Linardatos, E., Tell, R. A., & Rosenthal, R. (2008). Selective publication of antidepressant trials and its influence on apparent efficacy. *New England Journal of Medicine, 358*, 252–260. doi:10.1056/NEJMsa065779

Tversky, A., & Kahneman, D. (1974). Judgments under uncertainty: Heuristics and biases. *Science, 185*, 1124–1131. doi:10.1126/science.185.4157.1124

Twachtman-Cullen, D. (1997). *A passion to believe: Autism and the facilitated communication phenomenon*. Boulder, CO: Westview Press.

Tyner, S., Brewer, A., Helman, M., Leon, Y., Pritchard, J., & Schlund, M. (2016) Nice doggie! Contact desensitization plus reinforcement decreases dog phobias for children with autism. *Behavior Analysis and Practice, 9*, 54–57. doi:10.1007/s40617-016-0113-4

Uhls, Y. T., Michikyan, M., Morris, J., Garcia, D., Small, G.W., Zgourou, E., & Greenfield, P.M. (2014). Five days at outdoor education camp without screens improves preteen skills with nonverbal cues. *Computers in Human Behavior, 39*, 387–392. doi:10.1016/j.chb.2014.05.036

U.S. Department of Health and Human Services. Data from the National Health Interview Survey. December, 2012. Retrieved from http://www.cdc.gov/nchs/data/series/sr_10/sr10_256.pdf

U.S. Department of Health and Human Services, National Institutes of Health. (2009). Public welfare, protection of human subjects. Code of Federal Regulations: HHS Regulation 45 CFR, Part 46. Retrieved from http://www.hhs.gov/ohrp/humansubjects/guidance/45cfr46.html

Van Bavel, J. J., Mende-Siedlecki, P., Brady, W. J., & Reinero, D. A. (2016). Contextual sensitivity in scientific reproducibility. *Proceedings of the National Academy of Sciences, 113*(23), 6454–6459. doi:10.1073/pnas.1521897113

Vandell, D., Henderson, L. V., & Wilson, K. S. (1988). A longitudinal study of children with day-care experiences of varying quality. *Child Development, 59*, 1286–1292. doi:10.1111/j.1467-8624.1988.tb01497.x

Van Kleef, E., Shimizu, M., & Wansink, B. (2012). Serving bowl selection biases the amount of food served. *Journal of Nutrition Education and Behavior, 44*, 66–70. doi:10.1016/j.jneb.2011.03.001

Van Orden, K. A., Witte, T. K., Cukrowicz, K. C., Braithwaite, S. R., Selby, E. A., & Joiner, T. E. (2010). The interpersonal theory of suicide. *Psychological Review, 117*, 575–600. doi:10.1037/a0018697

Vazire., S., & Carlson, E. N. (2011). Others sometimes know us better than we know ourselves. *Current Directions in Psychological Science, 20*, 104–108. doi:10.1177/0963721411402478

Vedantam, S. (2016, June 7). How Stories Told of Brilliant Scientists Affect Kids' Interest in the Field. Transcript from *Morning Edition, National Public Radio.* Retrieved from http://www.npr.org/2016/06/07/481058613/how-the-stories-told-of-brilliant-scientists-affect-kids-interest-in-the-field

Vickery, T. J., Chun, M. M., & Lee, D. (2011). Ubiquity and specificity of reinforcement signals throughout the human brain. *Neuron, 72*, 166–177. doi:10.1016/j.neuron.2011.08.011

Waelde, L. C., Uddo, M., Marquett, R., Ropelato, M., Freightman, S., Pardo, A., & Salazar, J. (2008). A pilot study of meditation for mental health workers following Hurricane Katrina. *Journal of Traumatic Stress, 21*, 497–500. doi:10.1002/jts.20365

Wansink, B., & Kim, J. (2005). Bad popcorn in big buckets: Portion size can influence intake as much as taste. *Journal of Nutrition Education and Behavior, 37*, 242–245. doi:10.1016/S1499-4046(06)60278-9

Warner, J. (2008, January 7). Family meals curb eating disorders. *WebMD magazine.* Retrieved from http://www.webmd.com/parenting/news/20080107/family-meals-curb-teen-eating-disorders

Webb, E., Campbell, D., Schwartz, R., & Sechrest, L. (1966). *Unobtrusive measures: Nonreactive research in the social sciences.* Chicago, IL: Rand McNally.

Wechsler, D. (2004). *The Wechsler Intelligence Scale for Children* (4th ed.). London: Pearson Assessment.

Welsh, J. (2012, May 17). Parents are happier than non-parents. Live Science. Retrieved from http://www.livescience.com/20391-parents-happier-parents.html.

Whittaker, B. (2016, September 29). New California law prohibits all cell phone use while driving. KSBW8 News. Retrieved from http://www.ksbw.com/article/new-california-law-prohibits-all-cellphone-use-while-driving/4096079

Who Are the Happiest People in the World? *Chapter 5 opening headline.* Clifton, J. (2016, March 16). The happiest people in the world? Retrieved from http://www.gallup.com/opinion/gallup/189989/happiest-people-world.aspx

Wilson, B. A., & Wearing, D. (1995). Prisoner of consciousness: A state of just awakening following herpes simplex encephalitis. In R. Campbell, & M. A. Conway (Eds.), *Broken memories: Case studies in memory impairment* (pp. 14–30). Malden, MA: Blackwell.

Wilson, D. C. (2006, December). Framing the future of race relations. *Public Opinion Pros.* Retrieved from http://www.publicopinionpros.norc.org

Wilson, D. C., & Brewer, P. R. (2016). Do frames emphasizing harm to age and racial-ethnic groups reduce support for voter ID laws? *Social Science Quarterly, 97*, 391–406. doi:10.1111/ssqu.12234

Wilson, D. C., Moore, D. W., McKay, P. F., & Avery, D. R. (2008). Affirmative action programs for women and minorities: Support affected by question order. *Public Opinion Quarterly, 73*, 514–522. doi:10.1093/poq/nfn031

Wilson, T. D. (2011). *Redirect: The surprising new science of psychological change.* New York: Little, Brown.

Wolfers, J. (2014, October 31). How confirmation bias can lead to a spinning of wheels. *New York Times* (online). Retrieved from http://nyti.ms/1vnO7Az

Wood, J. V., Perunovic, E. W. Q., & Lee, J. W. (2009). Positive self-statements: Power for some, peril for others. *Psychological Science, 20*, 860–866. doi:10.1111/j.1467-9280.2009.02370.x

Yorio, N. (2010). Seven secrets of low-stress families. WebMD.com. Retrieved from http://www.webmd.com/parenting/features/seven-secrets-of-low-stress-families#1

Your Dog Hates Hugs (NYMag.com, 2016): *Chapter 1 opening headline.* Dahl, M. (2016, April 25). Your dog hates hugs. NYMag.com. Retrieved from http://nymag.com/scienceofus/2016/04/your-dog-hates-hugs.html

Zajonc, R. B., Heingartner, A., & Herman, E. M. (1969). Social enhancement and impairment of performance in the cockroach. *Journal of Personality and Social Psychology, 13*, 83–92. doi:10.1037/h0028063

Zappos.com. 61% Said This Shoe "Felt True to Size."

Credits

Frontmatter

Page ii: Hero Images/Getty Images; **p. viii:** Photo courtesy of the University of Delaware/Evan Krape photographer.

Part Opener I

Page 2: Dreamstime.

Chapter 1

Page 4 (left): bernatets photo/Shutterstock; **(right):** Tribune Content Agency LLC/Alamy Stock Photo; **p. 7:** AP Photo/Nati Harnik; **p. 8:** © A&E/Courtesy Everett Collection; **p. 11:** Georgijevic/Getty Images; **p. 12:** Harlow Primate Lab, Madison, WI; **p. 14:** © Walt Disney/Courtesy Everett Collection; **p. 15:** Deborah Netburn. © 2015 Los Angeles Times. Reprinted with Permission; **p. 16 (left):** Jeff Miller/University of Wisconsin–Madison; **(right):** Steve Liss/The LIFE Images Collection/Getty Images; **p. 19:** PHD Comics.com; **p. 20:** Jim Wilson/The New York Times/Redux.

Chapter 2

Page 24 (top): Alamy; **(bottom):** Courtesy of Tantrums, LLC; **p. 26 (top):** Courtesy of Vent.com; **(bottom):** sportpoint/Shutterstock; **p. 28:** Rue des Archives/Granger, NYC — All rights reserved; **p. 34:** Photo by Christina K. Betz; **p. 37:** Wavebreak Media ltd/Alamy; **p. 38:** BURGER/PHANIE/Getty Images/Canopy; **p. 40 (left):** AP Photo/Jose Luis Magana; **(right):** Ryan Collerd/The New York Times/Redux; **p. 43:** Bushman, Brad J., Does Venting Anger Feed or Extinguish the Flame? Personality and Social Psychology Bulletin. Sage Publications, 06/01/2002. © 2002, Society for Personality and Social Psychology, Inc. Reprinted by Permission of SAGE Publications; **p. 43 (inset):** Bushman, Brad J., Does Venting Anger Feed or Extinguish the Flame? Personality and Social Psychology Bulletin. Sage Publications, 06/01/2002. © 2002, Society for Personality and Social Psychology, Inc. Reprinted by Permission of SAGE Publications; **p. 44:** Photo by Beth Morling; **p. 49:** Photo by Ted Szczepanski; **p. 51 (top left):** NPR; **(top right):** Courtesy of ScienceDaily.com; **(bottom left):** Reproduced with permission. Copyright © 2017 Scientific American, a division of Nature America, Inc. All rights reserved; **(bottom right):** *Current Directions in Psychological Science.* Copyright © 2017 by the Association for Psychological Science. Reprinted by permission of SAGE Publications, Inc.

Chapter 3

Page 56 (left): Tim Graham/Getty Images; **(right):** momcilog/Getty Images; **(bottom):** Directphoto Collection/Alamy Stock Photo; **p. 61 (left):** Photo by Christina K. Betz; **(right):** Sean Gallup/Getty Images; **p. 75:** Schellenberg, G. (2004). Music lessons enhance IQ. Psychological Science, 15, 511–514. Copyright © 2004, Association for Psychological Science; **p. 78:** Joshua Resnick/Shutterstock; **p. 81:** CDC/Jessie Blount.

Part Opener II

Page 86: littleny/Shutterstock.

Chapter 4

Page 88 (left): Ryan Smith/Getty Images; **(right):** Oli Scarff/Getty Images; **(bottom):** littleny/Shutterstock; **p. 90:** National Archives and Records Administration, Southeast Region (Atlanta); **p. 91:** Paul J. Richards/AFP/Getty Images; **p. 92:** Courtesy Alexandra Milgram; **p. 93:** Courtesy Alexandra Milgram; **p. 95:** © Elizabeth Crews/The Image Works; **p. 98:** Copyright © 2017 American Psychological Association. Reproduced with permission. The official citation that should be used in referencing this material is "American Psychological Association. (2017). Ethical principles of psychologists and code of conduct (2002, amended June 1, 2010 and January 1, 2017). Retrieved from http://www.apa.org/ethics/code/index.aspx." No further reproduction or distribution is permitted without written permission from the American Psychological Association; **p. 101:** Diego Cervo/Fotolia; **p. 104:** Sathyanarayana Rao, T.S., & Andrade, C. (2011). The MMR vaccine and autism: Sensation, refutation, retraction, and fraud. Indian Journal of Psychiatry, 53, 95–96; **p. 106:** Used with permission from: Even Einstein struggled: Effects of learning about great scientists' struggles. Lin-Siegler et al. Journal of Educational Psychology. April 1, 2016. © 2016 American Psychological Association; **p. 108:** Courtesy PETA; **p. 109:** Courtesy Foundation for Biomedical Research; **p. 111:** Brendan O'Sullivan/Getty Images.

Chapter 5

Page 116 (top): Donatas Dabravolskas/Shutterstock; **(left):** James Doberman/Shutterstock; **(right):** Ingus Kruklitis/Shutterstock; **p. 121:** Vickery et al. (2011). Ubiquity and specificity of reinforcement signals throughout the human brain. Neuron, 72(1): 166–177, supplemental Figure S1, panel B. © 2011 Elsevier; **p. 132:** Table 2, p. 167, from Pavot, W., & Diener, E. (1993). Review of the Satisfaction With Life Scale. Psychological Assessment, 5(2), 164–172. doi:10.1037/1040-3590.5.2.164; **p. 133 (top):** GagliardiImages/Shutterstock; **(bottom):** Bruce Gifford/Getty Images; **p. 144:** Folio Images/Shutterstock; **p. 145:** James Doberman/Shutterstock.

Part Opener III

Page 150: Trio Images/Getty Images.

Chapter 6

Page 152 (top): Trio Images/Getty Images; **(left):** Photo by Christina K. Betz; **(right):** Monkey Business Images/Shutterstock; **p. 155:** Courtesy of Yelp; **p. 160:** Photo by Beth Morling; **p. 163:** NovaStock/Superstock; **p. 164:** Photo by Christina K. Betz; **p. 166:** Courtesy Matthias Mehl, University of Arizona; **p. 167:** Copyright 2013 by the American Psychological Association. Reproduced with permission. Campos et al., (2013). Positive and negative emotion in the daily life of dual-earner couples with children. Journal of Family Psychology, 27(1), 76–85. doi:10.1037/a0031413 No further reproduction or distribution is permitted without written permission from the American Psychological Association; **p. 168:** Copyright 2013 by the American Psychological Association. Reproduced with permission. Campos et al. (2013). Positive and negative emotion in the daily life of dual-earner couples with children. Journal of Family Psychology, 27(1), 76–85; **p. 170:** Mary Evans Picture Library/Alamy Stock Photo; **p. 171:** Reprinted with permission from Bowker et al. 2009, Naturalistic observations of spectator behavior at youth hockey games. *The Sport Psychologist*, 23(3) 301–316. © 2009 Human Kinetics, Inc.; **p. 173:** Spencer Grant/Science Source; **p. 177:** Image courtesy of Nicole Sugden and Margaret Moulson, Ryerson University.

Chapter 7

Page 178 (top): Fedor Eremin/Shutterstock; **(middle):** kozorog/Getty Images; **(bottom):** Zappos.com; **p. 182:** The Washington Post/Getty Images; **p. 183:** Daniel Acker/Bloomberg via Getty Images; **p. 186 (top):** Courtesy of Babycenter.com; **p. 186 (bottom):** © AAA 2016. Reprinted with permission; **p. 187:** Urbaniak, G. C., & Plous, S. (2015). Research Randomizer (Version 4.0) [Computer software]. Retrieved on January 20, 2017, from http://www.randomizer.org/; **p. 195:** dennizn/Shutterstock.

Part Opener IV

Page 200: Muslim Girl/Getty Images.

Chapter 8

Page 202 (left): ZenShui//Sigrid Olson/Getty Images; **(right):** LearningStockImages/Alamy Stock Photo; **(bottom):** Matthew Staver/The New York Times/Redux; **p. 214:** Juice Images/Alamy Stock Photo; **p. 216:** Mehl et al. Eavesdropping on Happiness: Well-Being Is Related to Having Less Small Talk and More Substantive Conversations. Psychological Science April 2010 21: 539–541, first published 2/18/10. Copyright © 2010, APS; **p. 229:** Shigehiro Oishi, et al., "The socioecological model of procommunity action: The benefits of residential stability," *Journal of Personality and Social Psychology*, Vol. 93(5), Nov. 2007, 831–844. Copyright 2007 by the American Psychological Association. Adapted with permission; **p. 231:** Sofi photo/Shutterstock.

Chapter 9

Page 236 (top): InspiredFootage/Getty Images; **(bottom):** Richard Cartwright/ABC via Getty Images; **p. 243:** asiseeit/Getty Images; **p. 254:** Dimitrios Pappas/Dreamstime.com; **p. 255:** Phovoir/Shutterstock; **p. 257:** pixelrain/Shutterstock.

Part Opener V

Page 270: Photo by Beth Morling.

Chapter 10

Page 272 (top): Photo by Beth Morling; **(bottom):** Andrew Scrivani/The New York Times/Redux; **Page 274:** Hongqi Zhang/Alamy Stock Photo; **p. 289:** Michael D. Mrazek et al. Psychological Science. Vol 24 (5), pp. 776–781, © 2013. Reprinted by Permission of SAGE Publications, Inc.; **p. 303:** Luka Lajst/Getty Images.

Chapter 11

Page 310 (top): Geoff Manasse/Getty Images; **(bottom):** Dorling Kindersley ltd/Alamy Stock Photo; **p. 324:** The Photo Works/Alamy Stock Photo; **p. 325:** Michael D. Mrazek et al. *Psychological Science*. Vol 24 (5), pp. 776–781, © 2013. Reprinted by Permission of SAGE Publications, Inc.; **p. 328:** Susan Chiang/Getty Images.

Chapter 12

Page 350 (top): Edward Frazer/Corbis; **(bottom):** Adrian Hancu/iStock Editorial; **p. 356:** Strayer, D. L., & Drews, F. A. (2004). Profiles in driver distraction: Effects of cell phone conversations on younger and older drivers. *Human Factors*, 46, 640–649. Photo courtesy David Strayer; **p. 381:** Photo by Eniko Kubinyi.

Part Opener VI

Page 386: cbpix/Getty Images.

Chapter 13

Page 388 (top): Elleringmann/laif/Redux; **p. 397:** Joe Dunckley/Shutterstock; **p. 399:** Hero Images/Getty Images; **p. 408 (left):** From NOVA ScienceNow, How Memory Works (http://www.pbs.org/wgbh/nova/body/corkin-hm-memory.html) © 1997–2017 WGBH Educational Foundation; **(right):** Henry Molaison, aged 60, at MIT in 1986. Photograph by Jenni Ogden, author of the book *Trouble in Mind: Stories from a Neuropsychologist's Casebook*; **p. 410:** Annese, J. et al. Postmortem examination of patient H.M.'s brain based on histological sectioning and digital 3D reconstruction. Nat. Commun. 5:3122 doi: 10.1038/ncomms4122 (2014); **p. 413:** Mendil/Science Source; **p. 417 (left):** Patrick Grehan/Getty Images; **(right):** © Maya Barnes Johansen/The Image Works.

Chapter 14

Page 424 (top): Mirko Macari/Shutterstock; **(left):** Barbara Davidson. © 2008 Los Angeles Times. Reprinted with Permission; **(right):** Benoit Decout/REA/Redux; **p. 427:** Jones et al. (2004). How do I love thee? Let me count the J's: Implicit egotism and interpersonal attraction. *Journal of Personality and Social Psychology*, 87, 665–683. © APA; **p. 435:** carlos cardetas/Alamy Stock Photo; **p. 436:** Jonathan Nourok/Getty Images; **p. 437 (headline):** © The Daily Star; **(photo):** Image Source/Getty Images; **p. 442:** Gallery Stock; **p. 445:** Masuda & Nisbett (2001), JPSP, 81, 922–934. © Takahiko Masuda, All rights Reserved; **p. 446:** Masuda & Nisbett (2001), JPSP, 81, 922–934. © Takahiko Masuda, All rights Reserved; **p. 449:** © Anoek Steketee.

Statistics Review: Descriptive Statistics

Page 477: Bushman, B. J., & Anderson, C. A. (2001). Media violence and the American Public. *American Psychologist*, 56, 477–489. © Copyright 2001 by Brad J Bushman & Craig A. Anderson.

Presenting Results: APA-Style Reports and Conference Posters

Pages 520–522: From *The Norton Field Guide to Writing*, *Third Edition* by Richard Bullock. Copyright © 2013, 2009, 2006 by W. W. Norton & Company, Inc. Used by permission of W. W. Norton & Company, Inc.; **p. 540:** Courtesy The College of Idaho.

Name Index

Fernbach, P. M., 164
Feshbach, S., 29, 31
Finch, S., 495
Finckenauer, J. O., 9
Finkelhor, D., 269
Finkle, C., 390
Foa, E. B., 48
Fode, K., 170, 172
Formann, A. K., 20
Fox, D. K., 414
Fraley, R. C., 432
Franklin, M. S., 9, 288, 325
Frey, D., 36

G

Gábor, A., 380
Gamer, M., 434
Ganesh, S., 455
Gásci, M., 380
Gay, P., 33
Geen, R. G., 31
Gernsbacher, M. A., 284, 523
Giancola, P. R., 351, 358, 359
Gilbert, D., 34
Gilbert, D. T., 431
Gillihan, S. J., 48
Gilovich, T., 37
Goldacre, B., 20–21
Gonzaga, G. C., 204
Goodman, J. K., 184
Gordon, A. M., 143–44, 145
Gottfredson, L. S., 135
Gould, S. J., 122, 133
Gray, F. D., 91
Green, B. L., 91
Greenberg, K., 302
Greenwald, A. G., 162
Griffin, S., 160
Grim, T., 235
Gross, J. J., 44
Guillory, J. E., 111
Gunn, R. L., 351

H

Ha, Y. W., 37
Hamedani, M. C., 444
Hamzelou, J., 455
Han, W. J., 250
Hancock, J. T., 111

Hanlon, C., 441, 442
Harlow, H., 12, 13, 14, 15, 280, 292, 440–41
Harms, W., 221, 223
Harsch, N., 164
Heine, S. J., 444, 447
Heingartner, A., 172
Heinz, A., 359–60, 361, 362, 363, 365f, 366, 370
Heinzen, T., 170
Heller, J., 91
Henderson, L. V., 355
Hendrick, C., 101
Henrich, J., 444f, 447
Herman, E. M., 172
Herskovits, M. J., 444
Hertwig, R., 102
Herzog, H. A., Jr., 108
Hill, P. L., 259
Hoffman, J. E., 46
Holmes, T. H., 120
Holt, J. C. D., 351
Hopkins, B. L., 414
Horwitz, J., 343
Howard, J., 380
Hsu, J., 267

I

Impett, E. A., 143–44
Inbar, Y., 430

J

Jewell, R. M., 184
Johansson, G., 447, 448f, 450, 455
Johnson, M. K., 390
Johnson, W., 122
Jones, J. H., 90, 91
Jones, J. T., 426, 427, 491, 492, 493, 494, 495
Jonson, A. R., 95
Judd, C. M., 160, 162

K

Kabat-Zinn, J., 9
Kagay, M., 157, 158
Kahneman, D., 33
Kaplan, R. M., 300
Katz, R. V., 91
Keltner, D., 121, 143–44

Kenny, D. A., 260, 262, 358, 481
Kensinger, E. A., 411
Kiene, H., 325
Kienle, G. S., 325
Kim, J., 466, 473, 474, 476
Kimmel, A. J., 97, 98, 102, 108, 109
King, G., 431
King, L. A., 343
Kirsch, I., 324
Klayman, J., 37
Klein, R. A., 431
Klein, O., 430
Klipker, K., 44
Kogan, A., 143–44
Kramer, A. D. I., 111
Krosnick, J., 160, 162
Kuhn, A., 291
Kushlev, K., 231
Ky, K. N., 20

L

LaBouff, J. P., 390, 391t, 396
Langer, E. J., 169, 172
Larsen, R. J., 160
Latané, B., 309
Lavallee, K. L., 391, 506t
Lawless, N. M., 455
Lee, D., 121f
Lee, J., 39
Lee, J. W., 384
Lelkes, Y., 160, 162
Levav, J., 392, 506t
Lichtenstein, D. R., 164
Liebler, A., 481
Likert, R., 155
Lillienfeld, S., 170
Lin, D. Y., 37
Linardatos, E., 436
Lin-Siegler, X. D., 80, 81, 101, 106f
Lohr, J. M., 29, 31
Lovaas, O. I., 284
Lucas, R. E., 343, 455
Luellen, J. K., 401
Luke, J. V., 184
Luna-Lucero, M., 80, 101, 106f
Lyubomirsky, S., 231, 343

M

Margraf, J., 391, 392, 393f, 397, 398, 400, 401–2, 403, 404, 506t
Markus, H. R., 183, 444
Marlowe, D., 162
Martino, S. C., 255
Marx, D. M., 160, 162
Masson, M. E. J., 48
Masuda, T., 445, 446
Mathur, U., 455
Matthews, A. M., 436
McCallum, J. M., 91
McCartney, K., 213
McKay, P. F., 159
McNulty, J. K., 355, 378, 523
Medeiros-Ward, N., 205
Meehl, P. E., 133
Mehl, M. R., 166, 173, 183, 189, 195–96, 205t, 206, 210, 216f, 217, 220, 221, 223, 225, 229, 343, 455, 506t
Mendelson, M., 138
Mende-Siedlecki, P., 430
Mendoza-Denton, R., 121
Meslin, E. M., 91
Metzger, M. M., 108
Meyer, A. H., 391, 506t
Meyers, E., 455
Miklósi, A., 380
Milgram, S., 92–94, 96, 101
Miller, D. P., 250
Miller, G. E., 418
Miller, N. E., 109
Milner, B., 408, 411
Mirenberg, M. C., 426, 427, 491
Mitchell, L., 437f
Miu, A., 255
Mock, J., 138
Moffat, N. J., 412
Mohamed-Ali, M. I., 177
Monahan, K., 255
Mook, D., 340, 441, 442
Moore, D. W., 159
Morris, D. H., 351
Moss, P., 422
Moulson, M. C., 177

Subject Index

double-blind studies, 323
driving
    cell phone use and, 352, 353, 355–57, 358, 364, 367, 368–69f, 372, 373, 374, 375–77, 379, 442, 443, 508, 509–10
    road rage, 185, 186f, 193
    texting and, 62, 69, 70, 73t

E

eating disorders, *see under* family meals
ecological validity (mundane realism), 439, 449, 450
effect size
    defined, 44, 211
    descriptive statistics for, 472–77
    meta-analysis and, 434–36
    sample size and, 489
    statistical significance and, 215–16
    statistical validity and, 211–14, 304–5
    Type II error and, 489
election polls, 184, 193, 196
electroencephalography (EEG), 122
empirical journal articles, 46–48
    components of, 46–47
    defined, 42
    example, 43f
    factorial designs in, 379
    mean and standard deviation in, 464–66
    reading with a purpose, 47–48
    on reliability and validity, 143–44
    on statistical significance, 216–17
empiricism (empirical method/empirical research), 5, 10–11
equivalent groups, posttest-only design, *see* posttest-only design
equivalent groups, pretest/posttest design, 288–90, 297
error, *see* margin of error of the estimate; measurement error; Type I error; Type II error
error variance, *see* noise
eta squared (h^2), 475
Ethical Principles of Psychologists and Code of Conduct, 98, 99t
ethics, 89–115
    in animal research, 105–9
    APA principles and standards, 98–109

Belmont Report, 94–97, 98, 99t, 108, 109
    core principles, 94–97
    debriefing, 93, 102–3, 112
    deception, 101–2, 112
    historical examples, 89–94
    informed consent, 95, 100–101, 110, 112
    IRBs and (*see* institutional review boards)
    in observational research, 173–74
    plagiarism avoidance (*see* plagiarism)
    quasi-experiments and, 404
    research misconduct, 103–5
    in reversal designs, 417
    thoughtful balance in, 110
Everything Guide to Narcissistic Personality Disorder, The (Lechan and Leff), 49
evidence-based treatments, 8
expanded rehearsal, 412–13, 416
expectancy effects, *see* observer effects
experience, 26–32
    comparison groups lacking, 26–28
    confounds in, 29
    research superiority to, 29–31
experimental demands, *see* demand characteristics
experimental realism, 449–50
experiments, 311–48
    defined, 75, 276
    how causal claims are supported by, 75–76
    longitudinal studies in lieu of, 242–43
    with more than one independent variable, 351–85 (*see also* factorial designs)
    null effects in (*see* null effects)
    with one independent variable, 351–52
    quasi- (*see* quasi-experiments)
    really bad, 312–13, 314f
    simple (*see* simple experiments)
    small-*N* (*see* small-*N* designs)
    threats to internal validity in, 312–27
external validity
    of association claims, 71, 226–29
    of causal claims, 78–79, 301–3
    defined, 70
    description, 72t

examples, 82, 232
    of frequency claims, 70, 179–80, 193–94
    importance of study and, 438–47
    interrogating, 193–97
    limit testing and, 357–58
    of multivariate correlational research, 264
    poor, 303
    in priorities, 79–80, 194–96
    probability sampling and, 191, 193–94, 302
    in quasi-experiments, 404
    the real world and, 449–50
    in small-*N* designs, 411, 418–19

F

Facebook study, 111–12
face validity, 134–35
facial electromyography (EMG), 121
facilitated communication (FC), 14
factorial designs, 355–82
    defined, 355
    identifying in reading, 378–82
    increasing the levels of independent variables, 371–72
    increasing the number of independent variables, 373–78
    independent-groups, 370
    interpreting results, 360–67
    limit testing with, 356–58
    mixed, 371
    theory testing with, 358–60
    3 × 4, 372, 373f
    three-way (2 × 2 × 2), 373–78
    2 × 3, 372
    2 × 2, 256, 367, 368–69f, 370
    variations in, 370–78
    within-groups, 370, 371f
factual knowledge, 299
faking bad, 162
faking good, 162
false positives, *see* Type I error
falsifiability, 14
family meals
    academic achievement and, 250–51, 252–53, 254
    dinner-table conversation, 167–68, 195
    eating disorders and, 66, 67, 76–77
fatigue effects, 294

for beta, 500–501
with correlation coefficient, 499–500, 501
defined, 479
F test, 496–99, 501
NHST (*see* null hypothesis significance testing)
samples, populations, and, 483–90
t test (*see t* test)
types of tests for, 490–501, 502–3t
information sources, *see* sources of information
informed consent, 95, 100–101, 110, 112
insensitive measures, 332, 342t
Institutional Animal Care and Use Committee (IACUC), 107, 109, 110
institutional review boards (IRBs), 99–100, 101, 110, 111, 174
instrumentation threats, 321, 327t, 329, 402
integrity (ethical standard), 98, 99t
intelligence
    conceptual definitions of, 135
    fMRI measures of, 122
    head circumference and (*see* head circumference)
    lead exposure and, 477
    music and, 20, 62, 66, 67, 73t, 74, 75–76, 78–79
intelligence tests (IQ tests)
    confirmation bias and, 36
    criterion validity of, 137
    as interval scales, 123
    as observational measures, 121, 122
    test-retest reliability of, 125, 130
    validity and reliability of, 142–43
interaction effects (interactions), 363–67
    crossover, 354, 366
    defined, 353
    intuitive, 353–55
    main effects compared with, 367, 368–69f
    methods of demonstrating, 363–66
    moderators shown by, 358
    spreading, 354
    theory testing with, 360
    from a three-way design, 373, 376–78
internal reliability (internal consistency)

application of, 126
correlation coefficient evaluation of, 130–31
defined, 125
example, 146
internal validity
    of association claims, 221–26
    of causal claims, 74–75, 76, 77, 78, 210, 306
    defined, 74–75
    description, 72t
    example, 82, 232
    in experiments, 281–86
    in longitudinal studies, 242
    in multivariate correlational research, 238
    in posttest-only design, 288
    in quasi-experiments, 396–404
    random assignment and, 191, 302
    in small-*N* designs, 410, 411, 413, 418
    study's method in establishing, 76
    theory-testing mode and, 440
    threats to, 312–27
    in within-groups designs, 294
    see also third variables
Internet polls, 185, 186f, 196
Internet ratings, 155, 164, 194
interrater reliability
    correlation coefficient evaluation of, 130
    definition and application of, 125
    example, 146
    of observational research, 171–72
    scatterplot evaluation of, 126–28
interrogating information, 8
    association claims, 71–73, 210–30
    causal claims, 73t, 74–79, 298–306
    claims, 68–80
    external validity, 193–97
    frequency claims, 69–70, 73t
    null effects, 330–45
interrupted time-series design, 394
interval scales, 123, 124t
introduction
    in empirical journal articles, 47
    in research reports, 507–10
intuition, 32–38
intuitive interactions, 353–55
inverse associations, *see* negative associations
IQ tests, *see* intelligence tests

IRBs, *see* institutional review boards
"it depends," 380–81

J

journal articles
    citing sources from, 523–24
    components of, 46–47
    empirical (*see* empirical journal articles)
    factorial designs in, 379
    mean and standard deviation in, 464–66
    peer-reviewed (*see* peer-reviewed sources)
    reading, 46–48
    on reliability, 131, 143–44
    review (*see* review journal articles)
    on statistical significance, 216–17
    on validity, 143–44
journalism, 17–21
    accuracy in, 19–21
    benefits and risks of coverage, 18–21
    importance of story, 18
    see also popular media
Journal of Educational Psychology, 80, 106f
judicial decision-making, 392–94, 398, 402, 403, 404, 405, 406
justice, *see* principle of justice
Justice Department, U.S., 9
Juvenile Justice and Delinquency Prevention Act of 1974, 9

K

kappa, 130
Kashdan, Todd, 31
known-groups paradigm, 137–39

L

Ladder of Life, 119, 120, 137, 139
Lancet, The, 104
large-*N* designs, 406, 407
Latin square, 296
leading questions, 156
Lechan, Cynthia, 49
Leff, Barbara, 49
levels, 58, 277
lie detectors, 137, 433
Likert scales, 155
Liker-type scales, 155
limit testing, 356–58
line graphs, 364, 365t

research
    applied, 16
    basic, 16
    claims not based on, 68
    database seach tips, 45t
    ethical standards for, 99–109
    experience *vs.*, 26–32
    finding in less scholarly places, 48–52
    finding scientific sources, 44–46
    intuition *vs.*, 32–38
    misconduct in, 103–5
    paying participants, 95, 110
    reading, 46–48
    translational, 16
    types of scientific sources, 42–44
research consumers, 6, 7–10
research producers, 6–7
research reports, 505–39
    abstract, 507
    citing sources, 522–24
    Discussion section, 514–16
    figures in, 513–14
    formatting, 516–17
    introduction, 507–10
    Method section, 510–12
    paraphrasing in (*see* paraphrasing)
    plagiarism, avoiding (*see* plagiarism)
    References section, 516, 523
    Results section, 512–14
    sample paper, 525–39
    tables in, 513–14
    title, 506–7
    writing style, 517–19
respect for persons, *see* principle of
    respect for persons
response sets (nondifferentiation),
    160–61
Responsible Conduct of Research, 97
restriction of range, 218–20
Results section
    in empirical journal articles, 47, 379,
        464
    in research reports, 512–14
Rethinking Positive Thinking
    (Oettingen), 49
reversal designs, 414–17
reverse-worded items, 160–61
review journal articles, 42–44, 433
    defined, 42
    reading with a purpose, 48
road rage, 185, 186f, 193

romantic relationships
    gratitude and longevity of (*see under*
        gratitude)
    positive attitudes in, 354–55, 378
Roper polling organization, 157
Rosenberg self-esteem inventory, 155
Rush, Benjamin, 26–28, 29, 35

S

samples
    biased, 181, 182–85
    defined, 180
    inference and, 483–90
    populations and, 180–81
    unbiased, 181, 186–91
    WEIRD, 447
sample size
    correlation coefficient and, 500
    effect size and, 489
    importance of, 196–97
    outliers and, 218
    statistical significance and, 215–16
    Type II error and, 488–89
    within-groups variability and, 339
    see also large-*N* designs; single-*N*
        designs; small-*N* designs
sampling, 179–99
    cluster, 188, 189
    convenience, 183–85, 191, 438, 439
    generalizability of, 179–92
    multistage, 188
    nonprobability (*see* nonprobability
        sampling)
    over-, 189
    probability (*see* probability sampling)
    purposive, 191–92
    quota, 192
    simple random, 187–88, 545–46
    snowball, 192
    stratified random, 188–89, 192
    systematic, 189, 546
sampling distribution
    of *F,* 497–98
    of *r,* 499–500
    of *t,* 492–93
SAT
    criterion validity of, 137
    statistical validity of, 218–20
Satisfaction with Life (SWL) scale, 131,
    132t

Scared Straight program, 8–10, 10, 33,
    343
scatterplots, 64–66, 468–70
    in bivariate correlational research,
        205–8
    defined, 64
    reliability evaluated with, 126–28
scientific literature, 433
scientific sources
    finding, 44–46
    types of, 42–44
scientists' stories, 66, 80–82
Secret Life of Pronouns, The
    (Pennebaker), 49
selection-attrition threats, 322
selection effects, 284–86, 312
    defined, 284, 326t
    examples, 326t, 328
    posttest-only design and, 288
    in quasi-experiments, 396–98
    within-groups designs and, 294
selection-history threats, 321
self-esteem
    praise and, 476
    self-talk and, 381–82
self-report measures, 122, 125, 126,
    130–31
    accuracy of, 163
    criterion validity of, 136–37
    described, 120–21
    of event memories, 163–64
    known-groups evidence for, 137–39
    meaningful responses on, 159–60
    observations compared with,
        168–69
    see also surveys and polls
self-selection, 185
semantic differential format, 155
September 11 attacks, 163–64
settings, 180
shared experience effects, 290–91, 292,
    294, 295, 300–301, 303, 305
shoe "fit true to size," 193, 194
"Silver Blaze" (Doyle), 34
simple experiments, 273–309
    examples of, 273–76
    interrogating causal claims in,
        298–306
    variables in, 276–78
    why causal claims are supported by,
        278–86